THE
COLLEGE
PRESS
NIV
COMMENTARY

1 & 2 KINGS

THE COLLEGE PRESS NIV COMMENTARY

1 & 2 KINGS

JESSE C. LONG, Jr.

Old Testament Series Co-Editors:

Terry Briley, Ph.D.
Lipscomb University

Paul Kissling, Ph.D.
Great Lakes Christian College

 COLLEGE PRESS
PUBLISHING COMPANY
Joplin, Missouri

Library of Congress Cataloging-in-Publication Data

Long, Jesse, 1953–
    1 & 2 Kings / by Jesse Long, Jr.
        p.   cm. — (The College Press NIV commentary. Old
    Testament series)
    Includes bibliographical references.
    ISBN 0-89900-882-8
    1. Bible. O.T. Kings—Commentaries.   I. Title: 1 and
2 Kings. II. Title: First & Second Kings. III. Title: First and
Second Kings. IV. Title. V. Series.
BS1335.53.L66 2002
222'.5077—dc21

                                                2002073899

A WORD
FROM THE PUBLISHER

Years ago a movement was begun with the dream of uniting all Christians on the basis of a common purpose (world evangelism) under a common authority (the Word of God). The College Press NIV Commentary Series is a serious effort to join the scholarship of two branches of this unity movement so as to speak with one voice concerning the Word of God. Our desire is to provide a resource for your study of the Old Testament that will benefit you whether you are preparing a Bible School lesson, a sermon, a college course, or your own personal devotions. Today as we survey the wreckage of a broken world, we must turn again to the Lord and his Word, unite under his banner and communicate the life-giving message to those who are in desperate need. This is our purpose.

ABBREVIATIONS

ABD . . . . .*Anchor Bible Dictionary*
ANET . . . .*Ancient Near Eastern Texts Relating to the Old Testament*
AUSS . . . .*Andrews University Seminary Studies*
BA . . . . . .*Biblical Archaeologist*
BAR . . . . .*Biblical Archaeology Review*
BETS . . . .*Bulletin of the Evangelical Theological Society*
BHS . . . . .*Biblia Hebraica Stuttgartensia*
CBQ . . . . .*Catholic Biblical Quarterly*
Dtr . . . . . .The Deuteronomist
DtrH . . . .The Deuteronomistic History
GA . . . . . .*The Gospel Advocate*
HTR . . . . .*Harvard Theological Review*
IEJ . . . . . .*Israel Exploration Journal*
JBL . . . . . .*Journal of Biblical Literature*
JETS . . . . .*Journal of the Evangelical Theological Society*
JSOT . . . . .*Journal for the Study of the Old Testament*
JSOTSup . .*JSOT Supplement Series*
KJV . . . . . .*Kings James Version*
LXX . . . . .*The Septuagint (Greek Translation of the Hebrew Bible)*
MT . . . . . .*The Masoretic Text (Hebrew Bible)*
NEA . . . . .*Near Eastern Archaeology*
NEAEHL .*The New Encyclopedia of Archaeological Excavations in the Holy Land*
NIV . . . . .*The New International Version*
NRSV . . . .*New Revised Standard Version*
SBL . . . . .*Society of Biblical Literature*
TA . . . . . .*Tel Aviv*
TB . . . . . .*Tyndale Bulletin*
VT . . . . . .*Vetus Testamentum*
ZAW . . . . .*Zeitschrift für Alttestamentliche Wissenschaft*

Simplified Guide to Hebrew Writing

Heb. letter	Translit.	Pronunciation guide
א	ʾ	Has no sound of its own; like smooth breathing mark in Greek
ב	b	Pronounced like English B *or* V
ג	g	Pronounced like English G
ד	d	Pronounced like English D
ה	h	Pronounced like English H, silent at the end of words in the combination āh
ו	w	As a consonant, pronounced like English V or German W
וּ	û	Represents a vowel sound, pronounced like English long OO
וֹ	ô	Represents a vowel sound, pronounced like English long O
ז	z	Pronounced like English Z
ח	ḥ	Pronounced like German and Scottish CH and Greek χ (chi)
ט	ṭ	Pronounced like English T
י	y	Pronounced like English Y
כ/ך	k	Pronounced like English K
ל	l	Pronounced like English L
מ/ם	m	Pronounced like English M
נ/ן	n	Pronounced like English N
ס	s	Pronounced like English S
ע	ʿ	Stop in breath deep in throat before pronouncing the vowel
פ/ף	p/ph	Pronounced like English P *or* F
צ/ץ	ṣ	Pronounced like English TS/TZ
ק	q	Pronounced very much like כ (k)
ר	r	Pronounced like English R
שׂ	ś	Pronounced like English S, much the same as ס
שׁ	š	Pronounced like English SH
ת	t/th	Pronounced like English T *or* TH

Note that different forms of some letters appear at the end of the word (written right to left), as in כָּפַף (*kāphaph*, "bend") and מֶלֶךְ (*melek*, "king").

Vowels in Hebrew (except where the ו is used to represent a vowel sound), are represented by "vowel points" added to the consonant. For example: הַ (*ha*, "the"). The letter *yod* (י, *y*) also becomes a *part of* certain vowel sounds, as in the conjunction כִּי (*kî*, "that"). Originally, Hebrew was written as "unpointed" text, with just the consonants. For convenience, the different vowel points are shown below on the letter Aleph (א).

אָ	ā	Pronounced not like long A in English, but like the broad A or AH sound
אַ	a	The Hebrew short A sound, but more closely resembles the broad A (pronounced for a shorter period of time) than the English short A
אֶ	e	Pronounced like English short E

א	ē	Pronounced like English long A, or Greek η (eta)
א	i	Pronounced like English short I
א	î	The same vowel point is sometimes pronounced like 'א (see below)
א	o	This vowel point sometimes represents the short O sound
א	ō	Pronounced like English long O
א	u	The vowel point ֻ sometimes represents a shorter U sound and
א	ū	is sometimes pronounced like the ו (û, see above)
'א	ê	Pronounced much the same as א
'א	ê	Pronounced much the same as א
'א	î	Pronounced like long I in many languages, or English long E
א	ə	An unstressed vowel sound, like the first E in the word "severe"
א, א, א	ŏ, ă, ĕ	Shortened, unstressed forms of the vowels א, א, and א, pronounced very similarly to א

PREFACE AND ACKNOWLEDGMENTS

My early memories of church include images of Old Testament stories. As one of my Sunday school teachers, my mother with "flannel-graph" lessons (she painted the backgrounds) reinforced the stories she had brought to life for me from infancy. I also vividly recall sermons my father preached from the Old Testament. He usually prefaced these sermons with a brief sketch of Old Testament history, which often included the statement: "This was followed by the period of the united kingdom for one hundred and twenty years, the divided kingdom for two hundred years, and Judah alone for another one hundred and fifty years." I can still remember the "points" in one of his sermons entitled "The Lost Book," a lesson on Josiah's discovery of the Book of the Law in the temple in Jerusalem. All of this my grandfather amplified, whose love for the Old Testament prophets lives on in the satisfaction I have when studying Hebrew Scripture.

A commitment to Old Testament study was further strengthened in graduate school with the influences of Drs. Herbert Huffmon, Paul Riemann, and Suzanne Richard, who introduced me to the larger world of the academic study of the Hebrew Bible. I will never forget walking home in the New Jersey snow (at Drew University) after one of Dr. Richard's classes in Syro-Palestinian archaeology and thinking, "How wonderful it is to be learning about the world of the Bible." In one of Dr. Riemann's classes I was first introduced to Robert Alter's "new book," *The Art of Biblical Narrative*. His class and that book changed the way I read Bible stories. Dr. Huffmon's sense of fairness and well-reasoned, rigorous approach to the text continues to influence my work.

The commentary itself is a product of fifteen years of teaching Hebrew narrative and Syro-Palestinian archaeology to undergraduate and graduate students at Southern Christian University and

Lubbock Christian University. As most teachers would concede, I have learned as much from the students that I have been blessed to have in my courses as they have learned from me. All of these influences have taught me something that I try to emphasize now in class, which I hope stands out in the commentary. The narratives of Scripture are fundamentally about the God of the story. One can never get too far off course, if he has a good sense of what the text is trying to say about the God of Israel and his purpose in the world. As a human product, the commentary will obviously have mistakes in both interpretation and presentation. An aspect of the human condition is that we are always in the process of learning more about him through the word that he has given us and in our experience of him in our lives. My prayer is that, in spite of its shortcomings, the commentary will, to borrow a phrase from a popular radio talk host, "make him look good" — give God glory and honor as the one who is the author of Israel's story and eternal life for all mankind!

Several have played an important role in the preparation of this commentary. I am indebted to Lubbock Christian University and a timely sabbatical to allow me to work exclusively on Kings. Drs. Ken Jones, Rod Blackwood, Don Williams, and Steve Joiner have especially been supportive. Their backing has enabled the project. Paul Holdorf, Bruce Gilstrap, Jack Gordon, and Jesse C. Long, Sr. read at least parts of the manuscript in progress and offered helpful comments. Conversations with Brandon Fredenburg about the literary dimension of Kings were stimulating for both of us. As a graduate assistant, Michael Martin helped me work through a literary reading of the story of the man of God from Judah in 1 Kings 13. Both undergraduate and graduate students in classes at LCU helped shape the discussion in the commentary of the story of kingship in Israel. Drs. Leon Crouch and Mark Sneed made significant contributions to the manuscript and provided an important sounding board for many of the ideas in the commentary. Tim Hadley was a special friend to read the manuscript and offer his expertise in Hebrew Scripture and as a copyeditor. The prayers of the university class at the South Plains Church of Christ were often felt in the early morning hours and difficult days of working on Kings.

One cannot complete a project like this one without the support of his family. My wife, JoAnn, and daughters, Laurel and Leah, have all sacrificed to see that "Dad's Kings project" move forward to its completion. JoAnn gave useful feedback as each section was completed, and our discussions on our morning walks helped crystallize important concepts in the interpretation of Kings. Her spiritual depth and understanding of the God of the story lies behind the discussion of Kings in this commentary. I would add that my parents, Jesse and Marilyn Long, have been a special source of encouragement during the work on this project.

My grandparents, Rex and Opal Turner, inscribed the first Bible I remember receiving, "To a grandson of whom we justly delight." I delight in their memory. They were a blessing from God to me. In a real way, the influence of my grandfather especially lives on in this work.

To the memory of Rex A. Turner, Sr., this commentary on 1 and 2 Kings is affectionately dedicated. A scholar, educator, and gospel preacher, his life was a blessing to thousands, especially as he encouraged young men to preach and give their lives in service to God. A loving grandson felt that encouragement. His spirit lives on in my love for the Old Testament and in the pleasure that I take in telling others about the God of Israel, "for whom and through whom everything exists" (Heb 2:10).

My grandfather would shift the focus back to Scripture, back to the author of life. To the God who is the "Builder" in this commentary project (see comments on 1 Kings 8 below), the God of Abraham, Moses, David, and my grandfather, I give all honor and praise:

"LORD, all that I have accomplished you have done for me; your name alone do I honor" (adapted from Isa 26:12-13).

INTRODUCTION

COMPOSITION

The composition of 1 and 2 Kings has generated much debate. The questions of author, date, and nature of the composition are complex. A detailed exposition of the issues involved would go well beyond the scope of this introduction. The following discussion will lay out some of the assumptions of this commentary's approach to Kings.

Current views of the composition of Kings have been most influenced by the publication of Martin Noth's seminal work on the Deuteronomistic History (abbreviated DtrH, Deuteronomy and Joshua through 2 Kings).[1] Scholars have generally viewed this literary corpus as a unified composition. In contrast with earlier approaches that set out to identify preliterary sources or viewed the separate books as individual compositions with redactional layers, Noth saw this material as a unified work of a single author, whom he named the Deuteronomist (Dtr). Dtr composed his theological history of Israel in the Babylonian exile, not long after the release of Jehoiachin from prison ca. 560 B.C. For Noth, the similar language and style of the various books suggest the unity of the composition. After Noth, other scholars, while accepting in broad outline Noth's thesis, have seen redactional layers in DtrH. One popular theory (the "Double Redaction" theory of Frank Moore Cross[2]) hypothe-

---

[1]For an English translation of the part of Noth's work dealing with DtrH, see Martin Noth, *The Deuteronomistic History*, JSOTSup 15 (Sheffield: JSOT Press, 1981; 2nd reworked ed., 1991). The original German edition was published in 1943. For more detailed summaries of the history of interpretation of DtrH, see Steven L. McKenzie, "Deuteronomistic History," in *ABD*; Flemming A.J. Nielsen, *The Tragedy in History: Herodotus and the Deuteronomistic History*, JSOTSup 251, Copenhagen International Seminar 4 (Sheffield: Sheffield Academic Press, 1997), pp. 85-97.

[2]Frank Moore Cross, *Canaanite Myth and Hebrew Epic: Essays in the History*

sizes that DtrH as it stands is composed of two separate editions, one from the time of Josiah and an updated version from the exile.

Aspects of Noth's thesis, particularly the view that Deteronomy is a product of the exile, are inconsistent with a conservative view of Scripture. It also does not necessarily follow that similar themes, theological slant, and literary style indicate that Joshua through 2 Kings is the product of a single author.[3] At the same time, however, a literary analysis of Kings suggests that the book is the product of an author, not a redactor(s).[4] Recognizing that sources were used and that works like Deuteronomy lie in the background of the composition, it is inconceivable that the sophisticated literary work that is Kings is the product of a redactor(s) who spliced together strands and episodes of pretexts to form the composition.

For example, the commentary on 1 Kings 20 below will show the storyteller using allusions to Deuteronomy 7:1-3 and the conquest of Jericho (Joshua 2, 6) to frame his account of Ahab's wars with Ben-Hadad and the subsequent judgment on Ahab by an unnamed prophet. Ahab displays mercy to and makes a covenant with Ben-Hadad, who had been dedicated (חֵרֶם, ḥērem) to Yahweh, as had the people of Jericho (cf. Deut 7:1-3). The allusions reinforce the judgment on Ahab and say that the king of Israel should have known better than to make a covenant with the dedicated-to-Yahweh king of Aram — as he should have known not to marry the Canaanite Jezebel. In Deuteronomy 7:1-3, Moses instructed Israel not to make covenants with, show mercy to, or marry the people of the land, who were to be totally destroyed (ḥērem). For purposes of this discussion, it is important to observe that the allusions in 1 Kings 20 cross pro-

---

of the Religion of Israel (Cambridge, MA: Harvard University Press, 1973), pp. 274-289.

[3]See James E. Smith, 1 & 2 Samuel, The College Press NIV Commentary (Joplin, MO: College Press, 2000), p. 17.

[4]For a critique of redactional views of DtrH, see Robert Polzin, Samuel and the Deuteronomist: A Literary Study of the Deuteronomistic History, Part 2: 1 Samuel (New York: Harper & Row, 1989), pp. 11-13; Nielsen, Tragedy in History, pp. 96-97; Burke O. Long, 1 Kings: With an Introduction to Historical Literature, vol. 9, The Forms of the Old Testament Literature (Grand Rapids: Eerdmans, 1984), pp. 16-21; Pauline A Viviano, "Glory Lost: The Reign of Solomon in the Deuteronomistic History," in The Age of Solomon: Scholarship at the Turn of the Millennium, ed. Lowell K. Handy (Leiden: Brill, 1997), pp. 336-337.

posed redactional boundaries, between a battle narrative and a prophet story, and indicate the narrative is a unified composition (see comments on 1 Kings 20). This example, which represents the use of only one technique in the composition, implies that Kings is the product of an author. The idea of a redactor is incompatible with the sophisticated use of allusion that characterizes this narrative.[5]

For the date of the book, Kings must have been written shortly after the release of Jehoiachin from prison in Babylon around 560 B.C. An exilic date means that the composition has been framed to address the situation of the exile.[6] As the inspired storyteller makes clear, sources were used to compose the history (e.g., "the book of the annals of Solomon" [1 Kgs 11:41], "the book of the annals of the kings of Israel" [14:19], and "the book of the annals of the kings of Judah" [14:29]), but the theological narrative is crafted to answer issues important to an exilic audience, the dominant question being: "How does one explain the fall of Jerusalem and the destruction of the temple in light of Yahweh's promise of an eternal throne for David (2 Samuel 7)?" Solomon's prayer at the dedication of the temple is one good place to see this dimension of the narrative. While the author indicates that his history is based on reliable sources (see comments on 1 Kgs 8:13), the episode is clearly retold for an exilic audience. The emphasis on prayer toward the temple (not sacrifices

---

[5]Serge Frolov's recent literary analysis of the succession narrative (i.e., much of 2 Samuel and 1 Kings 1–2) reflects current trends in the interpretation of DtrH and reinforces the position taken here. He concludes that the "subdivision [of DtrH] into fragmented narrative substrate and Deuteronomistic redactional layer(s) is not sufficiently warranted" ("Succession Narrative: A 'Document' or a Phantom?" *JBL* 12/1 [2002]: 104).

[6]A postexilic date for Kings DtrH, and much of the Hebrew Bible in the Hellenistic period is currently popular (see, e.g., Nielsen, *Tragedy*, p. 164), but unlikely (see, e.g., William G. Dever's critique of this position in *What Did the Biblical Writers Know and When Did They Know It? What Archaeology Can Tell Us about the Reality of Ancient Israel* [Grand Rapids: Eerdmans, 2001], pp. 273-276). A date for Kings in the early postexilic period is more plausible (so, e.g., Solomon's prayer is a call to pray toward a reconstructed temple in Jerusalem), but the fact that the conclusion of Kings does not know the edict of Cyrus (cf. 2 Chr 36:22-23; see Raymond B. Dillard and Tremper Longman III, *An Introduction to the Old Testament* [Grand Rapids: Zondervan, 1994], p. 161) and that passages like 2 Kgs 8:1-6 appear to offer hope that Israel's inheritance might be returned, imply an exilic date for the composition.

at the temple) would have particular meaning for the exiles (see comments on 1 Kings 8).[7] In the New Testament, a similar purpose explains some of the differences between the Gospel of John and the Synoptics. For example, the fact that there are no Sadducees in John may be reasonably explained when one recalls that the Gospel was written after the destruction of Jerusalem in A.D. 70, when the Pharisees dominated Judaism (the Sadducees receding into the background after the destruction of the temple). In this situation, John retells the story of Jesus in such a way that a polemic is set up between the ministry of Jesus and the Pharisees, who also represent the Jewish leaders of John's day. In his account, John selectively highlights the role that the Pharisees play in opposition to the ministry of Jesus, as the author of Kings highlights prayer in the account of the dedication of the temple.[8] The book of Chronicles also demonstrates how the same underlying history of Israel can be recast for another historical situation to answer additional questions. In the case of Chronicles, the composition is addressing for a postexilic audience whether Yahweh still cares for Judah. Recognizing an exilic audience for the story of Kings will help readers see many of the theological implications of the narrative.

The assumption of this commentary is that Kings was composed by a literary artist, an author, in the exile (probably in Babylon), sometime in the mid-sixth century B.C.[9] In light of this assumption, this person will be named "storyteller/narrator" (even in sections which are not dramatized) and "author/writer" through the course of the commentary.

---

[7]Gary N. Knoppers contends that Solomon's prayer is a late preexilic (i.e., from the time of Josiah's reforms) attempt to connect the king, the city, and the temple in a way that "bolsters the power of [the temple] by centralizing prayer" ("Prayer and Propaganda: Solomon's Dedication of the Temple and the Deuteronomist's Program," in *Reconsidering Israel and Judah: Recent Studies on the Deuteronomistic History*, ed. Gary N. Knoppers and J. Gordon McConville [Winona Lake, IN: Eisenbrauns, 2000], p. 374, cf. pp. 370-396). While he makes some cogent arguments, the most reasonable view is that 1 Kings 8 is framed for an exilic audience.

[8]See Raymond E. Brown, *The Gospel according to John (i-xii)*, The Anchor Bible, vol. 29 (New York: Doubleday, 1966), pp. lxx-lxxv.

[9]Cf. T.R. Hobbs, *2 Kings*, Word Biblical Commentary, vol. 13 (Waco, TX: Word Books, 1985), p. xxxiii; Burke O. Long, *1 Kings*, p. 21.

CHRONOLOGY

One important aspect of Kings that deserves special comment is chronology. The narratives of the kings of Judah and Israel are set in a chronological frame that provides structure to the composition. With each king, regnal notices give the length of the king's reign, a synchronism with the reign of the king in the corresponding kingdom, and for the kings of Judah the age of the king at his ascension to the throne. For the author of Kings, the attention to these details indicates his concern for chronology. However, the figures do not always add up.

There are in places inconsistencies between the lengths of reigns and the corresponding synchronisms.[10] For example, Pekah began his reign in the fifty-second and final year of the reign of Azariah of Judah and reigned twenty years (2 Kgs 15:27). Following the death of Azariah, Jotham reigned in Judah sixteen years (15:33), followed by his son Ahaz (16:2). However, Pekah was slain by Hoshea in the twentieth year of Jotham (15:30), and 2 Kings 17:1 says that Hoshea began to reign in the twelfth year of Ahaz of Judah. On the surface, these data are contradictory. In another type of discrepancy, the years in the regnal notations for the reigns of the kings in one kingdom do not always add up to the reigns of the kings in the other kingdom. For example, the total years for the reigns of the kings of Judah and Israel from the division of the kingdom in about 930 to the death of Ahaziah of Israel in the eighteenth year of Jehoshaphat (2 Kgs 3:1) should be the same, but the reigns for the kings of Judah add up to seventy-nine years and for the kings of Israel eighty-six years. In addition, on occasion there appears to be an inconsistency between the chronology in Kings and extrabiblical chronological information from surrounding states. In the records of Shalmaneser III, for example, references are made to Ahab's participation in the battle of Qarqar and twelve years later to tribute paid by Jehu. During the intervening period, the text in Kings documents the two-year reign of Ahaziah (2 Kgs 22:51) and the twelve-year reign of Joram (2 Kgs 3:1), which together eclipse the twelve years of the Assyrian records.

---

[10]For the following discussion, see Edwin R. Thiele, *The Mysterious Numbers of the Hebrew Kings*, rev. ed. (Grand Rapids: Kregel Publications; Zondervan, 1983), pp. 43-60; cf. Dillard and Longman, *Introduction*, pp. 156-159.

Some of the discrepancies can be explained by understanding how reigns were calculated in the ancient Near East. In the accession-year system (or postdating), the reign of the king was not counted until the first New Year following the king's ascension. In the nonaccession-year system (or antedating), the king's reign was figured from the first day of his kingship. Since in the nonaccession-year system the king's accession year is counted twice (as part of the reign of the preceding king and the beginning of the reign of the new king), this system of dating adds one year to each reign. To further complicate the issue, in some states the new year began in the month of Nisan in the spring, in others in the month of Tishri in the fall. In the text of Kings, there is evidence to suggest that Israel and Judah for much of the period of the divided kingdom employed different systems of reckoning reigns, while for brief periods their procedures were the same. Thiele argues that from the division of the kingdom Israel employed the nonaccession-year system until the reign of Jehoash. From his reign until the fall of Samaria, the accession-year system was used. In Judah, the accession-year system was the procedure from Solomon to the reign of Jehoram. Under the influence of the house of Ahab, the nonaccession-year system was employed from the reign of Jehoram to Joash. From the reign of Amaziah until the fall of Jerusalem, regnal counting followed the accession-year system. The two kingdoms apparently also began their regnal years at different times.[11]

Taking into account the additional year in the nonaccession-year system may resolve issues like some of the conflicting totals in the reigns of the kings of Judah versus the reigns of the kings of Israel. When the nonaccession-year counting is considered, the total reigns for the kings of Judah and Israel from the division of the kingdom to the death of Ahaziah are the same (seventy-nine years). Problems like the inconsistency between Kings and the record of Shalmaneser III for the period from the end of Ahab's reign to the reign of Jehu may also be resolved by factoring out the additional years. As a result, Ahaziah and Jotham ruled twelve actual years, which corresponds with the Assyrian records.[12] However, inconsistencies between the regnal notices and the synchronisms are often more difficult to

---

[11]Thiele, *Mysterious Numbers*, pp. 51-60.
[12]Ibid., pp. 49-51.

resolve. Thiele proposes coregencies (eight in all) and dual dating to solve such discrepancies. In the example of differences between the length of reigns and synchronisms cited above, the inconsistency in the statements about the length of Jotham's reign (that he reigned sixteen years [2 Kgs 15:33] and that he reigned twenty years [15:30]) may be explained by coregency. Thiele suggests the reasonable solution that Jotham was coregent with his son Ahaz during the last four years of his reign. But if this is accurate, it also means that the author of Kings is using "dual dating." The notation that Jotham reigned sixteen years must refer to his "official reign," whereas the reference to the twentieth year of Jotham encompasses his total reign, including the period when he was coregent with this father.[13]

Thiele's approach is not without its shortcomings. Some are uncomfortable with the fact that coregencies are usually inferred (not explicitly stated), and not everyone accepts the principle of dual dating.[14] In the final analysis, there is no approach that is completely satisfying. While perhaps overstating the case somewhat, Dillard and Longman maintain the chronological notations in Kings "remain something of an enigma."[15] Nevertheless, Thiele has contributed a plausible strategy for solving many, if not all, of the chronological difficulties in Kings. In the commentary below, specific issues of chronology will be addressed as they arise in the course of the discussion. The following chart is adapted from Thiele's outline of the chronology of the kings of Judah and Israel[16] and may be used for reference.

---

[13]Jotham apparently was also coregent with his father Azariah for about ten years (during the time that Azariah was smitten with leprosy), which was counted as part of Jotham's official reign. For a more in-depth discussion of the chronological issues surrounding the reigns of Jotham and Ahaz, and related issues (e.g., the difficulty with Pekah's twenty year reign in Israel), see ibid., pp. 118-138; and comments on 2 Kgs 15:27-28.

[14]See Hobbs, *2 Kings*, pp. xliii-xliv; Gershon Galil, *The Chronology of the Kings of Israel and Judah*, Studies in the History and Culture of the Ancient Near East, ed. B. Halpern and M.H.E. Weippert (Leiden: E.J. Brill, 1996), pp. 3-4; Dillard and Longman, *Introduction*, pp. 158-159.

[15]Dillard and Longman, *Introduction*, p. 159.

[16]Thiele, *Mysterious Numbers*, p. 10.

Dates of the Rulers of Judah and Israel

Judah	B.C.	Israel	B.C.
Rehoboam	930-913	Jeroboam I	930-909
Abijah	913-910		
Asa	910-869	Nadab	909-908
		Baasha	908-886
		Elah	886-885
		Zimri	885
		Tibni	885-880
		Omri	885-874
Jehoshaphat coregent	872-869	Ahab	874-853
Jehoshaphat total reign	872-848	Ahaziah	853-852
Jehoram coregent	853-848	Joram	852-841
Jehoram total reign	853-841		
Ahaziah	841	Jehu	841-814
Athaliah	841-835		
Joash	835-796	Jehoahaz	814-798
Amaziah	796-767	Jehoash	798-782
Azariah overlap with Amaziah	792-767	Jeroboam II coregency	793-782
Azariah (Uzziah) total reign	792-740	Jeroboam II total reign	793-753
Zechariah	753		
Shallum	752		
Menachem	752-742		
Jotham coregency	750-740	Pekah	752-732
Jotham official years	750-735	Pekahiah	742-740
Jotham total years	750-732		
Ahaz overlap with Jotham	735-732		
Ahaz official years	732-715	Hoshea	732-723
Hezekiah coregent[17]	*729-715*		
Hezekiah *sole reign*	715-686		
Manasseh coregent	696-686		
Manasseh total reign	696-642		
Amon	642-640		
Josiah	640-609		
Jehoahaz	609		
Jehoiakim	609-598		
Jehoiachin	598-597		
Zedekiah	597-586		

LITERARY ANALYSIS

In recent decades, scholars have rediscovered the literary dimension of the Old Testament. With the historical books (especially the

---

[17]Instead of coregency, Thiele posits an emendation by a late editor (at
2 Kgs 18:1-2,9-10) to explain apparent inconsistencies in the text (ibid., pp.
135-136, 174-176). For the possibility of a coregency with Ahaz, see the
introductory comments on 2 Kings 18–20.

Primary History, Genesis through 2 Kings), this has meant a deem-
phasis on historical questions and a turn toward issues of literary
composition and style. The result has been that Hebrew narrative
has emerged as an extremely well-crafted body of literature. In fact,
many have been taken aback by the sophisticated nature of Hebrew
storytelling. For that reason, the way biblical narratives are read has
changed. Instead of relegating the narrative sections of the Old
Testament to questions of history and background, for the more
overtly theological sections of Scripture, scholars and lay people
alike are reading these narratives more as stories (many in the
church have intuitively read biblical narrative this way for centuries)
— stories that are crafted for theological ends, to say something
about God's interaction with his creation in the story of Israel.
Robert Alter even avers it well may be that it is only in reading
Hebrew narratives as stories that readers are able "to see more clearly what they mean to tell us about God, man, and the perilously
momentous realm of history."[18]

As a result of the renewed emphasis on the literary dimension of
Scripture, narrative criticism of the Hebrew Bible has described the
techniques of storytelling employed by its authors. Adele Berlin
describes her work on the poetics of biblical narrative as an effort to
come up with the recipe (i.e., how the stories are told) for Bible stories.[19] Hermeneutically, if one has the formula for storytelling in
Scripture, he is going to be better able to discover the intent of the
author.[20] Understanding the methods used by the storyteller gives

---

[18]Robert Alter, *The Art of Biblical Narrative* (New York: Basic Books,
1981), p. 189.

[19]Adele Berlin, *Poetics and Interpretation of Biblical Narrative*, Bible and
Literature Series, vol. 9 (Sheffield: The Almond Press, 1983; reprint,
Winona Lake, IN: Eisenbrauns, 1994), p. 15 (page citations are to the orig-
inal edition).

[20]This view is not shared by everyone. Many place more emphasis on the
reader in interpretation and question whether one can determine the intent
of the author (see, e.g., Willem S. Vorster, "Readings, Readers, and the
Succession Narrative: An Essay on Reception," in *Beyond Form Criticism:
Essays in Old Testament Literary Criticism*, ed. Paul R. House, Sources for
Biblical and Theological Study, vol. 2 [Winona Lake, IN: Eisenbrauns,
1992], pp. 395-407). J.P. Fokkelman believes biblical texts were written to
stand on their own, without the need to appeal to the author and his situation. According to Fokkelman, what is needed for responsible interpreta-

direction to the reader and militates against the indiscriminate use (i.e., out of context) of Old Testament stories as "illustrations" for New Testament sermons. It will also undermine the tendency to spiritualize or moralize from Old Testament stories.[21] Hebrew narrative can be read on its own terms for determining what the inspired storyteller is saying about Israel's history for an audience in exile — and as sacred Scripture for subsequent generations of believers. Because of the large amount of story in the composition, these understandings are important for a commentary on Kings. In fact, one can view Kings as being composed of dramatized stories (e.g., the Elijah/Ahab narrative, 1 Kgs 16:29–22:40) that are set in a chronological frame.[22] Narrative criticism is essential for interpreting the stories, but even the frame (in which reigns are chronicled in exposition) displays "narrative" features. The narrator's voice continues in the expository sections (occasionally interspersed with dialogue), which are also characterized by the same indirect style of the dramatized stories. For example, in the chronological frame apparently inconsistent statements are often juxtaposed, leaving the reader to draw the appropriate, often ironic, inferences and conclusions (see, e.g., comments on 14:25-28). As in the dramatized stories, meaning is conveyed indirectly.

The discussion now turns to summarize some of the more important techniques of composition that appear in Kings.[23] The narrative

---

tion is a "competent reader" (*Reading Biblical Narrative: An Introductory Guide*, trans. Ineke Smit [Louisville, KY: Westminster John Knox Press, 1999], pp. 22-23). However, even if one considers the important role the reader plays in interpretation, meaning must be controlled by the text. Recognizing the sophisticated literary design in Hebrew stories directs the reader toward intentionality — since "design demands a designer!"

[21]See Sidney Greidanus, *The Modern Preacher and the Ancient Text: Interpreting and Preaching Biblical Literature* (Grand Rapids: Eerdmans, 1988), pp. 157-187.

[22]G. Michael Hagan, "First and Second Kings," in *A Complete Literary Guide to the Bible*, ed. Leland Ryken and Tremper Longman III (Grand Rapids: Zondervan, 1993), p. 184.

[23]For an introduction to narrative criticism of the Hebrew Bible, see Alter, *The Art of Biblical Narrative*; Berlin, *Poetics and Interpretation*; Fokkelman, *Reading Biblical Narrative*; Shimon Bar-Efrat, *Narrative Art in the Bible*, JSOTSup 70 (Sheffield: The Almond Press, 1989); Meir Sternberg, *The Poetics of Biblical Narrative: Ideological Literature and the Drama of Reading*, Indiana Studies in Biblical Literature (Bloomington: Indiana University Press, 1987);

of Naaman's healing and the subsequent affliction of Gehazi will illustrate many of the conventions that are discussed.[24]

Analysis of the recipe for Old Testament stories reveals that Hebrew narrative is scenic, moving from one scene to another with a scarcity of detail. Unlike modern forms of storytelling, there is little description of characters or scenes. When there is description, it is frequently significant. Readers are invited to create their own visual images, a technique which draws the reader into the story. Hebrew stories also display plot with narrative tension and structure (often in concentric [i.e., ABC/C′B′A′] or parallel [ABC/A′B′C′] patterns). Dialogue dominates, usually with two actors on the stage at one time. When dialogue appears, the pace of the narrative slows, and the narrated time corresponds with real time. The reader hears for himself; the story is not "told," but "shown." A careful reader takes notice when this happens, for, more often than not, the narrator will convey meaning in these dramatized scenes. In fact, one of the hallmarks of Hebrew narrative is its indirect style, where meaning is expressed obliquely through character speeches and actions — in other words, in a story. In the Naaman narrative (2 Kings 5), tension is created initially when Naaman is described as an Aramean leper, through whom Yahweh had given victory to Aram over Israel (5:1). Dialogue begins after only two verses of exposition, and the lack of detail in the narrative calls the reader to visualize the events of the story. A concentric structure begins with the introduction of the leper Naaman and ends with the leprous servant of Elisha, Gehazi (5:1,27).

Like other forms of good storytelling, the major characters in Hebrew narrative are often complex, true to life. Characters are developed by what they say (including inner speech) and do, what is said about them, and how they contrast/compare with other characters (or with themselves in other scenes). Often, character speeches and actions are ambiguous. The reader experiences the character as one does in real life, observing what they say and what they do — invited to draw evaluative conclusions about the character's persona in relation to other characters and the God of the story. Tension

---

David M. Gunn and Danna Nolan Fewell, *Narrative in the Hebrew Bible*, The Oxford Bible Series (Oxford: Oxford University Press, 1993).

[24]For a more detailed literary analysis of the Naaman narrative, see comments on 2 Kings 5.

created by the ambiguity may intensify when characters reflect different points of view.

Point of view is a technique the storyteller often uses for dynamic effect. In what they say and how they act, both major and minor characters reflect differing perspectives, which give the stories more depth. Also, like a camera, the narrator's telling eye often moves to narrate a story from different perspectives, sometimes in a panoramic view, at other times watching a character perform, even at times within a character revealing his inner thoughts (i.e., inner life). At all times, the omniscient narrator is in control. While a reader may question whether the statement of a character is true, statements by the narrator are reliable.[25] Whether in exposition or through character actions and dialogue, the narrator orchestrates events. He may even intentionally leave gaps in the story to further draw the reader into the narrative. Consequently, it is in and through the story that the narrator indirectly projects his own ideological point of view.[26] With Naaman, the storyteller highlights the contrasting perspectives of the various characters in the story and focuses especially on the point of view of Naaman. He even leaves a gap in the narrative as to Elisha's motivation for not receiving the Aramean, allowing the reader to see things from Naaman's point of view (5:9-12). The change in the foreign commander's perspective is a crucial aspect of the story. Through Naaman, the ideological point of view of the author is also verbalized: "there is no God in all the world except in Israel" (5:15).

Another hallmark of Hebrew storytelling is repetition. Repeated actions and speeches (by characters or by the narrator) may indicate

---

[25]Some question whether the narrator is always reliable (cf. David M. Gunn, "New Directions in the Study of Biblical Hebrew Narrative," in *Reconsidering Israel and Judah: Recent Studies on the Deuteronomistic History*, ed. Gary N. Knoppers and J. Gordon McConville, Sources for Biblical and Theological Study, vol. 8 [Winona Lake, IN: Eisenbrauns, 2000], pp. 566-577).

[26]In some narrative works, it is important to distinguish between the actual author and the implied author/narrator (also the actual audience and implied audience). For example, C.S. Lewis is the author of both *The Screwtape Letters* and *The Chronicles of Narnia*, but each one has a different narrator (analogy suggested by David Shelburne, a Lubbock Christian University graduate student). However, since this distinction is not made with Hebrew narrative (i.e., the Primary History), the author and the implied author/narrator, for all practical purposes, are one and the same.

emphasis. Sometimes dialogue is even repeated by the narrator, which may serve to highlight the statement or point of view of a character. Subtle changes in repeated phrases may also be significant. The repetition of key words (technically designated *Leitworter*), motifs, and themes is an especially important technique. Often the ideological stance of the narrative will not be too far from a cluster of repeated words or themes. In the story of Naaman, a "great/little" motif serves the storyteller to characterize Naaman, as the "great" commander is healed only when he becomes "little" in his own eyes and submits. His flesh becomes that of a "little" boy (5:14). This motif also calls attention to the important role that contrast often plays in Hebrew storytelling. The contrast between the "great" commander and the "little" girl (and the "great woman," the Shunammite, in ch. 4) establishes a frame for evaluating the character of Naaman and the change that he undergoes in the narrative. By the end of the story, however, the reader discovers that the most glaring contrast is between Naaman and Elisha's servant Gehazi. With structural irony,[27] the storyteller by contrast casts Gehazi as the outsider. At the end of the narrative, the servant of Elisha leaves unclean, with Naaman's leprosy (5:27).

The characterization of Gehazi illustrates another literary technique that the author of Kings uses for maximum effect. When Gehazi takes silver and clothing from Naaman and hides them in his house, he mirrors the actions of Achan, who took gold, silver, and clothing and hid them beneath his tent (Josh 7:19-21). The allusion frames the actions of Gehazi and serves to characterize him negatively. Later, when four lepers take gold, silver, and clothing from the Aramean camp and hide them (2 Kgs 7:8), both the story of Achan and Gehazi are actualized in such a way that their actions call attention to Yahweh's unseen actions in the story. According to Elisha's prophecy, the windows of heaven open, and the city of Samaria is blessed with bounty from the Arameans (7:1-2,17-20). When Gehazi emerges without leprosy in 8:1-6, the preceding scenes resurface to raise the hope of restoration for an exilic audi-

---

[27]Brandon L. Fredenburg delineates three kinds of irony in Hebrew Scripture, "verbal, dramatic, and structural," and describes how they are intentionally used in the Ahab narrative ("With Horns of Irony: The Implications of Irony in the Narrative of Ahab's Reign [1 Kings 16:29–22:40]," (Ph.D. diss., University of Denver and The Iliff School of Theology, 2003]).

ence. All of this is accomplished with the use of intratextual (within Kings) and intertextual allusions (with texts outside of Kings).

The use of allusion as a technique of composition is important for the overall purposes of the storyteller. Allusions to antecedent narratives enable the author of Kings to situate and frame characters and events in light of earlier stories in the sacred history. This has the effect of giving additional commentary on the story of kingship in Judah and Israel and guides the reader in interpretation.[28] In Kings, allusions frame characters (and their stories) as follows: Adonijah//Absalom; Solomon//Moses, and then Pharaoh in his harsh rule; Rehoboam//Pharaoh, as he follows in his father's footsteps; Jeroboam//Moses, and then Aaron as he sets up golden calves; Elijah//Joshua/Moses; Elisha//Elijah/Joshua; Ahab//Saul/Achan; Naboth//Achan, in the way he was executed; Gehazi//Achan; Hezekiah//David; Manasseh//Ahab; Josiah//Solomon/Moses, and Ahab when he humbles himself; Jehoiachin//Joseph, and Joash as the one who carries the Davidic promise (see comments on the various stories for specific allusions). The larger pattern suggests that the storyteller (in dialogue with Deuteronomy) deliberately set out to frame the story of kingship in Israel with the Exodus and conquest narratives. Israel lost her right to the land and was dispossessed like the Canaanites. In addition, the account of the house of Ahab and the subsequent decline and fall of Samaria frame the fall of Judah and Jerusalem.[29] As Joash survived the destruction of the

---

[28]Dennis Ronald MacDonald describes the "transvaluation" of aspects of Homeric epic in the *The Acts of Andrew*, where through allusion values in the earlier texts are replaced in the subsequent text ("Is There a Privileged Reader? A Case from the Apocryphal Acts," *Semeia* 71 [1995]: 32). While the author of Kings does not use antecedent texts in the same way as does the author of *The Acts of Andrew* (cf. pp. 30-33), the use of allusion in both documents appears to represent an ancient technique of composition.

[29]George Savran observes that the larger composition of 1 and 2 Kings is concentric, with the account of the Omride dynasty at the center of the composition ("1 and 2 Kings," in *The Literary Guide to the Bible*, ed. Robert Alter and Frank Kermode [Cambridge, MA: The Belknap Press of Harvard University Press, 1987], pp. 148-149). Since a concentric structure highlights what is at the center, the story of the Omrides stands out in Kings, in part for the defeat of Baal worship and the role of prophecy in Israel. But through the narrator's use of allusion, the account of the Omrides also frames the events to follow, which demonstrates a sophisticated literary strategy for Kings.

house of Ahab (which was linked to the house of David), so Jehoiachin survives the judgment on the house of David. When he is released from prison in exile, hope is rekindled that the promise to David of an eternal throne (2 Samuel 7) might yet be fulfilled.

The impact on reading is profound. Recognizing the literary dimension of Hebrew narrative, including Kings, suggests that meaning is usually found in reading the larger context. The text creates its own world for interpretation as speeches, actions, and statements by the narrator have meaning in context with other speeches, actions, and statements by the narrator — within Kings and in the larger canon. It also means that the underlying events are selectively retold in order to achieve theological goals. The ensuing commentary will demonstrate the sophisticated literary design of the narrative of Kings. However, recognizing this aspect of the composition does not preclude reading the narratives as good history. V. Phillips Long adeptly defends reading Hebrew narrative as both good literature and reliable history. In his discussion, he describes the dynamic interplay of what he names the three "impulses" of Hebrew narrative: history, literature, and theology.[30] The relationship between these three aspects of the text is represented in the following diagram:

The Dimensions of Hebrew Narrative

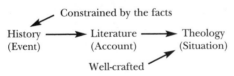

Describing Hebrew narrative as "representational" (as opposed to "nonrepresentational" art forms), Long believes that the authors of these narratives were "in some measure" constrained by the facts of Israel's history.[31] At the same time, however, they framed Israel's his-

---

[30]V. Phillips Long, "The Art of Biblical History," in *Foundations of Contemporary Interpretation*, ed. Moisés Silva (Grand Rapids: Zondervan, 1996), p. 327. Long is responding to Alter's characterization of Hebrew narrative as "fictionalized history" and "historicized fiction," p. 321; cf. Alter, *The Art of Biblical Narrative*, pp. 24-25).

[31]Ibid., pp. 325-327.

tory in a well-crafted account of events. The two ideas (i.e., good literature and reliable history) are not mutually exclusive. And, most important, even though they are cast as stories, these narratives are theological compositions, written for the purpose of addressing questions about Yahweh's relationship with Israel. The diagram brings out the dynamic relationship the text maintains with the underlying history (as the authors are "constrained" by the facts) and indicates that its theological purposes are enabled by the nature of the literature, as well-crafted narrative. Without the creative way the story of kingship is recounted in Kings, it would simply be a chronicle of selected events in the history of Israel. Instead, it is a brilliant literary composition and a theological masterpiece that answers fundamental questions about Yahweh's commitment to his people after the fall of Jerusalem.

In this commentary, these three dimensions of the text will be kept before the reader. The discussion will highlight the literary dimension of the narrative, which has too often been overlooked. At the same time, historical issues and background information from archaeology and Near Eastern studies will be discussed in order to maintain the important connection with the underlying events. But the goal is theological. Attention to the situation of an exilic audience will direct the modern reader to the questions of the narrative and, by extension, to important theological meanings for the people of God in any generation.

THEOLOGY

Recognizing that the narrative of Kings was skillfully written to address important theological questions for a Judean audience in exile enables a modern reader to draw out of the text several important themes. From this brilliantly conceived and well-executed story of kingship in Israel, the following theological issues stand out:

1) Kings is clearly a theodicy (i.e., an attempt to justify a troubling act of God), written in part to answer the question, "Why has the LORD done such a thing to this land and to this temple?" (1 Kgs 9:8). The answer in Kings is that Yahweh is not capricious; Israel and Judah are punished "because they have forsaken the LORD their God, who brought their fathers out of Egypt, and have embraced

other gods, worshiping and serving them—that is why the LORD brought all this disaster on them" (9:9).

2) This answer, however, creates tension in the composition. Jerusalem is destroyed, and the descendants of Israel are exiled because they have broken covenant with Yahweh — but what about Yahweh's promise to David that his house and his kingdom would be established and endure forever (2 Samuel 7)? This is the tension between the conditional Mosaic covenant and the unconditional Davidic covenant — the tension between law and grace. The Mosaic covenant provides the legal basis for the destruction of Jerusalem, but what about the covenant with David? An exilic audience knows what Yahweh has done to his house, the place where he caused his name to dwell. The underlying question of Kings is, "How can the covenant with David be unconditional? Will there be grace in the end for the exiles?"

3) In the process of wrestling with the tension between the two covenants, other theological issues emerge. One important theme that surfaces in the course of the story is the tension between the sovereignty of God and free will. While neat schemes of proof-texts may be marshaled to defend the complete sovereignty of God or, on the other hand, the free will the creator has bestowed on humans, the story of Kings affirms both ideas. Yahweh's sovereign will is established in the course of Israel's history, and the kings of Judah and Israel demonstrate free will in their choices to serve or not serve the God of Israel. This tension is maintained, for example, in the storyteller's account of Solomon's ascension to the throne (1 Kings 1-2). Indirectly, the narrator demonstrates that Solomon is Yahweh's choice — that the God of Israel is working to keep his promise to David. However, the distance the storyteller keeps between Yahweh and the actions of Solomon indicates that the king's executions (Adonijah, Joab, and Shimei; 1 Kings 2:13-46) to "establish" the kingdom "in his hand" are of his own volition.

4) An aspect of the tension between the sovereignty of God and free will is the question of how God works in the world. The narrative of Kings indicates that all of creation is at his disposal. In Kings, Yahweh works through and uses faithful kings (e.g., Josiah [2 Kings 23), unfaithful/wicked kings (e.g., Baasha [1 Kings 15:33-16:7]), overzealous kings (e.g., Jehu [2 Kings 9-10]), faithful prophets (e.g., Elijah [2 Kings 1]), overzealous prophets (e.g., Elijah [1 Kings 21]),

unfaithful/"foreign" prophets (e.g., the old prophet from Bethel [1 Kings 13], Zedekiah and Ahab's prophets [1 Kings 22]), lying prophets and lying spirits (e.g., Micaiah and the lying spirit [1 Kings 22]), foreign kings (e.g., Sennacherib [2 Kings 18–19]), and perhaps even foreign gods (e.g., Chemosh [2 Kings 3]) to do his bidding. The audience of Kings would be encouraged to know that Yahweh is Lord of history, the absolute ruler of heaven and earth who was in control of their situation in exile.

5) A prophet-fulfillment theme also runs through the narrative. Stories like the widow of Zarephath demonstrate the power of the prophetic word (1 Kings 17). The theme of the fulfillment of the word of Yahweh would be important for an exilic audience who, with the destruction of the temple and exile of the Davidic king, had reason to doubt God's promises.[32] At the same time, in the Elijah narrative especially, Kings introduces the idea of prophetic initiative and suggests that prophets of Yahweh are also flawed (1 Kings 17–19, 21; 2 Kings 1; see "Excursus: Elijah in Context, Literary Artistry for Theological Ends" below). Yet, even with imperfect prophets like Elijah, Yahweh's words (and the words of his prophet) are fulfilled. The question of true and false prophecy may also underlie stories like the man of God from Judah in 1 Kings 13 and Micaiah and the lying spirit in 1 Kings 22. If so, the storyteller reiterates the criteria laid out by Moses in the "law of the prophet" (Deut 18:14-22; cf. 1 Kgs 22:28). Moreover, in the account of Jehu's purge, the storyteller appears to address the misuse of the prophetic word, which still comes to pass. Jehu destroys the house of Ahab according to prophecy, but also appropriates the word of Elijah for his own political ends. Yahweh commends Jehu for carrying out his prophetic word and punishes the house of Jehu for his indiscretions (see comments on 2 Kings 9–10).

6) In line with the role the Mosaic covenant plays in Kings, the book of Deuteronomy lies behind the composition. Moses' speeches in Deuteronomy frame statements and stories in Kings, often with Deuteronomic language and themes. Dillard and Longman write, "[The writer of Kings] takes laws that are unique to the book of Deuteronomy as the spectacles through which he assesses the his-

---

[32]Dillard and Longman, *Introduction*, p. 164.

tory of the nation."[33] For example, the "law of the king" in Deuteronomy 17:14-20 serves as a frame for reading the account of Solomon's reign. When Solomon acquires horses, silver, gold, and wives, an informed reader recognizes that his actions run counter to the faithful king envisioned by Moses. But Kings (and the rest of DtrH) also provides commentary on Deuteronomy. When Elijah retreats to Sinai and then steps beyond the instructions of Yahweh in his judgment on Ahab (1 Kings 19, 21), the author of Kings extends (i.e., "applies") the "law of the prophet" in Deuteronomy 18:14-22. Even faithful prophets of Yahweh can speak presumptuously. A prophet of Yahweh must be careful to speak only the words of Yahweh (see "Excursus: Elijah in Context, Literary Artistry for Theological Ends" below).[34]

7) The author of Kings claims Yahweh alone is God. When, following the defeat of the prophets of Baal on Mount Carmel, the people cry, "The LORD—he is God!" (1 Kgs 18:39), and Naaman, after being healed of his leprosy, exclaims, "Now I know that there is no God in all the world except in Israel" (2 Kgs 5:15), the theological stance of the author is verbalized. A related aspect of God's nature is expressed when at the dedication of the temple Solomon says, "The heavens, even the highest heaven, cannot contain you. How much less the temple I have built!" (1 Kgs 8:27). With "name theology," Solomon explains Yahweh's presence in the house that he builds and calls on Yahweh to hear from heaven (8:29-30). A modern reader would say that Yahweh is omnipresent and omniscient. However, the theology of Kings is bigger than an apologetic claim about the supremacy of the God of Israel who rules (and hears) from heaven. The underlying message of the book is something more like the following: "Yahweh is not like the gods of the nations and should not be treated that way!" The mistake Israel and her kings make is in becoming like the nations they were to dispossess from the Promised Land. This happens when they emulate

---

[33]Ibid., p. 162.

[34]Gary N. Knoppers claims that Dtr's "use of Deuteronomy is sophisticated hermeneutically." He is "an independent author who often goes his own way" in his application of Deuteronomy to the history of Israel ("Solomon's Fall and Deuteronomy," in *The Age of Solomon: Scholarship at the Turn of the Millennium*, ed. Lowell K. Handy [Leiden: Brill, 1997], p. 409; see comments on 1 Kings 11:1-10).

Canaanite lifestyle and become enmeshed in idolatry. But their idolatry is not displayed primarily in worshiping other gods; it is in having an idolatrous attitude toward their own God, Yahweh. For them, he becomes just another god, an idol created in Israel's own image — who can be manipulated and controlled by appropriate ritual and religious service (see comments on 2 Kings 23). If Kings says anything about Israel's God, it says that he is not a God who can be directed, or over whom one can have power. Those who would call on the God of Abraham, Moses, and David must submit and listen to him!

8) The plot of Kings demonstrates that kingship, as an institution, does not deliver. But the underlying message is even more pointed. Not only does kingship not deliver, when a son of David is raised up who repents and faithfully restores the covenant, Yahweh's wrath is not assuaged. In Kings, Josiah is the loyal son, a Moseslike king who reestablishes the covenant with Yahweh. But even a righteous king is not able to undo the coming judgment. In a premature death, Josiah receives a measure of grace, but Judah and Jerusalem will experience the wrath of Yahweh (see comments 2 Kings 22–23). By implication, *repentance* and covenant *restoration*, in and of themselves, do not save. While Kings lauds the reformers among the kings of Judah (cf., e.g., 1 Kgs 15:9-15) and calls on an exilic audience to repent and turn to Yahweh (see comments on 1 Kings 13–14), the message of the book is that Yahweh is the one who saves. Recognizing that Moses said Yahweh would bring them back to the land and circumcise their hearts to love him (Deut 30:6), so an audience in exile must wait on Yahweh to deliver.

9) The release of Jehoiachin (meaning "Yahweh will establish") from prison at the end of the book indicates that there is grace in the end. Yahweh has not forgotten his promise to "establish" the throne of David forever (see comments on 2 Kgs 25:27-30). In the tension between the Mosaic and Davidic covenants, between law and grace, God's people should repent and look for grace. The Christian knows that, in due time, grace comes in David's greatest son, Jesus!

OUTLINE

BIBLIOGRAPHY

Aberbach, Moses, and Leivy Smolar. "Aaron, Jeroboam, and the Golden Calves." *JBL* 86 (June 1967): 129-140.

Ackerman, James S. "Knowing Good and Evil: A Literary Analysis of the Court History in 2 Samuel 9–20 and 1 Kings 1–2." *JBL* 109/1 (1990): 41-64.

Aharoni, Miriam, Ze'ev Herzog, and Anson Rainey. "Arad — An Ancient Israelite Fortress with a Temple to Yahweh." *BAR* 13/2 (March/April 1987): 16-35.

Aharoni, Yohanan. *The Land of the Bible: A Historical Geography*. 2nd ed. Philadelphia: Westminster, 1979.

Alter, Robert. *The Art of Biblical Narrative*. New York: Basic Books, 1981.

Appler, Deborah A. "From Queen to Cuisine: Food Imagery in the Jezebel Narrative." *Semeia* 86 (1999): 55-71.

Arav, Rami, Richard A. Freund, and John F. Schroder, Jr. "Bethsaida Rediscovered: Long-Lost City Found North of Galilee Shore." *BAR* 26/1 (Jan./Feb. 2000): 44-51, 53-56.

Avner, Uzi. "Sacred Stones in the Desert." *BAR* 27/3 (May/June 2001): 30-41.

Bar-Efrat, Shimon. "Literary Modes and Methods in the Biblical Narrative: In View of 2 Samuel 10–20 and 1 Kings 1–2." *Immanuel* 8 (Spring 1978): 19-31.

——————. *Narrative Art in the Bible*. JSOT Supplement Series 70. Sheffield: The Almond Press, 1989.

Barker, Margaret. "Hezekiah's Boil." *JSOT* 95 (2001): 31-42.

Beach, Eleanor Ferris. "The Samaria Ivories, Marzeah? and the Biblical Text." *BA* 56/2 (June 1993): 94-104.

Begg, Christopher T. "Unifying Factors in 2 Kings 1.2-17a." *JSOT* 32 (1985): 75-86.

Ben-Tor, Amnon. "Solomon's City Rises from the Ashes: Excavating Hazor, Part One." *BAR* 25/2 (March/April 1999): 26-37, 60.

Berlin, Adele. *Poetics and Interpretation of Biblical Narrative.* Vol. 9. Bible and Literature Series. Sheffield: The Almond Press, 1983. Reprint, Winona Lake, IN: Eisenbrauns, 1994.

Biran, Avraham. *Biblical Dan.* Jerusalem: Israel Exploration Society, 1994.

──────── . "Tel Dan: Biblical Texts and Archaeological Data." In *Scripture and Other Artifacts: Essays on the Bible and Archaeology in Honor of Philip J. King.* Ed. by Michael D. Coogan, J. Cheryl Exum, and Lawrence E. Stager. Pp. 1-17. Louisville, KY: Westminster John Knox Press, 1994.

──────── . "The Tel Dan Inscription: A New Fragment." *IEJ* 45/1 (1995): 1-18.

──────── . "Two Bronze Plaques and the *Ḥuṣṣot* of Dan." *IEJ* 49/1-2 (1999): 43-54.

Biran, Avraham, and Joseph Naveh. "The Tel Dan Inscription: A New Fragment." *IEJ* 45/1 (1995): 1-18.

Bleibtreu, Erika. "Grisly Assyrian Record of Torture and Death." *BAR* 17/1 (Jan./Feb. 1991): 52-61, 75.

Blenkinsopp, Joseph. "The Babylonian Gap Revisited: There Was No Gap." *BAR* 28/3 (May/June 2002): 36-38, 59.

Bloch-Smith, Elizabeth. "'Who Is the King of Glory?' Solomon's Temple and Its Symbolism." In *Scripture and Other Artifacts: Essays on the Bible and Archaeology in Honor of Philip J. King.* Ed. by Michael D. Coogan, J. Cheryl Exum, and Lawrence E. Stager. Pp. 18-31. Louisville, KY: Westminster John Knox Press, 1994.

Bodner, Keith. "Nathan: Prophet, Politician and Novelist?" *JSOT* 95 (2001): 43-54.

Bordreuil, Pierre, Felice Israel, and Dennis Pardee. "King's Command and Widow's Plea: Two New Hebrew Ostraca of the Biblical Period." *NEA* 61/1 (March 1998): 2-5, 7, 9-13.

Borowski, Oded. "Hezekiah's Reforms and the Revolt against Assyria." *BA* 53/2 (1995): 148-154.

Bowman, Richard G. "Narrative Criticism: Human Purpose in Conflict with Divine Presence." In *Judges & Method: New Approaches in Biblical Studies*. Ed. by Gale A. Yee. Pp. 17-44. Minneapolis: Fortress Press, 1995.

Brown, Raymond E. *The Gospel according to John (i-xii)*. The Anchor Bible, vol. 29. New York: Doubleday, 1966.

Brueggemann, Walter. *1 & 2 Kings*. Smyth & Helwys Bible Commentary. Macon, GA: Smyth & Helwys, 2000.

Cahill, Jane, Karl Reinhard, David Tarler, and Peter Warnock. "It Had to Happen — Scientists Examine Remains of Ancient Bathroom." *BAR* 17/3 (May/June 1991): 64-69.

Callender, Dexter E., Jr. "Servants of God[s] and Servants of Kings in Israel and the Ancient Near East." *Semeia* 83/84 (1998): 67-82.

Cogan, Mordechai. *1 Kings: A New Translation with Introduction and Commentary*. The Anchor Bible, vol. 10. New York: Doubleday, 2001.

_____ . "Sennacherib's Siege of Jerusalem: Once or Twice?" *BAR* 27/1 (Jan./Feb. 2001): 40-45, 69.

Cogan, Mordechai, and Hayim Tadmor. *II Kings: A New Translation with Introduction and Commentary*. The Anchor Bible, vol. 11. New York: Doubleday, 1988.

Cogan, Morton. *Imperialism and Religion: Assyria, Judah and Israel in the Eighth and Seventh Centuries B.C.E.* Missoula, MT: Society of Biblical Literature and Scholars Press, 1974.

Cohen, Rudolph, and Yigal Yisrael. "The Iron Age Fortresses at 'En Ḥaseva." *BA* 58/4 (Dec. 1995): 223-235.

_____ . "Smashing the Idols: Piecing Together an Edomite Shrine in Judah." *BAR* 22/4 (July/Aug. 1996): 40-45, 48-51, 65.

Cohn, Robert L. "Convention and Creativity in the Book of Kings: The Case of the Dying Monarch." *CBQ* 47 (1985): 603-616.

_____ . *2 Kings*. Berit Olam: Studies in Hebrew Narrative & Poetry. Collegeville, MN: A Michael Glazier Book, The Liturgical Press, 2000.

Conroy, Charles. "Hiel between Ahab and Elijah-Elisha: 1 Kgs 16,34 in Its Immediate Literary Context." *Biblica* 77, fasc. 2 (1996): 210-218.

Coote, Robert B. "Yahweh Recalls Elijah." In *Traditions in Transformation: Turning Points in Biblical Faith.* Ed. by Baruch Halpern and Jon D. Levenson. Pp. 115-120. Winona Lake, IN: Eisenbrauns, 1981.

Cross, Frank Moore. *Canaanite Myth and Hebrew Epic: Essays in the History of the Religion of Israel.* Cambridge, MA: Harvard University Press, 1973.

_____. "King Hezekiah's Seal Bears Phoenician Imagery." *BAR* 25/2 (March/April 1999): 42-45, 60.

Curtis, J.E., and J.E. Reade, eds. *Art and Empire: Treasures from Assyria in the British Museum.* New York: The Metropolitan Museum of New York, 1995.

Daviau, Michéle, and Paul-Eugéne Dion. "Moab Comes to Life." *BAR* 28/1 (Jan./Feb. 2002): 38-49, 63.

Dearman, J. Andrew. *Religion & Culture in Ancient Israel.* Peabody, MA: Hendrickson, 1992.

Deutsch, Robert. "First Impression: What We Learn from King Ahaz's Seal." *BAR* 24/3 (May/June 1998): 54-56, 62.

_____. "New Bullae Reveal Egyptian-Style Emblems on Judah's Royal Seals." *BAR* 28/4 (July/Aug 2002): 42-51, 60-62.

Dever, William G. "Archaeology and the 'Age of Solomon': A Case-Study in Archaeology and Historiography." In *The Age of Solomon: Scholarship at the Turn of the Millennium.* Ed. by Lowell K. Handy. Pp. 217-251. Leiden: Brill, 1997.

_____. "The Silence of the Text: An Archaeological Commentary on 2 Kings 23." In *Scripture and Other Artifacts: Essays on the Bible and Archaeology in Honor of Philip J. King.* Ed. by Michael D. Coogan, J. Cheryl Exum, and Lawrence E. Stager. Pp. 1-17. Louisville, KY: Westminster John Knox Press, 1994.

_____. *What Did the Biblical Writers Know and When Did They Know It? What Archaeology Can Tell Us about the Reality of Ancient Israel.* Grand Rapids: Eerdmans, 2001.

DeVries, Simon J. *1 Kings.* Vol. 12. Word Biblical Commentary. Waco, TX: Word Books, 1985.

Dillard, Raymond B., and Tremper Longman III. *An Introduction to the Old Testament.* Grand Rapids: Zondervan, 1994.

Finkelstein, Israel. "The Archaeology of the Days of Manasseh." In *Scripture and Other Artifacts: Essays on the Bible and Archaeology in Honor of Philip J. King*. Ed. by Michael D. Coogan, J. Cheryl Exum, and Lawrence E. Stager. Pp. 169-187. Louisville, KY: Westminster John Knox Press, 1994.

Fokkelman, J.P. *King David (II Sam. 9-20 & I Kings 2-2)*. Vol. 1. Narrative Art and Poetry in the Books of Samuel: A Full Interpretation Based on Stylistic and Structural Analyses. Assen, The Netherlands: Van Gorcum, 1981.

_____. *Reading Biblical Narrative: An Introductory Guide*. Trans. by Ineke Smit. Louisville, KY: Westminster John Knox Press, 1999.

Fouts, David M. "A Defense of the Hyperbolic Interpretation of Large Numbers in the Old Testament." *JETS* 40 (1997): 377-387.

Fredenburg, Brandon L. "When Prophets Lie and Kings Win: A Narrative-Critical Examination of First Kings 22:1-38." Paper presented at the Christian Scholars Conference, Lubbock Christian University, 22 July 1995.

_____. "With Horns of Irony: The Implications of Irony in the Narrative of Ahab's Reign (1 Kings 16:29-22:40)." Ph.D. diss., University of Denver and The Iliff School of Theology, 2003.

Freedman, David Noel, ed. *Anchor Bible Dictionary*. 6 vols. New York: Doubleday, 1992.

Frisch, Amos. "The Exodus Motif in 1 Kings 1-14." *JSOT* 87 (2000): 3-21.

_____. "The Narrative of Solomon's Reign: A Rejoinder." *JSOT* 51 (1991): 22-24.

_____. "Structure and Its Significance: The Narrative of Solomon's Reign (1 Kings 1-12:24)." *JSOT* 51 (1991): 3-14.

Fritz, Volkmar. "Temple Architecture: What Can Archaeology Tell Us about Solomon's Temple." *BAR* 12/4 (July/Aug. 1987): 38-49.

Frolov, Serge. "Succession Narrative: A 'Document' or a Phantom." *JBL* 121/1 (2002): 81-104.

Gal, Zvi. "Cabul: A Royal Gift Found." *BAR* 19/2 (March/April 1993): 39-44, 84.

Galil, Gershon. *The Chronology of the Kings of Israel and Judah*. Studies in the History and Culture of the Ancient Near East. Ed. by B. Halpern and M.H.E. Weippert. Leiden: E.J. Brill, 1996.

Garcia-Treto, Francisco O. "The Fall of the House: A Carnivalesque Reading of 2 Kings 9 and 10." *JSOT* 46 (1990): 47-65.

Garsiel, Moshe. "Puns upon Names as a Literary Device in 1 Kings 1–2." *Biblica* 72 (1991): 379-386.

Gileadi, Avraham. "The Davidic Covenant: A Theological Basis for Corporate Protection." In *Israel's Apostasy and Restoration: Essays in Honor of Roland K. Harrison*. Ed. by Avraham Gileadi. Pp. 157-163. Grand Rapids: Baker, 1988.

Gray, John. *I & II Kings: A Commentary*. 2nd ed. The Old Testament Library. Philadelphia: The Westminster Press, 1970.

Greidanus, Sidney. *The Modern Preacher and the Ancient Text: Interpreting and Preaching Biblical Literature*. Grand Rapids: Eerdmans, 1988.

Gregory, Russell. "Irony and the Unmasking of Elijah." In *From Carmel to Horeb: Elijah in Crisis*. Ed. by Alan J. Hauser and Russell Gregory. Pp. 91-169. JSOT Supplement Series 85. Sheffield: The Almond Press, 1990.

Gunn, David M. "New Directions in the Study of Biblical Hebrew Narrative." In *Reconsidering Israel and Judah: Recent Studies on the Deuteronomistic History*. Ed. by Gary N. Knoppers and J. Gordon McConville. 8:566-577. Sources for Biblical and Theological Study. Winona Lake, IN: Eisenbrauns, 2000. First published in *JSOT* 39 (1987): 65-75.

_____ . *The Story of King David: Genre and Interpretation*. JSOT Supplement Series 6. Sheffield: JSOT Press, 1978; reprint, 1982.

Gunn, David M., and Danna Nolan Fewell. *Narrative in the Hebrew Bible*. The Oxford Bible Series. Oxford: Oxford University Press, 1993.

Hagan, G. Michael. "First and Second Kings." In *A Complete Literary Guide to the Bible*. Ed. by Leland Ryken and Tremper Longman III. Pp. 182-192. Grand Rapids: Zondervan, 1993.

Hardeman, N.B. "Believing a Lie." In *Hardeman's Tabernacle Sermons*. 2:71-82. Nashville: McQuiddy Publishing Co., 1923.

Hauser, Alan J. "Yahweh versus Death — the Real Struggle in 1 Kings 17–19." In *From Carmel to Horeb: Elijah in Crisis*. Ed. by Alan J. Hauser and Russell Gregory. Pp. 9-89. JSOT Supplement Series 85. Sheffield: The Almond Press, 1990.

Heider, George C. *The Cult of Molek: A Reassessment*. JSOT Supplement 43. Sheffield: JSOT, 1985.

Herr, Larry G. "The Iron Age II Period: Emerging Nations." *BA* 60/3 (Sept. 1997): 114-151, 154-183.

Hicks, John Mark. *1 & 2 Chronicles*. The College Press NIV Commentary. Joplin, MO: College Press, 2001.

Hobbs, T.R. "2 Kings 1 and 2: Their Unity and Purpose." *Studies in Religion/Sciences religieuses* 13/3 (1984): 327-334.

_____. *2 Kings*. Vol. 13. Word Biblical Commentary. Waco, TX: Word, 1985.

Horn, Siegfried H. "The Chronology of King Hezekiah's Reign." *AUSS* 2 (1964): 40-52.

Huffmon, Herbert B. "The Covenant Lawsuit in the Prophets." *JBL* 78 (1959): 285-295.

Hurowitz, Victor A. *I Have Built You an Exalted House: Temple Building in the Bible in Light of Mesopotamian and Northwest Semitic Writings*. JSOT Supplement Series 115. Sheffield: Sheffield Academic Press, 1992.

Johnstone, William. "Guilt and Atonement: The Theme of 1 and 2 Chronicles." In *A Word in Season: Essays in Honor of William McKane*. JSOT Supplement Series 42. Ed. by J.D. Martin and P.R. Davids. Sheffield: JSOT Press, 1986.

Kissling, Paul J. *Reliable Characters in the Primary History: Profiles of Moses, Joshua, Elijah and Elisha*. JSOT Supplement Series 224. Sheffield: Sheffield Academic Press, 1996.

Kitchen, Kenneth A. *The Bible in Its World: The Bible & Archaeology Today*. Downers Grove, IL: InterVarsity Press, 1977.

_____. "How We Know When Solomon Ruled." *BAR* 27/4 (Sept./Oct. 2001): 32-37, 58.

_____. "Shishak's Military Campaign in Israel Confirmed." *BAR* 15/3 (May/June 1989): 32-33.

_____. "The Shoshenqs of Egypt and Palestine." *JSOT* 93 (2001): 3-12.

_____. "Where Did Solomon's Gold Go?" *BAR* 15/3 (May/June 1989): 30.

Klein, Lillian R. *The Triumph of Irony in the Book of Judges.* JSOT Supplement Series 68. Sheffield: The Almond Press, 1989.

Knoppers, Gary N. "Aaron's Calf and Jeroboam's Calves." In *Fortunate the Eyes that See: Essays in Honor of David Noel Freedman in Celebration of His Seventieth Birthday.* Ed. by A.B. Beck, et al. Pp. 92-104. Grand Rapids: Eerdmans, 1995.

_____. "Prayer and Propaganda: Solomon's Dedication of the Temple and the Deuteronomist's Program." In *Reconsidering Israel and Judah: Recent Studies on the Deuteronomistic History.* Ed. by Gary N. Knoppers and J. Gordon McConville. Pp. 370-396. Winona Lake, IN: Eisenbrauns, 2000. First published in *CBQ* 57 (1995): 229-254.

_____. "Solomon's Fall and Deuteronomy." In *The Age of Solomon: Scholarship at the Turn of the Millennium.* Ed. by Lowell K. Handy. Pp. 392-410. Leiden: Brill, 1997.

_____. "'There Was None like Him': Incomparability in the Books of Kings." *CBQ* 54/3 (July 1992): 411-431.

_____. "The Vanishing Solomon: The Disappearance of the United Monarchy from Recent Histories of Ancient Israel." *JBL* 116/1 (1997): 19-44.

Lasine, S. "The Riddle of Solomon's Judgment and the Riddle of Human Nature in the Hebrew Bible." *JSOT* 45 (1989): 61-86.

Lemaire, André. "Name of Israel's Last King Surfaces in a Private Collection." *BAR* 21/6 (Nov./Dec. 1995): 48-52.

_____. "The Tel Dan Stela as a Piece of Royal Historiography." *JSOT* 81 (1988): 3-14.

Lemche, Niels Peter, Thomas Thompson, William G. Dever, and P. Kyle McCarter, Jr. "Face to Face: Biblical Minimalists Meet Their Challengers." Interview by Hershel Shanks. *BAR* 23/4 (July/Aug. 1997): 26-42, 66.

Livingston, G. Herbert. *The Pentateuch in Its Cultural Environment.* 2nd ed. Grand Rapids: Baker, 1987.

Long, Burke O. "A Darkness between Brothers: Solomon and Adonijah." *JSOT* 19 (1981): 79-94.

_____ . *1 Kings: With an Introduction to Historical Literature.* Vol. 9. The Forms of the Old Testament Literature. Grand Rapids: Eerdmans, 1984.

Long, Jesse C., Jr. "Confirming a Highway to Heaven." *GA* 138/3 (March 1996): 34-36.

_____ . "God Doesn't Always Thunder." *GA* 132/12 (Dec. 1990): 32.

_____ . "God's Name Is Not Magic." *GA* 132/3 (March 1990): 53.

_____ . "Putting God in His Place." *GA* 132/2 (Feb. 1990): 37.

_____ . "Text Story & Sermon Story in Dialogue: On Preaching Bible Narratives." *Preaching* 12/4 (Jan./Feb. 1997): 19-23.

_____ . "When Clean and Unclean Aren't Always Black and White." *Preaching* 12/4 (Jan./Feb. 1997): 24-26.

Long, V. Phillips. "The Art of Biblical History." In *Foundations of Contemporary Interpretation.* Ed. by Moisés Silva. Pp. 281-429. Grand Rapids: Zondervan, 1996. First published as *The Art of Biblical History.* Vol. 5. Foundations of Contemporary Interpretation. Grand Rapids: Zondervan, 1994.

Lubetski, Meir. "King Hezekiah's Seal Revisited." *BAR* 27/4 (July/Aug. 2001): 44-51, 59.

MacDonald, Dennis Ronald. "Is There a Privileged Reader? A Case from the Apocryphal Acts." *Semeia* 71 (1995): 29-43.

Machinist, Peter. "The Transfer of Kingship: A Divine Turning." In *Fortunate the Eyes that See: Essays in Honor of David Noel Freedman in Celebration of His Seventieth Birthday.* Ed. by A.B. Beck, et al. Pp. 105-120. Grand Rapids: Eerdmans, 1995.

Manor, Dale W. "Worshiping Images and Figurines: Biblical and Anthropological Perspectives." Paper presented at the annual meeting of the American Schools of Oriental Research, Orlando, Florida, 19 November 1998.

Margalit, Baruch. "The Meaning and Significance of Asherah." *VT* 40/3 (1990): 264-297.

Mattingly, Gerald L. "Moabites." In *Peoples of the Old Testament World*. Ed. by Alfred J. Hoerth, Gerald L. Mattingly, and Edwin M. Yamauchi. Pp. 317-333. Grand Rapids: Baker Books, 1994.

McConville, J. Gordon. "1 Kings 8:46-53 and the Deuteronomic Hope." In *Reconsidering Israel and Judah: Recent Studies on the Deuteronomistic History*. Ed. by Gary N. Knoppers and J. Gordon McConville. Pp. 358-369. Winona Lake, IN: Eisenbrauns, 2000. First published in *VT* 42 (1992): 67-79.

_____. *Grace in the End: A Study in Deuteronomic Theology*. Studies in Old Testament Biblical Theology. Grand Rapids: Zondervan, 1993.

_____. "Narrative and Meaning in the Books of Kings." *Biblia* 70 (1989): 31-49.

Mettinger, T.N.D. *Solomonic State Officials: A Study of the Civil Government Officials of the Israelite Monarchy*. Coniectanea Biblia. Lund: Gleerup, 1971.

Meyers, Carol. "The Israelite Empire: In Defense of King Solomon." In *Backgrounds for the Bible*. Ed. by Michael Patrick O'Connor and David Noel Freedman. Pp. 181-197. Winona Lake, IN: Eisenbrauns, 1987.

Milgrom, Jacob. "Magic, Monotheism and the Son of Moses." In *The Quest for the Kingdom of God: Studies in Honor of George E. Mendenhall*. Ed. by. H.B. Huffmon, et al. Pp. 251-265. Winona Lake, IN: Eisenbrauns, 1983.

Millard, Alan R. "Assessing Solomon: History or Legend." In *The Age of Solomon: Scholarship at the Turn of the Millennium*. Ed. by Lowell K. Handy. Pp. 25-29. Leiden: Brill, 1997.

_____. "Does the Bible Exaggerate King Solomon's Golden Wealth?" *BAR* 15/3 (May/June 1989): 20-29, 31, 34.

_____. "King Solomon in His Ancient Context." In *The Age of Solomon: Scholarship at the Turn of the Millennium*. Ed. by Lowell K. Handy. Pp. 30-53. Leiden: Brill, 1997.

_____. "King Solomon's Shields." In *Scripture and Other Artifacts: Essays on the Bible and Archaeology in Honor of Philip J. King*. Ed. by Michael D. Coogan, J. Cheryl Exum, and Lawrence E. Stager. Pp. 286-295. Louisville, KY: Westminster John Knox Press, 1994.

_____. "Large Numbers in the Assyrian Royal Inscriptions." In *Ah, Assyria . . . : Studies in Assyrian History and Ancient Near Eastern Historiography Presented to Hayim Tadmor*. Scripta Hierosolymitana, 33. Ed. by M. Cogan and I. Eph'al. Pp. 213-222. Jerusalem: The Magnes Press, 1991.

_____. "Sennacherib's Attack on Hezekiah." *TB* 36 (1985): 61-77.

Miller, J. Maxwell. "Separating the Solomon of History from the Solomon of Legend." In *The Age of Solomon: Scholarship at the Turn of the Millennium*. Ed. by Lowell K. Handy. Leiden: Brill, 1997.

Miscall, Peter D. "Elijah, Ahab and Jehu: A Prophecy Fulfilled." *Prooftexts* 9 (Jan. 1989): 73-83.

Mitchell, T.C. *Biblical Archaeology: Documents from the British Museum*. Cambridge: Cambridge University Press, 1988.

Monson, John. "The New 'Ain Dara Temple: Closest Solomonic Parallel." *BAR* 26/3 (May/June 2000): 20-35, 67.

Montgomery, James A. *A Critical and Exegetical Commentary on the Books of Kings*. The International Critical Commentary. Edinburgh: T. & T. Clark, 1951.

Mullen, E. Theodore, Jr. "Crime and Punishment: The Sins of the King and the Despoliation of the Treasuries." *CBQ* 54/2 (April 1992): 231-248.

Murray, Donald F. "Of All the Years the Hopes — Or Fears? Jehoiachin in Babylon (2 Kings 25:27-30)." *JBL* 120/2 (2001): 245-265.

Na'aman, Nadav. "Cow Town or Royal Capital?: Evidence *for* Iron Age Jerusalem." *BAR* 23/4 (July/Aug. 1997): 43-47, 67.

_____. "Historical and Literary Notes on the Excavation of Tel Jezreel." *TA* 24 (1997): 122-128.

Nelson, Richard D. *First and Second Kings*. Interpretation: A Bible Commentary for Teaching and Preaching. Louisville: John Knox, 1987.

Nielsen, Flemming A.J. *The Tragedy in History: Herodotus and the Deuteronomistic History*. Pp. 85-97. JSOT Supplement Series 251, Copenhagen International Seminar 4. Sheffield: Sheffield Academic Press, 1997.

Noth, Martin. *The Deuteronomistic History.* 1943. Reprint, JSOT Supplementary Series 15. Sheffield: JSOT Press, 1981; 2nd reworked edition, 1991.

Olley, John W. "'Trust in the Lord': Hezekiah, Kings and Isaiah." *TB* 50/1 (1999): 59-77.

_____. "YHWH and His Zealous Prophet: The Presentation of Elijah in 1 and 2 Kings." *JSOT* 80 (1998): 25-51.

Olyan, Saul. "*Hăšālôm*: Some Literary Considerations of 2 Kings 9." *CBQ* 46/4 (Oct. 1984): 652-668.

_____. "2 Kings 9:31 — Jehu as Zimri." *HTR* 78/1-2 (1985): 203-207.

Oswalt, John, N. "'Golden Calves' and the 'Bull of Jacob': The Impact on Israel of Its Religious Environment." In *Israel's Apostasy and Restoration: Essays in Honor of Roland K. Harrison.* Ed. by Avraham Gileadi. Pp. 9-18. Grand Rapids: Baker, 1988.

Overholt, Thomas W. *Cultural Anthropology and the Old Testament.* Old Testament Library Series. Minneapolis: Fortress Press, 1996.

Parker, Kim Ian. "The Limits to Solomon's Reign: A Response to Amos Frisch." *JSOT* 51 (1991): 15-21.

_____. "Repetition as a Structuring Device in 1 Kings 1–11." *JSOT* 42 (1988): 19-27.

Pitard, Wayne T. *Ancient Damascus: A Historical Study of the Syrian City-State from Earliest Times until Its Fall to the Assyrians in 732 B.C.E.* Winona Lake, IN: Eisenbrauns, 1987.

Polzin, Robert. *Samuel and the Deuteronomist: A Literary Study of the Deuteronomistic History. Part 2, 1 Samuel.* New York: Harper & Row, Publishers, 1989.

Pritchard, James B., ed. *Ancient Near Eastern Texts Relating to the Old Testament.* Princeton: Princeton University Press, 1969.

Provan, Iain W. *1 and 2 Kings.* New International Biblical Commentary. Peabody, MA: Hendrickson , 1995.

_____. *1 & 2 Kings.* Old Testament Guides. Sheffield: Sheffield Academic Press, 1997.

Rahmani, L.Y. "Ancient Jerusalem's Funerary Customs and Tombs. Part 2." *BA* 44/3 (1981): 229-235

Roberts, Kathryn L. "God, Prophet, and King: Eating and Drinking on the Mountain in First Kings 18:41." *CBQ* 62 (2000): 632-644.

Rofé, Alexander. *The Prophetical Stories: The Narratives about the Prophets in the Hebrew Bible, Their Literary Types and History.* Jerusalem: The Magnes Press, 1988.

Sasson, Victor. "King Solomon and the Dark Lady in the Song of Songs." *VT* 39/4 (Oct. 1989): 407-414.

Savran, George. "1 and 2 Kings." In *The Literary Guide to the Bible.* Ed. by Robert Alter and Frank Kermode. Pp. 146-164. Cambridge, MA: The Belknap Press of Harvard University Press, 1987.

Schneider, Tsvi. "Six Biblical Signatures: Seals and Seal Impressions of Six Biblical Personages Recovered." *BAR* 17/4 (July/Aug. 1991): 26-33.

Sérandour, Arnaud. "King, Priest, and Temple." *NEA* 61 (March 1998): 6.

Shanks, Hershel. "Everything You Ever Knew about Jerusalem Is Wrong (Well, Almost)." *BAR* 25/6 (Nov./Dec. 1999): 20-29.

_____ . Review of *The Conquest of Lachish by Sennacherib,* by David Ussishkin. *BAR* 10/2 (March/April 1984): 48-65.

_____ . "Three Shekels for the Lord: Ancient Inscription Records Gift to Solomon's Temple." *BAR* 23/6 (Nov./Dec. 1997): 28-32.

Shea, William H. "Jerusalem under Siege: Did Sennacherib Attack Twice?" *BAR* 25/6 (Nov./Dec. 1999): 36-44, 64.

Simon, Uriel. "Minor Characters in Biblical Narrative." *JSOT* 46 (1990): 11-19.

Smith, James E. *1 & 2 Samuel.* The College Press NIV Commentary. Joplin, MO: College Press, 2000.

Smith, Mark S. "The Near Eastern Background of Solar Language for Yahweh." *JBL* 109/1 (1990): 29-39.

Sneed, Mark R. "A Middle Class in Ancient Israel." In *Concepts of Class in Ancient Israel.* Ed. by Mark R. Sneed. Pp. 53-65. Atlanta: Scholars Press, 1999.

Speer, Charles W. "A Study of Allusion in the 'Birth Narrative' of Luke's Gospel." Master's thesis, Lubbock Christian University, 1996.

Stager, Lawrence E., and Samuel R. Wolff. "Child Sacrifice at Carthage — Religious Rite or Population Control?" *BAR* 10/1 (Jan./Feb. 1984): 30-51.

Stern, Ephraim. "The Babylonian Gap Revisited: Yes There Was." *BAR* 28/3 (May/June 2002): 39, 55.

_____. "The Babylonian Gap: The Assyrians Impressed Their Culture on Israel . . . The Babylonians Left No Trace." *BAR* 26/6 (Nov./Dec. 2000): 45-51, 76.

_____. "The Many Masters of Dor, Part 2: How Bad Was Ahab?" *BAR* 19/2 (March-April 1993): 18-29.

Stern, Ephraim, ed. *New Encyclopedia of Archaeological Excavation in the Holy Land.* 4 vols. Jerusalem: The Israel Exploration Society & Carta; New York: Simon & Schuster, 1993.

Sternberg, Meir. *The Poetics of Biblical Narrative: Ideological Literature and the Drama of Reading.* Indiana Studies in Biblical Literature. Bloomington: Indiana University Press, 1987.

Stigers, Harold G. "The Interphased Chronology of Jotham, Ahaz, Hezekiah and Hoshea." *BETS* 9 (1996): 81-90.

Taylor, J. Glenn. "A Response to Steve A. Wiggins. 'Yahweh: The God of Sun?'" *JSOT* 71 (1996): 107-119.

_____. "Was Yahweh Worshipped as the Sun?" *BAR* 20/3 (May/June 1994): 52-61, 90-91.

Taylor, Joan E. "The Asherah, the Menorah and the Sacred Tree." *JSOT* 66 (1995): 29-54.

Thiele, Edwin R. *The Mysterious Numbers of the Hebrew Kings.* Rev. ed. Grand Rapids: Kregel Publications; Zondervan, 1983.

Turner, Rex A., Sr. *Daniel: A Prophet of God.* Montgomery, AL: Southern Christian University, 1993.

_____. *Teacher's Annual Lesson Commentary: On Uniform Bible Lessons for the Churches of Christ.* Vol. 55. Nashville: Gospel Advocate Co., 1976.

Ussishkin, David. *The Conquest of Lachish by Sennacherib.* Tel Aviv: Tel Aviv University, The Institute of Archaeology, 1982.

_____. "The Date of the Judaean Shrine at Arad." *IEJ* 38/3 (1988): 142-157.

_____. Interview by Hershel Shanks. In *Biblical Archaeology: From the Ground Down*. Written, directed, and hosted by Hershel Shanks. Biblical Archaeology Society. 1996. Videocassette.

Ussishkin, David, and John Woodhead. "Excavations at Tel Jezreel 1990–1991: Preliminary Report." *TA* 19 (1992): 3-56.

_____. "Excavations at Tel Jezreel 1994–1996: Third Preliminary Report." *TA* 24 (1997): 6-72.

Van Winkle, D.W. "1 Kings XII 25–XIII 34: Jeroboam's Cultic Innovations and the Man of God from Judah." *VT* 46/1 (1996): 101-114.

Vaughn, Andrew G. *Theology, History, and Archaeology in the Chronicler's Account of Hezekiah*. Atlanta: Scholars Press, 1999.

Viviano, Pauline A. "Glory Lost: The Reign of Solomon in the Deuteronomistic History." In *The Age of Solomon: Scholarship at the Turn of the Millennium*. Ed. by Lowell K. Handy. Pp. 336-347. Leiden: Brill, 1997.

Vorster, Willem S. "Readings, Readers, and the Succession Narrative: An Essay on Reception." In *Beyond Form Criticism: Essays in Old Testament Literary Criticism*. Ed. by Paul R. House. 2:395-407. Sources for Biblical and Theological Study. Winona Lake, IN: Eisenbrauns, 1992. First published in *ZAW* 98 (1986): 351-362.

Walsh, *1 Kings*. Berit Olam: Studies in Hebrew Narrative & Poetry. Collegeville, MN: A Michael Glazier Book, The Liturgical Press, 1996.

Waltke, Bruce K. "The Phenomenon of Conditionality within Unconditional Covenants." In *Israel's Apostasy and Restoration: Essays in Honor of Roland K. Harrison*. Ed. by Avraham Gileadi. Pp. 123-139. Grand Rapids: Baker, 1988.

Weinfeld, Moshe. "The Counsel of the 'Elders' to Rehoboam and Its Implications." In *Reconsidering Israel and Judah: Recent Studies on the Deuteronomistic History*. Ed. by Gary N. Knoppers and J. Gordon McConville. Pp. 516-539. Winona Lake, IN: Eisenbrauns, 2000. First published in *Maarav* 3/1 (1982): 27-53.

Wenham, John W. "Large Numbers in the Old Testament." *TB* 18 (1967): 19-53.

_____. "The Large Numbers of the Old Testament." In *Eerdmans Handbook to the Bible*. Rev. ed. Ed. by David Alexander and Pat Alexander. Pp. 192-193. Grand Rapids: Eerdmans, 1983.

Whitelam, Keith W. *The Just King: Monarchical Judicial Authority in Ancient Israel.* JSOT Supplement Series 12. Sheffield: JSOT Press, 1979.

_____ . "The Symbols of Power: Aspects of Royal Propaganda in the United Monarchy." *BA* 49/3 (1986): 166-173.

Wiggins, Steve A. "A Rejoinder to J. Glen Taylor." *JSOT* (1997): 109-112.

_____ . "Yahweh: The God of Sun?" *JSOT* 71 (1996): 89-106.

Williams, David S. "Once Again: The Structure of the Narrative of Solomon's Reign." *JSOT* 86 (1999): 49-66.

Willis, John T. *First and Second Samuel.* The Living Word Commentary on the Old Testament. Austin, TX: R.B. Sweet, 1982; Abilene, TX: ACU Press, 1984.

_____ . *Isaiah.* The Living Word Commentary on the Old Testament. Austin, TX: R.B. Sweet, 1980; Abilene, TX: ACU Press, 1984.

Wright, Christopher J.H. *God's People in God's Land: Family, Land, and Property in the Old Testament.* Grand Rapids: Eerdmans, 1990.

Yadin, Yigael. *Hazor: The Rediscovery of a Great Citadel of the Bible.* New York: Random House, 1975.

Younger, K. Lawson. "The Deportations of the Israelites." *JBL* 117/2 (1998): 201-227.

_____ . "The Fall of Samaria in Light of Recent Research." *CBQ* 61/3 (1999): 461-482.

1 KINGS 1

I. THE STORY OF SOLOMON (1:1–11:43)

A. SOLOMON BECOMES KING (1:1-53)

The opening scenes of 1 Kings (chs. 1–2) are at once a conclusion to preceding literary/historical trajectories and an introduction to events that follow. David is dying; two camps are vying for his throne; the younger of his two sons will ascend to the throne, squash perceived opposition, and establish the promised dynasty (2 Samuel 7). Because of imperfections already foreshadowed in these initial scenes, in its final chapters the dynasty will be exiled to Babylon.

All of this is accomplished with remarkable literary skill. Characters emerge from these scenes as real flesh-and-blood personalities. Allusion to earlier scenes, contrast between characters, rival points of view, and ambiguous actions and dialogue heighten the political intrigue that surrounds the main tension of the narrative: Who will become king in Israel?

But Israel's story is more than palace intrigue and political history. With consummate skill, the narrator introduces themes that will resurface through the course of the larger story. The nature of kingship in Israel, the role of Deuteronomy in the life of people and king, and the fulfillment of prophecy (although the prophetic voice itself is silent in these scenes) all underlie the twists and turns of the narrative of Kings.

Nevertheless, in "Act One" of this tragic drama, one question subtly overshadows all other concerns: Where is Yahweh in the story? In a narrative that must have been written, at least in part, to say that God has kept his promise to David (2 Samuel 7), God is silent. The omniscient narrator holds back, keeps quiet about how God moves in these events. Surely he is at work, but what is his point

of view? What does he think of the intrigue, the plotting, the elimination of enemies, and, perhaps most offensive, the fratricide in the
palace — brother taking the life of brother? How is God able to use
these imperfect people for his purposes?

Herein lies a primary theological issue of Kings: How is God's
sovereign will enacted with imperfect people and institutions? How
does God's will interface with free will, especially when Israel and
her kings choose another course? This is the real tension of Kings.
The answer will call attention to Yahweh's power and grace, for he
will remember his promise to Abraham, Isaac, Jacob, *and David* and
emerge as the sole hero of the story.

1. King David's Powers Wane (1:1-4)

These initial verses establish the frame for the political intrigue
that dominates the inaugural scenes in Kings. In particular, the
king's impotence forms the backdrop for rival factions to make
advances toward the throne. David's sexual incapacity may have precipitated these events. In the ancient Near East, the virility of the
king appears to have been associated with his perceived ability to
govern. In any case, David's physical condition symbolizes his political impotence in not already having publicly named an heir.

1:1-4 With exposition, the narrator sets the stage. **David** is **old**
and cannot **keep warm**. Unnamed servants suggest that a **young virgin** be sought out for the king. Their words define her role. In
Hebrew, "stand before the king" (**attend the king** in the NIV, v. 2)
is a typical way of describing one who will serve. However, the sexual overtones to their proposal stand out in the phrase "lie in your
bosom" (somewhat obscured by **lie beside him** in the NIV, v. 2).
"Lying with someone" is a Hebrew idiom for sexual intercourse (see,
e.g., the phrase used in the David and Bathsheba episode in 2 Sam
11:4,11; 12:11,24).

The narrator's use of the word "bosom" (חֵיק, *ḥêq*) alludes to
Nathan's parable of judgment against David.[1] In the parable, the ewe

---

[1] See James S. Ackerman, "Knowing Good and Evil: A Literary Analysis of
the Court History in 2 Sam 9–20 and 1 Kings 1–2," *JBL* 109/1 (1990): 41-
64. However, his suggestion that Bathsheba "snatched the kingship from the
bosom of David" is not supported by the context.

lamb slept in the bosom of the poor man (2 Sam 12:3). Although subtle, this allusion introduces an important contrast between the beautiful Abishag and the once desirable Bathsheba, the lamb who was taken into David's bosom. In the verses that follow, numerous allusions to events in the larger story will frame the turmoil in the palace and suggest antecedent causes for the mayhem. Principal among them, David's act of taking Bathsheba is the event that precipitates the disharmony in the royal family that resurfaces in the question of who will ascend to the throne.

This paragraph ends with the comment that "the king did not know her" (**the king had no intimate relations with her** in the NIV, v. 4). With this phrase, the narrator reinforces the sexual dimension of the servants' scheme and introduces the key word "know" (יָדַע, *yāda'*). In the verses that follow, David is characterized as impotent in other arenas. Even though king, he does not know what is going on in his kingdom.

2. Adonijah Wants to Be King (1:5-10)

1:5-6 Adonijah is introduced as the son of **Haggith**. Naming Adonijah's mother establishes the familial boundaries that frame the rivalry for the throne. Solomon's mother will play an important role in Adonijah's defeat — and ultimate death. Adonijah puts **himself forward** (נָשָׂא, *nāśā'*, "to lift up"), a verb that carries negative connotations for his character (cf. Num 16:3; Prov 30:32). In this way, the narrator also implies that David has not designated Adonijah as his successor. Adonijah's first words, **"I will be king,"** reinforce these early impressions.

By calling attention to Adonijah's retinue of **chariots** and **men to run ahead**, the narrator alludes to Absalom's failed attempt to usurp the throne of his father David (see 2 Sam 15:1). Also, the verb used by the narrator for the NIV's **never *interfered*** [עָצַב, *'āṣab*] **with him** is ironic, representing another allusion to the story of Absalom. In this context, it carries the idea of not causing pain in Adonijah, not reproaching him. In 2 Samuel 19:2 [3], the whole army mourned when they heard that David was grieving (*'āṣab*) for Absalom. The Hebrew word *'āṣab* appears only fifteen times in the Old Testament, three times in Samuel and once in Kings. The use of the word in this text appears to

intentionally recall David's reaction to the death of Absalom, a consequence that might have been averted if the king had reproached
Amnon for the rape of Absalom's sister. As with Absalom, David never
approached Adonijah to ask, **"Why do you behave as you do?"** David's
failure to discipline his sons characterizes his relationship with them
(see 2 Sam 13:21-38; 14:23-33). Not so subtly, the narrator adds that
Adonijah was very handsome and was born next after Absalom.[2] The
obvious resonance with Absalom's revolt (2 Samuel 15–19) situates
the narrative and guides the reader. Like his older brother,
Adonijah's actions may also be rebellious. In addition, the links with
the failed coup are foreboding for Adonijah's prospects of sitting on
his father's throne.

1:7-8 Adonijah shrewdly marshals support for his political purposes. He acquires the backing of **Joab**, the commander of the army,
and **Abiathar the priest** — two powerful figures who go back to
David's early days (see 2 Sam 2:13; 1 Sam 23:6).[3] However, another
camp of important figures is not with Adonijah. This faction included **Zadok the priest**, **Benaiah**, the captain of the palace guard (see
2 Sam 23:20-23), David's own court prophet **Nathan**, **Shimei**, "the
friend of the king,"[4] and **David's special guard.**

---

[2]Adonijah was the fourth son of David (2 Sam 3:2-5). Since Amnon and
Absalom are dead, and Kileab is missing and presumed dead, Adonijah is
the oldest living son of the king.

[3]Iain W. Provan suggests that the support for the two contenders to the
throne divides between those who go back to the time when David was in
Hebron and those who joined the regime in Jerusalem (*1 and 2 Kings*, New
International Biblical Commentary [Peabody, MA: Hendrickson, 1995], pp.
24-25). Jerome T. Walsh adds that Adonijah was born during David's time in
Hebron (2 Sam 3:4), while Solomon was born in Jerusalem. Solomon's camp,
according to Walsh, may represent a more "pluralistic and cosmopolitan
viewpoint" (*1 Kings*, Berit Olam: Studies in Hebrew Narrative & Poetry
[Collegeville, MN: A Michael Glazier Book, The Liturgical Press, 1996], p. 8).
Similarly, Walter Brueggemann views Solomon's faction as wanting to move
Israel into "international trade and prosperity" with important "theological
accommodations" (*1 & 2 Kings*, Smyth & Helwys Bible Commentary [Macon,
GA: Smyth & Helwys, 2000], p. 12; see pp. 21, 35, 41).

[4]As the NIV text note indicates, the Hebrew text may be corrupted here
(see John Gray, *I & II Kings: A Commentary*, 2nd ed., The Old Testament
Library [Philadelphia: Westminster Press, 1970], p. 79, note a). "Friend of
the king," a political appointment in Judah (cf. 1 Kgs 4:5), is a plausible
reading. In addition, the introduction of Shimei without any qualifiers seems
incongruent with the larger story, where Shimei, son of Gera, opposes David

1:9-10 The storyteller adeptly carries the reader to a sacrificial feast sponsored by Adonijah. The occasion of the feast is not given, but the location, important later in the story, is identified as **the Stone of Zoheleth near En Rogel**.[5] Adonijah's guest list is provocative. Echoes of Absalom's feast for Amnon (2 Sam 13:23-33) suggest ulterior motives. The double naming of the featured guests, **brothers** and **king's sons**, interjects suspense and highlights both the familial and political relationships dominating the situation. Naming the men of Judah who were royal officials reinforces the political nature of the occasion and adds to the intrigue.

Changing direction in verse 10, the narrator now names those not invited to the feast. The order is as important as the names on the list. **Nathan the prophet** will play a major role in the conspiracy to thwart Adonijah's desire for the throne. **Benaiah**, and David's **special guard**, will provide the military muscle to ensure Adonijah's defeat. Then with a skillful pen, the narrator pencils in, at the end of the list, **or his brother Solomon**. With this first reference to Solomon in the story,[6] the reader learns that all of the king's sons were invited to the feast, except this one. In a brief stroke, the storyteller has introduced the other contender for the throne and set the stage for the intrigue that must follow. Which of the two will be king in Israel?

3. Has Adonijah Become King? (1:11-14)

1:11-14 Nathan approaches Bathsheba and asks about Adonijah. The pace has slowed; dialogue now dominates. Nathan's speech is

---

(1 Sam 16:5-14; 1 Kgs 2:8-9,36-46). How could he support Solomon? Walsh suggests that this Shimei is the son of Ela mentioned in 1 Kgs 4:8 (*1 Kings*, p. 8, n 2). Provan argues that "you have *with you* Shimei . . ." in 1 Kgs 2:8 indicates that Shimei was in the camp of Solomon and, so, prefers not to amend the text in 1 Kgs 1:8 (*1 and 2 Kings*, p. 28). If Provan is correct, Solomon's actions against Shimei (2:36-46) are even more distasteful.

[5]En-Rogel appears to have been a spring south of Jerusalem where the Hinnom and Kidron valleys converge, just a few hundred yards from the Gihon spring (see W. Harold Mare, "Serpent's Stone [place]," in *ABD*; Gray, *I & II Kings*, p. 83).

[6]This is the first reference to Solomon since 2 Sam 12:24-25.

calculated to arouse fear in Bathsheba. **"Adonijah . . . has become king"** and her life and the life of her son are threatened. David is impotent; he doesn't *know* (*yāda'*) what has happened. Nevertheless, has Adonijah set himself up as king? The narrator has only revealed that Adonijah believes he will be king (v. 5) and has invited key political operatives to a feast. This charge may only represent Nathan's point of view, his reading of events.[7] In addition, did David **swear** to Bathsheba, **"Solomon your son shall be king after me"**? In the history from Joshua through 2 Kings, there is no record of such a promise. Also, in this larger narrative, Yahweh nowhere designates Solomon as David's successor.[8]

Yet, towering over this text is Yahweh's promise that he would establish a "house" for David and set one "from your own body" on the throne (2 Sam 7:1-17). The narrator will subtly reinforce the promise theme with the word **swear** (שָׁבַע, *šāba'*). Eight of the twelve times this word occurs in Kings are in the first two chapters of 1 Kings. The related noun "oath" (שְׁבֻעָה, *šᵉbū'āh*) appears in Kings only in 2:43. And how appropriate it is that Bathsheba plays an important role in these events. Her name means "daughter of swearing"(בַּת־שֶׁבַע, *bath-šeba'*).[9] Yahweh has sworn that David will have a son to sit on his throne, but has David sworn that it will be Solomon?

---

[7]Walsh suggests that Nathan's "spin" could be a fabrication (see *1 Kings*, p. 25). Fokkelman believes that Nathan is completing the task which he began in 2 Sam 12:25 and is therefore reliable. If this is correct, it would follow that Nathan and Bathsheba's appeal to an oath made by David is also credible (*King David [II Sam. 9–20 & I Kings 2–2]*, vol. 1, Narrative Art and Poetry in the Books of Samuel: A Full Interpretation Based on Stylistic and Structural Analyses [Assen, The Netherlands: Van Gorcum, 1981], p. 412). Suggesting that Nathan was probably fabricating as he had in the parable for David (2 Sam 12:1-7), Keith Bodner argues that the three Nathan episodes in Samuel–Kings (2 Sam 7:1-17; 12:1-15,24-25; 2 Kings 1:1-31) "reveal a prophet with a growing sense of divine purpose (even resorting to rather dubious means) in securing the throne for the specified son of the king" ("Nathan: Prophet, Politician and Novelist?" *JSOT* 95 [2001]: 43-54).

[8]In 1 Chr 22:9-10, Yahweh identifies Solomon as the promised son who would sit on David's throne. However, Chronicles is a separate literary composition, postdating Kings. The audience of Kings only knows that Solomon became king in place of his father David.

[9]For wordplay involving names in 1 Kings 1–2, see Moshe Garsiel, "Puns upon Names as a Literary Device in 1 Kings 1–2," *Biblica* 72 (1991): 379-386.

4. Bathsheba Approaches the King (1:15-21)

1:15 The "daughter of swearing" has an audience with the king, to remind him of an oath that she says he had made to her. Carefully, the narrator sets the scene for the reader. The old monarch is in his room, and Abishag is **attending him**. Bathsheba must have noticed the beautiful Abishag with her husband, the king. The queen herself was once desirable and in a similar position, lying in the bosom of the king (v. 2). Now, as she comes to replace David with her son Solomon, she sees all too vividly that the younger Abishag has replaced her.[10]

1:16-17 Bathsheba **bows low** with respect. David's response is curt, **"What do you want?"** The contrast between what she says and Nathan's instructions suggests that she is not just a puppet.[11] Her words are calculated,[12] but also reflect a relationship with the aging king. Nathan's question for David, "Did you not swear . . . ?" becomes in Bathsheba's mouth, **"You yourself swore to me your servant by the LORD your God."** The small change suggests personal knowledge and reinforces her claim for the reader.

1:18-20 Accepting Nathan's view of events, **"Adonijah has become king,"** Bathsheba charges the king with impotence: **"You, my lord the king, do not know** [*yāda*] **about it."** She then informs David of Adonijah's feast, carefully wording her report to arouse David against Adonijah and conjure up sympathy for Solomon. When she names Joab **the commander of the army**,[13] the king's blood pressure must have risen. Finally, she lets out that, even though all of the king's sons were invited, **"He has not invited Solomon, your servant."**

---

[10]Berlin, *Poetics and Interpretation*, pp. 27-28. Berlin also notes the "sad irony that the once virile David who could not restrain his passion is now oblivious to the young woman who 'lies in his bosom' to provide him with warmth" (p. 28).

[11]Robert Alter shows how Bathsheba expands Nathan's instructions, the differences between the two speeches in character for each one (*The Art of Biblical Narrative*, pp. 98-100).

[12]Notice her use of naming to show deference to the king: "my lord," "your servant," "my lord the king," and "Solomon your servant" (vv. 17-21).

[13]Her naming contrasts with the narrator's naming of Joab in verse 7 as "the son of Zeruiah."

1:21 Bathsheba's last word to the king — **"I and my son Solomon will be treated as criminals"** — is perhaps her most calculating comment. The NIV's "criminals" is in Hebrew (literally) "sinners" (חַטָּאִים, *ḥaṭṭā'îm*). Is she not deliberately conjuring up for the king the time when one of her sons died for David's sin (2 Sam 12:13,15-18)? Would she and another son suffer a similar fate, this time at the hands of a brother? On another level, the narrator makes one more subtle allusion to David's adultery, the event that set in motion this whole sordid affair.

5. Nathan the Prophet Approaches the King (1:22-27)

1:22-27 Nathan's words to the king are just as calculating, perhaps even more manipulative. To arouse David, he takes the course of a faithful servant who has been kept in the dark. In Hebrew, he begins not with a question but with a statement[14]: "You have **declared that Adonijah shall be king**." He then informs the king of events that support this observation. But some of the king's faithful servants were not invited to Adonijah's feast, beginning with **"me, your servant."** Again, last on the uninvited list is **your servant Solomon.** Nathan finishes with a question: "Have you done this **without letting his servants know** [*yāda'*] who would be king?" Nathan knows that David is impotent, that the king *doesn't know* about Adonijah's feast.

The prophet's slant on events surfaces when he adds that the commanders of the army had been invited and that they were all at the feast saying, **"Long live King Adonijah."** The narrator nowhere confirms this tidbit of information.

6. King David Confirms His Oath (1:28-31)

1:28-31 The king summons Bathsheba, who apparently left when Nathan entered, and affirms the promise that the "daughter of swearing" (*bath-šeba'*) said he had made to her (1:17). David *swears* (*šāba'*) an **oath**. He swears by Yahweh that he **will carry out today** the oath he had sworn by Yahweh to Bathsheba. Solomon would sit

---

[14]Walsh, *1 Kings*, p. 16.

on his throne. The impotent, aging king has been aroused. And the reader hears a familiar David. He swears by Yahweh, **"who has delivered me out of every trouble."**

7. King David Acts (1:32-37)

1:32-35 David summons supporters of Solomon. **Zadok** and **Nathan** will **anoint** (מָשַׁח, *māšaḥ*[15]) the new king, and **Benaiah** will provide military escort. Riding on the king's **mule** would indicate for observers the king's support for Solomon.[16] The anointing would take place at **Gihon**, the main source of water for Jerusalem — and not far from where Adonijah and his supporters are reveling.[17] Solomon would reign instead of David, although some type of co-regency may actually be under consideration here. He would be anointed **king** (מֶלֶךְ, *melek*) over Israel, but David adds that he has appointed Solomon as **ruler** [נָגִיד, *nāgîd*, "prince"] **over Israel and Judah.** Both Saul and David were anointed *nāgîd* over Israel (cf. 1 Sam 9:16; 10:1; 13:14; 25:40; 2 Sam 5:2; 6:21; 7:8). As is reflected in his speech and in contrast with Saul, David never forgets that Yahweh was *King* (*melek*) in Israel and that he was his anointed prince.[18]

---

[15]This word is the Hebrew verb form of the word from which derives the word Messiah.

[16]The Hebrew is (literally) "she-mule," found in the Old Testament only in this episode (vv. 33,38,44). Apparently, horses were not ridden at this time in Israel (see James A. Montgomery, *A Critical and Exegetical Commentary on the Books of Kings*, The International Critical Commentary [Edinburgh: T. & T. Clark, 1951], pp. 76-77). Simon J. DeVries adds that because of the law against crossbreeding (Leviticus 19:19), David's mule would be an expensive, imported animal (*1 Kings*, vol. 12, Word Biblical Commentary [Waco, TX: Word, 1985], p. 16).

[17]For the location of En Rogel see note 5.

[18]See John T. Willis, *First and Second Samuel*, The Living Word Commentary on the Old Testament (Austin, TX: Sweet, 1982; Abilene, TX: ACU Press, 1984), p. 138 (page citation is to the 1984 edition). Mordechai Cogan observes that the term *nāgîd* in Samuel and Kings (1 Sam 9:16; 10:1; 25:30; 2 Sam 5:2; 6:21; 7:8; 1 Kgs 1:35; 14:7; 16:2; 2 Kings 20:5) refers both to the crown prince and the king (*1 Kings: A New Translation with Introduction and Commentary*, vol. 10, The Anchor Bible [New York: Doubleday, 2001], p. 161).

1:36-37 Benaiah expresses the wish that Yahweh may **declare** (אָמַר, *'āmar*[19]) that it be so. On another level, Benaiah may be indirectly expressing the point of view of the narrator, that Yahweh would indeed establish Solomon's throne. Benaiah's statement can be translated, "The LORD, the God of my lord the king, *will* declare it." In any case, his statement calls attention to the fact that in the larger story Yahweh has not "declared" that Solomon would be king (see comments on 1:11-14). Benaiah concludes his wish with, "May Yahweh **make his throne even greater than the throne of my lord King David!**" — a desire that will be realized in the larger narrative.

8. Solomon Is Anointed King (1:38-40)

1:38-40 The loyal servants of the king set out to anoint **Solomon**. The narrator mentions for the first time the **Kerethites and Pelethites**, apparently the king's bodyguards under the command of **Benaiah** (cf. 2 Sam 8:18; 20:23).[20] At **Gihon**, **Zadok** anoints Solomon with the **horn of oil from the sacred tent**.[21] **All the people** follow the new king **rejoicing**, so loud that the earth shook. There is widespread support for Solomon among the people.

9. Jonathan Reports to Adonijah (1:41-49)

1:41-42 Adeptly, with the noise of the celebration, the narrator transitions the reader to Adonijah's **feast** at En Rogel. Joab hears the **sound of the trumpet** and asks about the uproar. As he is speaking, Jonathan arrives with news from the city. Again, the narrator subtly connects Adonijah with the story of Absalom. During Absalom's revolt, **Jonathan the son of Abiathar the priest** served as a messen-

---

[19]The NIV is reading the MT here (יֹאמַר, *yō'mar*). A few Hebrew manuscripts and the Syriac have "do it" (יַעֲשֶׂה, *ya'ăśeh*).

[20]The Kerethites and the Pelethites appear to have been Cretan and Philistine mercenaries (from the Sea Peoples) in David's service (see Cogan, *1 Kings*, p. 162; DeVries, *1 Kings*, p. 17; Provan, *1 and 2 Kings*, p. 29).

[21]The NIV adds "sacred" to qualify the tent that housed the ark of the covenant, which David escorted to Jerusalem (2 Sam 6:17). This tent should not be confused with the tabernacle at Gibeon (see 2 Chr 1:3-5).

ger for David at En Rogel (2 Sam 17:7). Ironically, this same messenger now carries intelligence to En Rogel for those who apparently would like to unseat David as king.[22]

1:43-45 The news is not good.[23] David has made Solomon king.
For the third time, the narrator recounts the details of Solomon's
anointing, this time through the reporting eye and ear of Jonathan.
Verses 44-45 relay the events that have transpired with remarkable
accuracy. The repetition reinforces the *reliability* of Jonathan as
messenger.

1:46-49 Jonathan continues with details that span beyond that
moment in time. He reports information of which it would be
impossible for him to have knowledge.[24] Temporally, verses 46-48
transpire after Jonathan's report, and presumably after the feast
breaks up. **Solomon** sits on **the royal throne**; the **royal officials**
come to congratulate the king; and **the king** bows **on his bed**.
Spatially, how could Jonathan, at that moment in time, know what
was occurring in the palace and in the king's bedchamber?[25]

Each of the three verses in question begins with וְגַם (*wᵊgam*,
moreover, v. 46; **also**, v. 47; untranslated, v. 48), perhaps indicating
later expansion. Against this view, Burke O. Long argues that *wᵊgam*
clauses appear to characterize messenger speeches in Samuel and
Kings (e.g., 1 Sam 4:17; 2 Sam 1:4; 2 Sam 11:24).[26] Another possibility is that in this instance the *wᵊgam* statements signal elaboration by

---

[22]Walsh, *1 Kings*, pp. 29-30.

[23]Walsh observes that Jonathan's first word (אֲבָל, *'ăbāl*, "Not at all!" in the
NIV) is similar in sound to (אָבַל, *'ābal*, "to mourn"); ibid., p. 28.

[24]See Cogan, *1 Kings*, p. 163; Walsh, *1 Kings*, p. 30.

[25]One could argue that there is a gap in time between the anointing at
Gihon and Jonathan's arrival at En Rogel, allowing for the events recorded
in verses 46-48. However, the text makes the point that the anointing and
Jonathan's arrival were simultaneous events. For the reader, the literary
antecedent of "the trumpet" (הַשּׁוֹפָר, *haššôphār*) that Joab hears is the anointing trumpet (בַּשּׁוֹפָר, *baššôphār*) of verse 39. Or perhaps Jonathan simply anticipates the events that follow, although the fact that he quotes David precisely argues against this solution. How could he anticipate the king's exact
words? Finally, Jonathan may be an unreliable messenger, who assists the
Solomon party by dispersing the followers of Adonijah with his exaggerated
report. Again, the role that the David quotation plays in the larger succession
story suggests that in the view of the storyteller, he is trustworthy.

[26]Burke O. Long, "A Darkness between Brothers: Solomon and
Adonijah," *JSOT* 19 (1981): 80-81.

the narrator for rhetorical effect. Does the use of *wᵊgam* in 1:46-48 cleverly connote the narrator's voice embedded within Jonathan's speech?[27] If so, the *wᵊgam* clauses would indicate to the original audience expansion by the storyteller, in this case providing information through Jonathan which is important to the plot.

Nevertheless, though *wᵊgam* may represent a subtle shift to information supplied by the narrator, that this information is framed by the situation of Jonathan's report suggests literary design. In fact, Jonathan's speech represents a common literary device. Information important for the reader is summarized and even telescoped in discourse. When this occurs, the character's words may directly reflect the narrator's point of view. In this instance, the narrator reports through Jonathan (in the *wᵊgam* clauses) dialogue from David. Indirectly, the reader hears David praise Yahweh for giving him a successor — clearly an allusion to God's promise to David in 2 Sam 7:5-16. Both David and the narrator see Solomon as the fulfillment of the oath Yahweh made to David to build him an eternal house.

Jonathan's speech is a good example of a passage where the "historical, literary, and theological impulses" in Scripture converge. There is no reason not to believe that the author in this case was *constrained by the historical facts*.[28] The details that are added in verses 46-48 have every appearance of being an accurate account of the events that transpired following the anointing of Solomon as king. For literary reasons, however, the inspired author has Jonathan convey this information (perhaps signaling expansion with *wᵊgam*). The theological impulse surfaces in David's speech. The aging king and the narrator believe that God has fulfilled his promise to David.

10. Adonijah Fears for His Life (1:50-53)

1:50-53 Afraid for his life, **Adonijah** goes to the sacred tent and grabs on to the **horns of the altar** for protection.[29] His action

---

[27]In 21:23, when Elijah appears as messenger to Ahab with a word of judgment, a similar *wᵊgam* statement may also signal the narrator's voice, interjecting a word of judgment on Jezebel (see comments on 21:23).

[28]See V. Phillips Long, "The Art of Biblical History," pp. 319-337.

[29]For examples of four-horned altars excavated in Iron Age Palestine, see Dever, *Biblical Writers Know*, pp. 176, 180-181, 188-190.

appears to reflect a common ancient Near Eastern belief that holy sites were places for asylum (cf. 2:28-30; Exod 21:12-14). Adonijah will only leave the tent if his brother **Solomon** swears (*šābaʿ*) not to kill him **with the sword**.[30] Solomon's first words in the narrative are a *promise* to Adonijah that if he proves to be a **worthy man** (a somewhat ambiguous phrase) and if no **evil is found in him** (also ambiguous), Adonijah will live. Later, Solomon will find pretense to take his brother's life (2:13-25).

These verses form the final scene in a section that displays a concentric structure. The central scene highlights David's oath in verses 28-31 as follows:[31]

> A. Adonijah maneuvers to take the throne (5-10).
> > B. Nathan reminds Bathsheba of the oath that Solomon would be king (11-14).
> > > C. Bathsheba and Nathan address David (15-27).
> > > > X. *David restates the oath to Bathsheba* (28-31).
> > > C′. The oath is fulfilled (32-40).
> > B′. Jonathan announces that Solomon is king (41-49).
> A′. Adonijah flees and is confronted by Solomon (50-53).

The pivotal role that David's oath plays in chapter one reinforces the *swearing/oath* motif that characterizes the first two chapters of 1 Kings.

---

[30]Nathan prophesied that David's house would be characterized by the sword (2 Sam 12:9-10; see comments on 1 Kgs 2:5-9; and "The Succession Story Viewed in Context").

[31]Fokkelman emphasizes the central role that David's oath structurally plays in this section. The following outline is adapted from *Narrative Art and Poetry*, pp. 364-367, 410.

1 KINGS 2

B. SOLOMON'S KINGDOM IS ESTABLISHED (2:1-46)

1. David Charges Solomon (2:1-9)

Nearing death, David gives his son Solomon a farewell charge (vv. 2-9)[1] that stands out as one of the more significant texts of these initial scenes in Kings. On the level of plot, David's instructions serve the story to reinforce his characterization and to set the stage for reading Solomon's actions as he secures his kingdom. On the level of theological meaning, the charge, with references to Deuteronomy, establishes a frame for evaluating the reigns of the kings who will follow David, yet it also introduces tension with the promise that Yahweh made to David that his throne would last forever (2 Samuel 7). This tension will continue through the narrative, for the story of Israel is fundamentally a chronicle of the failure of kingship.

2:1-4 David instructs Solomon to keep the Law of Moses. He appears to have in mind especially Deuteronomy 5:33–6:5 and 10:12-13. The "law of the king" in Deuteronomy 17:14-20 may also be in view. When the role of the Torah is seen in the larger story (see 1 Kgs 8:9,53,56; 2 Kgs 14:6; 18:6,12; 21:8; 23:25), the reader also hears in David's words the voice of the narrator. Deuteronomy, and David's speech, will serve as a foil for reading the narrative of Israel's kings. Later in the story, for example, the narrator says of Josiah, the king like David, that there was no king like him "who turned to the LORD as he did—with all his heart and with all his soul and with all his strength, in accordance with all the Law of Moses" (23:25).

When David mentions the promise that Yahweh made to him, he surely has in mind the promise of 2 Samuel 7 that God would set

---

[1]Commentators often see correspondence with similar "death-bed" speeches in Scripture (cf., e.g., Genesis 49; Deuteronomy 31–33; Joshua 23–24; 1 Samuel 12).

one of his sons on his throne and establish an eternal kingdom. However, there is not in 2 Samuel 7 exactly the conditional promise that David remembers here. Yahweh would "punish him [David's descendant(s)] with the rod of men," but he adds that his love would "never be taken away from him" (2 Sam 7:14-15). On the other hand, Psalm 132 expresses the same conditional promise David recalls to Solomon: "If your sons keep my covenant and the statutes I teach them, then their sons will sit on your throne for ever and ever" (v. 12). Resolving the apparent conflict, Bruce K. Waltke demonstrates that the unconditional covenants (on the pattern of ancient Near Eastern grants) in the Old Testament (i.e., Yahweh's covenants with Noah, Abraham, and David) have conditional elements. The covenant with David was based on David's righteous desire to build a house for his God and "a prior spiritual relationship," which by implication should be maintained. Yahweh also adopts David and his descendants ("I will be his father, and he shall be my son," 2 Sam 7:14), which is the basis for punishing rebellious sons. And even David himself suffers punishment for his sins in the affair with the wife of Uriah the Hittite. The effect of the conditional aspects of Yahweh's eternal and irrevocable covenant with David is that it establishes "the hope that Yahweh would raise up a loyal son."[2] In the same vein, Avraham Gileadi reasons that the unconditional and conditional aspects of the Davidic covenant "[leave] open the possibility of Yahweh's appointment of a loyal Davidic monarch in the event of a disloyal monarch's default."[3]

Nevertheless, the tension between the two *versions* of the covenant that Yahweh made with David (Yahweh's promise in 2 Samuel 7 and David's words to Solomon in 1 Kgs 2:1-4), even if it

---

[2]Bruce K. Waltke, "The Phenomenon of Conditionality within Unconditional Covenants," in *Israel's Apostasy and Restoration: Essays in Honor of Roland K. Harrison*, ed. Avraham Gileadi (Grand Rapids: Baker, 1988), pp. 130-132.

[3]Avraham Gileadi, "The Davidic Covenant: A Theological Basis for Corporate Protection," in *Israel's Apostasy and Restoration: Essays in Honor of Roland K. Harrison*, ed. Avraham Gileadi (Grand Rapids: Baker, 1988), p. 159. Referencing Hobbs, J. Gordon McConville also argues that the promise to David (2 Sam 7:1-17) may be implicitly conditional, "signal[ing] the discrepancy between expectation and performance in the life of the kings" ("Narrative and Meaning in the Books of Kings," *Biblia* 70 [1989]: 38; see Hobbs, *2 Kings*, p. xxiv).

is just surface tension, drives the larger narrative of Kings. God has declared that David's house would be eternal, but this unconditional aspect of the promise only lies in the background of Kings. The story of kingship in Israel is about how David's descendants *do not* faithfully **walk in his ways**.[4] The temple that David's son will build is destroyed at the end of the account, and a son of David is exiled to Babylon. Both author and reader know that the descendants of David do not remain loyal to Yahweh. The issue is not whether the promise is conditional; Yahweh clearly punishes the descendants of David for their unfaithfulness. The question is, how is Yahweh's promise to David unconditional? How will David's throne be established forever? For an audience in exile, this is the underlying question of the book of Kings — for the unconditional aspect of the Davidic covenant raises the hope that the fortunes of Israel could be restored.[5]

But the tension between the unconditional and conditional aspects of the covenant with David in Kings represents an even larger theological question.[6] It is in effect the tension between divine will and free will: God's purpose in history in the face of human choices. The road that Israel takes is fundamentally a matter of choice. Both Solomon and Jeroboam (and their descendants) choose to follow a course that leads them away from Yahweh. And this then becomes the tension between the need to punish Israel and her kings for unfaithfulness and the desire for them to receive the blessings of the covenant — the tension between law and grace. Ultimately, grace wins.[7] Yahweh will

---

[4]David asserts that his descendants should keep the Law of Moses and walk before Yahweh "with all their heart and soul," so that they will "prosper" (from שָׂכַל, *śākal*) and always have a man from the house of David on the throne (vv. 3-4). Of the kings of Judah in the larger story, Hezekiah and Josiah best meet these conditions. Hezekiah "does right in the eyes of Yahweh as his father David" and "prospers" ("was successful" in the NIV, from *śākal*; 2 Kings 18:3,7). Josiah follows Yahweh "with all his heart and with all his soul and with all his strength, in accordance with all the Law of Moses" (2 Kings 23:25).

[5]See Gileadi, "The Davidic Covenant," p. 159.

[6]Some scholars resolve the tension between the conditional and unconditional versions of God's covenant with David by saying that the promise for a son on the throne of Judah was unconditional, while ruling over the northern tribes was conditional. Provan argues that this is unlikely. The "throne of Israel" (v. 4) must refer to the United Kingdom as it does in 1 Kgs 8:20 and 10:9 (*1 and 2 Kings*, p. 35).

[7]See J. Gordon McConville, *Grace in the End: A Study in Deuteronomic Theology*, Studies in Old Testament Biblical Theology (Grand Rapids:

anoint a loyal son to sit on David's throne, and a descendant of David will be the Messiah who dies for the sins of the world!

2:5-9 The turn to vengeance in David's instructions appears to be inconsistent with his emphasis on keeping the law. On the surface, he moves from piety to personal revenge for wrongs done him during his reign. Yet, are his instructions motivated solely by personal concerns? Walsh describes David's speech as consisting of "platitudes and pragmatism": Solomon should "obey the law" and watch out for his enemies.[8] Provan adds that David's pragmatic approach is designed to secure for Solomon a unified kingdom. When the dying king describes Solomon as **a man of wisdom** (v. 9; cf. v. 6, the first time in Kings that he is named wise), his connotation is one who is shrewd and calculating.[9] David, the politician, is well aware of the forces in the kingdom that are working against a unified Israel.[10] In assassinating both **Abner** and **Amasa** (2 Sam 3:22-30; 20:8-22), **Joab** undermined overtures toward political reconciliation with northern opponents. As a member of the house of Saul (2 Sam 16:5-14; 19:15-23), **Shimei** would remain a threat to an Israel and Judah aligned under the rule of Solomon.

Viewed from another angle, however, personal issues clearly color David's words. All three characters remembered by David were in some way associated with **Absalom**'s rebellion. Does he not remember Joab as the one who, in defiance of his instructions, killed Absalom (2 Sam 18:4-17)? Afterwards, David tried to replace Joab as commander of his army with Amasa, Absalom's commanding officer, only to have Joab assassinate him (2 Sam 17:13; 19:25; 20:4-13). David also recalls that **"the sons of Barzillai . . . stood by me when I fled from your brother Absalom,"** and **"Shimei . . . called down bitter curses on me."**

In addition, David's words belie feelings of personal offense.[11] He begins with, **"You yourself know what Joab son of Zeruiah *did***

Zondervan, 1993), pp. 90-91, 121-122, 134-139; "Narrative and Meaning," 46-48; Provan, *1 and 2 Kings*, pp. 31-32.

[8]Walsh, *1 Kings*, pp. 38-39.

[9]This is David's sense whether he is being pragmatic or is motivated by personal revenge.

[10]Provan, *1 and 2 Kings*, p. 34.

[11]Fokkelman also sees David's instructions as being motivated by a desire for personal revenge (*Narrative Art and Poetry*, pp. 386-388).

to me" (v. 5). When he commands Solomon to dispatch **Shimei . . . to the grave *in blood*,** the reader hears David counter Shimei's charge that Yahweh was judging David because he was "a man of blood" (2 Sam 16:8).

The key word "swear" also surfaces here with consequence. David recalls his oath to Shimei, **"I swore to him by the LORD: 'I will not put you to death by the sword.'"** He then instructs Solomon to eliminate him **in blood.** The narrator may expect the reader to hear Nathan's words to David after the murder of Uriah: "The sword will never depart from your house" (2 Sam 12:10). So, David passes the sword on to his son Solomon.[12]

But even more telling, David's instructions to Solomon, whether uttered for political or personal reasons, call attention with appalling irony to the main failure of his life. The dying monarch says of Shimei, **"Do not consider him innocent."** When describing why Joab should die, he says, **"Shedding their blood in peacetime as if in battle, and with that blood stained the belt around his waist and the sandals on his feet."** Yet who of the characters in the story is guiltier than David of shedding innocent blood? Was he not the very one who instructed this same Joab to have killed in battle the innocent Uriah?

So, with his controlled use of irony, the narrator allows the inconsistencies in David's final words to Solomon, with all of their ambiguity, to characterize Israel's greatest king. David is a complicated character, sometimes a model of devotion to Yahweh, at other times as self-serving as any king in Israel. When he is humble and "giving," he receives the blessings of Yahweh. The "grasping" David suffers both personally and politically.[13] Both men surface in his dying words to the son who would continue his house. The kings who follow will prove less complex, sometimes devoted to the law, more often grasping for whatever political or personal gain they can attain. In spite of his weaknesses, David will overshadow subsequent

---

[12]Brueggemann also connects Nathan's oracle in 2 Sam 12:10 with the events in 1 Kings 1–2 (*1 & 2 Kings*, p. 40).

[13]David M. Gunn characterizes David's story as alternating between the public and private spheres and between episodes of "giving" and "grasping" (*The Story of King David: Genre and Interpretation*, JSOTSup 6 [Sheffield: JSOT Press, 1978; reprint, 1982], pp. 94-111 [page citations are to the reprint edition]).

rulers as the one whose heart was "fully devoted" to Yahweh (cf. 11:4; cf. 3:14; 9:4-5; 11:6,33,38).

2. David Dies, and Solomon's Kingdom Is Established (2:10-12)

2:10-12 David dies and is buried in the city that he had taken and made his capital (2 Sam 5:6-12). When the narrator says that David **rests with his fathers**, he is using an idiom for death, which originated in the custom of family-tomb burials. David, however, is the first of his lineage to be buried in Jerusalem. In Kings, the phrase may also indicate a peaceful death (see comments on 1 Kgs 22:40).[14] After supplying an abstract of the reign (see 2 Sam 5:1-5) and burial of the monarch, the narrator includes a final statement that deserves emphasis. Skillfully, he adds that Solomon's **rule was firmly** *established* (כוּן, *kûn*). His use of *kûn* ("establish") echoes the language of 2 Samuel 5:12; 7:12,13,16,26, and suggests a providential hand. Yahweh has kept his promise to David and placed Solomon on David's throne.[15]

3. Adonijah Asks for Abishag (2:13-18)

2:13-18 With naming (i.e., **the son of Haggith** and **Solomon's mother**) the narrator establishes the relationships that dominate this scene. **Adonijah**, the rival to Solomon's throne, approaches the Queen Mother with a request. When she asks, **"Do you come peacefully?"** (הֲשָׁלוֹם, *hăšālôm*), the narrator situates Adonijah with another usurper in Kings. Both Joram and Jezebel ask Jehu the same question before their demise (2 Kgs 9:22,31). Adonijah requests that he be given David's bedmate, **Abishag the Shunammite**. He prefaces his request with words that are at odds with the details already laid out by the narrator. **"All Israel looked to me as their king"** contrasts with "all the people" who went up after Solomon in 1:39-40. And **"The kingdom was mine . . ."** must reflect Adonijah's irrational, perhaps even arrogant, point of view. However, **it has come to him from the Lord** represents what must be the point of view of the narrator,

---

[14]Cogan, *1 Kings*, pp. 174-175.
[15]Provan, *1 and 2 Kings*, p. 37; see comments on 2:46 and "The Succession Story Viewed in Context."

that Solomon is Yahweh's choice to succeed David.[16] Again, the narrator indirectly affirms that God is working in these events.

4. Solomon Eliminates Adonijah (2:19-25)

2:19-21 The request for Abishag is couched in ambiguity. What motivates the king's older brother to request **Abishag**? Taking a concubine of the king appears to have been generally perceived as an attempt at a *coup d'état* (see 2 Sam 3:6-8; 16:20-22). Is Adonijah scheming for the kingdom, or simply infatuated with Abishag? Even more intriguing, why does Bathsheba relay his request to the king? Does she see an opportunity to remove her son's primary rival to the throne, or does she want Abishag, her husband's beautiful young companion, out of the palace?[17] The careful wording by both parties and subtle changes in the petition by Bathsheba (e.g., **"one small request"**) are calculating. Nevertheless, their motives remain elusive.

2:22-25 Solomon's reaction is less opaque. He views this appeal as an attempt to take his throne. In spite of the statement that Solomon's throne had been established (v. 12), the king feels threatened by Adonijah.[18] After declaring that he would not refuse his mother (note the repetition of "refuse" [vv. 16,17,20] suggesting emphasis), he *refuses* her request. The king's word is not reliable. Solomon has sworn to protect Adonijah, unless some "evil be found in him" (1:51-52). Does his brother's request warrant Solomon's response? Politically, perhaps Adonijah's imprudence demands such a harsh response. Morally, however, is the king's reaction appropriate from one who is Yahweh's anointed?

---

[16]Often in Hebrew narrative, characters (even minor characters) appear to represent the point of view of the storyteller (see Shimon Bar-Efrat, "Literary Modes and Methods in the Biblical Narrative: In View of 2 Samuel 10–20 and 1 Kings 1–2," *Immanuel* 8 [Spring 1978]: 22; Uriel Simon, "Minor Characters in Biblical Narrative," *JSOT* 46 [1990]: 18). For example, רָאָה (*rā'āh*, "to see") is the key word in the Abraham narrative, as is reflected when Abraham says to Isaac, "God himself will provide [*see* for himself/'see to it' (יִרְאֶה, *yir'eh*)] the lamb" (Gen 22:8). Hagar, a minor character, expresses the main theological idea of the story when she says, "I have now seen the One who sees me" (Gen 16:13).

[17]Berlin, *Poetics and Interpretation*, pp. 29-30.

[18]To a lesser degree, he also feels threatened by Joab and Shimei (Fokkelman, *Narrative Art and Poetry*, pp. 396-397, 408).

The double oath that Solomon utters indicts the king. Swearing in the name of Yahweh, he expresses the belief, already indirectly made by the narrator, that "[God] **has established** [*kûn*] **me securely on the throne of my father and has founded a dynasty** [literally, "house"] **for me as he promised.**" Solomon believes that Yahweh is keeping his promise to David (2 Samuel 7), although David's house is now "for me a house." However, if Yahweh has established Solomon on his father's throne, how is Adonijah a threat to Solomon? Since Cain and Abel, God has never sanctioned *brother* taking the life of *brother*, especially among his people Israel. Yahweh is keeping his promise to David, but does he condone Solomon's actions to *secure* the throne?

5. Solomon Exiles Abiathar (2:26-27)

2:26-27 Solomon now acts to remove a key supporter of Adonijah, **Abiathar the priest**. Abiathar escaped the massacre at Nob with the ephod and joined David's band of men being pursued by Saul (1 Sam 22:20-22; 23:6). He later served as priest with Zadok when David received the kingdom of Israel (2 Sam 8:17). Abiathar's exile to **Anathoth** fulfills **the word the Lord had spoken** to Samuel about the house of Eli (1 Sam 2:27-36).[19] Albeit, the statement that the "word of the LORD" was fulfilled is the only place in 1 Kings 1–2 where the narrator explicitly says that Yahweh sanctions an action!

6. Solomon Eliminates Joab (2:28-35)

2:28-33 When **Joab** hears what Solomon had done to Adonijah, he takes asylum in **the tent of the LORD. Benaiah** is sent to eliminate Joab. Apparently out of respect for the altar, he returns with a message from Joab. In response, **Solomon** gives a speech that recalls the deathbed charge from David to eliminate Joab because of bloodguilt (1 Kgs 2:5-6). However, the subtle ironies of this charge surface

---

[19]Since Abiathar was of the house of Eli (see 1 Sam 22:20), Zadok as his replacement (see v. 35 below) apparently is the "faithful priest" finally imagined by that prophetic word (1 Sam 2:35). Jeremiah, a priest from Anathoth, may have been a descendant of Abiathar (Jer. 1:1).

again to undermine Solomon's actions. **Joab** appears to have assassinated **Abner**, in part, out of personal revenge for the death of his brother Asahel (see 2 Sam 3:30). Yet, Joab also eliminated both Abner (as Israel's commanding officer) and **Amasa** (as Joab's replacement after the death of Absalom) for political reasons — as Solomon will eliminate Joab to secure his kingdom. The law of asylum (Exod. 21:12-14) only offers refuge to those who have caused accidental death. Does this justify Solomon's actions, which are clearly motivated by political concerns? The law also says that one is to be taken away from the altar, a "technicality" that Solomon overlooks.[20] And Solomon is also mistaken, for it is the guilt of his father that really lies behind these events, **the guilt of the innocent blood that Joab shed** on behalf of David (v. 31). The ghost of Uriah the Hittite rears his hoary head again!

2:34-35 As Joab had eliminated his rivals, Benaiah executes Solomon's command and kills Joab. Benaiah is placed in Joab's position as commander of the army. **Zadok** replaces **Abiathar** as priest.

7. Solomon Makes an Oath to Shimei (2:36-38)

2:36-38 Solomon sends for **Shimei**, a Benjamite from the house of Saul and a supporter of Absalom's rebellion (2 Sam 16:5-14). He was to stay in **Jerusalem** and not **cross the Kidron Valley**. In that direction was his home in the territory of Benjamin. These constraints on Shimei's freedom were no doubt designed to keep him from fomenting insurrection in an area where opposition to the new regime could materialize. Solomon *swears* that Shimei will bear responsibility for his own death if he violates this charge.

8. Solomon Eliminates Shimei; The Kingdom Is Established in Solomon's Hand (2:39-46)

2:39-41 Three years later, two of **Shimei's** servants flee to **Achish, king of Gath**, the same refuge David sought in fleeing from Saul. Five times in these verses, the narrator sounds the place to

---

[20]Provan, *1 and 2 Kings*, p. 42.

which Shimei goes to retrieve his slaves. **Gath** is in the opposite direction of the Kidron and Shimei's home in Benjamin. There is here no hint of subversive behavior.[21]

2:42-45 Solomon, to his own advantage, uses this event as a pretext to eliminate **Shimei**. The king craftily manipulates the facts by misquoting his earlier conversation with Shimei. There is no record that Solomon had forced Shimei to swear by Yahweh, and the king had not associated the death penalty with leaving Jerusalem. Shimei would die the day that he crossed the Kidron valley! On false charges, Solomon removes an "enemy" of the house of David by misconstruing an oath.[22] The king who overlooked the "letter of the law" on asylum when he dispatched Joab now uses the "letter of the law," a technicality, to remove another potential threat.[23] Also reflecting something of the character of Solomon, the king shifts the responsibility for the now imminent execution of Shimei (vv. 37,42-43) even to Yahweh: **"the LORD will repay you."**[24]

2:46 Benaiah is dispatched as executioner. The word פָּגַע (*pāgaʿ*, **struck down** in the NIV) surfaces again (in Kings only in 2:25,29,31,32,34,46) to reinforce the thematic brutality of Solomon's rise to power.[25] The narrator adds that rule is now **firmly established** [*kûn*] **in Solomon's hands** [literally, "in the hand of Solomon"]! The kingdom already given by Yahweh as fulfillment of the promise to David (surely the meaning of v. 12 above) is "established *in Solomon's hands*." The repetition of *kûn* ("establish") with the addition of "*in Solomon's hands*" suggests emphasis. With his own hands, Solomon has taken by cunning and scheming what had already been given. In a brief stroke, the narrator insinuates that the three executions (all recorded after v. 12) were the responsibility of Solomon, not Yahweh!

---

[21]Walsh, *1 Kings*, p. 62.

[22]These observations are based on Walsh's excellent treatment of this episode (ibid., pp. 60-65).

[23]Provan, *1 and 2 Kings*, p. 42.

[24]Walsh, *I Kings*, p. 64.

[25]Ibid., p. 65.

EXCURSUS

THE SUCCESSION STORY VIEWED IN CONTEXT
(1:1–2:46)

The introduction to the story of the Davidic monarchy is a brilliant literary composition that puts closure on historical lines that began in 1 and 2 Samuel and anticipates the episodes that follow by establishing the ideological construct for reading the larger story. This is accomplished with deft literary expertise. In particular, the inspired narrator's use of allusions with ironic effect, key words/ motifs, and an indirect, literary approach highlight the theological character of 1 and 2 Kings.

Resonance with earlier events in Samuel frames these introductory scenes and guides the reader in interpreting the events surrounding the succession of Solomon. For example, allusions to Absalom's rebellion color the reader's impressions of Adonijah and foreshadow his demise. The ironic effect of this technique is particularly significant as the image of David's adulterous affair with Bathsheba and the consequent cover-up and murder of her husband are conjured up. The description of Abishag's service reminds the reader of Uriah's ewe lamb who was taken into the king's "bosom" (1:2), and Bathsheba's statement that she and her son were in danger of being treated as "criminals" ("sinners" [חַטָּאִים, ḥaṭṭā'îm], 1:21) calls to mind the consequences of David's adultery (see above).

And these events *are a consequence* of the king's sin! When David passed judgment on the rich man in Nathan's parable, declaring, "He must pay for that lamb four times over" (2 Sam 12:6), he was passing judgment on himself. In the narrative, Adonijah would be the fourth son of David to die an unnatural death.[26] The theme of bloodguilt puts an exclamation point on this irony. Both David and

---

[26]See Ackerman, "Knowing Good and Evil," 49-51. Fokkelman demonstrates that the death of each of the four sons follows "the unjustified sexual possession of a woman (women)" and asserts that "it is clear as day" that David's sin began this cycle (*Narrative Art and Poetry*, pp. 413-414). The four are: the child born of David's "affair" with Bathsheba (2 Sam 12:15-23), Amnon (2 Sam 13:1-33), Absalom (2 Sam 18:1-18), and Adonijah (1 Kgs 2:13-25). It is not just a coincidence that many of the characters who take

Solomon excuse the assassination of Joab on the basis of bloodguilt (2:5-6,31-33), yet David, in the matter of Uriah the Hittite, is the one who bears the greater guilt. So, the storyteller adeptly affirms that David's transgression precipitated the sorry events surrounding the succession of his son Solomon to the throne.

The key word "swear/oath" (root שָׁבַע, *šb'*) further brings to light key theological themes in the story. On one level, swearing as a motif calls attention to the promise that Yahweh had made to David concerning the son who would rule in his place (2 Sam 7:1-17). This suggests that, even though God is not *on stage* in this story, he is a player. He will keep his promise to David. Yet, on another level, the two main actors are further characterized negatively with this thematic pattern. Both David and Solomon only "technically" keep their promises/oaths (see comments on 2:1-46). The contrast herein brought out between the character of Yahweh and his anointed rulers reinforces the question neatly set forward in the narrative: Is God's promise to David in 2 Samuel 7 conditional or unconditional? Will David's descendants enjoy the blessings of an eternal kingdom, or suffer the curses of a broken covenant as they disregard the "Law of Moses" (1 Kgs 2:3) and walk in their own way?

Also, the motif of peace/violence permeates this story. Solomon, whose name means "peace" (שְׁלֹמֹה, *š'lōmōh*), inherits the sword of his father David, as Nathan had prophesied (2 Sam 12:10; see comments on 2:5-9). He carries it well in his consolidation of power. The key word *pāga'* ("strike down," "attack") serves to underscore the violence that characterizes Solomon's rise to power and portends an ominous future for the dynasty of David. In the larger story, Solomon's prayer, "On David and his descendants, his house and his throne, may there be the LORD's peace forever" (2:33), will not be realized. Initially, Solomon will be blessed with a kingdom of peace, but adversaries will be raised up against him (see comments on 5:1-6; 8:54-61; 11:14-40). Before the curtain closes, the house of David will suffer ruthless acts of violence.[27]

With his indirect approach, the storyteller is better able to

---

the stage in this first act of Kings played a prominent role in preceding acts in Samuel that delineated the events following David's sin. In particular, note the role of Bathsheba, Nathan, Joab, Barzillai, Shimei, and Jonathan.

[27]Brueggemann, *1 & 2 Kings*, pp. 11, 22-23, 37, 39-40.

accomplish his theological purposes. Skillfully, the narrator indicates that Solomon is Yahweh's choice to sit on the throne of his father, fulfilling the promise to David in 2 Samuel 7:1-17. With the use of *kûn* ("establish") in 2:12 (see also 2:24,45,46), the narrator subtly connects the succession story with the promise in 2 Samuel 7:16 that "your throne will be established (*kûn*) forever."[28] Also, while the narrator never explicitly says that Solomon is Yahweh's choice, several characters clearly affirm his election. Through Benaiah (1:36-37), Adonijah (2:15), Solomon (2:24), and, above all, through David himself (1:48, by way of Jonathan), the narrator signifies Solomon as Israel's anointed king. When the reader remembers that Solomon is Jedidiah ("beloved of the LORD"; 2 Sam 12:25), Yahweh's hand in these events is confirmed.

At the same time, however, the narrator keeps his distance from the speech and actions of the major characters as they participate in the palace intrigue. Nathan and Bathsheba are calculating, perhaps even manipulative, in their interactions with the king. Even David displays the complexities of an all-too-human monarch. In his last breath, he admonishes Solomon to walk in the way of Yahweh and, in the same breath, councils him to eliminate political enemies who had done personal harm to David. Solomon carries out his father's wishes and removes his rival to boot — even after the narrator informs the reader "his rule was firmly *established*" (2:12). The executions of Adonijah, Joab, and Shimei (2:13-46) are all narrated after that important assertion. At no time does the narrator intimate that these actions are of Yahweh. The only act that the inspired storyteller explicitly associates with Yahweh is the banishment of Abiathar to Anathoth, "fulfilling the word the LORD had spoken at Shiloh about the house of Eli" (2:27).[29] After Solomon has done away with perceived adversaries, the narrator concludes his account with "the kingdom was now firmly *established in Solomon's hands*" (2:46). In a statement that parallels the

---

[28]Provan, *1 and 2 Kings*, p. 37.

[29]The prophet Nathan had by the word of Yahweh communicated the oracle of dynastic promise to David (2 Sam 7:8-17) and named Solomon Jedidiah (2 Sam 12:25). That he is, therefore, a major actor in the succession of Solomon, but bears no word from Yahweh concerning his election, reinforces the indirect literary style by which the narrator is able to affirm Yahweh's role and keep his distance from what the characters do. There is a prophet here but no word from Yahweh!

declaration in 2:12, the addition of (literally) "in the hand of Solomon" suggests that he was seizing power. Solomon was grasping a kingdom that had already been *established!*[30]

This accomplished use of literary technique enables the storyteller to bring out the tension between Yahweh's sovereign will and human choices. God fulfills his promise to David but is not responsible for the way Solomon establishes the throne *"in his hands"* (2:46). Recognizing this mollifies the discomfort that many feel when the young king executes his brother (and other enemies) and challenges the view that God participates in Solomon's immoral acts. Misconstruing this story, Richard Nelson even writes:

> Yahweh is an unindicted co-conspirator in the palace intrigue. As the Book of Kings unfolds, the reader will recognize Yahweh as a master of deception. . . . Perhaps it is offensive that no moral judgments are made on these shady characters, or worse, that the god of universal history should be involved in a sleazy harem intrigue. . . . Yahweh's plan and will must be effected, and for God, at least, the ends justify the means.[31]

This lack of literary sensitivity obscures an important theological message in Kings. In the opening act of his story, the narrator demonstrates that Yahweh's will is accomplished in spite of human weaknesses. He is behind the scenes, keeping his promise, but there is not anything here to suggest that he condones Solomon's purge.[32]

---

[30]Walsh observes that the "establish" statements in 2:12 and 46 form an *inclusio* for Solomon's executions. Verse 12 represents the narrator's point of view: the kingdom was *firmly established* in Solomon's hand. In verse 46, Solomon's point of view is reflected. This is achieved when "firmly" in verse 12 becomes "in his hand" in verse 46. (The NIV's "now firmly" in v. 46 is not in the Hebrew text.) Also, "rule" (מַלְכֻת, *malᵉkûth*) in verse 12 becomes "the kingdom" (הַמַּמְלָכָה, *hammamlākāh*) in verse 46. The narrator is asserting that Solomon is "consolidating his own sovereignty" (*I Kings*, p. 46). In a similar vein, Fokkelman maintains that 2:12 and 46 indicate that the consolidation of Solomon's reign was not a result of his purge. The king only feels more secure (*Narrative Art and Poetry*, pp. 390, 409).

[31]Richard D. Nelson, *First and Second Kings*, Interpretation: A Bible Commentary for Teaching and Preaching (Louisville: John Knox Press, 1987), p. 22; cf. Brueggemann, *1 & 2 Kings*, pp. 20-23.

[32]Lillian R. Klein argues that in Judges, Yahweh withdraws from Israel and the judges as they lose sight of him (*The Triumph of Irony in the Book of Judges*, JSOTSup 68 [Sheffield: The Almond Press, 1989], pp. 38, 46, 110-111, 158,

Herein lies the brilliance of 1 Kings 1 and 2 as an introduction to the book of Kings, even though in many ways it is as much a conclusion to the succession story that began in 2 Samuel.[33] The palace maneuvering and ruthless acts are an overture to what follows because the tension between Yahweh's promise, his sovereign will, and human free will, as expressed in the path that the monarchy in Israel takes, encompasses the larger story.[34] God's plan will often clash with the choices of Israel's kings as they decide not to walk in the way of Yahweh with all of their heart. The end will show the inadequacies of kingship. When this occurs, will there be judgment or grace for Israel, and what will come of Yahweh's promise of an eternal throne for David?

---

187). Scripture affirms that God works in the immoral acts of humans, without condoning those acts. Joseph's statement to his brothers, "You intended to harm me, but God intended it for good" (Gen 50:20), does not saddle God with their guilt.

[33]In his analysis of the succession narrative, Fokkelman has demonstrated the role 1 Kings 1-2 plays as a conclusion to the story of David (*Narrative Art and Poetry*, pp. 410-418). Others see chapters 1 and 2 as integral to the account of Solomon's reign (see, e.g., Kim Ian Parker, "Repetition as a Structuring Device in 1 Kings 1-11," *JSOT* 42 [1988]: 19-27.) Since the work of Leonhard Rost in the first half of the twentieth century, a cornerstone of Old Testament study has been the view that most of 2 Samuel 1-1 Kings 2 is a "Succession Narrative" which was incorporated into the Deuteronomistic History ("DtrH"; i.e., Joshua–2 Kings; see "Introduction: Composition"). However, more recent literary analyses have challenged this assumption. Serge Frolov avers that this "is a figment of scholars' imagination," the underlying document "a likely nonentity." A literary analysis suggests that these texts "are integral components of a composition tracing the developments that took place between the death of Saul and that of David and constituting in turn a chapter in the history of the Israelite monarchy." Instead of "redactors," those who created the history should be seen as "authors" ("Succession Narrative: A 'Document' or a Phantom," 103-104).

[34]See McConville, "Narrative and Meaning," 45. McConville also sees the divergence between God's will and human responsibility as significant in Deuteronomy (*Grace in the End*, pp. 160-162), the composition that especially lies behind the theology of Kings.

1 KINGS 3

C. YAHWEH GIVES SOLOMON WISDOM AND MORE
(3:1–5:18)

After the dramatized introduction where Solomon's throne is established and then secured in his hands, the storyteller narrates an account of Yahweh's promise to Solomon at Gibeon for wisdom, wealth, and honor (3:4-15). The remainder of the story will revolve around Solomon's use/misuse of these blessings from Yahweh (chs. 3–11). Again, the composition is carefully crafted, replete with both verbal and structural ironies that serve to characterize Solomon and highlight the character of his benevolent God. While dramatized scenes with dialogue appear (e.g., 3:16-28), exposition dominates, with a lengthy description of the construction of Solomon's temple and palace (6:1–7:51). Nevertheless, the account demonstrates a well-thought-out, ingenious use of archival (see 11:41 and comments on 8:8) and narrative material to represent faithfully the reign of Israel's most impressive, and in some ways most tragic, king.

1. Solomon's Reign Is Framed (3:1-3)

3:1 The narrator now frames the story of Solomon's reign. With echoes of Deuteronomy and shadows of what will come, these initial verses of exposition highlight key themes that will characterize Solomon's rule and further reinforce the negative portrayal of Solomon already suggested. The first thing said about Solomon forms a bookend with the judgment on his reign for marrying foreigners in 1 Kings 11:1-8 — and therein foreshadows the larger story. Solomon makes **an alliance** (חתן, *ḥtn*) with the king of Egypt by marrying Pharaoh's **daughter**.[1] The verb *ḥtn* ("become a son-in-law") also

---

[1]Victor Sasson believes that the "dark lady" of the Song of Songs (see 1:6)

appears in a passage that lies behind this story: "Do not *intermarry* [*ḥtn*] with them. . . . for they will turn your sons away from following me to serve other gods" (Deut 7:3; also in Josh 23:12; cf. Deut 17:17).[2] The narrator begins with what he will develop later. In the end, Solomon's foreign wives and their gods will turn his heart from Yahweh (1 Kgs 11:1-2).[3]

The new king's building projects are another important theme introduced in these verses. Fulfilling God's promise to David (see 2 Sam 7:13), Solomon is the son of David who builds **the temple of the LORD** (literally, "the house of Yahweh"). He also builds **his palace** (literally, "his house") and extends the **wall around Jerusalem**.[4] However, the order here is odd. The narrator lists *Solomon's house* before *Yahweh's house*, even though the following account records the construction of the temple before the palace. When the narrator informs the reader that the temple took only seven years to complete, and the palace thirteen years (1 Kgs 6:38; 7:1), Solomon's priorities are brought into question.[5] Is the storyteller carefully qualifying his portrayal of Solomon even as he prepares to narrate the outstanding request that the young king makes of Yahweh at Gibeon (3:4-15)?

3:2-3 Reflecting this thrust, each of the next two statements contains a caveat. With the use of רַק (*raq*) in verses 2 and 3b (**however** and **except** in the NIV), the narrator tempers Solomon's building successes. *Only*, the people are **still sacrificing at the high places** calls to mind that Israel was to worship at "the place the LORD your God will choose . . . to put his Name for a dwelling" (Deut 12:4). The people are unable to do so, **because a temple had not yet been built**

---

was Pharaoh's daughter ("King Solomon and the Dark Lady in the Song of Songs," *VT* 39/4 [Oct. 1989]: 407-414).

[2]The law of the king also warns against returning to Egypt (Deut 17:16; see Provan, *1 and 2 Kings*, p. 44). Walsh suggests that the language indicates Solomon had become subordinate to the Pharaoh (*1 Kings*, p. 70).

[3]A literary reading suggests Solomon sows "the seeds of his own destruction" (Provan, *1 and 2 Kings*, pp. 44-46; see Walsh, *1 Kings*, pp. 70, 85; contra Cogan, *1 Kings*, p. 189).

[4]That Solomon built the wall of Jerusalem probably means he extended the wall to enclose the temple mount, which lies just north of the city of David.

[5]See especially McConville, "Narrative and Meaning," 35.

for the Name of the LORD.[6] And even after the remarkable statement that Solomon loved Yahweh, the storyteller adds, *Only,* **he offers sacrifices and burns incense on the high places.** In the appraisal of the kings to follow, even for *good* kings, worship on high places will be enough to merit a negative assessment (see, e.g., 1 Kgs 15:14). Yet of no other king does the narrator say, "He *loved* Yahweh"! Nevertheless, even this statement will later resound with discord when the reader learns that Solomon *loves* many foreign women, who turn his heart after other gods (11:1-8).[7]

2. Solomon Asks for a Discerning Heart (3:4-15)

3:4-5 Solomon now makes an entrance as he worships at one of the high places.[8] At the great **high place** in **Gibeon**, the king sacrifices **a thousand burnt offerings**, and Yahweh appears to him **in a dream**.[9] In the ancient Near East, dreams were thought to be one way that the gods communicated with man. One could encourage such divine contact by ritual at holy sites (in the scholarly literature

---

[6]See ibid.

[7]Provan, *1 and 2 Kings*, pp. 45-46.

[8]In Chronicles, the story of Solomon begins with the young king's request for wisdom at Gibeon with some differences. While the episode in Kings emphasizes Solomon, the story in Chronicles, which is an abbreviation of the account in Kings, calls attention to "all Israel" (2 Chr 1:1-17). See John Mark Hicks, *1 & 2 Chronicles,* The College Press NIV Commentary (Joplin, MO: College Press, 2001), p. 261; cf. pp. 261-264.

The account of the reign of Solomon in Chronicles (2 Chr 1:1–9:31) differs markedly from the account in Kings, with a significant abridgment of the story in Kings for the Chronicler's theological purposes. John Mark Hicks summarizes that the Chronicler leaves out Solomon's sins and emphasizes his role as the temple-builder. In his typological approach, the Chronicler presents Solomon as a second David, David and Solomon as Moses and Joshua, and Solomon and Huram-Abi as the new Bezalel and Oholiab. Theologically, the building of the temple is a high point in redemptive history, representing Yahweh's presence in the postexilic community (*1 & 2 Chronicles,* pp. 257-259).

[9]According to Chronicles, the tabernacle and bronze altar of Bezalel were located at the high place in Gibeon (2 Chr 1:3-5). Gibeon has been identified with el-Jib, a village ca. 9 km. north of Jerusalem. For the results of excavations at the site, see James B. Pritchard, in *NEAEHL*.

styled "incubation").[10] Perhaps Solomon goes to Gibeon for such a purpose. These initial verses of exposition set the stage for the dream-sequence dialogue between Yahweh and Solomon (vv. 6-14), in which Solomon is granted wisdom from above.

3:6-9 The young king's response is extraordinary. He acknowledges the **great kindness** (חֶסֶד, *ḥesed*) that Yahweh had shown to his father David, and, apparently reflecting the narrator's point of view, describes his father as (literally) "walking faithfully, with a righteous and upright heart" (v. 6). Then Solomon again (cf. 2:24) expresses his belief that Yahweh had given David **a son to sit on his throne** and had made him king (another veiled reference to 2 Samuel 7). By naming, **your servant** and **little child**,[11] Solomon humbly presents himself as a novice who is unprepared for the responsibilities of state. But his deference is not hollow or contrived. Remarkably, he asks for a **discerning heart** (literally, "a *hearing* heart . . . to discern good and evil," v. 9), not for his own good, but **to govern this great people** Yahweh had chosen! Solomon's word choice, "a great people, **too numerous to count or number**" (v. 8), recalls the promise that Yahweh had made to Abraham (Gen 13:14-17) and further commends the king.

3:10 Strategically located at the center of this scene (see below), the omniscient narrator says that Yahweh is **pleased** with Solomon's selfless request. This is the first direct expression of God's attitude toward Solomon since Nathan named him Jedidiah ("loved by the LORD," 2 Sam 12:25).

3:11-14 Because Solomon had not asked selfishly, Yahweh promises to give him **a wise and discerning heart** and more. He would receive that for which he did not ask — **riches and honor** like no other king. On the level of event, Solomon's wisdom was directly related to his successes. Carol Meyers makes a reasonable case that his "unique gifts of wisdom and of successful diplomacy" sustained and expanded the empire built by David through conquest.[12] Yet,

---

[10]See Cogan, *1 Kings*, p. 190.

[11]Solomon was old enough to have fathered Rehoboam before becoming king (see 1 Kgs 11:42; 14:21).

[12]Carol Meyers, "The Israelite Empire: In Defense of King Solomon," in *Backgrounds for the Bible*, ed. Michael Patrick O'Connor and David Noel Freedman (Winona Lake, IN: Eisenbrauns, 1987), pp. 189, 195-197.

this promise is also conditional. As his father, the son must **walk** in
the way of Yahweh and **obey his statutes and commands** to live a
long life. With his reference to **David**, Yahweh himself reinforces
what Solomon expressed in verse 6. In spite of his weaknesses, the
father of the dynasty was faithful. He is the standard, based on criteria laid out in Deuteronomy (cf., e.g., 6:1-5; 17:14-20), for evaluating the reign of Solomon and the kings who will follow. The remainder of the story of Solomon will demonstrate how Yahweh keeps his
promise to Solomon and bring out the consequences of the king's
unfaithfulness for his own reign and for those of his house who
would sit on David's throne.

3:15 The scene ends where it began. Solomon is sacrificing burnt
offerings, only this time not on one of the high places. He sacrifices
before the "ark of Yahweh's covenant"[13] in Jerusalem. The contrast
is not coincidental. The concentric structure of this scene highlights
the central statement about God's pleasure with Solomon in element X (v. 10) and by contrast the place of sacrificing in the parallel elements A and A′ (vv. 4,15b).[14]

A. Solomon sacrifices at the great high place in Gibeon (4).
 B. Yahweh appears to Solomon in a dream and speaks (5).
  C. Solomon asks for a discerning heart (6-9).
   X. *The narrator declares that Yahweh was pleased* (10).
  C′. Yahweh promises Solomon a wise and discerning
       heart and more (11-14).
 B′. Solomon awakes and realizes that it was a dream (15a).
A′. Solomon sacrifices before the ark of Yahweh in Jerusalem
     (15b).

Solomon's actions before the ark in Jerusalem must reflect the
divine wisdom that God had promised.[15] In the ancient Near East,
kings are thought to get their wisdom from the gods, but
Deuteronomy 4:6-8 says that wisdom comes from keeping Torah — as

---

[13]The NIV's "the Lord's covenant" reflects בְּרִית־אֲדֹנָי (*bᵉrîth 'ădōnāy*, MT).
Other reliable manuscripts read "the LORD's covenant" (בְּרִית־יהוה, *bᵉrîth
YHWH*). This preferred reading corresponds to the NIV emendation in verse
10 to YHWH. In both cases, *'ădōnāy* ("Lord") must be a scribal replacement
for YHWH (see DeVries, *1 Kings*, pp. 46-47).

[14]The following outline is adapted from Walsh (*2 Kings*, p. 73), with
important modifications.

[15]See Provan, *1 and 2 Kings*, p. 49; Walsh *1 Kings*, p. 74.

does 1 Kings 3:14. In accord with the Law of Moses, Solomon is now worshiping in the place where Yahweh would cause his name to dwell (see Deuteronomy 12). The naming, "ark of Yahweh's covenant," reinforces the connection with Moses and Deuteronomy.

This divine wisdom is in stark contrast with the worldly wisdom Solomon employed in efforts to secure the throne. When David described him as wise (2:6,9), the meaning was "shrewd." The wisdom that Yahweh promises will discern good from evil (vv. 9,12). Even this divine wisdom, however, will conflict with the foolish choices Solomon makes. Yahweh may give wisdom, but Solomon, as each king in Israel, has free will to choose his own course.

3. Solomon Demonstrates His Wisdom (3:16-28)

3:16-23 The account of Solomon's reign now turns to an episode that demonstrates Yahweh has blessed David's son with wisdom from above. The king administers justice for the afflicted and saves a child. In the ancient world, women without husbands were at times forced into prostitution. Their situation draws no disrespect from Solomon.

The story itself is artfully crafted. In the Hebrew text, there is more ambiguity than appears in the NIV translation of these verses. **The first one** and **the first woman** (vv. 22,27) have been added to help the reader keep up with the skirmishing. The underlying text does not identify the two beyond "this woman" and "the other woman" and does not indicate that, as most assume, the first speaker is telling the truth. The result is a composition that draws the reader into the story. The reader views the scene from Solomon's point of view and feels the tension in the dilemma that is set before him. This serves to underscore the brilliance of the judge-king, who is able to discriminate far more than the reader can discern.[16]

3:24-27 Striking by its absence, there is no interrogation, no search for verification. Justice is determined by a ploy. By clearly

---

[16]Meir Sternberg, *The Poetics of Biblical Narrative*, pp. 166-169. For a good discussion of the issues of interpretation involved, see S. Lasine, "The Riddle of Solomon's Judgment and the Riddle of Human Nature in the Hebrew Bible," *JSOT* 45 (1989): 61-86.

human means, the king is able to ferret out what only God could see (cf. 8:39) — what was in the heart of the disputants before him.[17] In this way, and by contrast with the king who eliminated rivals in chapter 2, Solomon demonstrates that this wisdom is beyond what he had before. The king calls for a **sword**. However, this time he uses it for purposes other than from when he *shrewdly* (cf. 2:6,9) was securing the throne *in his hands* (see 1:51; 2:25,34,46).[18]

3:28 The scene closes with a note that expresses the point of the story. When the people hear the king's judgment, they know that Solomon has **wisdom from God** to govern justly. This is the righteous king envisioned in royal Psalm 72:

> Endow the king with your justice, O God,
>> the royal son with your righteousness.
> He will judge your people in righteousness,
>> your afflicted ones with justice. . . .
> He will defend the afflicted among the people
>> and save the children of the needy; . . .
> For he will deliver the needy who cry out,
>> the afflicted who have no one to help.
> He will take pity on the weak and the needy
>> and save the needy from death.
> He will rescue them from oppression and violence,
>> for precious is their blood in his sight (1-2,4,12-14).

---

[17]Lasine, "Riddle of Solomon's Judgment," 77.
[18]Provan, *1 and 2 Kings*, p. 52.

1 KINGS 4

4. Solomon Rules over All Israel (4:1-20)

4:1-6 The wisdom from above is now highlighted through exposition of Solomon's administrative proficiency. Commentators often see Egyptian parallels in the offices on this list.[1] If this is correct, Egyptian influence must have begun during the reign of David because, while perhaps more complex, Solomon's cabinet for the most part mirrors David's administration (cf. 2 Sam 8:15-18; 20:23-25). Officials over **the district officers** and **in charge of the palace**,[2] and a **personal advisor** (literally, "friend of the king"[3]), are additional administrators. While plausible, an Egyptian connection is somewhat speculative. In any case, Solomon's government, as David's, looks like the nations (cf. 2 Sam 8:15-18; 20:23-25).

In addition to bureaucratic offices, several of these officials reflect continuity with the previous administration. **Jehoshaphat son of Ahilud** and **Adoniram son of Abda** serve in the same positions as under David (2 Sam 8:15-18; 20:23-25). Also, Solomon's cabinet includes sons of **Zadok, Shisha**,[4] and **Nathan**. The notation that

---

[1]See, e.g., T.N.D. Mettinger, *Solomonic State Officials: A Study of the Civil Government Officials of the Israelite Monarchy*, Coniectanea Biblia (Lund: Gleerup, 1971), pp. 158-159; Brueggemann, *1 & 2 Kings*, pp. 43, 45, 58. That Solomon married the daughter of Pharaoh (3:1) lays a foundation for influence from Egypt, forbidden in Deut 17:16.

[2]The idiom in Hebrew is "over the house" (also translated "palace administrator" in 2 Kgs 10:5; 18:18,37; 19:2). Obadiah functions in this role for Ahab (1 Kgs 18:3). The title appears on seal impressions from the seventh-sixth centuries and in the Royal Steward Inscription from an Iron Age tomb in Silwan (probably the tomb of Shebna; cf. Isa 22:15-19; 2 Kgs 18:18); see Dever, *Biblical Writers Know*, pp. 206, 219-220.

[3]Hushai, "the friend of David," may have been a personal advisor to David (2 Sam 15:37; 16:16).

[4]"Shisha" may derive from an Egyptian title for the office of secretary.

Zadok and Abiathar (also priests of David, 2 Sam 20:25) served as priests is curious. When securing his throne, Solomon dismissed Abiathar and replaced him with Zadok (1 Kgs 2:26-27,35). The reference to **Azariah son of Zadok—the priest** in verse 2, must mean that Zadok's son had become high priest, but Solomon had exiled Abiathar to Anathoth (2:26-27). Since Abiathar's exile fulfilled the word of the LORD about the house of Eli (v. 27), this statement may be a subtle suggestion that Solomon's decisions are not always consistent with divine wisdom.[5] In the larger account of his reign, this theme emerges as a central message.

The fact that the chief priest **Azariah** is listed first in Solomon's cabinet, in contrast with the commander of the army in David's cabinet (2 Sam 8:15-18; 20:23-25), may represent a change in political influence that corresponds with the construction of the temple.[6] That the last official mentioned here is **Adoniram** who was over the **forced labor** may also be significant (v. 6; cf. 5:13-14; 9:15,21). Later, Adoniram will play a tragic role in the division of the kingdom (12:18). At this point, the organization of the king's cabinet indicates that Solomon wisely maintained continuity with his father's regime.

4:7-19 In spite of a general belief among scholars that **all Israel** (vv. 1,7) signifies the northern kingdom, the natural sense here and elsewhere in 1 Kings 1–11 is all of the twelve tribes, including both Israel and Judah.[7] Solomon's district officers[8] function as tax collec-

---

The individual called by the title here is probably David's secretary Seraiah (cf. 2 Sam 8:17; 20:25; 1 Chr 18:16). With a son named Elihoreph, he may also be an Egyptian (Mettinger, *Solomonic State Officials,* pp. 25-30).

[5]Apparently overlooking the narrator's statement in 1 Kgs 2:27 that Abiathar's exile was of the LORD, Provan believes that the note in verse 4 about Abiathar serving as a priest under Solomon indicates the divine wisdom that the king received in chapter 3 caused his reinstatement (*1 and 2 Kings,* p. 54). The reference to Zadok and Abiathar may be intended to record the priests who served only a short term at the beginning of Solomon's reign (Cogan, *1 Kings,* p. 202).

[6]Tomoo Ishida, "Solomon (person)," in A*BD.*

[7]Provan persuasively argues this point (*1 and 2 Kings,* pp. 55-56, 103-104; cf. Walsh, *1 Kings,* pp. 86-87).

[8]The NIV's "district governors" (נְצִיבִים, $n^e\hat{sib}\hat{im}$) in verse 7 follows a minority text that overlooks the majority reading "district officers" (נִצָּבִים, $ni\hat{ss}\bar{a}b\hat{im}$). It is also inconsistent with $ni\hat{ss}\bar{a}b\hat{im}$ in verses 5 and 27. This will be important when "governor" ($n^e\hat{sib}$) appears in verse 19 (Provan, *1 and 2 Kings,* p. 54).

tors who are responsible for provisioning the king and his house. Anomalies in the list of names are difficult to explain. A complete record includes proper name and patronym (i.e., father's name; e.g., **Baana son of Hushai**, v. 16). One name, **Ahimaaz** (v. 15), has no patronym, and five names are only patronyms (e.g., **Ben-Hur**; literally, "son of Hur"; see vv. 8-11,13). The last category of names is thought by some to represent Canaanite officials. Administrative lists from Ugarit include only patronyms for certain hereditary offices, and the patronym-only names from Solomon's list may overlap with annexed Canaanite territory. However, while plausible, this view remains speculative.[9] Also, the intrusive, complete record in verse 12, **Baana son of Ahilud**, undermines the alternate suggestion that these five names denote that the top right corner of the original list was torn.[10] It is noteworthy that two of Solomon's sons-in-law were overseers (vv. 11,15).

Perhaps more important are the geographical references that cross tribal boundaries. Solomon initiates what appears to be a new system of collecting taxes. However, commentators claim too much when they argue that the new king is consciously attempting to subvert traditional tribal loyalties. DeVries cautions that the system may represent seasonal production.[11] Each tax official was responsible for provisions for one month of the year. It would be natural to coordinate his month and geographical area with seasonal yields. Many also see the list as indicating that Solomon taxes only northern tribes. References to Judah and Jerusalem are missing from the list. Even so, Provan persuasively argues that verse 10 represents a district in Judah. **Socoh** only occurs in Scripture as a town of Judah (Josh 15:35,48; 1 Sam 17:1; 2 Chr 11:7); **Hepher** appears as a clan of Judah in 1 Chronicles 4:6; and Arab, with the same consonants as **Arubboth**, is listed as a town of Judah in Joshua 15:52. This reading would suggest that the last phrase in verse 19 (**He was the only governor over the district** in the NIV; literally, "There was one governor who was in the land"), which is sometimes interpreted as describing Judah,[12] should be understood as referring to Azariah in

---

[9]See Mettinger, *Solomonic State Officials,* pp. 120-121.

[10]DeVries, *1 Kings,* p. 68.

[11]Ibid., pp. 71-72.

[12]The LXX adds "in Judah," picked up by the NRSV, at the end of verse 19.

verse 5. He was the one **governor** (נְצִיב, *nᵉṣîb*, v. 19) over the district officers (נִצָּבִים, *niṣṣābîm*, v. 5).[13] In any case, the list highlights the role that taxation plays in Solomon's regime, echoing the warnings of Samuel in 1 Samuel 8:15-17.[14]

4:20 Notwithstanding the outline in the NIV (which places v. 20 in the next paragraph), verse 20 brackets the statement in verse 1 that **King Solomon ruled over all Israel**.[15] The result of governing with wisdom from above is that the people of **Judah and Israel** prosper and are **happy**. Again, Psalm 72 mirrors the narrator's point of view:

> Endow the king with your justice, O God,
>> the royal son with your righteousness.
> He will judge your people in righteousness,
>> your afflicted ones with justice.
> The mountains will bring prosperity to the people,
>> the hills the fruit of righteousness. . . .
> In his days the righteous will flourish;
>> prosperity will abound till the moon is no more
>>> (vv. 1-3,7).

The people also become **as numerous as the sand on the seashore**, which subtly alludes to the covenant Yahweh had made with Abraham (Gen 22:17; 32:12). Beyond his promises to David and Solomon (2 Samuel 7; 1 Kings 3), Yahweh is faithfully working to keep his oath to Abraham (cf. 2 Kgs 13:23)!

---

[13]Provan, *1 and 2 Kings*, pp. 56-57. For a different explanation of Solomon's twelve administrative districts, see Mettinger, *Solomonic State Officials*, pp. 111-127; Cogan, *1 Kings*, pp. 205-211. Cogan believes "Judah" appeared twice in verses 19-20, having dropped out of verse 19 due to scribal error (p. 211).

[14]In the context of defending a tenth-century state for Solomon, Dever posits archaeological identifications for the administrative centers in 1 Kings 4, demonstrating the plausibility of this list for the time of Solomon (*Biblical Writers Know*, pp. 138-144; following Yohanan Aharoni, *The Land of the Bible: A Historical Geography*, 2nd ed. [Philadelphia: Westminster, 1979], pp. 308-320).

[15]That verse 20 should be read with the preceding section is supported by the Hebrew text of chapter 4, which ends with verse 20.

5. Solomon Rules the Nations (4:21-25)

4:21-24[16] Many view the account of Solomon's reign as legendary and question whether he **ruled over** the expansive kingdom outlined here.[17] One issue that challenges the biblical description is that archaeologists have not recovered any inscriptions from Solomon's reign. If he were such a powerful monarch ruling over the empire described in Kings and Chronicles, one would expect, on the face of it, to find some record of his reign.[18] Alan Millard responds to this accusation by observing that only sixteen of one hundred and thirteen kings in the eastern Mediterranean region from 1000 to 600 B.C. are known from their inscriptions. In this light, he argues, "The absence of [inscriptions from] Solomon becomes less remarkable."[19] The fact is only very little has been recovered from ancient Palestine. The lack of epigraphic evidence from the reigns of David and Solomon is not unique.[20] From a more positive angle, Kenneth Kitchen argues, "The nature and extent of the mini-empire of David and Solomon is also unique to one time period, from about 1200 B.C. to about 900 B.C." Before this time, the Hittites and the Egyptians dominated geopolitics. After this period, the Assyrians and then the Babylonians and Persians exercised political control over the region. During the reign of Solomon, there was a vacuum in world politics that enabled the first and only Israelite empire.[21]

Solomon's dominion reaches to the expanse of the promise to Abraham (Gen 15:18; cf. v. 20): "To your descendants I give this

---

[16]The Hebrew versification does not correspond with the English text (English 4:21-34 = Hebrew 5:1-14; English 5:1-18 = Hebrew 5:15-32). References in this commentary follow the English versification. Where applicable, Hebrew versification may be added in brackets (e.g., 4:21[5:1]).

[17]For example, J. Maxwell Miller argues that "the biblical materials have a long and complex history of their own and the Solomon which they present is a largely legendary figure" ("Separating the Solomon of History from the Solomon of Legend," in *The Age of Solomon: Scholarship at the Turn of the Millennium*, ed. Lowell K. Handy [Leiden: Brill, 1997], p. 24).

[18]Ibid., pp. 14-15.

[19]Alan R. Millard, "King Solomon in His Ancient Context," in *The Age of Solomon: Scholarship at the Turn of the Millennium*, ed. Lowell K. Handy (Leiden: Brill, 1997), p. 46.

[20]Ibid., p. 48.

[21]Kenneth A. Kitchen, "How We Know When Solomon Ruled," *BAR* 27/4 (Sept./Oct. 2001): 37, 58.

land, from the river of Egypt[22] to the great river, the Euphrates." In
realization of the promise of "both riches and honor" for Solomon
(3:13), the nations from north Syria as far as **Tiphsah** to **Gaza** in
Philistia bring **tribute**. The king's **daily provisions** are staggering,[23]
and **peace**, a theme in the larger narrative (see "The Succession
Story Viewed in Context"), characterizes his reign. Once more,
Psalm 72 imagines such a ruler:

> He will rule from sea to sea
> > and from the River to the ends of the earth.
> The desert tribes will bow before him
> > and his enemies will lick the dust.
> The kings of Tarshish and of distant shores
> > will bring tribute to him;
> the kings of Sheba and Seba
> > will present him gifts.
> All kings will bow down to him
> > and all nations will serve him (8-11).

4:25 The people of **Judah and Israel** benefit from the divine
favor toward Solomon. Because their king rules the nations, there is
security and prosperity among them. **Each man under his own vine
and fig tree** intimates that these are blessings from Yahweh (see
Micah 4:4; Zech 3:7-10; cf. Hos 2:12; Joel 1:12). **During Solomon's
lifetime** reflects Yahweh's commitment to his people during
Solomon's reign. Later, the narrator will indicate that the king's
unwise choices will threaten Israel's security as adversaries are raised
up against him and his kingdom of peace (11:14-40).

---

[22]"The border of Egypt" corresponds with "the river of Egypt" (cf. 1 Kings
8:65) in the promise to Abraham. "The river of Egypt" is better identified
with the Nahal Bezor in the Sinai than the traditional Wadi el 'Arish (see M.
Görg, "Egypt, brook of," in *ABD*).

[23]Miller, among others, argues for a "less extensive and fabulous
Solomonic realm" ("Separating the Solomon of History," p. 24). Alan R.
Millard retorts that there is not anything in the narratives of Solomon's reign
or extrabiblical evidence from the tenth century to counter the claim of 4:24
[5:1] that Solomon ruled the region west of the Euphrates ("Assessing
Solomon: History or Legend," in *The Age of Solomon: Scholarship at the Turn
of the Millennium*, ed. Lowell K. Handy [Leiden: Brill, 1997], p. 27).

6. Solomon Multiplies Horses (4:26-28)

4:26-28 Solomon's hegemony over the nations must have been sustained by a large military. The substantial number of **chariot horses** (from Egypt and very expensive, 1 Kgs 10:28)[24] that his **district officers** provision suggests so, and at the same time interjects another sour note. Within this superlative description of Israel's most impressive monarch, the reader learns that Solomon maintained thousands of **horses**. An informed reader remembers the warning in Deuteronomy 17:16 that the king "must not acquire great numbers of horses for himself or make the people return to Egypt to get more of them." Yahweh blesses Solomon, but is the young king doing, in David's words, "what the LORD your God requires" (2:3)?

7. Solomon's Fame Spreads (4:29-34)

4:29-34 The narrator now explicitly asserts what he has shown: God gives Solomon **wisdom**. The wisdom from Yahweh leads to riches (vv. 22-23) and honor (vv. 31,34), which had also been promised (3:13). Solomon's wisdom surpasses men of renown (cf. Ps 88:1; 89:1; 1 Chr 2:6), beyond all the wisdom of **the East** and **Egypt**. This wisdom includes the **proverbs** and **songs** for which he is well known in Scripture (cf., e.g., Prov 1:1; S of S 1:1). Endowed with skills of observation in the natural sciences, **his fame spread**s. **Men of all nations**, **sent by all the kings of the world**, come to hear for themselves the wisdom of a *truly renaissance man*! The queen of Sheba's visit in 10:1-13 will reinforce the claim the narrator makes here.

On the surface, these claims appear hyperbolic, but in context they show how Yahweh keeps his promises to Solomon. They also bring into focus the subtle inconsistencies in the narrator's caricature of the king. The language lauding his wisdom is juxtaposed with

---

[24]The NIV is following the Codex Vaticanus and 2 Chr 9:25 with "four thousand" over "forty thousand" in the Hebrew text (MT) of 4:26. If teams of three horses per chariot were stabled together, four thousand stalls would correspond with the twelve thousand horses of the MT (see Walsh, *1 Kings*, p. 88; Cogan, *1 Kings*, p. 214; Hicks, *1 & 2 Chronicles*, p. 309).

the note about his chariots (4:26-28). If Solomon is so wise, able to discern good from evil (3:9), how does one explain his multiplication of horses?

1 KINGS 5

8. Solomon Prepares to Build Yahweh's House (5:1-18)

5:1-7 When **Hiram king of Tyre**[1] hears that Solomon rules in place of David, he sends **envoys** to the new king because (literally), "Hiram had love for David."[2] In this context, the language suggests that the two monarchs had a covenant/treaty relationship (cf. 2 Sam 5:11). The reader hears Solomon's communiqué in dialogue that conjures up again images of Yahweh's promise to David in 2 Samuel 7. He also hears Solomon put a favorable spin on David's failure to build a house for Yahweh. His father **"could not build a temple for the Name of the LORD his God until the LORD put his enemies under his feet"** (cf. Ps 110:1). Since now **"the LORD my God has given me rest on every side,"** Solomon is going to build a temple. However, an attentive reader remembers that it was only when "the LORD had given him rest from all his enemies around him" (2 Sam 7:1) that David asked to build a house for Yahweh. David's rest did not last (see 2 Sam 8:1-14; 10–11; 12:26-31; 15–20), just as the rest given by Yahweh to Solomon will not last. The kingdom of שָׁלוֹם (šālôm, "peace") in which **there is no adversary [שָׂטָן, śāṭān]"** will not be maintained. Because of foolish choices, Yahweh will raise up *adversaries* against Solomon (1 Kgs 11:14,23,25). That there is no **"disaster"** (פֶּגַע, pegaʻ) may also be ironic. This rare word calls to mind the violence that accompanied Solomon as he *secured* his throne, underscored in the narrative by the key word פָּגַע (pāgaʻ,

---

[1]Hiram I (a shortened form of Ahiram, "my [divine] brother is exalted") reigned ca. 970–936 B.C. (Cogan, *1 Kings*, p. 226).

[2]For the differences between the Kings version of Solomon's dealings with Hiram and the parallel account in 2 Chronicles 1–16, see Hicks, *1 & 2 Chronicles*, pp. 266-271.

"strike down," "attack;" in Kings only in 2:25,29,31,32,34,46; see "The Succession Story Viewed in Context").[3]

Solomon quotes, if not exactly at least in substance, Yahweh's promise to David (v. 5). Again, the narrator reinforces the connection between 2 Samuel 7 and Solomon's reign through a character. The king affirms that Yahweh has kept his promise to David that a son would sit on his throne and that Israel would have rest (see comments on 8:14-21). Solomon will now build a house for **the Name of the LORD** (2 Sam 7:11-13), an expression that has important theological implications for the author of Kings. Along with "Angel of Yahweh," "Face/Presence," and "Glory" (see, e.g., Gen 22:11-12; Exod 33:14-15; 1 Sam 4:18-22), the "Name of Yahweh" enables the inspired authors of the Primary History (Genesis through 2 Kings) to represent a transcendent deity who can also commune with Israel. By this use of metonymy (where the name of a part is used for the whole), Yahweh can be everywhere and also dwell in the house that David's son builds (see comments on 1 Kgs 9:27-30). Rest for Israel and a place for the Name of the LORD envisioned by Moses (Deut 12:5-26) and promised to David (2 Sam 7:11-13) are now to become a reality.

In order to obtain **cedars of Lebanon** for Yahweh's house, Solomon proposes that their men could work together, Solomon compensating with wages. **Hiram** praises Yahweh (something not unusual in the pagan ancient Near East [see, e.g., Num 22–24]) for the **wise son** he has given Israel.

5:8-9 Again, the reader hears Hiram's rejoinder as dialogue, personalizing the rapport between the two kings. His response to Solomon's overture, however, raises questions about the relationship between them. On the surface, the two men negotiate as equals, even though the narrator has made a point that all the nations from the border of Egypt to north Syria are subject to Solomon and pay him tribute (4:21-24). Is Solomon wisely making pretense at negotiating with a subordinate, or is this another case where the meaning on the surface is undermined by what Solomon actually does with the blessings Yahweh has given him? Hiram counters with an offer of **cedar *and* pine logs**. Only, his servants alone would supply the logs and float them to Israel. Instead of wages, Solomon should provision his **household**.

---

[3]Walsh, *1 Kings*, p. 99.

5:10-18 The narrator now outlines the results of the negotiations. Hiram supplies **all of the cedar and pine logs** Solomon needs, and Solomon provisions Hiram's house annually with an impressive **twenty thousand cors of wheat** and **twenty thousand baths of pressed olive oil**. In the context of these negotiations, the narrator states again that Solomon has wisdom from God, even though the deal appears at first to follow Hiram's counter offer. Then the reader learns (vv. 13-18) that Solomon's men do work alongside the men of Hiram in Lebanon, according to Solomon's initial proposal. When coupled with Hiram's dissatisfaction with Solomon's gifts in 9:10-14, this outcome suggests that Hiram in these dealings is the junior partner.[4]

Nevertheless, how wise is Solomon in these agreements? Walsh asks, "If Solomon is so wise, why does he agree to terms that so favor Hiram's interests and include such exorbitant annual costs?" He notes that the **20,000 cors of wheat** is a substantial portion of the only 33,000 cors of fine flour and meal that Solomon received annually (4:22), not to mention the **pressed olive oil**. Is the note about his wisdom in any way sarcastic?[5]

To the comment about Solomon's wisdom is appended an innocuous note that **peaceful relations** exist between the two kings, and they make **a treaty** (literally, "covenant"). However, Deuteronomy 7:1-4 forbids making covenants with and marrying the people of the land. While Hiram was not devoted to destruction as were the people of Jericho, the narrator will refer to Deuteronomy 7:1-4 in his condemnation of Solomon for marrying foreign wives, including, among other nations, Hiram's "nationality," the Sidonians (i.e., the Phoenicians; 11:1-2,5,33; see 5:6). Ahab will later be judged harshly for making a covenant with Ben-Hadad king of Syria and for marrying Jezebel, daughter of Ethbaal king of the Sidonians (16:31; see comments on 1 Kings 20–21). Again, there is more than appears on the surface in this noticeably nuanced presentation of Solomon's reign.

Also nuanced is the statement that **Solomon conscripted laborers from all Israel**. Most commentators have argued this text indicates Solomon forced Israelites into slave labor as part of his corvée

---

[4]Provan, *1 and 2 Kings*, p. 64.
[5]Walsh, *1 Kings*, pp. 98-99.

(unpaid, forced labor; in Hebrew מַס, *mas*), even though 1 Kings
9:20-23 makes the point that Solomon did not make slaves of the
children of Israel. Non-Israelites were conscripted into "his slave
labor force" (מַס־עֹבֵד, *mas 'ōbēd*; see below). As descendants of the
nations not exterminated by the first generation in the land, they
were to become slaves in Israel (9:20-21; cf. Josh 16:10; 17:13; Judges
1:28,30,33,35).[6] This distinction is based on the understanding that
Yahweh had delivered Israel from slavery in Egypt (Exodus 1–14;
Deut 7:8). The descendants of Abraham were to be slaves/servants
of Yahweh.[7]

Nevertheless, why does the storyteller wait until 9:20-23 to clarify
who in **all Israel** was forced into the *mas*? Perhaps the ambiguity created by the two statements about Solomon's corvée is intentional —
and consistent with the sophisticated literary design evidenced
throughout the presentation of Solomon's reign. While Solomon
never technically forced Israelites into permanent slavery, he apparently did cross the line in terms of his harsh rule over the people of
God. Mettinger explains the apparent inconsistency between 5:13
and 9:21-22 in the different terms used in the two texts. In 5:13, all
Israel is enrolled into the *mas*; in 9:21, the Canaanites are forced into
the *mas 'ōbēd* (the NIV's "slave labor force"). If *mas 'ōbēd* means "permanent labor force," Israelites were conscripted into temporary
labor and Canaanites into a permanent corvée.[8] So, by naming
Israelite conscription for the king's building projects *mas*, the narrator is consciously calling attention to Solomon's oppressive policies,
which were predicted by Samuel. The prophet described the enlist-
ment and taxation that were realized in Israel in the days of Solomon
(1 Sam 8:11-18),[9] and this statement about the *mas* anticipates the

---

[6]See Provan, *1 and 2 Kings*, p. 64.

[7]Dexter E. Callender, Jr., "Servants of God[s] and Servants of Kings in
Israel and the Ancient Near East," *Semeia* 83/84 (1998): 77-80.

[8]Mettinger, *Solomonic State Officials*, pp. 131-139. Cogan contends that the
use of *mas 'ōbēd* in Josh 16:10, when compared with the use of *mas* in Judg
1:30,33,35 and 2 Chr 8:8 and *mas 'ōbēd* in 1 Kgs 9:21, indicates that the two
are interchangeable (*1 Kings*, pp. 229-230, 303). However, overlap in the
range of meaning for these terms does not preclude subtle distinctions. If
Cogan is correct, the narrator is creating even more tension in his use of
mas – to characterize Solomon as an overbearing monarch.

[9]Callender distinguishes between "what Israel viewed as intolerable
'forced labor' and the general 'servile' (*'bd*) relationship between people as

tragic legacy Solomon's cruelty bodes for Israel. As a repressive regime develops, Israel is *returned to Egypt* (Deut 17:16; cf. Exod 1:11). In the end, the kingdom is divided because Rehoboam refuses to ease off of the labor policies of his father, who had beaten the people with whips (12:4-15). In 12:18, **all Israel**, led by Jeroboam who was in charge of the "labor force [סֵבֶל, *sēbel*] of the house of Joseph" (11:28), will stone **Adoniram**, who **was in charge of the forced labor** (*mas*, 5:14). Again, how wise was this most blessed of kings, who apparently built a glorious kingdom, not on his faith in the God who blessed him, but on the backs of the people he ruled?

The **craftsmen** that Solomon employs would ensure a magnificent temple, but one brief statement, apparently misconstrued in the NIV, may allude to misplaced priorities already suggested at the introduction to the account of Solomon's reign (3:1-3). **Two months at home** (v. 14) is (literally) "two months in his house." A work schedule of one month on and two months off would be generous, especially for the corvée, but doesn't square with the harsh work conditions suggested by the response of **all Israel** in 12:4-15. A more likely reading is that the forced labor spent one month working in Lebanon and two months working on *his house*, the palace that Solomon was building concurrently with the house for Yahweh (6:37–7:1).[10]

'servants' and king as 'lord.'" He believes that in 1 Sam 8:11-18, Samuel warns Israel of the dangers of such forced labor ("Servants of God[s]," 75-77). While Callender is correct to connect 1 Samuel 8 with the Kings references to Solomon's harsh policies, he misses the creative way the storyteller calls attention to these policies by naming the Israelite labor force *mas* and, at the same time, maintaining that Solomon never forced his countrymen into slavery (the *mas 'ōbēd*).

[10]Provan, *1 and 2 Kings*, p. 65. Walsh takes "his house" to refer to the temple (*1 Kings*, p. 100).

1 KINGS 6

D. THE PROMISE OF A HOUSE FOR YAHWEH IS FULFILLED (6:1–8:66)

1. Solomon Builds a House for Yahweh (6:1-38)

6:1 In the four hundred and eightieth year after the Israelites had come out of Egypt and **in the fourth year** of his reign, Solomon begins work on a house for Yahweh.[1] This note situates the building of the temple within the larger history of Israel and suggests a connection with Egypt and the Exodus. In the report to follow, allusions to the Exodus will bring out the importance of the temple and play a role in the overall characterization of Solomon.[2] The construction of the temple represents the fulfillment of everything Yahweh had promised for Israel (see, e.g., Deut 12:1-28). The Exodus calls to mind the oppression of the captivity in Egypt and Yahweh's deliverance. The kings of Israel were not to make Israel return that way again (Deut 17:16). Before he rests with his fathers, Solomon will set Israel on the course to Egypt. When all is finished, both Israel and Judah will "return to Egypt" — as they are led away to Assyria and Babylon (cf. Hos 8:13; 9:3).[3]

---

[1]If the fourth year of Solomon's reign were ca. 966/965 B.C., the four hundred and eighty years would date the Exodus to ca. 1445 B.C. (965 + 480 years = 1445). An alternate view would see four hundred and eighty as symbolic, representing twelve generations of forty years. At twenty years for the actual span of a generation, this would place the Exodus in the thirteenth century B.C. (965 + [12 x 20 = 240] = 1205). For a concise discussion of the issues involved in determining the date of the Exodus, see G. Herbert Livingston, *The Pentateuch in Its Cultural Environment*, 2nd ed. (Grand Rapids: Baker, 1987), pp. 43-52.

[2]See Amos Frisch, "The Exodus Motif in 1 Kings 1–14," *JSOT* 87 (2000): 3-21.

[3]The Chronicler also connects the construction of the temple to the bind-

6:2-10 The narrator now sketches a picture that will enable the reader to visualize[4] the grandeur of the house that Solomon builds for Yahweh.[5] What emerges is a temple that parallels in plan and iconography contemporary temples in Palestine and North Syria.[6] Tripartite, longroom temples[7] from as early as the first half of the second millennium B.C., like the temple described here, have been excavated at numerous sites (e.g., at Hazor in Israel and Tell Tainat in Syria).[8] The closest parallel to date is the 'Ain Dara temple in northern Syria. A longroom temple excavated between 1980 and 1985, this structure was contemporary with the Solomonic temple and features, for the first time, **side rooms** like those described in verses 5-6,8,10.[9] The fact that the Solomonic temple parallels this

---

ing of Isaac, when he mentions that the temple is constructed on Mount Moriah (Gen 22:2). For a discussion of this allusion in Chronicles, see Hicks, *1 & 2 Chronicles*, p. 273.

[4]This account contrasts with parallel building accounts in the ancient Near East which lack detailed descriptions (Victor A. Hurowitz, *I Have Built You an Exalted House: Temple Building in the Bible in Light of Mesopotamian and Northwest Semitic Writings*, JSOTSup 115 [Sheffield: Sheffield Academic Press, 1992], pp. 245-246).

[5]The description of the temple and its furnishings in 1 Kings 6–7 is replete with textual problems and difficult-to-translate, technical language, which, because of the limitations of space, this commentary will not attempt to unravel. The account of Solomon's temple construction in 2 Chr 3:1–5:1 is condensed to less than half the description in Kings. The Chronicler's version appears to be framed to emphasize the liturgical, not the architectural, aspects of the temple construction (Hicks, *1 & 2 Chronicles*, pp. 271-272; for the differences between the two accounts, see pp. 271-279).

[6]Defending the description in Kings of the Solomonic temple, Dever asserts, "Let me emphasize that *every single detail* of the Bible's complicated description of the Jerusalem temple can now be corroborated by archaeological examples from the Late Bronze and Iron Ages. There is nothing 'fanciful' about 1 Kgs. 6–8" (*Biblical Writers Know*, 155).

[7]Three-room structures with an entrance on the short axis, so that the long axis runs perpendicular to the entrance. The temple also parallels the tabernacle of Exodus (cf. Exodus 25–31, 35–40).

[8]See Volkmar Fritz, "Temple Architecture: What Can Archaeology Tell Us about Solomon's Temple," *BAR* 12/4 (July/August 1987): 38-49; Carol Meyers, "Temple, Jerusalem," in *ABD*. Dever indicates "nearly 30 examples" can be verified in the archaeological record (*Biblical Writers Know*, 145).

[9]The 'Ain Dara temple stood from 1300 B.C. to 740 B.C. For the parallels between the two temples, see John Monson, "The New 'Ain Dara Temple: Closest Solomonic Parallel," *BAR* 26/3 (May/June 2000): 20-35, 67; see Dever, *Biblical Writers Know*, 155.

Syrian temple type reinforces the Phoenician connection in the construction of Yahweh's house, through Hiram king of Tyre.

The house for Yahweh was a large structure (60 cubits long, 20 cubits wide, and 30 cubits high[10]) with a **portico** (אוּלָם, *'ûlām*) an additional 10 cubits in length at the entrance to the building. The main construction was divided into two rooms, a central hall (הֵיכָל, *hêkāl*[11]) 40 cubits in length and an inner sanctuary (דְּבִיר, *d^ebîr*) 20 cubits in length, which housed the ark of the covenant (vv. 16-19).[12] The temple's **side rooms**, evidenced at 'Ain Dara, wrapped around the building on three sides, three stories high with at least one entrance on the south. These rooms extended the width of the building to approximately thirty-five cubits and the length to more than seventy-seven cubits.[13] The NIV's **narrow clerestory windows** may have been false windows. At 'Ain Dara, at least two false, recessed windows were carved in the walls of the temple with figure-eight lattice patterns.[14] The dressed **blocks** used in the construction fit so well, not a sound of **an iron tool** is heard in construction.[15] Solomon completes the house, **roofing it with beams and cedar planks.**

---

[10]The NIV measurements in the text notes are based on the length of the short cubit (ca. 45 cm/18 in), as opposed to the longer Egyptian (or royal) cubit (ca. 52.5 cm/21 in). Second Chronicles 3:3 indicates that the short cubit was used in the construction of the temple. For a discussion of measurements in the temple construction, see Meyers, "Temple, Jerusalem," in *ABD*; Marvin A. Powell, "Weights and Measures," in *ABD*.

[11]The Hebrew *hêkāl* is also the word for temple or palace, although in this account the expression "house of Yahweh" is the designation for the temple. The *hêkāl* here is the NIV's "main hall." In 8:8,10, it is named "the Holy Place."

[12]See Heb 9:1-28 for the Christian interpretation of the symbolism of the tabernacle, and by extension Solomon's temple.

[13]The lower rooms were five cubits wide. Rooms on the upper stories were extended to six and seven cubits in width, apparently because of a construction technique where walls were reduced in thickness to allow for roof beams, an additional cubit for each floor. The width of this ancillary construction would be at least seven cubits (see Meyers, "Temple, Jerusalem," in *ABD*).

[14]Monson, "The New 'Ain Dara Temple," 34.

[15]Behind this statement lies the typical Phoenician ashlar masonry (i.e., dressed stone) of monumental construction, which is evidenced at numerous sites in Palestine in the tenth–ninth centuries B.C. (Dever, *Biblical Writers Know*, p. 147). The already-cut blocks were simply put in place.

6:11-13 The word of the LORD[16] comes to Solomon, with conditions for sanctioning the temple with his presence. Now, in dialogue, Yahweh *himself* refers to the promise that he had made to David (2 Samuel 7). That promise *was* conditional! If Solomon **"follows my decrees . . . and obeys them"** (literally, "walk[s] in them"; see Deut 5:33; 10:12-13; 17:19), Yahweh **"will live among the Israelites and will not abandon** them." The temple will be a symbol of Yahweh's commitment to David and represent his presence in Israel. He will dwell (שָׁכַן, *šākan*, the word from which "Shekinah" is derived) with them in this house. Yet in spite of Yahweh's choice, Solomon and his descendants will break their covenant with Yahweh. Both temple and kingship will be shattered. When this occurs, has Yahweh *abandoned* Israel and disregarded his promise to David?

6:14-38 Solomon built the temple and completed it serves as a transition to a more detailed description of the temple but also implies that Solomon pledged himself to the promise Yahweh makes. The house that he builds is glorious. The inside is covered in costly **cedar**, with **flooring of pine**, and is overlaid from top to bottom with **pure gold** (vv. 15,18,20-22,28,30,32,35). Sometimes thought to be an exaggeration, Millard demonstrates with ancient Near Eastern parallels the plausibility of the Kings description. For example, a shrine in king Tutankhamun's tomb was covered inside and out with pure gold, and pillars in front of the Temple of the Sacred Boat at Karnak (erected by Tuthmosis III) had unusual slits, apparently for attaching gold sheathing. Other features in this Egyptian temple also had slits for gold.[17]

The portrait of Yahweh's house in Kings calls attention to the **inner sanctuary** (*dᵉbîr*; vv. 16,19-22). It was apparently constructed as a square cube of 20 cubits of cedar (overlaid with gold) at the back of the building. Based on parallels with the 'Ain Dara temple, the difference in height between the inner sanctuary (20 cubits) and the central hall (30 cubits) probably means that the inner room was on

---

[16]This is the second time "word of the LORD" appears in Kings, the first time to Solomon directly (cf. 2:27). Later, the word of the LORD will play an important role in the prophetic commentary on the actions of Israel's kings.

[17]Alan R. Millard, "Does the Bible Exaggerate King Solomon's Golden Wealth?," *BAR* 15/3 (May/June 1989): 27-29, 31; idem, "King Solomon in His Ancient Context," 31-36.

a raised platform approached by steps,[18] although the description in Kings does not mention steps. In the inner sanctuary, **the Most Holy Place** (קֹדֶשׁ הַקֳּדָשִׁים, *qōdeš haqqŏdāšîm*, v. 16), **the ark of the covenant of the LORD** was positioned. The naming stands out, for the ark represents the covenant that Yahweh made with Israel and makes another connection with the Exodus imagery that lies behind this account. Stretching over the Ark of the Covenant is **a pair of cherubim**, of olivewood overlaid with gold and with wings that span the width of the room (vv. 23-28). In the ancient Near East, cherubim were composite beings with wings. They often accompanied deities and functioned as guardian-like figures (cf. Gen 3:24). On the ark itself is a pair of cherubim (Exod 25:18-22; 37:7-9), guarding the very throne of God on earth (see, e.g., 1 Sam 4:4).[19] Thrones in the ancient Near East were often decorated with cherubim figures (e.g., in the famous Megiddo Ivory scene where the Canaanite king sits on a throne carved with winged cherubim). However, the ark probably represents Yahweh's footstool (1 Chr 28:2; Ps 99:5; 132:7).[20]

The temple doors receive special attention (vv. 31,33-35). **The five-sided** and **four-sided jambs** probably connote the number of recesses in the frames.[21] Doors of olive and pine are decorated with **cherubim, palm trees, and open flowers**, as are the walls around the temple (v. 29). Ezekiel records that a two-faced cherub was carved between palm trees, with the face of a man toward the tree on one side and the face of a lion toward the tree on the other side (Ezek 41:18-20). In the ancient Near East, composite creatures were often portrayed beside trees (frequently the palm tree), feeding on or guarding the sacred tree. Solomon may have chosen this imagery to represent the temple as the Garden of Eden, Yahweh's dwelling on earth (Gen 3:24).[22]

Evidence of construction with alternating courses of stone and

---

[18]Monson, "The New 'Ain Dara Temple," 33.

[19]Carol Meyers, "Cherubim," in *ABD*.

[20]See C.L. Seow, "Ark of the Covenant," in *ABD*.

[21]Monson, "The New 'Ain Dara Temple," 34-35.

[22]Elizabeth Bloch-Smith, "'Who Is the King of Glory?' Solomon's Temple and Its Symbolism," in *Scripture and Other Artifacts: Essays on the Bible and Archaeology in Honor of Philip J. King*, ed. Michael D. Coogan, J. Cheryl Exum, and Lawrence E. Stager (Louisville, KY: Westminster John Knox Press, 1994), pp. 23-25.

wooden beams as in the **inner courtyard** (v. 36; cf. 7:12) has been discovered in the ninth-century-B.C. remains at Tel Dan.[23] What must have been an expensive feature serves to reinforce the extravagance of Solomon's house. The description of the temple ends with a note that Solomon **finish**es [from כָּלָה, *kālāh*] **in all its details** the construction of the temple in **seven years**. The verbal root for "complete/finish" (*klh*) ties 1 Kings 6:9,14,38 (and 7:1; 9:1) with Genesis 2:1 and the creation. This must symbolize, at least in part, that the house that was *finished* (vv. 9,14,38) was good, as was Yahweh's work in his seven days of creation (Genesis 1; cf. Rev 22:1-21).

---

[23]Avraham Biran, "Tel Dan: Biblical Texts and Archaeological Data," in *Scripture and Other Artifacts: Essays on the Bible and Archaeology in Honor of Philip J. King*, ed. Michael D. Coogan, J. Cheryl Exum, and Lawrence E. Stager (Louisville, KY: Westminster John Knox Press, 1994), pp. 7-8. This type of construction may have been for earthquake protection (Dever, *Biblical Writers Know*, pp. 147-148).

1 KINGS 7

2. Solomon Builds His House (7:1-12)

7:1-12 In contrast to the seven years to build Yahweh's house, Solomon spends **thirteen years** constructing *his house*. The Hebrew syntax, in fact, puts emphasis on the contrast (literally): "and his house, Solomon built." Does this indicate misplaced priorities (see comments on 3:1)?[1] And Solomon's house was as grand as the house for Yahweh. **The Palace of the Forest of Lebanon** calls attention to the amount of cedar used in its construction. As a key word in this section (occurring 17 times in chs. 5-7), the cedar from Lebanon reinforces the claim in the text that Yahweh blessed Solomon with wealth. However, the king's riches will also be a curse in Solomon's life and for Israel (see comments on chs. 10-11; cf. Deut 17:17).[2]

In his oracle against this very palace and the house of David, Jeremiah warns Zedekiah by the word of the LORD:

> I will send destroyers against you,
> > each man with his weapons,
> and they will cut up your fine cedar beams
> > and throw them into the fire (Jer 22:7).

To Jehoiakim, the prophet says:

> Woe to him who builds his palace by unrighteousness,
> > his upper rooms by injustice,
> making his countrymen work for nothing,
> > not paying them for their labor. . . .
> Does it make you a king
> > to have more and more cedar? (22:13,15)[3]

---

[1]Provan, *1 and 2 Kings*, p. 69; Walsh, *1 Kings*, pp. 105-106; contra Cogan, *1 Kings*, p. 257.

[2]See Brueggemann, *1 & 2 Kings*, p. 79.

[3]Jehoiakim was apparently building an opulent palace, which may have

Judah will go into exile, back to Egyptian captivity in Babylon, because of forsaking the covenant and serving other gods — and because her kings will pursue wealth and honor over righteousness and justice. The **Hall of Justice**, the throne room for the kings of Judah, will be burned for the injustice of the sons of David who sit on that throne (Jer 22:1-30; see 2 Kgs 24:1-17).

Solomon starts Israel on that path. The narrator inserts that Solomon builds a similar house for **Pharaoh's daughter, whom he had married**. The note that introduced his reign (3:1) resurfaces as a subtle reminder of the king's divided loyalties and foreshadows his demise (11:1-13). The mention of Solomon's Egyptian wife, consequently, casts a shadow over the description of his wealth. In this added blessing from Yahweh are seeds that will mature into heartache for Israel.

3. Solomon Furnishes Yahweh's House (7:13-51)

7:13-22 The Phoenician connection in the construction of the temple is strengthened when Solomon secures **Huram**[4] **. . . a man of Tyre and a craftsman in bronze** to manufacture the implements for the temple. Perhaps the most impressive of his numerous achievements were the two massive pillars flanking the entrance to the portico. Parallels from the temples at Tell Tainat and 'Ain Dara indicate that these were load-bearing pillars, not the freestanding columns usually envisioned.[5] The eighteen-cubit high bronze pillars were topped with impressive capitals five cubits in height. **Pomegranates**, an ancient Near Eastern fertility symbol, decorated the capitals, which resembled **lilies.** The so-adorned pillars therein imitate a floral

---

been excavated at Ramat Raḥel north of Bethlehem (see comments on 2 Kgs 23:36–24:7).

[4]The Hebrew is Hiram (חִירָם, ḥîrām, also in vv. 40,45). The variant Huram (חוּרָם, ḥûrām) occurs in 2 Chr 2:2,13; 4:11,16; see the NIV text note. Huram's role parallels the role that Bezalel played in the construction of the tabernacle (Exod 31:2-5). While verse 14 indicates that Huram's mother was "a widow from the tribe of Naphtali," the Chronicler claims that "his mother was from Dan" (2 Chr 2:13). One plausible explanation is that Naphtali represents a geographical identification and Dan a genealogical association (Hicks, *1 & 2 Chronicles*, p. 279).

[5]Monson, "The New 'Ain Dara Temple," 30, 33; cf. Cogan, *1 Kings*, p. 271.

pattern typical in ancient Near Eastern temple architecture.[6] Symbolizing the power of the God of Israel, Solomon names the pillars **Jakin** (יָכִין, *yākîn*, "he will establish") and **Boaz** (בֹּעַז, *bō'az*, "in strength"). These names probably represent the first words of prayers or blessings that honor Yahweh as the source of *security* and *strength*.[7] Jakin recalls the promise to David: "I *will establish* the throne of his [i.e., David's offspring] kingdom forever" (2 Sam 7:13).[8]

The size of the columns, along with most other features in the courtyard and temple, suggests that this house is constructed to accommodate an all-powerful deity. At 'Ain Dara, large three-foot-long footprints carved in the floor of the portico and threshold to the main hall probably represent the deity entering the temple. The massive columns in Yahweh's house flanked an entrance worthy of the God of Israel and creator of the cosmos.[9]

7:23-26 In the courtyard, at the southeast corner of the temple (v. 39), Solomon constructs an impressive **Sea of cast metal**, which also must have possessed cosmic symbolism. This enormous object, ten cubits across and five cubits high, is decorated with **gourds**, has a rim **like a lily blossom**, and rests on **twelve bulls** facing the four winds. While its function, from this description, is unclear (2 Chr 4:5 indicates it was for washing), its various features indicate that it also is symbolic. A relief of the Assyrian Sargon II (eighth century B.C.) shows two reservoirs on bulls' legs in front of the temple at Musasir. Other parallels, for example the temple of Marduk at Babylon, suggest that these basins represent the cosmic waters of chaos or the waters of life. Baal's victorious battle with *Yam* ("Sea") in the Ugaritic myths may represent a similar idea. Solomon's bronze sea, therefore, most likely epitomized Yahweh's sovereign power and rule over his creation.[10]

---

[6]Carol Meyers, "Jachin and Boaz," in *ABD*. For a concise discussion of the archaeological parallels with the description of the Solomonic temple, including Canaanite iconography, see Dever, *Biblical Writers Know*, pp. 144-157.

[7]See Bloch-Smith, "Solomon's Temple and Its Symbolism," p. 19.

[8]See Cogan, *1 Kings*, p. 264.

[9]Monson, "The New 'Ain Dara Temple," 26-28; see Bloch-Smith, "Solomon's Temple and Its Symbolism," p. 21.

[10]Carol Meyers, "Sea, Molten," in *ABD*; Bloch-Smith, "Solomon's Temple and Its Symbolism," pp. 20-21; see John Day, "Baal," in *ABD*.

7:27-39 The ten large **movable stands** (lavers) were situated five on the north side of the temple and five on the south side. Decorated with **lions, bulls and cherubim,** a few parallels, although not exact, have been found at Ras Shamra, Megiddo, and on Cyprus.[11] With regard to their decoration, the temple at 'Ain Dara included reliefs of lions, cherubim, and other figures, attending the house of the deity.[12] In 2 Chronicles 4:6, the lavers in the temple are described as basins for washing burnt offerings.

7:40-47 Huram makes **the basins and shovels and sprinkling bowls** for the temple service. An interesting example of religious accoutrements was uncovered in the sacred area at Tel Dan. Three iron shovels were exposed in eighth-century-B.C. layers beside a three-foot square altar. Associated ash with charred bone indicates that the shovels were used in a sacrificial setting.[13] A summary of the impressive bronze objects for the temple follows in verses 41-45, objects forged in the Jordan valley. There is so much, Solomon does not weigh the amount of bronze. Yet, noticeably absent from the list is the bronze altar described in 2 Chronicles 4:1 and 7:7 (cf. 1 Kgs 8:31,54,64; 9:25; 2 Kgs 16:14-15). David constructed an altar on the threshing floor of Araunah the Jebusite, the site of the temple, and in so doing consecrated the place for the temple that his son Solomon would build (2 Sam 24:18-25; 1 Chr 21:18–22:1). The narrator may want the reader to remember David's altar.[14]

7:48-51 The writer records that **Solomon also** constructs **all the furnishings** of gold for the temple, which are suitable for a superlative deity. Among the list of furnishings are the **golden altar** of incense located just before the inner sanctuary (6:22) and the **golden table,** of which the Chronicler indicates there were ten (2 Chr 4:8,19).[15] **The bread of the Presence** is (literally) "the bread of the faces." Like "the Name of Yahweh," *the Face of God* signifies the dwelling among the people of Israel of the transcendent God of

---

[11]Carol Meyers, "Laver," in *ABD*; Bloch-Smith, "Solomon's Temple and Its Symbolism," pp. 19-20.

[12]Monson, "The New 'Ain Dara Temple," 23.

[13]Avraham Biran, *Biblical Dan* (Jerusalem: Israel Exploration Society, 1994), pp. 192-196, Color Plate 33.

[14]Cogan suggests the altar is missing due to a textual omission during copying (*1 Kings*, p. 289).

[15]Cf. the description of the tabernacle furnishings in Heb 9:1-5.

creation (see comments on 5:5). **The lampstands of pure gold** were not the seven-branched, menorah candelabra of later periods, but seven-spouted, bowl-shaped lamps typical of Iron II sacred contexts.[16] The **gold sockets** for the doors of the temple are thought by some to reflect the imaginary character of this description. However, ancient Near Eastern parallels suggest that the surfaces of stone sockets in temples and palaces were sometimes overlaid with gold.[17] This impressive list is punctuated with the note that Solomon brings the objects **his father David had dedicated** to the temple (see 1 Chr 22:1-5). The reader remembers David's desire for a house for his God and hears again Yahweh's promise that David's son would build that house (2 Samuel 7).

---

[16]For a nice example, see Biran, *Biblical Dan*, Color Plate 25, p. 165.
[17]Millard, "King Solomon in His Ancient Context," p. 35.

1 KINGS 8

4. The Ark of the Covenant Is Brought to the Temple (8:1-13)

The report of Solomon's dedication of the house for Yahweh and the prayer that he offers on that occasion is one of the more important passages in 1 and 2 Kings (8:1-66). This text, especially, appears to reflect the theological point of view of the overall composition. Allusions to the Exodus and references to Yahweh's promise to David position the construction of the temple in the larger context of Israelite history and establish a framework for interpreting the tragic story that ensues. In addition, while the construction of the temple as a chapel for the king and even the events surrounding its dedication reflect the sociopolitical realities of Iron Age Palestine, the emphasis on the temple as a house of prayer to the God who hears from heaven suggests important theological distinctions for the role of this house in the life of the people. As with the preceding characterization of Solomon, there also may be subtleties in the representation that further color that portrait. Moreover, this section has figured prominently in discussions of the composition of Kings. In light of those who see various layers of composition here, it is important up front to see the literary unity of this section as is indicated by its concentric structure:[1]

---

[1]Adapted from Gary N. Knoppers, "Prayer and Propaganda: Solomon's Dedication of the Temple and the Deuteronomist's Program," 375. With recurring language, themes, and actions (in addition to structure), Knoppers demonstrates the literary unity of 1 Kings 8. He writes, "The intricate literary architecture of 1 Kings 8 militates against removing entire sections of this chapter as the work of later redactors and glossators simply on the basis of a shift in style or a change in topic" (p. 380).

A. Assembly (8:1-3)
  B. Sacrifice (8:5; ark brought to temple, 4-13)
    C. Blessing (8:14-21)
      D. Solomon's Stance (8:22)
        E. Invocation (8:27-30; keep your promise to David, 23-26)
          F. Three Petitions (for Yahweh to hear, 8:31-36)
            X. General Petition (for Yahweh to hear and forgive, 8:37-40)
          F'. Three Petitions (for Yahweh to hear, 8:41-51)
        E'. Invocation (8:52-53)
      D'. Solomon's Stance (8:54)
    C'. Blessing (8:55-61)
  B'. Sacrifice (8:62-64; festival observed, 65)
A'. Dismissal (8:66)

At the center of this structure appears the general petition that reflects the overall emphasis of Solomon's prayer (8:37-40). When Israel has broken covenant and a penitent spreads his hands toward this house in prayer, may Yahweh *hear from heaven*, his dwelling place, and forgive.

8:1-13 Solomon brings the **ark of the LORD's covenant** up from **the city of David** along with **the tent of meeting and all the sacred furnishings in it**[2] to the temple mount. The ceremonies, with sacrifices too many to be **recorded or counted**, reflect solemnity and respect for the ark of Yahweh (cf. 2 Sam 6:1-19). Apparently, Solomon waited eleven months from the completion of the temple to dedicate it during the Feast of Tabernacles (from the eighth month to the seventh month; see 6:38; 8:2; cf. Lev 23:34). This association with Tabernacles (cf. **tent of meeting**, v. 4) introduces an Exodus theme that clearly characterizes this account. Concerning the Feast of Tabernacles, Moses commanded, "For seven days celebrate the Feast to the LORD your God at *the place* the LORD will choose" (Deut 16:15). The narrator employs the key word **place**

---

[2]The "tent of meeting" (the tabernacle of Moses), up until the dedication of the temple, was located at Gibeon (cf. 3:4; 2 Chr 1:3; 5:4-5).

(מָקוֹם, *māqôm*)[3] to subtly reinforce that Yahweh is choosing Jerusalem and this house as a dwelling for his Name, as Moses had prophesied (Deut 12:1-28; see 1 Kgs 8:16,17,18,19,20,29,44,48). The parallel word מָכוֹן (*mākôn* "place/established place" [from כּוּן, *kûn*, "be established"], v. 13; in verses 39,43,49 used for God's dwelling in heaven) buttresses the "place" motif and connects it with the theme that Yahweh is *establishing* this house as he *establishes* a house/dynasty for David (see 2 Sam 7:12,13,16).

The ark is brought to the **Most Holy Place** (קֹדֶשׁ הַקֳּדָשִׁים, *qōdeš haqqŏdāšîm*) and is placed **beneath the wings of the cherubim**, the footstool of Yahweh's throne on earth (see comments on 6:14-38). With naming, **ark of the LORD's** *covenant* (vv. 1,6), and with his description of the contents of the ark, **the two stone tablets that Moses had placed in it at Horeb, where the LORD made a covenant with the Israelites,**[4] the narrator strengthens the connection with Moses' covenant and stresses continuity with the Exodus events. The correlation materializes as **the cloud** and **glory of the LORD** from the wilderness experience fill Yahweh's house (cf. Exod 13:21-22; 16:10; 19:9; 24:15-18; 33:9-10; 40:34-38). Dramatically, this incident demonstrates that Yahweh has accepted Solomon's house. Both the cloud and the Glory represent his presence (see comments on 5:5). In a vision, Ezekiel will later see the cloud and the Glory of the LORD, hovering above the winged cherubim, leave this temple for the "sin of the house of Israel and Judah" (Ezek 9:9–10:22). Isaiah envisions a time, however, when all mankind will see the Glory of the LORD, a time when Yahweh's presence will appear in a human house (Isa 40:1-5; see John 1:14-23).

The **poles** of the ark of the covenant **are still there today** (v. 8) indicates that the author must be using sources (cf., e.g., 11:41; 2 Kgs 14:19,29) to compose his account of the kings of Israel and Judah. The poles are there and can be verified, yet in 2 Kings 25:8-17, the temple is burned with fire and the objects in it are carried to Babylon. When Kings was written, there were no poles to be seen in

---

[3]Seven of twenty-eight occurrences of *māqôm* in Kings are in chapter eight (8:6,7,21,29,30[2],35).

[4]The word "covenant" is read by ellipsis. The Hebrew is "where Yahweh cut with the children of Israel." The underlying idiom is "Yahweh cut a covenant" (כָּרַת יהוה בְּרִית, *kārath YHWH bᵉrîth*; cf., e.g., Gen 15:18; Deut 5:3).

the temple; it was lying in ruins! The description of the temple and the report of its dedication must be based on earlier material. In 1 Kings 8:8, a fragment of that material is conspicuously left lying on the surface. As to its purpose, the note that the poles are still visible appears to function as an ancient form of documentation, verification that this is a reliable account.[5]

Solomon expresses his belief that Yahweh has chosen this house and prays that it will be **"a place [mākôn] for you to dwell forever"** (v. 13). The two words for "dwell" in Solomon's prayer stand out. He uses יָשַׁב (yašab) in verse 13, the common word for sitting/dwelling. In verse 12, שָׁכַן (šākan, "sojourn/dwell") serves as a direct link to God's promise to dwell among them (Exod 25:8; 29:45,46; 40:35). (The word for tabernacle, מִשְׁכָּן (miškān), is derived from šākan.) When Solomon mentions Yahweh's promise to dwell in a **dark cloud** (v. 12), he calls to mind Exodus 20:21; Deuteronomy 4:11; 5:22. But as the reader is aware, the story will sadly end with this house in ruins. At that time, with a brief stroke, the narrator connects those inglorious acts of judgment on Judah with Solomon's magnificent accomplishment: "The bronze from the two pillars, the Sea, and the

---

[5]See Provan, *1 and 2 Kings*, p. 77. How much of the account is preexilic and how much is later is difficult to determine. The role that the temple plays in the composition would perhaps suggest that a good portion of it is preexilic. However, the emphasis on exile and the temple as a house of prayer to a God who hears from heaven (8:27-53) points to an exilic (or perhaps even postexilic) time frame. Prayer in the direction of the temple (vv. 29,30,33,38,42,44,48) would be especially apropos to exiles in Babylon. But this must be kept in perspective. Hurowitz demonstrates that Solomon's temple dedication has preexilic parallels that include petitions to hear the king's prayer. For example, in an inscription at the restoration of the temples of Anu and Adad in Ashur, from well over a century before Solomon, Tiglath-pileser I says, "So may Anu and Adad faithfully turn to me. May they love the uplifting of my hands, may they hear my fervent prayer" (*I Have Built You an Exalted House*, pp. 69, 295, 298-300). These parallels suggest that Solomon's prayer must not be a wholesale creation of the exile. The account of Solomon is an inspired, selective, and reliable retelling (cf. a different retelling in 2 Chronicles) of the events of his reign for an audience that has experienced exile. Ancient Near Eastern analogies indicate that Solomon's prayer and his building projects are not out of place in the tenth century B.C. A literary analysis suggests that, while sources were used, Kings is a brilliantly conceived, unified composition of the exile that addresses theological issues raised by the destruction of the house of Yahweh, a house that is so eloquently described here (see "Introduction: Composition").

movable stands, which *Solomon had made* for the temple of the Lord" are broken up and taken to Babylon (2 Kgs 25:13-17).

And that ending, the destruction of Jerusalem and the temple that Solomon builds for Yahweh, may have its genesis here. In Solomon's prayer, he repeatedly calls attention to the fact that *he had constructed* the temple for Yahweh. **"I have indeed built"** recurs six times in the verses that follow (8:13,20,27,43,44,48; cf. 21,59) and appears to reflect a self-absorbed attitude that suggests that the temple may be as much about Solomon as the one who will dwell in the house that he builds (see comments on 8:31-51).[6] In the end, it may be that this spirit is what keeps this son of David from sustaining the devotion to Yahweh that characterized his father. And as the descendants of Solomon (and the kings of Israel) follow in his footsteps and become infatuated with prestige and power, the people of Israel will forget that Yahweh, not their kings, is the one who delivered them from Egypt, joined with them in covenant, and established a house for David in Jerusalem. Yahweh will not dwell in this house forever!

5. Solomon Blesses Israel (8:14-21)

8:14-21 Solomon blesses **the whole assembly** and in their presence explains the promise that Yahweh had made to his father David (2 Samuel 7).[7] What was suggested at the beginning of the composition (see comments on 1 Kings 1–2) is now made explicit, albeit from the mouth of the story's principle character, Solomon: God has placed Solomon on the throne of his father and has empowered him to build a house for his Name (see especially 2 Sam 7:13). Yahweh has kept his promise and in so doing is honoring the oath that David had made to build a temple (Psalm 132; 2 Sam 7:1-2).

But the first-person pronouns (vv. 20-21) also suggest that Solomon may be making political hay out of that oath. His words lift up the God of Israel, but they also validate his reign and the religious innovation that he introduces. When Israel builds a permanent

---

[6]See Walsh, *1 Kings*, p. 115.

[7]For the differences in the parallel account of Solomon's speeches in 2 Chr 6:1-42, see Hicks, *1 & 2 Chronicles*, pp. 284-292. The account in Chronicles affirms Yahweh's commitment to David and his presence in the postexilic community (p. 284).

house for their God, they become even more like the nations that surround them (see 1 Sam 8:4-22). Solomon wisely connects his new temple with the **"covenant of the LORD"** and "the deliverance from **Egypt**." Among the people, there must have been some resistance to his innovative changes. The participation of "the elders of Israel, all the heads of the tribes and the chiefs of the Israelite families" (v. 1) in the ceremonies reflects an effort to secure their endorsement and build consensus for the new house for Yahweh. And, when the cloud fills the temple, Yahweh himself endorses the change and consents to the house! The storyteller records these events to highlight both the relocation of the ark and the appearance of the cloud. For him, these are key events in the history of Israel, representing the end of one era and the beginning of another.[8]

However, the temple is a human convention that could distort the true nature of the God of all creation. Name theology resurfaces (vv. 16,17,18,19,20,29,33,35,41,42,43,44,48; see comments on 5:5; 8:27-30). Solomon has built a **"temple for the Name of the LORD"** to dwell, as Yahweh specified to David (2 Sam 7:13). Yet, Yahweh may be misrepresented in the very trappings of power that are symbolized in the magnificent house Solomon has constructed. Only when this same edifice lies in ruins, will Israel's kings learn that Yahweh and his temple are not objects to be manipulated and used for political ambitions.

6. Solomon Prays for Mercy (8:22-53)

8:22-26 Solomon begins his prayer by reminding Yahweh of **"your promise to your servant David my father"** (cf. vv. 24,25,26). No doubt, his position **before the altar of the LORD in front of the whole assembly of Israel** indicates that what he says is also for Israel's hearing. His posture, **spreading out his hands toward heaven** (cf. v. 54), reinforces a theological linchpin of this account: Yahweh hears from heaven. Other important theological ideas are also expressed. Yahweh keeps his **"covenant of love"** (literally,

---

[8]See Knoppers, "Prayer and Propaganda," pp. 382, 384. Knoppers observes that the ark is not mentioned again after 8:21 (p. 384).

"keeping covenant and mercy [חֶסֶד, *ḥesed*]") for those who serve him **"wholeheartedly"** (literally, "who walk before him with all of their heart" [cf. Deut 10:12]). And Solomon's version of the promise to David (2 Samuel 7), as remembered by David in 1 Kgs 2:3-4, is conditional: **"If only your sons are careful in all they do to walk before me."** Solomon calls on Yahweh to **"let your word that you promised your servant David my father come true."**[9]

8:27-30 In these verses, the theological dilemma introduced by the temple as a permanent dwelling for Yahweh is directly addressed: **"Will God really dwell on earth?"** If the heavens cannot contain him, **"how much less this temple I have built!"** Name theology resolves the tension. The transcendent Yahweh dwells in heaven, only his Name resides on earth. As Stephen argues, "The Most High does not live in houses made by men" (Acts 7:48). Continuing the same thought, he quotes the prophet Isaiah:

> "Heaven is my throne,
>   and the earth is my footstool.
> What kind of house will you build for me?
>   says the Lord.
> Or where will my resting place be?
> Has not my hand made all these things?" (Acts 7:49-50;
>   cf. Isa 66:1,2).

By metonymy, "Name of Yahweh" enables Israel to comprehend a transcendent deity who can commune with his people in the place that he chooses. (Another manifestation of God, "Face/Presence," also appears in this text in v. 28 [see comments on 5:5 and "Excursus: Solomon's Temple Viewed in Context"]). So, the house that Solomon builds becomes **the place** (vv. 29,30[2×]; see comments on 8:1-13) where Yahweh's relationship with Israel is mediated. Supplicants pray toward the temple. When this occurs, "May Yahweh keep his **eyes open toward this temple**, **hear from heaven**, and **forgive**" (cf. vv. 34,36,39,50). Remarkably, the emphasis here is not on sacramental cleansing through sacrifices at this *place*[10] but on

---

[9]The verb that Solomon uses here (in the NIV "let . . . come true") is אָמַן, *'āman*, from which derives the expression of acceptance "Amen" (see Deut 27:15-26).

[10]Deuteronomy 12:1-28 emphasizes sacrifice at the *place* Yahweh would choose.

efficacious prayer from penitents to a merciful God — from penitents who **pray toward this place**. For an exilic audience, this would
have special appeal.[11]

8:31-51 Solomon now enumerates specific circumstances in
which Yahweh should **hear from heaven and act**. The seven petitions by and large reflect the consequences/curses of breaking
covenant with Yahweh (Deut 28:15-68). The first three are requests
for Yahweh to administer justice (vv. 31-32, specifically in the matter
of "oaths before the LORD"; cf. Exod 22:10-12), bring Israel back
from captivity (vv. 33-34), and send rain (vv. 35-36) — when they turn
to him. The central petition is a more general call for Yahweh to
relent from various curses: "When a penitent heart spreads **out his
hands toward this temple** [cf. vv. 22,54]—**then hear. . . . Forgive and
act**" (vv. 37-40). In the final three petitions, Solomon calls on
Yahweh to hear the foreigner who prays toward the temple (vv. 41-
43), uphold the cause of the people when they go to war (vv. 44-45),
and show mercy when Israel is taken into captivity (vv. 46-51).

The emphasis on Yahweh's **"Name"** (vv. 33,35,41,42,43[2×],44,
48), that he should **"hear from heaven"** (vv. 32,34,36,39,43,45,49),
and that penitents should pray **"toward this temple"** (vv. 38,42,44,
48) reinforces the view of the temple already outlined above (see
comments on vv. 27-30). Another important theme emerges when
Solomon calls on Yahweh to show mercy toward his people when
because of their sins they are taken into exile (vv. 33-34; 46-51).
When they **"turn back to you"** (v. 33, i.e., "repent," שׁוּב, *šûb*; see
vv. 35,47[2×],48), Yahweh should **"forgive the sin of your people**
[v. 34; see vv. 30,36,39,50] **and bring them back"** (v. 34; literally,
"cause them to return," *šûb*). The play with *šûb* ("turn back," "bring
back"; vv. 33,34,35,47,48) introduces an important motif in Kings.
The message for an exilic audience is to repent — **"turn back to you
with all their heart and soul"** (v. 48; see Deut 6:5; 10:12; 2 Kgs
17:13) — and Yahweh may **"uphold their cause"** and perhaps *bring
them back* (*šûb*) to the land.[12] Wordplay with *šûb* and שָׁבָה (*šābāh*,

---

[11]Praying toward Mecca in Islam reflects a similar tradition. In exile,
Daniel prays toward Jerusalem (Dan 6:10).

[12]J.G. McConville demonstrates dialogue between 1 Kgs 8:46-53 and Deut
29:17-27; 30:1-10, and argues that because there is no mention of returning
to the land in verses 46-51, 1 Kings 8, in contrast with Deut 30:1-10, only

"carry into captivity"; vv. 46[2×],47[2×],48,50)[13] reinforces the view that this prayer is selectively retold for an exilic audience, who would be familiar with Moses' promise of *return* (*šûb*, a *second Exodus*) in Deuteronomy 30:1-10 (cf. Isa 11:10-16).

There is no one who does not sin (v. 46) sounds an ironic note. Even the king who is expressing these sentiments will not be able to keep from sinning against Yahweh. To be sure, his sins will bring on the division of the kingdom (11:1-40) and set Israel on a precipitous path. As suggested above (see comments on 8:1-13), that path may begin with **"I have built."** Six times in his recorded speeches/ prayers at the dedication of the temple the reader hears Solomon call attention to the temple "*I have built*" (vv. 13,20,27,43,44,48)![14]

8:52-53 Solomon ends his prayer with another reference to the Exodus.[15] The connection with **"your servant Moses"** and the deliverance from Egypt is an important matter for both Solomon and for an exilic author of Kings. Solomon names Moses and himself **"your servant,"** a link that would further validate the innovations he has made in building the temple. For someone in exile, remembering that Yahweh was a deliverer in Egypt would raise expectations that he might be the same for Israel again.[16]

---

envisions improved conditions while in captivity ("1 Kings 8:46-53 and the Deuteronomic Hope," in *Reconsidering Israel and Judah: Recent Studies on the Deuteronomistic History*, ed. Gary N. Knoppers and J. Gordon McConville [Winona Lake, IN: Eisenbrauns, 2000], pp. 358-369). However, the reference to return (with *šûb*) in verse 34 suggests that the author espouses a hope for both improved conditions and return to the land (see Provan, *1 and 2 Kings*, p. 81). If some had already returned to Judah (perhaps in an early postexilic context), an improved situation in captivity would still be a major concern and perhaps explain the emphasis.

[13]See Nelson, *First and Second Kings*, p. 54. The wordplay may be extended to *yašab* ("dwell," vv. 43,49; see Walsh, *1 Kings*, p. 114).

[14]See Walsh, *1 Kings*, p. 115.

[15]Connections with Moses and the Exodus permeate Solomon's prayer. For example, "your mighty hand and outstretched arm" (v. 42) recalls the language of deliverance in Exodus (see, e.g., Exod 6:1,6). Also, Jerusalem as the "chosen city" (vv. 16,44,48) echoes directly Moses' words in Deut 12:5,11,14,18,21,26.

[16]Frisch, "The Exodus Motif," 10.

7. Solomon Blesses Israel Again (8:54-61)

8:54-61 Having begun his prayer with references to the promise Yahweh had made to David, Solomon finally blesses Israel with a prayer that Yahweh will remember his promises to Moses. **Not one word has failed of all the good promises he gave through his servant Moses** recalls a similar statement by Joshua: "Not one of all the good promises the Lord your God gave you has failed" (Josh 23:14; cf. 21:43-45). As the God of Israel created a nation in Canaan from the descendants of Abraham and *gave them rest* (21:44; cf. Exod 33:14; Josh 1:13; 23:1), now he has established in Israel a royal house and a temple for his dwelling — **and given rest to his people Israel** (Deut 12:10; 1 Kgs 5:4; cf. 2 Sam 7:11). Yahweh has delivered on all of his promises. A reader familiar with the Joshua-Judges story, however, should see portents of ominous things to come. Yahweh gave Israel the land as a possession, but Israel did not take the land (Judg 2:17-36). They allowed the people of the land to remain and in the process became like their idolatrous neighbors (cf. Josh 23:12-13; Judg 2:20-23; 17–21). Yahweh has again fulfilled his word, but will Israel and her kings remain **fully committed to the Lord our God, to live by his decrees and obey his commands?** In the larger story, they are not able to keep Torah. Israel, like the nations who inhabited Canaan before them, will lose their right to the land. They will be disinherited from the possession promised to their fathers and will be sent into captivity — as it were, back to Egypt!

The language of verse 58 is from Deuteronomy: **"May he turn** [נָטָה, *nāṭāh*] **our hearts to him, to walk in all his ways and to keep the commands, decrees and regulations he gave our fathers"** (cf., e.g., Deut 5:31–6:1). These words, however, have a hollow ring when Solomon's life is viewed as a whole. The phrase **"turn our hearts to him"** appears again when the narrator says that Solomon's wives "turned [*nāṭāh*] his heart after other gods" (1 Kgs 11:4). There is no reason to believe that Solomon was insincere in his expressions of devotion at the dedication of the temple. But like the people of Deuteronomy 30:1-10, he and his descendants will be unable to keep the Law of Moses. Israel will have to experience the curses of the covenant in exile and wait for a time when Yahweh will *turn their hearts* to him — in the words of Moses: "The LORD your God will circumcise your hearts and the hearts of your descendants, so that you may love him with all your heart and with all your soul, and live" (Deut 30:6). Only a new covenant will enable hearts like this (see Jer 31:31-34).

There is also some irony in Solomon's words, when he says that **"your hearts must be *fully committed* to the LORD our God"** (v. 61). "Fully committed" (שָׁלֵם, *šālēm*) is a form of Solomon's name (שְׁלֹמֹה, *šᵉlōmōh*). The one who in many ways embodies the promises of Yahweh will be unable to *fully commit* his heart and will lead Israel along the way to exile. When this happens, when Yahweh "leaves and forsakes" them (v. 57), what will come of the unconditional promise to David — and the promise to the patriarchs? Will there be any grace left for the descendants of Abraham? Solomon prays that Yahweh will be merciful!

8. Solomon and the People Sacrifice and Celebrate (8:62-66)

8:62-66 The ceremonies end as they began (v. 5). Solomon and all Israel offer **sacrifices before the LORD**. The impressive number of offerings testifies both to the king's wealth and to his devotion. **Fellowship offerings** (literally, "peace offerings," שְׁלָמִים, *šᵉlāmîm*) are highlighted (vv. 63,64), reinforcing the theme of peace that symbolizes the rest that Yahweh has given Israel through Solomon (*šᵉlōmōh*; see comments on 5:4; 8:56). **The king and all the Israelites dedicated** [חָנַךְ, *ḥānak*] **the temple of the LORD**.[17] Israelites from the entire expanse of the kingdom given by Yahweh celebrate with Solomon the Feast of Tabernacles (see comments on 8:2). The day after, the people **bless the king** and are dismissed to their homes **joyful and glad in heart**. This spirit and the happy, contented state mentioned in 4:20, come from Yahweh, who is honoring his covenant with **his servant David**.

---

[17]The verb the narrator uses here, "dedicated" (*ḥānak*), is related to חֲנֻכָּה (*ḥᵃnukkāh*), a word used for the dedication of the altar of the tabernacle (Num 7:10,11,84,88) — and for the festival of Hanukkah. In the Gospel of John, Jesus at Hanukkah describes himself as the one who has been dedicated/set apart for Yahweh (John 10:36).

EXCURSUS

SOLOMON'S TEMPLE VIEWED IN CONTEXT

The account of the construction and dedication of the Solomonic temple in Kings plays a major role in the composition. The temple represents Yahweh's commitment to Israel. He is keeping his promises to Moses (8:56) and David (8:25). Yahweh has chosen Jerusalem as the place for his Name to dwell (cf. Deuteronomy 12; cf. 1 Kgs 8:16,44,48; 11:13,32) and has established a son of David to sit on Israel's throne and build him a house for a dwelling (2 Samuel 7). Continuity with the Exodus traditions lays a foundation for a new era in Yahweh's relationship with Israel, a relationship that now has its locus in the temple that Solomon builds. Nevertheless, the climactic conclusion of the story will see the devastation of Yahweh's house. The glorious house Solomon dedicates will be destroyed, and the grand furniture he constructs will be carried to Babylon (2 Kings 25). An exilic reader already knows the plot.

On the level of event, the construction of Yahweh's magnificent temple and the impressive Palace of the Forest of Lebanon represents a conscious attempt on the part of Solomon to validate his reign and further establish his sovereign authority over Israel and subordinate states. In other words, it represents a program of royal propaganda.[18] The use of symbol to validate the legitimacy of the state is well documented for the ancient Near East. Among the many ways that royal power could be communicated to subjects and to external nation states was through monumental architecture. Carol Meyers writes, "The elaborate temple building was the dramatic visual statement of Yahweh's legitimation of Solomonic rule. . . . The existence of the temple of Yahweh in the palace complex was the typical and effective Near Eastern manner for communicating to the

---

[18]Propaganda is not used here in the sense of manipulating a populace but as "the process by which a particular worldview (ideology) is disseminated to a specific audience" (Keith W. Whitelam, "The Symbols of Power: Aspects of Royal Propaganda in the United Monarchy," *BA* 49/3 [1986]: 166). The following discussion relies on his article (166-173); see also Meyers, "The Israelite Empire," pp. 188-197; idem, "Temple, Jerusalem," in *ABD*; Bloch-Smith, "Solomon's Temple and Its Symbolism," pp. 26-27.

palace officials as well as to foreign emissaries that the king was carrying out Yahweh's will in his dominion over Israel and all the conquered territories."[19] Along with his other impressive building projects, the temple-palace complex constructed by Solomon must represent a well-calculated plan of communicating royal wealth and prestige. To validate the regime, the sanction of the deity was essential. In Solomon's case, the size and symbolic representation of the temple and the elaborate ceremonies of dedication reflect efforts to reinforce the legitimacy of his reign. The sophisticated iconography of the temple would have communicated to all levels of society that Yahweh was present on the temple mount, a symbolic Garden of Eden in Israel (see comments on 6:14-38), and that he had *established* the royal house that had constructed such a grand temple. The massive columns Jakin and Boaz, for example, represent Yahweh as the source of *security* and *strength*, but they also intimate that the king who raised these pillars embodies that power as protector of temple and state. In fact, the word "Jakin" derives from the verb כּוּן (*kûn*, "establish"), a key word in the narrative of Solomon's rise to power. Yahweh *established* him on the throne of his father as he promised David (2 Samuel 7; see comments on chs. 1-2).

The storyteller's presentation of the temple reinforces the sociopolitical background of these events as in some sense reflecting royal propaganda. In addition to the detailed description of the temple, the rendering of the dedication portrays Solomon as using that occasion to validate his reign. In the presence of "the elders of Israel, all the heads of the tribes and the chiefs of the Israelite families," and "the whole assembly of Israel," the repeated references to Moses and the Exodus and to Yahweh's promise to his father David must have been calculated to confirm his rule with divine endorsements. Solomon's repeated phrase, "I have built," indicates his desire for Israel to see him as the recipient of divine favor.

This reading does not, however, in and of itself, undermine Solomon's actions or suggest that he was disingenuous; it merely brings out his worldview — a view that is consistent with the inspired author's point of view. In fact, the theology underlying 2 Samuel 7 reflects the political history that is implied in this account. Yahweh

---

[19]Meyers, "The Israelite Empire," p. 190.

promised David that he would establish a house for him (a royal lineage) and that his son would build a house (temple) in which his Name would dwell.[20] The wordplay with "house" (בַּיִת, *bayith*, 2 Sam 7:11-16) suggests that the two are intertwined. To build a lasting house/lineage meant constructing a house for Yahweh. When David asked to construct a house for his God, Yahweh responds by saying, in so many words, that there was no need for him to dwell in a house (2 Sam 7:5-7).[21] This is not something for which he asks. Nevertheless, when Yahweh chooses to build a house/dynasty for David, he also chooses to dwell in a permanent house! The two go hand in hand. The God of Israel must know that building a lasting house/dynasty for David, in the world of Iron Age Palestine, means authorizing David's son to build a house for his Name. A sociopolitical reading that stresses the *events* of state formation in Israel is consistent with the inspired, literary *account* of those events and actually strengthens its *theological* thrust. The dynamic interplay between event, account, and theology is herein impressively reinforced.

Recognizing the sociopolitical, human aspect of Solomon's temple construction also enables the reader to see the subtleties of the author's *account* of these events. The ironic retelling of Solomon's reign, including the construction and dedication of the temple, suggests that the text is not everything that it appears to be on the surface.[22]

---

[20]The "house of David" inscription from Tel Dan demonstrates the use of this phrase in Palestine in the ninth century B.C. (Avraham Biran, "The Tel Dan Inscription: A New Fragment," *IEJ* 45/1 [1995]: 1-18). The designation in Kings for the temple, "house of Yahweh," appears on a receipt for a contribution to the temple that may date as early as the late ninth century during the reign of Joash, or perhaps the seventh century B.C. from the reign of Josiah (Pierre Bordreuil, Felice Israel, and Dennis Pardee, "King's Command and Widow's Plea: Two New Hebrew Ostraca of the Biblical Period," *NEA* 61 [March 1998]: 2-5, 7, 9-13; Hershel Shanks, "Three Shekels for the Lord: Ancient Inscription Records Gift to Solomon's Temple," *BAR* 23/6 [Nov./Dec. 1997]: 28-32; see comments on 2 Kings 12). "House of Yahweh" also occurs on an ostracon (inscribed potsherd) from Arad (no. 18), which either designates the temple in Jerusalem or the sanctuary at Arad (see Dever, *Biblical Writers Know*, p. 181).

[21]In 1 Chr 22:6-10, David explains to Solomon that because he was a man of blood, Yahweh decreed that Solomon would build the temple and establish the dynasty.

[22]Brueggemann, as well, sees the presentation as ironic. The seeds for Solomon's downfall, especially his self-indulgence, are below the surface in

From one perspective, Solomon should be lauded for his efforts to establish a permanent dwelling for Yahweh in Jerusalem and for the extravagance that he showers on Yahweh's house. On another level, however, the seeds for Solomon's downfall are sown as he builds God's house and strengthens his hold on the throne. For example, the wealth from Yahweh that Solomon lavishes on the temple, symbolized by gold, plays a role in his ruin (see Deuteronomy 17).[23] Also, the honor and rest that he receives lead to political alliances that multiply wives and concubines, who "turn his heart after other gods" (1 Kgs 11:4). So, when Solomon prays that Yahweh might "turn our hearts to him," by irony the narrator calls attention to the inconsistencies in his reign. Human motivations are complex. Solomon may be sincere as he dedicates a house for Yahweh, but he is also self-serving. Remarkably, Yahweh responds to his devotion. In the end, however, a self-absorbed Solomon will be unable to live his professions!

The theological thrust of this complex portrayal deserves emphasis. At least three key ideas stand out in Solomon's temple construction and dedicatory prayers.[24] At the top of the list is the apparent inconsistency with building a dwelling for an omnipresent creator of the cosmos. Name theology is how Israel dealt with the tension inherent in a transcendent God dwelling in a house on earth (see comments on 5:5; 8:27-30). John N. Oswalt sees transcendence as the concept that separated Israel from her idolatrous neighbors, which he defines as "the idea that God was other than the psychophysical order of the universe; he was not accessible in or through it, and it was impossible to manipulate him by manipulating it."[25] Understanding transcendence precludes any attempt to

---

the account of his reign (*1 & 2 Kings*, pp. 70-71; see McConville, "Narrative and Meaning," 34). Walsh also highlights Solomon's "self-absorption" (see, e.g., *1 Kings,* p. 115). Missing the ironic nature of the composition, Pauline Viviano writes, "Where the Deuteronomistic historian has the opportunity to fault Solomon for his foreign marriages (1 Kgs 3:1) and buying horses from Egypt (1 Kgs 10:28-29), both of which are forbidden in the deuteronomic law (Deut 17:16-17), he does not do so" ("Glory Lost, p. 345).

[23]See Brueggemann, *1 & 2 Kings*, p. 103.

[24]See Nelson, *First and Second Kings*, pp. 59-60.

[25]"'Golden Calves' and the 'Bull of Jacob': The Impact on Israel of Its Religious Environment," in *Israel's Apostasy and Restoration: Essays in Honor of Roland K. Harrison*, ed. Avraham Gileadi (Grand Rapids: Baker, 1988), p. 14.

manipulate Yahweh through an idolatrous, magical approach to the almighty God of creation. Concerning the place of worship, Jesus said, "God is spirit, and his worshipers must worship in spirit and in truth" (John 4:24).

Further reflection suggests that Yahweh's agreement to allow his Name to dwell in a material house must be an accommodation.[26] The trappings of cedar and gold are in many ways inconsistent with the God of the egalitarian society of slaves that Moses led out of Egypt — and being "confined" to a permanent house increases the danger that Israel will misrepresent and attempt to manipulate him. Recognizing that the desire for a temple may also represent another way in which Israel becomes like the nations (1 Samuel 8) raises further questions about the temple. In order to establish a house/ dynasty for David, does Yahweh acquiesce to a permanent house of cedar and gold? For Christians, the incongruity of a God housed in a temple of gold with the image of the same God lying in a manger is difficult to reconcile. Yet, even this tension has important implications for understanding the nature of the God of Israel. While the trappings of wealth may represent an accommodation of sorts, an extravagant temple, where access to his presence is limited to an elite class, demonstrates the distance between Yahweh and man. A holy creator is so beyond human experience — "for there is no one who does not sin" (8:46) — that Solomon's temple does reflect one aspect of his nature. This is the same far-away, holy God who could not show his face to Moses (Exod 33:17-23). On the other hand, an infant God lying in a manger says that Yahweh is close; he is also nearby, available — the God with whom Moses conversed face to face (Exod 33:11). And this too is reflected in Solomon's prayer: "Hear the supplication of your servant and of your people Israel when they pray toward this place. Hear from heaven, your dwelling place, and when you hear forgive" (8:30). The dedication of Solomon's temple reminds the reader that Yahweh is both far away and near — a Holy God who delights in showing mercy to those who turn to him.

---

[26]Although perhaps overstated, Brueggemann recognizes the "dilemma of Solomon's temple," an "extravagant structure shot through . . . with awkwardness for Yahwism" (*1 & 2 Kings*, p. 97).

The emphasis on prayer toward the temple and the call for Israel to turn/repent (*šûb*) are the other key theological ideas in this account. Both suggest that the inspired narrator's report of Solomon's reign, based on records of what actually happened,[27] is selectively retold for Israel's situation in exile. Captives in exile would be comforted to hear Solomon pray for Yahweh to hear from heaven. They would also hear the call for Israel to *šûb* (repent). Perhaps their repentance will influence Yahweh to bring them back (*šûb*, 8:33-34). In dialogue with Deuteronomy 30, Solomon's prayer, then, becomes an exilic plea for mercy (8:28). The remaining story will draw out whether there will be *grace in the end*.[28]

---

[27]See the comments on 8:8 and "Introduction: Composition." The events of Solomon's reign are framed for theological meaning for Israelites who have witnessed the destruction of the temple and are in exile. Yet, while it is apparent that this account is written for an audience in exile, the story of the construction and dedication of the temple is at home in the time of Solomon, in the tenth century B.C. (see Hurowitz, *I Have Built You an Exalted House*, pp. 299-300; and Millard, "Solomon's Golden Wealth," 34). The reference to the poles of the ark in 8:8 indicates that there were sources and suggests that the author feels *constrained* by the facts. Again, the dynamic interplay between event, account, and theology emerges (see V. Philips Long, *The Art of Biblical History*, pp. 319-337.)

[28]This phrase is borrowed from McConville's well-reasoned construction of Deuteronomic theology. He demonstrates that an exilic hope characterizes the theology of Kings, although he believes this hope was muted by the realities of exile. Emphasizing 1 Kgs 8:46-53, he does not see a return to the land in Solomon's dedicatory prayers (*Grace in the End*, pp. 121-122, 134-139; see also "Narrative and Meaning," 46-48).

1 KINGS 9

E. SOLOMON IS BLESSED WITH TARNISHED TREASURES (9:1–10:29)

1. Yahweh Appears to Solomon Again (9:1-9)

9:1-9 When Solomon had completed his building projects, Yahweh **appears to him a second time, as he had appeared to him at Gibeon** (see 3:4-15). In his own words, the reader hears Yahweh say that he has **consecrated this temple** (9:3,7).[1] He has placed his **Name there forever.** Not only will his eyes be on this house, his **heart will always be there.** However, Yahweh's commitment is conditional (cf. 2:4; 3:4; 6:12). If Solomon and his sons walk before him as his father walked, Yahweh will keep the promise that he made to David. A descendant of David will forever sit on his throne in Jerusalem (2 Sam 7:16). Again, David is the standard by which the kings of Israel and Judah are measured (cf. 3:3,14; 11:4,6,34,38; 15:3,11; 2 Kgs 14:3; 16:2; 18:3; 22:2). However, if Solomon or his sons turn (*šûb*) from him and serve other gods, then Yahweh will **"cut off Israel from the land I have given them and will reject this temple I have consecrated for my Name."** Wordplay now underscores the extent of the devastation that will occur. **"Israel will then become a byword"** (מָשָׁל, *māšāl*). In Hebrew, *māšāl* is also the word for "proverb" and the consonants for "rule/have dominion/reign"

---

[1]At verse 3, the Chronicler departs from the account in Kings and adds to Yahweh's response to Solomon (2 Chr 7:12b-15) verses which reflect his own theological concerns. Often quoted, verse 14, in particular, reflects the theology of Chronicles: "If my people, who are called by my name, will humble themselves and pray and seek my face and turn from their wicked ways, then will I hear from heaven and will forgive their sin and will heal their land." For an excellent discussion of the significance of this verse for Chronicles, see Hicks, *1 & 2 Chronicles*, pp. 294-297.

(מָשַׁל, *māšal*). Yahweh placed Solomon on the throne of his father to have dominion (*māšal*, 4:21 [5:1]) over Israel and blessed him with wisdom to rule (*māšal*), with which he had written many proverbs (*māšāl*, 4:32 [5:12]). Yet, if he does not live by Torah and serve Yahweh, as did his father, the temple will become a ruin and Israel a *māšāl* ("byword") — a tragic *folly*[2] for a man with wisdom from God.

Again, the language is from Deuteronomy. For Israel's failure to keep Yahweh's covenant, Moses promised, "The LORD will drive you and the king you set over you to a nation unknown to you or your fathers. . . . You will become a thing of horror and an object of scorn (*māšāl*) and ridicule to all the nations where the LORD will drive you" (Deut 28:36-37). When this happens and Yahweh's house lies in ruins, all who pass by will ask, **"Why has the Lord done such a thing to this land and to this temple?"** Surely a burning issue for an audience in exile, this must represent, at least in part, the question of the book of Kings.[3] The move from singular to the plural forms in verses 6-9 (e.g., **"But if you** [pl.] **or your** [pl.] **sons turn . . ."**) may even represent Yahweh breaking narrative frame to give exhortations to readers in exile.[4] Why did Yahweh allow his house to be destroyed and in the process desert his people? In the mouth of those who pass the skeleton that was Solomon's imposing temple, Yahweh answers: **"Because *they* have forsaken the LORD their God, who brought their fathers out of Egypt, and have embraced other gods, worshiping and serving them."** And this must also represent the point of view of the storyteller. Yahweh has not forsaken his people; they have forsaken him! Free will explains Israel's plight in exile; they chose to serve other gods — but what about Yahweh's unconditional, eternal covenant with David (2 Samuel 7)? Is there hope for a return and for the restoration for which Solomon has prayed (8:33-34,46-53,57-58)?

---

[2]Provan, *1 and 2 Kings*, p. 60.

[3]In Hebrew narrative, characters often make statements or ask questions that represent major themes or issues of the composition (see comments on 2 Kings 3). For example, Gideon's question, "If the LORD is with us, why has all of this happened to us?" (Judg 6:12), represents the underlying issue of Joshua–Judges. Since God had blessed Israel with the land and promised that he would fight their battles, how does one explain their precarious situation among their ungodly neighbors?

[4]Walsh, *1 Kings*, pp. 117-118.

2. Solomon Builds His Kingdom (9:10-28)

9:10-28 At the end of twenty years of construction, during which time Solomon builds the house for Yahweh and the house for himself,[5] he gives twenty towns in Galilee to Hiram. The meaning of the name **Cabul** is enigmatic.[6] Zvi Gal believes he has found the area in the Galilee, excavating tenth-century-B.C. remains with Syro-Phoenician connections at Khirbet Ras el Zeitun, about one mile from the modern day village of Kabul.[7] That Hiram was upset with Solomon's gesture indicates that Solomon was the senior partner in their relationship (see comments on 5:1-12). To complete his building projects, Solomon makes **forced labor** (מַס, *mas*) of the people Israel **could not exterminate** (חָרַם, *ḥāram*; cf., e.g., Josh 6:21) from the land. **But Solomon** does **not make slaves of any of the Israelites**, albeit his rule apparently was excessively harsh (see comments on 5:13-14; 12:1-24).[8]

Solomon's building achievements are impressive. However, some scholars have questioned the accuracy of 1 Kings' portrayal of Israel in the tenth century B.C., suggesting that this description is an ideal construct of a later time. Conversely, monumental remains at **Hazor, Megiddo, and Gezer** support the description here. In particular, six-chambered gates at each site, generally dated to the tenth century, reflect Solomon's strategy of fortifying strategic locations to maintain control of his kingdom.[9] In fact, the archaeology of Hazor,

---

[5]The combined seven years for the temple and the thirteen years for the palace (6:38–7:1) do not preclude that the two buildings were constructed concurrently (see comments on 5:13). Grouping them together suggests that they were part of the same temple-palace complex.

[6]Cogan, *1 Kings*, pp. 299-300.

[7]Zvi Gal, "Cabul: A Royal Gift Found," *BAR* 19/2 (March/April 1993): 39-44, 84.

[8]For the differences in the parallel account of Solomon's other building activities in 2 Chr 8:1-16, see Hicks, *1 & 2 Chronicles*, pp. 299-302.

[9]See Larry G. Herr, "The Iron Age II Period: Emerging Nations," *BA* 60/3 (Sept. 1997): 123. Reinforcing the Solomonic dating, Amnon Ben-Tor dates the six-chambered gate and contemporaneous remains at Hazor to the last half of the tenth century ("Solomon's City Rises from the Ashes: Excavating Hazor, Part One," *BAR* 25/2 [March/April 1999]: 26-37, 60). For the debate over the tenth century in Palestine, see, e.g., Niels Peter Lemche, Thomas Thompson, William G. Dever, and P. Kyle McCarter, Jr., "Face to Face:

Megiddo, and Gezer, with monumental architecture and evidence of town planning, indicates for Dever that "10th century BCE Israel [was] not only 'urbanized,' but now under *centralized* political authority."[10] Ancient Near Eastern parallels with the description of the temple in 1 Kings (see comments on chs. 6–7) also demonstrate that the description of Solomon's "state building" and construction projects is not incompatible with what is known of the tenth century B.C. in the Levant.

The parenthetical reference that **Pharaoh king of Egypt** took Gezer and gave it as a **wedding gift to his daughter Solomon's wife** (vv. 16-17; cf. 3:1; 7:8; 11:1) may be indirectly corroborated in a battle scene on a monument of Pharaoh Siamun (979–960 B.C.). In a relief at the temple of Amun at Tanis, Siamun attacks an adversary who wields a double-headed ax with blades that are crescent shaped. The form of this ax suggests that the enemy is Philistine, a people of Aegean origin. The double crescent blade comes from the Aegean or Balkan regions. Kitchen suggests that the relief represents a campaign by Siamun against the Philistine coast. Siamun and Solomon may have set out to eliminate increasing Philistine influence on trade between Egypt and Israel. For his support, Solomon receives the strategic site of Gezer,[11] and perhaps Pharaoh's daughter. Some have argued that a marriage between the king of Israel and a daughter of

---

Biblical Minimalists Meet Their Challengers," interview by Hershel Shanks, *BAR* 23/4 (July/Aug. 1997): 26-42, 66; Gary N. Knoppers, "The Vanishing Solomon: The Disappearance of the United Monarchy from Recent Histories of Ancient Israel," *JBL* 116/1 (1997): 19-44; Dever, *Biblical Writers Know*, and references there. For a solid defense of David and Solomon's Jerusalem, see Nadav Na'aman, "Cow Town or Royal Capital?: Evidence *for* Iron Age Jerusalem," *BAR* 23/4 (July/Aug. 1997): 43-47, 67. The "house of David" inscription from Tel Dan (see n. 20, p. 134) clearly indicates there was an early Israel (Dever, *Biblical Writers Know*, pp. 128-129).

[10]William G. Dever, "Archaeology and the 'Age of Solomon': A Case-Study in Archaeology and Historiography," in *The Age of Solomon: Scholarship at the Turn of the Millennium*, ed. Lowell K. Handy (Leiden: Brill, 1997), pp. 226-227. Dever applies principles of state formation to the archaeological record of the tenth century in Israel and demonstrates "an Israelite state in the Iron IIA period," the age of David and Solomon (p. 251; see pp. 217-251; cf. Dever, *Biblical Writers Know*, pp. 124-157; Knoppers, "Vanishing Solomon," 39-41).

[11]Kitchen, "When Solomon Ruled," 35-36; see Cogan, *1 Kings*, p. 301.

the pharaoh of Egypt is implausible, even the type of story one would find in *The Thousand and One Nights*.[12] Many Old Testament scholars believe that the Egyptians did not give their daughters in marriage to foreigners, but Kitchen cites examples of such marriages from the tenth to the eighth centuries B.C.[13] Once more, extrabiblical sources indicate the story of Solomon is believable.

Solomon builds **store cities and the towns for his chariots and for his horses**. And after Pharaoh's daughter comes up to his palace, Solomon builds the enigmatic **supporting terraces** (vv. 15,24).[14] The references to Pharaoh's daughter (vv. 16,24) reinforce the important role that she plays in the negative characterization of Solomon. His wives will be his downfall (see comments on 3:1; 11:1-8). Nevertheless, the reference to Pharaoh's daughter in verse 24 is juxtaposed with the note in verse 25 that Solomon **fulfills [שָׁלֵם, *šālēm*] the temple obligations** (literally, "completed the house"; cf. 7:51). He completes the temple by inaugurating and participating in Israel's three annual feasts (see Exod 23:15-17; 34:23; Deut 16:16). Solomon has both deserving and undeserving qualities. The king also builds **ships at Ezion Geber**. With experienced sailors from Phoenicia, **they sail to Ophir** and bring back . . . **gold**.[15]

---

[12]Miller, "Separating the Solomon of History," p. 15. Millard counters, "Wherever the book [of Kings] can be checked against adequate records from other states, it can be seen to be a reliable record, keeping its own purpose and view in mind" ("King Solomon in His Ancient Context," p. 50).

[13]Kitchen, "When Solomon Ruled," 36-37.

[14]The "tripartite pillared buildings" at sites like Megiddo and Hazor, at one time thought to be stables constructed by Solomon, may not be stables and clearly date from the ninth century B.C. after Solomon. The stepped stone structure exposed on the City of David's eastern slope, thought by some to be the "supporting terraces" (מִלּוֹא, *millô'*, "fill/filling") mentioned here, was probably constructed before the United Monarchy (see Herr, "The Iron Age II Period," 138-139, 124-126; cf. W. Harold Mare, "Millo [place]," in *ABD*).

[15]The island of Jezîrat Far'ôn (Coral Island) in the gulf of Elath — with early Iron Age remains and underwater evidence of an artificial harbor — may be Ezion Geber (Meir Lubetski, "Ezion-Geber," in *ABD*). The best suggestions for Ophir are Arabia or East Africa; Ophir also can mean fine gold. From the eighth-century-B.C. Tel Qasile, Ophir occurs in a receipt on an inscribed potsherd: "gold of Ophir to Beth-horon. 30 shekels" (David W. Baker, "Ophir," in *ABD*; Millard, "King Solomon in His Ancient Context," p. 41). Millard speculates that "Solomon may have taken advantage of a 'lucky strike' in Ophir" (p. 42).

1 KINGS 10

3. The Queen of Sheba Visits Solomon (10:1-13)

10:1-9 The Queen of Sheba's visit[1] reinforces themes introduced prior to the description of the temple. The wisdom, wealth, and honor promised to Solomon (3:1-15) are all confirmed in this episode. In fact, the account of Solomon's reign displays a somewhat concentric structure in which elements recorded after the construction of the temple have parallels that appear prior to its construction. For example, 5:1-12 parallels 9:10-14; 5:13-18 parallels 9:15-23; and 4:29-34 parallels 10:1-13.[2] This arrangement highlights changes in Solomon's relationship to his blessings and calls attention to the inconsistencies in his life. The visit of the Queen of Sheba especially echoes themes from 4:29-34.

---

[1]Since Sheba was probably located on the southwest corner of the Arabian Peninsula, a region that played a major role in Iron Age trade, the Queen of Sheba's mission must have included trade negotiations (Stephen D. Ricks, "Sheba, Queen of," in *ABD*), although Cogan regards a commercial motive for the queen's visit as speculation (*1 Kings*, p. 315).

[2]Nelson, *First and Second Kings*, p. 63. For two different ways of viewing the structure of the account of Solomon (i.e., as two parallel stories [chs. 3–8, 9–11], or as a concentric structure with an emphasis on the construction and dedication of the temple [ch. 6–8]), see Parker, "Repetition as a Structuring Device," 19-27; idem, "The Limits to Solomon's Reign: A Response to Amos Frisch," *JSOT* 51 (1991): 15-21; Amos Frisch, "Structure and Its Significance: The Narrative of Solomon's Reign (1 Kings 1–12.24)," *JSOT* 51 (1991): 3-14; idem, "The Narrative of Solomon's Reign: A Rejoinder," *JSOT* 51 (1991): 22-24. Analyzing the two approaches, David S. Williams finds verbal evidence that indicates two parallel stories. However, important connections also reinforce themes highlighted in the concentric view, indicating "a fascinating web of connections, indicating a tightly woven account" ("Once Again: The Structure of the Narrative of Solomon's Reign," *JSOT* 86 [1999]: 49-66). Recognizing the ironic nature of the composition also suggests that it is more complex than two parallel accounts (favorable to Solomon [chs. 3–8] and unfavorable to Solomon [chs. 9–11]). In addition, the structure is also influenced by ancient Near Eastern literary patterns for temple building accounts,

When the reader hears the Queen of Sheba describe Solomon's grandeur (vv. 6-9), again, a minor character expresses the narrator's point of view (see n. 16, p. 77): "Yahweh has **delighted in you and placed you on the throne of Israel**" (cf. 2 Sam 12:25; 7:11-16). "In **wisdom**[3] **and wealth you have far exceeded the report I heard**" (see 1 Kgs 4:20-34). "**How happy your men must be**" (cf. 4:20; 8:66), evidencing the rest/peace that was promised (see comments on 5:1-6; 8:54-61). "**Because of the LORD's eternal love for Israel, he has made you king, to maintain justice and righteousness.**" It was because of Solomon's request for "discernment in administering justice" (3:11; cf. 3:28) that Yahweh promised to bless Solomon.

However, the Queen of Sheba does not mention the populace: "**How happy your men must be! How happy your officials, who continually stand before you and hear your wisdom!**" This is different from the emphasis in 4:20: "The people of Judah and Israel were . . . happy" (see also 4:25). The stress on luxury items and wisdom for Solomon's glory that characterizes 9:10–10:29, in contrast with the blessings of Yahweh that were used for the people of Israel in chapters four and five, suggests a shift toward the type of king of whom Samuel warned (1 Sam 8:11-18).[4] By the creative use of structural irony, Solomon is exposed as a self-indulgent leader who has lost sight of his divinely ordained role as shepherd of Israel.

In Israel, the ideal king is one who administers justice and righteousness for the disenfranchised (see Psalm 72; cf. Jer 22:2-3,13,15). Later, as Jerusalem stands on the precipice of ruin, Jeremiah predicts the coming of a righteous king: "'The days are coming,' declares the LORD, 'when I will raise up to David a righteous Branch, a King who will reign wisely and do what is just and right in the land'" (Jer 23:5). Since Solomon and his sons do not measure up to this standard, the promise of an eternal kingdom for David's son must ultimately refer to the Messiah (2 Sam 7:14-16). In the New Testament, Jesus mentions the "Queen of the South's" expedition to

---

for which Hurowitz establishes the following pattern: decision to build/divine approval, acquisition of materials, description of building process, dedication, dedication prayer, and conditional blessings and curses for the future king (*I Have Built You an Exalted House*, pp. 311-312).

[3]Three of the six references to Solomon's wisdom in this chapter occur in the Queen of Sheba's speech (vv. 4,6,7,8,23,24).

[4]Provan, *1 and 2 Kings*, pp. 84-87; Walsh, *1 Kings*, pp. 130-132.

hear the wisdom of Solomon and claims that "one greater than Solomon is here" (Matt 12:42; Luke 11:31).[5]

10:10-13 The narrator concludes his account of the Queen of Sheba's expedition to Jerusalem with a note about her gifts of **gold, large quantities of spices, and precious stones** (and a parenthetical reference on the precious materials brought in by Hiram's ships). Her gifts are pale in comparison with Solomon's wealth (10:14-29). Solomon reciprocates by giving her **all that she desired and asked for** (cf. 5:8-11[22-25]; 9:11). Officials from the nations journey to Jerusalem to "listen to Solomon's wisdom" (4:34).

4. Solomon Accumulates Wealth (10:14-29)

10:14-21 As in the description of the temple, these verses glitter with **gold**.[6] Solomon's wealth is symbolized by gold, highlighted by the **shields of hammered gold** and the **great throne inlaid with ivory and overlaid with fine gold**. Some have questioned the authenticity of this description, labeling it unabashed exaggeration. Millard, however, demonstrates the plausibility of this report with a range of parallels from the ancient Near East. For example, Solomon's golden shields correspond with "shields of gold" taken by soldiers of Sargon II of Assyria from the temple in Musasir (714 B.C.). The great throne has as a parallel the ivory-veneered, gold-plated throne of king Tutankhamun of Egypt (fourteenth century B.C.). Golden tableware has been discovered throughout the ancient Near East from the time of Ur and Ugarit to Alexander. Prosperous kings were expected to have such tableware and display their wealth ostentatiously. In terms of amounts of gold and its use in adorning Solomon's building projects, the description in Kings is not out of place in the tenth century B.C.[7]

---

[5]In one sense, Solomon is a type of the messianic king to come. However, there are also important contrasts between Solomon and Jesus (Yahweh's Messiah), not the least of which is their attitude toward possessions. Solomon stores treasures on earth (see comments below), while the Messiah teaches that treasures should be laid up in heaven (Matt 6:19-24; Luke 12:32-34). Jesus said, "Do not worry . . . not even Solomon in all his splendor was clothed like [the lilies of the field]" (Matt 6:29; see Luke 12:13-31); see Provan, *1 and 2 Kings*, pp. 100-102.

[6]"Gold" (זָהָב, *zāhāb*) occurs fourteen times in chapter ten.

[7]Millard, "Solomon's Golden Wealth," 21-29, 31, 34; idem., "King

10:22-25 Solomon has **a fleet of trading ships** that travel a far-reaching route and bring back exotic items every three years. The Hebrew wording is "ships of Tarshish" (אֳנִי תַרְשִׁישׁ, *'ŏnî tharšîš*), in this case probably signifying a type of ship for trade (cf. 1 Kgs 22:49; 2 Chr 9:21; 20:36-37).[8] Israel's king is **greater in riches and wisdom** than all other kings. **The whole world** comes, bearing gifts, to **hear the wisdom God** has **put in his heart**. Again, the storyteller reminds the reader that Solomon's wisdom is from God (cf. 3:28; 5:12). Everything that Yahweh promised Solomon (3:1-15) has come to pass in abundance, symbolized by the gold, silver (v. 27), and tribute. Nevertheless, for a careful reader, an ironic, dissonant chord sounds. In the Torah, Moses cautioned that the king "must not accumulate large amounts of silver and gold" (Deut 17:17).

10:26-29 The narrator's ironic approach continues when he notes that **Solomon's horses** are **imported from Egypt** (cf. 2 Chr 1:16-17).[9] An expensive horse and a chariot from Egypt are singled out to put an exclamation point on the king's actions. As already observed (see comments on 4:26-28), the law of the king prescribed, "The king, moreover, must not acquire great numbers of horses for himself or make the people return to Egypt to get more of them, for the LORD has told you, 'You are not to go back that way again'" (Deut 17:16). The narrator is consciously making a connection with Moses' instructions. Yahweh has kept his promises to Solomon, but has Solomon kept the charge to walk in the way of his father David and follow Moses' Law (cf. 2:2-4; 3:5-15; 6:11-12; 9:1-9)?

Solomon's Shields," in *Scripture and Other Artifacts: Essays on the Bible and Archaeology in Honor of Philip J. King*, ed. Michael D. Coogan, J. Cheryl Exum, and Lawrence E. Stager (Louisville, KY: Westminster John Knox Press, 1994), pp. 286-295; "King Solomon in His Ancient Context," pp. 36-41; see comments on 6:14-38.

[8]See David W. Baker, "Tarshish," in *ABD*. "Silver of Tarshish" appears on an ostracon (inscribed potsherd) from the seventh (or perhaps ninth) century B.C., apparently representing Tarshish as a place. While the exact location of Tarshish is debated, Jonah 1:3 and Ps 72:10 indicate that it was west of Israel (Bordreuil, Israel, and Pardee, "Two New Hebrew Ostraca," 4-5).

[9]For the view that Egypt (מִצְרַיִם, *miṣrayim*) was originally *Muzur/Musri* (מֻצְרִים, *muṣrîm*, cf. NIV text note) north of the Taurus Mountains, see Gray, *I & II Kings*, pp. 268-269; Cogan, *1 Kings*, pp. 321-322. However, this view is unnecessary and misses the significance of Egypt in the storyteller's ironic presentation of Solomon's reign (see Hobbs, *2 Kings*, pp. 84, 90-91).

1 KINGS 11

F. SOLOMON TURNS AWAY FROM YAHWEH (11:1-43)

1. Solomon's Wives Turn His Heart (11:1-13)

11:1-10 The narrator's oblique strategy of alluding to the law of the king (Deut. 17:14-20) in regard to Solomon's gold and horses from Egypt (1 Kgs 10:14-29) now becomes more direct. Solomon **loves many foreign women besides Pharaoh's daughter**. These wives were from the nations about which Yahweh had said, **"You must not intermarry [חתן, *ḥtn*; also in Deut 7:3; Josh 23:13; 1 Kgs 3:1] with them, because they will surely turn your hearts after their gods"** (see Exod 34:16; Deut 7:1-4). However, only one of the seven "devoted" nations of Deuteronomy 7:1 is mentioned among Solomon's list of wives (i.e., "the Hittites"). Apparently, the author of Kings is creatively applying Deuteronomy 7:1-4 and Joshua 23:11-13 to Solomon's foreign marriages. Before his death, Joshua admonished Israel: "So be very careful to love the LORD your God. But if you turn away [*šûb*] and ally yourselves [דבק, *dābaq*] with the survivors of *these nations that remain among you* and if you *intermarry* [*ḥtn*] *with them* and associate with them, then you may be sure that the LORD your God will no longer drive out these nations before you. Instead, they will become snares and traps for you, whips on your backs and thorns in your eyes, until you perish from this good land, which the LORD your God has given you" (Josh 23:11-13). The more general and somewhat ambiguous "these nations that remain among you" allows the author to expand Moses' original declaration beyond the seven nations that were designated for destruction.[1] Solomon violated the injunctions

---

[1]Gary N. Knoppers, "Solomon's Fall and Deuteronomy," pp. 399-401, 409. Hermeneutically, the author of Kings is combining the two passages and applying the underlying principle (i.e., foreign wives will turn Israel

of Moses and Joshua not to intermarry with the people of the land. Moses also charged, "[The king] must not take many wives, or his heart will be led astray" (Deut 17:17).

What was suggested before is now made explicit. Beginning with Pharaoh's daughter (1 Kgs 3:1), Solomon took many wives (**seven hundred wives of royal birth and three hundred concubines**[2]), and he **held fast** [*dābaq*] **to them in love**. Four times, the narrator employs a variant of "*turned* his heart" (נָטָה, *nāṭāh*; vv. 2,3 [NIV "led him astray"], 4,9). The reader hears Solomon at the dedication of the temple pray, "May [the LORD] *turn* [*nāṭāh*] *our hearts* to him, to walk in all his ways and to keep the commands, decrees and regulations he gave our fathers" (see comments on 8:58). Even though Yahweh had **appeared to him twice** (3:1-15; 9:1-9) and had commanded him not **to follow other gods** (9:6-9), **Solomon did not keep the LORD's command**!

To underscore Solomon's unfaithfulness, the storyteller deliberately uses language that is pregnant with broader meaning (as in "turn his heart" above). That Solomon "*held fast* [*dābaq*] to them in love" stands out. The verb *dābaq* is used in Deuteronomy to express faithfulness, "holding fast to Yahweh" (10:20; 11:22; 13:4[5]; 30:20). Joshua used the same language: "But you are to hold fast [*dābaq*] to the LORD your God, as you have until now. . . . But if you turn away and ally [*dābaq*] yourselves with the survivors of these nations that remain among you . . ." (Josh 23:8,12).[3] Instead of *clinging* to the God of his father David, Solomon *clings* to his foreign wives. Also, **as Solomon grew old . . . his heart was not** *fully committed* (שָׁלֵם, *šālēm*, a form of Solomon's name, *šᵉlōmōh*) recalls Solomon's prayer at the dedication that "your hearts must be *fully committed* [*šālēm*] to the LORD our God, to live by his decrees and obey his commands" (8:61). In addition, Solomon had described Yahweh as one who keeps covenant with those who (literally) "walk before you with all their heart" (8:23).

Yet, perhaps most difficult to reconcile, **on a hill east of Jerusalem, Solomon** *builds* **a high place** for Chemosh and one for "Molech"

---

away from God) to Solomon. In this way, Kings also serves as commentary on Deuteronomy.

[2]These numbers may be symbolic (cf. S of S 6:8-9).

[3]Knoppers, "Solomon's Fall," p. 401.

(v. 7).[4] Reflecting an important theme in the story, at least twelve times in the narrative the storyteller and the king himself reiterate that Solomon built the house for Yahweh (6:1,2,14,38; 8:13,20,27,43, 44,48; 9:1,10). The son of David who *built* the house for Yahweh's Name also *builds* high places for the gods of his foreign wives![5]

11:11-13 Yahweh speaks again to Solomon (see 3:4-15; 6:12-13; 9:1-9). Because the king had **"not kept my covenant and my decrees,"** Yahweh will **tear the kingdom away from Solomon** and give it to one of his servants. Yet, this would not happen in Solomon's lifetime: **"for the sake of David your father** [v. 12, "my servant" in v. 13], **I will not do it during your lifetime."** Yahweh's judgment on Solomon would be delayed. In the larger story, delayed retribution will characterize Yahweh's interaction with Israel and Judah.[6] For example, punishment for both Jeroboam and Ahab of Israel will happen during the days of their sons (see 14:1-19; 21:27-29; 2 Kgs 9:14-29; cf. 2 Kings 22–23), and the final judgment will be inflicted on Israel by Assyria (2 Kgs 17:1-23). For the composition of Kings, this has the theological effect of explaining how both Israel and Judah were dispossessed from the land because of the sins and evil influence of earlier kings. But the delay also subtly interjects an underlying theme of grace. Yahweh is patient to administer justice, offering his people the opportunity to *repent/return* (*šûb*). In 1 Kings 13:33, the narrator declares, "Even after this, Jeroboam did not change ["turn from/repent," *šûb*] his evil ways." Through Jeremiah, the word of Yahweh to "the house of Israel" makes clear: "If at any

---

[4]In verses 5 and 33 (also in 2 Kings 23:13), the NIV changes the original Milcom (מִלְכֹּם, *milkōm*) for Molech of verse 7 (מֹלֶךְ, *mōlek*), even though Molech in verse 7 is often dismissed as a confusion of Molech with Milcom, the god of the Ammonites (see George C. Heider, "Molech [Deity]," in *ABD*). While the exact nature of these cults is unclear, there is no compelling reason to make this change (see Provan, *1 and 2 Kings*, p. 93; Cogan, *1 Kings*, pp. 327-328).

[5]Later, Josiah will tear down Solomon's high places (2 Kings 23:13).

[6]Gary N. Knoppers argues that these "transgenerational punishments" characterize the composition of Kings and contrast with the Chronicler's more cyclical "sequence of punishments and rewards." From the perspective of Deuteronomy, "it is a mark of divine leniency to impose the punishment due to the father upon the son." This approach allows the author of Kings to contrast "David's positive precedent in Judah with Jeroboam's negative precedent in Israel" ("Solomon's Fall and Deuteronomy," pp. 405-409).

time I announce that a nation or kingdom is to be uprooted, torn
down and destroyed, and if that nation I warned repents [*šûb*] of its
evil, then I will relent and not inflict on it the disaster I had planned"
(Jer 18:7-8). For an exilic audience, *delayed destruction/retribution*
offers the possibility of *delayed deliverance*. This hope is reinforced
when Yahweh declares that "for the sake of David my servant," one
tribe will remain for Solomon's son.

The language in 11:1-13 resonates with the opening scene of
Solomon's reign (3:1-15), after he had established his kingdom.
Structurally, 3:1-15 and 11:1-13 sport numerous connections that
ironically reinforce the failures of Solomon's reign. Pharaoh's
daughter is mentioned in 3:1 and 11:1. High places appear in
3:2,3,4, while high places to other gods are built in 11:7. Perhaps
most significant, 3:3 says, "Solomon showed his love for the LORD by
walking according to the statutes of his father David." By contrast,
in 11:1-2 the narrator says the king **loved many foreign women!**
Again, in 3:10 Yahweh was pleased with Solomon's request, and in
3:14 he said, "If you walk in my ways . . . as David your father did, I
will give you a long life." The narrator records in 11:6 that "Solomon
did evil in the eyes of the Lord; he did not follow the Lord as David
his father had done." In both texts, Yahweh speaks to Solomon. At
Gibeon, he tells Solomon that his blessings are conditional — if he
obeys, "as David your father did, I will give you a long life" (3:14). In
11:11-13, Yahweh announces that since Solomon has disobeyed, **"I
will most certainly tear the kingdom away from you."**[7]

The effect of these connections is to call into question Solomon's
wisdom. Yahweh promised Solomon "a wise and discerning heart"
(3:12), which he demonstrates in the episode of the two prostitutes
(3:16-28). Nevertheless, how wise is the king who is portrayed here
— marrying foreign women (see Deut 7:1-4) and building high places
for their gods? Yahweh has given Solomon wisdom from above,
along with both wealth and honor. Exercising free will, Solomon disregards the source of his many blessings and chooses his wives over
the God of his father David and his people Israel.

---

[7]See Frisch, "Structure and Its Significance," 11-12; Walsh, *1 Kings*,
pp. 136, 138.

2. Yahweh Raises Up Adversaries against Solomon (11:14-40)

11:14-25 One consequence of Solomon's apostasy is that Yahweh raises up adversaries[8] against him. In 5:4[18], Solomon boasted to Hiram, "The LORD my God has given me rest on every side, and there is no *adversary* or disaster." The kingdom of שָׁלוֹם (*šālôm*), promised by Yahweh (2 Sam 7:10-11), is broken by Solomon's unwise choices. Ironically, the three adversaries, Hadad the Edomite, Rezon, and Jeroboam, structurally parallel the three adversaries Solomon removed in the beginning to *establish* his reign (2:13-46).[9] Also, Hadad the Edomite conjures up images of Moses, and the description of Rezon calls to mind King David.

Like Moses, Hadad is taken in by Pharaoh and becomes a member of his family (cf. Exod 2:1-10). Later he goes to Pharaoh and requests, **"Let me go, that I may return to my country"** (cf., e.g., Exod 5:1). Like David, Rezon flees from his king and leads a band of brigands (cf. 1 Samuel 22–30). Later he becomes king in Damascus (cf. 2 Sam 2:4) and is an adversary to Israel **as long as Solomon lives.**[10] These allusions reinforce with an exclamation point the claim of the text. Yahweh was behind Solomon's troubles. As he was with Moses and David, he is with Hadad the Edomite and Rezon. Hadad, from Edom in the south, and Rezon, from Damascus in the north, plague Solomon's idyllic reign.[11]

11:26-40 Also, **Jeroboam son of Nebat rebels against the king.** Following the formula for introducing the kings of Judah, Jeroboam's mother is mentioned (see, e.g., 14:21). Yet, he is (literally) "a servant of Solomon who raised his hand" against the king. As Saul and David before him, he is described as a **man of standing** (1 Sam 9:1; 16:18), whom Solomon placed **in charge of the whole**

---

[8]Adversary in Hebrew is שָׂטָן (*śāṭān*). Only later does its range of meaning broaden to encompass the evil one, Satan (see Job 1:6–2:7).

[9]Parker, "Repetition as a Structuring Device," 21-22.

[10]This phrase is (literally) "all the days of Solomon." That Rezon may have been a threat to Solomon from early in his reign is not inconsistent with an apostasy in his old age. While Solomon's heart was turned to other gods when he was old (11:4), the seeds for his departure were apparently sown from near the beginning of his reign. The phrase could also mean "the rest of his life" (Provan, *1 and 2 Kings*, pp. 96-97; Cogan, *1 Kings*, p. 334).

[11]Walsh, *1 Kings*, pp. 140-141; see Frisch, "The Exodus Motif," 12-13.

labor force [*sēbel*] of the house of Joseph. The fact that Jeroboam is placed over the "labor force" (סֵבֶל, *sēbel*; from *sābal*, "carry/bear") of Ephraim and Manasseh will resurface when, after the death of Solomon, the kingdom is rent because of the oppressive policies of the house of David (see comments on 5:10-18; 12:1-24).

While the frame stories of Hadad the Edomite and Rezon say that God raised them up as adversaries, reinforcing this idea with allusions to Moses and David, with Jeroboam the narrator introduces a prophetic voice that sanctions rebellion as judgment on Solomon. Through the word of **Ahijah the prophet of Shiloh**, Yahweh initiates insurrection against his anointed. **Wearing a new cloak** (שַׂלְמָה, *śalmāh*), Ahijah meets Jeroboam **on the way** (דֶּרֶךְ, *derek*[12]) and *tears* **it into twelve pieces**, offering the future king ten pieces. Ahijah speaks for Yahweh: **"I am going to tear [**קָרַע, *qāraʿ*] **the kingdom out of Solomon's hand and give you ten tribes."** The symbolism here is difficult to miss. Saul *tore* (*qāraʿ*[13]) Samuel's robe, which symbolized the kingdom that was *torn* from him and given to one of his neighbors (1 Sam 15:27-28). So, as Ahijah's *śalmāh* ("robe") is *torn*, so will Solomon (*šᵉlōmōh*) be rent, his kingdom *torn* from his hand.

"But for the sake of my servant David and the city of Jerusalem" Solomon would retain one tribe.[14] Yahweh will do this **"because they have forsaken [**עָזַב, *ʿāzab*] **me and worshiped** other gods." This calls to mind Solomon's prayer that Yahweh not leave (*ʿāzab*) them, and Yahweh's promise not to abandon (*ʿāzab*) them, if Solomon follows his decrees (8:57; 6:13; cf. 9:9). The change to plural (**"***they* **have forsaken me"**[15]) suggests that Solomon has led Israel away from God:

---

[12]In the story of Jeroboam, *derek* will play an important thematic role.

[13]Occurring six times in verses 11-31, *qāraʿ* ("tear") functions as a key word, in part, to connect the dynastic prophesies of Samuel and Ahijah.

[14]In this symbolic act, the numbers do not add up. Only eleven pieces of the cloak are allocated. Most suggest that the ambiguous role that Benjamin plays in the larger narrative is a plausible solution. In 12:21-23, Judah *and Benjamin* follow Rehoboam. Yet, when Jeroboam establishes a high place in Bethel, a city of Benjamin, he is exercising political control over Benjamin (12:28-33; cf. Josh 18:21-22). From another angle, the tribe of Simeon apparently assimilated with Judah. Their inheritance was within the territory of Judah (Josh 19:1; cf. 21:9; Judg 1:3), perhaps accounting for the missing piece (cf. Cogan, *2 Kings*, pp. 340, 355).

[15]While some ancient versions have the singular "he has forsaken me"

"*They* **have not walked in my ways, nor done what is right in my eyes, nor kept my statutes and laws as David, Solomon's father, did**." Once more, the language is from Deuteronomy (e.g., 5:33–6:2; 10:12-13). Solomon and Israel have broken covenant with Yahweh.

Again, **"for the sake of David my servant, whom I chose and who observed my commands and statutes,"** Solomon's son will receive one tribe — **"so that David my servant may always have a lamp before me in Jerusalem, the city where I chose to put my Name."** "For David and for Jerusalem" echoes themes in the preceding account, in particular the promises to Moses and David (Deuteronomy 12, 2 Samuel 7). Jeroboam will become king in Israel. Solomon's son will retain one tribe for the sake of David — and for the unconditional promise of Yahweh that David's throne would "endure forever before me" (2 Sam 7:16).

And Yahweh's promise to Jeroboam is the same as his promise to David (2 Samuel 7). He will build Jeroboam an **"enduring** *house*" (NIV "dynasty") as he **built for David.** However, the promise to Jeroboam is conditional. The new king of Israel must **"do whatever I command you and walk in my ways and do what is right in my eyes by keeping my statutes and commands."** As Yahweh *was with* Moses (Exod 3:12), Joshua (Josh 1:5), Gideon (Judg 6:16), and David (2 Sam 7:9), he promises Jeroboam, **"I will be with you."**

Yahweh will **humble David's descendants because of this, but not forever.** Perhaps the most important words in this drama, especially for an audience in exile, are **but not forever.** To David, Yahweh promised, "When [his son] does wrong, I will punish him with the rod of men, with floggings inflicted by men. But my love will never be taken away from him, as I took it away from Saul" (2 Sam 7:14-15). The oath to David may still prove to be unconditional. The God of Israel has *torn* the kingdom from Solomon as he did from Saul, but Yahweh's love will remain with the descendants of David. There may yet be grace — hope for the return for which Solomon prayed (8:33-34).

As Moses fled from Pharaoh to Midian (Exod 2:15), Jeroboam, ironically, flees to **Shishak** (Shoshenq I) in Egypt. The king of Israel tries **to kill Jeroboam,** but the divinely sanctioned insurgent remains in Egypt until Solomon's death (see 12:2).

(see NIV text note), the more difficult plural in the Hebrew text (MT) is preferred.

3. Solomon Sleeps with His Fathers (11:41-43)

11:41-43 Perhaps the writer feels as the Queen of Sheba, he has told "not even half" (10:7) of Solomon's **wisdom** and accomplishments. Everything Solomon did is **written in the book of the annals of Solomon**, probably an archival source for the author's story. Solomon reigns **forty years** and is succeeded by **Rehoboam his son**.

The dates for his reign can be inferred from extrabiblical sources. If Siamun was the father-in-law of Solomon as some believe, the Pharaoh's relief commemorating his assault on the Philistines situates the beginning of Solomon's reign ca. 970–960 B.C. (see comments on 9:16-17). Shoshenq I's (i.e., the biblical Shishak) campaign into Palestine (ca. 930–925 B.C., the fifth year of Rehoboam; cf. 1 Kgs 14:25-26; 2 Chr 12:1-9) would put the death of Solomon somewhere ca. 930 B.C. But the reign of Solomon can be nailed down more exactly with the aid of two records from Shalmaneser III of Assyria. His Monolith Inscription records Ahab's participation in the battle of Qarqar in 853 B.C., and an annalistic inscription from the eighteenth year of his reign documents tribute from Jehu to Shalmaneser in 841 B.C. (probably also reflected on the Black Obelisk of Shalmaneser [see comments on 2 Kgs 10:32-33]). Since the length of the reigns of Ahab's two sons Ahaziah and Joram was twelve years (22:51; 2 Kgs 3:1; nonaccession-year system = 12 actual years), Ahab must have died shortly after the battle of Qarqar; Jehu ascended the throne shortly before 841 B.C. Working back from these dates and the biblical references to the reigns of the kings of Israel and Judah (78 yrs from the death of Ahab in 853/852 B.C.), the Kingdom of Solomon was divided in 931/930 B.C., at the ascension of Rehoboam to the throne of Israel following the death of Solomon. Since Solomon reigned forty years (v. 42), he must have ascended the throne in 971/970 B.C.[16]

A careful reader may linger over the length of his reign. Yahweh had promised Solomon, "If you walk in my ways and obey my

---

[16]Kitchen, "When Solomon Ruled," 32-37, 58; idem, "The Shoshenqs of Egypt and Palestine," *JSOT* 93 (2001): 11; Thiele, *Mysterious Numbers*, pp. 67-78; Galil, *Chronology of the Kings*, pp. 14-15. Dever works back from the campaign of Shishak (ca. 930–925 B.C.) to posit a date of 975 B.C. for the ascension of Solomon ("Archaeology and the 'Age of Solomon,'" p. 239; *Biblical Writers Know*, pp. 134-135).

statutes and commands as David your father did, I will give you a long life" (3:14; see 6:12-13; 9:4-5). The conditional promise offered the young king *a long life*. Solomon lived a long life with a full reign of forty years, even though he did not walk in the ways of David his father (11:4,6,33). The resolution can only be that it was when he was already old that his heart was finally turned to other gods (11:4; see 9:4-8). Since he was already blessed with a long life, the consequence now must be that the kingdom will be *torn* from him in the days of his son.

Solomon's turn to other gods happened later in life, but the ironic presentation of his reign suggests that he foolishly made unwise choices along the way. The seeds of his destruction were sown as he used the blessings of Yahweh (wisdom, wealth, and honor) to build *for himself* a magnificent kingdom — on the backs of the people he ruled (as the following episode will bear out [12:1-25]). Yahweh kept his promises, and then some. But, much like Israel in the story of Joshua and Judges, Solomon did not rely on the God of his forefathers, allowing his kingship to become like the nations (1 Samuel 8). What Solomon had spent a lifetime building will be broken, and, unfortunately for Israel, his reign will set them on the road to captivity in Egypt again (see comments on 2 Kgs 25; cf. Deut 17:16).

The story of Solomon functions in the larger composition of Kings as a paradigm for interpreting the actions of the kings who follow. Solomon's father, David, is the ideal standard. Solomon is the king who took Yahweh's blessings and made them a curse. For God's people in exile, the story of this king's tragic reign explains why they had been abandoned and, at the same time, offers hope that Yahweh may be their savior once more.

1 KINGS 12

II. THE STORY OF JEROBOAM'S APOSTASY (12:1–14:20)

The story of Jeroboam begins according to Ahijah's prophecy (11:29-39). As a result of the folly of Solomon's son, the kingdom is given to Jeroboam, who emerges as a Moseslike figure raised up by Yahweh to deliver Israel from the oppressive rule of Solomon. The Exodus imagery is not coincidental, but the promise of Jeroboam's rebellion turns sour. The young king does not walk in the way of Yahweh's servant David and chooses another course. Like Aaron, Jeroboam uses the golden calf to represent Yahweh before the people. "Jeroboam as Moses" becomes "Jeroboam as Aaron."[1] He establishes houses of worship to rival Yahweh's house in Jerusalem and alters the form and substance of Israelite worship. The course that he chooses will lead Israel to ruin (see 2 Kgs 17:7-23).

A. JEROBOAM RECEIVES THE KINGDOM (12:1-24)

1. Israel Asks Rehoboam for Relief (12:1-5)

12:1-5 Rehoboam goes to **Shechem** to be coronated king of Israel. That he had to travel to Shechem reflects the political rivalries that existed in Israel from well before the division of the kingdom. David was made king over all Israel seven years after he became king over Judah in Hebron (2 Sam 2:1-4; 5:1-5). Shechem was an important center during the period of Joshua–Judges (see, e.g., Josh 24:1-27) and was located in the hill country of Ephraim (cf.

---

[1]Provan, *1 and 2 Kings*, p. 103. For parallels between the Jeroboam narrative and the Exodus story see Frisch, "The Exodus Motif," 13-18.

1 Kgs 12:25; Josh 21:21), perhaps the dominant tribe in the north.[2] By accenting Rehoboam's anticipated coronation in Shechem, the narrator intimates an already weakened monarchy. Rehoboam has to travel to Shechem to gain the support of the northern tribes. They do not come to Jerusalem. Political forces are at work to undermine the new king's authority.

On hearing that Rehoboam would become king, **Jeroboam**, who is in exile in Egypt (11:40), **returns**[3] to Israel. He is summoned to the coronation. Jeroboam and **the whole assembly of Israel** approach Rehoboam with an appeal **to lighten the harsh labor and the heavy yoke** Solomon had put on them. The language echoes Israel's hard treatment by Pharaoh in Egypt. "Harsh labor" (עֲבֹדָה קָשָׁה, *'ăbōdāh qāšāh*) appears in the Old Testament only six times, two of which occur in the parallel accounts of Israel's request to Rehoboam (12:4; 2 Chr 10:4). Three other references refer to bondage in Egypt (Exod 1:14; 6:9; Deut 26:6).[4] By extension, the people's words highlight Solomon's coercive policies and characterize him as another Pharaoh (see comments on 5:13-14; 9:20-23). Rehoboam directs them to **come back** ("return," *šûb*) in three days, apparently to give him time to formulate an answer. Jeroboam and all Israel will *come back* (*šûb*) in three days but will not *return* (*šûb*) to his rule. Instead, like Moses, Jeroboam will lead Israel from under Solomon's heavy yoke.

2. Rehoboam Listens to His Young Friends (12:6-15)

12:6-7 Rehoboam consults the elders who had served his father. They answer that he must become a servant of the people. "If you will become a **servant** and **serve** them, **they will always be your servants**" (cf. 2 Chr 10:7). The elders are not saying that he should be manipulative — "Say what the people want to hear." Ancient Near Eastern parallels indicate that **give them a favorable answer**

---

[2]Hosea calls Israel "Ephraim" (see, e.g., Hos 4:17). For the location and summary of excavations at Shechem, see Edward F. Campbell, "Shechem: Tell Balâtah," in *NEAEHL*.

[3]The verb יָשַׁב (*yašab*) may be read "he returned" or "he remained" (see the NIV text note). "He returned" parallels 2 Chr 10:2, is plausible in this context, and introduces the word *šûb* ("return"), a key word in the Jeroboam narrative.

[4]Frisch, "The Exodus Motif," 13.

(literally, "speak to them good words/deeds") means make appropriate formal agreements, in this case, to relieve the people's burdensome plight.[5] While the elders' answer may be contrived, for what obviously is a difficult situation, this view of kingship is consistent with the description of the ideal king in Psalm 72 and the king/leader as shepherd in Ezekiel 34, who should "take care of the flock" (v. 3). Ezekiel adds that the sheep "were scattered [sent into exile] because there was no shepherd" (v. 5). Following in the footsteps of his father, Rehoboam will lose the kingdom, in part, for not being a shepherd to Israel — a servant king. Both Israel and Judah will be scattered because of the dearth of such leadership among God's anointed kings.

12:8-11 Rehoboam rejects the advice of the **elders** and turns to the **young men** (literally, "boys") with whom he had grown up. His words to them are a mirror to the underlying man. When he repeats the request of the people, he selectively leaves out the strong, passionate language and promise to serve in the people's request. In his mouth, their petition becomes simply **"lighten the yoke."** Identifying with "his friends," he says, **"How should *we* answer these people who say *to me* . . . ?"** Unaware of the gravity of the situation, he apparently sees the throne as a "God-given" right and as a means for personal benefit. The response of his peers is crude. **"My little finger is thicker than my father's waist,"** although a technically accurate translation, in idiomatic Hebrew probably means something like, "My male organ is thicker than my father's waist."[6] By including their vulgar remark, the narrator clearly situates this immature group and lays bare the character of Rehoboam, who will listen to their advice. They recommend that Rehoboam take a hard stand: **"I will make it even heavier . . . and scourge you with scorpions."**

12:12-15 Taking the advice of his young friends, **the king answers the people harshly**. He does, however, exercise some restraint. Rehoboam omits the vulgar remark but takes their hardline stand. The new regime will make the burden on the people **even**

[5]Moshe Weinfeld, "The Counsel of the 'Elders' to Rehoboam and Its Implications," in *Reconsidering Israel and Judah: Recent Studies on the Deuteronomistic History*, ed. Gary N. Knoppers and J. Gordon McConville (Winona Lake, IN: Eisenbrauns, 2000), pp. 530-539.

[6]See Cogan, *1 Kings*, pp. 348-349.

heavier. Rehoboam's arrogant folly is clearly revealed. He becomes another Pharaoh who will "make the work harder" for Israel (Exod 5:9). The narrator now breaks frame. This **turn of events** is from Yahweh.[7] Rehoboam's foolish act fulfills **the word of the LORD** spoken by the prophet **Ahijah** to **Jeroboam son of Nebat.** To reinforce this affirmation, the narrator frames a scene where Jeroboam is only a silent actor. He is an essential part of the plot, yet he speaks only as part of the group, "the whole assembly of Israel" (v. 3). Yahweh breaks up the nation he had established not with superior military forces led by a worthy insurgent. He breaks up the kingdom with the same foolish spirit that led Israel to this point in the first place. Solomon's self-indulgent folly resurfaces in his son and shatters the impressive empire he had built.

3. Rehoboam Rejects Israel's Request (12:16-24)

12:16-19. The people react: **"What share** ["portion" (חֵלֶק, *ḥēleq*)] **do we have in David, what part** ["inheritance" (נַחֲלָה, *naḥălāh*)] **in Jesse's son? To your tents, O Israel!"**[8] The language mirrors Sheba's call when Israel deserted David, sometime after Absalom's rebellion. Only the men of Judah remained with David (2 Sam 20:1-2). **Rehoboam** rules the sons of Israel living in **Judah.** No doubt to reinforce the hard line that he had taken, Rehoboam sends out **Adoniram,** who was **in charge of the forced labor** (*mas*; see 4:6; 5:14 and comments on 5:14).[9] **All Israel stones** Adoniram to death. Adoniram's role in the story, as the overseer of Solomon's *mas*, reinforces the author's contention (by inference) that Solomon has taken Israel back to Egypt. Rehoboam escapes to Jerusalem. Israel remains **in rebellion to the house of David.**

---

[7]Peter Machinist demonstrates that "this turn of events [סִבָּה, *sibbāh*]" is a technical term to indicate a change in political rule (cf., e.g., 2:15; 1 Chr 10:13-14; "The Transfer of Kingship: A Divine Turning," in *Fortunate the Eyes That See: Essays in Honor of David Noel Freedman in Celebration of His Seventieth Birthday,* ed. A.B. Beck, et al. [Grand Rapids: Eerdmans, 1995], pp. 105-120).

[8]*Ḥēleq* and *naḥălāh* are important words in the Ahab narrative (see comments on 1 Kings 21 and 2 Kings 9).

[9]If this is the same Adoniram who was over David's corvée (*mas*, 2 Sam 20:24), he is now an old man (Cogan, *1 Kings,* p. 350).

12:20-24 In another assembly, **Jeroboam** is made king **over all Israel**. Many scholars argue "all Israel" in Kings refers to the northern kingdom. This enables the view that the promise to David of an eternal kingdom in 2 Samuel 7 only entails the tribe of Judah. The conditional aspect of the promise (1 Kgs 2:2-4) applies to the northern kingdom. Verse 20 is an important passage for this interpretation. While attractive, this approach does not fit the plain meaning of "all Israel" in most contexts (see comments on 4:7) and undermines the theological thrust in the tension between the conditional and unconditional aspects of the promise to David (see comments on 2:1-4). In this context, the narrator is indicating that Jeroboam by consensus of the assembly at Shechem becomes king of all Israel. However, the political reality (and divine intention; cf. 11:13,32,36) is that Rehoboam retains control over Judah (12:20).[10] In fact, in Jerusalem he is able to muster **the whole house of Judah and the tribe of Benjamin—a hundred and eighty thousand fighting men** to go up against Israel.[11] They set out to **regain** ["bring back/cause to return," *šûb*] **the kingdom for Rehoboam the son of Solomon**. With naming (by reference to Rehoboam as "son of Solomon"), the narrator keeps before the reader that this man was the son of the king who had wisdom from God (also v. 23).

The **word of God** comes through the prophet **Shemaiah the man of God**, rendered as direct speech to Rehoboam and the people of Judah: **"Do not go up to fight against your brothers . . . . Go home** ["return," *šûb*] **. . . for this is my doing."** Again, this time in Yahweh's own words, the narrator indicates that the schism is from God. To their credit, the house of Judah and tribe of Benjamin **obey the word of the LORD and** *go* **home** ("return," *šûb*).

B. JEROBOAM SINS AGAINST YAHWEH (12:25-33)

12:25-27 The story of Jeroboam's reign begins with a building notice that, although brief, parallels the account of Solomon's building projects. Jeroboam **fortifies** [literally, "builds"] **Shechem** as his capital and from there *builds up* **Peniel**. The narrator then moves to

---

[10]Provan, *1 and 2 Kings*, pp. 105-106.
[11]For the distribution of tribes between Israel and Judah see n. 14, p. 154.

establish the tension that will drive the remainder of the Jeroboam narrative with inner speech, represented in Hebrew narrative as dialogue. **Jeroboam thought to himself** is (literally) he "said in his heart." Although the rendering in the NIV is technically accurate, "said in his heart" has important implications for characterizing Jeroboam's apostasy. While disobedient to the Law of Moses, his sin is above all a matter of the heart. He reasons, "The **kingdom** may **revert** ['return,' *šûb*] **to the house of David**." "If they go up to **the temple of the LORD in Jerusalem, they will again give their allegiance** [literally, "the *heart* of this people will *return* (*šûb*)"] **to their lord . . . will kill me and return** [*šûb*] **to King Rehoboam**." Ironically, with the word "return" (*šûb*) the narrator brings out that both kings want to avoid the consequences of the division. Rehoboam set out to "regain ["bring back/cause to return," *šûb*] the kingdom" and was told to "go home" ("return," *šûb*). Jeroboam was afraid that if the people "return" (*šûb*) to Jerusalem, their hearts would "return" (*šûb*) to Rehoboam.[12] As Solomon's insecurity motivated him to *establish* his kingdom *in his hands* (see comments on 2:13-46), Jeroboam's words, and his actions to follow, belie an insecurity that masks a lack of trust in Yahweh and his prophetic word (see 11:29-40).[13]

12:28-30 One of the key words from the preceding scene resurfaces here. As Rehoboam sought council, Jeroboam now seeks **advice** (יָעַץ, *yā'aṣ*, "to advise"; 12:6,8,9,13; cf. "advice," עֵצָה, *'ēṣāh*; 12:8,13,14) and foolishly makes **two golden calves**. Echoes of Aaron's sin at the foot of Sinai emerge when Jeroboam quotes almost verbatim Exod 32:4,8: **"Here are your gods, O Israel, who brought you up out of Egypt."** By allusion, the storyteller now portrays Jeroboam not as a Mosaic deliverer from pharaonic oppression but as an Aaronlike figure who sponsors an alternate view of Yahweh.[14] He set up one calf **in Bethel, and the other in Dan**, to

---

[12]Gary N. Knoppers, "Aaron's Calf and Jeroboam's Calves," in *Fortunate the Eyes That See: Essays in Honor of David Noel Freedman in Celebration of His Seventieth Birthday,* ed. A.B. Beck, et al. (Grand Rapids: Eerdmans, 1995), pp. 97-98.

[13]See Walsh, *1 Kings,* p. 172; Provan, *1 and 2 Kings,* p. 109.

[14]Moses Aberbach and Leivy Smolar identify thirteen connections between the Aaron and Jeroboam golden calf narratives. They conclude that the "interdependence of these narratives" is explained in either of two ways: The Zadokite priesthood of Jerusalem retold the Aaron narrative to

counter the temple in Jerusalem and frame the borders of his kingdom. This becomes **a sin** not only for Jeroboam but also for the people who travel **as far as Dan to worship**.[15]

While it is obvious that the inspired author views Jeroboam's act as idolatrous, from a human perspective Jeroboam does not do anything that Solomon did not do when he built a temple for Yahweh in Jerusalem — which also was a radical innovation in the religious life of Israel. Bull calves often symbolized male deities in ancient Near Eastern iconography, yet there is evidence to suggest that the image could also represent the pedestal of the deity, who comes down to reside on the image.[16] Solomon's cherubim in the Holy of Holies appear to reflect a similar notion. The ark of the covenant is best understood as Yahweh's footstool. In trying to counteract Solomon's innovations in Jerusalem, Jeroboam looked to Aaron for traditions that for some in Israel must have been more "conservative" than the permanent temple that Solomon built. Bethel may have been the home of Aaronide priests (and traditions associated with the brother of Moses; see Judg 20:26-28). Also, according to the book of Judges (in a rather negative assessment) the priesthood of Dan went back to the grandson of Moses (see Judg 18:30-31).

---

discredit the cultic practices of the north, or Jeroboam intentionally set out to emulate Aaron ("Aaron, Jeroboam, and the Golden Calves," *JBL* 86 [June 1967]: 129-140). The latter view respects the integrity of the text and is the reading that is presented here.

[15]Avraham Biran has uncovered Jeroboam's high place at Tel Dan. While no golden calf remains, excavators found ample evidence of the religious ritual practiced at this location. Among the features uncovered were a large platform, adjacent buildings, installations for water rites, a horned altar for incense, and remains of a large sacrificial altar from the time of Jeroboam II (eighth century B.C.). The stratigraphy of the sacred area indicates significant construction in the tenth (Jeroboam), ninth (Ahab), and eighth (Jeroboam II) centuries B.C. (see Biran, *Biblical Dan*, pp. 159-233). For excavations at Bethel, see James Leon Kelso, "Bethel," in *NEAEHL*. A jasper seal found at Megiddo with a roaring lion and the inscription "Shema, servant of Jeroboam" is now thought by some to date to the reign of Jeroboam I, instead of Jeroboam II (see Cogan, *1 Kings*, p. 382).

[16]At Arslan Tash near the Euphrates, for example, excavators uncovered an Assyrian basalt stela from the time of Shalmaneser III (ninth century B.C.) on which was carved a male deity in Assyrian dress wielding thunderbolts and standing on the back of a bull as a pedestal. The thunderbolts and bull probably signify a storm god. Baal in the period of the divided kingdom was a storm god (see Cogan, *1 Kings*, pp. 358, 363).

Jeroboam can be seen as setting up shrines to Moses and his brother Aaron. Apparently, Aaron was not viewed in some northern traditions in the same negative light as in other circles — and in the
account of Aaron's apostasy in the book of Exodus (ch. 32).[17]
Political necessity often encourages a "reevaluation" of history and
the appropriation of earlier, even unpopular traditions.

That Jeroboam names his sons Nadab and Abijah ("Yahweh is
my father"; cf. 14:1,20), the names of Aaron's sons, Nadab and
Abihu ("He is my father"; cf. Exod 6:23), cannot be a coincidence.
Also, the theophoric element "Yah/Jah" (for Yahweh) in Abijah's
name stands out. Jeroboam is a follower of Yahweh. There is not
anything in this text to indicate that he set up shrines to foreign
gods.[18] The new king is consciously reenacting the life of Aaron in
service to Yahweh. When he excludes Levites from the priesthood,
he is not attacking worship to Yahweh but remembering the role
that they played in exterminating those who had participated in
Aaron's rebellion (Exod 32:25-29). In his mind, Jeroboam must have
set out to establish a "more conservative" cult for Yahweh that
would be anchored in Exodus traditions and rival Solomon's grand
temple in Jerusalem.

Nevertheless, the inspired author of Kings sees the new king's
changes as an ultimate act of apostasy. Jeroboam does not follow the
Law of Moses (see below) and misrepresents Yahweh. While the
king of Israel may have viewed the golden calves as pedestals and
seen his innovations as no different from what Solomon did, his
actions reflect a different view of God. Jeroboam presents the calves
to Israel as *"gods, who brought you out of Egypt"* (12:28). In his
prayer, Solomon asserts that Yahweh brought Israel out of Egypt: "I
have provided a place there for the ark, in which is the covenant of
the LORD that he made with our fathers when he brought them out
of Egypt" (8:21; cf. vv. 16,51,53). He also affirms in the presence of
Israel that it is the Name of Yahweh that dwells in the house that he
built (see, e.g., 8:20). Never does any author of Scripture "equate"
the ark of the covenant or the cherubim with God![19] Jeroboam mis-

---

[17]See ibid., pp. 358-359, 363.

[18]See John N. Oswalt, "'Golden Calves' and the 'Bull of Jacob'," p. 12.

[19]Knoppers, "Aaron's Calf," p. 101; see pp. 98-104; Provan, *1 and 2 Kings*,
pp. 111-112.

represents Yahweh by overlooking his transcendence — Yahweh is not accessible through physical means.[20] In this way, the king's idolatrous cult exposes his desire to manipulate both the people of Israel and the God who had made him their king. Jeroboam breaks the first two commandments of the Law and substitutes man-made images for Yahweh, the true God of Israel who *brought them out of Egypt* (Exod 20:2-4). In the larger story of Kings, the high places of Israel and Judah represent apostasy, in part because they foster a false conception of Yahweh.[21]

12:31-33 In addition to the golden calves, **Jeroboam** *builds* **shrines on high places** [literally, "*house*[s] of high places"], makes **priests from all sorts of people** (who were not even from the tribe of Levi; cf. Deut 18:1-8), **institutes a festival . . . like the festival held in Judah** (in the **eighth month**), and **offers sacrifices on the altar**. The language calls attention to the contrast with Solomon, who *built* a *house* for Yahweh and dedicated the temple at the Feast of Tabernacles in the seventh month (cf. Deut 16:15). Contrary to the Law of Moses, Jeroboam has altered worship to Yahweh, in terms of the place of worship, the object of worship, the time of worship, and the priesthood of worship.[22] He has not kept "my statutes and commands, as David my servant did" (11:38).

The narrator uses repetition in these verses to reinforce the calculating way Jeroboam goes about reshaping religion in Israel. "He instituted/made/did" (עָשָׂה, *ʿāśāh*) occurs six times in verses 28-33 to demonstrate that the king is the primary actor. In contrast with Aaron in Exodus 32, who was pressured by the people, Jeroboam is deliberate in reviving Aaron's apostasy.[23] The festival that he institutes is held in **a month of his own choosing**. The underlying Hebrew is (literally) "which he devised in his heart."[24] Again, while

---

[20]See Oswalt, "'Golden Calves and the 'Bull of Jacob,'" pp. 13-17.

[21]Hobbs argues that in the course of the composition the high places "eventually become symbols for apostasy" because they represent the worship of foreign gods (*2 Kings*, p. 232). Cogan correctly observes that most of the references to high places in Kings reflect "the illicit worship of YHWH" (*1 Kings*, p. 184).

[22]Rex A. Turner, Sr., *Teacher's Annual Lesson Commentary: On Uniform Bible Lessons for the Churches of Christ*, vol. 55 (Nashville: Gospel Advocate Co., 1976), p. 24.

[23]Knoppers, "Aaron's Calf," pp. 97-101.

[24]Following the *qere* ("what is read") in the margin of the Hebrew text (MT).

he is disobedient in breaking the commandments of Moses, what he does is fundamentally a matter of the heart (12:26,27,33; see Deut 6:5; 10:12-13). Jeroboam does this by choice! Also with repetition, the storyteller emphasizes that the king himself worships on the high place at **Bethel** (vv. 29,32[2×],33; cf. 13:1). The emphasis on Bethel sets the stage for the scene that follows. The king is dedicating the shrine at Bethel during the festival that he institutes, when the prophet from Judah arrives with a curse for the new altar.[25]

---

[25]Jeroboam also sets Israel and Judah on separate sociocultural trajectories, which are reflected in the material remains of Iron II Palestine. In pottery, shekel-weights, pillar-base figurines, and *lmlk* (לְמֶלֶךְ) jar handles, by the ninth–eighth centuries B.C., there is a clear cultural/political border between Israel and Judah. Dialectical differences between north and south (e.g., names in the north ending in *-yaw* [יו] and names in the south ending in *-yāhû* [יהו]) reinforce this observation (Dever, *Biblical Writers Know*, pp. 129-130). The new king in the north also changed the calendar in Israel: the beginning of the year from 1 Nisan to 1 Tishri and regnal reckoning from postdating to antedating — all for the purpose of cementing the division between the two kingdoms (Galil, *Chronology of the Kings*, p. 15).

1 KINGS 13

C. THE PROPHET FROM JUDAH CURSES THE ALTAR IN BETHEL AND IS CURSED (13:1-34)

1. The Word of the Lord Is Delivered in Bethel (13:1-10)

13:1-3 One of the more unusual stories in all of Scripture begins innocently enough with the **word of the LORD** in the mouth of **a man of God** from **Judah**. By the end of the story, the man of God himself will be cursed by the word of the LORD and will be outlived by the king who causes Israel to sin. As he readies to make an offering at the altar he has constructed in Bethel, **Jeroboam** is interrupted by a prophet who speaks in the name of Yahweh. The repetition of "the word of the LORD" (vv. 1,2) in the narrator's voice, with **"this is what the LORD says"** (i.e., "thus says Yahweh") in the mouth of the prophet, introduces a key theme in the narrative and indicates that the message is reliable. "Word of the LORD" occurs ten times in chapter 13. Walsh observes that the phrase "by the word of the LORD" appears seven times in this chapter, with only five other occurrences in the Hebrew Bible. He adds that beginning with the story of Jeroboam, the word of Yahweh takes on a more important role in Kings. While Yahweh speaks directly with Solomon, he only speaks through the prophetic word to Jeroboam, a pattern that will characterize his interaction with the kings of Israel and Judah to follow.[1]

The prophet foresees a son of David named **Josiah** who will desecrate this very altar with the bones of the **priests of the high places who now make offerings here** (see 2 Kgs 23:15-18). Nelson calls attention to the fact that the curse of the man of God sets up a contrast between Jeroboam and Josiah — one the quintessential evil

---

[1]Walsh, *1 Kings*, pp. 191, 204.

king, the other a king like David.[2] In fact, the link between the oracle from the man of God and 2 Kings 23 unifies 1 and 2 Kings.[3] In
the episode at Bethel, the man of God also gives a **sign, "The altar
will be split apart and the ashes on it will be poured out."**

13:4-10 The king stretches **out his hand** to have the prophet
seized. His hand shrivels, and he is not able to **pull it back** ("cause
[it] to return," *šûb*). Then, **the altar** is split apart, and **its ashes** pour
out according to the sign from the man of God by the *word of
Yahweh*.[4] Jeroboam petitions the prophet to **intercede**, that his hand
be **restored** ("cause to return," *šûb*), which the man of God does.
Demonstrating the power of the prophet, the king's hand is *restored*
(*šûb*) and becomes **as it was before**. In response, the king invites the
man of God to his **home** for a meal and offers him a **gift**. The
prophet from Judah declines, even for **"half your possessions, I
would not go with you, nor would I eat bread or drink water here**
[literally, "in this *place* (מָקוֹם, *māqôm*)"]**." He was "commanded by
the word of the LORD: 'You must not eat bread or drink water or
return [*šûb*] by the way [דֶּרֶךְ, *derek*] you came.'"**

In dialogue, the narrator has introduced at least three of the
story's key words. Jeroboam asks that his hand be *restored* (*šûb*). The
man of God refuses to eat or drink in this *place* (*māqôm*), and he had
been commanded not to *return* (*šûb*) by the *way* (*derek*) he came.
Reinforcing this in exposition, the narrator finishes the scene: **So he
took another road** (*derek*) **and did not return** (*šûb*) **by the way** (*derek*)
he had come *to Bethel*.

2. The Prophet from Judah Is Deceived (13:11-19)

13:11-14a An **old prophet**[5] living in Bethel has **sons** who attend

---

[2]Nelson, *First and Second* Kings, p. 92.

[3]Walsh, *1 Kings*, p. 177.

[4]Verses 3,5 are viewed by Walsh as parenthetical statements. He suggests
that in verse 3 the narrator breaks frame to describe the sign for the reader. Jeroboam may not have been present when the sign was given. He translates verse 5 as an aside to confirm the reliability of the author's claim. "The
altar *has been* torn down," and the evidence is in Bethel. While his reading
of verse 3 is likely, his translation in verse 5 is not demanded by Hebrew
grammar or context (see ibid., pp. 178-179).

[5]"Prophet" and "man of God" are often used interchangeably in Hebrew

the dedication and are witnesses to what the man of God from Judah did and **what he had said to the king**. The prophet asks, **"Which way [*derek*] did he go?"** They show him **the road** (*derek*) that he took, and he rides after him. With brief exposition and selective dialogue, the narrator introduces an important character, yet he leaves a large gap with respect to this man and his motivations. Only enough is said to raise questions: Why did the old prophet stay away from the dedication ceremonies? Does this mean that he is a prophet of Yahweh who is more sympathetic with Jerusalem and uncomfortable with Jeroboam's innovations at Dan and Bethel? Why does he want to find the man of God from Judah? Why does the narrator emphasize that the sons told him "what [the man of God from Judah] had said to the king"? Since the man of God's words to the king concerned eating *in this place*, does the old prophet deliberately set out to lead the prophet astray? Does he want to thwart the man of God's mission, so that his own burial would not be desecrated, as one who also officiated at Jeroboam's high places? While the gap draws the reader even further into the story, answers to these questions are apparently not important to the storyteller. What is important is what the old prophet does, as the remaining scenes will demonstrate.

13:14b-19 The old prophet from Bethel finds the man of God from Judah sitting under a tree. Their meeting is reported with dialogue. The prophet from Bethel, aware of the man of God's conversation with the king, extends an invitation: "Come home with me and eat." The man of God from Judah responds as he had to king Jeroboam: "I cannot eat or drink *in this place* [*māqôm*]. The word of Yahweh told me, 'You must not eat *there* or *return* [*šûb*] by the *way* [*derek*] you came!'" The old prophet from Bethel answers that he too is **a prophet**, and, **"An angel said to me by the word of the LORD: 'Bring him back** ["cause him to turn/return," *šûb*] **with you to your house so that he may eat bread and drink water.'"** By the *word of Yahweh*, an angel had said, "*Bring him back* [*šûb*]!" The narrator then breaks frame to add, **He was lying to him.**[6] Accepting the prophet's

---

Scripture. In chapter 13, the narrator uses the two terms to distinguish between the two unnamed characters in the story.

[6]On the surface, there is some ambiguity in this statement. Who lied, the old prophet or the angel? If the angel lied, the story deals more with true

word, the man of God from Judah *returns* (*šûb*) with the prophet from Bethel to his house.

3. The Word of the Lord Judges the Prophet from Judah (13:20-25)

13:20-25 At the prophet from Bethel's table, **the word of the LORD** comes not to the man of God from Judah but **to the old prophet who had brought him back** ("caused him to turn/return," *šûb*). He cries out to the man of God, **"This is what the LORD says: 'You have defied the word of the LORD and have not kept the command the LORD your God gave you. You came back** ["returned," *šûb*] **and ate bread and drank water *in the place* [*māqôm*] where he told you not to eat or drink.'"** The prophet's **body** would not be **buried** with his fathers. The prophet "who had brought him back" ("caused him to turn/return," *šûb*) sends him on his way. **A lion** meets **him** [literally, "found him"] **on the road** (*derek*) and kills him. His body is thrown on the road (*derek*). Almost like sentries, both the donkey and the lion in an unnatural posture stand over the body, which is **reported** in the city.

4. The Prophet from Bethel Buries the Man of God (13:26-32)

13:26-32 When the prophet who had brought him back ["caused him to turn/return," *šûb*] **from his journey** [literally, "from the way/road," *derek*] hears about the body, he knows that it is **"the man of God who defied the word of the LORD."** The old prophet from Bethel finds the **body** that had been **thrown down on the road** (*derek*). The **lion** had not eaten the body or attacked the donkey, indicating that this was of Yahweh. He *brings* the body *back* ("caused it to

---

and false prophecy, as the story of Micaiah in chapter 22. However, since in the larger composition, Jeroboam's "lie" (i.e., his misrepresentation of Yahweh in the form of the golden calves) leads Israel astray, it is better to read this as saying that the old prophet (like Jeroboam) lied to the prophet from Judah (see below).

return," *šûb*) and buries him in his own tomb.[7] Mourning for the man of God, the old prophet commands his sons on his death to bury him beside the man from Judah. Ironically, the prophet who *caused the death* of the man of God affirms the veracity of the prophet's word. The old prophet has *turned*, repented (in contrast with Jeroboam; see below), and now expresses the truth he has witnessed: **"For the message he declared by the word of the LORD . . . will certainly come true."** The irony that the old prophet from Bethel speaks this word demonstrates the power of the word of Yahweh!

The word of the man of God from Judah comes to pass. In 2 Kings 23:15-18, Josiah will demolish Jeroboam's high place at Bethel and burn human bones on the altar to defile it. The tomb of the prophet from Judah and the old prophet from Bethel will be left undisturbed. To reinforce the connection between the word against Jeroboam and Josiah's reform, in addition to the prophetic voice of the man of God from Judah, the narrator will even call to mind the old prophet's words: "Just as he had done at *Bethel*, Josiah removed and defiled all *the shrines at the high places* that the kings of Israel had built *in the towns of Samaria*" (2 Kgs 23:19; cf. 1 Kgs 13:32).[8]

5. Jeroboam Does Not Repent (13:33-34)

With the affirmation of the old prophet from Bethel (v. 32), an unusual story ends on an ironic note and reinforces the truth of the word of Yahweh. However, unanswered questions loom. Where is the justice in the death of the man of God while the old prophet, who lied to the prophet from Judah, gets off without even a reprimand? Does obedience to Yahweh so overshadow anything else that

---

[7]Tombs from the period of the monarchy typically were rock-cut, multi-roomed chambers lined with benches for multiple, family burials. The tomb of the old prophet could easily accommodate both prophets (see Herr, "The Iron Age II Period," 129, 141, 146, 161-162).

[8]Walsh, *1 Kings*, p. 189. When the narrator has the old prophet mention "the towns of Samaria," he is employing an anachronism for effect on a reader in a situation well after these events. The city of Samaria was not built until the reign of Omri (16:23-24) and so was not a designation for Israel until much later. With the intentional connection between 13:32 and 2 Kings 23:19, the storyteller is obviously writing after the fall of the northern kingdom.

God will compromise even the most basic sense of justice to punish an otherwise worthy man?

13:33-34 The storyteller now offers some direction, gives a clue for reading the story of the man of God from Judah. **Even after this, Jeroboam did not change** ["repent/turn/return," *šûb*] **his evil ways** [*derek*]. The story is not about the man of God from Judah; it is about Jeroboam! The narrative of the man of God from Judah and the old prophet from Bethel serves as an object lesson for Israel, in Jeroboam's day and for an exilic audience.[9] Like the old prophet, Jeroboam caused Israel to turn (*šûb*) from the way (*derek*) of Yahweh to the way (*derek*) he had chosen. In fact, the old prophet three times in the story is named "the prophet who brought [the man of God] back" ("caused him to return/turn," *šûb*; vv. 20,23,26). In verse 26, the narrator even describes him as "the prophet who brought him back ["caused him to turn/return," *šûb*] from the way [*derek*]" — exactly the thing Jeroboam did to Israel (and Judah; see below). And even after the death of the man of God, he continued in his sin, consecrating **anyone** as priest. **This was the sin of the house of Jeroboam that led to its downfall** (cf. 12:30-31; Exod 32:30-31). In the larger story, in fact, one refrain characterizes the reign of Jeroboam and the influence that he had on the course of Israel's history. Jeroboam the son of Nebat was the king *who caused Israel to sin!*[10]

The storyteller has crafted a literary work of art, which establishes a framework for reading the story of Israel's kings and the kings of Judah who follow the same path (see 2 Kgs 17:19). Jeroboam is portrayed as the one responsible for Israel's ultimate demise. Lacking faith in Yahweh, Jeroboam in his insecurity consciously set out on a course away from the Law of Moses. His deliberate acts (e.g., brought out with the verb "to do" [*'āśāh*]; see comments on 12:31-33) precipitate the message from the man of God from Judah. The narrator establishes Jeroboam as guilty of disobedience. In the comparison between Jeroboam and Rehoboam, for example,

---

[9]The fact that both the man of God and the old prophet are unnamed supports this interpretation. If the personal names of these two historical figures were given, the story would not have the effect that it does in context with Jeroboam's apostasy. The story would then be more about them than commentary on Jeroboam's reign.

[10]See 14:16; 15:26,30,34; 16:2,19,26; 21:22; 22:52[53]; 2 Kings 3:3; 10:29,31; 13:2,6,11; 14:24; 15:9,18,24,28; 17:21; 23:15.

Jeroboam is the disobedient king. To Rehoboam, Yahweh says do not go up (עֲלֵה, 'ālāh) and return (šûb). Rehoboam and the people of Judah and Benjamin obey (12:24). In contrast, Jeroboam commands Israel not to go up ('ālāh) to Jerusalem (12:28). He makes gods he claims brought up ('ālāh) Israel from Egypt (12:28) and ascends ('ālāh) the altar to make sacrifices (12:33). The narrator provides closure for the comparison when he says that Jeroboam did not return (šûb) from his evil ways (13:33).[11]

By his use of key words, the narrator further highlights the importance of obeying and turning back to Yahweh. With way/road (derek), the narrator keeps before the reader the word of God through Ahijah that Jeroboam must, "Do whatever I command you and walk in my ways [derek]." Derek occurs twelve times in the story of the man of God from Judah. It also figures six times in the refrain, "walking in the ways [derek] of Jeroboam and in the sin he had committed and had caused Israel to commit" (1 Kgs 16:19; see 15:25-26,34; 16:2,19,26; 22:52[53]). In the same way, the phrase "in this place [māqôm, 13:8,16,22]" calls attention to Jeroboam's sin. As he dedicates an altar in Bethel, the reader recalls the place Yahweh had chosen for his Name to dwell – Jerusalem (Deuteronomy 12; 1 Kings 8; see comments on 8:1-13). In contrast with Jeroboam, Solomon dedicated the temple that he built with the blessing of Yahweh.

The most important word in the story is "return" (šûb).[12] Šûb occurs twenty-eight times in chapters 12 and 13. This is 24 percent of its occurrences in all of 1 and 2 Kings. The concentration indicates emphasis. Often, key words in Hebrew narrative in some way encapsulate the message of the story, as appears to be the case here. Jeroboam turned (šûb) from the way of Yahweh. The man of God from Judah was commanded to return (šûb) by another way, but the old prophet brought him back ("caused him to return," šûb) to his home in Bethel. Even after all of this, Jeroboam did not repent (šûb). The word for repentance in Hebrew is šûb! Jeroboam caused Israel to turn from Yahweh and did not repent when shown the error of his way. When his premeditated course for Israel ends in Assyrian

---

[11]D.W. Van Winkle, "1 Kings XII 25–XIII 34: Jeroboam's Cultic Innovations and the Man of God from Judah," *VT* 46/1 (1996): 110.

[12]Nelson also sees "way/road" (*derek*) and "turn/return" (*šûb*) as key words in chapter 13 (*First and Second Kings*, pp. 84, 87).

captivity, the narrator will say, "The LORD warned Israel and Judah through all his *prophets and seers*: 'Turn ["repent," *šûb*] from your evil ways [*derek*]. Observe my commands and decrees, in accordance with the entire Law that I commanded your fathers to obey and that I delivered to you through *my servants the prophets*'" (2 Kgs 17:12-13). The man of God from Judah is one of the first of Yahweh's prophets with a message of repentance for Israel.

The story of the man of God from Judah demonstrates the necessity of reading contextually. If the story is read in isolation, without regard to its role in the larger composition, the reader may miss the focus of the narrative.[13] Some scholars have done this by seeing the story as primarily about true and false prophecy. While true and false prophecy may be an underlying issue, especially as it resonates with other stories in Kings (e.g., 1 Kings 22), this is not the storyteller's primary concern. In the end, God's word in the mouth of both the man of God and the old prophet comes true (affirming Deut 18:14-22), and the man from Judah should have known not to accept any word that violated the law/command he had been given.[14] Nevertheless, in context, the true/false prophecy theme also directs the reader to avoid the sin of Jeroboam.

Others misread the story when, again viewing it in isolation, they fail to see the grace in the narrative. A legalistic mind-set can see this story as a proof text for being justified by law: "Look at what happened to the man of God from Judah. He was judged for believing a lie." And the story *does* say as much. The old prophet lied, and the prophet from Judah suffered the consequences.[15] Like Jeroboam,

---

[13]The key word *šûb* demonstrates a literary connection between chapters 12 and 13, including the story of Rehoboam's foolish disregard for the advice of his older advisors. In fact, "advise/advice" (*yā'aṣ*/*'ēṣāh*; see comments on 12:28-30) connects the Rehoboam and Jeroboam narratives. Jeroboam also sought *advice* before changing worship in Israel (12:28). In addition, is it just a coincidence that the "old/young" advisors theme in 12:6-15 continues in chapter 13 with the *old* prophet from Bethel, whose advice to the man of God ends in disaster?

[14]Van Winkle, "Jeroboam's Cultic Innovations," 106-107. For a discussion of interpretations of 1 Kings 13, including true and false prophecy, and the need to see the larger parameters of the story, see pp. 101-114. Cogan writes that the story seems to acknowledge "the devious ways of divine justice" (*1 Kings*, p. 374).

[15]N.B. Hardeman's sermon, "Believing a Lie," emphasizes this aspect of

the man of God disobeyed the law. He had defied the word of the LORD and had not "kept the law/commandment [מִצְוָה, *miṣwāh*]" which Yahweh commanded him (13:21; cf. 11:38).[16] If God would punish the prophet from Judah, he would punish Jeroboam — and Israel and Judah — for disobedience.

Part of the story's brilliance is that it upholds the necessity of keeping the law, but also bears witness to Yahweh's grace toward Israel. This text is bigger, more balanced than appears at first glance. There is not just law here. Jeroboam is the one who should have been killed by the lion, yet he was allowed to live. Yahweh gives him an opportunity to *turn* (*šûb*) and allows Israel to continue for two hundred years before suffering the consequences of Jeroboam's sin. So, the larger narrative demonstrates the divine patience of Yahweh and his love for Israel. Delayed retribution is a theme in Kings that actually reveals the many mercies of the God of Israel. Judgment is sure, but Yahweh is ready to relent if Israel will *repent* (*šûb*; see Jer 18:7-10 and comments on 11:11-13). Also, Jeroboam's premeditated act was not just a matter of disobeying commandments; it was a matter of the heart (see comments on 12:25-27,31-33). In his lack of faith in Yahweh, his disobedience was a deliberate choice.

A careful look at the narrative demonstrates that it is a story of grace. The events are parabolic, a lesson for Jeroboam, for Israel and Judah, and for an exilic audience. If one follows in the sin of Jeroboam, the consequences will be dire. The man of God lost his life, and "the sin of the house of Jeroboam led . . . to its destruction from the face of the earth" (13:34). An audience in Babylon would see the symbolism in the fact that the man of God was from Judah. At the hand of Nebuchadnezzar in the early sixth century B.C., Jerusalem suffered the same fate as Samaria because they also walked in the sins of Jeroboam (2 Kgs 17:19). Yet, in the same breath the story is a call for repentance: "Even after this, Jeroboam did not *change* ["repent," *šûb*; 13:33]." And every call for repentance is an expression of grace. The message for an audience in exile is "*šûb* ["repent"], keep the law, and love Yahweh with all of your heart!"[17]

---

the story of the man of God from Judah (in *Hardeman's Tabernacle Sermons*, vol. 2 [Nashville: McQuiddy Publishing Co., 1923], pp. 71-82).

[16]Van Winkle, "Jeroboam's Cultic Innovations," 111.

[17]Nelson also sees the story as a message for an exilic audience to "turn/repent" (*First and Second Kings*, p. 89).

1 KINGS 14

D. AHIJAH PROPHESIES AGAINST JEROBOAM (14:1-20)

The final episode in the story of Jeroboam is well crafted. After a brief statement introducing the problem that drives the plot (the king's son is ill, v. 1[1]), the narrator builds suspense with drama (vv. 2-6) that leads to the heart of the episode, Ahijah's indictment and judgment of Jeroboam's house (vv. 7-16). Exposition that includes a burial note at the end (vv. 17-20) establishes the word of the prophet Ahijah and reinforces a prophecy-fulfillment theme that runs through 1 and 2 Kgs and ties the various stories together.

14:1-3 Following the introductory note, the storyteller allows the reader to overhear **Jeroboam**'s conversation with his **wife** about their son. Tension is created when Jeroboam directs his wife to **disguise** herself and seek out **Ahijah the prophet** in **Shiloh** with gifts. Why does the king propose the disguise? Jeroboam acknowledges that Ahijah was the prophet who told him that he **would be king** and expresses confidence in the word of the prophet when he adds, **"He will tell you what will happen to the boy"** (cf. 2 Kgs 1:2-4).[2] However, the reader is aware that Jeroboam has taken another *way* since meeting Ahijah on the road (*derek*, 11:29-39). In view of the king's apostasy, the deception must represent a damaged relationship with Ahijah and with the God who had made him king.

14:4-6 Jeroboam's wife (literally) "arose, and went, and came." The eye of the narrator's camera watches her. She never speaks, but

---

[1]In verse 1, the NIV's "At that time" may be misleading. Ahijah's blindness and age (v. 4) suggest that some time has transpired since the events of the preceding chapters. Walsh suggests "There came a time when" would better fit the context (*1 Kings*, p. 193).

[2]Abijah's age is not indicated. Jeroboam and the narrator name him נַעַר (*na'ar*, "boy"; vv. 3,17), a term that could refer to a young man. Ahijah names him יֶלֶד (*yeled*; v. 12, "boy" in the NIV), usually indicating a "child."

hears the word of Ahijah the prophet. Her presence personalizes the judgment on Jeroboam's house. Adding that, because of his age, Ahijah **could not see**, the narrator lets the reader overhear Yahweh inform the prophet that Jeroboam's wife is coming in disguise. In the larger story, a disguise motif recurs with king Ahab, another king who influenced Israel for evil (cf. 20:35-43; 22:29-40). Neither Jeroboam nor Ahab is able to escape Yahweh's judgment. The blind prophet then *hears* **the sound of her footsteps at the door**. In what at first appears odd, he meets her with recognition and says, **"I have been sent to you with bad news."** The child's illness and the mother's errand to Shiloh are of God. In reality, Ahijah is being sent to her. Jeroboam's wife cannot disguise herself. She and her husband are unmasked. Though blind, the prophet sees and knows. Yahweh is in control!

14:7-9 The prophet speaks for Yahweh, **the God of Israel**, in first person: **"I raised you up . . . and made you a leader** [נָגִיד, *nāgîd*, "prince"] **over my people Israel."** The words resonate with Yahweh's message to David through the prophet Nathan (2 Sam 7:8). Only, Jeroboam is no David. King David was told that Yahweh would make his name great (v. 9); Jeroboam is indicted for crimes against Yahweh. Also, the language reminds the reader that Yahweh is king in Israel. Like Saul, David, and Solomon (1 Sam 9:16; 10:1; 2 Sam 7:8; 1 Kgs 1:35), Jeroboam was made *prince* (*nāgîd*) over Israel (see comments on 1:35).

The words that follow echo Ahijah's first meeting with Jeroboam (11:29-39). The two meetings bookend the story of Jeroboam and the connections between them provide a framework for the oracle of judgment that ensues. Yahweh **tore the kingdom** (11:29-32; cf. 1 Sam 15:27-29) from the house of Solomon and gave it to Jeroboam, but Jeroboam did not follow Yahweh **"like my servant David . . . with all his heart"** (11:37-39). In contrast with David, Jeroboam has **done more evil** than all the kings **who lived before** and is guilty of idolatry, of making **other gods**, even **idols made of metal**. The same language appears in the description of Aaron's sin, which Jeroboam revives (Exod 32:4,8).[3] Yahweh is aroused, angry

---

[3]Both אֱלֹהִים (*'ĕlōhîm*, "gods") and מַסֵּכָה (*massēkāh*, "cast image") appear in Exod 32:4,8 and 1 Kings 14:9 (cf. 2 Kgs 17:16).

that Jeroboam has turned his back on the one who had made him *prince* over Israel (cf. 1 Kgs 14:15; 2 Kgs 17:11,17).

14:10-13 Because of Jeroboam's sin, Yahweh will **bring disaster on the house of Jeroboam**. Yahweh's speech is graphic. **Every last male** (literally, "the one who urinates against the wall"; cf. 16:11; 21:21; 2 Kgs 9:8) will be cut off. The house of Jeroboam will be like **dung** that is burned up as fuel. **Dogs** and **birds** will devour his descendants, which means they will perish in times of political upheaval. Members of the house of Jeroboam will not go to the family tomb in peace. And, when Jeroboam's wife **sets foot in the city, the boy will die.** However, **all Israel will mourn** for the boy. He will be **the only one** of Jeroboam's sons who will be buried, because Yahweh has found in him (literally) "a **good** thing." But what "good thing" does Yahweh see in this son of Jeroboam? The ambiguity is provocative — and calls attention not to the boy but to Yahweh. The God who judges is also the God who searches out righteous hearts, even in the house of Jeroboam (cf. 1 Chr 28:9; Ps 7:9). While surely a sign of Yahweh's judgment on Jeroboam, the child's death will also be an act of grace.

14:14-16 The prophet now looks into the future, even to Israel's ultimate humiliation. Yahweh **will raise up for himself a king** who will **cut off** the house of Jeroboam.[4] Ahijah speaks of Baasha son of Ahijah of the tribe of Issachar who will assassinate Nadab and eliminate Jeroboam's whole family (15:27-30). But Jeroboam's apostasy will have far-reaching consequences. As Moses predicted (Deut 29:25-28; cf. 28:64-68), Yahweh will **strike Israel, uproot** them from the **land** he had given them, and **scatter** them beyond the Euphrates. In a similar invective, Hosea warns his generation that the "calf-idol of Samaria" would be broken into pieces and the people of Israel would "return to Egypt and eat unclean food in Assyria" (Hos 8:5-6; 9:3). An exilic audience would see Ahijah's words as explaining their plight. Both Israel and Judah do not keep the commandments of Yahweh and lose their right to the land (see 2 Kgs 17:1-23).

That they also made **Asherah poles**, representing the mother

---

[4]The last part of verse 14 (in the NIV, "This is the day! What? Yes, even now") is almost untranslatable as it stands in the Hebrew text and may represent a later scribal note.

goddess,[5] puts an exclamation point on their idolatry and suggests the direction in which Jeroboam's sin led Israel. Asherah was a consort/wife of El and Baal who at times was apparently worshiped in Israel as a consort of Yahweh. At Kuntillet 'Ajrud in the Sinai desert, an inscription on a potsherd (from the eighth century B.C.), with an accompanying drawing of three figures, refers to "Yahweh and his Asherah" (יהוה ואשרת, *YHWH . . . w'šrth*). (A similar inscription has been found in a tomb at Khirbet el-Qôm near Hebron.) The 'Ajrud inscription reads, "I have blessed you by Yahweh of Samaria and by his consort" (*'šrh*). While there has been some disagreement on the relationship between the drawing and the inscription, two of the three figures now appear to represent Yahweh and his consort, probably the goddess Asherah.[6] That the inscription labels the figures "Yahweh *of* Samaria and his consort/'Asherah'" brings to life this text (14:15), which associates "Asherah poles" with Israel/Samaria.

It is unclear if representations of a mother goddess were made by Jeroboam. The verb is plural: "They [Israel] made Asherah poles." The note probably encapsulates Jeroboam's influence on Israel. What began with him developed into full-scale idolatry. However,

---

[5]Contra the NIV text note, the Hebrew *'ăšērāh* can mean the wooden symbol of the mother goddess (as in 14:15) or the name of the goddess Asherah (e.g., 18:19). For a balanced treatment of Asherah in the ancient Near East and the Old Testament, see John Day, "Asherah (deity)," in *ABD*. Joan E. Taylor makes the case that the "Asherah pole" was a living tree that was pruned, representing the fertility goddess as the tree of life ("The Asherah, the Menorah and the Sacred Tree," *JSOT* 66 [1995]: 29-54).

[6]See Baruch Margalit, "The Meaning and Significance of Asherah," *VT* 40/3 (1990): 274-278. Impacting the question of whether "Asherah" signifies the goddess or simply a cultic artifact that in its various forms (e.g., the drawing and inscription at 'Ajrud, Asherah poles, or figurines) represented cultic talismans (i.e., charms), William Dever argues, "Whether 'a/Ashera' at 'Ajrûd means the goddess herself or merely her symbol as an 'agent of blessing' that could be invoked alongside Yahweh, it was the widespread perception of the goddess's *reality* in ancient Israel that gave the symbolism its efficacy. . . . Thus Asherah was thought of as the consort of Yahweh, or at least a 'hypostasis' of him, a personified aspect" (*Biblical Writers Know*, pp. 185-187). Dale W. Manor argues that in the ancient world there would not have been a differentiation between the symbol (i.e., artifact) and the deity ("Worshiping Images and Figurines: Biblical and Anthropological Perspectives" [paper presented at the annual meeting of the American Schools of Oriental Research, Orlando, Florida, 19 November 1998], 19-21).

there is not anything in the account of Jeroboam's apostasy to suggest that he was worshiping *foreign* gods. Baal, for example, is not mentioned (cf. 16:32-33). The "other gods, idols made of metal" (v. 9) are the golden calves representing Yahweh. And even if he did make symbols of a mother goddess, the idols probably represented Asherah as a consort of Yahweh. The contrast with Solomon stands out. Solomon built high places for the gods of his foreign wives, but Jeroboam builds high places with idols for Yahweh. In so doing, the king of Israel misrepresents God by introducing an idolatrous view of Yahweh to Israel. In this way, Jeroboam commits a great sin and **causes Israel** to sin, a refrain that from this point on will characterize the history of Israel (see comments on 13:33-34).

14:17-18 The story of Jeroboam closes with the narrator's voice. His eye once more follows the wife of Jeroboam. With only enough detail to draw the reader into the story, Jeroboam's wife carries the brief scene. Again, she (literally) "arose, and went, and came" (cf. v. 4) to Tirzah, Jeroboam's capital.[7] **As soon as she stepped over the threshold of the house** ties this concluding scene with the beginning when Ahijah "heard the sound of her footsteps at the door" (v. 6). When her son hears the sound of his mother's footsteps at the door, the only one in the house of Jeroboam in whom something good could be found dies. Ironically, she is the harbinger of death for her son, as Jeroboam brought death to Israel. *All Israel* mourns his death, **as the LORD had said through his servant the prophet Ahijah**. A prophecy-fulfillment theme that will characterize the larger narrative demonstrates that Yahweh's sovereign word will be enacted regardless of human choices.

14:19-20 In a final notation, the narrator avows that **the other events** in Jeroboam's reign are recorded in **the book of the annals of the kings of Israel**, probably court records at the author's disposal. The story that he tells is reliable, based on official records. A concluding formula records that Jeroboam reigned **twenty-two**

---

[7]Jeroboam's first capital appears to have been Shechem and then perhaps Peniel/Penuel during the campaign of Shishak (1 Kings 12:25). Tirzah has been identified with Tell el-Far'ah (North), although the identification is still uncertain (Dale W. Manor, "Tirzah [place]," in *ABD*). For a summary of the excavation of Iron Age levels at the site, see Alain Chambon, "Far'ah, Tell-(North): Late Bronze Age to the Roman Period," in *NEAEHL*.

years, not the forty years of a blessed reign. He **rested with his fathers** (i.e., was buried in the family tomb) implies a peaceful death. Judgment on his house is delayed to the time of his son. The theme of delayed retribution first emerging in Kings with Solomon now resurfaces with Jeroboam (see comments on 11:11-13; 13:33-34).[8] Jeroboam's son **Nadab** becomes king in his place.

III. SOME KINGS OF JUDAH AND ISRAEL (14:21–16:28)

A. KINGS OF JUDAH ARE BOTH GOOD AND BAD (14:21–15:24)

The storyteller now skillfully transitions to the chronological frame into which the major stories of Kings (e.g., Solomon, Jeroboam, and the Elijah narrative) are structurally set. The effect of this arrangement is to provide a framework for seeing clearly the major actors in a tragedy that portrays Israel as spiraling toward ruin and exile.[9] Before the story slows down again to show the interaction between Ahab and Elijah (16:29 ff.), the narrator will give a synopsis of the reigns of Rehoboam, Abijah, and Asa in Judah along with Nadab, Baasha, Elah, Zimri, and Omri in Israel. His technique is to present the reign of one king and subsequent kings of the same kingdom until the death of the corresponding king in the north or south. Then, the narrator backtracks to pick up the story of the other kingdom (see, e.g., 15:25). The effect of this synoptic presentation is to imply that, even though the kingdom is politically divided, this is one story.[10]

The accomplishments of each king are sandwiched between introductory and concluding formulas. The account of the king's reign begins with the name of the king, the name of his father/the preceding king, the regnal year of the corresponding king in Israel or Judah (during the divided kingdom), the age when he became king, the length of his reign in which capital, and for the kings of Judah his mother's name. Following a theological appraisal with a

---

[8]Knoppers, "Solomon's Fall and Deuteronomy," pp. 406-409.
[9]Hagan, "First and Second Kings," p. 184.
[10]Nelson, *First and Second Kings*, p. 99.

list of accomplishments and/or sins, a concluding formula mentions the source for information on the king's reign, indicates the place of his burial, and identifies the king's successor. There are exceptions to this pattern, especially for the kings of Israel.

1. Rehoboam Does Evil in the Eyes of Yahweh (14:21-31)

14:21 Rehoboam is **forty-one** when he becomes king, and he reigns **seventeen years in Jerusalem**. By means of contrast, the narrator calls attention to Jeroboam's sanctuaries in Bethel and Dan when he adds that Jerusalem was the city Yahweh had **chosen** for his **Name** to dwell (cf. 8:16,44,48; 11:13,32,36; Deuteronomy 12). To Rehoboam's mother's name, the storyteller adds that **she was an Ammonite**. The Chronicler gives additional information about Rehoboam's family (2 Chr 11:18-23) and his building activities (11:5-17). The supplementary information includes the note that priests and Levites from the northern kingdom immigrated to Judah because Jeroboam and his sons rejected them as priests to Yahweh (vv. 13-17).

14:22-24 When he evaluates the reign of Rehoboam, the narrator focuses on the people of **Judah**. As with Jeroboam and Israel, Yahweh's **anger** has been aroused by their sin, even **more than their fathers had done** (cf. 14:9). *They* set up **high places, sacred stones and Asherah poles**. High places are precincts for sacrifice and worship; sacred stones usually (although not always) represent male deities;[11] "Asherah poles" most likely were wooden symbols/images of a goddess, probably the mother goddess.[12] **On every high hill and under every spreading tree** recalls the language of Deuteronomy 12:2-3 and indicates the extent of Judah's idolatry and disregard for the Law of Moses (cf. 2 Kgs 16:4; 17:10). The traditional understanding of קָדֵשׁ (*qādēš*), reflected in the NIV translation **male shrine prostitutes**, has been questioned by recent scholarship. While the feminine קְדֵשָׁה (*qᵊdēšāh*) may refer to shrine prostitutes (cf. Hos 4:14), *qādēš* appears to have reference to a priestly functionary asso-

---

[11]In pairs, stone pillars may represent male and female deities (see Uzi Avner, "Sacred Stones in the Desert," *BAR* 27/3 [May/June 2001]: 30-41.)

[12]Jeremiah sarcastically reverses the male and female symbols: "They say to wood, 'You are my father,' and to stone, 'You gave me birth'" (Jer. 2:27).

ciated with pagan religious practices.[13] Contrary to the covenant
Yahweh had made with the descendants of Abraham, the people of
Judah participate **in all the detestable practices of the nations the
LORD had driven out before the Israelites**. Yahweh drove out the
Canaanites because of their "detestable practices," their wickedness
(see, e.g., Deut 7:25-26; 12:29-31; 18:9-13; cf. 2 Kgs 16:3; 21:2,11).
When the people of Judah and Israel become like the nations, they
will also be dispossessed from the land.

14:25-28 In the fifth year of Jeroboam, Shishak king of Egypt
goes up against Jerusalem. He takes **treasures** from the house of
Yahweh and the palace as tribute. At the temple of Amun in Thebes,
a hieroglyphic relief with place names records Shishak's (i.e.,
Shoshenq I) campaign into Palestine (ca. 925 B.C.) and therein confirms his devastation of both Israel and Judah. While the storyteller
here selectively describes only Shishak's impact on Judah, the inscription records numerous sites in Israel that were also destroyed by the
Pharaoh of Egypt — in spite of the fact that Shishak had acted as
Jeroboam's protector (11:26-40). A fragment of a stela found at
Megiddo, which was inscribed with cartouches of Shishak, also
demonstrates the Egyptian pharaoh's presence in Palestine.[14] In order
to save Jerusalem, Rehoboam gives to Shishak as tribute the **gold
shields** that **Solomon had made** for the Palace of the Forest of
Lebanon (10:16-17). The king of Judah replaces them with **bronze
shields**, carried ceremonially by the royal **guard** each time the king
goes to the temple. Juxtaposed with the description of Judah's idolatry, the narrator no doubt intends the reader to see how far Judah has
fallen — because of the sins of Rehoboam and the people of Judah.

---

[13]See Elaine Alder Goodfriend, "Prostitution," in *ABD*; Karel van der
Toorn, "Cultic Prostitution," in *ABD*; Cogan, *1 Kings*, p. 387; and comments
on 2 Kings 23:4 ff.

[14]Kenneth A. Kitchen, "Shishak's Military Campaign in Israel Confirmed,"
BAR 15/3 (May/June 1989): 32-33; see also Donald B. Redford, "Shishak
(person)," in *ABD*. Jerusalem is not mentioned on the temple of Amun
reliefs, but one row of place names is completely missing, not to mention
the fact that Rehoboam paid off Shishak with tribute (Kitchen, "The
Shoshenqs," 11). For the significance of Shishak's campaign into Palestine
for the debate over the existence of Israel in the tenth century B.C., see
Dever, *Biblical Writers Know*, pp. 134-138.

Having reasserted Egyptian control over Canaan, following the death of Solomon, Shishak returns to Egypt with Solomon's gold.[15]

In this instance, the contrast with the Chronicles' account of the reign of Rehoboam illustrates the less direct, inductive style employed by the author of Kings. In his characterization of Rehoboam's reign, the Chronicler is much more straightforward: "Because they had been unfaithful to the LORD, Shishak king of Egypt attacked Jerusalem" (2 Chr 12:2). Then, he adds the word of Shemaiah the prophet against Rehoboam and the leaders of Judah: "This is what the LORD says, 'You have abandoned me; therefore, I now abandon you to Shishak'" (v. 5). The invasion of Judah by the Pharaoh of Egypt is punishment from Yahweh! As a result of the prophet's invective, the king and the leaders of Judah humble themselves; God relents; and Jerusalem is saved. However, Shishak takes the treasures of the temple and palace, including Solomon's shields of gold, as tribute. The Chronicler adds, "Because Rehoboam humbled himself, the LORD's anger turned from him, and he was not totally destroyed. Indeed, there was some good in Judah" (12:12; cf. vv. 1-12). For his purposes, the inspired author of Kings omits the Judean King's repentance (see comments on 15:16-24). Also, he expects the reader to draw appropriate inferences. The brief account of Shishak's invasion, without the oracle from Shemaiah, is simply sandwiched beside the evaluation of Rehoboam's reign. The reader is left to draw the conclusion, made explicit in 2 Chronicles 12, that Shishak's invasion was judgment from Yahweh. In Kings, the loss of temple treasures, whether by invasion, tribute, or to secure the services of a foreign monarch, is a negative event that foreshadows the destruction of Jerusalem and the house that Solomon built for Yahweh (cf. 15:17-19; 2 Kgs 12:18-19; 14:11-14; 16:7-9; 18:13-16; 24:10-13).[16]

14:29-31 The concluding formula corroborates the author's claims. The **other events** in the reign of Rehoboam are recorded in

---

[15]What happened to Solomon's gold? Kitchen suggests that it went to the temples of the gods and goddesses of Egypt in the time of Shishak's son, Osorkon I. Within about a year of Shishak's death, he was succeeded by his son, who subsequently donated as much as 383 tons of gold and silver to his gods. Part of this sum may have come from the temple in Jerusalem ("Where Did Solomon's Gold Go?" *BAR* 15/3 [May/June 1989]: 30).

[16]E. Theodore Mullen, Jr., "Crime and Punishment: The Sins of the King and the Despoliation of the Treasuries," *CBQ* 54.2 (April 1992): 231-248.

the **book of the annals of the kings of Judah**. He adds that there was **continual warfare between Rehoboam and Jeroboam**. Even though Rehoboam obeys the word of the prophet Shemaiah and does not go up against Jeroboam at the division of the kingdom (12:22-24), the narrator implies that he (and Jeroboam) did not accept the political division of Israel decreed by Yahweh. In fact, there will be hostilities off and on between Judah and Israel throughout the period of the divided kingdom. Rehoboam dies and is buried **with his fathers** (in the royal tomb) in the **City of David**.[17] When he names Jerusalem the "City of David" (here and with each burial through the reign of Ahaz), the storyteller subtly reminds the reader of Yahweh's promise to keep one tribe "so that David my servant may always have a lamp [i.e., a descendant] before me in Jerusalem" (11:36; cf. 15:4; 2 Sam 7:12-16). Then, in a brilliant addendum, the narrator mentions again that Rehoboam's mother **was an Ammonite**. The repetition (see v. 21) suggests broader overtones. The influence of Solomon's foreign wives (11:1-8) goes on! Rehoboam's son **Abijah**[18] sits on the throne of Judah after his death.

---

[17]Rock-cut tombs at the southern end of the City of David have been identified as the tombs of the kings of Judah. However, subsequent quarrying and no material remains make secure identification virtually impossible. Other sites have been suggested with little evidence for support (see L.Y. Rahmani, "Ancient Jerusalem's Funerary Customs and Tombs. Part 2," *BA* 44/3 [1981]: 229-235).

[18]The Hebrew text has Abijam (also in 15:1,7-8). The LXX and 2 Chr 12:16 read Ahijah (see the NIV text note).

1 KINGS 15

2. Abijah Follows in His Father's Footsteps (15:1-8)

15:1-8 Rehoboam's son **Abijah** continues down the path his father walked, to which his short **three**-year reign testifies. Abijah's **heart** is **not fully devoted to the LORD his God** as had been the **heart of David**.[1] Again, David is the standard by which the kings of Judah are judged. The narrator follows this assertion by reinforcing the promise that Yahweh made to Jeroboam through the prophet Ahijah, and by extension the promise made to David (2 Samuel 7). Using the technique of repetition, he reiterates Ahijah's pledge that, for the sake of David, Yahweh is leaving **a lamp in Jerusalem** (see 11:36; cf. 2 Sam 7:12-16). This will stand in stark contrast with Israel, which will experience two assassinations and one forced royal suicide (15:25–16:28) before the more stable Omride dynasty comes to the throne. In spite of the course that Rehoboam and his son Abijah have taken, Yahweh is keeping an heir of David on the throne in Jerusalem — for Abijah's great-grandfather David **had done what was right . . . all the days of his life** (see 11:33,38; 14:8). But the storyteller adds a significant caveat — **except in the case of Uriah the Hittite**. David was righteous but not perfect. What the narrator had declared with irony in his introduction (see comments on chs. 1–2) is now stated explicitly in the only reference to Uriah the Hittite in Kings. Even the paragon of righteous kings was flawed!

War between the house of **Rehoboam** and the house of **Jeroboam** becomes a theme in the narrative, with two notes for emphasis in verses 6-7 (cf. 14:30). The Chronicler adds an account of a battle between Abijah and Jeroboam (2 Chr 13:3-21) and asserts

---

[1]The Chronicler's appraisal of the reign of Abijah is more positive (2 Chr 13:1–14:1).

that God delivers Israel into the hand of Judah (v. 16). The additional material results in a decidedly more positive evaluation of this Judean king. However, Abijah is the only king in Chronicles who does not receive a formal appraisal, which perhaps indicates an ambiguous presentation of his reign, leaving open the door for the characterization of Abijah in Kings.[2] After Abijah's death, **Asa his son succeeds him as king**.

3. Asa Walks in the Way of David (15:9-24)

15:9-15 With Asa, the narrator introduces a theme of reform that will serve as another connector in the larger story.[3] As one of the reforming kings of Judah,[4] his reign stands out. In contrast with his father and grandfather, **Asa** does **what was right in the eyes of the LORD, as his father David had done**. His **forty-one** year reign bears witness to his character, but his efforts at reform especially mark him as one of the good kings of Judah. In particular, Asa tears down the idols his fathers had made and **deposes his grandmother Maacah[5] from her position as queen mother**, apparently a rank of importance in the Judean royal court (cf. 2:13-25). His grandmother had set up a **repulsive** image/symbol of the goddess **Asherah**,[6] and Asa, as Josiah later, cuts it down and **burns it in the Kidron Valley**[7] (cf. 2 Kgs 23:6).

---

[2]Hicks, *1 & 2 Chronicles*, pp. 332-333.

[3]McConville, "Narrative and Meaning," 42-46.

[4]Asa (15:9-24), Jehoshaphat (22:41-50), Hezekiah (2 Kings 18–20), and Josiah (22:1–23:30) are the four royal reformers in the history of Judah (Turner, *Teacher's Annual Lesson Commentary*, p. 56). One could also add the early years of Joash, during the days of Jehoiada the priest (2 Kings 12:2).

[5]The Hebrew reads "mother." The NIV translation reflects the view that Maacah, the mother of Abijah (15:2), remained in the position of queen mother after the death of her son. However, since Abijah reigned only three years, it is also possible that Maacah was the mother of both Abijah and Asa. Provan's view that Asa may have been the child of an incestuous union between Abijah and his mother is not, other than this note, indicated in the text (see Provan, *1 and 2 Kings*, p. 126).

[6]Consistently translating *'ăšērāh* as "Asherah pole," the NIV translation is misleading. A better rendering would be, ". . . because she made a disgraceful image (מִפְלֶצֶת, *miphleṣeth*) for Asherah (לָאֲשֵׁרָה, *lā'ăšērāh*). Asa cut the disgraceful image down and burned it in the Kidron Valley."

[7]The Kidron Valley lies on the eastern side of the City of David. These objects were taken outside the city for obliteration.

Yet, this Judean son of David is not the ideal monarch. **Asa's heart** is **fully committed to the LORD all his life,** *only* **he** does **not remove the high places**. In the eyes of the storyteller, this is a black mark on his reign. Later kings will be assessed in part on this fundamental criterion (see 22:44; 2 Kgs 12:3; 14:4; 15:4; 15:35; 16:4; 21:3; cf. 1 Kgs 3:2-3). Jerusalem was the place Yahweh had chosen for his Name to dwell for worship (1 Kings 8; Deuteronomy 12). High places promote an idolatrous view of Yahweh (see comments on 12:14-16; 2 Kings 23). By contrast, Hezekiah (2 Kgs 18:4) and Josiah (23:8,13,15,19) will later stand out as model kings for removing high places from the land. At the same time, Asa's devotion is evident when he brings into the temple **the silver and gold and the articles he and his father had dedicated** to Yahweh.

15:16-24 Not removing high places is not the only black mark on the reign of Asa king of Judah. **Baasha king of Israel** makes an incursion into Judah and fortifies **Ramah**, just a few miles north of Jerusalem. In a defensive move, Asa takes **all the silver and gold** from **the LORD's temple** and from **the palace** and uses them to persuade **Ben-Hadad** of Syria to make a **treaty** (literally, "covenant") with Judah against Israel. In a section of exposition, part of the chronological frame into which the dramatized stories of Kings are placed (see comments on 14:21-31), Asa's communiqué to Ben-Hadad is represented as dialogue. This serves to highlight Asa's overture and suggests that this episode is not insignificant. The narrator continues in exposition to recount the outcome. Ben-Hadad accepts Asa's offer and sends his army against Israel.[8] Baasha withdraws to **Tirzah**, the capital of Israel. Asa uses Baasha's building materials to build up Geba and Mizpah, surely a humiliation to Baasha.

Again, the account of the reign of Asa in Chronicles (2 Chr 14:2–16:14) sheds light on the indirect style employed by the author of Kings (see comments on 14:25-28).[9] According to the Chronicler, Hanani the seer said to Asa, "Because you relied on the king of Aram [Syria] and not on the LORD your God, the army of the king of Aram has escaped from your hand. . . . You have done a foolish

---

[8]The region taken by Ben-Hadad is roughly the same as the area that will be taken by Tiglath-Pileser in the eighth century (v. 20; cf. 2 Kings 15:29).

[9]For a discussion that brings out the Chronicler's nuanced presentation of Asa's reign, see Hicks, *1 & 2 Chronicles*, pp. 340-358.

thing, and from now on you will be at war" (16:7-9). Later, the kings
of Israel and Judah will appeal to Assyria for deliverance — with disastrous results for both. Asa was so upset that he put the prophet in
prison (v. 10). In the Kings account, there is no prophet, no oracle
against Asa. The author of Kings allows the book of Deuteronomy
to frame Asa's covenant with the king of Syria. In Deuteronomy 7:2,
Moses commanded Israel concerning the idolatrous people of the
land: "Make no treaty with them, and show them no mercy." Ahab
will be judged harshly for making a covenant with another Ben-
Hadad king of Syria (see comments on 5:26 and ch. 20).

In addition, in Kings the loss of gold and silver by tribute or conquest from the house of Yahweh serves as a negative event in the
reign of a king of Judah. At the end of the story, the valuable objects
dedicated to Yahweh will be carried to Babylon as the temple itself
is destroyed (cf. 14:25-28; 2 Kgs 12:18-19; 14:11-14; 16:7-9; 18:13-16;
24:10-13).[10] Instead of turning to Yahweh for deliverance, Asa takes
gold and silver that he and his father had dedicated to Yahweh and
sends them as a *bribe* (שֹׁחַד, *šōḥad*, literally, "bribe"; "gift" in the NIV,
v. 19) to Ben-Hadad. Toward the end of the larger story, Ahaz will
offer a similar bribe (*šōḥad*) to Tiglath-Pileser (2 Kgs 16:8). With
regard to Asa, the narrator relates these events without comment.
Asa's bribe and covenant with Ben-Hadad are simply juxtaposed
with the positive note that he had dedicated silver and gold and
other objects for the temple.

In a final blot on his reign, the narrator notes that **in his old age**,
Asa's **feet** become **diseased**,[11] no doubt a trial from Yahweh for his
lack of faith. In his more direct approach, the Chronicler adds,
"Even in his illness he did not seek help from the LORD"
(2 Chronicles 12). In Kings, the narrator records that Asa was buried
with his fathers in the City of David.[12] Asa is a good king, a

---

[10]Mullen, "Crime and Punishment," 231-248.

[11]Since "foot/feet" can be an idiom in Hebrew for the genital area, some
believe that Asa may have acquired a venereal disease. More likely, with the
rich diet of a king, he simply developed gout (see DeVries, *1 Kings*, p. 191).

[12]The Chronicler adds that Asa was buried in "a tomb he had cut for himself in the City of David" (2 Chr 16:14). For the Chronicler, evil kings apparently were not buried in the royal cemetery (cf., e.g., 2 Chr 21:19-20; 24:25;
26:23; 28:27); see Elizabeth Bloch-Smith, "Burials," in *ABD*. The author of
Kings makes no such distinctions.

reformer, who was not able to remain faithful. In the larger story, even reform will not be enough to save the lamp that Yahweh left in Jerusalem for David.[13]

B. KINGS OF ISRAEL FOLLOW IN THE SINS OF JEROBOAM (15:25–16:28)

1. Baasha Rises Up against the House of Jeroboam (15:25-32)

15:25-32 In his synoptic presentation of Judah and Israel, the narrator now transitions to the kings of Israel who rule during the reign of Asa of Judah. **Nadab son of Jeroboam** follows **in the ways of his father**. In verse 26, the narrator repeats a statement from Ahijah's oracle against the house of Jeroboam (14:16, that he restates with emphasis in v. 30), which will resurface as a refrain in the larger story of Israel's kings (see comments on 13:33-34). Nadab continues in his father's sin, **which he had caused Israel to commit**. As a result of his father's sin (v. 30), **Baasha son of Ahijah of the house of Issachar** assassinates Nadab and **succeeds him as king**. On taking the throne, the new king eliminates **Jeroboam's whole family**. The narrator then stresses that this happened **according to the word of the LORD given through his servant Ahijah the Shilonite** (14:6-16). The kings of Israel and Judah have free will to take their own course but cannot escape the judgment of the word of Yahweh. In a final note, the narrator calls attention again to the warfare between Asa of Judah and Baasha of Israel (see 15:16-22).

---

[13]See McConville, "Narrative and Meaning," 42-46.

1 KINGS 16

2. Baasha Walks in the Way of Jeroboam (15:33–16:7)

15:33–16:6 Resembling the dynasty he replaces, **Baasha** does evil in the sight of Yahweh. He *also walks* **in the ways of Jeroboam and in his sin, which he had caused Israel to commit** (see 15:26,30). To reinforce the judgment that is incurred on the house of Baasha, the narrator breaks exposition once more (cf. 15:19) to let the reader hear a character speak. Through the prophet **Jehu, the word of the LORD** comes against Baasha in language that is familiar. **"I lifted you up . . . and made you leader"** [נָגִיד, *nāgîd*, "prince," see comments on 1:32-35; 14:7-9], **"I am about to consume"** [בָּעַר, *bā'ar*, "burn"], and **"dogs will eat . . . and birds of the air will feed"** mirror the oracle against Jeroboam by Ahijah the Shilonite (14:7,10-11). In addition, the reader hears again, but this time in prophetic dialogue for further emphasis, the refrain that already characterizes the Kings of Israel after Jeroboam: Baasha **"walks in the ways of Jeroboam and causes my people Israel to sin"** (see comments on 13:33-34; 15:25-32). Baasha's fate will be the same as Jeroboam, in whose path he also is leading Israel.

16:7 With repetition that emphasizes the word of Yahweh, the storyteller concludes the account of the reign of Baasha and adds a note that reinforces one of the main theological ideas in Kings. The "word of the LORD" comes against the house of Baasha through the prophet Jehu because he had become like Jeroboam. Then, almost in passing, the narrator adds **and also because he destroyed it** [i.e., Jeroboam's house].[1] Baasha is judged, in part, for doing something

---

[1]Some argue that in v. 7 the preposition עַל, (*'al*, "concerning," "also because" in the NIV) should be translated "in spite of." The sense would then be that Baasha was punished for becoming like Jeroboam, *in spite of the fact that* he carried out Yahweh's judgment on the house of Jeroboam (see

that was an "act of God," at least in the sense that Ahijah prophesied that Jeroboam's house would be destroyed. In Kings, Yahweh's sovereign will is accomplished in spite of human weaknesses/sins and sometimes through them. The narrator's brief comment reinforces the implications of the indirect way he recounted the events surrounding Solomon's rise to power. Yahweh was keeping his promise to David that one of his offspring would sit on his throne (2 Samuel 7), yet the narrator keeps his distance from what Solomon does to secure the throne *in his hands*. Yahweh does not condone Solomon's egregious acts to consolidate his power (see comments on ch. 2). And Yahweh does not condone what Baasha does to the house of Jeroboam, even though this is "according to the word of the LORD given through his servant Ahijah the Shilonite" (15:29). Perhaps Baasha goes beyond the word of Yahweh in manner or extent. However, the narrator does not qualify his statement in any way. Turner explains that Yahweh often uses the wicked to punish the wicked, as the accounts of Jeroboam, Baasha, and Zimri bear out (also Assyria and Babylon against Israel and Judah).[2] Baasha is punished, in part, for his role in destroying the house of Jeroboam.

3. The Dynasty of Baasha Is Consumed (16:8-14)

16:8-14 The prophet Jehu's judgment against the house of Baasha is fulfilled in the short two-year reign of **Elah son of Baasha**. **Zimri**, one of the king's chariot commanders, assassinates Elah while he is **getting drunk in the home of Arza**, the overseer of his palace (perhaps suggesting a larger conspiracy).[3] On ascending the throne in Tirzah, Zimri eliminates **the whole family of Baasha**. The language resonates with the oracle against Jeroboam. **A single male** is in Hebrew an idiom (literally, "the one who urinates against the

---

Montgomery, *Commentary on the Books of Kings*, p. 282; Gray, *I & II Kings*, p. 361). While this reading alleviates the tension created by this verse, the traditional translation in the NIV is consistent with the theological point of view of the author of Kings (see below). Cogan views v. 7 as secondary (*1 Kings*, pp. 409-410).

[2]Turner, *Annual Lesson Commentary*, pp. 34-36.

[3]DeVries, *1 Kings*, p. 197. Jezebel will sarcastically refer to Jehu as Zimri just before her death (2 Kgs 9:31).

wall") that appears in Kings only in judgment oracles (first against Jeroboam [14:10] and later Ahab [21:21; 2 Kgs 9:8]; cf. 1 Kgs 16:11). Once more, **the word of the LORD** comes to pass, this time through **the prophet Jehu.** Yahweh is **provoked** because of **their worthless idols** (literally, "vanities, worthless things"; cf. 16:26; 2 Kgs 17:15). The royal house in Israel is yet again removed because of the sins of Baasha and his son — and because they *caused Israel to sin.* The allusion to Jeroboam, who is not mentioned in this paragraph, is clear. The house of Baasha also follows in the way of Jeroboam the son of Nebat — and incurs the same judgment.

4. Zimri Is Replaced by Omri (16:15-20)

16:15-20 The political turmoil in Israel continues. **Zimri** only lasts **seven days. Encamped near Gibbethon** (see 15:27), when the army hears about the *coup d'état,* they proclaim **Omri, the commander of the army,**[4] as king over Israel and under his leadership besiege Tirzah. When Zimri realizes he has no chance to prevail, in an apparent suicide he **sets the palace on fire around him.** The narrator explains that he dies because of his sins and because he also *walks* **in the ways of Jeroboam and in the sin he had committed and had caused Israel to commit** (see comments on 13:33-34; 15:25-32). Yet, what could Zimri do in only seven days to warrant such condemnation? For the inspired narrator, his violent death surely justifies such an appraisal. Zimri also is guilty, as was Baasha (v. 7), of unlawful violence against the royal house. In only seven days, Zimri had done enough to display the character of Jeroboam.

---

[4]Since the narrator only describes Omri as "commander of the army" and does not list his patronym ("son of so-and-so"), some believe that he may have been a foreign mercenary of Canaanite extraction (see Gray, *I & II Kings,* pp. 364-365). While this view is consistent with the overtures the house of Omri apparently makes toward Canaanite culture, Cogan remarks that it is "overdone to make Omri out to be a foreigner . . . simply on the basis of name etymology" (*1 Kings,* pp. 416, 418).

5. Omri Prevails and Becomes King (16:21-28)

16:21-28 Not everyone accepts **Omri**. One faction **supports Tibni of Ginath**, and the other faction **supports Omri** for king in Israel. In fact, the chronological markers in the text indicate that there are two kings, Tibni and Omri, in Israel for a time. In 16:15, the narrator records that it was in the *twenty-seventh* year of Asa of Judah that Zimri assassinates Elah and in turn takes his own life at the advance of Omri on Tirzah (see vv. 8-18). In 16:23, Omri ascends the throne in the *thirty-first* **year of Asa king of Judah** and reigns *twelve years*. But, the narrator notes in 16:29 that Omri dies in the *thirty-eighth* year of Asa, suggesting only a *seven-year* reign. The storyteller's terse style in this section (the chronological frame) leaves the reader to sort out the apparent discrepancy. Omri's twelve-year reign must have included the period of time that he and Tibni were rival claimants to the throne of Israel. He reigns as sole ruler of Israel for only seven years.[5]

The brief synopsis of Omri's reign does not reflect the important place that he held in the political history of Israel. Up until he came to the throne, no king was able to establish a secure dynasty. The house of Omri, however, rivals the dynasty of Jehu for longevity in Israel (Omri, ca. 44 yrs.; Jehu, ca. 89 yrs.).[6] In the Assyrian annals, Jehu is even called the "son of Omri," and, as late as the eighth century B.C., Tiglath-Pileser III and Sargon II name Israel "Omri-Land."[7] In terms of political initiative, Omri apparently set out to move Israel into the mainstream of Canaanite culture and to a position of leadership among the surrounding nation states. For political reasons (reminiscent of Solomon), Omri probably arranged the marriage between Ahab and Jezebel, daughter of Ethbaal king of the Sidonians (v. 31). Later, the house of Omri will be joined to the house of David in Judah when Jehoram son of Jehoshaphat marries a daughter of Ahab (Athaliah; 2 Kgs 8:16-18). Such a conciliatory position toward Judah may have begun with Omri to strengthen his hand against Damascus.[8]

---

[5]See Thiele, *Mysterious Numbers*, pp. 85, 88-90; cf. Galil, *Chronology of the Kings*, p. 22.

[6]See Thiele, *Mysterious Numbers*, p. 217.

[7]*ANET*, pp. 280, 281, 284, 285.

[8]For a good summary of the reign of Omri with implications from biblical and secular sources, see Winfried Thiel, "Omri (person)," in *ABD*.

Having successfully besieged his own capital in Tirzah (16:15-18), Omri chooses to move his capital. He purchases a hill in the central hill country from **Shemer** and builds the royal city of **Samaria**. Strategically situated on both north-south and east-west trade routes, the location was also easily defended. This is evidenced by the fact that although the city was besieged on at least a couple of occasions (cf. 1 Kings 20; 2 Kgs 6:24–7:20), the walls were not breached until the *three-year* Assyrian siege that ended in 721/720 B.C. (cf. 2 Kgs 17:5; cf. 15:14,25). Excavations at the site (Sebastiyeh) have exposed fortifications and a palace that date from the time of Omri. Sophisticated building techniques are evidenced with well-dressed ashlar masonry with header and stretcher construction. Along with prestige items like ivory plaques that display Phoenician motifs, the material remains testify to the Phoenician influence on the house of Omri (as in Solomon's building projects).[9]

The other events of Omri's reign must have included military campaigns. Mesha king of Moab records on the famous "Mesha Stone" (or "Moabite Stone") that "Omri, king of Israel, he humbled Moab many years" and adds that "Omri had occupied the land of Medeba, and [Israel] had dwelt there in his time and half the time of his son [Ahab], forty years."[10] Without doubt, much more could be written about Omri, but the storyteller is not primarily interested in political/military history. His concern is theological. Omri **sins more than all those before him** and **walks in the ways of Jeroboam . . . and in his sin, which he had caused Israel to commit** (see comments on 13:33-34; 15:25-32). Again, Yahweh is aroused to **anger** because of his sin and Israel's **worthless idols** (literally, "vanities, worthless things"; cf. 16:13; 2 Kgs 17:15).

At first glance, **Omri** *rests* *with his fathers* appears to imply that he was buried in the family tomb. However, the phrase must have become a euphemism for death (perhaps a peaceful death), since the king **was buried in Samaria**, the city he founded, and not in the family tomb. The same language is used for the burial of David of Bethlehem in Jerusalem (2:10). **Ahab** succeeds his father as king.

---

[9]James D. Purvis, "Samaria, (place)," in *ABD*; see Nahman Avigad, "Samaria (City)," in *NEAEHL*.

[10]*ANET*, p. 320 (see comments on 2 Kings 3).

With Omri, another dynasty comes to the throne in Israel. Will this house suffer a similar fate to the two that have already been judged? Parallels between Jeroboam and Baasha and their sons establish a pattern that creates an expectation for the reader that this line of kings may also incur Yahweh's wrath. Both Jeroboam and Baasha rule just over two decades; both receive similar judgment oracles; their sons Nadab and Elah each reign two years; Nadab is assassinated while on campaign at Gibbethon; when Elah is assassinated, the army is again/still encamped at Gibbethon (16:15); and both assassins annihilate the respective royal houses.[11] When the narrator in the next paragraph says that Ahab's evil exceeds all who reigned before him, the reader can anticipate the dynasty's ultimate downfall. Elijah will announce a similar judgment on the house of Omri (21:17-24). Later, Micah will say to Judah,

> You have observed the statues of Omri
>   and all the practices of Ahab's house,
>   and you have followed their traditions.
> Therefore I will give you over to ruin
>   and your people to derision;
>   you will bear the scorn of the nations (Micah 6:16).

IV. THE STORY OF ELIJAH AND ELISHA VERSUS THE HOUSE OF AHAB (16:29–2 KINGS 12:21[22])

A. ELIJAH CHALLENGES AHAB (16:29–19:21)

1. The Reign of Ahab is Framed (16:29-34)

16:29-33 The regnal formula for the reign of Ahab starts out as with other kings. **Ahab son of Omri** begins his reign over Israel **in the thirty-eighth year of Asa** of Judah. As in the previous accounts, a theological assessment of Ahab's reign follows. However, in this instance the narrator uses this pattern as a transition to the dramatized story of Elijah and Ahab (17:1 ff.). The concluding formula for Ahab's reign does not appear until 22:29-40.

---

[11]Walsh, *1 Kings*, p. 220.

As the kings of Israel before him, Ahab is judged an evil king. That he does **more evil** to provoke Yahweh to anger is repeated for emphasis (vv. 30,33). Since the same thing is said of his father Omri (16:25; and the narrator twice names Ahab "son of Omri" [vv. 29,30] to reinforce the connection), the narrator is indicating that during Ahab's reign there is a noticeable progression further away from Yahweh. Ahab **considers it trivial** to continue in the **sins of Jeroboam**. Going beyond Jeroboam's apostasy, he marries **Jezebel daughter of Ethbaal king of the Sidonians**[12] and worships **Baal**. While Solomon built *high places* for foreign gods, and Jeroboam set up calf-idols to represent Yahweh, Ahab *builds* a **temple** [literally, "house"] **of Baal** in Samaria.[13] He also sets up a symbol of **Asherah**, in this instance the consort of Baal (see comments on 14:14-16). Ahab probably also worships Yahweh. In antiquity, it was common for one to worship numerous deities concurrently, and the king gives his sons Yahwistic names, Ahaziah and Jehoram.[14] Nevertheless, the story of Ahab is framed to emphasize the king's foreign idolatry, which, with Jezebel, he sanctions in Israel. In spite of Moses' injunction in Deuteronomy 7:3-4 not to intermarry with the people of the land "for they will turn your sons away from following me to serve other gods," Ahab marries a "Canaanite" wife. His idolatrous acts follow suit.

This is the first reference to Baal in Kings. Like Solomon (cf. 11:1), Ahab takes a Sidonian wife and allows her to lead him and Israel further into apostasy. Josephus[15] records that Ethbaal (meaning "Baal exists") was also a priest of Astarte, perhaps explaining Jezebel's aggressive posture toward Canaanite religion. The form of Jezebel's name in the Hebrew text may represent a parody. The name originally meant, "Where is the Prince [*'izĕbūl*]?" It is derived from the epic of Baal's battle with *Mot* ("death"). When Baal is

---

[12]A seal has come to light that may have belonged to Jezebel. It is carved in Phoenician style and includes the paleo-Hebrew letters לשֶׁz (לבז׳, *yzbl*, "Jezebel"; see Ephraim Stern, "The Many Masters of Dor, Part 2: How Bad Was Ahab?" *BAR* 19/2 [March-April 1993]: 25, 28).

[13]Cogan comments that Ahab's construction of a temple for Baal is no different from Solomon's construction of high places for his foreign wives, "a courtesy to his foreign wife in accord with the accepted norms of international diplomacy" (*1 Kings*, p. 423).

[14]Ibid.

[15]Josephus, *Jewish Antiquities*, 8.13.2.

defeated by *Mot* and is taken to the underworld, the god of rain "neglects the furrow of his tillage." The search is made for Baal: "Where is the Prince, Lord of Earth?"[16] In the Hebrew rendering of Jezebel's name, "prince" (*zĕbūl*) appears to be vocalized as "dung" (*zebel* signifies dung in Arabic; cf. 2 Kgs 9:37),[17] surely representing the author's negative view of Israel's Sidonian queen and her influence on Israel. Idolatry in the northern kingdom of Israel now takes the form of worshiping foreign gods.

16:34 The building note that concludes the introduction to Ahab's reign strikes an ominous chord for the future of his house and also introduces a motif that will dominate the story of Elijah that follows. During Ahab's reign, **Hiel of Bethel** rebuilds **Jericho**. With his **firstborn** and his **youngest**, he lays **its foundations** and sets up **its gates**. Since Jericho was inhabited after the time of Joshua (see, e.g., Judg 1:16; 2 Sam 10:5), the statement must mean that Hiel rebuilt Jericho's fortification walls.[18] Less certain is what is meant by the loss of his two sons. In Hebrew, the NIV's **at the cost of** is simply "*with* Abiram his firstborn" and "*with* Segub his youngest." The language may reflect the ancient Near Eastern practice of child sacrifice (as a foundation deposit) to secure divine favor for important building projects or (as implied in the NIV) the accidental death of his sons during construction.

That this happened **in accordance with the word of the LORD spoken by Joshua** indicates that the narrator's purpose is not just to record what happened. His claim is that these events are the fulfillment of the word of Yahweh. In fact, the Hebrew of verse 34b ("He laid . . . Segub") is almost verbatim from Joshua's curse on Jericho in Joshua 6:26b. The narrator has only added the names of Hiel's sons to the curse (two words in Hebrew: בַּאֲבִירָם, [*ba'ăbîrām*, "with Abiram"] and בִּשְׂגוּב [*biśgûb*, "with Segub"]). The effect is to create a prophecy-fulfillment theme that will dominate the episodes that follow. For Ahab, Joshua's curse will loom as a dark shadow over his house. In the end, Ahab's sons will suffer a similar fate to Hiel's firstborn and youngest (2 Kgs 1:1-18; 9:14–10:17).[19]

---

[16]*ANET*, p. 141.

[17]See Gale A. Yee, "Jezebel (person)," in *ABD*.

[18]See Gray, *I & II Kings*, p. 369.

[19]For some similar observations and an excellent discussion of the literary

The *word of Yahweh* will be the key motif in the account of Elijah and Ahab. However, in Joshua 6, there is no "word of the LORD" recorded. Joshua curses the city of Jericho on his own initiative.[20] The curse comes to pass because Joshua as a servant of God represents Yahweh. Joshua's word is the word of Yahweh. In the story that ensues, the issue of prophetic initiative will resurface in the speech and actions of Elijah who as a prophet acts as a representative of the God of Israel.

---

connections between 1 Kgs 16:34 and the stories of Elijah and Elisha, see Charles Conroy, "Hiel between Ahab and Elijah-Elisha: 1 Kgs 16,34 in Its Immediate Literary Context," *Biblica* 77, fasc. 2 (1996): 210-218.

[20]Paul J. Kissling makes a similar observation (*Reliable Characters in the Primary History: Profiles of Moses, Joshua, Elijah and Elisha*, JSOTSup 224 [Sheffield: Sheffield Academic Press, 1996], pp. 114-115).

1 KINGS 17

2. Elijah Declares a Drought (17:1-7)

17:1-7 The prophet **Elijah the Tishbite, from Tishbe in Gilead** (in northern Transjordan) is introduced with a word for Ahab king of Israel, announcing a drought. There will be no **"dew or rain . . . except at *my* word!"** Then **the word of the LORD** comes to Elijah and commands him to *hide* **in the Kerith Ravine** [literally, "river of cutting"], **east of the Jordan** (perhaps near his home in Gilead). There, he would have water to **drink**. Yahweh has **"ordered [צָוָה, *ṣāwāh*] the ravens to feed you** [literally, "*sustain* you," כּוּל, *kûl*; cf. v. 9] **there."** Already, the narrator has introduced themes that will dominate in the scenes that follow. The underlying tension of the story through chapter 18 revolves around the drought that was brought on Israel by Elijah. The theme of eating and drinking (sustaining) will tie together several scenes as well (17:1-6,7-16; 18:1-15,41-42; 19:3-9).[1] Also, in subsequent episodes, both the word of the prophet and the word of Yahweh will be prominent themes. It stands out initially that the drought comes from Elijah. Yahweh responds to the threat created by Elijah's promise by *hiding* the prophet east of the Jordan.

God commands, and Elijah obeys. As Yahweh orders the ravens and the widow of Zarephath (in the following scene, v. 9), so he directs Elijah. As a faithful prophet, Elijah follows. In a remarkable economy of words, the narrator underscores Elijah's obedience, as the parallel structure (with a minor variation, switching b' and c') of these verses bears out:

---

[1] Deborah Appler demonstrates the important role that eating plays as a motif in the narrative of Ahab and Jezebel ("From Queen to Cuisine: Food Imagery in the Jezebel Narrative," *Semeia* 86 [1999]: 55-71).

A. "There will be no rain, except at my word" (v. 1).
   B. The word of Yahweh comes and commands (v. 2).
      a. "Go the Kerith Ravine and hide" (v. 3).
      b. "Drink from the brook" (v. 4).
      c. "I have commanded the ravens to feed you" (v. 4).
   B'. Elijah does according to the word of Yahweh (v. 5).
      a'. Elijah goes to Kerith Ravine (v. 5).
      c'. Ravens bring bread and meat (v. 6).
      b'. Elijah drinks from the brook (v. 6).
A'. The brook dries up because there is no rain (v. 7).

The prophet obeys, and his word comes to pass. The very brook sustaining Elijah dries up **because there had been no rain in the land.** Nevertheless, Yahweh will continue to take care of Elijah.

3. Elijah Is Sustained by a Widow (17:8-16)

17:8-16 Once more, the reader hears the word of Yahweh direct Elijah, this time to **Zarephath of Sidon.** In an in-your-face tactic, Yahweh will provide for Elijah on Jezebel's home turf (cf. 16:31), in a city of Sidon! Yahweh has **"commanded** [*ṣāwāh*] **a widow . . . to *supply*** [*kûl*, literally, *"sustain"*; cf. v. 4] **you with food."** When Elijah approaches the city, he meets a widow **gathering sticks**, an encounter that was surely not by happenstance. The Hebrew suggests as much (and that this event is narrated from Elijah's point of view) with a *hinnēh* clause: **"When he came to the town gate**, there, *at that moment* [הִנֵּה, *hinnēh*], **a widow was there gathering sticks"** (v. 10). She apparently does not know that she has been "commanded" to provide for the prophet. Elijah takes the initiative. He asks her for **a little water** and a **piece of bread**. Her first words acknowledge **"the LORD your God."** Does she recognize a follower of Yahweh/an Israelite by his dress, or is this a sign for Elijah that she is the widow designated by Yahweh? Whichever is the case, she claims that she has nothing to give. At that very moment, she is preparing a meal for herself and her son, **"that we may eat it—and die."**

The word of Yahweh appears in dialogue with Elijah (v. 8) but also surfaces in the mouth of the prophet: **"For this is what the LORD, the God of Israel, says: . . ."** (v. 14). Yahweh speaks to prophets and through them. As Elijah obeyed Yahweh, the widow obeys the word of Elijah, and his words come to pass. The narrator establishes the prophet's words with a technique that is common in Hebrew narrative (see comments on 16:34). He simply repeats Elijah's dialogue with only minor changes (in this case a change in tense): **The jar of flour was not used up and the jug of oil did not run dry** (cf. v. 14). To this, the storyteller appends a summary statement, which associates the word of Yahweh with the prophet's words — **in keeping with the word of the Lord spoken by** [literally, "by the hand of"] **Elijah**. This statement reminds the reader of Elijah's reference to himself in verse 1, **"except at my word,"** but the narrator is also connecting these events with the reference to Joshua in 16:34. **"In keeping with the word of the LORD spoken by Elijah"** is in Hebrew verbatim the same as **"in accordance with the word of the LORD spoken by** [literally, "by the hand of"] **Joshua."** Only, Elijah is substituted for Joshua. In the story of Elijah to follow, there will be numerous allusions to Moses and Joshua. With the reference to Joshua in 16:34 (that is associated with Elijah in 17:16), the narrator introduces a Moses/Joshua paradigm that will serve as a construct for reading and interpreting Elijah's story. As Joshua (and Moses) served Yahweh, so Elijah stands in a special place as his representative in Israel.

4. Elijah Raises the Widow's Son (17:17-24)

17:17-18 A complication arises. The **son of the woman** with whom Elijah is staying stops breathing. His mother blames Elijah: **"Did you come to remind me of my sin and kill** [literally, "cause to die," from מוּת, *mûth*] **my son?"** Do her words reflect normal suspicions in a culture of prophetic/shamanlike characters, or do they represent some dishonesty on her part in the way that she initially presented her situation to Elijah? For example, she is named "the mistress of the house," perhaps indicating some financial means (reflected in the NIV's **the woman who owned the house**).[2] The narrator only gives enough information about her to draw the reader further into the story. How could such a thing happen with Elijah in the house?

---

[2]See Kissling, *Reliable Characters*, pp. 116-117.

17:19-20 The child's mother blames Elijah; Elijah blames Yahweh. The prophet takes the child to his room and **lays him on his bed**. He then cries out to Yahweh, **"O LORD my God, have you brought tragedy** [literally, "brought evil"] **upon this widow I am staying with, by causing her son to die** [*mûth*]**?"** Elijah charges Yahweh with killing (cf. v. 18) the widow's son. A sensitive reader is taken aback by such a bold accusation. It even appears on the surface to be somewhat self-centered, as he names his hostess, "the widow, with whom *I am staying.*" Later, Elijah will make other statements that will call to mind this scene and characterize the prophet of Yahweh as one who is somewhat egotistical (see comments on ch. 19).

17:21-23 Elijah **stretches himself out** on the widow's son **three times** and asks Yahweh to return his spirit/breath (נֶפֶשׁ, *nephes̆*) to him. In this behavior (cf. Elisha's similar miracle in 2 Kgs 4:8-37), the prophet acts more like a shaman than prophets of a later time (e.g., the eighth-century prophets Amos, Hosea, Isaiah, and Micah). The trappings of his miracle are also somewhat different from the miracles of Jesus that were actualized more by his spoken word (however, cf. Mark 7:33; 8:23; John 9:6). Perhaps this reflects the world of ninth-century-B.C. Palestine, a world of "witch doctors" and shamans. Yahweh is working through a prophet who mirrors cultural norms and expectations, yet Elijah is no magician. He is able by divine power to bring the dead to life.[3]

In an important statement for the larger story, the narrator says that **the LORD hears Elijah's cry** (literally, "heard/obeyed Elijah's voice" [קוֹל, *qôl*]). This declaration stands out. After a description of Yahweh's response to Joshua's request that the sun stand still, the narrator in Joshua 10:14 declares, "There has never been a day like it before or since, a day when the LORD listened to a man [literally, "heard/obeyed the voice (*qôl*) of a man"]." In another allusion to Joshua in the Elijah narrative, the storyteller carefully calls attention to the special relationship Yahweh has with the prophet. Later, "voice" will reappear as an important key word in Elijah's confrontation with the prophets of Baal (ch. 18) and with Yahweh on

---

[3]For a discussion of similar anthropological issues in the Elijah and Elisha narratives, see Thomas W. Overholt, *Cultural Anthropology and the Old Testament*, Old Testament Library Series (Minneapolis: Fortress Press, 1996), pp. 24-68.

Mount Horeb (ch. 19). The child's **life** (*nepheš*) **return**s, and Elijah carries him to his mother alive![4]

Alan J. Hauser argues that the real struggle in 1 Kings 17–19 is Yahweh versus death. In this scene, Yahweh demonstrates his power over death. In chapter 18, Yahweh battles Baal, a god in Canaanite mythology who seasonally is defeated by death (Mot) as drought overcomes the land. Yahweh defeats both Baal and Mot (drought) and triumphs, demonstrating that he even has power over death.[5]

17:24 Ignoring the emotion that must have overwhelmed the widow of Zarephath, the narrator closes the curtain on Elijah's sojourn in Sidon with her simple statement about the prophet. Indirectly, through her dialogue, he thus communicates what must be the reason behind the way he portrays these events as he does. She exclaims, **"Now I know that you are a man of God and that the word of the LORD from your mouth is the truth."** So, the scene closes with a proclamation that once more connects the word of Yahweh and the word of the prophet. A careful reader recalls Elijah's promise that there would not be dew or rain "except at [literally, *the mouth of*] my word," demonstrating an inclusion with verse 1.[6] Elijah is a prophet who, like Joshua, represents Yahweh. Yahweh listens to his voice and enables the prophet's words to come to pass. This important chapter establishes a frame for reading the remaining scenes in this act of Kings. Yahweh will again listen to the voice of the prophet and uphold his word (ch. 18). However, in subsequent scenes, the reader will have cause to question whether every word in the mouth of this prophet is true (see comments on chs. 19 and 21).

---

[4]There are echoes of Elijah's miracle in Luke 7:11-17 (see also Heb 11:35). When inaugurating his ministry in Nazareth, Jesus refers to the widow of Zarephath and challenges the prejudice of the people (Luke 4:25-26; see comments on 2 Kings 5).

[5]Alan J. Hauser, "Yahweh versus Death — The Real Struggle in 1 Kings 17–19," in *From Carmel to Horeb: Elijah in Crisis*, ed. Alan J. Hauser and Russell Gregory, JSOTSup 85 (Sheffield: The Almond Press, 1990), pp. 11-89.

[6]Walsh, *1 Kings*, pp. 227, 232.

1 KINGS 18

5. Elijah Meets Obadiah (18:1-15)

18:1-2 After almost three years, **the word of the LORD** comes again to Elijah. The reader hears Yahweh speak. As in two previous scenes, Elijah is told to **"Go"** (הֲלֹךְ, *hālak*; see 17:3 [literally, *"Go* from this place"* for the NIV's "leave here"]), this time to **"present yourself to Ahab"** because Yahweh is about to **send rain on the land.** In Hebrew, the language of the command is repeated, "Elijah goes [*hālak*] to *present himself* to Ahab" (v. 2). Once more, Elijah obeys the word of Yahweh, although no additional directions are given to the prophet. The narrator adds that **the famine** is **severe in Samaria.**

18:3-6 Obadiah is introduced as the official who was over Ahab's house, yet he is described as **a devout believer** (literally, "one who feared Yahweh exceedingly"). As Yahweh had hidden Elijah, Obadiah had hidden one hundred prophets by fifty to a cave when **Jezebel was killing** [כָּרַת, *kārath*, "cutting"; cf. 17:3] **off the LORD's prophets.** Obadiah *sustained* (*kûl*; cf. 17:4,9) the prophets of Yahweh with bread and water. The reader hears the allusion to Yahweh's provisions for Elijah, with the theme of eating and drinking (17:1-16). Has Yahweh commanded Obadiah to provide for the prophets as he commanded the ravens and the widow of Zarephath to provide for Elijah? Ahab and Obadiah divvy up the countryside as they look for **grass,** so they would not have to **kill** [*kārath*, "cut"] the king's **animals.** Jezebel has been *cutting* prophets. Ahab does not want to *cut* his animals. Yahweh sustained Elijah in the "river of cutting" (17:3). But, does the king have the same concern for his subjects? Ahab is concerned about *sustaining* animals, while Obadiah has been *sustaining* prophets of Yahweh!

18:7-15 While Obadiah is out searching for grass, Elijah suddenly appears. Obadiah falls on the ground with respect and says, **"Is it**

really you, my lord Elijah?" The prophet orders Obadiah, **"Go tell**
your master [literally, 'your lord'], **'Elijah is here.'"** Does "your lord"
indicate sarcasm in Elijah's voice? The two are acquainted. Obadiah
recognizes Elijah, and Elijah knows that Obadiah is in the service of
Ahab. Nevertheless, Obadiah's posture is one of complete deference
(cf., e.g., "my lord," vv. 7, 13; "your servant," vv. 9, 12), even though
Obadiah interprets Elijah's request as a death sentence.

Robert Alter believes the contrast between the lengthy, stammering
speech of Obadiah (vv. 9-14) and the succinct reply by Elijah (v. 15; the
technique of "contrasting dialogue") dramatizes the character differences between the two. Obadiah comes across as a righteous man who
has acted on conscience but who is also "an ordinary man with under-
standable fears and hesitations."[1] Through Obadiah's speech, the reader learns that Ahab has been searching among the surrounding nations
for Elijah. He also hears again that Obadiah is devout. Obadiah repeats
what the narrator has already said. He has (literally) *"feared Yahweh*
from his youth" (cf. v. 3). The reader also hears from Obadiah's own
mouth how he hid and *sustained (kûl)* one hundred prophets by fifty to
a cave when Jezebel was killing off Yahweh's prophets (cf. v. 4). This
technique of repeating in dialogue what has already been said in exposition (or vice versa) is common in Hebrew narrative.[2] In this case, the
repetition serves to reinforce the characterization of Obadiah. There is
no doubt that he is both a courageous and righteous man (although he
is afraid to approach Ahab for Elijah), who embodies the meaning of
his name Obadiah ("servant of Yahweh"). Later, the contrast between
Obadiah and Elijah, when Elijah is forced to confront Jezebel's wrath,
will ironically serve to characterize Elijah negatively (see comments on
ch. 19).[3]

---

[1]Alter, *The Art of Biblical Narrative*, p. 73.

[2]Robert Alter calls this "dialogue-bound" narration (ibid., p. 65).

[3]When Walsh describes Obadiah as representing the "ambivalence" that
characterizes Israel as they waver between the two deities, he misses the significance of this repetition (Obadiah's courage against Jezebel) and miscon-
strues the important role that Obadiah plays in the story (*1 Kings*, pp. 242-
243; 260, 263; cf. John W. Olley, "YHWH and His Zealous Prophet: The
Presentation of Elijah in 1 and 2 Kings," *JSOT* 80 [1988]: 36-37). For the contrast between Elijah and Obadiah, see Russell Gregory, "Irony and the
Unmasking of Elijah," in *From Carmel to Horeb: Elijah in Crisis*, ed. Alan J.
Hauser and Russell Gregory, JSOTSup 85 (Sheffield: The Almond Press,
1990), pp. 105-106, 112.

Obadiah objects that the **"Spirit of the LORD"** may carry Elijah away. He is afraid that when he informs Ahab, "Elijah is here," the prophet will not be found anywhere, and he will lose his life. The phrase "Elijah is here" (הִנֵּה אֵלִיָּהוּ, *hinnēh 'ēliyāhû*) appears four times in this scene (vv. 7,8,11,14). The first instance is not reflected in the NIV's "Elijah met him" (literally, "Elijah at that moment/suddenly was there to meet him"). In verse 7, the phrase may suggest the miraculous if not simply sudden appearance of Elijah. The repetition seems to reinforce the fact that just as he appeared, he may as quickly disappear (v. 12).[4]

Obadiah's words are prophetic. His statement foreshadows what will later happen to Elijah. At the close of his ministry, the prophet is carried to heaven in a whirlwind (2 Kgs 2:11). Prophets from Jericho ask to search for Elijah, saying, "Perhaps the Spirit of the LORD has picked him up and set him down on some mountain or in some valley" (2:16). Obadiah is afraid that the prophet will disappear now as before. For almost three years, he has been missing. Elijah promises to *present himself* to Ahab that very day, as Yahweh commanded (18:1).

6. Elijah Battles the Prophets of Baal (18:16-46)

18:16-19 Indicating who has the upper hand in this situation, Ahab goes to meet Elijah. The king labels the prophet **"you troubler of Israel,"** suggesting that Elijah had brought devastation on Israel as did Achan in the days of Joshua.[5] Elijah retorts, **"I have not made trouble for Israel. But you and your father's family** [literally, "house"] **have."** Ahab had disobeyed **the LORD's commands** and **followed the Baals**. Through Ahab's allusion to Achan, Deuteronomy surfaces again. In fact, Ahab's sin of worshiping other gods puts

---

[4]Walsh adds that Obadiah may be upset with Elijah's request because "Elijah is here" literally means, "Behold, Yahweh is my God!" — something that certainly would anger Ahab (*1 Kings*, p. 240).

[5]Of nine occurrences of the verb עָכַר (*'ākar*, "to trouble") in the Hebrew Bible, three appear in the Achan narrative (Josh 6:18[2×]; 7:25) and two in the interaction between Ahab and Elijah (1 Kgs 18:17-18). The place where Achan was stoned was named the Valley of Achor (עָכוֹר, *'ākôr*, "trouble" [Josh 7:24]).

Achan's indiscretion to shame (cf. Deut 7:1-11,25-26). The drought that ravaged Israel was appropriate for a nation that had broken covenant with Yahweh (Deut 28:24).

Apparently on his own initiative,[6] Elijah orders Ahab to gather the people of Israel on Mount Carmel along with the **prophets of Baal** and the **prophets of Asherah who eat at Jezebel's table**. The reference to "the prophets of Asherah" may be a scribal addition. Prophets of Asherah are not mentioned in the contest that follows. However, Jezebel is not mentioned in the contest either (until ch. 19). The absence of the prophets of Asherah may correspond with her absence at Mount Carmel.[7] The invitation is to a great contest, a duel of popular deities, Yahweh and Baal, for the hearts of the people of Israel.

18:20-24 When the people and prophets assemble on Mount Carmel, Elijah challenges Israel with a charge that resonates with Joshua's call to choose Yahweh over the gods of the land (Josh 24:15). The prophet's choice of words is simple, yet provocative: **"How long will you waver** [from פָּסַח, *pāsaḥ*] **between two opinions? If the LORD is God, follow him; but if Baal is God, follow him."** The verb that Elijah uses to suggest the idea of *wavering* between the two deities is unusual. It is the verb form (*pāsaḥ*, only used seven times in the Hebrew Old Testament) of the word for Passover (פֶּסַח, *pesaḥ*; cf. Exod 12:13, 23, 27).[8] The fact that the narrator later (v. 26) uses this uncommon word to describe the antics of the prophets of Baal suggests that Elijah's word selection is intentional. Israel's vacillation made a mockery of Yahweh and the Exodus, the salvation event that formed the nation. The choice is straightforward. If Yahweh proves to be God, follow him; if Baal, then follow him! The people do not (literally) "answer him a word."

In spite of the fact that the reader is well aware of at least one

---

[6]See Gregory, "The Unmasking of Elijah," p. 104; Kissling, *Reliable Characters*, pp. 99-100, 113, 118, 122-23, 143.

[7]Walsh observes that, like Yahweh and Obadiah, Jezebel is also sustaining prophets (*1 Kings*, p. 238). Kissling notices that Elijah does not invite Jezebel (*Reliable Characters*, p. 107).

[8]Walsh adds that this word group also carries the nuance of being lame ("hobbling," 2 Sam 4:4) and is a disqualification for a priest of Yahweh (Lev 21:18), which has negative connotations for both Israel and for the prophets of Baal (1 Kgs 18:20,26) in this contest (*1 Kings*, p. 245).

hundred prophets of Yahweh who were kept alive by Obadiah (vv. 1-15), Elijah claims to be the only prophet of Yahweh remaining: **"I am the only one of the LORD's prophets left."** On the surface, Baal's **four hundred and fifty prophets** leave Elijah at a disadvantage. Disregarding the odds, Elijah lays out the conditions of the contest. The prophets of Baal and then Elijah will prepare a sacrifice without setting it on fire. Calling on their respective gods, **"the god who answers by fire—he is God."** In designing this duel, Elijah displays the immense faith that characterizes this important man of God.[9] The prophet is confident that the true God of Israel will be able to consume the sacrifice and overcome his chief rival. Elijah has also chosen to battle Baal on his terms, allowing him to use his most effective weapon, lightning. Mythological texts from Ras Shamra (the ancient city of Ugarit) describe Baal as a storm god who rides the clouds and controls the seasons by providing rain, which enables the fertility of both land and animal. When Baal speaks, his voice (in Ugaritic *ql*, in Heb. קוֹל [*qôl*]) of thunder rocks the mountains:

> Baal opens rifts in the clouds,
> Baal gives forth his holy voice [*qlh*],
> Baal discharges the utterance of his lips;
> His holy voice (*qlh*) convulses the earth,
> . . . the mountains quake" (restored text; see *ANET*, p. 135).

But Yahweh's voice (*qôl*) also shakes the earth and even shatters cedars (Psalm 29). Elijah's contest would settle once and for all which of the two dueling deities is truly God. The people this time answer, (literally) "the word is good" (cf. v. 21).[10]

18:25-29 The prophets of Baal prepare their sacrifice and call **on the name of Baal** until noon, shouting, **"O Baal, answer us!" But there** is **no response.** The NIV obscures the artistry in the composition. The Hebrew reads, "There was no *voice* [*qôl*[11]]; there was no

---

[9]Kissling believes Elijah puts Yahweh in a bind. To save face in Israel, he has no choice but to respond to his prophet (*Reliable Characters*, pp. 122-123).

[10]Jesse C. Long, Jr., "God Doesn't Always Thunder," *GA* 132/12 (Dec. 1990): 32.

[11]In Hebrew, *qôl* is the word for "voice," "thunder," and "sound." The narrator is using verbal irony in wordplay to subtly undermine the worship of Baal in Israel.

one to answer" (v. 26). There is no *voice of thunder* from the powerful god of the storm! The narrator then employs the word that Elijah
used to describe Israel's wavering. The prophets of Baal **dance**
[*pāsaḥ*] **around the altar**. Their perverse *dancing* ("springing/pass-
ing over") is the same as Israel's foolish "dancing" between the two
opinions. Both these prophets and Israel are blind to the one God
who could answer, the God who had delivered Israel at "Passover"
in the Exodus (see comments on v. 21).

Elijah cajoles the prophets of Baal to (literally) "call out in a louder *voice*" (*qôl*; vv. 27,28). With high sarcasm, he muses that perhaps
their god was occupied. His language is more than crude. **"Perhaps
he is . . . busy"** may be rendered, "Perhaps . . . he *has gone to the privy*"
(v. 27).[12] The prophets "call out in a louder *voice*" (*qôl*, v. 28), cut
themselves **as was their custom**, and **continue their frantic prophesying**[13] until evening. But, again, "there is no *voice*" (*qôl*, v. 29) —
there is no voice of thunder, no one to hear. Baal, the god of thunder and lightning, fails his test. He is unable to put fire to the sacrifice. He is, in fact, no god at all!

18:30-35 Elijah enjoins **all the people** to approach him. As the
narrator describes the action, the reader watches Elijah work. The
detail retards the pace and builds suspense as the scene progresses.
Elijah repairs **the altar of the LORD**, which presumably was
destroyed during the purge described by Obadiah (18:1-15). With
twelve stones, the prophet rebuilds the altar **in the name of the
LORD**. The narrator interjects that the stones represent the tribes of
Israel, which he associates with Jacob's wrestling match at the Jabbok
(Gen 32:22-32). His statement reminds the reader of Israel's ances-
try and in this way their identity as the people of Yahweh. With this
parenthesis, the narrator also mentions once more **the word of the
LORD**, already established as a key motif in this story (see comments
on ch. 17) — which, however, is noticeably absent in the episode on
Mount Carmel (occurring only in 18:1,31). The twelve stones of the
altar also call to mind the altar of twelve pillars that Moses built at
the foot of Horeb and the memorial stones that Joshua set up at the

---

[12]See Cogan, *1 Kings*, p. 441.

[13]The use of the word "prophesy" (נָבָא, *nābā'*) in this context suggests that
ecstatic behavior may have characterized prophetic behavior in the ninth
century B.C. (cf. 1 Sam 10:1-13; 19:18-24).

Jordan (Exod 24:4; Josh 4:1-24), intimating another connection with Moses/Joshua (see comments on 16:34). Elijah saturates the altar and sacrifice with water (*twelve* jars full) to reinforce the improbability of the powerful demonstration that follows.

18:36-37 For the first time in the story, the narrator names Elijah a prophet.[14] His relationship with Yahweh will be demonstrated in the events that follow. One assumes that Elijah prays to Yahweh in the presence of the people and for their benefit, naming him **the God of Abraham, Isaac and Israel**. His word choice, "Israel" instead of "Jacob," suggests what the narrator spells out for the reader in verse 31 — the God of their ancestors was the one who made Israel's very identity possible. Elijah reminds the people of that relationship. His prayer is that they will know that **"you are God in Israel."** Yahweh, not Baal, reigns in Israel! But Elijah adds, **"and that I am your servant and have done all these things at your command."**[15] The NIV obscures an important phrase in this sentence. Elijah says (literally), "*and at your word*, I have done all of these things" (v. 36). The reader recalls the important role the word of Yahweh has played in Elijah's story. Finally, the prophet calls on Yahweh to act, using the very words of the prophets of Baal: **"Answer me, O LORD, answer me"** (cf. v. 26). Elijah reiterates that this is so that Israel "will know that you, O LORD, that you are God." The people should also know that **"you are turning their hearts back again."** This is a mighty contest. The spoils for the victor are the hearts of the people of Israel.

18:38-40 As in the death of the widow's son, Yahweh listens to the *voice* of Elijah (cf. 17:22). **The fire of the LORD** consumes the sacrifice, and even the very stones of the altar, licking up the water in the trench that Elijah dug. Witnessing the power of the *voice/thunder* of God, the people fall on their faces and proclaim, **"The LORD—he is God! The LORD—he is God!"** Elijah's prayer has been answered (vv. 36,37), and his name realized. In Hebrew, "Elijah" (*ʾēlîyāhû*) means "Yahweh is God" (or "Yahweh is my God"). Once more, a character's name carries symbolic meaning for the biblical story,

---

[14]Elijah describes himself as one of the prophets of Yahweh (v. 22), and the widow of Zarephath named him "a man of God" (17:24).

[15]Kissling observes there is a faithful servant nearby, and he is Obadiah (meaning "Servant of Yahweh"), not Elijah (*Reliable Characters*, p. 120).

suggesting Yahweh's providential hand in the lives of the players in Israel's grand narrative (see comments on 1:1-14; 18:7-15). Elijah has the prophets of Baal carried down from Carmel to the Kishon and **slaughtered** there. The narrator's choice of words is significant. The verb that he employs (שָׁחַט, *šāḥaṭ*, "to slaughter") is often used as a technical term for *slaughtering for sacrifice*, occurring, for example, in the instructions for Passover in Exod 12:6 (cf. 2 Kgs 10:7,14; 25:7). The prophets who were *dancing* ("springing/passing over," *pāsaḥ*; see comments on vv. 21,26) around their altar to Baal are now sacrificed to free Israel from the slavery of idolatrous worship.

18:41-46 Elijah commands Ahab, **"Go, eat and drink, for there is the sound [*qôl*] of a heavy rain."** On the basis of parallels between the covenant renewal in Exodus 24:3-11 (see especially vv. 9-11) and the narrative account of the contest on Mount Carmel, Kathryn L. Roberts argues that verse 41 implies the renewal of Israel's covenant with Yahweh. Ahab is sent to eat and drink (a communal meal), and so validate the covenant with Yahweh. The God who sustained Elijah with *food* and *water* now restores covenant and provides for his people.[16] And, as he listened to Elijah's *voice* (*qôl*), he will now precipitate the *sound* (*qôl*) of rain in Israel (cf. 18:1). In a strange, symbolic act reminiscent of stretching out three times over the widow's son (see comments on 17:21), Elijah with his head between his knees (perhaps in prayer) sends his servant **seven times** to look out over the sea. The seventh time, the servant reports, **"A cloud as small as a man's hand is rising from the sea."** For Elijah, an unsurpassed stalwart of faith, even a small cloud is enough to know that Yahweh is about to send rain. Ahab is told to hurry back before the rains mire his travel. The sky grows black, the winds pick up, and **a heavy rain** begins. Ahab sets out in his chariot, and **the power of the LORD** seizes Elijah, enabling him to **run ahead of Ahab** to Jezreel (the location of Ahab's winter palace, not far from Carmel).

Even though Elijah was an ordinary man, he prayed, and it did not rain (17:1-7). He prayed once more, and it rained (18:41-46). Such was the power of his faith — that Yahweh listened to the *voice* of his prophet (17:22; 18:36-46; see Jas 5:16-18).

---

[16]Kathryn L. Roberts, "God, Prophet, and King: Eating and Drinking on the Mountain in First Kings 18:41," *CBQ* 62 (2000): 632-644.

1 KINGS 19

7. Elijah Retreats to Mount Horeb (19:1-18)

19:1-4 Ahab tells **Jezebel everything Elijah had done**. Through a messenger, she speaks to Elijah, **"May the gods deal with me . . . if by this time tomorrow I do not make your life like that of one of** [the prophets Elijah had slaughtered]." Afraid for his life,[1] the great warrior for Yahweh retreats from the perceived threat. In contrast with Obadiah, who in the face of Jezebel's threat hid prophets, Elijah runs. The discrepancy with the faith that he displayed on Mount Carmel could not be greater. In the **desert**, the prophet prays for Yahweh to **"take my life."** He adds, **"I am no better than my ancestors."** Perhaps Elijah expected Ahab and Jezebel, the advocates for Baal worship in Israel, to be overthrown. His dejection parallels that of Moses in Numbers 11:14-15, but the contrast with his earlier claim to stand alone in Israel is conspicuous. In defeat, he sees himself as no better than anyone else[2] and appears to blame himself for not delivering Israel from Baal.

19:5-9a As God sustained the prophet in the Kerith Ravine and in Zarephath (and as Obadiah fed prophets with *food* and *water* [18:4,13]), Yahweh again provides. Another messenger appears,[3] touches Elijah, and says, **"Get up and eat."** The **angel of the LORD** twice feeds the exhausted prophet.[4] The words **cake of bread** and

---

[1]As the NIV text note indicates, the Hebrew consonants may be read as "Elijah *was afraid*" or "Elijah *saw*." That Elijah was *afraid* fits the context and, as the more difficult reading (indicating that the great prophet was afraid), is preferred (see Cogan, *1 Kings*, p. 450).

[2]Olley, "YHWH and His Zealous Prophet," 38-39.

[3]In Hebrew, angel and messenger are the same word (מַלְאָךְ, *mal'āk*).

[4]Robert B. Coote suggests that when the angel feeds Elijah, Yahweh is answering the prophet's request to take his life: "Eat, and keep your *nepeš* ['life']" ("Yahweh Recalls Elijah," in *Traditions in Transformation: Turning*

jar connect this provision with the story of the widow (*cake of bread*, 17:13; *jar/jug*, 17:12,14,16), as *eating* and *drinking* continue a motif established at the beginning of Elijah's drought (17:1 ff.).[5] Yahweh provides for his prophet as he would provide for Israel, were they not worshiping other gods.

Allusions to the story of Hagar with Ishmael in the wilderness of Beersheba (Gen 21:14-19) serve as an important frame for Elijah. Hagar puts Ishmael under a bush and sobs in the desert. Under a bush, Elijah prays for death. Yahweh "heard the *voice* [*qôl*] of the boy" (21:17), as he hears/obeys the voice of Elijah. For both, Yahweh provides. The God of Elijah is a God who sustains — who delivers, even when his servants cannot see him clearly.

In the strength of that food, Elijah journeys **forty days and forty nights** to **Horeb, the mountain of God**.[6] The allusion to Moses is intentional. Moses was on the mountain of God "forty days and forty nights" when he saw Yahweh's glory (Exod 24:18; 34:28). As Yahweh appeared to Moses on Mount Horeb (33:12–34:9), so he will appear to Elijah. But Elijah is no Moses. He does not even measure up to Obadiah. Confronted with Jezebel's threat, Elijah flees to Horeb and hides in a *cave* (v. 9a). By contrast, in the peril of Jezebel's purge, Obadiah hid one hundred prophets by fifty to a *cave* (18:4,13). Ironically, the courageous prophet, who saw himself as the only remaining, faithful defender of Yahweh ("I am the only one of the LORD's prophet's left" [18:22]), is now himself hiding *in a cave!*[7]

19:9b-10 The dominant motif of the story's early scenes emerges once more. The *word of Yahweh* appears to Elijah, but this time asks, **"What are you doing here, Elijah?"**[8] A careful reader hears the

---

Points in Biblical Faith, ed. Baruch Halpern and Jon D. Levenson [Winona Lake, IN: Eisenbrauns, 1981], p. 117).

[5]With consummate literary skill, the narrator even frames the miracle on Mount Carmel with this motif: "The fire of Yahweh fell and *devoured/consumed* [אָכַל, *'ākal*, "to eat"; "burned up" in the NIV] the sacrifice, the wood, the stones and the soil" (18:38).

[6]"Horeb" is the same as Mount Sinai (see "G.I. Davies, "Sinai, Mount [place]," in *ABD*). It stands out that "Horeb" is the usual designation for the mountain of God in Deuteronomy, which lies behind Kings (cf. especially Deut 18:16, the "prophet like Moses" passage that echoes the themes of 1 Kings 18–19; see "Excursus: Elijah in Context").

[7]Gregory, "The Unmasking of Elijah," p. 112.

[8]Walsh believes that this question means that Yahweh expected Elijah to

irony. Elijah prayed on Mount Carmel that the people would know that he had "done all these things [literally] *at your word*" (18:36). Now, the word of Yahweh asks why he is on Horeb, hiding in a cave. Overlooking their apparent repentance (18:39-40), the self-centered prophet blames Israel. Claiming to have been **zealous** for Yahweh, he charges, **"The Israelites have rejected your covenant, broken down your altars, and put your prophets to death with the sword."** The spirit that he displays stands apart from Moses, who on the same mountain prayed for Yahweh to forgive Israel (see Exod 34:8-9). The reader also hears again, **"I am the only one left"** (cf. 18:22). Elijah's point of view is that he is the only faithful servant of Yahweh remaining in Israel.

19:11-14 The word of Yahweh commands the prophet to **"stand on the mountain in the presence of the Lord, for the Lord is about to pass by** [עָבַר, *'ābar*]**."** The language connects this event with Yahweh's appearance to Moses in Exodus 33–34. In that text, Yahweh "*passed by*" (*'ābar*) Moses, and the great deliverer of Israel was able to see God's backside (Exod 33:19,22-23; 34:6). Before this, Yahweh appeared to Moses on the mountain with thunder (*qôl*) and lightning, and Yahweh descended in fire as the earth trembled (Exod 19:16-25). Now, Elijah, who has described himself as one who "stands in the presence of Yahweh,"[9] is directed to *stand in Yahweh's presence* as he passes by. Still hiding with his cloak over his face, he steps to the mouth of the cave. As in Moses' theophany, Yahweh comes down in a storm, but this time he is not in the **wind**, the **earthquake**, or the **fire**.

The NIV translation obscures what occurs next. "A calm, quiet *voice*" (*qôl*, the NIV's **gentle whisper**) appears.[10] The irony is deafening. Yahweh listened to the *voice of Elijah*, when he brought the widow's son to life and consumed Elijah's offering with fire (1 Kgs

---

be somewhere else. The journey the Angel of Yahweh has in mind for the prophet (v. 7) is back to his prophetic ministry, not to Horeb (*1 Kings*, p. 272).

[9]This phrase is a Hebrew idiom for service, which the NIV translates "whom I serve" in 17:1 and 18:15.

[10]Coote sees an allusion in the word "quiet" (דַקָּה, *daqqāh* "thin/small") to manna in Exod 16:14, which is described as being *daq* ("thin"). So, the story addresses the prophet who is to feed the people "the *qôl* . . . *daqqāh*, the mannalike, life-giving word of Yahweh" ("Yahweh Recalls Elijah," p. 119).

17:22; 18:36-38). Now, in contrast with the *thundering voice* on Mount Carmel, a *quiet voice* whispers.[11] When Elijah hears the voice, he finally ventures out of the cave. His reluctance to "stand in Yahweh's presence" (v. 11) may represent a desire to resign his position as prophet.[12] The voice asks (as did the word of Yahweh, v. 9), **"What are you doing here, Elijah?"** The prophet answers, word for word, as before: **"I have been very zealous for the LORD . . . I am the only one left, and now they are trying to kill me too."** The display on the mountain has not altered the self-absorbed prophet's point of view. Israel has forsaken Yahweh, and Elijah is the only faithful one remaining.

19:15-18 Yahweh speaks to Elijah. The prophet is charged with anointing **Hazael** and **Jehu** as kings of Syria and Israel, along with **Elisha son of Shaphat** as a prophet. With the sword this trio will kill all who dare to threaten the prophet.[13] Elisha will **succeed** [him] **as prophet** [literally, "as prophet *instead of you*"]. Yahweh's commander in the battle against Baal is being replaced. Then, almost as if in passing, Yahweh adds, **"Yet I reserve [שָׁאַר, šā'ar] seven thousand in Israel—all whose knees have not bowed down to Baal and all whose mouths have not kissed him."** Elijah is not the only one! The prophet who claimed, "I alone am left" (18:22; 19:10,14), should know that there are many in Israel who have not surrendered in the heat of battle, many with the faith of servants like Obadiah. A remnant (שְׁאֵרִית, šᵊ'ērîth) in exile would be encouraged to remain faithful, like Yahweh's servant Obadiah (see comments on 2 Kgs 19:1-7,29-34; 25:8-13; 22-26).

A careful reader recalls statements in the story that reinforce this characterization of Elijah. The narrative begins with "there will be

---

[11]Frank Moore Cross argues that this story signals "the beginning of a new era in [Yahweh's] mode of self-disclosure," in which the God of Israel is not known in terms of the traditional storm theophany but through his word (*Canaanite Myth*, pp. 190-194).

[12]Walsh believes that Elijah is resigning as prophet of Yahweh (*1 Kings*, p. 277).

[13]While Elijah is discouraged with the turn of events following the contest on Carmel, he has set in motion currents that will lead to the demise of authorized Baal worship in Israel. Through political means, Jehu in 2 Kings 9–10 will overthrow the house of Ahab and stamp out Baal in Israel (see Provan, *1 and 2 Kings*, pp. 146-147).

neither dew nor rain . . . *except at my word*" (17:1). Later, the reader
hears Elijah say to Yahweh, "Have you brought tragedy also upon
this widow *I am staying with*, by causing her son to die?" (17:20). On
Mount Carmel, he prays, "Let it be known today . . . that *I am your
servant* and have done all these things at your command/word"
(18:36). With "*I alone am left*" (18:22; 19:10,14), one suspects that
Elijah has an all too high view of his own self worth.[14] Rereading the
story, the reader also stops to question the widow's assertion that
Elijah's words are true (17:24).[15] While the text demonstrates that
the word of the LORD always comes to pass, not every word in the
mouth of this prophet is true. Elijah is not the only faithful servant
of Yahweh in Israel! In this sense, Elijah is presumptuous (cf. Deut
18:14-22).

Perhaps the inspired storyteller intends the reader to think once
more of Moses. When instructed to speak to the rock at Kadesh, in
anger Moses struck the rock, saying, "Must *we* bring you water out of
this rock?" Yahweh performed a miracle for Moses but judged him
and Aaron for not honoring him as holy in the sight of the people
(Num 20:1-13).[16] Elijah honors Yahweh in the presence of the people
(18:36-37),[17] but also wants God to acknowledge him before Israel.
Elijah appears to be too concerned with his own position. In fact, the
prophet's retreat to Horeb should not be explained as simply an
onset of depression at the strain of the great contest and his disap-
pointment at the turn of events. His words and actions belie someone who sees himself as too much at the center of Yahweh's work in
Israel. Remarkably, as with Moses, Yahweh listens to the voice of the
prophet and honors him before the people. Nevertheless, as Elijah
cowers in a cave on Horeb in retreat, Yahweh reprimands the
prophet. He commissions Elijah once more, but also subtly puts him

---

[14]See Gregory, "The Unmasking of Elijah," pp. 102-104, 123-124.

[15]Kissling argues that a second-time reader is able to see the narrative's
subtleties, which call into question the reliability of Elijah (*Reliable
Characters*, pp. 96-148).

[16]For an overview of interpretations of Num 20:1-13, which argues Moses'
sin was attributing the miracle to himself, see Jacob Milgrom, "Magic,
Monotheism and the Son of Moses," in *The Quest for the Kingdom of God:
Studies in Honor of George E. Mendenhall*, ed. H.B. Huffmon, et al. (Winona
Lake, IN: Eisenbrauns, 1983), pp. 251-265.

[17]Does Elijah have in mind the story of Moses striking the rock (18:36-37)?

in his place. Yahweh directs him to anoint a successor and, to paraphrase, says, "Elijah, get up and get to work! And, by the way, you are not my only servant. There are countless numbers [seven-thousand is symbolic] in Israel who have not bowed down to Baal!"

8. Elisha Is Called to Follow Elijah (19:19-21)

19:19-20 Traveling from Mount Horeb, Elijah finds **Elisha son of Shaphat**, who is **plowing**, and puts **his cloak around him**. Elisha follows after Elijah and asks if he can **kiss** his parents farewell. The reference to kissing connects Elisha with Yahweh's "seven thousand, whose knees have not bowed down to Baal and whose mouths have not *kissed* him" (v. 18). Elisha must be one of the faithful in Israel. Elijah's response is curious: **"Go back. . . . What have I done to you?"** The reader wonders the same. What has Elijah done to Elisha? The prophet has been commanded to anoint Elisha as prophet in his place. Does handing over his cloak represent an "anointing," or is this just the abrasive Elijah the reader has seen a glimpse of in his interaction with Obadiah (cf. 18:7-15)? Or, is it possible that since an anointing scene is missing, the storyteller is suggesting that Elijah is only reluctantly obeying Yahweh's directive? In the larger narrative, there is no indication that Elijah formally anoints his successor. Elisha dons the cloak as successor only after it falls from Elijah at his ascension (2 Kgs 2:11-14).[18] Beyond this, Elisha is left to carry out the other two parts of Yahweh's directive. In 2 Kings 8:7-15, Elisha — not Elijah — journeys to Damascus to inform Hazael that he would be king in Syria. Also, it is Elisha — not Elijah — who sends one of a company of prophets to *anoint* Jehu as king over Israel (2 Kgs 9:1-13).[19]

In any case, the story of Elijah's confrontation with the prophets of Baal does not end where it began. In the initial scenes, in the Kerith Ravine and at Zarephath, there is no doubt that when Yahweh speaks Elijah obeys. The story ends, however, with direc-

---

[18]Kissling says, "If he retained it literally he did not keep it metaphorically." Further, he reasons that Elisha becomes "successor-designate, not his successor," forcing Elijah to continue his prophetic ministry. Elisha then becomes the reason for Elijah's "partial rehabilitation" (*Reliable Characters*, pp. 151, 153-154).

[19]See ibid., pp. 125, 144-145.

tives that are never carried out by the prophet. This does not take away from the faith that Elijah displays when he orchestrates and carries out the contest on Mount Carmel. There is no greater demonstration of belief in Yahweh in the Old Testament. Elijah's retreat to Horeb and subsequent inaction do, however, say that this prophet, like other great men in Scripture, is only human. Later, an overzealous Elijah will even step beyond the word of Yahweh (see comments on 21:17-29).

19:21 In a masterful stroke, the narrator closes the curtain on this story by narrating a brief scene that both introduces the character of Elisha and puts closure on a motif that runs through the whole of the narrative. Elisha takes **his yoke of oxen and slaughters** [זָבַח, zābaḥ, "slaughter for sacrifice"] **them**. Using his **plowing equipment** as fuel to boil the meat (probably with the sense of "boiling a sacrifice"; see, e.g., Exod 12:9), he gives it **to the people**. That the story closes with plowing is hopeful for an Israel ravaged by drought. But even more, after sacrificing his livelihood,[20] Elisha gives the meat to the people, and they eat a meal that may be a fellowship offering.[21] The story's eating and drinking motif ends with the people eating. As Yahweh provided for Elijah, he will provide for Israel. Elisha, in particular, will emerge as a prophet whose ministry will benefit the ordinary people of Israel. The scene closes with Elisha **follow**ing Elijah to become **his attendant** (שָׁרַת, šārath), as Joshua served Moses (see, e.g., Exod 24:13 [with šārath]).

---

[20]Jesus apparently refers to Elisha in Luke 9:62, when he says, "No one who puts his hand to the plow and looks back is fit for service in the kingdom of God." In the kingdom of God, one's commitment must be greater than that of the prophet Elisha.

[21]See Walsh, *1 Kings*, p. 280.

EXCURSUS

ELIJAH IN CONTEXT:
LITERARY ARTISTRY FOR THEOLOGICAL ENDS

The story of Elijah's contest with the prophets of Baal on Mount Carmel is one of the best examples in 1 and 2 Kings of the sophistication of Hebrew narrative. This extremely well-crafted narrative employs many of the techniques of Hebrew storytelling to achieve important theological ends. For example, the storyteller skillfully uses contrast/oblique commentary, especially between Obadiah and Elijah and between Elijah and Moses, to characterize Elijah and suggest that there is more to the story than appears on the surface. Also, key words/motifs, like "the word of Yahweh," function as signposts for reading the ideological level of the narrative, for, above everything else in the story, the word of Yahweh in the life of both Elijah and Israel is one of the story's primary concerns.

The narrator especially uses irony to maximum effect.[22] For example, irony negatively characterizes Elijah when he cowers *in a cave* on Horeb, as the reader remembers that Obadiah hid prophets *in a cave* from Jezebel. Since irony implies design, recognizing the ironic patterns allows the reader to see the author's intended meanings. In particular, the ironic contrast between Elijah and Moses lays open the major weakness of the prophet. When Yahweh *passes by* Elijah on Horeb, the prophet responds by reproaching the people of Israel (19:10,14). When Yahweh *passed by* Moses on Horeb, he prayed, "Forgive our wickedness and our sin" (Exod 34:9). From this contrast, Walsh concludes, "Where Moses continued in his dedication to the people and considered his own unique closeness to Yahweh primarily as a function of Yahweh's devotion to his people, Elijah became more self-absorbed and finally came to see himself in opposition to the people Yahweh expected him to serve as a prophet."[23]

For an original audience, allusions to the epic battle the storm god Baal has with death (Mot) also color the narrative with an iron-

---

[22]Gregory demonstrates the sophisticated use of both verbal and situational irony in the Elijah narrative ("The Unmasking of Elijah," pp. 91-169).

[23]Walsh, *1 Kings*, pp. 288-289; see also Gregory, "The Unmasking of Elijah," p. 145.

ic tint, suggesting that Yahweh is the true God of the storm and even master over death. In addition, the verbal play with "voice" (as with "the word of Yahweh") enables the storyteller to subtly comment on the actions of Elijah, but at the same time allows him to reveal important ideas about the God of Israel. Through his *voice of thunder*, the people learn that "Yahweh — he is God!" But Elijah also learns something about God. He learns that God does not always thunder. More often, he works as a *calm, quiet voice*, in the lives of men and women, who, like the seven thousand, are just faithful![24]

The way the various features are plotted reinforces the artistry of the composition and again suggests levels of meaning beyond the surface events of Elijah's life, as the following outline bears out:

Structure of the Elijah-on-Mount Carmel Narrative:
Concentric Structure with Framing, Parallel Segments

16:29-34 Introduction to Ahab's reign: Joshua's curse introduces the "word of Yahweh."

17:1-24 Scenes that establish the frame for reading the story.

"Rain" A. *Elijah speaks*: "It will not rain, except at *my word*."

"Word of YHWH" B. Yahweh *sustains* Elijah (Kerith Ravine and Zarephath).

C. Elijah embodies the *word of Yahweh* (the key word in the narrative).

"Voice" D. Yahweh listens to the *voice of Elijah* (17:22; Elijah raises the widow's son.)

E. **18:1-15.** In the face of Jezebel, Obadiah hides prophets in caves.

F. **18:16-19.** Elijah confronts Ahab.

"At your word" "Voice" X. **18:1-40.** Elijah orchestrates the battle of the "Storm Gods." (Yahweh listens to the *voice of Elijah*. Elijah claims: "I alone am left." "I have done all these things *at your word*.")

"Rain" F'. **18:41-46.** Elijah tells Ahab that it will rain. (He prays for rain.)

E'. **19:1-4.** In the face of Jezebel, Elijah runs for his life. (He hides in a cave on Horeb [9:9,13]).

19:5-18 Scenes that provide commentary on the actions of Elijah and the nature of the word of Yahweh.

"Word of YHWH" B'. The Angel of Yahweh *sustains* Elijah.

C'. The *word of Yahweh* appears and speaks to Elijah: "What are you doing here?" "I alone am left."

"Voice" D'. The *voice of Yahweh* appears and speaks to Elijah: "What are you doing here?" "I alone am left."

A'. *Yahweh speaks*: "There are seven thousand who have not bowed down to Baal." ("Elijah, you are not the only one!")

19:19-21 Conclusion and transition: The people eat. Elisha is commissioned.

---

[24]Jesse C. Long, Jr., "God Doesn't Always Thunder," 32. Olley makes a similar point and underscores how this message would be appropriate for an exilic audience. In exile, Israel should expect "the provision of Yahweh" and know that he is not always "confrontational." He also worked "through a widow in Zarephath and an Obadiah in Ahab's court" ("YHWH and His Zealous Prophet," 51).

The structure and the rhetorical devices employed in this sophisticated design uphold important theological themes. The story's
concentric structure (in the body of the narrative) calls attention to
the confrontation on Mount Carmel, which is at the center of the
outline (item "X"). No doubt, an important reason for the story is
that it demonstrates that Yahweh is the one, true God, in contrast
with false gods like Baal. The parallel segments ("B C D" and "B' C'
D'") that frame the story, establish "the word of Yahweh" and
"voice" as important motifs and in turn ironically employ them to
put Elijah in his place. The overall design suggests that the author is
also making an important statement about prophecy in Israel.

With respect to prophecy, the story clarifies the relationship
between the prophet and Yahweh. The introduction of "the word of
Yahweh spoken by Joshua son of Nun" in the frame verse, 16:34, on
close inspection, suggests that prophetic initiative plays an important role in that relationship.[25] There is no word from Yahweh in
Joshua 6:26-27. Joshua is the one who curses Jericho, and his curse
becomes the word of Yahweh (see comments on 16:34). Elijah also
assumes some initiative when he calls for a drought, performs the
miracle of the jar of flour and jug of oil, prays for the widow's son,
lays out the dramatic contest on Carmel, and prays for rain. Yahweh
responds to the prophet's initiatives and *listens to/obeys* his voice (see
especially 17:22; 18:36-38). The widow's statement, "Now I know
that you are a man of God and that the word of the LORD from your
mouth is the truth" (17:24), denotes not only that the prophet
speaks the words that Yahweh puts in his mouth (cf. Deut 18:18-19),
but that Yahweh also establishes the word of the prophet. Yahweh
continues to care for him and honors the prophet's word (and/or
actions),[26] even when the prophet, as in the case of Elijah, is somewhat self-consumed. Again, the parallel between Elijah and Moses'
indiscretion at Kadesh is helpful. Moses and Aaron strike the rock
and do not acknowledge God. Yahweh upholds their action, and
reprimands them afterwards (Num 20:1-13).

---

[25]Kissling correctly highlights Elijah's initiative but does not directly
address the implications of this observation for understanding the nature of
prophecy in Israel (*Reliable Characters*, pp. 96-148; cf. 113-115; 118-119; 122-
123).

[26]See Olley, "YHWH and His Zealous Prophet," 48-49.

Prophetic narratives like this one indicate that the prophet of Yahweh is not simply a megaphone or a sound system for God. While often called on to relay the very word of Yahweh, the prophet is more than a messenger. He is Yahweh's representative, the one who speaks for Yahweh, yet who also embodies and enacts Yahweh's word in the world. Therefore, it is paramount that the prophet of Yahweh submit to divine direction. This understanding of prophecy does not contradict the Chronicler's view that the prophetic word comes by the Spirit of God (cf. 1 Chr 12:18; 28:12; 2 Chr 15:1; 20:14).[27] Yahweh's Spirit enables a man to speak for God, but does not override free will. For example, in Israel's early history several of the Judges did "unfaithful" things, even after the Spirit of Yahweh came upon them: The Spirit of Yahweh came upon Gideon, and he asked for another sign (Judg 6:34-40); the Spirit of Yahweh came upon Jephthah, and he made a rash vow (11:29-31); and the Spirit of Yahweh came upon Samson, and he went to see a woman (13:25–14:1). God's presence is always mediated by human will.[28] In addition, prophetic initiative is not inconsistent with Peter's statement that prophecy "never had its origin in the will of man" (2 Pet 1:20-21). When the prophet submits to the will of God (in what he says and does), the Holy Spirit is able to work, so that the prophet's message is not his own interpretation but the very word of Yahweh. The story of Elijah on Mount Carmel and its surrounding scenes are framed to reinforce this important biblical principle — the man of God must submit to the will of Yahweh!

The submissive relationship between the prophet and the word of Yahweh is further reinforced with the motifs "word of Yahweh" and "voice" and with the several allusions to Moses in the story,[29] suggest-

---

[27]See Hicks, *1 & 2 Chronicles*, p. 385.

[28]See Richard G. Bowman, "Narrative Criticism: Human Purpose in Conflict with Divine Presence," in *Judges & Method: New Approaches in Biblical Studies*, ed. Gale A. Yee (Minneapolis: Fortress Press, 1995), pp. 17-44.

[29]Walsh outlines numerous allusions to Moses in this narrative. For example, the manna and quail stories in Exodus 16 and Numbers 11 appear to lie behind 1 Kings 17, and the journeys of Moses and Elijah are similar, fleeing the wrath of a king, living in a foreign land, returning to challenge the king, and traveling to Horeb to experience a theophany (see *1 Kings*, pp. 285-289). In addition to Moses, Gregory outlines allusions to Deborah (Judges 4), Hagar (Genesis 21), Jacob (Genesis 32), Gideon (Judges 6), and Jonah ("The Unmasking of Elijah," pp. 138-147).

ing that this narrative also serves as commentary on Deuteronomy 18:14-22. In the dialogue between Deuteronomy and Kings, the teachings of Moses often provide a context for reading Kings, but the stories in Kings may also amplify the words of Moses. In Deuteronomy 18, Moses prophesies of the prophet like him who would come. Ultimately, Jesus is the prophet of whom Moses speaks, but the principles in this passage apply to all prophets raised up to be spokesmen for Yahweh. The allusions to Moses in the Elijah narrative suggest that Elijah is (and also sees himself as) a prophet-like-Moses for Israel.[30] In addition, "voice" is an important word in both texts (cf. Deut 18:16), and Yahweh's words to Moses ("I will put *my words* in his mouth, and he will tell them everything I command him" [v. 18]) reflect themes in the Elijah narrative (cf. 1 Kgs 17:24: "the word of the LORD *from your mouth* is the truth"). This pattern clearly suggests a connection between these texts.[31] While Elijah is not the presumptuous, false prophet described by Moses (Deut 18:20), even a prophet of Yahweh must be careful to speak only the words of Yahweh. Nevertheless, prophets of Yahweh are also human (cf. 1 Kings 13). In the story of Naboth's vineyard, Elijah will alter the word of Yahweh in an overaggressive response to Ahab. Even then, Yahweh upholds the word of his prophet (see comments on 21:17-29).

---

[30]Walsh entertains whether Elijah is the prophet-like-Moses of Deut 18:15-19 and concludes that the contrasts between the two indicate that Elijah is "almost the equal of Moses" but "ultimately fail[s] to meet the standards Moses set" (*1 Kings*, p. 288).

[31]Apparently, one reason Elijah joins Moses on the Mount of Transfiguration is that for Israel he dramatically prefigured Jesus as the prophet-like-Moses who would come (see Luke 9:28-36). The author of the Elijah narrative is consciously making a connection between Moses and Elijah.

1 KINGS 20

B. AHAB BATTLES THE KING OF ARAM (20:1-43)

1. The King of Aram Picks a Fight with Ahab (20:1-12)

20:1-12[1] In Hebrew narrative style, escalating tensions between the king of Israel and the **king of Aram** are represented through dialogue. As in the diplomatic negotiations between Solomon and Hiram king of Tyre (5:1-9), the dialogue appears in the form of messages between the two monarchs.[2] In fact, the phrase **"this is what Ben-Hadad says"** (vv. 2,5; i.e., "thus says Ben-Hadad") is the formula for messenger speech often employed by prophets ("thus says Yahweh"). In the scenes that follow, the prophet as messenger with a word from Yahweh will play an important role (see vv. 13,14,28, 42). Ben-Hadad wants to **search** (חָפַשׂ, *ḥāphaś*) Ahab's palace, indicating that he suspects that Ahab is hiding something. In verse 38, יִתְחַפֵּשׂ (*yithḥappēś*, from *ḥaphaś*) is the verb form used by the narrator

---

[1] In the Greek text, the chapters that describe the Aramean wars (chs. 20–22) are coupled after the story of Naboth's vineyard, so that the order is 21, 20, and 22. On the surface, this is appealing, with stories of Elijah followed by stories of Ahab's wars with Aram. But this arrangement does not appreciate the literary impact of the Hebrew narrative structure, which sets the story of "a paradigmatic prophet" over against "a paradigmatic conflict between the monarchy and the prophetic movement" (Walsh, *1 Kings*, p. 316, n. 1; for an opposing view, see Wayne T. Pitard, *Ancient Damascus: A Historical Study of the Syrian City-State from Earliest Times until Its Fall to the Assyrians in 732 B.C.E.*, [Winona Lake, IN: Eisenbrauns, 1987], p. 118). Also, the principle of textual criticism that the more difficult reading would be the preferred reading would adopt the Hebrew order. The Greek rearrangement reflects a superficial understanding of the composition.

[2] The army of Ben-Hadad may have been camped in the Jordan valley at the city of Succoth. As the NIV text note indicates, סֻכּוֹת (*sukkôth*) in vv. 12,16, may be translated "tents" or "Succoth."

to say that the prophet "disguised himself." Provan perceptively sees
the story begin "with Aramean inability to see through Ahab's 'disguise,'" and end "with Ahab's inability to see through a prophetic
disguise." In chapter 22, Yahweh "will all too easily see through
[Ahab's] disguise."[3]

Walsh demonstrates that the concentric structure of verses 1-12
centers on Ahab's audience with the elders in verses 7-8:[4]

> A. NARRATIVE INTRODUCTION (20:1)
>> B. FIRST EXCHANGE OF MESSAGES
>>> i. Ben-Hadad to Ahab (20:5-6)
>>>> C. AHAB CONSULTS THE ELDERS (20:7-8)
>>> ii. Ahab's reply (20:9)
>> B'. THIRD EXCHANGE OF MESSAGES
>>> i. Ben-Hadad to Ahab (20:10)
>>> ii. Ahab's reply (20:11)
> A'. NARRATIVE CONCLUSION (20:12)

To Ahab's credit (reflecting a more positive characterization of
Ahab), the king **summons all the elders of the land** in order to
obtain their counsel.[5] They advise him not **"to agree to his
demands."** Ahab returns a diplomatic reply (v. 9), but the relationship between the two kings deteriorates to taunts. Ben-Hadad
employs a curse (v. 10, **"May the gods deal with me . . ."**) that was
used by Jezebel in the preceding story (19:2), and Ahab with braggadocio uses an idiom to say, in effect, "Don't celebrate your victory
until you have fought the battle" (v. 11). Nevertheless, Ahab comes
across as a rather weak figure, a vassal of the Aramean king. Narrated from Ahab's point of view, Ben-Hadad appears to be picking
a quarrel.

2. Ahab Defeats the King of Aram (20:13-34)

20:13-21 An unnamed **prophet** (literally, "a certain prophet")
approaches Ahab. His appearance buttresses the point that was

---

[3]Provan, *1 and 2 Kings*, p. 155.
[4]Walsh, *1 Kings*, p. 294.
[5]Ibid., p. 297.

made in the preceding narrative that Elijah, who is noticeably absent from this story — and is nowhere anointing — was not the only faithful prophet in Israel.[6] As his messenger, the unnamed prophet bears a word from Yahweh. The formulaic **"this is what the LORD says"** sets up a contrast with the messengers of Ben-Hadad who spoke to Ahab in the preceding scene (cf. vv. 3,5). As the story progresses, this contrast will reinforce an underlying question: Will Ahab submit to Ben-Hadad or to Yahweh? The prophet as messenger speaks for Yahweh in first person: **"I will give** [the army] **into your hand today, and then you will know that I am the LORD."** Even as the people learned on Mount Carmel that "Yahweh, he is God," so Ahab, who was present at that contest, must know that the God who delivers Israel is Yahweh (cf. v. 28)![7]

The prophet answers Ahab's concerns and gives him directions for the battle.[8] The **young officers** may have been professional soldiers.[9] The narrator sets the stage for Yahweh's deliverance. Ben-Hadad and his subordinate kings (probably from surrounding city-states) pass the time in preparation for battle **getting drunk**. Walsh suggests that Ben-Hadad's orders to his scouts in verse 18 (**"If they have come out for peace, take them alive; if they have come out for war, take them alive"**) represent the "muddled thought" of someone under the influence.[10] Yahweh works with military stratagem and even through human vice. Led by the young officers, Ahab and Israel rout the overconfident Ben-Hadad and the army of Aram. The

---

[6]Provan, *1 and 2 Kings*, p. 151; see Kissling, *Reliable Characters*, p. 127, n. 34; p. 128, n. 35.

[7]Provan calls attention to this theme in Exodus (e.g., Exod 6:7; 7:5; 10:2) and observes that Ahab and Israel are being reminded that Yahweh is the same God who delivered their ancestors (*1 and 2 Kings*, p. 152).

[8]The question, "Who will *start* [אָסַר, *'āsar*, "bind"] the battle?," would be better translated, "Who will complete the battle?" (Walsh, *1 Kings*, p. 300; Provan, *1 and 2 Kings*, p. 155).

[9]See John W. Wenham, "Large Numbers in the Old Testament," *TB* 18 (1967): 50; DeVries, *1 Kings*, p. 249. Provan believes that they were "untrained lads," a feature that would highlight the miraculous nature of the victory (*1 and 2 Kings*, p. 155).

[10]Walsh, *1 Kings*, p. 301. Walsh also outlines "a brilliant example of literary art" in vv. 16-19, where the narrator represents the simultaneous actions of the army of Israel and Ben-Hadad's camp (pp. 300-301; see also Nelson, *First and Second Kings*, p. 133).

miracle is that Israel is able to overcome insurmountable odds. From one perspective, it is also a "miracle" that Yahweh works in behalf of the idolatrous Ahab. Or, is it simply the *miracle* of God's grace, which will be extended to Ahab in other ways (see comments on 21:25-28)?

20:22-28 Yahweh's prophet counsels Ahab to **"strengthen your position."** When the next military season comes around, the king of Aram will once more attack. Ben-Hadad's advisors counsel him to engage the army of Israel on level ground because, **"Their gods are gods of the hills."** A similar point of view was expressed in the days of Joshua when Israel felt insecure about fighting the Canaanites on the coastal plain, where iron chariots were formidable (cf. Josh 17:16-18; Judg 1:19). Once more as messenger ("thus says Yahweh," v. 28), the man of God speaks for Yahweh, **"Because the Arameans think the LORD is a god of the hills and not a god of the valleys, I will deliver this vast army into your hands, and you** [plural in Hebrew] **will know that I am the LORD."** The Arameans will learn that Yahweh is not a localized deity who only dwells in the hills of Samaria. However, the point of Yahweh's action is so that Ahab and all Israel will learn that Yahweh is the God of Israel and all creation (cf. v. 13)!

20:29-34 The battle is joined and Israel, according to traditional English translation, inflicts **one hundred thousand casualties** on Aram. Those surviving the battle retreat to **Aphek,**[11] where a fortification wall collapses on **twenty-seven thousand** soldiers. From every indication of the size of armies, cities, and fortifications in Iron Age Palestine, these numbers are implausible.[12] According to John Wenham, the source of the problem with Old Testament numbers probably rests, at least in part, on the confusion of two words with the same consonants (אֶלֶף, *'lp*).[13] Since in biblical Hebrew words

---

[11]The location of Aphek, probably in or near Aramean territory, is in dispute (see Rafael Frankel, "Aphek [Place]," in *ABD*).

[12]Less than 3,000 people were killed in the World Trade Center terrorist attack (11 September 2001).

[13]Wenham, "Large Numbers in the Old Testament," 19-53; for a concise summary, see idem, "The Large Numbers of the Old Testament," in *Eerdmans Handbook to the Bible*, rev. ed., ed. David Alexander and Pat Alexander (Grand Rapids: Eerdmans, 1983), pp. 191-192; see also Hicks, *1 & 2 Chronicles*, pp. 28-30.

were written only with consonants, the words אֶלֶף (*'eleph*) and אַלֻּ[ו]ף (*'allûph*) could be misread. The usual word for thousand, but also for a "military company" or a "family/clan" (1 Sam 10:19), is *'eleph*; *'allûph* carries the connotation of "chief" or "commander" (Exod 15:15) — and, Wenham argues, a professionally trained and armed soldier. If he is correct, in the battle with Ben-Hadad, Israel put in the field a small professional force that was augmented by seven thousand of the common people. This army killed *one hundred* Aramean professional soldiers. *Twenty-seven* more professional soldiers died when the wall of Aphek fell.[14] If these numbers are not in some way symbolic,[15] an alternate reading would be one hundred, and twenty-seven, *companies* of soldiers.

The collapse of the wall at Aphek resonates with the fall of the wall at Jericho, both of which happened on the seventh day (see Josh 6:15-20).[16] While at first a link between the two appears only to be a possibility, a careful reader remembers that the storyteller has framed the narrative with the note that Hiel rebuilt the fortifications of Jericho (16:34). Additional allusions in the verses that follow will secure a clear connection between the conquest narrative and the account of Ahab. Hiding within the city of Aphek, Ben-Hadad's officials advise him to allow them to approach the king of Israel in a posture of contrition[17] to plead for his life. They preface their advice with, **"We have heard that the kings of the house of Israel are merciful** [חֶסֶד, *ḥesed*]**."** At Jericho, Rahab asked the spies for *ḥesed* ("mercy"; Josh 2:12,14). When Ahab receives the advisors (now messengers), they pick up on Ahab's words (**"He is my brother"**) and bring Ben-Hadad out of hiding. Of all things, Ahab invites the vanquished king to **come up** (עָלָה, *'ālāh*) into his chariot. Walsh notices

---

[14]Wenham, "Large Numbers in the Old Testament," 50.

[15]Provan connects the 7,000 "Israelites" (v. 15) with the 7,000 who had not bowed to Baal (19:18), suggesting that this number represents a "remnant" (*1 and 2 Kings*, pp. 155-156; see also Brueggemann, *1 & 2 Kings*, p. 248). The evidence from Assyrian royal inscriptions suggests to David M. Fouts that these numbers may represent a type of figurative language, literary or scribal hyperbole, which does not embarrass the text's historicity ("A Defense of the Hyperbolic Interpretation of Large Numbers in the Old Testament," *JETS* 40 [1997]: 377-387).

[16]Provan, *1 and 2 Kings*, p. 153; contra Cogan, *1 Kings*, p. 467.

[17]An explanation for the "ropes around our heads" (v. 31) is allusive. For suggestions, see Gray, *I & II Kings*, pp. 429-430.

that Ben-Hadad's campaigns to "go up" ('ālāh, vv. 1,26) against Israel were thwarted by Yahweh, until Ahab invites him to *come up* ('ālāh) and become a partner.[18] Ben-Hadad offers back cities of Israel taken by his father and **market areas** [חוּצוֹת, ḥûṣôth] **in Damascus**. At Tel Dan, Avraham Biran may have uncovered evidence of similar bazaars from the time of the Omride dynasty.[19] The king of Israel postures. If they could cement an agreement in a **treaty**, a covenant (בְּרִית, bᵊrîth), Ahab would let the king of Aram go free. An alert reader recalls the trouble that Saul got into when he saved king Agag of the Amalekites alive (1 Sam 15:1-34) — in contrast with Joshua, who killed the *banned*, Amorite kings who hid in the cave at Makkedah (Josh 10:16-28). Nevertheless, Ahab sells Ben-Hadad freedom for some cities in the north and bazaars in Damascus. He makes *a covenant* with Ben-Hadad,[20] as the spies made an agreement with Rahab at Jericho and as Joshua made a covenant with the Gibeonites (Josh 2:1-24; 9:1-26).[21]

3. The Word of Yahweh Condemns Ahab (20:35-43)

20:35-37 In one of the more puzzling stories in Scripture, **one of the sons of the prophets**[22] asks a **companion** to **strike** him. The reader is aware that this request comes **by the word of the LORD**, information that is not shared with the companion, who must also be one of the sons of the prophets. When he refuses, the prophet declares, **"Because you have not obeyed the LORD** [literally, "the

---

[18]Walsh, *1 Kings*, p. 309.

[19]At least two superimposed buildings just outside the gate, dating from the ninth century, may have been "ḥuṣṣot." In one building, two bronze plaques were uncovered that are etched with north Syrian cultic scenes (Avraham Biran, "Two Bronze Plaques and the *Ḥuṣṣot* of Dan," *IEJ* 49/1-2 [1999]: 43-54).

[20]Since Ahab was already a vassal, Cogan says Ahab "renegotiated" the treaty (*1 Kings*, p. 469).

[21]Making covenants with the people of the land who were devoted to destruction is one of the underlying themes of the book of Joshua, as the story of the Gibeonites bears out (cf. Deut 7:2; see comments on 1 Kgs 20:35-43).

[22]This phrase suggests that there were "guilds" or "schools" for prophets (see comments on 2 Kgs 2:1-17).

voice of Yahweh"], **as soon as you leave me a lion will kill you."**
"The word of Yahweh" and "the voice of Yahweh" converge as in the
preceding story of Elijah. On his way, a **lion** *finds* (מָצָא, *māṣā'*) the
man and mauls him, as a lion *found* (*māṣā'*) the man of God from
Bethel who disobeyed the word of Yahweh (13:20-24).[23] In fact, the
unusual phrase "by the word of Yahweh" (v. 35) appears seven times
in chapter 13, suggesting a close relationship between these stories.[24]
The prophet *finds* another man who obediently strikes and wounds
the man of God.

The dialogue between the two prophet stories once more raises
the question of Yahweh's fairness. The old prophet lied to the man
of God at Bethel, and the companion in this story does not know
that the prophet's word is from Yahweh. Where is the justice in
either of these occurrences? How does one explain the prophet's
harsh word to his companion? Only the unfolding of events will clarify the meaning. As in the story of the man of God from Judah, this
prophet story will also serve as commentary on the actions of the
king of Israel (see comments on ch. 13). When the final act is finished, Ahab's story will have been as much about Yahweh's grace as
his justice.

20:38-43 Disguising himself with **his headband** [or bandage]
down over his eyes, the prophet waits for Ahab. The disguise will
allow him to enact a parable of judgment for the unsuspecting king
of Israel. Ironically, Ahab will later disguise himself to avert Yahweh's
judgment (22:30), in much the same way that the wife of Jeroboam
wore a disguise to secure a favorable word from Ahijah (14:1-20).
When the king passes by, the prophet detains him and acts out his
ruse about a captive who escaped. With very little to go on, Ahab
passes judgment in words that are thick with irony: **"You have pronounced** [your sentence] **yourself."** But Ahab is the very one who
allowed the captive Ben-Hadad, king of Aram, to escape. His own
words indict him. The prophet removes his disguise, and the king
recognizes him as one of the prophets. Whether the prophet had
previously brought a word to Ahab is only speculation. As the story
began (vv. 2,5), the scene closes with messenger speech. With a word

---

[23]The verb *māṣā'* probably has the sense of "happen upon/meet unexpectedly" (Cogan, *1 Kings*, p. 371).

[24]Walsh, *1 Kings*, p. 314.

from Yahweh, the prophet passes judgment on Ahab: **"This is what the LORD says: You have set free a man I had determined should die** [literally, "a man I dedicated/banned" (אִישׁ־חֶרְמִי, *'îš ḥermî*)]**."** In the end, Ahab acquiesced to the king of Aram, rather than obey Yahweh. Ben-Hadad was *dedicated* (חָרַם, *ḥāram*) to Yahweh in *holy war* – in the same way the inhabitants of Canaan were *dedicated* (*ḥāram*) during the conquest (cf. Deut 20:10-20). He also sold himself to the riches of Canaanite culture as Achan disobeyed and took *dedicated* (*ḥāram*) objects from Jericho (Josh 7:1-26). Ahab is now the one who *troubles* Israel (see comments on 18:17).[25] The verdict in the prophet's ploy now becomes the sentence for the king: **"It is your life for his life"** (cf. v. 39). The king of Israel returns home **sullen and angry**, a state the reader will see him in again when he does not get what he wants in the matter of Naboth's vineyard (21:4-5).

The constellation of allusions to Israel's formative history establishes a definitive relationship between the story of the battle with Ben-Hadad and the conquest of Canaan. The use of חֵרֶם (*ḥērem*), in particular, establishes the author's intent to make this connection. The Hebrew *ḥāram/ḥērem* is one of the key words in the conquest narrative, occurring twenty-five times (in its verb and noun forms) in the book of Joshua. Including this text (v. 42), it appears in Kings only three times. In 9:21, the verb is used when Solomon forces into his corvée (unpaid, forced labor) those who escaped Joshua's *ban*. In 2 Kings 19:11, *ḥāram* occurs in a letter from Sennacherib to Hezekiah, outlining how the Assyrians had *totally destroyed* all the nations. Its use in the prophet's judgment of Ahab (v. 42) indicates that the allusion to the fall of Jericho when the wall at Aphek collapses on Ben-Hadad's troops (v. 30) must be intentional. The author also intends the reader to recall that when Saul saved king Agag, an Amalekite was also under the *ban* (*ḥāram/ḥērem* occurs eight times in 1 Samuel 15). This arrangement illustrates a literary technique that characterizes the indirect and masterfully layered composition that is Kings. As already demonstrated with the allusions to Absalom's revolt in the Solomon narrative and the allusions to Moses in the Elijah on Carmel narrative, earlier episodes in the life of Israel frame many of the stories in Kings. This allows the author

---

[25]Provan, *1 and 2 Kings*, pp. 151, 153. Provan describes Ahab as "'the troubler of Israel,' the Achan and the Saul of the northern monarchy" (p. 151).

to make subtle, and often more powerful, theological claims about the events he is relating.

This pattern of allusions also offers direction in reading the difficult-to-interpret story about the companion who would not strike the prophet on command (vv. 35-37). Allusions to the conquest narrative actually connect more precisely with the text that lies behind the story of the fall of Jericho. In Deuteronomy 7:1-3, Moses commanded Israel concerning the nations in the land to 1) "destroy them totally" (*ḥāram*), 2) "make no treaty ["covenant," *bᵉrîth*] with them," 3) "show them no mercy," and 4) "not intermarry with them." Each of these features appears in the Ahab narrative: 1) Ben-Hadad is *dedicated* (*ḥāram*) to Yahweh (v. 42); 2) Ahab makes a treaty/covenant (*bᵉrîth*) with Aram (v. 34); 3) Ahab shows the king of Aram mercy (*ḥesed*, v. 31); and 4) Ahab marries the Sidonian Jezebel (16:31), a figure who will play a sinister role in the story of Naboth's vineyard to follow (ch. 21). Just as the companion of the prophet was not told that the word was from Yahweh, so Ahab is not told that Ben-Hadad was *dedicated* (*ḥāram*) to Yahweh. There is nothing in 1 Kings 20 that records a *ban* on the king of Aram. But Ahab should have known — he should have known from the teachings of Moses and stories of Joshua and Saul.[26] In this way, the story of the prophet's companion provides a key for interpreting Ahab's reign. This is in much the same way that the story of the man of God from Judah provides commentary on the reign of Jeroboam.[27] The companion should have obeyed the prophet, and Ahab veered off course by not obeying the word of Yahweh that had been given by the prophet Moses.

The story's well-designed pattern of allusions, along with the "disguise" and "messenger" motifs, also argues for the unity of the narrative. Even Walsh, who is sensitive to the literary sophistication of Hebrew narrative, accepts the common position that verses 1-34

---

[26]Provan writes, "Ahab should have read the past in the present. He ought to have known the implications of [violating the requirements of] holy war" (ibid., p. 154). Nelson suggests that the king *and the reader* "should have known about this ban all along" (*First and Second Kings*, p. 136).

[27]The points of contact between the two prophet stories reinforce this observation (see comments on vv. 35-37). Walsh argues that the connections between vv. 35-37 and chapter 13 indicate that Ahab followed in the sin of Jeroboam (*1 Kings*, p. 314).

represent a positive view of Ahab and verses 35-43 a rather negative view that was appended at a later date.[28] However, the numerous allusions to the conquest narrative appear by verses 29-30 and continue on through verse 42, tying together the "positive" and "negative" parts of the story. The narrator's use of words from the root *ḥpś* in verses 6 and 38, and twice in 22:30,[29] not only connects the introduction and concluding scenes in the Ahab and Ben-Hadad account, but also ties the prophetic judgment in verses 41-43 with the defeat of Ahab in chapter 22. The narrative's important messenger motif, highlighted by the messenger formula "thus says 'so-and-so'" in verses 3,5,13,14,18, and 42, is also clearly woven into the fabric of chapter 20. In addition, the narrative is framed in such a way that the reader identifies with Ahab (so the positive portrayal) and then is caught off guard by the reversal at the end — Ahab has violated the ban![30] This does not represent separate stories stitched together, just good storytelling. Again, these features demonstrate that the narrative is a unified composition of high literary art.

---

[28]Walsh avers that vv. 35-43 are "juxtaposed as an alternative rather than a corrective" (ibid., p. 313; cf. pp. 313-315).

[29]There is only one other occurrence of *ḥpś* in Kings (2 Kgs 10:23).

[30]See Nelson, *First and Second Kings*, pp. 135-136.

EXCURSUS

AHAB'S WARS WITH ARAM

The confrontation between the Ben-Hadad (Aramaic = Bir-Hadad) of chapters 20 and 22 and Ahab is historically problematic. Ben-Hadad I, son of Tab-Rimmon son of Hezion, ruled in Damascus in the first part of the ninth century B.C. He is the Ben-Hadad of 1 Kings 15:16-22. Extrabiblical sources clearly identify another Ben-Hadad son of Hazael, who reigned at the end of the ninth through the first part of the eighth century. In 2 Kings 13, this Ben-Hadad held sway over Israel until Jehoash, with Elisha's blessing, removed the Aramean hold over Israel. Many scholars have questioned whether there was a Ben-Hadad reigning in Damascus during the time of Ahab and his sons (1 Kings 20–2 Kings 8). They argue that these stories are actually from the reign of Ben-Hadad son of Hazael. The narratives have been incorrectly attributed to the time of Ahab. Rationale for this position includes the following: 1) there is no Ben-Hadad from extrabiblical sources who can be securely placed in this period; 2) the Assyrian records identify the king of Aram during the time of Ahab as Adad-idri (Hadadezer); 3) Ahab was not originally named in chapters 20 and 22; and 3) the characterization of Ahab in these stories as weak does not fit the extrabiblical portrait of this Israelite king.[31]

Against this view, there are reasons to accept the biblical account as it stands. Most decisive to the proposed reconstruction is the fact that the episode in which Ben-Hadad is assassinated in 2 Kings 8:7-15 cannot be attributed to Ben-Hadad, son of Hazael (since this king is assassinated by Hazael).[32] One inscription of Shalmaneser III of Assyria supports the biblical account of Hazael's rise to power. The

---

[31]Pitard, *Ancient Damascus*, pp. 114-125; for a convenient overview of his position, see idem, "Ben-Hadad (Person)," in *ABD*.

[32]The fact that Jehoshaphat accompanies Ahab into battle (1 Kings 22) also undermines this interpretation. If the battle at Ramoth-Gilead is moved to the time of Jehoash, Amaziah would be the Judean king in the story (cf. 2 Kings 14). The hostile relationship between these two kings does not match the cooperation between Israel and Judah in 1 Kings 22. Cogan argues, "If Jehoshaphat is original to the story line in 1 Kgs 22, the appearance of Ahab in both 1 Kgs 20 and 22 is primary" (*1 Kings*, pp. 471-472).

relevant passage reads, "Adad-idri died [or: disappeared]. Hazael, the son of a nobody, seized the throne."[33] The implication is that Adad-idri is the king of Aram who is assassinated in 2 Kings 8, a king who also went by the name Bir-Hadad (Heb. = Ben-Hadad). By implication, Adad-idri is the Aramean king who battled Ahab in 1 Kings 20 and 22.[34] "Ben-Hadad" was a throne name that could be applied

---

[33]Pitard, *Ancient Damascus*, p. 135; cf. *ANET*, p. 280. Pitard's attempt to dismiss this text is unconvincing. He argues that since Shalmaneser's description of his battles in this inscription is an abbreviated summary that has "been telescoped into highly reduced accounts and portrayed as if they were a single campaign" (p. 136), it follows that the implied connection between the death of Adad-idri and Hazael is suspect. A son of Adad-idri, named Bir-Hadad (= Ben-Hadad), was most likely the king who was assassinated. He reasons that either 2 Kings 8 is in error in naming Ben-Hadad (in the place of Adad-idri) as the king who was assassinated, or, Pitard's preference, Shalmaneser's inscription is in error in suggesting that Adad-idri is the king who was assassinated. It was actually his son, a heretofore unknown Bir-Hadad (p. 133). Requiring fewer mental gymnastics, there is no reason not to accept both texts as reliable accounts of the same incident. The Adad-idri of the Shalmaneser inscription is the same person as the Ben-Hadad (= Ben-Hadad II) of 2 Kings 8 (see Cogan, *1 Kings*, p. 474; Mordechai Cogan and Hayim Tadmor, *II Kings: A New Translation with Introduction and Commentary*, vol. 11, The Anchor Bible [New York: Doubleday, 1988], pp. 78-79), who is eliminated by Hazael. In fact, the Assyrian account reinforces the basic plot of the story in Kings, when it names Hazael a "nobody" (not discussed by Pitard) who usurps the throne of Aram. While it is not impossible that Adad-idri's son was actually the one assassinated by Hazael, it is conjecture that he even had a son named Bir-Hadad. The natural reading is that 2 Kings 8 is a more detailed report of what is alluded to in the inscription of Shalmaneser III. Also, if Pitard is correct, there is "virtually no information in the biblical sources about Damascus during the time of the Omride Dynasty" (p. 124), even with the significant role Aram plays in the story. Pitard comes to this conclusion in spite of the fact that the biblical account appears to be reliable in describing the relationship between Moab and Israel, per the Mesha Stela, and the archaeology of Jezreel suggests that the stories associated with that site are also trustworthy (see Nadav Na'aman, "Historical and Literary Notes on the Excavation of Tel Jezreel," *TA* 24 [1997]: 124). In this context, it seems incredulous to claim that there is not even a memory of Ahab versus Aram in the biblical story. Cogan writes, "The two battles between Israel and Aram-Damascus in 1 Kgs 20, and the associated one in 1 Kgs 22 can be accommodated within the reign of Ahab" (*1 Kings*, p. 473; cf. pp. 462, 471-474).

[34]Cogan and Tadmor argue, "Ben-Hadad, foe of Ahab . . . is identical with Adad-idri of Assyrian inscriptions" and name him Ben-Hadad II (*II Kings*, pp. 78-79; see Cogan, *1 Kings*, p. 472).

to any king of Aram.[35] The name means "Son of Hadad." Hadad is
the proper name of the Canaanite storm god who is designated Baal
("lord") in Hebrew Scripture. In fact, the author of Kings may have
chosen to use the throne name Ben-Hadad in place of Adad-idri for
literary reasons. There is some irony in the fact that Ahab, who
introduced Baal worship into Israel (see comments on 16:29-34), is
warring with a "Son of" the storm god "Hadad" (i.e., Baal).[36]

In regard to Ahab, he is only named three times in the Hebrew
text of 1 Kings 20 (vv. 2,13,14),[37] in contrast with "Ben-Hadad"
whose name occurs thirteen times. However, this does not necessarily mean that Ahab's name has been appended to stories that
were originally written about another king of Israel. A literary reading suggests there is design behind the naming. In chapter 20, the
way the two kings are named is reversed. Ahab is named "Ahab"
three times (vv. 2,13,14) and "king of Israel" thirteen times (vv. 2,4,7,
11,13,21,22,28,31,32,40,41,43). Ben-Hadad is named "Ben-Hadad"
thirteen times (vv. 1,3,5,9,10,16,17,20,26,30,32,33[2×]) and "king of
Aram" four times (vv. 1,20,22,23).[38] A contrast is set up between the
"king of Israel" and "Ben-Hadad," which, as indicated above, means
"Son of the storm god Hadad." The battle continues between the
God of Israel, represented by Ahab, and the god of the Canaanites,
represented by the king of Aram. This contrast reinforces the call
for Ahab and Israel to "know that I am Yahweh" (vv. 13,28). From
another angle, Ahab appears in chapter 20 on an international stage

---

[35]See DeVries, *1 Kings*, p. 248.

[36]The Melqart Stela found near Aleppo mentions a "Bir-Hadad [= Ben-
Hadad], the son of [ ], the king of Aram" who has been identified with the
three proposed Ben-Hadads in Kings and a couple of other suggestions. In
a new translation of this inscription, Pitard argues that this Bir-Hadad was a
king of northern Syria and not a king of Damascus (*Ancient Damascus*, pp.
138-144). In any case, the appearance of another "Ben-Hadad" reinforces
the suggestion that this name was a common name for Kings in Syria, and
apparently a throne name for Adad-idri.

[37]The translators of the NIV have inserted the other occurrences of
"Ahab" (cf. vv. 10,15,33,34).

[38]"The kings of the house of Israel" refers to Ahab in v. 31. In two places
for each king, the appellations are combined, "Ahab king of Israel" (vv. 2,13)
and "Ben-Hadad king of Aram" (vv. 1,20), leaving only one occurrence of
"Ahab" by itself and two occurrences of "Ben-Hadad" alone. These details
strengthen the observation that there is an intentional pattern here.

as king of Israel, so the predominance of this appellation in the text. In the preceding and following scenes, where "Ahab" is more frequent, he is portrayed in less formal and even personal situations. By the use of naming, at least in part, the narrator is able to characterize Ahab in both the political and personal aspects of his life. In both arenas, the king of Israel comes up short in his relationship with Yahweh.[39]

As the story continues, the narrator will use naming to suggest more than appears on the surface. In chapter 22, the contrast is set up between "the king of Israel" and "Jehoshaphat" (meaning "Yahweh has judged") in a way that highlights Yahweh's judgment of Ahab king of Israel.[40] In 2 Kings 1 and the Elisha narratives, the kings of Israel are usually not named, except in framing statements. This may indicate that the Elisha narratives represent a separate source used by the author of Kings, but does not imply that these stories have been indiscriminately attached to the reigns of Israel's kings. Again, a literary explanation should also be considered. As the digression from Yahweh continues, the kings of Israel become minor characters, almost stereotypes, in the dramatized scenes they occupy, especially in confrontation with the prophet of Yahweh. Hobbs observes that naming in the text of the Mesha Stela appears to parallel naming in 2 Kings 3. In Mesha's inscription, after the first mention of Omri and his son in line seven, Moab's chief rival is simply referred to as "the king of Israel" or "Israel."[41] The monument is inscribed to honor the king of Moab (who speaks in first person after naming himself), not the king of Israel — as the prophet is the major character in the Elisha narratives. In the account of the kings of the northern kingdom, with exceptions like Jehu, who is wielding Yahweh's sword of judgment on the house of Ahab,[42] the name of the king is almost irrelevant; one king could be substituted for another, as the kings continue in the sins of Jeroboam. The chrono-

---

[39]For an important example of naming as a literary device with implications for the composition of Kings, see the story of Joash in 2 Kings 11–12 (especially the comments on 11:4-11).

[40]Since Ben-Hadad is only a minor character in chapter 22, he is named "king of Aram" (see comments on 22:1-5).

[41]Hobbs, *2 Kings*, p. 33.

[42]It seems to be significant that Jehu is named "Jehu son of Jehoshaphat son of Nimshi" (see comments on 2 Kgs 9:1-5).

logical frame maintains the dynastic succession from king to king, but in the narratives each king is like the one before, if not worse.

More challenging is the observation that the narrative's characterization of Ahab does not mesh with what is known of this Israelite king from extrabiblical sources. Without doubt, the Omride dynasty was one of the more successful regimes in the history of the northern kingdom (see comments on 16:21-28), and Ahab appears to have been an important player in the political arena of his day. The Mesha Stela indicates that Israel held hegemony over Mesha king of Moab during Ahab's reign (see comments on 2 Kings 3), but the battle of Qarqar, in particular, appears to be at odds with the description of Ahab in 1 Kings 20. In the Monolith Inscription, Shalmaneser III records Ahab's participation in a south-Syrian coalition of forces that faced him on the Orontes. Ahab apparently supplied two thousand chariots (more than any other single member of the coalition) and ten thousand foot soldiers to the combined forces.[43] However, in 1 Kings 20, Ahab is portrayed as weak, even a vassal of the king of Aram, with few military resources. The army of Israel is "like two small flocks of goats" (v. 27) up against the massive army of Aram. Also, when the advisors of Ben-Hadad put forward that "Israel's god is a god of the hills and not a god of the valleys," they are suggesting military strategy (v. 24). Israel was apparently less adept at chariot warfare than her Canaanite neighbors (cf. Judg 1:19). Israel's military strength as reflected in 1 Kings 20 appears to contradict the implications of the Monolith Inscription.

The contradiction, however, is only on the surface. The characterization of Ahab and his military in 1 Kings 20 is caricature, in the sense that the relative strength of forces is the issue. The army of Israel is "like two flocks of goats" only in contrast with Aramean forces and must reflect a degree of hyperbole. The story is framed to say that the odds are against Israel. Yahweh is the one who delivers Ahab. The military strategy underlying the comment by Ben-Hadad's advisors that "Israel's gods are gods of the hills" does not mean that Ahab has no chariots, only that Aram would be "stronger on the plains" (v. 23). When one factors in the fact that Assyrian records were at times exaggerated,[44] the differences between 1 Kings

---

[43]*ANET*, p. 279.
[44]See Alan R. Millard, "Large Numbers in the Assyrian Royal

20 and the Monolith Inscription appear to be overemphasized. In addition, the covenant/treaty between Ben-Hadad (Adad-idri) and Ahab (v. 34) probably represents the beginning of Ahab's role in the coalition that opposed Shalmaneser at Qarqar.[45] In the coalition, Adad-idri was the dominant partner. His name appears first, as the leader of the coalition, in each of his four campaigns against Shalmaneser (853, 849, 848, and 845 B.C.).[46] The Ben-Hadad of 1 Kings 20 is certainly in character with this leader of Aram. When Ahab makes a covenant with the king of Aram, he graduates from vassal to partner, albeit a junior partner. The treaty enabled Ahab to build up his military forces, including chariotry, in order to participate in the coalition to the degree that he did.[47] First Kings 22:1 indicates Ahab had almost three years to strengthen his military before the battle of Qarqar, which occurred in 853 B.C., just before the end of his reign (1 Kings 22).[48] Apparently, the battle itself was a stand-

---

Inscriptions," in *Ah, Assyria . . . : Studies in Assyrian History and Ancient Near Eastern Historiography Presented to Hayim Tadmor*, Scripta Hierosolymitana, 33, ed. M. Cogan and I. Eph'al (Jerusalem: The Magnes Press, 1991), pp. 213-222; Fouts, "A Defense of the Hyperbolic Interpretation," 383-386.

[45]Pitard objects that the treaty between Israel and Aram is improbable because of the reference to Ben-Hadad's father taking cities from Ahab's father (20:34). This does not fit with "what is known about Omri, that he could have been under Aramaean domination to the extent assumed by this passage" (*Ancient Damascus*, p. 116). However, Pitard and others are guilty of extrapolating from limited evidence. Controlling cites along the border does not mean domination, as the situation along the Golan Heights even today indicates. Also, in the days of Ben-Hadad son of Tab-Rimmon, Damascus apparently held the upper hand in the region as is demonstrated by Asa's appeal to Ben-Hadad for security (15:16-22). A more balanced view from all of the available evidence is that in the southern Levant in the first half of the ninth century B.C., there are two leading states — and the struggle between the two is faithfully represented in the story of Kings.

[46]Pitard, *Ancient Damascus*, p. 130.

[47]Cogan argues 1 Kings 20 could have been from an early stage in Ahab's reign before building up his forces (*1 Kings*, p. 474).

[48]The date of 853 B.C. for the battle of Qarqar is one of the benchmarks for unraveling the chronology of the divided kingdom. Another inscription of Shalmaneser III mentions Jehu offering tribute to the king of Assyria in 841 B.C. (probably represented on the Black Obelisk). Since Ahaziah and Joram together reigned twelve years after the death of Ahab and before the succession of Jehu, Ahab must have died shortly after the battle of Qarqar (853 – 12 = 841 B.C.). See comments on 11:41-43; 10:32-33 and Thiele, *Mysterious Numbers*, pp. 76-77.

off, even though Shalmaneser takes credit for defeating the coalition. After Qarqar, Ahab appears to have taken advantage of a weakened Aramean king to take back Ramoth Gilead in the Transjordan.[49] This scenario no doubt explains Ben-Hadad's vindictive attitude toward Ahab (22:31-33). The king of Aram ordered his chariot commanders, "Do not fight with anyone, small or great, except the king of Israel." Ahab broke his treaty with Aram and risked the coalition when he attacked Ben-Hadad at Ramoth Gilead.

Also, in terms of characterization, there is no reason to believe that Kings misrepresents Ahab. The purpose of the narrative is not political history. If so, it admittedly falls short. The battle of Qarqar, one of the more significant events of the ninth century B.C., and Ahab's participation in the battle are not mentioned in the Kings account. The selective retelling of Ahab's reign in Kings calls attention to his relationship with Yahweh. The stories that are recorded characterize him as weak in order to say something ultimately about him spiritually. Apparently, Ahab was easily influenced. Yet, his characterization is also more complex than appears on the surface. Ahab may be seen as manipulative in chapter 21, and, in chapter 22, the king of Israel comes across as a strong, controlling monarch (see "Excursus: The Reign of Ahab"). And even if he was docile in some of his relationships, this does not preclude successes in other ventures, especially with a queen like Jezebel behind the throne. The account of his reign and his wars with Aram are consistent with the extrabiblical data and indicate that Ahab had opportunity to restore the fortunes of Israel, with Yahweh fighting his battles (ch. 20). Ironically, his choice to covenant with a king that had been *devoted* (*ḥāram*) to Yahweh in the end leads to his downfall.

---

[49]The battle at Ramoth Gilead must have taken place in 852 B.C. (Cogan, *1 Kings*, p. 498).

I KINGS 21

C. AHAB TAKES POSSESSION OF NABOTH'S VINEYARD
(21:1-29)

1. Ahab and Jezebel Murder Naboth for His Vineyard (21:1-16)

21:1-7 Near Ahab's winter palace in Jezreel lies the **vineyard belonging to Naboth the Jezreelite**, which Ahab covets for a **vegetable garden**. Naboth refuses to sell it to Ahab, for exchange or for silver, because the parcel of land is **"the inheritance** [נַחֲלָה, *naḥălāh*] **of my fathers."** Apparently, Naboth does not think it appropriate for his inheritance to fall into the hands of king and state. Tribal lands were to remain in the possession of the clan, even to be redeemed in the year of jubilee (cf. Lev 25:23-34; Num 36:1-12).[1] On another level, Naboth introduces a motif that participates once more in the connections between the story of Ahab and the conquest narrative. The land of Canaan was given to Israel as an *inheritance* from Yahweh (see, e.g., Deut 4:38; 12:9; 20:16; Josh 11:23).[2]

---

[1]Christopher J.H. Wright articulates the relationship between land in Israel and the "theological self-understanding of the nation in its relationship with Yahweh." When Ahab and Jezebel take Naboth's inheritance, they move "far beyond mere social injustice to Naboth and his family" and bring about the "direct involvement of God" (*God's People in God's Land: Family, Land, and Property in the Old Testament* [Grand Rapids: Eerdmans, 1990], pp. 151-159).

[2]If "plot of ground" (חֵלֶק, *ḥēleq*; cf. 2 Kings 9:26) is read instead of "wall" (חֵל, *ḥēl*) in v. 23, per the NIV text note, there is one more connection with "land theology" and the conquest narrative (cf. Deut 12:12; 14:27 where "plot" and "inheritance" [*naḥălāh*] occur in tandem [Nelson, *First and Second Kings*, p. 141]). Cogan believes "wall" is a correction of an original *ḥēleq*, in order to bring "the prophecy in line with the reported place of Jezebel's death in 9:33, nearby the wall of Jezreel" (*1 Kings*, p. 482). The best manuscripts read "by the wall of Jezreel" (see comments on 2 Kgs 9:36-37).

Israel possesses the land at his pleasure, so is constrained to abide by his will. In fact, Israel metaphorically represents Yahweh's vineyard, for which he labored (cf. Isa 3:13-15; 5:1-7; John 15:1-17). When Ahab takes the inheritance of Naboth to turn it into a vegetable garden,[3] he undermines this reality. But his actions symbolize even more. In the larger narrative, the king of Israel takes from Yahweh the vineyard that had been entrusted to him for safekeeping and turns it into an idolatrous land.

As in the preceding episode, Ahab returns home **sullen and angry** (cf. 20:43). In verse 4, the narrator repeats for emphasis Naboth's words: **"I will not give you the inheritance of my fathers."**[4] Like a child who has not gotten his way, the king lies on his bed **sulking**, refusing even **to eat**. Entering the scene with no fanfare, the narrator names **Jezebel** simply **"his wife"** (vv. 5,7,25), to underscore the relationship between the two. The queen asks Ahab, **"Why are you so sullen? Why won't you eat?"** In response, Ahab recaps his exchange with Naboth, with an important omission. The king leaves out the reason for Naboth's refusal. For Jezebel, the Jezreelite's response becomes a snub with an obstinate, **"I will not give you my vineyard."** Ahab may be more the manipulator than the passive, childlike character who appears at first glance.[5] The queen sarcastically asks if this is the way a king acts and orders, **"Get up and eat! Cheer up. I'll get you the vineyard of Naboth the Jezreelite."** Jezebel names Naboth "the Jezreelite," as have the narrator and Ahab (vv. 1,4,6), which calls attention to his *inheritance* in Jezreel (cf. 15,16 [literally, "to take possession of the vineyard of Naboth *the Jezreelite*"]). Jezebel proceeds to orchestrate the sordid events that follow.

21:8-14 In **Ahab's name** and with **his seal**, the queen sends a letter to **the elders and nobles who live in Naboth's city with him**. The

---

[3]On the basis of the description of Egypt as a "vegetable garden" (Deut 11:10), some believe "vegetable garden" (v. 2) may ironically represent Egypt (Provan, *1 and 2 Kings*, pp. 157-158; Nelson, *First and Second Kings*, p. 141).

[4]Walsh believes that the subject of "and he said" (v. 4; obscured in the NIV, which attributes the statement once more to Naboth) is Ahab, so that Ahab is "muttering" Naboth's words on his way home (*1 Kings*, p. 319). In any case, the repetition of Naboth's statement establishes a frame for identifying important omissions when Ahab describes his exchange to Jezebel below.

[5]For a helpful discussion of Ahab's omissions and the implications for characterization, see ibid., pp. 320-321, 327.

naming ("who lived . . .") suggests that these men probably knew
Naboth (also v. 11), a fact which indicts their participation in
Jezebel's immoral scheme. The contents of her dispatch are represented as dialogue. In contrast with Obadiah (18:1-15), the elders
and nobles acquiesce and arrange for charges against Naboth. To
underscore their compliance, the narration follows almost verbatim
the contents of Jezebel's letter. The **scoundrels**[6] accuse Naboth of
blasphemy (cf. Lev 24:10-23; Exod 22:28). Literally, they charge him
with *"blessing* [בָּרַךְ, *bārak,* with the opposite meaning of "curse"; also
v. 10] **God and king**," in this instance, ironically suggesting that this
injustice is being perpetrated on a righteous man.[7] But the irony
goes even deeper. No doubt, **two** scoundrels are chosen and Naboth
is stoned **outside the city**, in order to give the appearance of adher-
ence to the law (cf. Deut 19:15-21; Lev 24:13-16) — by which, however, they are breaking the ethical and moral demands of the
covenant.[8] Also, the **day of fasting** and the disposition of Naboth
outside the city are ironically calculated to distance the community
from Naboth's sin (Deut 21:1-9).[9] Yet, the ambiguity in the text
about who actually stones Naboth suggests that all are guilty, the elders and nobles, the people, and the scoundrels who charge Naboth
with blasphemy.[10] Much like Achan in the days of Joshua (Josh 7:24-
26), Naboth is stoned to death — only this time for the greed of
another.

---

[6]Nothing is said about who these men are. They may have been some of
the poor, who are bought for this dastardly deed. In a way, everyone is
"bought" by Jezebel, especially Ahab, "who sells himself to do evil" (21:20).

[7]Hebrew sensibilities preclude using the expression *"curse* God." See, e.g.,
Job 1:5; 2:9, where *bārak* occurs with the same connotation.

[8]Provan notes that the elders were the "guardians of justice" (cf., e.g.,
Deut. 19:11-14) and observes that idolatry "inevitably leads to abandonment
of righteousness," which is clearly reflected in 21:25-26 (*1 and 2 Kings*,
pp. 158-159).

[9]Keith W. Whitelam, *The Just King: Monarchical Judicial Authority in
Ancient Israel*, JSOTSup 12 (Sheffield: JSOT Press, 1979), pp. 179, 181.

[10]Walsh argues that the scoundrels are the subject of v. 13b and therefore
the ones who lead the way in stoning Naboth. The scoundrels then report
to Jezebel (the letter was from Ahab), implying that they are plants from the
queen (*1 Kings*, pp. 324-325). While plausible, Walsh acknowledges that "the
people" (v. 13) could be the subject of "they took him . . . and stoned him,"
and the elders and nobles, though grammatically removed from v. 14, in
terms of narrative flow could also be the subject of "sent word to Jezebel."

Missing from this account is how Ahab was legally able to take possession of Naboth's property after his death. Second Kings 9:26 implies that Naboth's sons were also executed (perhaps as Achan's family, Josh 7:24-26). Without heirs, his *inheritance* (*naḥălāh*) should have been given to a brother, or "to the nearest relative in his clan, so that he may *possess* [יָרַשׁ, *yāraš*] it" (Num 27:8-11; cf. Lev 25:8 ff.; Deut 25:5-10). An interesting ostracon (i.e., inscribed potsherd, from the ninth [or perhaps seventh] century B.C.) has come to light from the antiquities market that illustrates Israel's inheritance laws. The ostracon represents a request to an unnamed official from a widow whose husband died without children. She asks, "[Let] your hand [be] with me and entrust to your maidservant the inheritance [*nḥlh*, the first occurrence of this word outside the Hebrew Bible] about which you spoke to 'Amasyahu [perhaps her husband]. As for the wheat field that is in Naamah, you have [already] given [it] to his brother." She has apparently been promised (and is making formal request for) part of the inheritance (or at least the use of it), even though she has no legal right to the property.[11] Her petition indicates that "the state" had some role in inheritance disputes. Jezebel apparently eliminates (and/or discourages) all claimants to the property of Naboth,[12] so that Ahab, as head of state, can take possession of the choice vineyard.

21:15-16 When Jezebel receives the communiqué that Naboth is dead, she enjoins Ahab, **"Get up and take possession [*yāraš*] of the vineyard of Naboth the Jezreelite that he refused to sell you."** Her word choice conjures up once more the conquest narrative. "Take possession" (*yāraš*) is one of the key words of the conquest (see, e.g., Deut 7:1,17; Josh 1:11,15) and also of this well-crafted account. In Kings, *yāraš* occurs only ten times, five times in this story

---

Would the authorities in Jezreel have complied so readily to the order from the king had they not known that Jezebel was behind the scene? The ambiguity appears to be intentional.

[11]Bordreuil, Israel, and Pardee, "Two New Hebrew Ostraca," 3,7,9-13; Shanks, "Three Shekels for the Lord," 28-32.

[12]This text may indicate that the king could confiscate the property of someone who was executed, although biblical law makes no such allowance (Provan, *1 and 2 Kings*, p. 160). Whitelam reasons that the meager evidence makes this conclusion tentative (*The Just King*, pp. 175-176).

(vv. 15,16,18,19,26).[13] In Deuteronomy 25:19; 26:1, the two important words of this narrative, "inheritance" (*naḥǎlāh*) and "possess" (*yāraš*), appear together. Yahweh gave Israel the land "to *possess* as an *inheritance*." In the verses that follow, "taking possession" will play an important role in assessing Ahab and his reign. On hearing the news of Naboth's death, the compliant king, who characteristically follows orders (e.g., 18:19-20,41-42), "gets **up and** goes **down to take possession** [*yāraš*] of [literally] the vineyard of Naboth the Jezreelite."

The narrator leaves an interesting gap at this point in the narrative. Jezebel only tells Ahab that Naboth is dead. The king does not inquire into the circumstances. Does he not know about the stoning (or care to ask), or has he been a participant all along in this affair? Does the reader see, once more, a passive Ahab, or one who has been more actively involved in these events than appears on the surface? Either way, he is not the righteous king of Psalm 72, who upholds justice and defends the oppressed — and will be held accountable for the murder of Naboth the Jezreelite (v. 19).[14]

2. The Word of Yahweh Censures Ahab and Elijah (21:17-29)

21:17-24 The word of Yahweh comes once more to Elijah. The man of God is directed to **"Go down to meet Ahab king of Israel, who rules in Samaria.[15] He is now in Naboth's vineyard, where he has gone to take possession** [*yāraš*] **of it."** Irony in these instructions ties together the preceding scenes and Yahweh's response. Jezebel told Ahab to "Get up [קוּם, *qûm*] and eat!" (v. 7) and "Get up [*qûm*] and take possession of the vineyard" (v. 15). Yahweh commands Elijah to (literally) "Get up [*qûm*] and go down to meet Ahab king of Israel,"[16] suggesting by contrast that Elijah obeys Yahweh, while Ahab has chosen to obey his wife Jezebel. Also, the repetition

---

[13]Four of the five other ocurrences in Kings refer to Yahweh *dispossessing* (the *Hiphil* form of *yrš*) the nations during the conquest (14:24; 2 Kgs 16:3; 17:8; 21:2).

[14]See Walsh, *1 Kings*, p. 326.

[15]The Hebrew reads, "who is in Samaria." Since Ahab is taking possession of Naboth's vineyard in Jezreel, the sense must be something like the NIV translation, "who reigns in Samaria."

[16]Brueggemann, *1 & 2 Kings*, p. 259.

of "to take possession" (*yāraš*), this time in the mouth of Yahweh, reinforces *taking possession* as a theme in the narrative. Elijah is to say to Ahab, **"This is what the LORD says** [i.e., "Thus says Yahweh"]: **Have you not murdered a man and seized** [*yāraš*, "taken possession of"] **his property?"**[17] Then Yahweh repeats, apparently for emphasis, the messenger formula: **"Say to him, '*This is what the LORD says*: In the place where dogs licked up Naboth's blood, dogs will lick up your blood—yes, yours!'"** Ahab's involvement in the death of Naboth the Jezreelite will not go unpunished. There will be life for life (cf. Num 35:31; Deut 19:21)!

When the prophet encounters Ahab, the king ironically exclaims, **"So you have found me, my enemy!"** Earlier, Ahab was the one looking for Elijah (18:1-15). The king acknowledges what the text has already made clear, that he is an adversary of Yahweh's prophet. The statement may also reflect some guilt on Ahab's part and perhaps an attempt to avoid Elijah after the Mount Carmel contest. Elijah explains that he has appeared **"because you have sold yourself to do evil in the eyes of the LORD."** The narrator will pick up Elijah's words when he characterizes Ahab's reign at the end of the scene (vv. 25-26). Without prefacing his remarks with the standard messenger formula ("thus says Yahweh"), Elijah launches into Ahab in first person as Yahweh: **"I am going to bring disaster . . . because you have provoked me to anger and have caused Israel to sin."** The oracle of judgment borrows from the oracles against Jeroboam and Baasha, the judgment against Jeroboam serving as its model (cf. 14:1-16; 16:1-4). Notably, "caused Israel to sin" (v. 22) suggests that Ahab has followed in the sin of Jeroboam (see comments on 13:33-34), even though he went beyond Jeroboam by introducing Baal worship into Israel (cf. 16:29-34). Concerning his queen, whom Elijah never addresses personally,[18] the prophet says, **"Dogs will devour Jezebel by the wall of Jezreel"** (which comes to pass in 2 Kgs 9:30-37). "Eating/not eating" continues as a theme (i.e., vineyard, vegetable garden, not eating, fasting, and now

---

[17]The prophetic judgment here (and in 20:35-43) indicates that in Israel the king was above the law. The only recourse for monarchical abuse of power was divine authority (Whitelam, *The Just King*, pp. 167-181).

[18]Kissling, *Reliable Characters*, p. 131.

devouring) that ties together the various scenes in this story.[19]
Elijah's words are an indictment on Ahab's entire house. All of his
descendants, and his idolatrous queen, will perish in the political
turmoil that the prophet says will come (see comments on 14:10-13).

Verses 23-24 may represent the narrator's voice.[20] Since there are
no quotation marks anywhere in the Hebrew Bible, it is not always
easy to distinguish between dialogue and the narrator's voice. The
judgment on Jezebel begins with וְגַם (w°gam, "and also"; see comments on 1:46-49), switches to third person ("the LORD says"), and
prefaces the narrator's obvious aside in verses 25-26. Jehu confirms
a word from Elijah that Jezebel would be devoured by dogs in the
plot of ground that belonged to Naboth (2 Kgs 9:36-37). However,
Jehu may remember an oracle that was given on another occasion,
which the narrator inserts here in his voice, to round out the
prophetic condemnation of Ahab's family. Jezebel also receives
divine condemnation.

On closer examination, Elijah's words once more are brought
into question. Twice, Yahweh instructs his prophet to say, "thus says
Yahweh" (v. 19), yet Elijah prefaces his word with no such messenger formula. Instead, with no signal, he assumes the divine voice and
in first person commences to pass judgment on Ahab (vv. 21-22). To
top it off, his message is not what Yahweh instructed him to give.
While the judgment that he speaks mirrors similar oracles to
Jeroboam and Baasha, he says nothing about dogs licking up Ahab's
blood **"in the place where dogs licked up Naboth's blood."**[21] In his
zeal for Yahweh (cf. 19:10,14) and righteous indignation over the
sins of the king of Israel, Elijah passes judgment on the entire house
of Ahab, even though Yahweh has said nothing about Ahab's
house.[22] Nevertheless, Yahweh's designs on Ahab will, at least in

---

[19]See Nelson, *First and Second Kings*, p. 140; Appler, "From Queen to
Cuisine," 55-71.

[20]See Walsh, *1 Kings*, pp. 331-332; Nelson, *First and Second Kings*, p. 143.

[21]Kissling demonstrates that Elijah changes Yahweh's directive in terms of
both content and form (*Reliable Characters*, p. 131; cf. pp. 127-132 for an
excellent discussion of Elijah's initiative in this instance). Olley asks if Elijah
"has taken initiative to embellish on behalf of YHWH?" ("YHWH and His
Zealous Prophet," 43).

[22]Kissling, *Reliable Characters*, p. 110. The fact that Yahweh later modifies

part, come about. After the battle of Ramoth Gilead, the dogs lick up the blood of the killed-in-action king of Israel. However, Yahweh's word to Elijah does not *exactly* come to pass. The dogs lick up the king's blood not in the vineyard of Naboth the Jezreelite, but at a pool in Samaria, where prostitutes bathe (22:37-38).[23] At that point, the narrator adds, "as the word of Yahweh had said" (v. 38) — not "as the word of Elijah had said." In 2 Kings 10:17, the storyteller narrates events that happen "according to the word of the LORD *spoken to Elijah*," suggesting that the storyteller is distinguishing the word of Yahweh from the word of Yahweh through Elijah (cf. 17:24). Does Yahweh's word not come to pass in all of its details because, at least in part, Elijah never speaks the prophecy?[24] Yahweh's intention for Ahab comes to pass — a life for a life — but the dogs lick up the king's blood in Samaria (22:38). The man of God appears here as a prophet who is going beyond his directive, as the word of Yahweh to Elijah will intimate at the end of the chapter.[25]

Elijah's judgment oracle (v. 28), but sustains his own personal judgment on Ahab (v. 19; cf. 22:34-38), reinforces this reading (p. 130).

[23]Nelson frames this inconsistency as "a mistake in prediction or sloppy fulfillment on God's part" (*First and Second Kings,* p. 138), while DeVries argues that this indicates the king of chapter 22 was not Ahab, but Joram (*1 Kings,* p. 257). Provan plausibly resolves the discrepancy by translating מָקוֹם (*māqôm,* "place") as "instead of" (cf. Hos 1:10) in 21:19: "*Instead of* dogs licking up Naboth's blood, dogs will lick up your blood — yes, yours!" (*1 and 2 Kings,* p. 160). However, a literary explanation has more promise. When Joram's death is viewed as symbolically representing (and fulfilling the oracles about) the death of Ahab, dogs licking up Ahab's blood in Samaria indicates incomplete fulfillment, which finally receives closure when Joram is thrown on "the field that belonged to Naboth the Jezreelite" (see comments on 2 Kgs 9:24-26).

[24]The fact that Yahweh alters Elijah's word to come to pass in the days of Ahab's son (v. 29) impacts the fulfillment of the prophetic statements in chapter 21 (see comments on 2 Kgs 9:24-26).

[25]An alternate reading would assume that Elijah received additional instructions from Yahweh. First Kings 21:19 simply summarizes Yahweh's judgment on Ahab, the language of which is not repeated in the annotated oracle that follows. If Jehu is describing this scene to Bidkar in 2 Kgs 9:25-26, a reader may assume that there is more than appears on the surface in 21:17-24. However, this view overlooks the repetition of the messenger formula in Yahweh's address to Elijah and its absence in his word to Ahab — and the clear, albeit restrained, reprimand that Elijah receives at the end of the chapter (see below).

21:25-26 Using Elijah's own words (v. 20), the storyteller breaks frame (vv. 23-24 may also be in the narrator's voice; see above) with a parenthetical statement that characterizes the reign of Ahab: **"There was never a man like Ahab, who sold himself to do evil . . . , urged on by Jezebel, his wife."** Like Achan at Jericho, the king of Israel sold himself for possessions, to the Aramean king for a treaty, and for the vineyard of Naboth the Jezreelite. His ruthless wife Jezebel was the evil influence behind his turn away from Yahweh. The narrator adds, **"He behaved in the vilest manner by going after idols, like the Amorites the LORD drove out** [*yāraš*, "dispossessed"] **before Israel."** The storyteller's language cements the correlations between the story of Ahab and the conquest narrative and reveals the author's theological point of view. As brought out in the comments on chapter 20, in direct opposition to Moses' instructions (Deut 7:1-4), the king of Israel 1) failed to destroy Ben-Hadad king of Aram, who was *dedicated* (*ḥāram*) to Yahweh, 2) showed him mercy, 3) made a treaty/covenant with him, and 4) took as his queen the Sidonian Jezebel. Concerning such marriages, Moses forewarned Israel: "They will turn your sons away from following me to serve other gods" (7:4). This is what happened to Ahab. Disobeying the Law of Moses, the king of Israel went after the **idols** of the people of the land and, in the process, became one of them — **like the Amorites the LORD** *drove out* **before Israel.** The same language will later be used to explain how Manasseh (the southern kingdom's Ahab) led Judah into captivity (2 Kgs 21:11). For an exilic audience, the accounts of Ahab and Manasseh explain why they have been *dispossessed* from the land of their *inheritance*.

21:27-29 In verses that are often missing when the story of Ahab is retold, the storyteller narrates Ahab's response to Elijah's condemnation. **"When Ahab heard . . ."** are the same words that preface the king's trek to Jezreel in verse 16.[26] Only, now a penitent king tears **his clothes, puts on sackcloth, and fasts**. Lying in **sackcloth**, he walks around **meekly**. The contrast with his behavior at the beginning of the story could not be greater. When Ahab could not get

---

[26]Walsh, *1 Kings*, p. 335; Nelson, *First and Second Kings*, pp. 142-143. Olley demonstrates that vv. 27-28 are integral to the composition, when he observes that vv. 16,27 are parallel with vv. 17,28 ("YHWH and His Zealous Prophet," 43).

what he wanted from Naboth, he went around "sullen and angry," and he would not eat. Now, the king of Israel walks around "meekly," and he fasts! The word of Yahweh comes again to Elijah: **"Have you noticed how Ahab has humbled himself before me? Because he has humbled himself, I will not bring this disaster in his day, but I will bring it on his house in the days of his son."** When Yahweh says that Ahab "humbled himself" (כָּנַע, *kānaʿ*), he uses a word employed elsewhere in Kings only of Josiah (2 Kgs 22:19).[27] Ahab "repents," and Yahweh extends grace to the disobedient king. Yahweh then qualifies the word of Elijah. The **disaster** on Ahab's **house** will happen **in the days of his son** (cf. 2 Kgs 9:14-29). In the same way, judgment will be postponed for Judah until the days of Josiah's son Zedekiah (see comments on 2 Kgs 22–23; 25:27-30). Delayed retribution represents Yahweh's many mercies in Kings.

At first glance, it seems odd that this part of the Ahab story should end with a word to Elijah and no additional message for Ahab. Yahweh does not direct Elijah to carry this word to the contrite king. The scene ends abruptly, suggesting that Elijah, not Ahab, is the focal point at the end of the story. As in the theophany on Mount Horeb (19:9-18), this penitent-king episode ends with Yahweh speaking to Elijah. At Horeb, Yahweh put Elijah in his place by saying, in effect, "You are not the only one; there are seven thousand who have not bowed down to Baal" (v. 18). When this scene ends, Yahweh puts the prophet in his place with a rhetorical question: "Have you noticed how Ahab has humbled himself before me?" The overzealous prophet of Yahweh was apparently a man who was much more comfortable with the fire of Yahweh than with his amazing grace — who was surprised, with many modern readers, that mercy was extended even to a wicked king like Ahab.[28]

Remarkably, Yahweh still honors the word of his prophet. While Yahweh alters Elijah's word by saying that the judgment on Ahab's *house* (the part that Elijah added[29]) would happen in the days of the king's son, when the word comes to pass the narrator will say that

---

[27]Chronicles, however, takes up *kānaʿ* ("to be humble") as a major theme (see, e.g., 2 Chr 33:10-13,19).

[28]Olley wonders if "the narrator is leaving the reader to assume that Elijah does not like the message [of grace]?" ("YHWH and His Zealous Prophet," 43).

[29]See Kissling, *Reliable Characters*, p. 130.

Ahab's family was destroyed "according to the word of the LORD spoken to Elijah" (2 Kgs 10:17).[30] As Yahweh's representative, Elijah passes judgment on the abominable acts of the house of Ahab in language that mirrors the condemnation of the two previous regimes in Israel. However, the prophet misuses "prophetic initiative" (see comments on 16:34 and "Excursus: Elijah in Context") when he goes beyond the direct instructions Yahweh had given him. Yahweh modifies Elijah's word, but upholds the judgment that the man of God pronounced on the house of Ahab. The prophet's word is the word of Yahweh, which comes to pass. With the rhetorical question at the end of the story, Elijah is subtly reprimanded, and continues to learn more about Yahweh. Having already seen that Yahweh does not always thunder (see "Excursus: Elijah in Context"), he now knows that the awesome fire of Yahweh may be turned aside, if only for a time, by his incomparable grace. In exile, those who had been *disinherited* from the land would be encouraged by Yahweh's grace toward Ahab.

---

[30]In 2 Kgs 9:6-10, an unnamed prophet gives an oracle of judgment on the house of Ahab in language similar to Elijah's oracle, although he does not receive this word from either Yahweh or Elisha. The prophet goes beyond Elisha's instructions, reinforcing the idea of prophetic initiative, but, unlike Elijah, his word does not conflict with a specific directive from Yahweh.

1 KINGS 22

D. YAHWEH'S WORD AGAINST AHAB COMES TO PASS
(22:1-40)

1. Micaiah Prophesies Ahab's Death (22:1-28)

22:1-5 For three years, hostilities between Israel and Aram are in abeyance. When **Jehoshaphat king of Judah** visits Ahab in Samaria, **the king of Israel** proposes a campaign[1] to retake from Ben-Hadad the strategic Ramoth Gilead in the Transjordan.[2] Not until verse 20, and then again only in his death notice (vv. 39-40), is the king of Israel named "Ahab." The king of Judah is named "Jehoshaphat" (meaning "Yahweh has judged") twelve times in the story. In chapter 20, the contrast in naming between Ahab and Ben-Hadad called attention to an important theological aspect of the narrative — the battle was between Yahweh's king and the "son of the storm god Hadad" (see comments on 20:1-12). In this story, the interplay between the "king of Israel" and "Yahweh judges" bolsters the

---

[1]In Chronicles, Ahab *urged* (סות, *sûth*) Jehoshaphat (2 Chr 18:2), the same verb the Chronicler uses when Satan *incites* (*sûth*) David (1 Chr 21:1) to take a census (Hicks, *1 & 2 Chronicles*, 367).

[2]For many scholars, chapter 22 began as a battle report that was later augmented with prophet-story additions (see, e.g., DeVries, *1 Kings*, 265-266), yet there are reasons to believe that it is a composition with its own integrity, including "a typical and unifying literary skeleton" (Burke O. Long, *1 Kings*, p. 233). Also, the above discussion of chapter 20 suggests that the developmental view of ch. 22 (and also ch. 21 with a similar "prophet narrative," vv. 17 ff.) is unlikely. In ch. 20, the storyteller's allusions to the conquest narrative and Deut 7:1-4 demonstrate that the account of Ahab's battles with Ben-Hadad, with both a "prophet narrative" and "battle report," is a unified composition (see comments on ch. 20). For the question of whether this battle report belongs to the reign of Ahab, see Cogan, *1 Kings*, p. 496; and "Excursus: Ahab's Wars with Aram."

underlying theme of the narrative. Yahweh judges Ahab for what he has done as king of Israel.[3] Since he is only a minor character in this story, the king of Aram is not named Ben-Hadad in chapter 22 (see comments on 20:1-12). **"I am as you are . . ."** (cf. 2 Kgs 3:7) may indicate that a covenant relationship now exists between Israel and Judah.[4] Following the division of the kingdom, there was conflict between the two emerging nation states (see v. 44; cf. 14:30; 15:6-7, 16-22). The Chronicler explains that Jehoshaphat's relationship with Ahab is secured with a marriage alliance between the two (2 Chr 18:1). The narrator in Kings has been silent about this development. If the king of Judah is acting on treaty obligations,[5] apparently as the inferior partner,[6] his actions are more easily explained. Jehoshaphat asks Ahab to **seek counsel of the LORD** (literally, "seek the word of Yahweh"), which suggests to the reader that he is a righteous king (cf. v. 43).

22:6-9 The king of Israel *gathers* (קָבַץ, *qābaṣ*) **the prophets—about four hundred men**. The number connects this story with the contest on Carmel, where Ahab *gathered* (*qābaṣ*) four hundred and fifty prophets of Baal, who were taken by Elijah to the Kishon and executed (18:20,22,40).[7] In contrast with the Mount Carmel narrative, the four hundred prophets are not named. Are they prophets of Yahweh or Baal — or the four hundred prophets of Asherah who were absent on Mount Carmel (cf. 18:19)? Perhaps they are prophets who are qualified practitioners for various deities (like Balaam, Num 22–24)? Their words may give them away. The four hundred prophets declare that **"the Lord** (אֲדֹנָי, *'ădōnāy*[8]) **will give it into the king's hand."** Only after Zedekiah speaks in the name of Yahweh

---

[3]Also, the formal "king of Israel" intimates more distance than the personal "Jehoshaphat," who as a righteous king is in a closer relationship with Yahweh.

[4]The language could also represent court etiquette (Cogan, *1 Kings*, p. 489).

[5]Hicks suggests "a mutual defense obligation" (*1 & 2 Chronicles*, p. 367).

[6]See Walsh, *1 Kings*, 344; Brueggemann, *1 & 2 Kings*, pp. 275-276.

[7]Provan notices other numerical links with earlier scenes: 7,000 in 19:18 and 20:15; and 32 in 20:1 and 22:31 (*1 and 2 Kings*, p. 166).

[8]The Hebrew MT reads *'ădōnāy* ("Lord"), while other manuscripts read YHWH ("LORD"). The MT may reflect a scribal change to *'ădōnāy*, more appropriate in the mouths of the false prophets of Ahab. However, in v. 12 the same prophets prophesy in the name of Yahweh, not *'ădōnāy*. The literary explanation offered here is sufficient reason to follow the MT.

(v. 11) do these prophets affirm that Yahweh ("the LORD") will give victory to the king (v. 12) — suggesting they are following his lead and are not prophets of Yahweh. Also, Ahab's prophets may be practiced at equivocating. Not only is "Lord" ambiguous, they do not specify which king will triumph.[9] Perhaps Jehoshaphat is able to see through their veiled speech.

Ahab's question to the prophets recalls the inquiries made by the people of Israel in the war with Benjamin (Judg 20:1-28). In that story, inquiring of Yahweh was only a formality, the people "as one man" (vv. 1,8,11) having already decided their course of action. As in the divine council scene to follow, Yahweh deceptively counseled Israel to attack. Only after two defeats did they approach Yahweh with fasting and appropriate offerings. Phinehas (v. 28) asked Ahab's question (1 Kgs 22:6): **"Shall I go to war . . . or shall I refrain?"** In both stories, the answer is **"Go"—"for the Lord will give it into the king's hand"**/"for tomorrow I will give them into your hands" (v. 6/Judg 20:28). However, in Judges 20:28, Yahweh has finally decided to fight for Israel. In the battle against Aram, Yahweh will defeat the armies of Ahab and Jehoshaphat.

Continuing the ambiguity concerning Ahab's prophets, Jehoshaphat's question to Ahab (v. 7) may be translated: **"Is there not a prophet of the LORD here whom we can inquire of?"** (NIV), or "Is there no other prophet of the LORD here . . . ?" (*NRSV*).[10] Either way, the king of Judah specifically asks for a prophet of Yahweh, and his question suggests that he has some concerns about the prophetic word the two kings are receiving. Ahab acknowledges that there is one other prophet, **"through whom we can inquire of the LORD,"** but this prophet **"never prophesies anything good about me, but always bad."** In the war with Ben-Hadad, Ahab has received favorable messages from prophets (ch. 20), but he has also received oracles of judgment (chs. 20, 21). In fact, the reader anticipates the entrance of Elijah the Tishbite and is somewhat surprised by the introduction to **Micaiah son of Imlah.**[11] The fact that another prophet of Yahweh pronounces evil concerning Ahab reinforces the judgment in preceding scenes and establishes expectations for the

---

[9]For the ambiguities in their speech, see Walsh, *1 Kings*, p. 345.

[10]See Provan, *1 and 2 Kings*, p. 165.

[11]Walsh makes a similar observation (*1 Kings*, p. 346).

message of doom that surely must follow. King Ahab sends for the prophet Micaiah.

22:10-14 The scene with the two kings seated on their thrones outside the **gate of Samaria**[12] with **prophets prophesying before them** most likely was a common occurrence. At Tel Dan, archaeologists uncovered in the outer courtyard of the city gate a low platform with corresponding column bases that probably supported a canopied throne.[13] Such a throne may have held the image of a deity, representing a high place in the gate (cf. 2 Kgs 23:8), or it may have been the place where the king sat for judgment or for occasions like what is represented in this text. What appears at first to be incidental information, the kings were **dressed in their royal robes**, will turn out to be important to the plot in the battle which follows. One king will wear his robes, and the other will disguise himself in order to counter the word of a prophet (vv 29-40). In the presence of the two kings, the prophets of Ahab are *prophesying*, suggesting not that they are giving oracles but that they are involved in some kind of ecstatic behavior (cf. 1 Sam 10:9-11; 19:18-24). Another allusion to the prophets of Baal who also were "prophesying" as they jumped about their altar (18:26-29) seems probable.

Zedekiah son of Kenaanah emerges as their leader. The **iron horns** that he fashions are appropriate for representing Yahweh or Baal, each one often portrayed with bull imagery (see comments on 12:25-33), and may reflect a form of sympathetic magic (cf. Jer 28:10-14). Zedekiah's name with the Yahwistic ending *yāh* (יְהוּ, *yāhû* in v. 24, represented by –iah in English) suggests that he is a prophet of Yahweh. However, his patronym, **son of Kenaanah**, adds to the ambiguity already introduced in the story. In Hebrew, Kenaanah (כְּנַעֲנָה, *kᵊnaʿănāh*) has the same consonants as Canaan (כְּנַעַן, *kᵊnaʿan*). Zedekiah is a son of Canaan, which no doubt insinuates that he could not be a true prophet of Yahweh.[14] Nevertheless, he prefaces his pronouncement with the messenger formula for Yahweh, **"This is what the Lord says"** and speaks for him, **"With these** [iron horns]

---

[12]The word translated "the threshing floor" (גֹּרֶן, *gôren*) in the NIV may simply refer to an open place outside the gate.

[13]Biran, *Biblical Dan*, pp. 238-241.

[14]Walsh suggests that this ambiguity may reflect the situation in Israel where the differences between the worship of Yahweh and the worship of Baal are blurred (*1 Kings*, p. 347, n. 5).

you will gore the Arameans until they are destroyed." This time naming Yahweh, **all the other prophets** prophesy, **"The LORD will give it into the king's hand"** (cf. Judg 20:28). The **messenger** sent to secure Micaiah[15] relays that the prophets speak **as one man** (cf. Judg 20:1,8,11) and cautions him to give a similar, favorable message. As already implied, this suggests that Ahab prefers prophets who are "yes-men." Micaiah answers that he can only speak **"what the LORD tells me"** (cf. Deut 18:18).

22:15-18 When Micaiah arrives, Ahab asks the prophet the same question he had posed to his prophets, except that he now frames it in the plural: **"Shall *we* go up . . . "** (cf. v. 6).[16] Including Jehoshaphat in his intentions may be calculated to predispose Micaiah to offer a favorable message. The stratagem appears to work. Micaiah's response mirrors the word of the prophets (v. 12): **"Attack and be victorious . . . for the LORD will give it into the king's hand."** However, King Ahab is not swayed. There must have been something in the prophet's intonation that smacked of sarcasm, indicating that he was not telling the truth. Ahab breaks in, **"How many times must I make you swear to tell me nothing but the truth in the name of the LORD?"** The phrase "in the name of Yahweh" stands out. According to Moses, it is a prerequisite for a message from Yahweh (Deut 18:19,22). Micaiah will speak in the name of Yahweh (1 Kgs 22:17,19-23), as have Zedekiah and the group of four hundred prophets (vv. 6,11-12). Which one, Micaiah or Ahab's prophets, speaks for Yahweh? The prophet sees **"all Israel scattered on the hills like sheep without a shepherd."** He adds, **"These people have no master"**[17] — meaning Israel will be defeated, and her king killed. Ahab blames the word on the prophet, who always prophesies **"only bad"** about the king.

22:19-23 Micaiah prefaces his speech with an oracle formula, **"Hear the word of the LORD"** (cf., e.g., Isa 1:10; Jer 2:4; Hos 4:1),

---

[15]Micaiah also bears a Yahwistic name, with the meaning, "Who is like Yahweh?"

[16]In v. 15, the NIV is inconsistent, translating the last part of the phrase in the singular, following a Greek reading, while translating the first part of the phrase in the plural. The Hebrew (MT) is plural in both instances.

[17]"Master" is plural in Hebrew. Walsh suggests that this could intimate the "plural of rank" or that Jehoshaphat could also die in battle (*1 Kings*, p. 349), which does not occur.

but does not speak for Yahweh in first person. In his third person report, the prophet sees the throne room of heaven with **all the host of heaven** surrounding the throne (cf. Job 1:6-12) — in much the same way the kings of Israel and Judah are seated on their thrones outside the gate of Samaria. Micaiah reports seeing one spirit offer to become **a lying spirit in the mouths** of the king's prophets, in order to **entice** [פָּתָה, *pāthāh*] **Ahab into attacking Ramoth Gilead and going to his death there**. The NIV obscures the playful ambiguity in Yahweh's request (v. 20): "Who will entice Ahab to go up and *fall upon* [as "enjoin the battle at" or as "die in battle at"] Ramoth Gilead?" As the story plays out, both meanings will prove to be true. Yet, nowhere does the narrator confirm the prophet's vision; it is all reported speech. Micaiah claims, **"The LORD has put a lying spirit in the mouths of all these prophets,"**[18] and announces, **"The LORD has decreed disaster** [literally, 'evil'] **for you."** Yahweh will return Ahab's evil back onto the disobedient king, who has already been *enticed* (*pāthāh*) to worship other gods (see Deut 11:16).

So, adjures the prophet, Yahweh is *deceiving* Ahab. Ironically, the king's prophets *are* speaking for Yahweh, but not the truth. While initially disconcerting for modern readers, this role for Yahweh is not inconsistent with stories that lie in the background of this text.[19] Already noted is the narrative in Israel's past where Yahweh twice advised the children of Israel to go up against the men of Benjamin, both times allowing Israel to be defeated (Judg 20:1-35). There also are allusions in the Ahab story to the reign of Saul.[20] Like Ahab, Saul extended mercy to a king who had been *devoted to destruction* (1 Samuel 15; see comments on 1 Kgs 20:35-43). In addition, as Ahab *inquired* (דָּרַשׁ, *dāraš*, 22:5,7,8) of "his prophets" before the battle of Ramoth Gilead, Saul *inquired* (*dāraš*, 1 Sam 28:7) of the medium of Endor before the battle of Mount Gilboa, *disguising himself* (חָפַשׂ, *hāphaś*, v. 8) in order to obtain a vision from her. Ahab will try

---

[18]Because "spirit" in the Hebrew text carries the article (i.e., "the spirit"), Walsh suggests that this is "the spirit of Yahweh" (ibid., p. 351).

[19]A "lying spirit" is also not inconsistent with New Testament teaching. In 2 Thess 2:11-12, Paul indicates that God sends those who do not accept the truth "a powerful delusion so that they will believe the lie" (see Hicks, *1 & 2 Chronicles*, pp. 371-372).

[20]For parallels between Ahab and Saul, see Provan, *1 and 2 Kings*, pp. 163-165.

to elude the word of Micaiah by *disguising himself* (*ḥāphaś*, 1 Kgs 22:30) in the battle of Ramoth Gilead. These connections reinforce another that sheds light on Micaiah's "lying spirit." An evil spirit from Yahweh, a spirit that is not unlike the lying spirit that deceives Ahab, troubled the character of Saul (cf. 1 Sam 16:14-16,23; 18:10; 19:9). In both cases, Yahweh uses a malevolent spirit to bring down a king of Israel who has chosen his own way.

22:24-28 Zedekiah **slaps** Micaiah **in the face** and sarcastically asks, **"Which way did the spirit from the LORD go?"** Micaiah retorts that Zedekiah **will find out on the day** he goes **to hide in an inner room**, recalling the Aramean king who hid in an inner room *in defeat* (1 Kgs 20:30). King Ahab commands that Micaiah be held in Samaria until after the battle. His order is prefaced by the standard messenger formula ("This is what the king says"), which by contrast sets his word against the word of the prophet of Yahweh. When Ahab concludes his decree with "until I return safely [literally, 'in peace']," he may be trying to counteract the word announced by Yahweh's prophet.[21] In prison, Micaiah will suffer with a fare of **bread and water**. At the beginning of the Ahab narrative, Obadiah hides prophets of Yahweh and feeds them bread and water. Now at the end, one of Ahab's false prophets will hide in defeat. In confinement, a prophet of Yahweh will be served bread and water — perhaps intimating that, as a representative of Yahweh, he also will be *sustained*, and his word upheld.

Micaiah has the last word: **"If you ever return safely, the LORD has not spoken through me."** The prophet exits, reminding the king and people of the only true test of a prophet. Once more there is resonance with Deuteronomy. Moses affirmed, "If what a prophet proclaims in the name of the LORD does not take place or come true, that is a message the LORD has not spoken" (Deut 18:21). After having applied the law of the prophet (18:14-22) to the prophet Elijah, who steps just beyond the command of Yahweh (see "Excursus: Elijah in Context," and comments on 21:17-29), the storyteller concludes Ahab's reign with a scene that explains how to identify a false

---

[21]Brandon L. Fredenburg, "When Prophets Lie and Kings Win: A Narrative-Critical Examination of First Kings 22:1-38" (paper presented at the Christian Scholars Conference, Lubbock Christian University, 22 July 1995), p. 13.

prophet, one who speaks presumptuously. While the text infers that it is not always easy to determine a true prophet from a false one (with lying spirits and true prophets who lie, etc.), the bottom line is, "Does the prophet's word come to pass?" If so, Yahweh has upheld the prophet's word; he speaks for God!

Micaiah adds, **"Mark my words, all you people!"** — a statement that is exactly the same as the opening words in the book of Micah (a form of the name Micaiah; see Micah 1:2). Even though there are reasons to believe the phrase is a later addition, the book of Micah is an appropriate backdrop for the story of Micaiah.[22] In Micah 1:2-7, the eighth-century Micah foresees the fall of Samaria because of idolatry: "I will make Samaria a heap of rubble, a place for planting vineyards. . . . All her idols will be broken to pieces" (vv. 6-7). If the reference to Micah belongs to the original composition (in the period of the exile), the storyteller ironically ends Micaiah's dialogue with an allusion to the eighth-century prophet's invective against Israel, which in effect moves beyond the defeat of Ahab to the fall of Samaria. But the prophet's words stand out for another reason. In Micaiah's parting comment, an important detail withheld is finally revealed. There is an audience of "the people" who witness this exchange. In fact, a careful rereading of the story indicates that much of it is told from the point of view of an onlooker (who is able to overhear conversations), of someone in the audience that day (see especially the narration in vv. 10 ff.). As the people on Mount Carmel were challenged to consider who really is God, Yahweh or Baal, so the crowd gathered at the gate of Samaria is challenged to consider who really speaks for Yahweh. An audience in exile, the actual audience of this text, already knows the outcome. The defeat of Ahab foreshadows the final destruction and exile of Israel and Judah — each of whom forgot who speaks for Yahweh.

---

[22]Provan, *1 and 2 Kings*, p. 166. The phrase is not in important Greek texts (the Codex Vaticanus or the Lucianic recension), and many believe it is a later, marginal note (see Gray, *I & II Kings*, p. 447; Cogan, *1 Kings*, p. 493). If it is a scribal addition, the reference to Micah is not inappropriate. Also, without the connection to Micah or the Greek variants, there would be no reason to question Micaiah's words. His statement works well in the composition as it stands.

2. Ahab Is Killed at Ramoth Gilead (22:29-40)

22:29-38 The **king of Israel and Jehoshaphat** go out to reacquire **Ramoth Gilead**, located across the Jordan in the territory of Gad. A city of refuge and the center of one of Solomon's administrative districts (see Josh 20:8; 1 Kgs 4:13), Ramoth Gilead was an important Israelite town on the northern border that now is in Aramean hands.[23] Less concerned with political/military history, the storyteller does not indicate when the king of Aram took the city. When relations between the two were last cited, there was a treaty between Damascus and Samaria. However, the king of Aram may not have kept his promise to return the cities his father had taken (20:34).[24] Ahab proposes that Jehoshaphat go into battle dressed in his **royal robes**, while he **disguise**s himself. The king of Israel may know about Ben-Hadad's designs to get him (v. 31). He also wants to frustrate the oracle Micaiah has uttered against him, which suggests something about his worldview. In Canaanite religion, manipulating prophets and deities was a matter of course.

The ploy almost works. Ben-Hadad's forces have been ordered to go after Ahab alone, no doubt reflecting bitter feelings because the king of Israel, a member of Ben-Hadad's military coalition, has attacked the Arameans (see "Excursus: Ahab's Wars with Aram"). Mistaking Jehoshaphat for the king of Israel, Ben-Hadad's **chariot commanders** attack the king of Judah. When the king cries out, they recognize their mistake and turn away. In the account in Chronicles, Jehoshaphat cries out to Yahweh, who delivers the king by drawing the enemy away (2 Chr 18:31-32). Then, an unidentified soldier, **at random**, draws **his bow** and lets fly an arrow that just happens to **hit the king of Israel between sections of his armor** — the king who had *disguised* himself for safety (cf. 1 Kgs 20:35-43). The reader knows, however, that this was not just by happenstance. Just three years before, Ahab had defeated Aram by the word of Yahweh, inflicting "heavy losses [מַכָּה, *makkāh*] on the Arameans" (20:21). Now, **the blood from his wound** [*makkāh*] flows **onto the floor of the chariot**.

In the evening, the king dies. Like sheep without a shepherd

---

[23]Many identify Ramoth Gilead with Tell Ramith, located 7 km south of Ramtha (see Patrick M. Arnold, "Ramoth-Gilead [Place]," in *ABD*).

[24]Walsh, *1 Kings*, p. 343.

(v. 17), the army disperses. Ahab is **brought to Samaria** and **buried** there. With his blood pooled up in the bottom, the king's chariot is washed **at a pool in Samaria (where the prostitutes bathed)**. Dogs **lick up his blood, as the word of the LORD had declared**. Provan argues that there is no need to translate זֹנוֹת (*zōnôth*, "prostitutes," v. 38) with the unusual connotation of "weapons" (as in the NIV text note) because of possible connections with Deuteronomy 23:17-18 [18-19], where Israel is commanded not to bring the wages of a prostitute or (literally) a "dog" ("male prostitute" in the NIV) into the house of Yahweh to pay a vow. Coupling prostitutes and dogs in verse 38, "remind[s] the reader, by association of ideas, of the whole idolatrous career that has brought Ahab to this ignominious end."[25] All of this happens according to the word of Yahweh, who informed Elijah that as the dogs licked up the blood of Naboth, so dogs would lick up the blood of Ahab (21:19). That this takes place in Samaria and not Jezreel indicates that Yahweh's work is not yet complete. Final closure will come in the death of Ahab's son Joram in Jezreel, which will symbolically represent the death of Ahab (see comments on 1 Kgs 21:19; 2 Kgs 9:24-26). Three different prophets have given a word of judgment to Ahab (20:35-43; 21:17-28; 22:1-28).[26] As Micaiah son of Imlah, the last of the three, had prophesied, the king of Israel does not return alive (22:17,28).

22:39-40 The concluding formula for Ahab's reign now appears (cf. 16:29-34). The narrator avers that the details of Ahab's building exploits can be found in the **annals of the kings of Israel**. That more is not said about his building projects underscores that the storyteller's concerns are theological. Archaeology has demonstrated that Ahab was one of the more prominent kings of the northern kingdom (see comments on 20:1-12). Numerous sites in northern Israel were **fortified** in the ninth century. At Samaria, Beth-Shean, Hazor, Dan, Jezreel, and Dor, archaeologists have uncovered substantial fortifications, and other structures like the Megiddo stables, that most likely were constructed by Ahab.[27] For example, the fortified

---

[25]Provan, *1 and 2 Kings*, p. 164.

[26]Peter D. Miscall, "Elijah, Ahab and Jehu: A Prophecy Fulfilled," *Prooftexts* 9 (Jan. 1989): 74-75.

[27]Stern, "How Bad Was Ahab?" 24-29; see Dever, *Biblical Writers Know*, pp. 163-164, 239-241.

acropolis at Jezreel, excavated in 1990–91 by David Ussishkin, with a casemate wall (a double wall with connecting walls forming interior "rooms," typical of Iron Age Palestine) and towers dates solely to the ninth century B.C.[28] Also, approximately five hundred fragments of ivory plaques (decoration for furniture) were exposed in the ruins of the palace at Samaria, directly confirming the reference to Ahab's palace **inlaid with ivory**. It was a building with costly furniture adorned with ivory.[29]

The last phrase in the concluding formula (i.e., **Ahab rested with his fathers**) usually indicates a peaceful death. In the book of Kings, Ahab is the only king dying a violent death of whom this statement is made. Typically, the note about Ahab has been viewed as inappropriate to the plot of the prophetic narrative and battle story to which it forms a conclusion, reflecting compositional layers.[30] A literary explanation is more helpful.[31] Ahab's violent death and peaceful burial correspond with the prophetic word concerning his demise. The king of Israel would fall at Ramoth-Gilead (22:20); however, the destruction of his house, foretold by Elijah, would come to pass in the days of his son (21:29). Ahab dies on the field of battle and is buried in Samaria, yet his lineage continues. In context, the burial notice calls attention to the prophetic word of delay in retribution on the house of Ahab. In addition, the language resonates with the account of the death of Josiah at the end of the book. Josiah also dies a violent death on the field of battle and is carried in a chariot back to Jerusalem where he is buried (2 Kgs 23:29-30). While the phrase "rested with his fathers" does not appear in his burial notice, the prophetess Huldah conveys this word of Yahweh to Josiah: "I

---

[28]David Ussishkin and John Woodhead, "Excavations at Tel Jezreel 1990–1991: Preliminary Report," *TA* 19 (1992): 3-56; idem., "Excavations at Tel Jezreel 1994–1996: Third Preliminary Report," *TA* 24 (1997): 6-72; see Dever, *Biblical Writers Know*, pp. 239-241.

[29]See Dever, *Biblical Writers Know, pp.* 237-239. Further illustrating Canaanite influence on the house of Ahab, Eleanor Ferris Beach demonstrates that the ivories from Samaria represent the entire range of motifs that decorated the ceremonial furniture used in certain religious feasts, like the מַרְזֵחַ (*marzēaḥ*) of Amos 6:4-7 ("The Samaria Ivories, *Marzeaḥ*, and Biblical Text," *BA* 56/2 [1993]: 94-104).

[30]See Cogan, *1 Kings*, pp. 495-496.

[31]Also, Galil demonstrates that there are exceptions in the regnal formulas (*Chronology of the Kings*, pp. 34-35).

will gather you to your fathers, and you will be buried in peace" (22:20). The death of Ahab foreshadows the death of Josiah. Both Ahab and Josiah die in battle and are buried "in peace." Both humble themselves before Yahweh (1 Kgs 21:27-29; 2 Kgs 22:19), and retribution is delayed (see comments on 2 Kings 23; 25:27-30). For the house of Ahab, it comes in the days of Ahab's son Joram (cf. ch. 9). For the house of David, it comes in the days of Josiah's son Zedekiah (cf. ch. 25). At Ahab's death, **Ahaziah his son** becomes king in his place.

EXCURSUS

THE REIGN OF AHAB (16:29–22:40)

The account of Ahab's reign is interwoven with the career of the prophet Elijah. In fact, the first episodes of the story (chs. 17–19) revolve more around Elijah than Ahab, who is only a minor character. In the second half of the narrative (chs. 20–22), the roles are reversed. Ahab as king of Israel is the major player, the prophet Elijah receiving only a limited, though important, part in two scenes that conclude the act of Naboth's vineyard. In each of the three chapters where Ahab is the protagonist, there is also a prophetic judgment oracle against the king of Israel.[33] With two contrasting stories (the story of Elijah and the story of Ahab), the structure allows the author to make an important theological point about Ahab's role in introducing the worship of foreign gods into the northern kingdom. As Walsh brings out, "The single focus is the struggle between Yahweh and Baal for the loyalties of Israel and its royal house."[34] But the structure also enables the storyteller to highlight the significant role that prophetic discourse plays in the dynamic of Yahweh's judgment on Israel's kings. In this vein, he is also able to reinforce the basic teaching of Deuteronomy 18:14-22, that the word of Yahweh in the mouth of the true prophet is something that comes to pass. However, even prophets of Yahweh are human. Providing commentary on Deuteronomy 18, the narrative also says that any prophet who would presume to speak in the name of Yahweh must submit to his word (see "Excursus: Elijah in Context"). Yet, even then, Yahweh is able to use imperfect prophets (e.g., Elijah), even false prophets (e.g., Ahab's four hundred), for his purposes.

One of the more interesting features of this story is the characterization of Ahab, a tragic figure in Old Testament narrative. While extrabiblical data indicate that he was a politically significant king of Israel (see comments on 20:1-12), a surface reading of the text suggests that the king was weak. In fact, Ahab often appears rather

---

[33]For an excellent discussion of the structure of the Elijah and Ahab stories, see Walsh, *1 Kings*, pp. 361-365.

[34]Ibid., p. 364.

docile, acting at the direction of others (cf., e.g., 18:19-20; 21:15-16). Nevertheless, the amount of narrative time that his reign receives indicates that he was one of the more important monarchs in the history of Israel. And, instead of a docile figure, the king can also be seen as passively aggressive. In particular, ambiguities in the matter of Naboth's vineyard indicate that he is a complex character. His actions can be read as being manipulative. Surely he knows how Jezebel will react to Naboth's snub. And why doesn't the king ask how Naboth dies? Perhaps he is more involved than the surface details indicate (see comments on 21:1-16).

Brandon Fredenburg suggests that a controlling monarch dominates his scenes in chapter 22.[35] That Ahab's prophets are "yes-men" illustrates this character flaw and the style of his rule. In fact, the king is so concerned with controlling people and events that he cannot accept Micaiah's first word and demands that the prophet tell him "nothing but the truth in the name of the LORD" (v. 16), even though the truth will offset the favorable word he has received. In a final attempt to exercise control over Micaiah and his god Yahweh, Ahab imprisons the prophet and disguises himself in battle. He disguises himself to frustrate the word of Yahweh, which is able to overcome even the schemes of powerful kings like Ahab. Fredenburg writes, "Similar to King Midas, everything Ahab tries to control ends up controlling him,"[36] especially the God he has chosen to oppose. Yet, even with all his foibles, Ahab still has the capacity to humble himself, an act that Yahweh acknowledges when he extends to this wicked king a measure of grace (21:28).

Nevertheless, however one wishes to characterize Ahab, his controlling nature in chapter 22 suggests more than characterization. It also reflects his worldview and the depths to which idolatry permeates his reign. The sin of idolatry is not just the sin of worshiping other deities. At its core, it is the sin of trying to control one's own life and world, a man becoming his own god. For the people of Israel, this meant trying to control Yahweh for their own benefit and purposes. This worldview is reflected in Ahab's confrontation with

---

[35]Fredenburg, "When Prophets Lie and Kings Win," p. 15. Walsh argues that there is a progression in the characterization of Ahab to the negative portrayal in chapter 22 (*1 Kings*, pp. 362-363).

[36]Fredenburg, "When Prophets Lie and Kings Win," p. 15.

Micaiah. Ahab believes he can manipulate prophets and overcome
oracles (e.g., in his disguise), in the same way that appropriate sacrifices and burnt offerings could appease the gods and secure blessings for him and his people. In other words, Ahab has an idolatrous
view of Yahweh (see comments on 14:14-16). The text clearly spells
out that the king of Israel and his Sidonian wife Jezebel are responsible for leading Israel further into idolatry, institutionalizing the
worship of Baal and Asherah in Israel (see, e.g., 2 Kgs 10:28-29). But,
like Jeroboam before him, his principal sin is located in his view of
Yahweh. To him, the God of Israel is just another one of the gods
of the land. In the account of Ahab's reign, the inspired storyteller
demonstrates that Yahweh is God of Israel and in relation to him
there is no other. Yet, tragically, when given the opportunity to
know and experience this God and his mercy, Ahab chooses to sell
himself to the gods of the land and to the pleasures that he thinks
they can offer him. In the end, he is defeated by his idolatry.

The account of Ahab's reign also illustrates the important technique of allusion for ironic effect that characterizes Hebrew storytelling. With a creative use of allusion, Ahab becomes another Saul
who, like the first king of Israel, is removed as king by defeat on the
field of battle. Ironically, like Saul, Ahab is mortally wounded by an
archer (1 Sam 31:3; 1 Kgs 22:34-37; cf. 2 Kgs 8:28-29; 9:15,21-28).
Later, when the prophecy of the fall of the house of Ahab comes to
fruition, Ahab's son Joram suffers a similar fate (2 Kgs 9:24-26).
Ahab's reign mirrors the tragic reign of Israel's first king. But the
web of allusions also indicates that Ahab broke covenant with
Yahweh. When Ahab sells himself for the vineyard of Naboth the
Jezreelite, he becomes Achan, who out of greed disobeyed the law
of חֵרֶם (ḥērem, i.e., the regulations concerning things "devoted" to
Yahweh). He directly disobeyed the words of Moses (Deut 7:1-4)
when he married Jezebel and in his dealings with Ben-Hadad (see
comments on ch. 20). By compromising with Canaanite culture,
Ahab becomes enmeshed in idolatry and, ironically, in the end turns
out to be ḥērem ("devoted to destruction") to Yahweh (cf. 1 Kgs
20:42). For an audience in exile, the message is to put off the gods
of the land in which they have been scattered and return to Yahweh.

E. JEHOSHAPHAT AND AHAZIAH ARE CONTRASTED
(22:41–2 KINGS 1:18)

1. Jehoshaphat Walks in the Ways of His Father (22:41-50)

The storyteller now returns to his chronological frame and to the southern kingdom. Jehoshaphat was briefly on stage in the preceding drama, but kings of Judah have not been addressed since 15:9-24, when the reign of Jehoshaphat's father Asa was reviewed. The account of Jehoshaphat in Kings is considerably different from the Chronicler's version of his reign (2 Chr 17:1–21:1), which includes numerous events that are overlooked by the author of Kings. Writing for a postexilic audience, the Chronicler's purpose, in part, is to demonstrate that Yahweh is still devoted to his people. His presentation of Jehoshaphat (which is a significant part of his composition) paints a nuanced portrait of the king, negatively characterizing his treaty with the house of Ahab while praising his devotion to Yahweh.[37] Hicks contends that in this way, "Chronicles can extol Jehoshaphat's virtues while also anticipating the coming darkness his actions fostered. . . . The postexilic community sees in his reign not only the reason for their own previous exile, but also the hope of restoration."[38]

The author of Kings has no such grand design. For his purposes, Jehoshaphat is a minor character, though a generally faithful king. Jehoshaphat does not have his own drama, appearing with Ahab (ch. 22) before this summary section and afterwards in a flashback with Joram son of Ahab (2 Kings 3). In his indirect style, the storyteller asks the reader to situate the king in the larger story. Contrast with Ahaziah accentuates his righteous character, but allusions to Solomon and contrast with the "golden age" of Israel indicate that he does not quite measure up to the standard set by David's son. Framed by the larger narrative, even good kings cannot avert the calamity that is coming. In this way, Jehoshaphat foreshadows Josiah, the faithful reformer who most closely mirrors David, yet who is also unable to alter Judah's course.[39]

---

[37]Hicks, *1 & 2 Chronicles*, pp. 358-360.
[38]Ibid., p. 360.
[39]See McConville, "Narrative and Meaning," 45-46.

22:41-44[40] Following the forty-one-year reign of his father, **Jehoshaphat son of Asa** becomes **king in Judah** and reigns **twenty-five years**. The length of his reign suggests the blessing of Yahweh and a measure of stability in Judah not attained in the northern kingdom.[41] Jehoshaphat **walks in the ways of his father**, as Ahaziah "walk[s] in the ways of his father and mother" (v. 52[53]). Only, Jehoshaphat does **what is right in the eyes of the LORD**, while Ahaziah does "evil in the eyes of the LORD" (v. 52[53]). This contrast suggests important moral and theological distance between the two kings, but Jehoshaphat is not perfect. Like his father before him (15:14), he does not remove the **high places**, and **the people** continue **to offer sacrifices and burn incense there**. A similar situation existed before Solomon built the temple (3:2). For the author of Kings, now that there is a place where Yahweh has caused his name to dwell, there is no excuse for worshiping at the high places (cf. Deut 12:4 ff.; see comments on 15:9-15).

Without comment, the narrator adds, **Jehoshaphat was also at peace** [literally, "made peace"] **with the king of Israel**. On the surface, this appears to be a noble achievement. His father Asa had made a covenant with Ben-Hadad to foil the advances of Baasha (see comments on 15:16-24), but now there is peace between Israel and Judah. The kingdom of שָׁלוֹם (šālôm, "peace") that Solomon was given by Yahweh may be attainable again. On more careful reflection, however, peace with the house of Omri portends ominous things for the descendants of David. The narrator's statement is framed by the preceding story, where the coalition under Ahab and Jehoshaphat was defeated by Ben-Hadad, and, more importantly, by the God of Israel who determined that Ahab should die. In 2 Kings 3, Jehoshaphat will accompany Ahab's son Joram against Mesha of Moab with inconclusive results, but the marriage alliance between the two houses (cf. 2 Chr 18:1) will eventually put the abominable Athaliah on the throne of Judah (2 Kings 11). To clarify Yahweh's view of this union, the Chronicler adds a scene where Jehu the seer condemns Jehoshaphat for his alliance with Ahab: "Should you help

---

[40]The English and Hebrew versification differ slightly in this section. Verse 43 in English equals vv. 43-44 in Hebrew, with the result that the English vv. 44-50 equals the Hebrew vv. 45-51.

[41]Provan, *1 and 2 Kings*, p. 167.

the wicked and love those who hate the LORD?" (2 Chr 19:2). In his inductive style, however, the author of Kings lets the reader judge Jehoshaphat (see comments on 14:25-28; 15:16-24). The forewarning in Deuteronomy 7:1-4 not to make covenants with those who are *ḥērem* ("devoted to destruction") to Yahweh may apply to the kings of Israel who also become *ḥērem* to Yahweh.

22:45-50 Following the general pattern for the concluding remarks on the reign of a king (see comments on 14:21-31), the reader anticipates a burial notice to appear shortly after the note about Jehoshaphat's achievements, which are **written in the book of the annals of the kings of Judah**. The unexpected list of "accomplishments" that follows should be understood as characterizing his reign. Admirably, he continued the reform that was begun by his father. The note that **there was then no king in Edom** may be taken as explaining how the king of Judah was able to build a fleet at **Ezion Geber**, which was at times controlled by Edom (cf. 9:26). This implies that Jehoshaphat was consciously trying to restore the fortunes of Judah to the glories of Solomon, even to the point of sending **trading ships** to **Ophir for Gold** (cf. 9:26-28).[42] The use of the word **deputy** (נִצָּב, *niṣṣāb*) further connects this information with Solomon who had **district officers** (נִצָּבִים, *niṣṣābîm*; 4:5; cf. 4:27[5:7]; 5:16[30]; 9:23). The implication is that Jehoshaphat has placed a governor over Edom.[43] Nevertheless, a wrecked fleet on the rocks of Ezion Geber indicates that the king of Judah is unable to restore the kingdom of Solomon.[44]

The details of Jehoshaphat's disagreement with **Ahaziah son of Ahab** are clouded. The text may be read as indicating that Ahaziah offers to aid Jehoshaphat when his fleet is wrecked. However, Chronicles records that Jehoshaphat entered into a joint venture with Ahaziah to build seafaring ships at Ezion Geber. In response to this agreement, the prophet Eliezer son of Dodavahu of Mareshah says to Jehoshaphat, "Because you have made an alliance with Ahaziah, the LORD will destroy what you have made." According to Chronicles, Judah's alliance with the king of Israel is the reason the ships are wrecked (2 Chr 20:35-37). Jehoshaphat's refusal probably

---

[42]Walsh, *1 Kings*, pp. 366-367; see Provan, *1 and 2 Kings*, p. 168.

[43]Provan, *1 and 2 Kings*, pp. 169-170.

[44]Walsh, *1 Kings*, 367; Provan, *1 and 2 Kings*, pp. 168.

follows the prophet's invective.[45] But, what in Chronicles is a blot on Jehoshaphat's record, in Kings becomes part of the positive assessment of his reign. Even though the king of Judah was the junior partner (i.e., vassal) in his alliance with Israel (an implication of the preceding story), there comes a time when he is able to refuse a northern king and "throw off Judah's subservience to Israel,"[46] apparently at the condemning word of a prophet of Yahweh (per 2 Chr 20:35-37). The account of Jehoshaphat's reign ends on an affirming note. After his death, his son **Jehoram** rules over Judah in his place.

2. Ahaziah Walks in the Ways of His Parents (22:51-53)

22:51-53 "Like father, like son" and "like mother, like son" epitomizes the life and reign of Ahaziah. The contrast with Jehoshaphat is striking. Only reigning **two years** in Samaria, he persists in the sins of his parents — and **in the ways of Jeroboam son of Nebat, who caused Israel to sin**. The refrain that characterizes the kings of Israel goes on (see comments on 13:33-34). But beyond the sin of Jeroboam, like his father Ahab, this king of Israel **worships Baal**, provoking **the LORD, the God of Israel, to anger**. Second Kings 1:1-18 continues the account of his reign with the story of Yahweh's judgment on another king who chooses to serve other gods.

---

[45]For other possibilities, see Hicks, *1 & 2 Chronicles*, pp. 391-392.
[46]Walsh, *1 Kings*, 367; see Brueggemann, *1 & 2 Kings*, p. 276.

2 KINGS 1

3. Ahaziah Hears the Word of Yahweh from Elijah
(2 Kings 1:1-18)

1:1-4 Demonstrating an artificial break between 1 and 2 Kings,[1] the account of the reign of Ahaziah of Israel, as part of the larger story of the house of Ahab, continues. The opening statement, **After Ahab's death, Moab rebelled**, foreshadows the more detailed narration of the campaign by Joram and Jehoshaphat against Moab in 3:1-27 (cf. especially v. 5) and negatively colors Ahaziah's reign. The kingdom of Omri and Ahab is unraveling.[2] The son of Ahab injures himself in a fall from **his upper room**. His father "fell" in battle at Ramoth Gilead (see comments on 1 Kgs 22:20). Ignobly, the son falls through some type of latticed, window construction. The king sends messengers to inquire (דָרַשׁ, *dāraš*) of **Baal-Zebub, the god of Ekron**, about his recovery.[3] Whereas Jeroboam sent his wife to the prophet Ahijah to inquire (*dāraš*) about the recovery of Abijah (1 Kgs 14:5), Ahaziah is now inquiring of a foreign god.[4] Since **Baal-**

---

[1]The original Hebrew text of Kings was apparently one composition. The division of the work into 1 and 2 Kings was introduced in the LXX (see Cogan and Tadmor, *II Kings*, p. 22).

[2]Hobbs, *2 Kings*, p. 7.

[3]Christopher T. Begg argues that a "sending/messenger motif," the "unfolding revelation of Elijah's identity," the "exemplification of stances towards Elijah and their consequences," and the "*ʿālāh/yārad*-terminology" in chapter 1 indicate a unified composition and "suggest a reexamination of the long-standing supposition that vv. 9-16 represent a secondary interpolation within a preexisting narrative" ("Unifying Factors in 2 Kings 1.2-17a," *JSOT* 32 [1985]: 75-86).

[4]Robert L. Cohn notices four stories in Kings with the pattern of the dying king who sends messengers to inquire of a prophet about his fate (Jeroboam [1 Kings 14], Ahaziah [2 Kings 1], Ben-Hadad [2 Kings 8], and Hezekiah [2 Kings 20]). He labels this pattern a type-scene ("Convention and Creativity

Zebub (בַּעַל זְבוּב, *ba'al z³bûb*) literally means "lord of the flies," the naming appears to be a parody on an epithet for Baal (בַּעַל זְבוּל, *ba'al z³bûl*, "Prince-Baal," or "Baal is prince").[5] The storyteller is satirically calling attention to Ahaziah's folly (cf. Matt 10:25; 12:24; Mark 3:22; Luke 11:15-19 — where "Beelzebub" is used for Satan).

The king of Israel sends **messengers** (מַלְאָכִים, *mal'ākîm*) to inquire, and Yahweh sends his "messenger" (מַלְאָךְ, *mal'āk* = **angel**) to Elijah. Embedded in this correspondence is the underlying plot of the story, the contest between the king of Israel and King Yahweh.[6] The Angel of Yahweh commands the prophet (literally), "Arise, go up to meet the messengers of the king of Samaria." In 1 Kings 21:18, the word of Yahweh directed Elijah (literally), "Arise, go down to meet Ahab." The parallel wording must be intentional, suggesting comparison between the two stories. In this episode, the prophet Elijah will more faithfully represent Yahweh than in the matter of Naboth's vineyard (see comments on 1 Kgs 21:17-28). The Angel of Yahweh appears only four times in Kings (1 Kgs 19:7: 2 Kgs 1:3,15; 19:35). Three out of four of the angel's appearances are to Elijah, elevating the stature of this man of God among the prophets of Yahweh. The specific instructions to Elijah stand out. Literally, the king would not "come down" (יָרַד, *yārad*; occurring twelve times in ch. 1; vv. 4,6,9,10,11,12,14,15,16) from the bed he had "ascended/climbed up on" (עָלָה, *'ālāh*; occurring eight times in ch. 1; vv. 3,4,6, 7,9,13,16; in addition to the *upper* room, עֲלִיָּה ['*ălîyāh*], v. 2). A motif of going up/coming down permeates this chapter. Also, again Elijah is instructed to repeat the messenger formula, **"this is what the LORD says"** (cf. 21:19).

---

in the Book of Kings: The Case of the Dying Monarch," *CBQ* 47 [1985]: 603-616), a literary convention suggested for Hebrew narrative by Alter (*Art of Biblical Narrative*, pp. 47-62). However, the numerous differences between the stories argue against a type-scene. More likely, kings' inquiring of prophets about medical problems was a common occurrence, which the storyteller with allusion and analogy highlights for his theological purposes.

[5]Baal-Zebub could also be the original name of a health deity who had control over flies and various diseases. Another view translates Zebub as "flame" (i.e., "Baal of the flame"), which would correspond with the fire motif in this story, although there is little support for this reading (see Walter A. Maier III, "Baal-Zebub [deity]," in *ABD*; Hobbs, *2 Kings*, p. 8; Cogan and Tadmor, *II Kings*, p. 25).

[6]Brueggemann, *1 & 2 Kings*, p. 284.

1:5-8 The prophetic message reaches the king indirectly through his own messengers. Their report is verbatim what the angel had instructed Elijah, only Elijah apparently begins his oracle with the messenger formula ("Thus says Yahweh"), and he directs the message solely to the king instead of the messengers (cf. **"you [pl.] are going off"** [v. 3] with **"you [sing.] are** *sending"* [v. 6]). These minor variations suggest that the storyteller is portraying Elijah as faithfully repeating the word of the Angel of Yahweh.[7] This dramatically contrasts with how Elijah represented the word of Yahweh in 1 Kings 21 (see comments on 21:17-28).

When the king asks about the messenger, he uses an unusual word. He asks about the **manner** (מִשְׁפַּט, *mišpaṭ*) of the man. The usual word for "judgment," *mišpaṭ* interjects an ironic element. Ahaziah is asking about the man of God who has pronounced *judgment* on the king. When the messengers describe the prophet's appearance, he recognizes Elijah. The narrator leaves a gap here. Has Ahaziah received oracles from Elijah before or only heard about the prophet from his father? Their response adds more irony. In Hebrew, the man of God is described as a בַּעַל שֵׂעָר (*ba'al śē'ār,* "a lord of hair") **with a leather belt**. Perhaps this signifies **a garment of hair**, as the NIV translates this phrase. More likely, it indicates Elijah was "a hairy man," in contrast with Elisha who was apparently bald (cf. 2:23).[8] In any case, in Hebrew there is wordplay with "Lord [*ba'al*] of the Flies" and "Lord [*ba'al*] of the hair,"[9] calling attention to the sarcasm already introduced in the story.

1:9-15 Elijah again appears on a mountain (הָהָר, *hāhār*; cf. 1 Kgs 18:19,20; 19:8,11), which is probably Mount Carmel.[10] In the New

---

[7]Kissling, *Reliable Characters*, p. 136.

[8]In Matt 3:4 and Mark 1:6, John the Baptist, who comes in the spirit of Elijah, is described as wearing a garment of camel's hair and a leather belt (see Provan, *1 and 2 Kings*, p. 170). The tradition that Elijah wore a hairy coat probably developed from the mantle associated with him (see 1 Kgs 19:13,19; 2 Kgs 2:8,13,14; cf. Zech 13:4) in the intertestamental period (Cogan and Tadmor, *II Kings*, p. 26; Hobbs, *2 Kings*, p. 10).

[9]Robert L. Cohn, *2 Kings*, Berit Olam: Studies in Hebrew Narrative & Poetry (Collegeville, MN: A Michael Glazier Book, The Liturgical Press, 2000), p. 6, n. 6.

[10]In Hebrew, the word "mountain" is definite, which may indicate this association (Hobbs, *2 Kings*, p. 10). Olley outlines the parallels between the events in 1 Kings 18–19 and 2 Kings 1. For example, in each Elijah calls

Testament, this mountaintop prophet will join Moses on the "mount of transfiguration" (cf. Matt 17:1-8; Mark 9:2-8; Luke 9:28-36). The king sends **a captain** with his men to bring down Elijah. The captain commands Elijah, **"Come down!"** So, the match is set between the power of the prophet, who said that the ailing king would not "come down" (*yārad*, vv. 4,6) from his bed, and the power of the king, who commands the prophet to "come down" (*yārad*) from the mountain.[11] Once more, Elijah calls *down* (*yārad*) **fire** from heaven (cf. 1 Kgs 18:38). Yahweh listens to the voice of Elijah (1 Kgs 17:22). Fire *comes down* (*yārad*) and devours ("eats," אָכַל, *'ākal*; cf. 18:38) the captain and his **fifty men**, demonstrating that Elijah is a man of God.

The scene is repeated, except the king tries to further impress the prophet with his authority. The second messenger prefaces his speech with the messenger formula, **"this is what the king says."** Elijah should, "*Come down* [*yārad*] **at once**!" This time, **the *fire of God***[12] *comes down* (*yārad*) and devours the captain and his men. The **third captain** recognizes the power of the prophet and approaches the man of God with deference. His point of view, echoed, for example, when he names himself and his men **"your servants,"** is the attitude that Ahaziah should have. The Angel of Yahweh instructs Elijah, **"Go down [*yārad*] with him."** Not without cause, the angel adds, **"Do not be afraid of him."** In spite of the great faith that Elijah displayed on Mount Carmel, the reader has seen him retreat in fear and run for his life (cf. 1 Kgs 19:3).[13] Elijah *goes down* (*yārad*) with the captain to confront the king.

1:16-18 The narrator reports only the word of the prophet. For the third time, the reader hears the word of the Angel of Yahweh. Again, there are only minor variations from the angel's instructions.[14] For example, this time Elijah asks, "Is it because there is no God in Israel for you *to inquire of his word*?" (cf. v. 3). The small devi-

---

down fire from heaven on the mountain, probably Carmel ("YHWH and His Zealous Prophet," pp. 44-45).

[11]See Cohn, *2 Kings*, p. 6.

[12]"Of God" is missing in some manuscripts and may appear here because of a copyist's error (dittography), where the phrase is confused with "man *of God*" in the first part of the verse (Hobbs, *2 Kings*, p. 3).

[13]See Olley, "YHWH and His Zealous Prophet," 44. Kissling believes that Elijah displays more confidence in 2 Kings 1 (*Reliable Characters*, p. 112).

[14]Kissling, *Reliable Characters*, p. 136.

ations from the original word, in the report of the messengers (v. 6) and then from Elijah (v. 16), give the message an aura of spontaneity in the dynamic of the human situation. However, the judgment itself, "You will not *come down* [*yārad*] from the bed you have *ascended* [*'ālāh*], but you will surely die," is word for word the same in each of the three versions of the oracle. Elijah has given the king the word of Yahweh without any addenda.[15] In this way, Kissling maintains the prophet has changed: "The scrupulous accuracy with which Elijah performs authorized actions is notable in light of past performance."[16] The narrator appends, **So** [Ahaziah] **died, according to the word of the LORD that Elijah had spoken** (cf. 1 Kgs 17:16). In the fire from heaven and the death of the king, Yahweh has affirmed that Elijah is a man of God.[17] The reader can say again with the widow of Zarephath, "Elijah is a man of God, and the word of Yahweh from his mouth is the truth" (cf. 17:24).

The story's structure highlights the word that Elijah gives:[18]

A. Ahaziah falls and inquires of Baal-Zebub (v. 2).
   B. The Angel of Yahweh sends Elijah with a word for the king's messengers (vv. 3-4).
      C. Messengers deliver the word (vv. 5-8).
         X. Captains confront Elijah (vv. 9-14).
   B'. The Angel of Yahweh sends Elijah with the word to Ahaziah (v. 16).
      C'. Elijah gives the word to Ahaziah (v. 16).
A'. Ahaziah dies (v. 17).

In this arrangement, the parallel scenes (e.g., A and A', etc.) stand out and underscore the word of judgment for Ahaziah, which comes to pass.

But the reader may be somewhat confused by these events. With the death of Ahab's son, one would expect Elijah to say something about the end of Ahab's house.[19] That he does not reinforces the

---

[15]Olley, "YHWH and His Faithful Prophet," 45.

[16]Kissling, *Reliable Characters*, pp. 136-137. But Kissling argues that his change is incomplete. Elijah never confronts Jezebel and does not carry out two of the assignments that Yahweh gave him on Horeb (pp. 138, 145).

[17]See Nelson, *First and Second Kings*, p. 157.

[18]Adapted from Cohn, *2 Kings*, p. 5.

[19]See Provan, *1 and 2 Kings*, p. 169.

reading that this Elijah is more compliant than the overzealous prophet who cursed the house of Ahab in Jezreel. However, Yahweh did say that Elijah's oracle would happen in the days of Ahab's son (1 Kgs 21:29). Where is Yahweh's judgment on the house of Ahab? The narrator has withheld information from the reader. For dramatic effect, he waits until this point to inform the reader that Ahaziah has **no son**. Another son of Ahab will sit on the throne in Samaria. Like his father, Ahaziah served other gods and received his reward, but the judgment of Yahweh on Ahab's house is yet to come.

The note that **Joram** succeeded Ahaziah in the **second year of Jehoram son of Jehoshaphat of Judah** is missing in the LXX.[20] If it is genuine, it appears to conflict with 3:1, where Joram son of Ahab becomes king of Israel in the eighteenth year of Jehoshaphat. To further confuse the situation, in 8:16 the text says that Jehoram of Judah becomes king in the fifth year of Joram son of Ahab. Thiele offers a plausible explanation. The reigns of Jehoshaphat and his son must overlap. If Jehoshaphat made his son coregent when he joined Ahab in the campaign to recover Ramoth Gilead (the seventeenth year of Jehoshaphat; cf. 1 Kgs 22:51), then it would follow that Joram became king in Samaria in the second year of the coregency of Jehoram of Judah (2 Kgs 1:17), which was the eighteenth year of Jehoshaphat's reign. Jehoram son of Jehoshaphat became sole regent of Judah in the fifth year of Joram son of Ahab, at the death of his father Jehoshaphat (8:16).[21] After the regnal note, the narrator closes in his usual pattern. The other events of Ahaziah's reign are written in **the annals of the kings of Israel**.

---

[20]Hobbs argues that there is reason to view it as an insertion (*2 Kings*, pp. 3-4).

[21]Thiele, *Mysterious Numbers*, 63, 99-100. Galil calls Thiele's hypothesis "one of the less objectionable proposals," but believes the dual dating is unlikely, preferring "to assume that this datum [1:17] is erroneous, and that it is one of the very few data in the Bible which were corrupted for some reason" (*Chronology of the Kings*, pp. 39-40).

2 KINGS 2

F. ELIJAH IS REPLACED BY ELISHA (2:1-25)

1. Elijah Is Taken Up to Heaven (2:1-18)

2:1-6 The transition from the ministry of the prophet Elijah to his successor is placed by the narrator outside the regnal record of the kings of Israel, and so stands out in the larger narrative.[1] The well-crafted transition story also serves, at the same time, as a conclusion to the account of Elijah and an introduction to the narrative of Elisha. The narrator begins by saying Yahweh is **about to take Elijah up** [הַעֲלוֹת, *ha'ălôth*, "cause to go up," from *'ālāh*] **to heaven in a whirlwind**, allowing the reader to share the **point of view** of the characters in the story. Intriguingly, the storyteller does not inform the reader how the players know what Yahweh is about to do. Perhaps it is simply because they are prophets and "sons of prophets" (**company of prophets** in the NIV). Tension is created with the seemingly mindless route on which Elijah leads Elisha. The pair travels from **Gilgal** to **Bethel** to **Jericho** and across the **Jordan**. Although scholars disagree, the Gilgal mentioned here is probably not the Gilgal east of Jericho where Israel encamped after crossing the Jordan (Josh 4:19). That **they** *went down* **to Bethel** suggests that the two prophets began their journey from a Gilgal in the hill country, probably located between Bethel and Samaria to the north (perhaps Jiljulieh, 12 km north of Bethel).[2] The parallel trek that Elisha takes on his return (vv. 14-24) gives the episode a symmetrical, concentric structure that reinforces the conclusion that Elisha replaces

---

[1]Brueggemann, *1 & 2 Kings*, p. 293.

[2]Wade R. Kotter, "Gilgal (place)," in *ABD*. If this is the Gilgal near the Jordan, as many assume, the zigzag, circuitous route reinforces Elisha's determination to remain with Elijah, most likely to secure his position as the prophet's successor (Kissling, *Reliable Characters*, pp. 157-159).

Elijah[3] and highlights the translation of Elijah to heaven in verse 11 (item "X," at the center of the outline).[4]

AA. On the mountain (probably Carmel) and in Samaria (ch. 1)
    (Elijah is a man of God!)
  A. To Bethel (vv. 1-3)
    B. To Jericho (vv. 4-5)
      C. To the Jordan (v. 6)
        D. Company of prophets witnesses (v. 7)
          E. Crossing the Jordan (v. 8)
            F. Asking for succession (v. 9)
              G. "If you see me" (v 10)
                X. Elijah taken (v. 11)
              G'. "Elisha saw" (v. 12)
            F'. Receiving succession (v. 13)
          E'. Crossing the Jordan (v. 14)
        D'. Company of prophets witnesses (v. 15)
      C'. At the Jordan, searching (vv. 16-17)
    B'. At Jericho (vv. 18-22)
  A'. At Bethel (vv. 23-24)
    (Elisha is a man of God, like Elijah!)
AA'. To Mount Carmel and Samaria (v. 25)

Elijah's behavior is curious. He appears to be trying to rid himself of the prophet he has been told should replace him (1 Kgs 19:16). The repetition heightens the tension. At each directive to **"Stay here,"** Elisha answers his mentor with an oath and adds, **"I will not leave you"** (vv. 2,4,6). Also, Elisha's attempt to silence each company of prophets interjects more mystery. Does this suggest a strained relationship between the two prophets, or is Elisha afraid that something will happen to interfere with his efforts to obtain a blessing from Yahweh's prophet? Kissling believes that Elisha's response indicates a degree of self-interest on his part.[5] In any case,

---

[3]Kissling, *Reliable Characters*, p. 156.

[4]T.R. Hobbs has influenced this outline, although he does not structure his arrangement around location ("2 Kings 1 and 2: Their Unity and Purpose," *Studies in Religion/Sciences religieuses* 13/3 [1984]: 327-334; *2 Kings*, pp. 17-19). While he demonstrates compositional unity, his outline is somewhat forced when it comes to the relationship between chapters 1 and 2 (see below).

[5]Kissling, *Reliable Characters*, pp. 157-159.

Elijah's aloof manner is out of character with the aggressive, forth-right personality the reader first comes to know.[6] Does this change reflect an attempt on Elijah's part to test Elisha, or is he reluctant to pass the baton on to Elisha as his successor? Nelson sees a "motif of testing," including a test of "loyalty," a "test of a last request," and a "test of seeing" (vv. 2-10).[7] Yet, if this is all a test, why has Elijah already been told to anoint Elisha as prophet in his place (1 Kgs 19:16)? Has he taken it on himself to "'pre-qualify' a man whom Yahweh has already chosen to replace him"?[8] While in one way out of character, Elijah's detached demeanor parallels his somewhat abrasive interaction with Elisha at their first meeting (see comments on 19:19-21). And, the great man of God has yet to formally anoint Elisha to replace him, in spite of Yahweh's instructions. In this framework, Elijah looks reluctant to hand over his power and posi-tion, especially when compared with the transfer of leadership from Moses to Joshua, which this story parallels (see Deut 31:1-29; 34:9).[9] Kissling even wonders if Elijah is "complying ["with Yahweh's direc-tive"] in such a way that his own role is given more importance than Yahweh originally gave it"[10] — a response that is in character with the self-centered prophet who saw himself as the *only* faithful servant remaining in Israel (19:10,14).

2:7-10 The **fifty men of the company of the prophets** (also fifty in vv. 16,17) connect this story with the bands of fifty men in chap-ter 1 (vv. 9-14). The phrase "company of prophets" (literally, "sons of prophets") occurs only eleven times in the Old Testament, all in Kings and, excepting 1 Kings 20:35, all in the Elisha stories (2 Kgs 2:3,5,7,15; 4:1,38[2×]; 5:22; 6:1; 9:1). Although the evidence is sparse, the expression may refer to a guild or "school" of prophets, who were led first by Elijah then Elisha (perhaps assuming the title of "father" of the group [cf. v. 12; 13:14]).[11] The miracle that Elijah

---

[6]Alexander Rofé interprets Elijah's actions as reflecting "withdrawal from the present world and apathy." While the prophet was never before "neu-tral or vacillating," he is now resigned to what is about to happen (*The Prophetical Stories: The Narratives about the Prophets in the Hebrew Bible, Their Literary Types and History* [Jerusalem: The Magnes Press, 1988)], pp. 47-48).

[7]Nelson, *First and Second Kings*, p. 159.

[8]Kissling, *Reliable Characters*, p. 146.

[9]Olley, "YHWH and His Zealous Prophet," 45-46.

[10]Kissling, *Reliable Characters*, p. 146.

[11]For the view that they were "lay supporters" of Elisha, see Hobbs,

performs, parting the Jordan with **his cloak**, mirrors both the parting of the Red Sea by Moses and of the Jordan when Joshua led Israel into Canaan. **The two of them cross over on dry ground** [חָרָבָה, *ḥārābāh*], as did Israel at the Red Sea and at the Jordan (Exod 14:21; Josh 3:17; 4:18).

After crossing, Elijah asks, **"What can I do for you before I am taken from you?"** Elisha wants to **"inherit a double portion of your spirit."** In this request, is he asking for double Elijah's prophetic powers, or is he asking to be his successor? In the larger story, Elisha outstrips Elijah in the number, variety, and magnitude of his miraculous deeds.[12] However, in Deuteronomy, "double portion" signifies succession, the right of the firstborn (cf. 21:15-17). If Elisha is asking to be Elijah's successor, which seems likely,[13] his mentor's response (**"You have asked a *difficult* thing"**) raises a flag. Yahweh has already indicated that Elisha would replace Elijah. Perhaps the narrator wants the reader to see that Elijah is the one trying to be *difficult*.[14] In any case, Elijah leaves this choice to Yahweh: **"If you see me when I am taken from you, it will be yours."**

2:11-13 As the two are **walking along and talking together**, they are **separated** by **a chariot of fire and horses of fire**. Once more, Elijah is associated with fire (cf. 1 Kgs 18:38; 2 Kgs 1:9-15). The prophet *goes up* (*'ālāh*) to heaven in a **whirlwind** (סְעָרָה, *s°'ārāh*, "storm," often associated with Yahweh; cf., Job 38:1; 40:6; Isa 29:6; Jer 30:23), even though Yahweh was not in the storm on Horeb (cf. 1 Kgs 19:9-18). Signifying that his request will be granted, the narrator says that Elisha *sees* the ascension and cries out, **"My father! My father! The chariots and horsemen of Israel!"** The same exclamation will be voiced at Elisha's death, demonstrating at the end of his life that, undeniably, he embodied the spirit of Elijah (2 Kgs 13:14). In distress, Elisha tears **his own clothes**, an expression of grief that also symbolizes his eminent transition from his old life. He takes up the **cloak that had fallen from Elijah** (cf. the repetition for emphasis in v. 14), the same cloak Elijah threw around him following

---

2 Kings, pp. 25-27. Turner sees this phrase as denoting schools for prophets (*Annual Lesson Commentary*, pp. 50-52, 57).

[12]Kissling, *Reliable Characters*, pp. 162, 191-195.

[13]See Hobbs, *2 Kings*, p. 21; cf. Cogan and Tadmor, *II Kings*, p. 32.

[14]Olley, "Yhwh and His Zealous Prophet," p. 46.

the great prophet's descent from Mount Horeb (1 Kgs 19:19; cf. 19:13). Apparently, Elisha was not allowed to wear it long.[15] Elijah never formally anoints Elisha (see comments on 19:16)! Falling from the prophet as he is taken into heaven, the cloak of Elijah is taken up by Elisha. With it he also takes up his mentor's prophetic ministry.

2:14-15 But the real test of succession comes now. Can Elisha replicate the miracle of the crossing? He strikes the water of the Jordan with Elijah's cloak, asking, **"Where now is the LORD, the God of Elijah?"** Elisha is calling on Yahweh to take action for him as he did for Elijah. The underlying Hebrew in verse 14 indicates that Elisha, following his entreaty, strikes the water again. After he calls on Yahweh and strikes a second time, Yahweh responds.[16] The waters are divided as before, and Elisha, like Joshua, crosses the Jordan as the successor to Elijah, the servant of Yahweh. As Yahweh was with Joshua, he will be with Elisha. Even the name Elisha ("God/my God saves") is a variant of the name Joshua ("Yahweh saves").[17] The company of prophets from Jericho witnesses the event, and proclaims what they have seen: **"The spirit of Elijah is resting on Elisha."**

2:16-18 From the company of prophets, **fifty able men** (cf. fifty in 1:9-15) offer to search for Elijah. They speculate, in much the same way as Obadiah (1 Kgs 18:12), that **"Perhaps the Spirit of the LORD has picked him up and set him down on some mountain or in some valley."** They apparently believe Yahweh has buried Elijah somewhere on the other side of the Jordan. The allusion to Moses, who was buried across the Jordan on Mount Nebo is unmistakable (Deut 34:1-9). Elisha gives in to their persistence. After **three days** of searching, they do not find the prophet. Elisha, who *saw* him ascend, retorts, **"Didn't I tell you not to go?"** Clearly, the prophet Elisha has out-of-the-ordinary perception that confirms he is Elijah's successor (cf. 6:15-17).[18]

---

[15]Kissling, *Reliable Characters*, pp. 125, 151, 153-154.

[16]Cohn, *2 Kings*, p. 15. Contra Kissling (*Reliable Characters*, p. 162), this does not mean that Elisha has to work harder than Elijah to perform the miracle. More likely, the retelling faithfully represents the experience of a man whose new powers are untried.

[17]Provan, *1 and 2 Kings*, p. 173.

[18]See Kissling, *Reliable Characters*, pp. 177-178.

EXCURSUS

THE TRANSLATION OF ELIJAH IN CONTEXT

When Elijah is taken to heaven in a whirlwind, the narrator's characterization of the prophet as less than perfect raises an important question. If Elijah was so self-willed, how does one explain his translation to heaven? The initial response to this question is that heroes in Scripture are human. Other than the Messiah himself, Bible characters are flawed, painted with strokes that bring to light foibles as well as faithful traits. The same is true of Elijah. A reader cannot see him cowering in a cave on Mount Horeb and keep him on a superhuman pedestal. But the previous discussion of prophetic initiative (see comments on 1 Kgs 16:29-34 and "Excursus: Elijah in Context") tempers the prophet's indiscretions.[19] Elijah is strong-willed and in some ways overzealous, at times crossing the line and stepping ahead of Yahweh (see comments on 1 Kings 21). However, the initiative that he displays is not out of place in the dynamic relationship between Yahweh and his prophet. When Elijah does not carry out Yahweh's instructions exactly (21:17-28), his disobedience is qualified by the fact that as Yahweh's representative (filled with his Spirit), it was also his prerogative to judge the house of Ahab. And in the end his judgment was appropriate. Even though Yahweh modified the prophet's word (21:27-28), Jehu vigorously acted out Elijah's prophecy on the descendants of Ahab, apparently with Yahweh's blessing (cf. 2 Kgs 10:17,30).[20]

One must also consider Elijah's faith. The faith that he displays when he initiates the contest on Mount Carmel is without parallel in Scripture.[21] When James acknowledges Elijah as "a man just like us"

---

[19]Prophetic initiative moderates an overly negative appraisal of Elijah (contra Kissling, *Reliable Characters*, pp. 96-148; Olley, "YHWH and His Zealous Prophet," 25-51).

[20]Although, Yahweh does not condone the way Jehu carries out the judgment on the house of Ahab (see comments on 2 Kings 9–10).

[21]Later, Elisha surpasses Elijah in the extent of his miraculous deeds (Kissling, *Reliable Characters*, pp. 162, 191-195). However, Elijah is the forerunner, blazing a trail for and enabling (in part by example) the mighty things Elisha is able to accomplish. Also, the circumstances of Carmel are unique. Elijah challenges Ahab and his prophets at the high point in the

(Jas 5:17-18), it becomes apparent that there was not anything special about the man Elijah, but his faith. He prayed, and *Yahweh responded*. And the prophet *was human*. The faith that he displayed on Carmel (1 Kings 18) is in a measure negated by the lack of faith that surfaces on Horeb (1 Kings 19). Yet, Yahweh was able to use his single-minded commitment and passion, in spite of his weaknesses, in powerful ways. In the final analysis, though, as is usually the case in Bible stories, Elijah's translation says more about Yahweh than it does Elijah.

Elijah was special, but he was not taken into heaven because of even a pretense of perfection.[22] Yahweh was able to take Elijah's faith and use him for his purposes in the world. When one steps back and looks at the larger story of Scripture, Yahweh is using Elijah to lay out a framework of expectations for the prophet-like-Moses who would come (Deut 18:14-22). Allusions to Moses establish Elijah as such a prophet, but both Moses and Elijah typify the Messiah who comes. Together, they embody the faith and spirit of the promised one. For these reasons, both figures accompany Jesus on the mount of transfiguration (cf. Matt 17:1-13; Mark 9:2-13; Luke 9:28-36). In addition, Elijah foreshadows what is to come in at least two other ways. He is both the forerunner, preparing the way for the Messiah, and a type of the Messiah himself.[23] As Elijah prepares the way for Yahweh's ultimate victory over Ahab's house in the days of Elisha, so John the Baptist, in the spirit of Elijah, will prepare the way for God's ultimate victory in Jesus (cf. Mal 4:1-6; Luke 1:11-17; Matt 11:1-19; 17:11-13; Mark 9:11-13; John 1:19-34). And, Elijah's miraculous power and single-minded commitment to Yahweh also prefigure the life of the Messiah.[24] All of these connections come together and are reinforced in Elijah's ascension to heaven in a

---

battle between Yahweh and Baal. The contest on Mount Carmel (and Elijah's role in it) remains unequaled.

[22]The example of Enoch does not contradict this observation. The somewhat ambiguous description of Enoch as one who "walked with God" and was "taken away" does not imply perfection (see Gen 5:21-24).

[23]See Charles W. Speer, "A Study of Allusion in the 'Birth Narrative' of Luke's Gospel," (master's thesis, Lubbock Christian University, 1996), pp. 97-102.

[24]Provan has an excellent summary of the ways the story of Elijah in Kings is used in the New Testament (*1 and 2 Kings*, pp. 178-180). For example (p. 179), Elijah is a "type of Jesus" in these ways: Angels minister to Jesus in the desert (1 Kgs 19:5-8; Matt 4:1-11); Jesus opposes "Beelzebub" (1 Kgs

whirlwind, which foreshadows the ascension of the Messiah and the victory over the forces of evil that event will signify.

18:20-40; 2 Kgs 1:2-17; Matt 12:22-28; Luke 11:14-20); Jesus works similar miracles (1 Kgs 17:7-24; Matt 14:13-21; 15:29-39; Luke 7:11-17); and Jesus ascends to heaven (2 Kgs 2:11; Acts 1:2).

2. Elisha Blesses the Waters of Jericho (2:19-22)

At first glance, the two episodes that conclude chapter 2 (vv. 18-22,23-25) appear simply to inaugurate the ministry of Elisha. However, themes from chapter 1 and allusions to earlier texts give these stories greater meaning. Hobbs demonstrates the unity of chapters 1-2, with correspondences that link them and indicate larger design.[25] For example, the descriptions of Elijah ("hairy," 1:8) and Elisha ("bald," 2:23) are the only physical descriptions of prophets in the Old Testament, suggesting an intentional association.[26] But the design in the narrative goes beyond 2 Kings 1-2. Conroy notices a connection between 1 Kgs 16:34, and the reference to Hiel of *Bethel* who rebuilt the walls of *Jericho* at the cost of two sons, and 2 Kings 2, where Bethel (vv. 2[2×],3,23) and Jericho (vv. 4[2×], 5,15,18) are key locations. He argues that this structure links the Elijah and Elisha cycles of stories. Each prophet plays a role in the death of a son of Ahab (Elijah and Ahaziah [2 Kings 1], Elisha and Joram [2 Kings 9]).[27] The first stories about the ministry of Elisha occur at Jericho and Bethel.

2:19-22 The **bad water** and **unproductive land** at Jericho may have resulted from the curse that Joshua placed on that site (1 Kgs 16:34).[28] The particulars of Elisha's remedy resonate with Elijah's antics when he stretched himself out over the widow's son three times (see comments on 1 Kgs 17:21-23). Also, Moses' first miracle following the Red Sea crossing was turning the bitter waters of Marah sweet (Exod 15:22-27).[29] At Yahweh's direction, Moses threw

---

[25]Hobbs, "2 Kings 1 and 2," 327-334; *2 Kings*, pp. 17-19.

[26]Hobbs, "2 Kings 1 and 2," 332. While his observations are generally sound, Hobbs puts forward a concentric structure for chapters 1-2 that is forced. For example, the physical descriptions of the prophets occur in elements B and A′ in his outline (not B and B′ or A and A′). Also, he connects 1:9-15 with the key word "come down" and 2:23-25 with the key word "go up," and with a "test of authority" in each scene, when "go up" is a key word that runs through chapter 1, and also appears in 2:1,11. This compels him to rearrange the scenes in chapter 1 to make his outline work (i.e., 1:9-15,1-8,16-18). It is better to see chapter 1 as connected to chapter 2 in a more general, less structured way.

[27]Conroy, "Hiel between Ahab and Elijah-Elisha," 215.

[28]Ibid., 216.

[29]Cohn, *2 Kings*, p. 17; Cogan and Tadmor, *II Kings*, p. 37.

a piece of wood into the water. Another allusion positions the stories of Elijah and Elisha in the shadow of Moses and Joshua. However, Elisha's words stand out more than his actions. The prophet prefaces his remarks with the messenger formula, **"This is what the LORD says,"** and speaks for Yahweh in first person, **"I have healed this water . . . ."** The narrator closes the scene by saying that the water remained pure, **according to the word Elisha had spoken**. The prophet has brought a blessing to the inhabitants of Jericho, and his word comes to pass, carries power, as did the word of Elijah (cf. 1 Kgs 17:7-24).

3. Elisha Curses Jeering Children (2:23-25)

2:23-25 The scene where Elisha curses the youths who mock him in Bethel is a difficult story to reconcile with Christian sensibilities. In fact, the NIV tries to soften the effect of the story in the underlying Hebrew with "youths" instead of "*little* boys/youths" (נְעָרִים קְטַנִּים, *nᵊʿārîm qᵊṭannîm*) in verse 23 and "children" (יְלָדִים, *yᵊlādîm*) in verse 24. Christian sensibilities aside, a contextual reading indicates that there is more here than comes to light in just a cursory evaluation. Since in the larger story of Kings Bethel is a center of rebellion against Yahweh (cf. 1 Kings 13), the narrator probably intends a level of symbolic meaning. One could easily imagine children from Bethel jeering a true prophet of Yahweh. Also, what the "youths" say stands out. They call Elisha "baldhead," which automatically suggests contrast with Elijah, who is styled hairy in 2 Kings 1:8 (see comments on 1:7-10). So, when they exclaim, **"Go on up [**'*ālāh*]**, you baldhead,"** a careful reader thinks of Elijah, who *went up* ('*ālāh*) to heaven in a whirlwind (vv. 1,11). The motif established in chapter 1 one reappears. In context, the "youths" are cajoling Elisha to go up like Elijah. And the reader remembers that king Ahaziah was to go up on his bed and not come down (see comments on 1:1-6). Hobbs sees a parallel with the captains who challenge the authority of Elijah and order him to "come down" (1:9-15).[30] As Elijah called down fire from heaven, Elisha brings she-bears out of the woods. The taunt does not just concern Elisha's appearance. The children are discounting

---

[30]Hobbs, "2 Kings 1 and 2," 332.

his authority and calling for the *downfall* of Yahweh's prophet. It follows that their actions are an affront not just to the man Elisha but also to the prophet as a representative of Yahweh.

At the same time, there is undeniably a human dimension to Elisha's action. In some way, the prophet probably takes the jeering personally. Kissling argues that Elisha's curse is precipitated because he believes that the children are saying that he does not "measure up to his predecessor." He also contends that since they are children, the narrator is intimating that Elisha is, to some degree, "morally inferior to Elijah."[31] A comparison with Elijah in 1:9-15, however, vindicates the prophet Elisha. On the mountain, Elijah also saw his authority challenged by Ahaziah and the captains with their companies of soldiers. When the third captain asks Elijah to "have respect for my life and the lives of these fifty men" (all innocent, as probably were the other two companies of fifty men), Elijah's moral compass could also be challenged. The text even suggests that Elijah's "curse" (i.e., calling down fire from heaven) was motivated out of fear (v. 15). When comparing the two scenes (1:9-15 and 2:23-25), it is difficult to see how Elisha's actions are any different from those of Elijah. In any case, Yahweh upholds the word of both prophets. To flout a representative of Yahweh is to flout God himself.

This episode connects the story of Elisha with Joshua in another way. The narrative where Joshua cursed Jericho by the word of Yahweh (1 Kgs 16:34; cf. Josh 6:26) stands in the background of this narrative.[32] As Yahweh listened to the voice of Joshua (Josh 10:14) and to the voice of Elijah (1 Kgs 17:22), he listens to the voice of Elisha. On his own initiative, the prophet curses the rebellious children of Bethel **in the name of Yahweh. Two** [she-]**bears** come out of the **woods** and maul **forty-two** of the boys.[33] Elisha has the ear of Yahweh and embodies the spirit of Elijah. In the name of Yahweh, he is able to bring blessings (vv. 19-22) and call down curses (vv. 23-25).[34] The prophet continues to **Mount Carmel**, Elijah's home base, and then on to **Samaria**, no doubt to continue the campaign against the house of Ahab (cf. ch. 1).

---

[31]Kissling, *Reliable Characters*, pp. 166-167, 195.

[32]Conroy, "Hiel between Ahab and Elijah-Elisha," 216.

[33]Forty-two may be a symbolic number for victims (cf. 2 Kgs 10:14). See Nelson, *First and Second Kings*, p. 161; Cogan and Tadmor, *II Kings*, p. 38.

[34]Cohn, *2 Kings*, p. 17; Provan, *1 and 2 Kings*, p. 174; Brueggemann, *1 & 2 Kings*, p. 299.

2 KINGS 3

G. MOAB REBELS AGAINST ISRAEL (3:1-27)

3:1-3 The storyteller returns to his report of the kings of Israel.[1]
Joram[2] is the second **son of Ahab** to reign in Israel, and he reigns
twelve years.[3] As the kings before him, he does **evil in the eyes of
the LORD,** but he was not as wicked as his parents, Ahab and Jezebel.
In fact, even with the Queen Mother in the background, Joram takes
down **the sacred stone of Baal that his father had made.** Standing
stones were often set up as objects of veneration in the ancient Near
East, representing various deities. Later, Jehu will demolish "the
sacred stone" in the temple of Baal in his effort to rid Israel of Baal
worship (10:26-27). If this is the same stone, Joram only dismantles
the sacred object. The strength of the Baal cult in Israel during the
time of Jehu suggests that Joram's reform is only modest at best.[4]
Whatever the intensity of his reform, **he** clings [דָּבַק, *dābaq*] **to the**

---

[1]As in other places in Kings, some scholars have seen an underlying "literary prehistory" to chapter 3. Hobbs maintains, "There might well be some
literary artistry at work which can be appreciated by examining the story in
its present form" (*2 Kings*, p. 32). The following discussion intends to call
attention to that artistry, which demonstrates both authorial intent and the
unity of the composition.

[2]The Hebrew is "Jehoram" (יְהוֹרָם, *yᵉhôrām*), an alternate spelling of
"Joram" (יוֹרָם, *yôrām*). Both spellings occur for Joram son of Ahab and for
Jehoram son of Jehoshaphat, without any discernible pattern (although, see
comments on 8:25-27). To avoid confusion, the NIV spells the name of the
king of Israel "Joram" and the king of Judah "Jehoram," a scheme that will
be maintained in this commentary, regardless of the spelling in the underlying Hebrew text.

[3]For a discussion of the chronological issues raised by "the eighteenth
year of Jehoshaphat," see comments on 1:16-18.

[4]Nelson, *First and Second Kings*, p. 165. Provan sees Joram "tolerating the
Baal cult" (*1 and 2 Kings*, p. 181).

sins of Jeroboam, which he had caused Israel to commit. The storyteller uses the same verb to describe Solomon's commitment to his foreign wives ("Solomon held fast [*dābaq*] to them in love," 1 Kgs 11:2; cf. *dābaq* in 2 Kgs 18:6). In the case of Jeroboam and Baasha, the sins of Jeroboam (and the accompanying idolatrous view of Yahweh represented by the golden calves) were enough to warrant divine judgment.

3:4-8 As a vassal of Israel, **Mesha king of Moab** supplied the kings of the house of Omri with tribute, which took the form of products from the pastures of Moab.[5] After the death of Ahab, Mesha **rebels against the king of Israel**. The fact that this statement (v. 5) is verbatim a repetition of the framing statement in 1:1 suggests that politically this was a significant development for the house of Ahab. In spite of the reference to the revolt in 1:1, the narrator says in verse 6 that **at that time** [the time of the revolt] **King Joram** prepares for a military campaign to restore Moab. Perhaps Mesha has done something to precipitate the aggressive response by Joram.[6] The king of Israel asks **Jehoshaphat king of Judah** to join him against Moab. His reply (**"I am as you are . . ."**) mirrors his own response to Joram's father Ahab when summoned to participate in the battle of Ramoth Gilead (1 Kgs 22:4). The formulaic rejoinder suggests that Judah is still a vassal of Israel,[7] although Jehoshaphat did exercise his muscles against Ahaziah (22:48-49). More important, the correspondence between the two battle stories establishes a framework for reading the account of the campaign against Moab. In the following scenes, questions raised about the prophet Elisha and the role Yahweh plays in the story will be answered by recognizing parallels between the two accounts. Jehoshaphat recommends that they approach Moab from the south, **through the Desert of Edom**. Apparently, the king of Edom is a vassal of Judah (1 Kgs 22:47).

---

[5]The word used to describe the king of Moab (נֹקֵד, *nōqēd*, "sheep breeder") appears elsewhere in the Old Testament only in Amos 1:1. The use of *nōqēd* in Amos suggests that the prophet was not a simple shepherd (cf. 7:14). He may have owned flocks of sheep.

[6]Contra Cohn, who sees this as a contradiction (*2 Kings*, p. 20). Gerald L. Mattingly believes that Israel did not immediately march on Moab because of preoccupation with an Assyrian threat that continued after the battle of Qarqar ("Mesha, [person]," in *ABD*).

[7]Cogan and Tadmor, *II Kings*, p. 44.

The revolt of Moab against Israel is corroborated in the famous Mesha Stela (also called the Moabite Stone) on which is an inscription from this same Mesha king of Moab. Discovered in the Transjordan at Dhiban in 1868, the inscription stimulated interest in Bible lands as the first extrabiblical text to directly mention events in the Bible. It remains the longest inscription from Iron Age Palestine. Dating from the mid-ninth century B.C., the campaign of Joram outlined in Kings is not specifically mentioned in the inscription (however, see below). Nevertheless, the inscription does give an overview of the general state of relations between Israel and Moab following the battle of Qarqar (and the death of Ahab at Ramoth Gilead) and the ensuing breakup of the coalition of states that controlled the region. Concerning the house of Omri, the inscription reads in part:

> As for Omri, king of Israel, he humbled Moab many years (lit., days), for Chemosh was angry at his land. And his son (or "sons") followed him and he also said, "I will humble Moab." In my time he spoke (thus), but I have triumphed over him and over his house, while Israel hath perished for ever! (Now) Omri had occupied the land of Medeba, and (Israel) had dwelt there in his time and half the time of his son (Ahab, or "sons"), forty years; but Chemosh dwelt there in my time.[8]

In the inscription, Mesha claims to have taken the Israelite cities of Ataroth and Nebo, slaughtering their inhabitants for Chemosh. He describes the conquest of Nebo in terms of holy war: "And Chemosh said to me, 'Go, take Nebo from Israel!' So I went by night and fought against it from the break of dawn until noon, taking it and slaying all, seven thousand men, boys, women, girls and maidservants, for I had devoted them to destruction (חרם, ḥrm) for (the god) Ashtar-Chemosh. And I took from there the [. . .] of Yahweh, dragging them before Chemosh."[9] He also claims to have defeated the king of Israel "while he was fighting against me" at Jahaz. Perhaps these incursions into Israelite territory are the occasion that precipitated the response of Joram. If Moab had secured and fortified its northern border with Israel, Joram's strategy of attacking from the south through Edom makes strategic sense. The inscription does

---

[8]*ANET*, p. 320.
[9]Ibid.

mention a successful military campaign to the south "against Hauronen" that could correlate with the invasion, but this is speculative.[10] In the inscription, Mesha praises his god Chemosh for saving Moab and causing him "to triumph over all my adversaries."[11]

3:9-12 The alliance of three kings sets out to attack Moab from the south, but without enough **water** falters in the desert. The **king of Israel** laments, **"Has the LORD called us three kings together only to hand us over to Moab?"** His remark takes the reader aback. When did Yahweh call this alliance to go up against Moab? Apparently, information has been withheld from the reader. When Jehoshaphat asks for a prophet of Yahweh (**"Is there no prophet of the LORD here, that we may inquire of the LORD through him?"**),[12] the reader recalls once more the campaign of Ahab and Judah against Ben-Hadad. This is the same question Jehoshaphat asked before that battle, when he realized that Ahab's prophets were simply parroting the wishes of the king (1 Kgs 22:7). On the analogy of that scene, the reader assumes that this campaign was also inaugurated and blessed with a similar prophetic word. In the ancient Near East, it was common to ask for the favor of the gods through prophets and diviners before taking on an enemy in battle. Once more, Jehoshaphat has reason to question the king of Israel's prophets. The army's present situation suggests their mission is doomed, and Yahweh is not with them. The reader suspects that a lying spirit may have enticed them to go up against Moab. Perhaps Yahweh will defeat Joram's plans so that he dies on the battlefield like his father Ahab.[13]

---

[10]Hobbs, *2 Kings*, pp. 40-41; Cogan and Tadmor, *II Kings*, p. 51.

[11]*ANET*, p. 320. For a concise overview of the inscription and its significance, see J. Andrew Dearman and Gerald L. Mattingly, "Mesha Stele," in *ABD*; Gerald L. Mattingly, "Moabites," in *Peoples of the Old Testament World*, ed. Alfred J. Hoerth, Gerald L. Mattingly, and Edwin M. Yamauchi (Grand Rapids: Baker, 1994), p. 327. For the first Moabite temple discovered in Palestine, in which Chemosh may have been worshiped, see Michéle Daviau and Paul-Eugéne Dion, "Moab Comes to Life," *BAR* 28/1 (Jan./Feb. 2002): 38-49, 63.

[12]Cohn emphasizes the contrast between Joram and Jehoshaphat, who seeks Yahweh (*2 Kings*, p. 21).

[13]Provan makes this connection but misses the gap the narrator leaves for an initial word from prophets as in 1 Kings 22. He wonders how Jehoshaphat could go off without consulting prophets (*1 and 2 Kings*, p. 182).

An officer of the king of Israel, not the king, points out that **Elisha son of Shaphat** is nearby. In subsequent stories, individuals on the social periphery will have knowledge of and access to Elisha.[14] The statement that Elisha **used to pour water on the hands of Elijah** is unique in the Old Testament. Most assume that it is an idiom to say he was a servant or understudy of Elijah. It may also relate to the present crisis. The troops and animals need water. The narrator leaves a "blank" as to how it happens that Elisha is nearby, although it is doubtful that he was traveling with the army. The text simply says that they **went down to him**. To his credit, Jehoshaphat recognizes Elisha and knows, **"The word of the LORD is with him."**

3:13-19 Elisha expresses animosity toward Joram: **"Go to the prophets of your father and the prophets of your mother."** Paradoxically, Joram repeats his exclamation (v. 10) that *Yahweh* has called them together — **"to hand** [them] **over to Moab."** The prophet declares that if it were not for **"the presence of Jehoshaphat king of Judah,"** he would not even acknowledge the king of Israel. Then Elisha does something bizarre for the average modern reader. He calls for a **harpist** to assist him in receiving a revelation from Yahweh. This apparently reflects a sociocultural dimension to prophecy in the ninth century B.C., where ecstatic, trancelike behavior (sometimes brought on by music) may be associated with the prophetic voice (cf. 1 Sam 10:5-11; see comments on 1 Kgs 17:21-23).[15] And Yahweh responds to Elisha's overture. The inspired narrator says that **while the harpist was playing, the hand of the LORD came upon Elisha** (cf. 1 Kgs 18:46).

In his oracle, Elisha twice uses the messenger formula, **"This is what the LORD says,"** and speaks for Yahweh in first person. Yahweh will deliver the army and its animals from their dire situation. The desert will miraculously become **"a valley** [i.e., 'wadi'] **full of ditches."** Without **wind or rain**, water will appear in the desert. The prophet then changes to third person (perhaps his own words[16]) to say, "Yahweh **will also hand Moab over to you."** In language that

---

[14]Ibid., p. 185.

[15]See Cogan and Tadmor, *II Kings*, p. 45; for a concise discussion of ecstasy in Old Testament prophecy, see Helmer Ringgren, "Ecstasy," in *ABD*.

[16]Highlighting the deception in the oracle, Kissling sees the change to third person and to Elisha's voice as important in the prophet's characterization as "unreliable" (*Reliable Characters*, pp. 75, 179, 181-187, 189-190).

calls to mind holy war,[17] the alliance will destroy the cities and resources of Moab, which will include cutting down **every good tree**, stopping up **all the springs**, and ruining **every good field with stones**. Some argue that Elisha's words contradict Moses' injunction not to cut down every tree when laying siege to a city (Deut 20:19-20). However, Israel was not to fell fruit trees, so they would have food to sustain an army away from home, a stipulation that does not fit this situation. In Moab, they are in close proximity to Israelite settlements and resources in the Transjordan.[18]

3:20-25 About the time for offering the sacrifice, an appropriate time for divine intervention, water miraculously appears **from the direction of Edom**. Yahweh has kept his word to deliver the army and its animals. The narrator now backtracks to set the scene for battle. The Moabites were aware of the advancing army. Troops were mustered (**young and old, who could bear arms**) and **stationed on the border**,[19] but the invading army had apparently outflanked Moabite ranks because the defenders are described looking east, into the sun. In the glare of the sun, they mistakenly think the water is blood: **"Those kings must have fought and slaughtered each other."** Yahweh's deliverance with water also becomes the means for "handing Moab over." Moab attacks **the camp of Israel** only to find the army waiting. They retreat, and **the Israelites invade the land**, slaughtering the Moabites. Noticeably, the alliance is named Israel in the battle report, probably reflecting Moab's point of view. Joram is the leader of the alliance, and Moab has rebelled against the house of Ahab.

For the most part, Elisha's words come to pass. There are, however, important differences between his oracle (v. 19) and the way the narrator describes Israel's invasion of Moab (v. 25). "Every fortified city and every major town" becomes simply **the towns** (or "cities"), and in the fulfillment of the prophecy the order changes from cities, trees, springs, and fields to cities, fields, springs, and trees. The reversed order prepares the reader for a surprise. The narrator moves from cities in reverse order back to one city. In spite of Elisha's prophecy,

---

[17]See Nelson, *First and Second Kings*, p. 167.

[18]Hobbs, 2 Kings, p. 37.

[19]The southern border of Moab was the Zered (i.e., the Wadi Hasa). See Herr, "The Iron Age II Period," 150.

Israel was not able to take **Kir Hareseth**,[20] one of the fortified cites of Moab. The storyteller relays these events, however, in such a way that Elisha's words are upheld. The prophet said that the alliance would *smite* (נָכָה, *nākāh*, v. 19; in the NIV "overthrow") the cities of Moab. In verse 25, the narrator states that Israel *tore down* (הָרַס, *hāras*; in the NIV "destroyed") their cities, except for Kir Hareseth. Then, he adds that slingers surrounded the city and **attacked** [*nākāh*, "smote"] **it**. Elisha's words ("You will *nākāh* every fortified city . . .") technically are true — in terms of details, if not in outcome.[21]

3:26-27 Holed up in Kir Hareseth, the king of Moab with **seven hundred swordsmen** tries **to break through to the king of Edom**. He either believes that the king of Edom would be more sympathetic or sees an area of weakness in that part of the battle line. Failing in that attempt, he moves to a last-resort maneuver to win victory over Israel and save his throne. Mesha offers **his firstborn son, who was to succeed him as king**, as **a sacrifice** [literally, "a whole burnt offering"] **on the city wall**. In response to the king's sacrifice, there is great **fury** [קֶצֶף, *qeṣeph*, "wrath"] **against Israel**. The alliance **withdraws and returns to their own land**. Mesha is saved. As Joram himself will be saved from the besieging Arameans (6:24–7:20) and Hezekiah from the Assyrians (18:9–19:37),[22] so Mesha is rescued from the hand of Israel.[23] Ironically, Joram's words are true. Yahweh has given them over "to the hand of Moab" (vv. 10,13).[24]

But what of Elisha's prophecy? This shocking reversal at the end of the story raises questions about his oracle. Also, key to unraveling the story, what is the "fury against Israel"? There is ambiguity in the text concerning this wrath. Is it the wrath of Jehoshaphat and the king of Edom against Joram, or perhaps the wrath of Yahweh? It

---

[20]Kir Hareseth may be the modern site of Kerak on the King's Highway in Jordan, a defensible location with steep slopes on three sides, although exact identification is uncertain (see Ernst Axel Knauf, "Kerak," in *ABD*; Cogan and Tadmor, *II Kings*, p. 46).

[21]Provan notices the repetition of *nākāh* to say that Elisha's words did come to pass (*1 and 2 Kings*, p. 186).

[22]Nelson, *First and Second Kings*, p. 168.

[23]Mesha's name means "salvation." Mattingly suggests that Mesha may have been named by his parents in hopes that he would deliver Moab from Israel, or his name may simply represent the common belief in Moab that Chemosh was a savior ("Mesha," in *ABD*).

[24]Provan, *1 and 2 Kings*, p. 183.

could even be the wrath of Moab's god Chemosh, who in Mesha's view must have won the day. The context would suggest that there was indignation against Joram, one assumes from Jehoshaphat, over what this untoward mission had led to, reprehensible human sacrifice to a foreign deity. Even though the alliance held the upper hand, this provocative act caused them to retreat. But the writer appears to be doing more than explain the coalition's retreat. The word that the narrator uses for wrath (*qeṣeph*; "fury" in the NIV) is regularly used for the wrath of God (cf., e.g., Num 18:5; Deut 29:27; Josh 9:20; 22:20).[25] Since the point of view of the storyteller is that Yahweh is the only true God (cf. 1 Kgs 20:28), it is unlikely that he means to say that Mesha was delivered because of the wrath of Chemosh.[26] More likely, in addition to explaining Israel's withdrawal, the narrator uses *qeṣeph* to say that Yahweh has defeated Joram (cf. 5:1). The resonance between this story and Ahab's ill-fated campaign against Ben-Hadad frames the narrator's words. While Joram has not met his fate on the battlefield, he has been defeated in much the same way as was his father. In fact, in a rather brilliant way, the narrator records Joram asking the question of the narrative: "Has the LORD called us three kings together only to hand us over to Moab?" (v. 10; emphasized by repetition in v. 13b) — to which the final scene answers, "Yes!"[27] The word of Yahweh has thwarted Joram's misguided efforts to maintain the regional dominance of his fathers.[28]

Recognizing how this story fits into the larger narrative explains the role of the prophet. Through the lens of the Ahab/Jehoshaphat battle narrative, Elisha is Micaiah.[29] He has enticed Joram to attack

---

[25]Cogan and Tadmor, *II Kings*, p. 47.

[26]Cohn wonders if v. 27 reflects Moab's point of view (*2 Kings*, p. 24). Nelson entertains the attractive suggestion that the text is saying that Yahweh uses gods like Chemosh (*First and Second Kings*, pp. 169-170).

[27]The king's statement can be read as a lament ("Alas, the LORD has called us . . . to hand us over to Moab!"), with the same effect (as in v. 13b).

[28]This contextual reading offers more than Brueggemann, who concludes, "The narrative leaves us hanging, without resolution" (*1 & 2 Kings*, p. 315).

[29]Kissling incisively sees the connection between Elisha and Micaiah, but to maintain his view of Elisha as an "unreliable" character, he dismisses it as an "option [that] should not necessarily be ruled out completely" (*Reliable Characters*, p. 186; see pp. 181-187).

Moab. At the same time, the narrator goes out of his way to say that Elisha's words are technically true. Only, the prophet's word is not the whole truth. Elisha does not explain (as Micaiah explained) what Yahweh is doing. In spite of the fact that Joram is not as bad as his parents, Yahweh has not forgotten Elijah's word of judgment on Israel. Unwittingly, the king twice verbalizes the point of the story — Yahweh called the three kings together to hand them over to Moab (vv. 10,13). The anger of Yahweh continues against the house of Ahab.[30] The reader can anticipate that Joram will die like his father.

---

[30]Hobbs observes, "The downward trend in the fortunes of the nation continues under Joram." The king's "apostasy brings with it defeat" (2 Kings, pp. 33, 38).

2 KINGS 4

H. ELISHA PERFORMS MIRACLES FOR THE SMALL AND GREAT (4:1–8:6)

1. Elisha Rescues a Widow (4:1-7)

The four episodes that follow demonstrate that Elisha has the spirit of Elijah and is a man of God who speaks for Yahweh (2:9; cf. 1 Kgs 17:16,24). In fact, each of the four narratives in some way mirrors the story of Elijah and the widow of Zarephath:

Oil multiplies (vv. 1-7)   //   Oil and flour multiply (17:13-16)
Son raised (vv. 8-37)   //   Son raised (17:17-24)
Flour plays a role (vv. 38-41)   //   Flour plays a role (17:13-16)
Bread multiplies (vv. 42-44)   //   Bread multiplies (17:13-16; cf. v. 13)

However, these stories are framed to commend something in Elisha's prophetic ministry that does not characterize Elijah's career. Elisha reaches out to those who do not possess power or prestige and even to those on the periphery of society: a widow, a bereaved woman, poor prophets, and "the people."[1] In each story, a problem is solved by the prophet for the benefit of these representatives of the powerless in Israelite society. The fact that nameless recipients of God's grace are not important characters reinforces this emphasis.[2] In this way, Elisha personifies the meaning of his name (אֱלִישָׁע, *'ĕlîšā'*, "God/my God saves") and prefigures the Messiah, not only as a miracle worker, but also as one whose mission includes the outcast of society (cf. Luke 4:16-19).

---

[1] The story of the widow of Zarephath is one exception, although Elijah was directed to the widow by Yahweh (cf. 1 Kgs 17:9).

[2] For good summaries of how verbal connectors and themes tie these Elisha stories together, see Nelson, *First and Second Kings*, pp. 170-171; Hobbs, *2 Kings*, pp. 45-46, 49.

4:1-7 The brief story about the widow of **a man from the company of the prophets**, who is trying to save her orphaned sons, especially portrays Elisha in the role of administering justice to the oppressed. In a patriarchal society, a woman without a male patron is virtually powerless.[3] So, caring for the widow and orphan comes to signify in Scripture social justice and the divine character that Yahweh expected of Israel (see, e.g., Isa 1:17; cf. Jas 1:27). As already delineated, this is the kind of justice (wisdom from above) that should characterize Israel's kings and will define the Messiah: "He will defend the afflicted among the people and save the children of the needy" (Ps 72:4; see comments on 1 Kgs 3:28). The widow's situation is precarious. Although regulated by law (Exod 21:2-11; Deut 15:12-18; Lev 25:39-46), unbridled debt slavery becomes an egregious offense in Israel that was condemned by the prophets (e.g., Amos 2:6; 8:6). By the time of the return from exile, almost twenty percent of the Israelite population are slaves (see Neh 5:1-13).[4] Without a redeemer, her sons will become **slaves** of the **creditor**.

The remedy resonates with Elijah's miracle of providing for the widow of Zarephath (1 Kgs 17:7-24) but has one interesting difference, secrecy. The widow is to **shut the door** when she pours the **oil into all the jars**. Later, Elisha will close the door when he raises the Shunammite's son (v. 33).[5] When all the jars are filled, **the oil stops flowing**. She has enough to pay her **debts** and provide for her sons. The widow's situation and point of view are changed. In the last verse of the story, the narrator for the first time names Elisha **the man of God** (v. 7). Although in the narrator's voice, he is subtly

---

[3]Brueggemann, *1 & 2 Kings*, p. 319.

[4]Assuming women and children are included in the figures, Ezra 2:64-65 records that 17.3% of the returnees were slaves (Mark R. Sneed, "A Middle Class in Ancient Israel," in *Concepts of Class in Ancient Israel*, ed. Mark R. Sneed [Atlanta: Scholars Press, 1999], p. 60). For helpful discussions of debt slavery in Israel, see pp. 58-63; Callender, "Servants of God(s)," 74-75. Sneed even maintains that because the "patrimony" (i.e., property) would go back to the clan of her husband, widows (and orphans without claim to patrimony) were in a worse situation than slaves (p. 60).

[5]Hobbs asserts that "secrecy and private miracles" characterize Elisha's prophetic ministry (*1 Kings*, p. 52). However, there is not enough correspondence to suggest that this foreshadows the messianic secret of the Gospel narratives.

representing a change in her point of view.[6] In verse 1, the widow named the prophet "Elisha." Although her request obviously reflects reverence for the prophet, by the end of the story she knows by experience that Elisha is a *man of God*.

2. Elisha Blesses a Woman from Shunem (4:8-37)

4:8-17 One day, Elisha travels to **Shunem**, a town in the hill country of Issachar (Josh 19:18), and stops to eat with a **well-to-do woman**. The phrase "one day" marks important transitions in the story (vv. 8,11,18).[7] The Shunammite is literally named "a great woman" (אִשָּׁה גְדוֹלָה, *'iššāh gᵊdōlāh*), with the nuance of a person of wealth. By the end of the story, however, there will be reason to believe that the narrator intends more in this designation than financial means. Apparently, the prophet traveled a circuit (cf. v. 38) that on occasion put him at Shunem. The woman asks her husband to build **a small room on the roof**, so that Elisha would have a place to stay. The furnishings are modest but more than adequate for the itinerant prophet. These minor details will serve the narrator later when the woman places her dead son on Elisha's bed. Throughout the story, the Shunammite takes initiative. Her husband is only a minor character, an agent who by contrast highlights his wife's faith in the prophet Elisha. Also, in contrast with the widow of Zarephath, the Shunammite knows early on that Elisha is **a holy man of God** (cf. 1 Kgs 17:7-24).[8]

On one trip through Shunem ("one day," v. 11), the man of God asks his servant **Gehazi** to **"Call the Shunammite."** Gehazi appears for the first time. The role of obedient servant that he plays in this story contrasts with his characterization in the following narrative (ch. 5). She "stands **before him**," the posture of an obedient servant.

---

[6]The point of view of characters is often represented in the narrator's voice. See, e.g., Gen 38:15 ff, where Judah's point of view is reflected in the pronouns the narrator uses to name Tamar. Judah thinks she is a prostitute and sees her as an impersonal "she," "her," etc. (see Berlin, *Poetics and Interpretation*, pp. 60-61).

[7]Cohn, *2 Kings*, p. 28; Nelson, *First and Second Kings*, p. 173.

[8]Cohn, *2 Kings*, p. 28. This is the only time in the Old Testament a prophet is described as "holy" (Cogan and Tadmor, *II Kings*, p. 56).

Elisha does not speak to her directly. Perhaps social mores dictate such formal interaction. **What can be done for you?** mirrors Elisha's question to the widow in the preceding story (v. 2). **Can we speak on your behalf to the king or the commander of the army?** indicates that Elisha has influence in high circles. He may have earned some political clout during the campaign against Moab (ch. 3). The Shunammite demurs, **"I have a home among my own people."** She is content with what she has. Ironically, she will later stand before the king and ask for the return of her property (8:1-6). Gehazi observes that she is childless, and **her husband is old.** In language that calls to mind Yahweh's promise that Sarah would have a son (cf. Gen 17:21; 18:10-15),[9] Elisha declares, **"About this time next year, . . . you will hold a son in your arms."** The woman demurs once more, **"Don't mislead** ["deceive"] **your servant."** Again, allusion to an earlier narrative guides the reader; however, the focus here is not the promised son. It is the messenger![10] As Yahweh's word to Abraham and Sarah came true (Gen 21:1-2), so does the word of Elisha, who speaks as Yahweh. The Shunammite conceives and bears a son, exactly **as Elisha told her.**

4:18-30 Without transition, the narrator carries the reader to **one day** after the child has grown (v. 18). In the field with his father, his head begins to hurt. He is taken to his mother and dies in her lap. Without any insight into her emotional response, the eye of the storyteller's camera watches the Shunammite. She acts. Verbs dominate. She *goes up*, *lays* the boy **on the bed of the man of God**, *shuts* **the door**, and *goes out* (v. 21). She asks **her husband** for permission to make the trek to Carmel. His response (**"It's not the New Moon or the Sabbath"**) may indicate that pilgrimages were made only on feast days.[11] His comment also adds to her characterization as a faithful follower of the prophet. It apparently was not uncommon for her to visit the prophet on feast days. Without informing her husband of the death of the child, she retorts, "Good-bye!" (שָׁלוֹם, šālôm, **"It's all right"** in the NIV). She, not the servant, saddles the donkey,

---

[9]Brueggemann demonstrates a relationship between the promise to Sarah and to the Shunammite (*1 & 2 Kings*, p. 322).

[10]See Cohn, *2 Kings*, p. 29.

[11]See Hobbs, *2 Kings*, pp. 51-52; Provan, *1 and 2 Kings*, p. 189.

directing the young man not to **slow down** without direction. **So she set out and came to the man of God at Mount Carmel**.

From Elisha's point of view, the reader sees her coming.[12] Elisha directs Gehazi to intercept the Shunammite and ask, **"Are you all right? Is your husband all right? Is your child all right?"** In Hebrew, these questions represent a common greeting with *šālôm* ("peace"; הֲשָׁלוֹם, *hăšālôm*, "are [you] well?"), but Elisha is genuinely concerned to see her approaching. Surprisingly, she answers *šālôm* (**"Everything is all right"** in the NIV), even though things are *not well*.[13] The repetition of *šālôm* (cf. her response to her husband in v. 23) suggests larger meaning. Her curt behavior both to her husband and to Gehazi reveals a single-minded resolve to reach the man of God. Social norms aside, at Carmel she grabs the prophet's **feet**. Gehazi tries to push her aside, but Elisha recognizes that **"She is in bitter distress, but the LORD has hidden it from me and has not told me why."** While the prophet can be clairvoyant (cf. ch. 5), he can only see what Yahweh allows him to see. The woman finally speaks with penetrating words for Elisha, but, unlike Elijah, the prophet does not blame Yahweh (cf. 1 Kgs 17:20). He acts. Gehazi is directed to run ahead with Elisha's **staff** to resuscitate the boy. In contrast with his instructions before, the prophet's servant is not to greet (בָּרַךְ, *bārak*) anyone. The Shunammite, now named **the child's mother** to call attention to her point of view, exclaims, **"As surely as the LORD lives and as you live, I will not leave you."** Remarkably, she quotes Elisha's words to Elijah at his ascension (2:2,4,6).[14] Her unwavering commitment to Elisha may remind him of his own belief in Elijah.[15] He follows her to Shunem.

4:31-37 Arriving ahead of Elisha, Gehazi places the staff **on the boy's face**. In words that echo Baal's response to his prophets on Mount Carmel, the narrator says **there was no sound or response** (cf. 1 Kgs 18:26,29). The obvious link with the prophets of Baal[16] negatively portrays Gehazi and foreshadows the curse he will later

---

[12]Cohn, *2 Kings*, p. 31.

[13]See Brueggemann, *1 & 2 Kings*, p. 323.

[14]Hobbs describes this repetition as "literary genius, and irony" (*2 Kings*, p. 48), but he offers no suggestion as to its exegetical significance.

[15]Cohn, *2 Kings*, p. 32.

[16]See Provan, *1 and 2 Kings*, p. 188.

receive. Cohn misses the point of the allusion when he claims that by extension it also associates Elisha with the "ineffectual prophets of Baal."[17] On the contrary, it establishes an important contrast between Gehazi and Elisha (which will be further spelled out in the story of Naaman to follow, ch. 5). Elisha (as did Elijah) will succeed where Gehazi (and the prophets of Baal) failed. But regardless of characterization, on the level of plot the echo increases the tension in the story. Will Elisha be able to raise the child? Will Yahweh listen to the voice of Elisha, as he listened to the voice of his servant Elijah (1 Kgs 17:22)?

Elisha finds **the boy lying dead on his couch**. He shuts the door and **prays to the LORD**, a parallel to Elijah's prayer that Yahweh "let this boy's life return to him" (1 Kgs 17:21). Resonance with Elijah's miracle frames this account, yet to create suspense, the narrator describes the action in somewhat greater detail (e.g., **mouth to mouth, eyes to eyes**, etc.). Will Yahweh respond to Elisha's prayer? The prophet paces the floor.[18] Raising the dead is the quintessential, most challenging demonstration of the power of Yahweh. Elijah stretched himself over the boy three times; Elisha does so only twice.[19] But the narrator uses a different verb for Elisha. Instead of מָדַד (*mādad*), for *stretching out* over the boy, he uses the word that described Elijah bending down (גְּהַר, *gāhar*) with his head between his knees as he prayed for rain (1 Kgs 18:42).[20] Perhaps the story-teller also wants to connect Elisha's actions with Elijah's prayer for rain. The parallels with Elijah's "death-bed miracle" in Zarephath suggest that the storyteller is affirming that Yahweh also listens to the voice of Elisha. The resonance also underscores Elisha's faith in Yahweh. The author of Hebrews affirms that "through faith . . .

---

[17]Cohn, *2 Kings*, p. 33.

[18]There is not anything in the narrative to suggest the narrator intends to convey a difference in powers between Elijah and Elisha, unless it is to say that Elisha's powers surpass those of his mentor. Elijah stretches himself over the widow's son three times, and Elisha stretches himself over the Shunammite's son twice (contra Kissling, *Reliable Characters*, p. 196).

[19]For a discussion of the shamanlike behavior in the miracles of Elijah and Elisha, see comments on 1 Kgs 17:21-23.

[20]Cohn suggests that this word "may indicate a final prostration over the boy which collects the energy that Elisha has created and transfers it to the dead child" (*2 Kings*, p. 33).

women received back their dead, raised to life again" (11:33,35) — in this case through the faith of both Elisha and the Shunammite.

Yahweh responds. The boy **sneezes seven times and opens his eyes**. The number seven must symbolically reinforce the miraculous nature of what has happened. The scene closes with the boy's mother, a "great woman" (*'iššāh gᵉdōlāh*, v. 8), once more at the **feet** of Elisha — only this time in a posture of veneration. The prophet has both given her a son and restored him to life, by the power of Yahweh. In the end, everything is *šālôm*!

3. Elisha Salvages Stew for a Company of Prophets (4:38-41)

4:38-41 Returning to Gilgal (for location, see comments on 2:1-6) in a time of **famine**, Elisha appears once more in association with a **company of prophets** (see comments on 2:7-10). "Company of prophets" ties together three of the episodes in this section (vv. 1-7, vv. 38-41, vv. 42-44). The famine appears to be the one mentioned in 8:1, where Elisha informs the Shunammite that Yahweh had decreed a seven-year famine against the land.[21] Indirectly, the story exposes how such acts of judgment affected the righteous poor. The community of prophets is left to scavenge for **herbs**. Apparently without any culinary inclinations, one prophet retrieves wild **gourds** and adds them to the community **stew**. When they begin eating, Elisha hears, **"O man of God, there is death in the pot!"** But the prophet knows what to do. **Flour** is added to offset the bitter (and perhaps toxic) taste.[22] The prophet is able to transform something inedible into nourishing food. Perhaps indicating why this story has been preserved, Elisha directs, **"Serve it *to the people* [the prophets' families?] to eat."** Elisha began his prophetic ministry feeding others. When the prophet was called to follow Elijah, he sacrificed his oxen, cooked the meat, and "gave it *to the people*" (1 Kgs 19:21). The narrator concludes, **there was nothing harmful in the pot.**

---

[21]Provan, *1 and 2 Kings*, p. 189; Nelson, *First and Second Kings*, p. 171.

[22]If the text has reference to wild gourds that grow in the region, they are not toxic, only bitter (Cohn, *2 Kings*, p. 53; Nelson, *First and Second Kings*, p. 174; cf. Cogan and Tadmor, *II Kings*, p. 58). No remedy is tendered for the ones who consumed some of the stew.

4. Elisha Multiplies Bread for the People (4:42-44)

4:42-44 A man from **Baal Shalishah**[23] arrives with **twenty loaves of barley bread baked from the first ripe grain, along with heads of new grain** for **the man of God**. The gift must represent an offering of firstfruits in appreciation for some relief from the famine. Once more, Elisha directs, **"Give it to the people to eat"** (cf. v. 41). His servant (the reader thinks of Gehazi) balks, **"How can I set this before a hundred men?"** Elisha repeats his directive and says, **"This is what the LORD says: 'They will eat and have some left over.'"** For the first time in this collection of miracle stories (ch. 4), Elisha speaks in the name of Yahweh. The people eat and have *some left over*. The narrator adds, **according to the word of the LORD**. This miracle and the three that precede it are enabled by the word of Yahweh, which resides in Elisha (cf. the widow of Zarephath's statement in 1 Kgs 17:24) — and are performed for the people of God!

Elisha's miracle of the multiplication of loaves resonates with Moses, who brought manna from heaven (Exodus 16),[24] but also looks forward to the Messiah's miracle of feeding the thousands. In each gospel narrative, Jesus multiples loaves (and fish) to feed a large crowd, with basketfuls *"left over"* (see, e.g., Luke 9:17). John even adds that the loaves were of barley (6:8). These allusions recommend additional connections with the ministry of Jesus. When the prophet raises the Shunammite's son, he prefigures the Messiah raising the dead (cf. Mark 5:21-24,35-43; Luke 7:11-17; John 11:17-31). And Elisha's compassion for the women (one poor and in need, the other wealthy but in need[25]) and the poor prophets in these stories foreshadows Jesus' ministry for those on the periphery, for the "poor" and "oppressed" (Luke 4:18-19).[26] Is it too much to add that the connection the narrator makes between Elisha's deeds of compassion and the word of Yahweh (v. 44) also prefigures the prophet who would come, "a prophet, powerful in *word* and *deed* before God and all the people" (Luke 24:19)?

---

[23]The city may be identified with Khirbet Sirisya, overlooking the Sharon plain (Gary A. Herion, "Baal-Shalishah [place]," in *ABD*).

[24]See Brueggemann, *1 & 2 Kings*, pp. 326, 329.

[25]See Cohn, *2 Kings*, p. 25.

[26]Luke's account of Jesus' announcement of his mission (4:24-27) includes references to Elijah and Elisha (Speer, "A Study of Allusion," 97). For helpful discussions of the connections between Elisha and the New Testament, see Provan, *1 and 2 Kings*, p. 190; Hobbs, *2 Kings*, pp. 54-55.

2 KINGS 5

5. Elisha Blesses a Syrian Commander (5:1-27)

5:1-2 The narrator sets the stage for the story of Naaman with an economy of words that is noteworthy. In these initial verses, the storyteller introduces the main character and supplies the information that establishes the story's primary tension. Naaman is described in glowing terms. He is named **commander of the army of the king of Aram**[1] and is portrayed as highly esteemed by **his master** the king. He is a **great man** and a **valiant soldier**. Only, he is a leper. With one word in Hebrew (מְצֹרָע, *mᵉṣōrāʿ*, "one who is leprous"[2]) appended to a string of accolades, the narrator artfully creates the character feature that will carry the plot.[3] Enough is said to give the reader the

---

[1]Provan observes that a foreigner theme is another connection with the widow of Zarephath story (1 Kgs 17:17-24), reinforcing the idea that Yahweh is a God "also of foreigners" (*1 and 2 Kings*, p. 191).

[2]Both participle (from צָרַע, *ṣāraʿ*; vv. 1,11,27) and noun forms (צָרַעַת, *ṣāraʿath*; vv. 3,6,7,27) appear in the Naaman story. The range of meaning for this word is broader than the English word "leprosy," encompassing a wide variety of skin diseases. Whatever the exact malady, for the audience of this narrative *ṣāraʿ/ṣāraʿath* would signal ceremonial uncleanness (cf. Lev 13-14; see ibid., p. 194; contra Hobbs, *2 Kings*, pp. 63, 68). On a literary level, the Syrian commander is unclean, as is Gehazi when he receives Naaman's disease. When Gehazi acquires the disease and then resurfaces in chapter 8 without any mention of leprosy, the reader should not look for "degrees of leprosy" to explain away the tension. That important gap in the story calls attention to Yahweh's role in the narrative (see below and comments on 8:1-6). For concise discussions of *ṣāraʿath* in the biblical world, see David P. Wright and Richard N. Jones, "Leprosy," in *ABD*; Cogan and Tadmor, *II Kings*, p. 63.

[3]The editors of *BHS* with the Lucianic recension suggest deleting "valiant soldier" as a scribal emendation to smooth out what appears to be awkward construction with "but he had leprosy." However, the reading in the MT ("He was a valiant soldier, but had leprosy") is better explained as literary

essential details, but only just enough. The particulars are left for
the reader to fill in. With a dearth of description, typical of Hebrew
narrative, the reader is invited to create his own images of the man
of prestige and privilege who acquires a socially unacceptable disease. The storyteller frames the tale and evokes these images with a
few brief strokes.

The frugal use of language also enables the reader to identify
narrative design. The description of Naaman as a "great man"
(אִישׁ גָּדוֹל, 'îš gādôl) stands out in this regard. This epithet is fraught
with ambiguity yet clearly connects the story with the preceding
Shunammite episode.[4] Does "great" mean important, rich, a man of
position? This uncertainty adds depth to the characterization of
Naaman and calls to mind the Shunammite who is also named
"great" ('iššāh gᵊdōlāh, "a great woman"; "a well-to-do woman" in the
NIV; see comments on 4:8-17). That both characters receive blessings and serve in their respective stories to highlight the actions of
the prophet Elisha suggests an overarching plan. Later, when other
parallels between the two come to the surface, the Shunammite will
provide an important character contrast for interpreting the foreign
commander, Naaman, and Elisha's servant, Gehazi. The central role
the adjective "great" plays in the story is further emphasized by contrast when the young Israelite slave is literally named the "*little* girl"
(נַעֲרָה קְטַנָּה, na'ărāh qᵊṭannāh, **young girl** in the NIV).[5]

These introductory verses also establish the story's underlying
tension. Yahweh **had given victory to Aram** by way of Naaman. In
the eyes of his king, Naaman was esteemed for this triumph. An
Israelite would have another point of view. In the larger narrative,
Aram had defeated a coalition of forces from Israel and Judah at
Ramoth Gilead. In that battle, King Ahab was killed, according to
the word of Yahweh (1 Kgs 22:29-40; cf. 20:42; 21:19). Was this the
victory Yahweh granted Aram? If so, what was Naaman's role? Was
he the one who orchestrated the triumph, or perhaps even the

---

technique that dramatically brings out the disparity in "the mighty man of
valor" who is also a "leper" (see Hobbs, *2 Kings*, p. 57).

[4]See Provan for additional parallels between the Shunammite and
Naaman stories (*1 and 2 Kings*, p. 195).

[5]Jesse C. Long, Jr., "Text Story & Sermon Story in Dialogue: On
Preaching Bible Narratives," *Preaching* 12/4 (Jan./Feb. 1997), 19.

anonymous Aramean who let the arrow fly that pierced Israel's king?[6] The lack of closure teases the reader. At the same time, Yahweh's role in an Aramean victory over Israel (1 Kings 22) establishes the broader parameters of the story. The tension also moves the story forward. The reference to **bands from Aram** that raid Israel and capture a "little" girl reinforces this tension. Naaman owns an Israelite slave. For the storyteller's audience, these features vilify Naaman. In addition, a pious reader in exile must view it as poetic justice that this Aramean hero becomes an "unclean" leper. The narrator's word choice also recommends contrast between Naaman, who is (literally) "before [לִפְנֵי, liphnê] his lord" (**in the sight of his master** in the NIV), and the little girl, who is "before [liphnê] Naaman's wife" (**served Naaman's wife** in the NIV).[7]

5:3-4 Dialogue, the hallmark of Hebrew narrative, first appears in the mouth of the Israelite slave girl. She informs her mistress, Naaman's wife, of the **prophet who is in Samaria** who could **cure** [אָסַף, 'āsaph[8]] **him of his leprosy.** Her unexpected counsel, however, runs counter to the tension so far created in exposition. Natural animosities and prejudices are subverted in her gesture of good will. With this obvious incongruity, the narrator's restraint in commenting on her action further highlights her role in the story. How many preachers have lingered at "her doorstep" and lauded her as a heroine worthy of emulation? Yet, she functions on the level of plot only as an agent. No explanation is given for her display and nothing else is said about her. She serves not only Naaman's mistress; she serves the story in a minor role as an essential element in the plot.

On another level, however, the action of the young girl from Israel highlights the story's narrative art. Her performance calls attention to the account's underlying irony.[9] A victorious Aramean commander turns, of all places, to Israel for help. In this, a young

---

[6]Josephus (*Antiq.* Xv.5) and the Targum on 2 Chronicles 18 claim Naaman killed Ahab (see Hobbs, *2 Kings*, p. 63).

[7]Cohn, *2 Kings*, p. 36.

[8]The verb *'āsaph* is used to describe Miriam's readmission to the community after she was healed of her leprosy (Cogan and Tadmor, *II Kings*, p. 65).

[9]Uriel Simon maintains that minor characters may "further the plot" or "clarify another character." Also, some minor characters "lend the narrative greater meaning and depth." He believes that the minor characters in the Naaman story separate into two groups whose attitudes toward the prophet

Israelite captive aids him. But more important (and representing a fundamental characteristic of Hebrew storytelling), the unnamed "little" girl serves as a contrast for evaluating the principle characters. She is the foil for putting other players in perspective. Readers are drawn to her, even though she is painted with a minimum of detail, in part because she diverges from other individuals in the story. In particular, as the narrative's moral touchstone, she comments on Gehazi, the self-centered and greedy servant of the prophet Elisha (see below).

By the careful use of naming, the narrator also outlines important relationships. **His master** and **her mistress** are appropriate for the character roles in the world of the story. That the narrator chooses to detail these in both exposition and dialogue, however, calls attention to the story's master-servant associations. Master-servant roles are even accented in dispatch (see v. 6 below). The slave girl, Naaman, and Gehazi all enact servant roles. This servant feature operates as further backdrop for interpreting character actions and speeches. Later, when Elisha says to Naaman, "As surely as the LORD lives, *whom I serve*, I will accept nothing!" (v. 16), the narrator's underlying ideological point of view is verbalized. Yahweh is Lord in Israel, and the prophet Elisha is his servant.

5:5-8 The **king of Aram** blesses the commander's trip to Israel. Later, the prophet in Israel will bless Naaman's return, in spite of his acknowledged role in the Aramean "thunder-god cult" (5:18-19). The command to "go" (הָלַךְ, *hālak*) ties together the key scenes involving the Aramean commander. Elisha tells Naaman to **"Go, wash"** and **"Go in peace"** (*hālak*, 5:10,19). Naaman goes to Israel bearing impressive gifts of **silver, gold,** and **clothing,** and a **letter** from the king. Consonant with the prominence of dialogue in Hebrew narrative, the letter is voiced as direct speech from king to king.

In an expression of anguish, the **king of Israel** tears **his robes** (בְּגָדִים, *bᵉgādîm*, "clothes"). Twice mentioned in the story, by the narrator in exposition and in dialogue by Elisha (vv. 7,8), this act reflects the divergent perspectives of the royal houses. **"See how he is trying to pick a quarrel with me"** calls attention to the political

do not correspond with the reader's expectations. Their "opposing attitudes to their respective national groups" call attention to the contrast between Naaman and Gehazi ("Minor Characters," 14-16).

tensions already suggested in the narrative. This response is similar to the reaction of Joram's father Ahab to Ben-Hadad's aggressive behavior (1 Kgs 20:7). Joram assumes similar Aramean aggression, which may be an accurate assessment, since the king conspicuously does not mention the prophet in his letter.[10] The act of tearing his clothes also introduces a motif of clothing that links the king in Israel with both Naaman, who bears gifts of silver, gold, and *clothing*, and Gehazi, who takes and hides silver and *clothing*. Clothing is not just incidental to the plot. In subsequent episodes, it will resurface. The king will again tear his *clothes* (6:30-31), and four lepers will take and hide from the Arameans silver, gold, and *clothing* (7:8). Thus, an apparently insignificant feature ties together what appear to be disparate scenes and again suggests overarching design.

"Am I God? Can I kill and bring to life?" focuses attention once more on the narrative's ideological level of meaning. In the preceding chapter, Elisha, "the man of God," brought life by raising the Shunammite's son. The prophet, as Yahweh's servant, is the real source of power in Israel. Underlying the dialogue's ironic accent is the narrative's recurring tension between prophet and king — and by extension between Yahweh and king. In the context of the larger narrative, the king's lack of knowledge stands out. King Joram obviously does not have Yahweh's power over life and death (cf. Deut 32:39); he does not even know to turn to Yahweh's prophet, in marked contrast with the captive slave girl. Later, when the king tears his clothes again (6:30-31), he utters an oath to put Elisha to death, the source of the power and life of Yahweh in the land.[11] Can this be anything but indirect judgment on the spiritual state of the monarchy in Israel?

"Have the man come to me and he will know that there is a prophet in Israel" resonates with earlier texts. The prophet Elijah prayed on Mount Carmel that the people might know "that you are God in Israel and that I am your servant" (1 Kgs 18:36). To Elijah, the widow of Zarephath exclaimed, "Now I know that you are a man of God and that the word of the LORD from your mouth is the truth" (1 Kgs 17:24). In the Shunammite narrative, the storyteller high-

---

[10]Provan, *1 and 2 Kings*, p. 191.

[11]Provan observes that Joram will be "belatedly enlightened" about the deeds of Elisha in 8:1-6 (ibid., p. 192).

lights her single-minded intent to get to "the man of God" with news of the death of her son. The slave girl hoped that Naaman might see "the prophet who lives in Samaria" (v. 3). Later, Naaman stands before the prophet and says, "There is no God in all the world except in Israel" (v. 15). Through dialogue, and with exposition and character actions, the narrator demonstrates that the prophet represents the God of Israel. Even the Aramean leper comes to know the God of "all the world" by way of that prophet. How characters respond to the prophet, for the narrator, also reveals attitudes toward the prophet's God, Yahweh.

5:9-14 Naaman arrives with an entourage of **horses and chariots** and (literally) "stands in the doorway of the house of Elisha" (**stopped at the door** in the NIV). An unnamed messenger meets the commander. Several details again call to mind the story of the Shunammite and place the two characters in association. As Naaman, she stood in the doorway of the prophet ("stood before him," 4:12; and "stood in the doorway," 4:15; Naaman "stood before him," 5:15) and, at least initially, communicated with him through an intermediary. Only, the prophet plays no favorites. Naaman is not given any special consideration. The narrator records, "Elisha sent a messenger to say [literally, 'saying'] to [Naaman] . . ." (v. 10). When the reader recalls that a similar thing is said concerning the prophet's interaction with the king ("[Elisha] sent [the king] this message [literally, 'saying'] . . ." [v. 8]), he realizes King Joram receives the same treatment as the Syrian commander. If anything, those who are not in positions of authority are treated by the prophet with more respect (see comments on ch. 4). The foreign leper is instructed once more to "go" — **"Go, wash yourself . . . and you shall be cleansed."** Provan suggests that since Naaman apparently sees prophets as magicians who have control of the "gods" (evidenced by "wave his hand over the spot," v. 11), Elisha's unexpected directive to "wash" may be designed to deemphasize the prophet and call attention to Yahweh, not Elisha.[12]

The **rage** with which Naaman responds to the "impertinence" of the prophet is not surprising. By calculated use of gapping and dialogue, the point of view of the Aramean is highlighted, and his reaction does not appear unreasonable. Explanation for Elisha's

---

[12]Ibid., p. 193.

brusque treatment of the foreign visitor is noticeably absent. The reader may view this gap as a character flaw, consistent with earlier actions of the prophet, or something all too appropriate for the Aramean, for one who displays such a prejudicial attitude toward Israel. Surely the king also deserves the treatment he receives from Elisha. Nevertheless, however one reads the enigmatic actions of the prophet, most readers can identify with Naaman's response — for, as Naaman, the reader is also left to judge the unexpected action (or lack of action) on the part of the prophet. The reticence of the narrator, with respect to Elisha's behavior, allows the reader to see things from Naaman's point of view.

In dialogue, Naaman's point of view, even his inner thoughts (**"I thought . . ."**), is verbalized. The foreign commander apparently understood Elisha to mean ritual cleansing. In his exclamation in verse 12 (**"Couldn't I wash** [רָחַץ, *rāḥaṣ*] **in** [the rivers of Damascus] **and be cleansed** [טָהֵר, *ṭāhēr*]**?"**), "wash" and "be clean" stand out. Both terms figure prominently in the purification rituals of Leviticus (cf., e.g., 14:8-9 [*rāḥaṣ*]; 13:6,13,34; 14:4,11 [*ṭāhēr*]).[13] At the same time, the lengthy diatribe reveals more than a disgruntled "patron" whose expectations are unrealized. Underlying prejudices and a haughty spirit come to the surface as the commander stomps off in a rage. The reaction of the foreign official may well justify for the reader the prophet's behavior, but more important is how through dialogue the narrator opens and lays bare the character of Naaman. In addition, by naming, **"call on the name of the LORD *his god*,"** the narrator subtly reveals Naaman's point of view toward the God of Israel, a view the reader will see change in the course of the narrative.

Naaman's servants approach the commander and give a more reasoned view of Elisha's instructions: **"If the prophet had told you to do some great [*gādôl*] thing, would you not have done it? How much more, then when he tells you, 'Wash and be cleansed!'"** The *"great"* man (5:1) is asked to do something that is in his eyes servile.[14] Notice that Naaman's servants, like the Israelite slave girl, act with wisdom, in contrast to Naaman and Israel's king Joram. Servant roles again are accented and are even subtly lauded. On hearing the prophet's remedy, Naaman goes **away angry**. Then, after accepting

---

[13]Ibid., pp. 192, 195.
[14]Jesse C. Long, "Text Story & Sermon Story," 19.

the advice of his servants, and to his credit, he goes **down and dip**s. The storyteller advances the plot with simple, unadorned exposition. The reader is left to fill in the gaps, imagine details, and feel the emotion that must have engulfed the repentant Aramean.

At this point, the language mirrors the typical Hebrew prophecy-fulfillment formula, where repetition demonstrates the power of the word of Yahweh.[15] The messenger informs Naaman, "Go, wash yourself seven times in the Jordan, and your flesh will be restored and you will be cleansed" (v. 10). In exposition, the narrator chronicles, **He went down and dipped himself in the Jordan seven times, as the man of God had told him** [literally, "according to the word of the man of God"]**, and his flesh was restored** [שׁוּב, *šûb*] **and became clean like that of a young** [קָטֹן, *qāṭōn*, "little"] **boy**. The simple repetition of Elisha's instructions marks a miracle. The additional "like that of a [little] boy" highlights the change, while "according to the word of the man of God" identifies the source. This rhetorical style finds a direct parallel with Elijah and the widow of Zarephath (1 Kgs 17:8-24). Elijah told the widow, "For this is what the LORD, the God of Israel, says: 'The jar of flour will not be used up and the jug of oil will not run dry until the day the LORD gives rain on the land'" (7:14). The narrator records, she "did [literally] according to the word of Elijah . . . the jar of flour was not used up and the jug of oil did not run dry, in keeping with the word of the LORD spoken by Elijah" (vv. 15-16). After Elijah raised her son, the widow exclaimed, "Now I know that you are a man of God and that the word of the LORD from your mouth is the truth" (v. 24). In part, the Naaman episode says the same of Elijah's successor, Elisha.

The narrator's restraint in describing the miracle serves to highlight the basic elements of the plot. Naaman obeyed the prophet and was healed. Yet, although brief, the storyteller's choice of words sets additional tessarae that bring into focus an important motif in the narrative's mosaic. The man's flesh becomes like that of a "little boy" (נַעַר קָטֹן, *na'ar qāṭōn*). The parallel with "little girl" (*na'ărāh q³ṭannāh*) suggests a motif with "great/little" that connects charac-

---

[15]Meir Sternberg cites Gen 1:3 as the first example of this technique, where repetition "settle[s] any lingering doubt about the causal link between performative and performance" (*Poetics of Biblical Narrative*, p. 108; see pp. 104-109).

ters (i.e., the Shunammite, Naaman, and the little girl) and provides a thematic anchor for the story.[16] Instead of doing some *great* thing, Naaman, who was *great* in the eyes of his king, followed the advice of a *little* girl, his own servants, and an uncommon prophet. His diseased flesh became like that of a *little* boy. The foreign commander becomes truly *great*, like the Shunammite, when he takes on the point of view of the *little* girl toward the prophet Elisha and his God Yahweh.[17] In an epilogue to the Shunammite narrative, the king says, "Tell me all the *great* things Elisha has done" (8:4). "Great/little" reinforces the foreign commander's change in point of view, his humble submission that ended in healing, and stresses the deeds of the prophet in Israel.[18]

That Naaman could dip in the Jordan and **be cleansed** (*ṭāhēr*) introduces another key word in the story (vv. 10,12,13,14). The use of *ṭāhēr* with leprosy signals an underlying theme of ceremonial uncleanness for the leprous Aramean (see Leviticus 13–14). Though, as a foreigner, Naaman could never be "clean" in the eyes of an Israelite audience. Nevertheless, "clean/unclean" serves as an important frame for interpreting the reversal at the end of the story (see below).

5:15-19a Naaman and his retinue "return" (*šûb*, **went back** in the NIV) to the prophet. Wordplay calls attention to the commander's trek back to speak to Elisha. The narrator also employs *šûb* to describe Naaman's healing: "his flesh was restored [literally, "returned," *šûb*]" (v. 14).[19] Cohn believes that *šûb* (vv. 10,14,15) is thematic in this story, signifying Naaman's conversion, his "turning."[20] If so, the symbolism is intended for the exiles, who are called to *šûb* ("return") to Yahweh (see comments on 1 Kings 13) — ironically in this instance, like the foreign Naaman.

The commander once more stands **before** the prophet (see comments on v. 9). Only, this time he stands as one who is *clean*, no longer afflicted with leprosy. His dialogue also reflects a change of

---

[16]Several commentators mention the play on "great/little" (see, e.g., Provan, *1 and 2 Kings*, p. 195; Cohn, *2 Kings*, p. 38).

[17]Commenting on the wordplay with "little girl" and "little boy," Brueggemann describes the slave girl as "earnest of what the general will become through the ministry of Elisha" (*1 & 2 Kings*, p. 334).

[18]Jesse C. Long, "Text Story & Sermon Story," 20.

[19]See Nelson, *First and Second Kings*, pp. 178-179.

[20]Cohn, *2 Kings*, pp. 38-39.

heart. He names himself **"your servant"** and expresses belief in Yahweh, the God of Israel! He even asks for **"as much earth as a pair of mules can carry"** for **burnt offerings and sacrifices** back home. The request represents the Near Eastern belief that deities were local gods who protected the land of their worshipers (cf. 1 Kgs 20:23).[21] The Aramean wants some Israelite soil to build an altar of earth (cf. Exod 20:24-26) and incur the blessing of Israel's God Yahweh.[22] Naaman's petition is ironic. Before his cleansing, he denigrated the land of Israel and its rivers, which could not compare with the rivers of Damascus.[23] His worldview has changed. In gratitude, Naaman offers **a gift** to the prophet Elisha, who with an oath (**"as surely as the LORD lives"**) refuses to take (לָקַח, lāqaḥ, v. 16; **accept** in the NIV) anything as a servant of Yahweh. The commander **urges** the prophet, but Elisha does not relent. He is only *the servant* of the God who healed Naaman. Yahweh is the source of blessing in Israel! Later, Elisha's rejection of Naaman's gift will resurface in judgment against the greed of Elisha's own servant Gehazi.

Repetition and contrasting dialogue serve to bring out Naaman's reticence when he makes his request of the prophet. The reader hears, **"But may the LORD forgive your servant for this one thing: When my master enters the temple of Rimmon to bow down and he is leaning on my arm and I bow there also—when I bow down in the temple of Rimmon, may the LORD forgive your servant for this."** The commander is almost like a child who knows that what he wants is inappropriate.[24] Rimmon (with the probable meaning of "thunderer") is an epithet for the god Hadad, the proper name for the Canaanite god Baal ("lord"; cf. Zech 12:11).[25] "Leaning on my arm" is an idiom for an official role in the service of the king (cf. 7:2,17). The reader may also hear an echo: "Yet I reserve seven thousand in Israel — all whose knees have not bowed down to Baal"

---

[21]See Cogan and Tadmor, *II Kings*, p. 67.

[22]"Now I know that there is no God in all the world except in Israel" indicates that the God of Elisha remains an Israelite God in the mind of Naaman.

[23]Cohn, *2 Kings*, p. 38.

[24]Cogan and Tadmor describe his dialogue as "halting speech" (*II Kings*, p. 65).

[25]Walter A. Maier III, "Hadadrimmon (deity)," in *ABD*; Cogan and Tadmor, *II Kings*, p. 65.

(1 Kgs 19:18). Elisha, in contrast with Naaman's stammering speech, simply blesses the foreigner's request: **"Go in peace"** (לְשָׁלוֹם לֵךְ, *lēk lᵊšālôm*).[26]

In the world of the story and for an audience in exile, the prophet's words, though brief, stand out. "Go in peace!" anoints the Aramean's request with divine approval. In the Samuel birth narrative, Eli sanctioned Hannah's request for a son: "Go in peace, and may the God of Israel grant you what you have asked of him" (1 Sam 1:17). Elisha's shorter response is no less significant. Hannah's reaction, "her face was no longer downcast" (1:18), calls attention to her faith response. Naaman's awakening belief in the God of Israel having already been expressed in dialogue, these brief words of blessing highlight the actions of the prophet and call to mind the underlying tension of the story — Yahweh's prophet heals and blesses an outsider.

Resonance with surrounding scenes indicates that the narrator is featuring the blessing. In the preceding Shunammite story, the greeting that dominates the narrative further connects her story with Naaman. Elisha's servant Gehazi approached her with the greeting: "Are you all right? Is your husband all right? Is your child all right?" (with *hăšālôm*, "are [you] well?"). The Shunammite responded, "Everything is all right" (*šālôm*; see comments on 4:26). In the scene that follows this interaction between Naaman and Elisha, the Aramean greets Gehazi with "Is everything all right?" (הֲשָׁלוֹם, *hăšālôm*). Gehazi responds, "Everything is all right" (*šālôm*, "Yes"; see comments on v. 21 below). The attention given the ordinary, everyday greeting/blessing in these scenes indicates a pattern. Naaman's conversation with Elisha even reinforces the role of the blessing in the story: "Please accept now a gift [בְּרָכָה, *bᵊrākāh*, "a blessing"] from your servant" (v. 15).[27] The Aramean has received a blessing from the prophet in Israel and wants to return the favor with a blessing of presents. The narrator records that the prophet refused the gift but blessed his request without explanation — "Go

---

[26]In 1 Kgs 8:41-43, Solomon asks Yahweh to be gracious toward the foreigner who prays toward the temple (Provan, *1 and 2 Kings*, p. 196).

[27]When Elisha sent Gehazi to "resuscitate" the Shunammite's son, he told his servant not to "greet" (*bārak*, "bless") anyone, and, "If anyone greets [*bārak*] you, do not answer" (4:29).

in peace" (*lēk lᵊšālôm*) — however incongruent his action appears to
Israelite sensitivities, or uncomfortable it might make an exilic reader under foreign domination.

5:19b-24 In these verses, the narrator exposes the true character
of Elisha's servant. In contrast with his master, Gehazi takes gifts and
uses deception to acquire favors that were rejected by Elisha. He
even swears with the same oath as Elisha (**"as surely as the LORD
lives,"** cf. v. 16) that he will "take [*lāqaḥ*, **"get"** in the NIV] **something
from him.**" That Elisha swore *not to take* (*lāqaḥ*, v. 16) from Naaman
accentuates the night-and-day contrast between the two.[28] Gehazi may
have reasoned that the goods were probably taken from Israel as
booty in the first place, but for the storyteller, his actions are unacceptable.[29] **He urged** [פָּרַץ, *pāraṣ*] **Gehazi** also connects this scene with
Elisha's unwillingness to accept payment from Naaman (v. 16) and
further highlights the contrast between these two players in the
drama. By naming, the storyteller also ironically contrasts Gehazi
with Naaman. Gehazi is the "boy/young man [**the servant** in the
NIV] **of Elisha the man of God.**" Yet, Naaman, who is now like "a little boy" (v. 14) is in spirit more the servant of Elisha than is Gehazi.[30]
As the prophet's designated "servant," Gehazi's actions are surprising. His reported inner speech adds to his negative characterization.
Only twice in the narrative does the storyteller record the inner
speech of characters.[31] In both cases, the hidden, underlying man is
brought out. The reader is able to see Naaman's arrogance and
Gehazi's greed. When Gehazi names the commander **"Naaman, this
Aramean,"** the reader detects beneath-the-surface prejudices that
reverberate with the underlying tension of the story. Gehazi's attitude parallels Naaman's initial view of Israel (and the river Jordan)
and deviates markedly from the spirit reflected in the actions of both
Elisha and the slave girl toward the foreign commander.

In a scene subsequent to the Naaman story (7:3-20), as Samaria

---

[28]Cohn, *2 Kings*, p. 40.

[29]Jesse C. Long, Jr., "When Clean and Unclean Aren't Always Black and
White," *Preaching* 12/4 (Jan./Feb. 1997): 25.

[30]Provan, *1 and 2 Kings*, p. 196.

[31]Both examples of inner speech are prefaced in Hebrew by "and he said"
(וַיֹּאמֶר, *wayyōʾmer*; vv. 11,20), exemplifying the primacy of dialogue in
Hebrew narrative. Naaman's speech also includes (literally), "And I said/
thought . . ." (v. 11).

lies under Aramean siege and is ravaged by famine, four lepers, in a desperate attempt at self-preservation, make their way from the city to the enemy camp. They find the camp deserted. Yahweh had caused the Arameans to hear the sound of chariots and horses, and the army fled in fear. After eating and drinking, the four take "silver, gold, and clothes." They carry the goods away and hide them (7:8). On their return to take additional items, they come to their senses: "We're not doing right. This is a day of good news and we are keeping it to ourselves" (7:9). Parallels with the story of Naaman are striking. Both scenes are tied together by leprosy. Israel and Aram are again in conflict. A careful reader notices that Naaman brought *silver, gold,* and *clothing* (v. 5) with him on his venture into Israel. Gehazi took **a talent of *silver* and two sets of *clothing*** and put them in his house (v. 22), apparently to hide them from his master. Provan suggests that his modest request was calculated not to arouse suspicion.[32] In verse 24, verbs dominate, enabling the reader to watch the coverup. Gehazi **came, took, put away,** and **sent.**[33]

In the larger canon, these scenes conjure up the image of Achan and the disheartening defeat at Ai. Achan coveted and took *silver, gold,* and *clothing* – "a beautiful robe from Babylonia, two hundred shekels of silver and a wedge of gold weighing fifty shekels" (Josh 7:21). These connections ironically suggest another, symbolic level of meaning.[34] Gehazi's greed reenacts the sin of Achan (as did the sin of Ahab; see comments on 1 Kgs 20:35-42; 21:25-26). Associations already established between Gehazi's meeting with Naaman and the Shunammite story — **"Is everything all right?"** (vv. 21-22; see above) — now also appear to be symbolic. The Shunammite sought healing for her son; Gehazi is greedily looking for material gain.[35] Everything is not *šālôm* ("all right") with Elisha's servant.[36]

5:25-27 Gehazi now stands **before his master** as Naaman and the Shunammite stood in his presence in earlier scenes (4:12; 5:15). However, the language is intentionally not the same. Gehazi (literal-

---

[32]Provan, *1 and 2 Kings*, p. 193.

[33]Cohn, *2 Kings*, p. 41.

[34]This is another example of the writer's use of allusion with ironic effects for theological ends.

[35]Hobbs, *2 Kings*, p. 61.

[36]Brueggemann writes that Naaman "moves from leprosy to well-being," while Gehazi "moves from well-being to leprosy" (*1 & 2 Kings*, p. 337).

ly) "stands *unto/against* [אֶל, *'el*] his lord," not *before* (לִפְנֵי, *liphnê*) him, suggesting an air of confrontation.[37] Elisha described himself as "standing before Yahweh" (v. 16; literally, "before whom I stand," "whom I serve" in the NIV) before refusing the commander's offer of gifts. The contrast is striking. Gehazi stands in stark contrast to the man of God. His dishonesty has been found out. As the clairvoyant prophet miraculously "heard" of the king's distress, he now reports seeing Gehazi's meeting with Naaman. How the prophet was able to hear and see is a subtle gap that further draws attention to the prophet. Elisha asks, **"Is this the time to take money** [literally, "*silver*"]**, or to accept** *clothes*, **olive groves, vineyards, flocks, herds, or menservants and maidservants?"** The prophet's rhetorical question resonates with Samuel's diatribe to Israel about the excesses of the monarchy (see 1 Sam 8:10-18). Gehazi only took *silver* and *clothing*, but in so doing he embodies the greed that characterizes kingship in Israel,[38] the very thing Elisha is battling as he reaches out to the disenfranchised (see comments on ch. 4). For the storyteller, Gehazi has chosen to cast his lot with Ahab, who also imitates the sin of Achan (see above). Even so, the time will come for Israel to take "booty," only this comes when the "floodgates of heaven" are opened (7:2,19). Yahweh will deliver Samaria from the Arameans and continue to be the source of blessing in Israel.

The narrative ends in irony. Naaman's leprosy now clings to Elisha's own servant. In the first verse of the narrative, Naaman is named a leper (מְצֹרָע, *mᵉṣōrāʿ*). In the final verse, Gehazi leaves **Elisha's presence** (literally, "from before [*liphnê*] him"; see comments on vv. 1-2) a leper (*mᵉṣōrāʿ*), **as white as snow** (cf. Exod 4:6; Num 12:10). In his desire for personal gain, Gehazi asks for a gift from Naaman and receives the Aramean's leprosy from Elijah. In the story, a Gentile is blessed, and a Jew is cursed. The unclean is now clean, the clean unclean. The story closes with a snow-white leper and a once-stained commander on his way with godspeed to his king and the house of an Aramean thunder god.[39]

---

[37]Cohn, *2 Kings*, p. 41; Hobbs, *2 Kings*, p. 67.

[38]Nelson describes Gehazi as "faithlessly greedy whereas Naaman is faithfully generous" (*First and Second Kings*, p. 180).

[39]Jesse C. Long, "Text Story & Sermon Story," 20.

For an exilic audience, this startling reversal would hit close to home. Nelson suggests that many exiles were "under intense syncretistic pressure," in the same way Christians in the New Testament "agonized over eating meat offered to idols."[40] While one suspects that this may have been an issue for some, the story's central irony suggests another aim. A foreign commander from an ungodly nation is blessed, and an Israelite is cursed. Many in exile would have no qualms about taking advantage of "an Aramean" (cf. v. 20). Yet, by contrast, the unnamed "little girl" *in exile* represents the point of view of the storyteller. Natural animosities and prejudices must be subverted to Yahweh's will and work among the nations. He is also God of "all the world." Jesus uses the story in this way when he counters Jewish prejudices toward outsiders in his hometown of Nazareth: "There were many in Israel with leprosy in the time of Elisha the prophet, yet not one of them was cleansed — only Naaman the Syrian" (Luke 4:27).[41] As Jeremiah urged the exiles to pray for Babylon (Jer 29:7), so the author of Kings subtly cautions the same audience to accept the judgment of Yahweh. Each character in the story plays a servant role (see above), as does the reader in exile. The exiles must remember that Yahweh is the one who *restores* (*šûb*) and that *returning* (*šûb*) to him means displaying the character of the God they serve, especially when scattered among the nations. "There is no God in all the world except in Israel" (v. 15), and he can be *worshiped* and *served* even in exile.

---

[40]Nelson, *First and Second Kings*, p. 183.

[41]See Jesse C. Long, "When Clean and Unclean," 25; idem, "Text Story & Sermon Story," 22. Brueggemann calls attention to parallels between Jesus' healing of the ten lepers and the story of Naaman (Luke 17:17-19). Jesus' dismissal of the one, foreign leper who returned reverberates with Elisha's dismissal of Naaman in 5:19 (*1 & 2 Kings*, p. 338).

2 KINGS 6

6. Elisha Makes an Axhead Float (6:1-7)

6:1-7 To remind the reader that Elisha's prophetic ministry was just as much about the small as the great, the insignificant as well as the politically powerful, the storyteller relates another brief episode of Elisha and one of the sons of the prophets (cf. 4:1-7,38-41,42-44), before recording the prophet's dealings with the kings of Israel and Aram.[1] This narrative also parallels the problem-solution pattern of the miracle stories in chapter 4. In this story, Elisha accompanies **the company of the prophets** to the Jordan to secure construction materials. The NIV's **"a place for us to live"** misrepresents their intention to build a larger assembly building for meetings with the prophet (a better translation: "a place to meet/sit [with you]," v. 2; cf. v. 1). The recurring word "place" (מָקוֹם, *māqôm*; vv. 1,2,6) serves to highlight the miracle in verse 6 and connects this story with the one that follows, in which Elisha knows the "place" where the king of Aram encamps (vv. 8,9,10).[2] One of the prophets loses an **iron** (בַּרְזֶל, *barzel*) "tool" in the Jordan. **Axhead** is an interpolation from the context. Iron was a precious metal and therefore expensive for the poor. Its loss engendered anxiety, for **it was borrowed.** When shown the "place" where it fell in the Jordan, Elisha throws a stick at that spot, and the iron floats to the surface. Once more, Elisha performs a miracle by throwing (cf. 2:19-22; 4:38-41)[3] and demonstrates that he wields the power of Yahweh for the poor.

---

[1]See Provan, *1 and 2 Kings*, p. 197.
[2]Cohn, *2 Kings*, pp. 43-44.
[3]Hobbs, *2 Kings*, p. 73.

7. Elisha Captures the Army of Aram (6:8-23)

6:8-14 The narrative now turns to international affairs. **The king of Aram** is once more at war with Israel.[4] Ben-Hadad (see v. 24) sets up camp at various **places** (*māqôm*; see above) within Israel. Miraculously, **the man of God** informs king Joram of the Aramean's whereabouts. The lack of specificity allows the narrator to underscore that this is a recurring scene. Elisha is protecting Israel from Aramean aggression. Not accepting Elisha's declaration, **the king of Israel** checks *the place* and confirms the prophetic word. Elisha avoids the Arameans, which angers Ben-Hadad. Believing there must be a spy among them, the king of Aram asks, **"Will you not tell me** [from נָגַד, *nāgad*] **which of us is on the side of the king of Israel?"** His question introduces the key word "tell/report" (the causative form of *nāgad*, "to be conspicuous"; vv. 11,12, 13), which links this story with the siege of Samaria narrative to follow (cf. 7:9,10,11,12,15). One of his "servants" ("officers" in the NIV) informs the king, **"Elisha, the prophet who is in Israel, tells** [from *nāgad*] **the king of Israel the very words you speak in your bedroom."** Once more, *servants* know more than their masters about the prophet Elisha (cf. 3:11; 5:2-3,13; cf. 7:13).[5] "The prophet who is in Israel" continues a theme from the story of Naaman (5:3,8).

The king of Aram commands his servants to "Go and see [**'Go, find out . . .'** in the NIV] **where** [Elisha] **is**." The king's dialogue interjects the key word "see" (רָאָה, *rā'āh*), which serves as a primary motif in this story and the one to follow. King Joram will also command his chariot drivers to "Go and see" (7:14). The storyteller artistically employs "seeing" as a vehicle for expressing the narrative's theological level of meaning (see below). The **report** returns ("is told/reported" [from *nāgad*]); he is in Dothan, a city located approximately 16 km north of Samaria.[6] The king sends a massive military force **with horses and chariots** to surround the fortified site, for the

---

[4]Some scholars date these events to the eighth century B.C. and the time of Hazael, but there is no reason not to believe that this story and the following siege narrative belong to the time of Joram (see ibid., pp. 76-77, 79; and "Excursus: Ahab's Wars with Aram").

[5]See Provan, *1 and 2 Kings*, p. 185.

[6]For identification, location, and summary of excavations at Tell Dothan, see William G. Dever, "Dothan (place)," in *ABD*.

purpose of capturing just one man, Ben-Hadad's nemesis and
Israel's prophet, Elisha.

6:15-17 The scene with **the servant** [מְשָׁרֵת, *mᵉšārēth*] **of the man
of God** who awakens to see the army of Aram surrounding the city
vividly brings out Yahweh's commitment to the prophet Elisha. The
narrator uses a new, unusual word for "servant" (*mᵉšārēth*, v. 15a),
intimating that this servant is not Gehazi. The reader sees the army
once more, **with horses and chariots**, but this time through the eyes
of the frightened servant. He sees (with הִנֵּה, *hinnēh*; see below) the
army and exclaims, **"Oh, my lord, what shall we do?"** Elisha's point
of view is different. He calms his servant, **"Don't be afraid,"** and
adds, **"Those who are with us are more than those who are with
them."** The prophet **prays** [cf. 4:33], **"O LORD, open his eyes so he
may see** [*rā'āh*]," and his servant sees [*rā'āh* and *hinnēh*; see below]
the horses and chariots of fire all around Elisha. Like Elijah, the
prophet now commands the army of God (cf. 1:9-15; 2:11-12).

6:18-19 As the Arameans advance, Elisha prays they will be strick-
en **with blindness** (סַנְוֵרִים, *sanwērîm*). This rare word for sudden
blindness occurs elsewhere in the Old Testament only in Gen
19:10[11], where angels strike the men of Sodom with blindness.
Yahweh once more answers Elisha's prayer. The Arameans become
blind, **as Elisha had asked** (literally, "according to the word of
Elisha"). In a somewhat confused state, they are led by the man of
God to Samaria. Since the army is able to follow Elisha to Israel's
capital city, their blindness must have been more a state of disori-
entation.[7] Perception impaired, they are unable to see clearly.

6:20 On entering the city, Elisha prays once more, asking
Yahweh **"to open the eyes of these men so they can see** [*rā'āh*]."
Their eyes are opened by Yahweh; **they look** [*rā'āh*], **and there they
are** [*hinnēh*], **inside Samaria**. Cohn comments on the use of *hinnēh*
in these scenes (vv. 15,17,20).[8] This difficult to translate term (consistently translated "behold" in the KJV) often signals a shift in point
of view, even "to internalize the viewpoint" of a speaker.[9] In this
instance, *hinnēh* calls attention to the point of view of the servant
and the Aramean army. Each one has a change in perception. The

[7]Provan, *1 and 2 Kings*, p. 199.
[8]Cohn, *2 Kings*, p. 46.
[9]Berlin, *Poetics and Interpretation*, pp. 62-63.

resonance between verses 17 and 20 has the same effect. With almost verbatim repetition, the narrator describes how Elisha's servant and the Aramean army are both enabled with sight ("LORD, open his eyes . . . ," v. 17; "LORD, open the eyes of these men . . . ," v. 20). The reader is able to see that Elisha's *insight* comes from Yahweh, who listens to the prophet.

Cohn sees a concentric structure to this story that, on careful inspection, highlights Elisha's prayers and Yahweh's response:[10]

A. Aramean raids are thwarted by Elisha's insight (vv. 8-10).
   B. The king of Aram is made aware of Elisha's insight
      (vv. 11-14).
      C. [Elisha prays (v. 17), and] Yahweh opens the eyes of
         the servant (vv. 15-17).
         X. [Elisha prays (v. 18), and] Yahweh blinds the
            army. Elisha leads it to Samaria (vv. 18-19).
      C'. ["LORD, open the eyes of these men" (v. 20), and]
          Yahweh opens the eyes of the army (v. 20).
   B'. The king of Israel sees, feasts, and dispatches the army
       (vv. 21-23a).
A'. Aramean raids cease (v. 23b).

In narrative elements C, X, and C', the focal scenes in this concentric structure, Elisha prays, and Yahweh responds.

6:21-23 An exuberant king Joram addresses Elisha with respect (**"my father"**) and wonders if he should **kill** Elisha's captives. He may not want to make the same mistake his father Ahab made, when he allowed Ben-Hadad to escape, a foreigner who had been devoted to destruction by Yahweh (see comments on 1 Kgs 20:31-43).[11] Elisha answers that the army should be watered and fed. The prophet may reason that annihilating Ben-Hadad's army would lead to fierce retaliation against Israel. A **great feast** is prepared for the Arameans. After **eating and drinking**, they are allowed to return to their king. This gracious treatment of Israel's archenemy results in the cessation of Aramean raids into Israel. On one such raid, the "little girl" who served Naaman's wife was taken from Israel (5:2). In

---

[10]Adapted from Cohn, *2 Kings*, p. 44 (words in brackets added by the author).

[11]Provan, *1 and 2 Kings*, p. 198; see Nelson, *First and Second Kings*, p. 187.

spite of the good will, however, the relaxation of tensions between Israel and Aram will not last long.

8. The Siege of Samaria Is Lifted by a Word from Elisha (6:24–7:20)

6:24-25 Each of the next three verses (vv. 24-26) in Hebrew begins with וַיְהִי (*wayᵉhî*), "and it happened."[12] With this term, the narrator transitions from the story of Elisha's "victory" over Aram and sets the stage for the Aramean siege of Samaria. After an unspecified length of time, **Ben-Hadad**[13] advances against Samaria and lays **siege** to the city. Will this be the end of Joram and the house of Ahab, as has been prophesied? Perhaps Yahweh will give Ben-Hadad and his commander Naaman another victory (see 5:1)? The siege leads to **famine**, so severe that **a donkey's head sold for eighty shekels of silver, and a fourth of a cab**[14] **of seed pods** [literally, "dove's dung"] **for five shekels**. "Dove's dung" may show how desperate the inhabitants of Samaria are for food, or it may highlight the shortage of fuel in the city. The term may have been a common appellation for inedible husks (so the NIV's "seed pods").[15] In any case, the note on black-market prices for less-than-appetizing items graphically shows how hopeless the situation is in Samaria.

6:26-29 In the poignant scene where King Joram is addressed by one of his suffering subjects as he walks **along the wall**, the city's plight is even more graphically brought out. When the anonymous woman cries out, she employs the usual word for "salvation": **"Help [יָשַׁע, *yāšaʿ*, "save"] me."** The king blames God. He says, in effect, "If Yahweh will not save you, how do you expect me to save you?" He

---

[12]Cohn, *2 Kings*, p. 49.

[13]This is the only time either the king of Aram or the king of Israel is identified in this narrative, but does not mean that these stories were indiscriminately appended to the account of Joram's reign. A literary reading suggests that the naming of characters in this story is calculated to highlight the role of the prophet Elisha (see "Excursus: Ahab's Wars with Aram").

[14]This is the only reference to the "cab" (*qab*) as a unit of measure in Hebrew Scripture. In postexilic times, the cab was one-sixth of a seah. However, Old Testament measures of capacity are difficult to define with certainty (see Marvin A. Powell, "Weights and Measures," in *ABD*).

[15]See Cogan and Tadmor, *II Kings*, p. 79; Gray, *I & II Kings*, p. 522.

asks, **"Where can I get help for you? From the threshing floor? From the winepress?"** In the midst of the siege, there is no grain from the threshing floor or wine from the press. The question the king asks next (**"What's the matter?"** literally, "What is to/for you?") is in essence the same question Elisha asked the Shunammite: "What can be done for you?" (4:13).[16] There is only one word difference in Hebrew (עָשָׂה, *'āśâ*, "be done"). The contrast is glaring. Elisha knows Yahweh and wields his power to rescue and bless. Even his name Elisha (אֱלִישָׁע, *'elîšā'*) means "God/my God saves." The king does not know Yahweh and can only blame God and curse the prophet.

Without a twinge of remorse, the woman describes eating her own **son**. Not unheard of in times of siege, she believes an injustice has been done to her because a friend did not carry through with her bargain to eat her son the following day. Resonance with the story where Solomon demonstrates wisdom from Yahweh in judging the dispute between two prostitutes is intentional. The king of Israel is once more asked to pass judgment over a child. Only, one of Solomon's disputants was pleading for life; this woman is pleading for death. And the woman expects the king to take her side.[17] Aghast at this turn of events, the reader can see the depths to which Israel has come, where a call for an impartial hearing is itself a perversion of justice!

An exilic audience would know the horror. Similar incidents happened in the Babylonian siege of Jerusalem (cf. Lam 2:20; 4:10; Ezek 5:10). Moses foresaw this scene when he outlined the curses of Israel's covenant with Yahweh: "The most gentle and sensitive woman among you . . . intends to eat [the afterbirth of her womb and the children she bears] secretly during the siege and in the distress that your enemy will inflict on you in your cities" (Deut 28:56-57). In exile, the descendants of Abraham should know that their hardships, past and present, were brought on by a broken covenant.

6:30-31 The king reacts by **tearing his robes**. In the preceding chapter, he tore his clothes on receiving the letter from Ben-Hadad about Naaman (5:7). Now, the king of Aram has besieged Samaria, and Joram believes that all is lost. When he tears his clothes, the people see **sackcloth** underneath his outer garments. With the

---

[16]Hobbs, *2 Kings*, p. 80.
[17]Cohn, *2 Kings*, p. 50.

clever addition of this apparently insignificant detail, the storyteller masterfully interjects some ambiguity into his characterization of Joram. Sackcloth suggests an attitude of mourning and a posture of humiliation and repentance before God. When Joram's father Ahab "put on sackcloth and fasted," Yahweh responded by altering the oracle of judgment that Elijah had made against his house (1 Kgs 21:27-29). Nevertheless, in the very next verse Joram mirrors his mother Jezebel, who sought to take the life of Elijah (1 Kgs 19:2), when he calls for the **head of Elisha son of Shaphat** with an oath.[18] The king blames Elisha for allowing Ben-Hadad's army to return to Damascus. Elisha fed and watered them, and now the king and his subjects are starving to death — to the point that they are eating each other. The king of Israel goes through the motions of repentance but does not have an accompanying faith in Yahweh, or his prophet Elisha, as a deliverer.

6:32-33 Sitting in his house with **the elders**, Elisha *sees* (**"Don't you** *see* [*rā'āh*] **. . . ?"**) that the king has sent a messenger to make his **head** like the "*head* of a donkey" in the market (v. 25). Since the army of Aram surrounds Samaria, Elisha must have a residence within the city. That "the elders" are **sitting with him** indicates the prophet has support from the respectable elements of Israelite society. Elisha names Joram a **murderer**. He has miraculously heard the king's exclamation **"to cut off my head"** (cf. v. 31). The prophet directs the elders to hold the door against the messenger and adds, **"Is not the sound of his master's footsteps behind him?"** The language calls to mind the prophet Ahijah, who heard "the sound of her footsteps," after Yahweh informed the prophet that the wife of Jeroboam was coming (1 Kgs 14:5-6). For his part, Joram acts like he believes that removing the prophet will eliminate the real source of Israel's problem. Reflecting a more mechanistic view of religion, the king, like his father Ahab, apparently thinks that by controlling prophets he can control the God of Israel and her destiny (cf. 1 Kgs 22:1-28).[19]

In verse 33, the narrator telescopes events for dramatic effect and interjects some uncertainty about who is speaking. The NIV

---

[18]Provan notices the parallels with Joram's parents (*1 and 2 Kings*, pp. 200-201). For the significance of the sackcloth in this story, see also Nelson, *First and Second Kings*, p. 189.

[19]See Provan, *1 and 2 Kings*, p. 201.

adds **the king** in order to clarify the ambiguity in the underlying Hebrew text. Without the emendation, the reader is unsure if the messenger speaks for the king, or if the king himself, whose footsteps could be heard behind the messenger, speaks to Elisha. In fact, initially, the speech sounds like it comes from Elisha: **"This disaster is from the LORD."** It is only after **"Why should I wait for the LORD any longer?"** that the reader realizes that these are the words of the king (so the addition of "the king" in the NIV). This creative use of ambiguity has the effect of underscoring Joram's lack of faith in Yahweh. The king no longer believes that the God of Israel will deliver Samaria. Ironically, the reader suspects that Joram may be right — Yahweh is punishing Israel — and wonders if this will be the end of the house of Ahab (cf. 1 Kgs 21:29).

2 KINGS 7

8. The Siege of Samaria Is Lifted by a Word from Elisha (6:24–7:20) (Continued)

7:1-2 Elisha responds with a word from Yahweh. He begins with a double formula for an oracle: **"Hear the word of the LORD"** (cf. 1 Kgs 22:19; 2 Kgs 20:16; Isa 1:10) and **"This is what the LORD says"** (see comments on 1 Kgs 21:19). The prophet announces, **"About this time tomorrow, a seah of flour will sell for a shekel and two seahs of barley for a shekel at the gate of Samaria."** The exorbitant prices of the siege will be alleviated when the markets of Samaria overflow with food. The king did not wait long enough; Yahweh will deliver Israel on the morrow! Also, the reader surmises that Elisha's oracle preserves his head for at least one more day.

But the narrator has one more surprise. The reader now learns that the king is not alone. **The officer on whose arm the king was leaning** (the same language Naaman uses to describe his relationship with the king of Aram; cf. 5:18) is also present and snaps, **"Look [*hinnēh*], even if the LORD should open the floodgates** [literally "windows"] **of the heavens, could this happen?"** Ominously for the king's "right-hand man," the prophet answers, **"You will see** [הִנְּכָה רֹאֶה, *hinnᵉkāh rō'eh*] **it with your own eyes . . . but you will not eat any of it!"** The seeing motif resurfaces (with *hinnēh* and *rā'āh*). Because the unnamed official is unable to *see* Yahweh as a savior, he will *see* but not experience Samaria's deliverance.

7:3-8 The scene changes to the city gate. **Four men with leprosy** [מְצֹרָעִים, *mᵉṣōrā'îm*] reason that their chances are as good with the Arameans as with the famine inside the city. Their disease connects them with the story of Naaman, on which the curtain closed with Gehazi being cursed with the Aramean's leprosy (*mᵉṣōrā'*, cf. 5:1, 27). Rabbinic tradition conjectures they were all sons of

Gehazi.[1] Elisha said the leprosy would "cling to [Gehazi] and to [his] descendants forever" (5:27). Perhaps one of the four is Gehazi himself? Far from idle speculation, the storyteller has left a subtle, but important gap in the narrative. In the world of the story, Gehazi is antecedent to the lepers who appear in this scene. As the narrative progresses, other parallels will reinforce the connections between them.

At dusk (v. 5), the lepers venture to **the camp of the Arameans**. When they reach **the edge of the camp**, they *see* (v. 5; *hinnēh*, not represented in the NIV; see comments on 6:20) that **not a man was there**. Parenthetically in verses 6-7, the narrator with a flashback explains that Yahweh[2] caused the army **to hear the sound of chariots and horses and a great army** (cf. 2 Sam 5:24). The Arameans perceive (v. 6; *hinnēh*, **"Look"** in the NIV) that **"the king of Israel has hired the Hittite and Egyptian[3] kings to attack us!"** Again, perception/misperception dominates the story. Ironically, the Arameans **abandon their tents** and flee *at dusk* (v. 7), the same time the *lepers* set out to the camp of Aram (v. 5). Provan suggests that there is wordplay here in Hebrew with *mᵉṣōrāʿîm* ("lepers," v. 8) and מִצְרַיִם (*miṣrayim*, "Egyptians").[4] The army of Aram believes that the lepers are the Hittites and Egyptians. With wordplay and repetition ("at dusk," vv. 5,7), the storyteller is able to drape the lepers' statement in verse 4 with verbal irony: "Let us go and *fall upon* [נָפַל, *nāphal*; **"surrender"** in the NIV] the camp of Aram." "Fall upon" is a Hebrew idiom for attack (cf. 1 Kgs 22:20, "attacking [*nāphal*] Ramoth Gilead"). The carefully worded narrative insinuates that by the power of Yahweh, the Arameans flee at the sound of the four advancing lepers. Yahweh delivers Samaria with lepers! The outcast/cursed become the vehicle for God's salvation. An exilic audience would be encouraged. Perhaps Yahweh will be able to use the cursed in exile in a similar way?

---

[1]See Hobbs, *2 Kings*, p. 90.

[2]The MT reads "Lord" (אֲדֹנָי, *ʾădōnāy*) in v. 6; other manuscripts read Yahweh (יהוה, *YHWH*).

[3]The tendency to amend the text to Musrites (מֻצְרִם, *muṣrîm*, from a region in northern Syria) instead of Egyptians (*miṣrayim*) is unnecessary. "Musri" often refers to Egypt in the Assyrian annals (Hobbs, *2 Kings*, pp. 84, 90-91; see Cogan and Tadmor, *II Kings*, p. 82; cf. Gray, *I & II Kings*, pp. 520, 524-525; Cogan, *1 Kings*, pp. 321-322).

[4]Provan, *1 and 2 Kings*, pp. 201-202.

The edge of the camp in verse 8 bookends the flashback (in v. 5), as the storyteller returns to the lepers. They enter one tent and devour food and drink. They also take booty, **silver, gold and clothes**, and go off and **hide** the spoils of Yahweh's victory over Aram. A careful reader recalls that Naaman brought *silver, gold,* and *clothing* with him from Aram (5:5), and Gehazi took *silver* and *clothing* from the Aramean and hid the goods in his house (5:25). Censuring his servant, Elisha asked, "Is this the time to take *silver,* or to accept *clothes* . . . ?" Gehazi then received Naaman's leprosy from Elisha. Now, in a moment of triumph over Aram that has been enabled by the God of Elisha, it is time to take *silver, gold,* and *clothing*! The four lepers enter **another tent**, *take*, and *hide*.

7:9-13 In contrast with Gehazi, the lepers realize that they are **not doing right** and should **report** [from *nāgad*] **this to the royal palace**. The verb root נגד (*nāgad*, in the causative sense of "tell/report") functions as a theme word for these final scenes in the narrative (vv. 9,10, 11,12,15) and forms a bridge with earlier scenes, where the king of Aram is told (6:11,12,13 — see discussion there) about Israel's prophet Elisha. The lepers return to the gate and **call out** [קָרָא, *qārā'*, "cry out"] **to the city gatekeepers** atop the wall. Hobbs suggests that all of the "shouting" in this scene indicates the lepers were "quarantined."[5] Their report mirrors the narrator's description of the preceding events (vv. 5,7), minus the booty the four were able to take and hide (v. 8).

The news is **reported** [again *nāgad*] **within the palace**, but the king is skeptical. He suspects that the empty camp is trickery; Ben-Hadad is trying to draw him out in the open so that his forces can **get into the city**. Though perhaps appropriate caution for a commander-in-chief, the king's response calls attention to his lack of faith in Yahweh and his prophet. Elisha had *told* Joram that there would be deliverance from the famine (v. 1), but the king is unable to see beyond the situation. One of the king's *servants* ("officers" in the NIV) suggests a reasonable course of action. They should send some men to reconnoiter the enemy camp — **"to find out what happened** [literally, 'and we will *see* (רָאָה, *rā'āh*)']." Another servant appears wiser than his master (cf. 5:13).

---

[5]Hobbs, *2 Kings*, p. 90.

7:14-16 Two chariots with their horses are selected, and the king tells **the drivers** to (literally) "go and see [*rā'āh*]" (**"Go and find out what has happened"** in the NIV). The king's command connects this scene with Ben-Hadad in the preceding episode, who told his servants to (literally) "go and see [*rā'āh*] where he is" (6:13). The king of Aram sent to find the whereabouts of the prophet Elisha; the king of Israel is sending to find out if the word of the prophet is true. The messengers discover the road down to the Jordan **strewn with the clothing and equipment** the Arameans discarded in flight. They **return and report** (from *nāgad*) to the king. Cohn observes that the reader at this point has seen the Aramean flight from five different viewpoints: the narrator, the Arameans, the lepers, the king, and the messengers.[6] When the messengers return, once more there is reporting (see comments on 6:8-14), and once more the word of Elisha is found to be reliable (cf. 6:10). The storyteller recounts that the people rush out and **plunder the camp of the Arameans** and reports the market prices in Samaria that day: **A seah of flour** is **sold for a shekel, and two seahs of barley** are **sold for a shekel**. Word for word (cf. 7:1), all of this comes to pass (literally) "according to the word of Yahweh" (**as the LORD had said** in the NIV).

7:17 With dramatic irony, the storyteller now records that the **officer on whose arm** [the king] **leaned** was placed by the king **in charge of the gate**. This is the same officer who doubted the word of Yahweh through the prophet Elisha (v. 2): "Even if the LORD should open the floodgates of the heavens, could this happen?" In charge of the gate, he is unable to participate in the plunder and is **trampled** in the gate by the people as they rush to take what Yahweh has given from the Arameans. The narrator adds that **he died, just as the man of God had foretold when the king came down to his house**. The word of Yahweh and the word of the prophet are one and the same (see comments on 1 Kings 17).

For the exiles, the storyteller is also saying something about faith in Yahweh. With a creative use of seeing as a motif, the narrative's ideological point of view is graphically expressed. The people of God should look and see beyond their immediate circumstances. The officer of the king was unable to see that Yahweh could open the windows of heaven for Israel and save Samaria. King Joram

---

[6]Cohn, *2 Kings*, p. 53.

suffers from the same form of myopia. He cannot see beyond the siege, for which he blames Yahweh. His religious posturing, reflected in undergarments of sackcloth, must have been more formality than real devotion. He could see no reason to *wait* any longer on Yahweh for deliverance (6:33).[7] An exilic audience must wait and, ironically, have the faith of Naaman, who also "leaned on the king." His flesh was *restored* (שׁוּב, *šûb*, "returned") when he trusted in the word of the prophet and dipped in the Jordan. He came to know that "there is no [other] God in all the world" (5:15). In exile, the captives must have faith in the word of the same God, who is in control of events, who can save even with a small band of lepers, and who has promised to rescue them. They must keep their eyes open, watch, and *wait* for Yahweh's deliverance.

7:18-20 Some have argued that verses 18-20 are a later addition to the story.[8] While repetition is a hallmark of Hebrew narrative, the storyteller usually invites the reader to make connections and draw conclusions from the speeches and actions of the characters in the story.[9] These verses quote once more Elisha's prophecy of lower market prices (v. 1; cf. v. 16) and the officer's statement about the windows of heaven (v. 2), along with Elisha's response that he would not eat any of the spoils (v. 2). Referring to the narrator's similar comment in verse 17, the last verse adds, **"And that is exactly what happened to him, for the people trampled him in the gateway, and he died."** At first glance, the repetition appears to be serious overkill.[10] However, if these verses are original, the storyteller may have deliberately chosen a repetitive, almost sermonic style to establish some contrast with the opaque, more indirect approach of the final scene of this section to follow. As the text stands, the

---

[7]This is in stark contrast with Hezekiah, who in a similar situation trusts in Yahweh to deliver him (see 2 Kgs 19:14-19).

[8]Hobbs, who defends the integrity and unity of the siege narrative, argues persuasively that vv. 18-20 are a secondary addition. The latter part of v. 17 is also somewhat "clumsy" (*2 Kings*, pp. 85, 88), which implies that the end of this story is difficult to assess.

[9]For example, meaning is conveyed indirectly through the widow's voice when she sums up the meaning of Elijah's miracles in Zarephath: "Now I know that you are a man of God and that the word of the LORD from your mouth is the truth" (1 Kgs 17:24).

[10]Nelson uses the phrase "thudding repetition" (*First and Second Kings*, p. 191).

concluding verses of the siege narrative have the effect of emphasizing the word of Yahweh through the prophet, which always comes
to pass. In the following scene, the Shunammite will have her land
and possessions returned. As an audience in exile wonders if their
land and possessions will also be returned, they can know that
Yahweh's word of deliverance in the mouth of his prophet Moses
will also come to pass: "When you and your children return to the
LORD your God . . . then the LORD your God will restore your fortunes and have compassion on you and gather you again from all the
nations where he scattered you" (Deut 30:2-3).

2 KINGS 8

9. The Shunammite Reports on Elisha's Great Deeds (8:1-6)

To put some closure on his account of Elisha's miracles for the great and small, the storyteller revisits perhaps the greatest of Elisha's miracles, when he brought back to life the Shunammite's son (4:8-37). Contrary to the view that this scene has been haphazardly appended to a collection of miracle stories, there is obvious, deliberate design to the composition. From 3:1, the story alternates between the prophet's dealings in international to local, even personal affairs:

A. The campaign against Moab (3:1-27)
   B. The widow's oil, the Shunammite's son, death in the pot, and feeding the 100 (4:1-44)
A. The Aramean leper (5:1-27
   B. A floating axhead (6:1-7)
A. The Aramean army trapped by Elisha and the siege of Samaria (6:8–7:20)
   B. The Shunammite's property returned (8:1-6).

The pattern will continue. In the subsequent episode, Elisha "anoints" Hazael as king of Aram, before anointing Jehu as king in Israel to bring judgment on the house of Ahab.

In addition, the resonance between Gehazi and the lepers who all *take and hide* from the Arameans demonstrates how episodes are consciously tied together in a web of connections. In the final episode, "the *great* things Elisha has done" (v. 4), in particular, brings together the parallel themes of Elisha's involvement with the politically powerful and the weak and powerless. "Great" functions as a key word in the Naaman story (see comments on ch. 5) and characterizes the miracle of the Shunammite's son (cf. 4:8 where the Shunammite is also named "great"). The narrator's use of the word "great" in this final scene shows that the storyteller is skillfully weaving together a tapestry of scenes. Gehazi appears in both key stories and lies in the shadows of the lepers' assault on the Aramean army. Also, the role that *šûb* ("return") plays in this concluding scene highlights an important theme in the larger composition.

8:1-3 With naming, **the woman whose son he had restored to life** (vv. 1,5), the narrator succinctly recalls the miracle — in such a way that Elisha's role is emphasized (see below). Intimating the prophet's genuine concern for the Shunammite, the narrator records in dialogue Elisha's instructions for her to leave Israel because of a **famine** from Yahweh. This may be the famine mentioned in 4:38-41, a broader famine that the localized devastation wrought by the siege of Samaria (6:24–7:20). Since it is from Yahweh, it probably represents punishment for breaking the Mosaic covenant (cf. Deut 28:16-18). That the famine would last for **seven years** indicates its severity, and perhaps the gravity of Israel's rebellion. The Shunammite does (literally) "according to the word of the man of God" and sojourns in Philistia with her family, although her husband is not mentioned and may be deceased. **At the end of the seven years**, she returns (*šûb*, "come back" in the NIV) **from the land of the Philistines** and makes a claim on **her house and land**. Ironically, she approaches the king with her petition. Earlier, through his servant **Gehazi**, Elisha had asked the Shunammite if he could "speak on your behalf to the king." She responded, "I have a home among my own people" (4:13). She now approaches the king to ask that her home be returned.

8:4-6 The king asks Gehazi, **the servant of the man of God**, to relate "all the great things Elisha has done." Is it just coincidence that as Gehazi recounts **how Elisha restored the dead to life** the Shunammite comes with her petition? With הִנֵּה (*hinnēh* indicated by **just as** in the NIV), the storyteller indicates Gehazi's surprise at the "coincidence." Then he names her once more **the woman whose son Elisha had brought back to life** (cf. v. 1), and Gehazi informs the king, **"This is the woman . . . and this is her son whom Elisha restored to life."** Four times now in this brief account, it has been repeated that Elisha is the one who brought the Shunammite's son to life. The woman's son evidences the *great things* Elisha has done.

The Shunammite recounts the story to the king, who is displaying a change in attitude toward Elisha. In the preceding episode,

Joram sought to sever the prophet from his head (6:31). One assumes Elisha's deliverance of Samaria has changed his disposition toward the man of God. The action the king initiates on the woman's behalf also contrasts dramatically with his parents, who unjustly confiscated the property of Naboth the Jezreelite (1 Kings 21).[1] A reader unfamiliar with the end of the story may wonder, with Joram's altered persona, if perhaps the promised judgment of Yahweh will be averted. Sadly, this change of heart will not be enough to alter the judgment that is coming on the king who could not wait on Yahweh (6:33), a sentence that hangs over the house of Ahab (cf. 1 Kgs 21:29). Joram assigns the Shunammite's case to an official and instructs him, **"Give back [šûb] everything that belonged to her, including all the income from her land from the day she left the country until now."** Her house and land, including the earnings from the property during the time she was sojourning in a foreign land, will be *returned* (*šûb*).

Recognizing the deliberate, albeit less than direct, character of the account of Elisha's miracles suggests that the narrator has consciously left an important gap in this concluding episode. How is it that Gehazi appears with the king? He is named "the servant of the man of God" and enters the scene in audience with Joram, even though Elisha cursed Gehazi with the Aramean commander's leprosy: "Naaman's leprosy will cling to you and to your descendants *forever*" (5:27). Some maintain that his leprosy must have been of the type that did not affect social intercourse.[2] Yet, the concern that Naaman displays for his illness and the clean/unclean motif that the narrator massages in the story of the Aramean argue against such a reading (see comments on 5:1-4). No distinction is made in the story between the leprosy of Naaman and Gehazi, and the leprosy of the four in the siege of Samaria narrative, who appear to be quarantined (see comments on 7:9-13). The narrator nowhere indicates that Gehazi was cured of his leprosy. Is it possible that the storyteller intends for the reader to wonder about Gehazi? Perhaps he was one

---

[1]Hobbs, *2 Kings*, p. 101; Brueggemann, *1 & 2 Kings*, p. 369.

[2]Kissling argues that either Gehazi's leprosy only made him ceremonially unclean, or the story of Naaman happened after 8:1-6. The effect on the reader is that perhaps "Elisha's predictions are inaccurate" (*Reliable Characters*, pp. 187-188).

of the four lepers, and perhaps after the deliverance of Yahweh, Elisha healed them? If so, the author is moving from the direct, repetitive style of 7:18-20 to his typical, more indirect approach that asks the reader to participate in the reading.

The role that the word *šûb* plays in the final scene suggests that this is his strategy. The Shunammite returns (*šûb*) from a foreign land, and her house and land (with the income from the property generated in her absence) are *returned* (*šûb*) to her. When Naaman was healed from his leprosy, the narrator chose the word *šûb* to describe the change: "His flesh was *restored* [*šûb*] and became clean like that of a young boy" (5:14). For an audience in exile, this word already stands out in the larger narrative (see comments on 1 Kgs 13:33-34) and implies that they too may yet experience Yahweh's salvation. As the Shunammite's house and land were *returned* to her, so their land may yet be *returned* to them. And, as Naaman's flesh was *restored* and made clean, perhaps they will be *restored* and made clean to again enjoy the blessings of Yahweh.[3] Gehazi's appearance in this scene raises the possibility that his flesh was also *restored* (*šûb*). The judgment of Yahweh, which is about to be unleashed on the house of Ahab, is not *forever*! The gracious promise to David of an eternal throne may yet be realized (cf. 2 Sam 7:12-16; 1 Kgs 11:39). The exiles should have faith in Yahweh's promises and wait for his salvation (2 Kgs 6:33).

I. THE HOUSE OF AHAB COMES TO AN END (8:7–10:36)

1. Elisha "Anoints" Hazael (8:7-15)

8:7-9 On hearing that the prophet Elisha is in Damascus, **Ben-Hadad king of Aram** sends Hazael to inquire about the king's illness. Once more, a king queries a prophet concerning a sickness. Earlier, Ahaziah inquired of Baal-Zebub of Ekron about his injury (1:1-6; cf. the somewhat parallel stories of Jeroboam [1 Kings 14]

---

[3]Hobbs also believes Gehazi may have been cured, which for him prefigures the restoration of Joash (chs. 11–12) and the return and restoration of Judah (*2 Kings*, pp. 101, 105).

and Hezekiah [2 Kings 20]).[4] At least Ben-Hadad has enough respect
for the prophet of Yahweh to inquire of Elisha. Like Naaman, Hazael
arrives bearing gifts, this time **forty camel-loads of all the finest
wares of Damascus**. The size of the gift reflects the esteem Ben-
Hadad must have for Elisha. There is no mention of whether Elisha
accepts the gifts (cf. 5:16). Hazael stands **before him**, as had the
Shunammite, Naaman, and Gehazi (4:12; 5:15,25), and with deference that must reflect Ben-Hadad's point of view says, **"Your son
Ben-Hadad king of Aram has sent me to ask, 'Will I recover from
this illness?'"**

8:10 Elisha's response has generated plenty of discussion. The
prophet is intentionally deceptive in what he declares to Hazael:
"Go and say *to him* [לֹ֗ו, *lô*]**, 'You will** *certainly recover***'; but the LORD
has revealed to me that he will in fact die** [literally, *"certainly die"*]**.'"**
In light of this seeming ethical difficulty, the Hebrew text (MT) at an
early date apparently was emended to eliminate the tension this creates for the characterization of Elisha: "Go and say, 'You will certainly *not* (לֹא, *lō'*) recover'" (see the NIV text note). The NIV is following the *qere* (the corrected text in the margin, *lô* ["to him"]),
which, as the more difficult reading, is preferred.[5] But how does one
reconcile a prophet of Yahweh using tactics like this to manipulate
this messenger and meddle in Aramean politics? Kissling reasons
that this demonstrates that Elisha is not a completely reliable character.[6] Since in other stories, like Joram's campaign against Moab,
the prophet is less than forthright, this view of Elisha is plausible. A
careful reading of the Elijah narrative also indicates that prophets
are flawed (see, e.g., comments on 1 Kings 19). Nevertheless, there
appears to be another level of meaning that mollifies Elisha's behavior. His deception is no different from Micaiah's initial, *lying word* to
Ahab: "Attack and be victorious" (1 Kgs 22:15).[7] To explain his
word, Micaiah recounts a scene in heaven where a *lying spirit* volun-

---

[4]There is no reason to label these inquiry stories as a type-scene (see n. 4
on p. 281; cf. Cohn, "Convention and Creativity," 603-616; idem, *2 Kings*,
pp. 59-60).

[5]See Cogan and Tadmor, *II Kings*, p. 90.

[6]Kissling, *Reliable Characters*, pp. 168-171, 198-199.

[7]Nelson sees a parallel in Elisha's lie ("certainly recover") and truth ("certainly die") and Micaiah's lie (1 Kgs 22:15,17) that was followed by the truth,
Ahab would perish (*First and Second Kings*, p. 193).

teers to *entice* Ahab to battle (22:19-23). Does the reader now hear a *lying prophet entice* Hazael to assassinate the king of Aram?[8] In verse 13, Elisha informs Hazael that he will become king in Aram.

If this interpretation is correct, there is some irony in the fact that Yahweh through the prophet Elisha instigates the death of Ben-Hadad. This is the king who led the Arameans in the battle at Ramoth Gilead in which king Ahab lost his life. A careful reader remembers that, because of the covenant Ahab initiated between the two kings, Ahab died in the place of Ben-Hadad, who was devoted to destruction (חֵרֶם, *ḥērem*) by Yahweh (see comments on 1 Kgs 20:42). A *lying spirit* enticed Ahab to join the battle against Ben-Hadad. Now, a *lying prophet* entices Hazael to assassinate Ben-Hadad.[9] In fact, the concentric structure of this paragraph emphasizes the prophet's interaction with Hazael, which precipitates the death of Ben-Hadad:[10]

A. Ben-Hadad is ill (v. 7).
    B. Hazael is commissioned (v. 8).
        C. Hazael goes to Elisha (v. 9a).
            X. Elisha entices Hazael (v. 9b-13).
        C'. Hazael returns to Ben-Hadad (v. 14).
    B'. Ben-Hadad receives Hazael (v. 14).
A'. Ben-Hadad dies at the hands of Hazael (v. 15).

As in the case of Baasha and Zimri (1 Kgs 15:25–16:20), Yahweh uses Ben-Hadad to punish Ahab, but in the end the king of Aram is devoted to Yahweh and gets what he deserves. The "anointing" of Hazael is another example of how the storyteller uses an earlier episode to frame a story with ironic results. In this way, Yahweh is shown again to be working in history, this time in the affairs of Israel's rival Aram — ultimately for the purpose of punishing his people.

---

[8]The connections between 1 Kings 22 and 2 Kings 3 indicate that the story of Micaiah and Ahab's battle with Ben-Hadad frames Joram's campaign against Moab. In Joram's assault on Mesha of Moab, Elisha is a *lying prophet*, in the sense that he "entices" Joram to proceed but does not give Joram the *whole truth* (see comments on 2 Kings 3). These two stories form the interpretive context for situating Elisha's words to Hazael and suggest that Elisha is *enticing* Hazael to assassinate Ben-Hadad.

[9]Brueggemann avers that Elisha "evoked the coup of Hazael" (*1 & 2 Kings*, p. 374).

[10]Adapted from Cohn, *2 Kings*, p. 60.

8:11-13 The scene with the staring is somewhat ambiguous. Hazael is obviously the subject of "he [the NIV inserts **Hazael**] **felt ashamed.**" If he is also the subject of "he stared at him," his fixed gaze is in reaction to the prophet's contradictory statements. If the prophet is staring, it either represents trancelike behavior associated with the additional vision he receives (v. 13, "the LORD has shown me"), or, more likely, a tactic to judge the reaction of Hazael.[11] Elisha **weep**s at what he sees in Hazael's future. This man, even though only a messenger,[12] will **become king of Aram** and bring great evil on Israel. Through the prophet Elisha, Yahweh is raising up another *adversary* against his people (cf. 1 Kgs 11:14-40) and bringing about events that he initiated in the days of Elijah. The prophet is in effect obeying the as yet *unfulfilled* directive to Elijah that he anoint Hazael as king over Aram. Shortly, he will complete the charge when he has Jehu anointed as king over Israel (2 Kgs 9:1-13).[13] They will both wield the sword of Yahweh against Israel (1 Kgs 19:15-17; 2 Kgs 8:11-12; 9–10; 13:3,22) — and even the house of David (9:27-28; 10:12-14; 12:18[19]), for which Aram will be punished (Amos 1:3-5). Up to this point, Elisha has been, for the most part, a vehicle of salvation, appropriate for his name (אֱלִישָׁע, *'ĕlîšā'*, "God/my God is salvation"). When he entices Hazael and "anoints" Jehu, however, he personifies his patronym ("son of Shaphat"="son of judgment," 1 Kgs 19:19).[14]

8:14-15 When Hazael returns to Ben-Hadad, he reports only Elisha's initial, deceptive statement: **"You [will] certainly recover."** Gray argues that there is no actual assassination in verse 15. The

---

[11]Cf. Hobbs, *2 Kings*, p. 102; Nelson, *First and Second Kings*, pp. 193-194; Cogan and Tadmor, *II Kings*, p. 90; Gray, *I & II Kings*, pp. 531.

[12]One extrabiblical reference to Hazael corresponds with his statement that he is "a mere dog" (v. 13) and implies the historical accuracy of this event. Shalmaneser III records that "Hazael, a commoner ['son of a nobody'] seized the throne [of Adad-idri (Hadadezer=Ben-Hadad)]" (*ANET*, p. 280; Pitard, *Ancient Damascus*, p. 135). Cogan and Tadmor connect the inscription with the "anointing" of Hazael in 2 Kings 8 and date the coup to 845–841 B.C. (*II Kings*, p. 92). For a discussion of the historicity of Israel's wars with Aram, including the significance of this text for determining the identity of Ben-Hadad, see "Excursus: Ahab's Wars with Aram."

[13]Turner suggests that the anointing of Jehu may have been delayed because of the "genuine repentance of Ahab" (*Annual Lesson Commentary*, p. 54).

[14]See Provan, *1 and 2 Kings*, p. 204.

king's body is discovered the next morning when the mosquito netting, which was dipped in water for a cooling effect, is removed. He does allow, however, that assassination is a "possible interpretation" of this verse.[15] While Shalmaneser's reference to Hazael does not describe the king's death, it does suggest a violent overthrow of the former regime.[16] The usual reading of this verse as an assassination also fits the context. Hazael is *enticed* by the word of the prophet to eliminate his master Ben-Hadad — and in this way is "anointed" king of Aram. The vision that Elisha receives ("Yahweh has shown me," vv. 10,13) comes to pass. And even in this there is hope. If Yahweh can establish the kings of the nations to wield his sword of judgment, perhaps he can establish kings to enact his many mercies.

2. Jehoram of Judah Is Defeated by Edom (8:16-24)

8:16-17 Consistent with his synoptic presentation of the reigns of the kings of Israel and Judah, the storyteller returns to the intervening kings of Judah before narrating the fall of the house of Ahab, even though Joram has not yet seen Yahweh's judgment. It turns out that the narrator takes this course because the fortunes of the two kingdoms are entwined. The two houses have been united in marriage, and Ahaziah, the son of Jehoram of Judah, will also experience Yahweh's wrath at the hands of Jehu (9:14-29). The chronological note that Jehoram began to reign **in the fifth year of Joram son of Ahab king of Israel** appears to conflict with statements in 1:17 and 3:1 that Joram of Israel became king in the second year of Jehoram son of Jehoshaphat king of Judah and in the eighteenth year of Jehoshaphat king of Judah. A reasonable solution is that Jehoram and his father Jehoshaphat were coregents until the fifth year of Joram of Israel. Jehoram then reigns **in Jerusalem eight years** as sole ruler of Judah.[17] Thiele believes that the fifth year of Joram is also the year of Jehoshaphat's death. The phrase **when Jehoshaphat was king of Judah** clouds the situation somewhat.[18]

---

[15]Gray, *I & II Kings*, pp. 528, 532.

[16]*ANET*, p. 280; Hobbs, *2 Kings*, p. 102.

[17]Thiele, *Mysterious Numbers*, pp. 99-101; see comments on 1:16-18.

[18]Ibid., p. 100.

Missing in some manuscripts, it could be a scribal addition, but Gray suggests that Jehoshaphat abdicates the throne in the fifth year of Joram and dies the following year.[19] More important is Thiele's observation that beginning with Jehoram's reign Judah adopts from Israel the nonaccession-year system of calculating reigns (in which reigns are counted from the first day the king ascends to the throne; see "Introduction: Chronology").[20] This corresponds with the new relationship between the two nations. Through marriage, the house of Ahab now holds sway over the throne in Jerusalem. If correct, the influence of the northern kingdom on Judah even extends to reckoning the reigns of the kings.

8:18-19 For the first time, the storyteller directly associates a king of Judah with the sins of Israel. The language, **He walked in the ways of the kings of Israel, as the house of Ahab had done**, echoes the refrain that characterizes the kings of Israel: ". . . walked in the ways of Jeroboam son of Nebat, who caused Israel to sin" (see comments on 1 Kgs 13:33-34). The Chronicler adds that the new king "put all his brothers to the sword" (2 Chr 21:4) and includes a letter to Jehoram from the prophet Elijah that says, in part, "You have led Judah and the people of Jerusalem to prostitute themselves, just as the house of Ahab did" (v. 13). Jehoram's apostasy must have included the worship of Baal, against which Elijah labored (cf. 2 Kgs 11:18).[21] Later, in explaining why Israel is taken into Assyrian captivity, the author of Kings will say that Judah (literally) "walked in the statutes/practices of Israel which they practiced" (17:19). In the larger story, this explains, at least in part, why even Judah is exiled and Jerusalem destroyed. This evil influence is brought directly on Judah when Jehoram marries **a daughter of Ahab**. No doubt, this union was arranged by Jehoshaphat when entering into a covenant of peace with the house of Ahab (1 Kgs 22:44). But an innocent marriage for the purpose of strengthening ties between the two nations turns disastrous for the house of David.

Yet, the narrator makes a point of saying that because of David Yahweh **was not willing to destroy Judah**. Yahweh promised to

---

[19]Gray, *I & II Kings*, p. 532, n. a.

[20]Thiele, *Mysterious Numbers*, pp. 58, 100-101.

[21]For a discussion of Elijah's letter including the chronological issues raised by its setting in the reign of Jehoram, see Hicks, *1 & 2 Chronicles*, pp. 396-397.

maintain a lamp for David and his descendants forever. David's house and kingdom would be established forever (1 Kgs 11:36; 15:4; the Chronicler specifically mentions Yahweh's "covenant with David" [2 Chr 21:4; cf. 2 Sam 7:16]), but the reader knows the rest of the story. Like Israel, Judah will be ravaged. The city of Jerusalem will be destroyed, and the temple of Yahweh will lie in ruins. So, the storyteller's statement has the effect of introducing once more the theme of delayed retribution (see comments on 1 Kgs 11:11-13).[22] Yahweh is patient with Judah for the sake of David. While his sword of judgment will soon fall on the joined-in-marriage houses of Ahab and David and in the end on both Israel and Judah, an exilic reader is reminded of Yahweh's unconditional, eternal covenant with the house of David.

8:20-22 In spite of Yahweh's patience with Judah, the course of events indicates that Solomon's kingdom of peace continues to unravel (as Omri's kingdom unravels during the reigns of Ahaziah and Joram; see comments on 1:1-4; and ch. 3).[23] Jehoshaphat attempted to restore the fortunes of the house of David by building a fleet of ships to sail to Ophir, a project that was not realized (1 Kgs 22:48-49). However, during his reign, **Edom** remained a vassal of the king of Judah (1 Kgs 22:47; 2 Kings 3). Jehoshaphat's son Jehoram apparently does not have the political or military muscle to maintain that dominance over Edom. In his days, Edom **rebels against Judah and sets up its own king**. When Jehoram tries to squash the revolt, he is ambushed and barely escapes with his life. Edom remains in rebellion, and **Libnah revolts at the same time**. Libnah was a Levitical city of Judah, perhaps a Canaanite city incorporated into the tribe (Josh 15:42; 21:13).[24] Jehoram is unable to control even his own territory. The Chronicler adds that this was because "Jehoram had forsaken the LORD the God of his fathers" (2 Chr 21:10).

---

[22]Cohn suggests that the connotation is "not yet" (*2 Kings*, p. 63). The Chronicler emphasizes the immediate judgment on Jehoram in a Philistine and Arab invasion of Judah (in which booty is carried away from the palace, including the king's wives and sons) and an "incurable disease of the bowels" (2 Chr 21:4-20).

[23]Hobbs, *2 Kings*, p. 7; Provan, *1 and 2 Kings*, p. 206.

[24]By the time of the reign of Hezekiah, Libnah is again under the control of Jerusalem (2 Kgs 19:8). While the identity of Libnah is uncertain, there are reasons to suggest Tell Bornat, ca. 8 km NE of Lachish, as the location of the site (John L. Peterson, "Libnah [place]," in *ABD*).

8:23-24 The account of Jehoram's reign closes with the standard formula. **The other events** in his reign are recorded in the **annals of the kings of Judah**. At his death, he is **buried with them in the City of David**, although the Chronicler says he was not buried in the tombs of the kings, a sign for him that Jehoram was a wicked king (2 Chr 21:20).[25] **Ahaziah his son** becomes king in his place.

3. Ahaziah Joins Joram of Israel against Hazael (8:25-29)

8:25-27 Ahaziah son of Jehoram begins to reign **in the twelfth year of Joram son of Ahab**.[26] He reigns only **one year**. Subtly, the narrator is intimating the judgment that is to come. Since Joram son of Ahab reigns only twelve years (3:1), the note about Ahaziah's one-year reign portends ominous things for both houses.[27] He then moves to establish a direct link between the two kingdoms, which lays a foundation for what is to come. The king's mother is **Athaliah, a granddaughter of Omri** — and therefore a daughter of Ahab king of Israel. As the storyteller now prepares to narrate the fall of the house of Ahab, Athaliah is called by name (cf. 8:18). A grandson of Ahab is king of Judah and **walks in the ways of the house of Ahab**. Then for emphasis, the storyteller mentions one more time that Ahaziah **was related by marriage to Ahab's family**.[28] Another marriage negatively affects the people of Yahweh (cf. 1 Kgs 11:1-4; 16:31-33).[29] The house of Ahab now occupies the throne of David. A careful reader takes notice. If the anger of Yahweh is about to consume the house of Ahab, what will happen to the promise of an eternal house for David?[30]

---

[25]For the Chronicler, "with them" must mean in the same city (Hicks, *1 & 2 Chronicles*, p. 399).

[26]Second Kings 9:29 says that Ahaziah became king in the eleventh year of Joram (see comments on 9:29).

[27]Provan, *1 and 2 Kings*, p. 207.

[28]The Hebrew may be interpreted as saying Ahaziah was also a son-in-law (חָתָן, *ḥāthan*) to the house of Ahab (cf. 1 Kgs 3:1), although *ḥāthan* may also mean "related to" as is indicated by the translation in the NIV (see Hobbs, *2 Kings*, p. 104).

[29]Provan, *1 and 2 Kings*, p. 206.

[30]Hicks, *1 & 2 Chronicles*, p. 401.

The close ties between the two houses surface in the names of the reigning monarchs. Ahab's sons are Ahaziah and Joram. Jehoshaphat names a son Jehoram (a variant of Joram), and, as this paragraph indicates, a son named Ahaziah succeeds Jehoram of Judah. Clearly, these reigning relatives are named after each other. This situation is confusing for a modern audience but is actually somewhat more confusing in Hebrew. The two variant spellings "Jehoram" (יְהוֹרָם, $y^ehôrām$) and "Joram" (יוֹרָם, $yôrām$) are both used for the respective kings, north and south, without any discernible pattern.[31] The following chart represents the Hebrew spelling employed in naming these kings of Israel and Judah:

King of Israel		King of Judah
	22:51	Jehoram
Jehoram	1:17	Jehoram son of Jehoshaphat
Jehoram son of Ahab	3:1	
Jehoram	3:6	
Joram son of Ahab	8:16	Jehoram king of Judah
	8:21	Joram
	8:23	Joram
	8:24	Joram
Joram son of Ahab	8:25	Jehoram king of Judah
Joram (2) son of Ahab	8:28	
Joram (2) son of Ahab	8:29	Jehoram king of Judah
Joram (2)	9:14	
Jehoram	9:15	
Joram (2)	9:16	
Jehoram	9:17	
Jehoram (2) king of Israel	9:21	
Jehoram	9:22	
Jehoram	9:23	
Jehoram	9:24	
Joram son of Ahab	9:29	
	11:2	Joram
	12:19	Jehoram

---

[31]The spelling may represent vocalization (e.g., the shorter spelling for names in construct, with an inseparable preposition, or preceded by the direct object marker), but there are noticeable exceptions. The NIV spells the name of the king of Israel "Joram" and the king of Judah "Jehoram," a format used here to avoid confusing the two (see n. 2, p. 299 and the NIV text notes for 8:21; 9:15).

This haphazard arrangement is not without design. The confusion is intentional, and the effect reinforces an underlying theological message.[32] Because of the intermarriage between the two houses and the evil influence of the house of Ahab on the house of David, the two are interchangeable. Joram is Jehoram; Jehoram is Joram — and Judah has become Israel! With a creative use of naming, the storyteller reinforces an important thrust in the composition. When Judah through the evil influence of the house of Ahab becomes like Israel, they also incur the wrath of Yahweh (cf. 17:19).

8:28-29 Ahaziah king of Judah joins **Joram son of Ahab** to fight against **Hazael king of Aram at Ramoth Gilead**, as Ahaziah's grandfather Jehoshaphat joined Ahab against Ben-Hadad, the battle in which the king of Israel experienced the wrath of Yahweh (1 Kgs 22:29-39). The Chronicler adds that the king's advisors from the house of Ahab counseled him to join Joram in battle (2 Chr 22:4-5). With the indicators already scattered through the narrative on the Omride dynasty, the reader wonders if perhaps now Yahweh will complete his judgment on the house of Ahab (see 1 Kgs 21:29). The results of the battle reinforce this suspicion. Joram is **wounded** [נָכָה, *nākāh*, "struck"] and **returns to Jezreel to recover from the wounds** [מַכִּים, *makkîm*] **the Arameans had inflicted** [*nākāh*] **on him at Ramoth Gilead, in his battle with Hazael king of Aram**. Ahaziah visits him **because he had been wounded** [חֹלֶה, *ḥōleh*, "made weak/ injured," from *ḥālāh*]. Intentionally, the language recalls the death of Ahab. The Hebrew words *nākāh, makkāh* [pl. -*îm*], and *ḥālāh* all appear in the description of Ahab's demise at the hand of Ben-Hadad king of Aram (1 Kgs 22:34-35). It is not just coincidence that Joram is *wounded* at Ramoth Gilead — as was his father. The following narrative will even suggest other parallels. When Ahaziah goes down to Jezreel to visit his *wounded* uncle, the stage is set for the purge of Jehu.

---

[32]The fact that there are other variant spellings of names without any clear pattern (e.g., "Hezekiah" [18:1] and "Yehezekiah" [20:10]) does not take away from this observation.

2 KINGS 9[1]

4. Jehu Is Anointed King of Israel (9:1-15)

9:1-5 Elisha commissions one from **the company of the prophets** (see comments on 2:7-10) to **Ramoth Gilead** to anoint **Jehu son of Jehoshaphat, son of Nimshi** as king of Israel. There is some irony in the fact that Jehu is the son of a "Jehoshaphat" ("Yahweh has *judged*").[2] Another Jehoshaphat (son of Asa, king of Judah) played a role in Yahweh's *judgment* on Ahab at Ramoth Gilead (1 Kings 22; see "Excursus: Ahab's Wars with Aram"). This "son of judgment" is Yahweh's choice to bring final judgment on the house of Ahab. That Jehu is in Ramoth Gilead with a group of **army officers** (vv. 4,11) indicates that the God of Israel is about to initiate a military coup. As in the case of Hazael, Yahweh is designating someone who has the means to depose the reigning regime. Elisha's instructions stand out. The prophet is to take a **flask and pour the oil on his head and declare, "This is what the LORD says: I anoint you king over Israel"** (v. 3). The directive resonates with the anointing of Saul, especially the "flask" of oil that appears only in the Saul and Jehu stories (cf. 1 Sam 9:27–10:1).[3] As with Saul, Jeroboam, and Baasha, Yahweh is the one who sets up and brings down kings in Israel.

---

[1]Saul Olyan argues that the key words שקע (*šqʻ*, "mad/crazy") and שלם (*šlm*, "peace/well being"), which cross over proposed compositional boundaries, undermine the two-source theory of the composition of chapter 9 and indicate it is a unity ("*Hăšālôm*: Some Literary Considerations of 2 Kings 9," *CBQ* 46/4 [Oct. 84]: 654-659).

[2]Jehu is named by Yahweh and the lookout atop the wall in Jezreel "Jehu son of Nimshi" (1 Kgs 19:16; 2 Kgs 9:20). Jehu's grandfather may have been a person of note, so the unusual patronym for Jehu, "son of [his grandfather] Nimshi." That Elisha and the narrator name him "Jehu son of Jehoshaphat, the son of Nimshi" (9:2,14) calls attention to the name Jehoshaphat ("Yahweh has judged").

[3]Provan, *1 and 2 Kings*, p. 209.

9:6-10 When Jehu is anointed, the narrator names the man Elisha has commissioned **the young man, the prophet.** He is more than a messenger; he is a man of God who also speaks for Yahweh. Perhaps this explains why he goes beyond the instructions of Elisha. His expansive statement may be a function of prophetic initiative and/or the Spirit of Yahweh working in the prophet (see "Excursus: Elijah in Context"). In contrast with Elijah in 1 Kings 21:19-24, he prefaces the oracle with "thus says Yahweh," although he inserts "Yahweh, *the God of Israel*" and adds that Jehu would be king over *"Yahweh's people* Israel" (v. 6). As he begins, these minor changes give the prophet's performance a human dimension and emphasize Yahweh's relationship with Israel, even though, apparently on his own initiative, he goes well beyond Elisha. However, there may be another way to read the prophet's lengthy expansion. When Jehu summarizes the words of the prophet for his companions, he quotes Elisha exactly: **"This is what the LORD says: I anoint you king over Israel"** (v. 12). The repetition may be a clue that the prophet's oracle is not an expansion — an indirect way of indicating that the prophet's instructions from Elisha included what appears at first glance to be added by the prophet. For purposes of narrative flow, the storyteller records only the basic thrust of the mission from Elisha, allowing the reader to hear the entire oracle in the mouth of the prophet. When Jehu summarizes what has happened, he repeats the essential message. Yahweh has anointed him king over Israel.[4]

The oracle itself resonates with Ahijah's oracle against Jeroboam (1 Kgs 14:7-16; cf. 16:1-3) and, more importantly, with Elijah's prophecy against Ahab and Jezebel (1 Kgs 21:20-24). In particular, **"I will cut [כָּרַת, *kārath*[5]] off from Ahab every last male** [literally, "the one who urinates against the wall"; cf. 1 Kgs 14:10; 16:11; 21:21] **in Israel—slave or free. I will make the house of Ahab like the house of Jeroboam son of Nebat and like the house of Baasha son of Ahijah"** is a quotation from Elijah (21:21-22), when he went beyond the directions of Yahweh to curse the whole house of Ahab. And there is a word for Jezebel, **"Dogs will devour her on the plot [חֵלֶק, *ḥēleq*] of ground at Jezreel,"** which also echoes Elijah's prophecy

---

[4]See ibid., p. 212.

[5]"Cut" (*kārath*) is a key word in the Elijah and Ahab narrative (see comments on 18:3-6). Now Yahweh will *cut* off the house of Ahab as he promised.

(21:23-24).[6] These connections link this prophet's word directly to Yahweh's work against Baal worship in Israel during the time of Ahab. The prophet utters not just the instructions of Elisha – his words are the word of Elijah,[7] who was originally commissioned to anoint Jehu as king of Israel (1 Kgs 19:15-18).

Ahab humbled himself in the presence of Yahweh's anger, and Elijah's word was delayed (1 Kgs 21:27-29). Now, Yahweh is about to establish the word of his prophet, which he said would happen in the days of Ahab's son: "I will bring [disaster] on [Ahab's] house in the days of his son" (21:29). Consequently, the God of Israel *will* **"avenge the blood of my servants the prophets[8] and the blood of all the LORD's servants shed by Jezebel."** Without doubt, this invective includes Yahweh's servant Naboth (1 Kings 21), along with all the prophets who were murdered by Jezebel (18:4,13). For these sins, the *house* of Ahab will fall. Francisco O. Garcia-Treto has demonstrated that "house" functions as a key word in this story (and in Kings), occurring eighteen times in 2 Kings 9 and 10.[9] That the *house of Ahab* – which now includes a descendant in the *house of David* who sits on the throne in Jerusalem – will fall is ominous for both kingdoms. It also reaches beyond the ninth century to the time when the *house of David* will experience another, similar judgment. When describing the sins of Manasseh, the inspired storyteller will say, "The LORD said through *his servants the prophets*: . . . 'I will stretch out over Jerusalem the measuring line used against Samaria and the plumb line used against *the house of Ahab*. I will wipe out Jerusalem as one wipes a dish, wiping it and turning it upside down'" (21:10,13).

9:11-15 Jehu at first tries to keep the news to himself. The company of officers wants to know: **"Is everything all right [הֲשָׁלוֹם,**

---

[6]In 1 Kgs 21:23, Elijah's recorded words are "by the wall of Jezreel," not "on the plot of ground at Jezreel" (see comments on 9:36-37).

[7]Cohn, *2 Kings*, p. 66.

[8]The phrase "my/his servants the prophets" will appear again in 17:13,23 (cf. 21:10; 24:2), with the emphasis on how Israel rejected Yahweh's prophets. The prophet Jeremiah, in particular, uses this phrase to bring out how God's people in rejecting his messengers rejected him (see Jer 7:25; 26:5; 29:19; 35:15; 44:4; cf. Ezek 38:17; Zech 1:6).

[9]He also makes the connection between this text and 2 Kgs 21:10-13 (Francisco O. Garcia-Treto, "The Fall of the House: A Carnivalesque Reading of 2 Kings 9 and 10," *JSOT* 46 [1990]: 47-50, 61).

hăšālôm; see comments on vv. 16-23]? **Why did this madman** [מְשֻׁגָּע,
mᵉšuggā', from *šāga'*[10]] **come to you?**" When he finally shares the
word of the prophet, **"I anoint you king over Israel,"** his comrades
respond by acknowledging him as king: **"Jehu is king!"** Then, in
verse 14 the narrator breaks frame to say that Jehu **conspires** (קָשַׁר,
qāšar; cf. 10:9) against Joram. Following on the heels of the anointing scene, this statement indicates that Yahweh initiates the conspiracy that follows. The word *qāšar* was also used of Baasha and
Zimri (1 Kgs 15:27; 16:9,16,20). Later, kings will be overthrown, in
both Israel and Judah, without the direct intervention of Yahweh (cf.
2 Kgs 12:21; 14:19; 15:10,15,25,30; 21:23,24).

To reestablish the context for what follows, the narrator now
repeats that Joram and Israel were **defending Ramoth Gilead
against Hazael king of Aram.**[11] Joram has returned to Jezreel to
recover from **the wounds** [מַכִּים, *makkîm*] **the Arameans had inflicted** [*nākāh*] **on him in the battle with Hazael king of Aram**. The repetition brings back into focus that Joram has been wounded at
Ramoth Gilead like his father Ahab. The double reference to Hazael
in verses 14-15 has the effect of reminding the reader that Yahweh
has anointed Hazael as an "*adversary*" against Israel. Both Hazael (at
Ramoth Gilead) and Jehu (at Jezreel) participate in Yahweh's judgment on the house of Ahab. In verse 15b, the storyteller returns to
the scene in Ramoth Gilead where Jehu's fellow officers proclaim
him king. Jehu responds to their gesture by saying, in effect, "If you
really feel this way, don't let anyone escape to tell Joram in Jezreel."

5. Jehu Assassinates Joram and Ahaziah (9:16-29)

9:16-23 Jehu sets out from Ramoth Gilead, in the Transjordan,
for Jezreel. The narrator repeats once more that Joram is in Jezreel,

---

[10]"Madman" (*mᵉšuggā'*) is probably a pejorative moniker for a prophet,
which derives from the ecstatic behavior prophets on occasion display (see
Jer 9:26; Hos 9:7; cf. 1 Sam 10:1-13; 19:18-24).

[11]The fact that there is no reference to Israel retaking Ramoth Gilead following 1 Kings 22 does not undermine the historical accuracy of this
account. Ramoth Gilead was a border town that probably changed hands
numerous times, and the primary purpose of Kings is not to give a complete
account of the history of Israel (see Hobbs, *2 Kings*, p. 116).

now **resting** (literally, "lying there"), and adds, again, that his nephew, **Ahaziah king of Judah**, is visiting him there (cf. 8:29). The pace of the action slows as Jehu approaches Jezreel. In this scene, the perceptual point of view alternates between those in Jezreel (the lookout atop one of the towers and Joram within the walls) and the messengers and Jehu on the approach to the city. The lookout sees Jehu coming, although he does not yet know his identity. The naming, **Jehu's troops** (literally, "Jehu's multitude"), lets the reader know that Jehu is not alone; he approaches in force. The detailed narration of the two messengers sent to intercept the approaching band further retards the action and creates suspense. Within Jezreel, the suspense builds as to the identity and mission of the approaching force. For the reader, who knows more than the participants in Jezreel, the suspense surrounds the actions of Jehu. How will he accomplish the charge Yahweh has given him?

The question that dominates this scene, **"Do you come in peace [*hăšālôm*]?"** resonates with the query of Jehu's comrades when the prophet left in haste (v. 11): "Is everything all right [*hăšālôm*]?" When the lookout recognizes that **"the driving is like that of Jehu son of Nimshi**, who **drives like a madman** [from *šāgaʻ*]" (v. 20), the reader hears another subtle connection with the scene where Jehu is anointed, in which the prophet is labeled a "madman" (*mᵉšuggāʻ*).[12] Is Jehu, then, *driving* like a prophet? While he may not be a madman in the sense of a prophet, he is accomplishing the word of Yahweh![13] In the reported dialogue between Jehu and the messengers, and finally between Jehu and Joram, "Do you come in peace [*hăšālôm*]?" carries additional symbolic meaning. This common greeting (*hăšālôm*, "Are [you] well?") functioned as a motif in the Shunam-

---

[12]David Ussishkin, the excavator of Tel Jezreel, imagines a scout spotting Jehu driving madly up the Jezreel valley from Gilead to the east and claims that the archaeological expedition to Jezreel uncovered the tower from which the lookout saw Jehu (interview by Hershel Shanks, in *Biblical Archaeology: From the Ground Down*, writ., dir., and host. by Hershel Shanks, Biblical Archaeology Society, 1996, videocassette). Na'aman writes, "The place of the city [of Jezreel] in the prophetical narratives that refer to Ahab and Joram corresponds exactly with the results of excavations" ("Notes on the Excavation of Tel Jezreel," 124).

[13]Recognizing the role *šgʻ* (vv. 11,20) plays in the narrative, Olyan says, "Both the prophets and Jehu are instruments of Yahweh's restoration of *šālôm*" ("*Hăšālôm*," 663).

mite and Naaman narratives to suggest another level of meaning, the well-being of the characters in the story (see comments on chs. 4–5). With this in the background, the repetition of *hǎšālôm* (nine times in ch. 9; vv. 11,17,18[2×],19[2×],22[2×],31) suggests emphasis and indicates a similar nuance.[14] When Joram meets Jehu in **the plot of ground that belonged the Naboth the Jezreelite**, the king wants to know from his commander who has arrived from the front if everything is all right.[15] Yet, the narrator has framed the story to suggest another connotation. Everything is not all right in Israel! When Jehu responds to Joram, **"How can there be peace** [מָה הַשָּׁלוֹם, *māh hašālôm*] **. . . as long as all the idolatry** [literally, "prostitution"; cf. Hos 1:2; 2:2,4; 4:12; 5:4] **and witchcraft** [cf. Isa 47:9,12; Micah 5:11; Nahum 3:4] **of your mother Jezebel abound?"** (v. 22), his dialogue surely represents the ideological point of view of the storyteller. There can be no peace, no well-being, when idolatry (elsewhere linked with prostitution and witchcraft; cf. Micah 5:10-15[9-14]) flourishes in Israel! As Joram flees from the plot that belonged to Naboth and warns **Ahaziah**, the reader knows that the word of Yahweh is about to fall on the house of Ahab, which includes the kings of both Israel and Judah.

9:24-26 The death of Joram echoes the death of his father Ahab.[16] As Joram flees, **Jehu** draws **his *bow* and *strikes* Joram *between* the shoulders. The arrow pierces his heart and he slumps down in his *chariot*.** The parallels between the death of father and son are conspicuous. In the battle with Ben-Hadad over Ramoth Gilead, an anonymous Aramean drew his *bow* (קֶשֶׁת, *qešeth*) and *struck* (יַכֵּה, *yakkeh*, from *nākāh*) Ahab *between* (בֵּין, *bên*) sections of his armor (1 Kgs 22:34-35). Jehu draws his *bow* (*qešeth*) and *strikes* (from *nākāh*) Joram *between* (*bên*) his shoulders. In another parallel, Ahab charged his chariot driver to "wheel around ["turn (הֲפָךְ, *hāphak*) your hand"]" (1 Kgs 22:34), and Joram "turned about ["turned (*hāphak*) his hand"] and fled" (2 Kgs 9:23).[17] Each one dies in his *chariot* (רֶכֶב/מֶרְכָּבָה, *merkābāh/rekeb*). When the reader recalls that each

---

[14]Olyan also views *šālôm* (and the question *hǎšālôm*) as a key word in the story, arguing that the violence that Jehu perpetrates on the house of Ahab is for the purpose of restoring *šālôm* (ibid., 660-668).

[15]Provan, *1 and 2 Kings*, p. 213.

[16]Ibid., p. 210.

[17]Hobbs, *2 Kings*, p. 117.

king was accompanied in battle by a king of Judah (Jehoshaphat with Ahab and Ahaziah son of Jehoshaphat with Joram) and that both father and son were *wounded* (received a wound/wounds, *makkāh/ makkîm*) at *Ramoth Gilead*, he realizes that there is larger design in the narrative (see "Parallels between the Deaths of Ahab and Joram"). Jehu's command to **Bidkar, "Throw him on the field that belonged to Naboth the Jezreelite,"** whom Ahab had murdered for the very same field (1 Kings 21), reinforces the resonance and indicates that, through a creative use of allusion, the storyteller is demonstrating the power of the word of Yahweh.

To Elijah, Yahweh said that dogs would lick up the blood of Ahab in the place where Naboth's blood was spilled (1 Kgs 21:19). However, Elijah never delivered this part of his instructions, and his prophecy was postponed to the days of Ahab's son. (Elijah broadened the prophecy to Ahab's house, which Yahweh altered to the days of his son; see comments on 1 Kgs 21:17-29). That dogs licked up Ahab's blood in Samaria, not Jezreel, was a signal that Yahweh's prophetic word was incomplete (see comments on 1 Kgs 22:37-38). Joram's death completes the prophecy. Symbolically, in his death Joram represents Yahweh's judgment on Ahab. When the king dies in his chariot at the hands of Jehu, he is Ahab. His body is thrown on the plot that belonged to Naboth, and Elijah's word and Yahweh's full intentions are fulfilled to the letter. Delayed retribution for the house of Ahab reflects Yahweh's mercy (1 Kgs 21:27-29), but his judgment is enacted — his word comes to pass![18]

Parallels between the Deaths of Ahab and Joram
(1 Kgs 22:34-38 and 2 Kgs 8:28-29; 9:14-15,23-26)

Ahab	Accompanied by Jehoshaphat of Judah	Received a *wound* (*makkāh*) at Ramoth Gilead	"Drew his bow [*qešeth*]"	"*Hit* [struck (*nākāh*)] the king"	"*Between* [*bên*] the sections of his armor"	"*Turn* [*hāphak*] your hand"	Dies in his *chariot* (*rekeb*)
Joram	Accompanied by Ahaziah of Judah	Received *wounds* (*makkîm*) at Ramoth Gilead	"Drew his bow [*qešeth*]"	"*Shot* [struck " (*nākāh*)] Joram	"*Between* [*bên*] the shoulders"	"*Turned* [*hāphak*] his hand"	Dies in his *chariot* (*rekeb*)

---

[18]On the pattern of the Ahab narrative, delayed retribution will be an important theme in the story of Josiah and the release of Jehoiachin at the end of the book (see comments on 2 Kgs 22:15-20; 23:29-30; 25:27-30).

Ahab	Dogs licked up his blood *in Samaria*		**Fulfills 1 Kings 21:19**
Joram	Body thrown on the field of Naboth *in Jezreel*		**Joram = Ahab**

When Jehu commands Bidkar to throw the body of Joram on the plot of ground that had belonged to Naboth, the reader hears new information from Jehu. Jehu and Bidkar were riding behind king Ahab when "Yahweh **made this prophecy** [מַשָּׂא, *maśśā'*[19]] **about him: 'Yesterday I saw the blood of Naboth and the blood of his sons, declares the LORD, and I will surely make you pay for it on this plot of ground, declares the LORD.'"** The narrator has chosen to withhold information until this crucial point in the story. The reader now learns that in addition to the message from the prophet who was sent from Elisha, Jehu has had another occasion to hear Yahweh's intentions for the house of Ahab. Jehu's memory of the oracle (it may represent a free paraphrase[20]) implies that Naboth's sons were also murdered in Jezreel, as Achan's entire family was executed in the days of Joshua (Josh 7:24-26). The narrator has Jehu relay the prophecy at this point in the story because it reinforces what is about to happen. With the wrath of God, Jehu executes a son of Ahab, ironically, on the very *plot* of ground where Naboth and his sons were murdered by Ahab and Jezebel.

When he hears the conversation with Bidkar, the reader at first thinks of Elijah. However, Jehu does not credit this prophecy to Elijah as he does elsewhere. In the next scene, Jehu ascribes the prophecy concerning Jezebel to Elijah (9:36; see 10:10; cf. 1 Kgs 21:23-24). The ambiguity as to the source of the prophecy may be intentional. In his references to the prophetic word in the Ahab story, since the judgment on Ahab (ch. 21), the storyteller appears to be differentiating between the word of Elijah and the word of Yahweh. In 1 Kings 17, he clearly made the point that the word of Yahweh and the word of the prophet were one and the same, in the sense that Elijah spoke for God and Yahweh upheld the word of the prophet. But after Elijah stepped ahead of Yahweh in his judgment

---

[19]Appearing only here in Kings, "prophecy/oracle" (*maśśā'*, elsewhere only in 2 Chr 24:27 and the prophetic literature [e.g., Isa 31:1]) may reinforce the notion that Jehu's language represents his own memory of the oracle (see below).

[20]Hobbs, *2 Kings*, p. 113. Miscall regards Jehu's prophetic references as "self-serving interpretations" ("Elijah, Ahab and Jehu," 79; see below).

on the wicked king, the storyteller distinguishes between the two. When Ahab's blood is licked up in Samaria, not Jezreel, for example, the narrator says that this was according to the word of Yahweh, referring to Yahweh's instructions to Elijah in 21:19, which Elijah did not relay to Ahab. The purpose of this distinction becomes clear in 2 Kings 10:17, where after the elimination of Ahab's entire family the narrator says, "[Jehu] destroyed them, according to the word of the LORD spoken *to Elijah*." The reference is to Yahweh's word to Elijah in 1 Kings 21:29 that, because Ahab repented, he would "bring [this disaster] on [Ahab's] house in the days of his son." When the reader sees that by allusion Jehu kills Joram as Ahab and throws him on the plot in Jezreel that belonged to Naboth, the strategy becomes clear. The narrator is demonstrating how both Yahweh's original (1 Kgs 21:19) and altered word (21:29), along with the word of the prophet Elijah (21:20-24), come to pass in every detail. Ironically, the storyteller distinguishes between the two in the end to demonstrate that they are the same — both Elijah's word (judgment on Ahab's entire house) and Yahweh's word (in the days of Ahab's son) come to pass.

9:27-28 Ahaziah king of Judah also experiences Yahweh's wrath. Seeing what happened to Joram, Ahaziah turns and runs from Jehu. He flees **in his chariot** and makes his way south, but is overtaken and wounded **on the way to Gur near Ibleam**. The king of Judah escapes to the fortified site of **Megiddo** (west of Jezreel, though probably his intended destination) where he dies.[21] His body is taken to Jerusalem, and he is buried **with his fathers in his tomb in the City of David**. The Chronicler explicitly says what the author of Kings implies in his indirect, narrative style: "Through Ahaziah's visit to Joram, God brought about Ahaziah's downfall" (1 Chr 22:7).[22]

The now famous "house of David" inscription, the fragments of which were discovered at Tel Dan in 1993 and 1994, may add information not considered by the storyteller to be germane to the

---

[21]Hobbs, *2 Kings*, p. 118. For the location of Beth Haggan, Ibleam, and Gur, see Adam Zertal, "Gur (place)," in *ABD*.

[22]The Chronicler's description of the death of Ahaziah differs in terms of details with the account in Kings. The Chronicler may be providing a broader view of events (cf. 1 Chr 22:7-9), whereas in Kings the particulars of Ahaziah's flight are central (see Hicks, *1 & 2 Chronicles*, pp. 401-402).

account[23] and, at the same time, reinforces an implication of his narrative. Most likely, Hazael set up the Aramaic inscription in Dan, when Aram, sometime after the coronation of Jehu (perhaps much later), took control of a portion of northern Israel. This indirectly corroborates the note in 10:32-33 that through Hazael Yahweh reduced the size of Israel. The inscription, in part, reads as follows:

> Hadad made me king. And Hadad went in front of me . . . [and] I slew [seve]nty kin[gs], who harnessed thou[sands of cha]riots and thousands of horsemen (or horses). [I killed Jeho]ram son of [Ahab] king of Israel, and [I] killed [Ahaz]iahu son of [Jehoram kin]g of the House of David. And I set [their towns into ruins and turned] their land into [desolation . . . .[24]

Reflecting Hazael's point of view, the inscription says that Hadad made him king, whereas the biblical text claims that Yahweh through his prophet Elisha "anointed" him king of Aram. The inscription also claims that Hazael, not Jehu, assassinated Joram and Ahaziah. While the inscription may well reflect events not delineated by the author of Kings (though unlikely, Jehu may have been in some way an agent of the king of Damascus), Hazael is probably claiming credit for something in which he had no direct part.[25] In any case, the claim in the inscription that Hazael was responsible for the death of Joram and Ahaziah matches the literary pairing of Hazael and Jehu in the death of the kings of Israel and Judah in Kings. Joram was wounded by Hazael at Ramoth Gilead and killed by Jehu at Jezreel, the king of Judah losing his life at the same time. However, according to the account in Kings, these events were set in motion by Yahweh, the God of Israel!

---

[23]Dever writes that the inscription "supplies new information that seems to differ with the biblical accounts. Yet it does confirm significant Aramaean victories over northern Israel in the mid-ninth century, of which the southern writers and editors seem to have been aware, however sketchy the accounts finally produced for their own purposes in 2 Kings" (*Biblical Writers Know*, p. 167; see below).

[24]Avraham Biran and Joseph Naveh, "The Tel Dan Inscription: A New Fragment," *IEJ* 45/1 (1995): 13.

[25]André Lemaire believes the inscription may have been engraved twenty or thirty years after the events and probably represents "boasting" on the part of Hazael ("The Tel Dan Stela as a Piece of Royal Historiography," *JSOT* 81 [1988]: 10-11).

9:29 The note that Ahaziah's reign began **in the eleventh year of Joram** appears to be out of place and contradicts the introductory note that indicated the king of Judah began to reign in the twelfth year of Joram. In fact, the concluding formula for the reign of the king is replaced by the first part of the usual introductory formula (9:29), which differs from the original introduction (8:25, eleventh year instead of twelfth year). Provan believes that the note was added to clarify how both kings die at the same time, when Joram reigned twelve years and Ahaziah one year.[26] However, if Thiele is correct that the "twelfth year" of 8:25 was calculated on the nonaccession-year system that Ahaziah adopted from Israel, and the "eleventh year" of 9:29 represents the accession-year system that was used in Judah before the house of Ahab came to the throne,[27] then the storyteller may be reinforcing an underlying theme – that Ahaziah perishes as a result of his relationship with Israel. Is it just coincidence that the account of Ahaziah's reign is bookended by two almost identical regnal notices, one reflecting the nonaccession-year system of Israel and the other the accession year system formerly used in Judah? The narrative of Ahaziah's death at the hands of Jehu ends, not with the usual concluding formula, but with a reminder that the house of Ahab affected even chronology in Judah.

6. Jehu Eliminates Jezebel (9:30-37)

9:30-35 When Jehu enters Jezreel, he is greeted by the picture of **Jezebel**, with **eyes** painted (literally, "painted her eyes with antimony [פוּך, *pûk*]") and **hair** coiffured, **look**ing **out of a window**. With this image, the narrator uses allusion once more to satirically comment on the role that Jezebel played in the decline and ultimate fall of Israel. Only, this time (as in the allusions to the epic of Baal in the Elijah on Mount Carmel story, 1 Kings 18) the allusion is not to antecedent biblical stories but to Canaanite mythology and a "woman at the window" motif (cf. 2 Sam 6:16; Judg 5:28-30). The

---

[26]Provan, *1 and 2 Kings*, p. 213.

[27]Thiele, *Mysterious Numbers*, p. 101. Galil believes Thiele's solution is too complicated, but does not offer a satisfactory solution (*Chronology of the Kings*, p. 38).

scene of a woman with an Egyptian coiffure looking out of a banis-
tered window is common on carved ivories from the ninth and
eighth centuries B.C. The motif represents a goddess (or a temple
prostitute) looking out of a window, in what may be an enticing
pose. It is more than ironic that the wicked queen who sponsored
goddess worship in Israel (cf. 1 Kgs 18:19) meets her end by being
thrown out of a window — it is poetic justice!

Jezebel's aggressive, manipulative character also appears to be
reflected in her death scene. Like a prostitute, she may have prepared herself to sexually entice Jehu (cf. Ezek 23:40-49), although
her actions probably reflect an arrogant, in-your-face posture as the
Queen Mother who challenges the authority of the conspirator.[28]
She displays a belligerent spirit as she names Jehu, **"Zimri,**[29] **you
murderer of your master."** Zimri assassinated Elah son of Baasha
and reigned only seven days (1 Kgs 16:8-20). Jezebel is in effect saying, "As usurper, you will get what you dish out!" Ironically, her
father-in-law Omri is the one who led the insurrection against Zimri.
(When Shallum assassinates Zechariah of the house of Jehu [15:10-
12], Jezebel's forecast is realized.) There is also irony in her question, **"Have you come in peace** [הֲשָׁלוֹם, *hăšālôm*]**?"** This is the question Joram asked when Jehu approached Jezreel (see comments on
9:17-22).[30] The madman of God does not come in peace. The graphic image of the queen's blood spattering **the wall and the horses as
they trample her** conjures up images of another goddess, the blood-
thirsty goddess Anat. Only, this time the goddess/queen gets what
she deserves. There may also be the rather crude connotation that
Jezebel's blood is like urine, from the idiom for a male, "the one
who urinates against the wall" (cf. 1 Kgs 14:10; 16:11; 21:21; 2 Kgs
9:8). In verses to follow, Jezebel will be described as dung, and the
house of Baal will become a latrine.[31]

---

[28]Cohn, *2 Kings*, p. 70; Saul M. Olyan, "2 Kings 9:31—Jehu as Zimri," *HTR*
78/1-2 (1985): 204-206.

[29]Olyan suggests that "Zimri" may function as wordplay on a root for his
name, זָמַר (*zāmar*, "to prune a vineyard"). So, ironically, Jehu is pruning the
house of Ahab from Yahweh's vineyard, the very house that had taken the
vineyard of Naboth the Jezreelite ("Jehu as Zimri," 206-207).

[30]Bathsheba asked the same question of Adonijah (1 Kgs 2:13). However,
his intentions for the throne were thwarted.

[31]Francisco O. Garcia-Treto, "A Carnivalesque Reading of 2 Kings 9 and
10," 54, 58.

When Jehu eats and drinks (perhaps symbolizing a funerary meal), while Jezebel is being eaten,[32] the theme of eating and drinking (and providing), which dominated the Elijah narrative, resurfaces.[33] But now an agent of Yahweh eats and drinks at the death of the one who tried to eliminate the prophets of Yahweh in Israel. Since the woman at the window motif also appears to have been associated with the Canaanite funerary meal (the מַרְזֵחַ [marzēaḥ]; cf. Amos 6:7; Jer 16:5), the storyteller may also be suggesting that in destroying the personified image of the woman at the window, Jehu "denies the necessary memorial rites to the murdered kings and queen mother."[34] His feasting also portrays him as a rather callous character, which is reinforced as his story progresses.

Jehu names Jezebel **"that cursed woman"** but shows her the respect due a **"king's daughter"** when he sends a detail **to bury her**. It may be symbolic that they find only **her skull, her feet, and her hands**, perhaps in a sacrificial sense. The meager remains may also represent the goddess Anat, sister and lover to Baal, who in the Ugaritic myths wore a necklace of heads and a belt of hands. If so, these body parts symbolize the Canaanite goddess who, along with Baal in scenes to follow, is dealt a deadly blow by Jehu. Tragically for Israel, the wound is not fatal. In the end, Israel will not be able to rid herself of the evil influence of Ahab and Jezebel.[35]

9:36-37 When Jehu is told that little remains of Jezebel, he responds by saying that this happened according to the word of Yahweh **that he spoke through Elijah the Tishbite** and quotes the prophet, although his memory is not exactly what the narrator recorded in 1 Kings 21:23-24. Neither Elijah nor the prophet who anointed Jehu mentions that **Jezebel's body** would **be like refuse on the ground**. This may represent withheld information or indicate that Jehu is prone to remember the word of Yahweh to his own

---

[32]Cohn, *2 Kings*, p. 70.

[33]Deborah A. Appler observes that a form of "to eat" (אָכַל, *'ākal*) appears forty-four times in the Jezebel narrative ("From Queen to Cuisine," 56).

[34]Eleanor Ferris Beach, "The Samaria Ivories," 100-103.

[35]For a discussion of the sacrificial nature of Jezebel's death and the connections between Jezebel and the goddess Anat, see Appler, "From Queen to Cuisine," 64-68. Appler contends that, with the symbols of the goddess Anat (i.e., Jezebel's skull and hands), the power of the goddess remains after the death of Jezebel (p. 68).

advantage.[36] There may be wordplay between refuse/dung and the name Jezebel (*zebel* means dung in Arabic, a language closely related to Hebrew),[37] which, if correct, represents the queen once more as excrement (cf. v. 33).[38] The reference to the **plot at Jezreel** is thematic. "Plot" (חֵלֶק, *ḥēleq*, "share of property/plot," in 9:10,36,37; and חֶלְקָה (*ḥelqāh*), "portion of a field/plot," in 9:21,25,26[2×]; see below) serves as a key word in this story to call attention to the irony that both Joram (symbolically as Ahab) and Jezebel die in Jezreel, where Naboth was murdered.

The connection between verse 36 and Elijah's recorded prophecy concerning Jezebel is difficult. The text in 1 Kings 21:23 reads, "Dogs will devour Jezebel *by the wall of* Jezreel" — instead of "on the plot of ground at Jezreel" (v. 36). While some manuscripts read "plot of ground" in 1 Kings 21:23, the best manuscripts read "by the wall of" (see comments on 21:23). Provan's suggestion is attractive, that in 2 Kings 9:33,36, the storyteller is intimating that Jezebel died both by the wall of Jezreel ("her blood spattered the wall") and on the plot of ground that belonged to Naboth, and that Elijah said both things (cf. 1 Kgs 21:23; and the anointing prophet's "Elijah-esque " word in 2 Kgs 9:10). This is plausible, if Jezebel's window opened on the wall of the city (cf. Josh 2:15), overlooking the plot of ground that belonged to Naboth.[39] In any case, through the words of Jehu and the details of his narration, the storyteller is vividly demonstrating that the word of the prophet Elijah was fulfilled.

[36]Miscall, "Elijah, Ahab and Jehu," 79. Provan believes that Jehu's statement is implied in Elijah's earlier prophecy about the dogs eating Jezebel (*1 and 2 Kings*, p. 212).

[37]Montgomery, *Commentary on the Books of Kings*, pp. 291, 407.

[38]Cohn, *2 Kings*, p. 71.

[39]Provan, *1 and 2 Kings*, p. 211; cf. Cogan and Tadmor, *II Kings*, pp. 112-113.

2 KINGS 10

7. Jehu Eliminates the Seventy Sons of the House of Ahab (10:1-11)

10:1-5 Jehu now turns to purge the remaining members of the **house of Ahab.**[1] **Seventy sons** probably symbolizes "a full house," a large number of descendants.[2] He sends a **letter** to officers in Samaria, including **officials of Jezreel**, who may have represented the city in the capital. The reference to Jezreel helps establish their complicity in the events that follow.[3] The letter also goes to the **elders** and (literally) "*supporters* of Ahab."[4] Jehu challenges the leaders of Samaria, who according to Jehu have a military advantage, to choose the **"best [טוֹב, ṭôb, "good"] and most worthy [יָשָׁר, yāšār, "right"] of your master's sons"** as king to confront him. The wording stands out. Later, Yahweh will use the same language to commend Jehu (v. 30). Also, **"your master's sons"** (vv. 2,3) and **"your master's house"** (v. 3) insinuate that their allegiance is still to Joram, even though the former king is not identified. Nowhere in chapter 10 is Joram named, which subtly reinforces that this judgment is on the house of Ahab.

---

[1]There is no reason to view chapter 10 as reflecting various compositional layers. As it stands, the narrative is a coherent, unified composition (see Hobbs, *2 Kings*, p. 126).

[2]Cogan and Tadmor, *II Kings*, p. 113.

[3]As the NIV text note indicates, some versions read "to the officials of the city" instead of "to the officials of Jezreel," an emendation that misses the important implication of this reference to Jezreel.

[4]The translation "guardians of Ahab's children" does not reflect the underlying Hebrew text. "Children" appears in some important Greek manuscripts but is missing in the MT. The word אֹמְנִים ('ōmnîm, "guardians" in the NIV) is a form (plural participle) of אָמַן ('āman, the word for "giving confirmation/support" — from which derives "amen" in English (see Provan, *1 and 2 Kings*, p. 217; Hobbs, *2 Kings*, p. 122).

Terrified, the important political leaders in Samaria, now including **the palace administrator** and **the city governor**, acquiesce and
defer to Jehu. They name themselves **"your servants"** and call on
him to (literally) "do what is good [*tôb*] in your eyes" (v. 5). They will
not anoint anyone king to confront the usurper. In the scenes to follow, Jehu will do "what is good in his eyes" when he destroys the
house of Ahab with a vicious brutality unsurpassed in Scripture. But
the officials' response also interjects a question that dominates the
narrative for a careful reader. Jehu's purge is "good" in his own eyes,
but is it "good," in terms of method and extent, in the eyes of the
narrator, and, more importantly, in the eyes of Yahweh?

10:6-8 In a second letter that is reminiscent of the letter Jezebel
sent to the elders and nobles in Jezreel (1 Kgs 21:8-14), Jehu challenges the leaders of Samaria, as he did the eunuchs who were in the
window with Jezebel (9:32-33): **"If you are on my side . . . take the
heads⁵ of your master's sons and come to me in Jezreel by this
time tomorrow."** Again naming the princes "your master's sons,"
the underlying test of allegiance is clear. It is time for the men of
Israel to choose Jehu or the house of Ahab, which the reader knows
also means Yahweh or Baal. **The leading men of the city** further
qualifies the influential men who act on Jehu's letter and by repetition (mentioned in vv. 1,5,6) emphasizes they are "partners in
crime" with Jehu, as were the leading men of Jezreel with Jezebel in
the death of Naboth. The emphasis on the leaders of Samaria and
Jezreel also has the effect, though, of characterizing Jehu, whose
coercive, manipulative acts are clearly meant to portray his persona
and regime. **When the letter arrives, these men . . . slaughter all
seventy of** the princes, **put their heads in baskets, and send them
to Jehu in Jezreel.** The word the narrator uses for slaughter (שָׁחַט,
šāḥaṭ) also has the technical meaning of "slaughter for sacrifice"
(also in v. 14; see comments on 1 Kgs 18:40; 2 Kgs 25:7), which reinforces an underlying theme that the house of Ahab is devoted to
destruction to Yahweh (see comments on 1 Kgs 20:24). In the manner of an Assyrian king, and no doubt to terrify the populace, Jehu

---

⁵Hobbs believes that "heads" (רָאשֵׁי, *ro'šê*) is intentionally ambiguous, since
the term may also mean leaders (*2 Kings*, p. 127). If so, this is another example of Jehu's cunning.

stacks the heads **in two piles at the entrance of the city gate** in Jezreel.[6]

10:9-11 The following morning, Jehu addresses the people of Jezreel: **"You are innocent** [צַדִּקִים, *ṣaddiqîm*, "just/righteous"]. **It was I who conspired** [קָשַׁר, *qāšar*] **against my master and killed him; but who killed all these?"** The usurper acknowledges his role in the death of their king, and craftily insinuates the participation of the people in his *conspiracy* (see comments on 9:14).[7] Then, even though he knows the role his own letter has played in coercing the leaders to assassinate the descendants of Ahab, he credits Yahweh with killing them: **"Know then, that not a word the LORD has spoken against the house of Ahab will fail. The LORD has done what he promised through his servant Elijah."** In this way, he claims divine authority for his deeds and uses "the display of bloody heads at the city gate to justify the slaughter of whoever remain[s] of the house of Ahab in Jezreel."[8]

Once more, Jehu associates his actions with the word of Yahweh (cf. 9:25-26,36-37). But, the calculating, somewhat underhanded way he construes the death of the seventy before the people of Jezreel suggests the possibility that he is also manipulating the word of Yahweh for his own benefit. Miscall argues that Jehu "remembers the past well and adapts his assertions about it to fit his present purposes."[9] For example, when Jehu uses the word חֶלְקָה (*ḥelqāh*) for "field/territory" in Joram's death (9:25-26) and חֵלֶק (*ḥēleq*) with the sense of "property in the city" for Jezebel's death (9:36-37), he appears to be remembering the word of Yahweh to fit the circumstances.[10] It is striking that, except for 10:17, Jehu, and not the reliable narrator, interprets the word of Yahweh — and even remembers prophetic oracles the reader has no way of confirming in detail (9:25-26,36-37). At the same time, the statement by the narrator in 10:17 that Jehu "destroyed [all who were left of Ahab's family]

---

[6]See Erika Bleibtreu, "Grisly Assyrian Record of Torture and Death," *BAR* 17/1 (Jan./Feb. 1991): 52-61, 75; Cogan and Tadmor, *II Kings*, p. 113.

[7]Brueggemann writes that Jehu "bind[s] them irreversibly to himself" (*1 & 2 Kings*, p. 396).

[8]Cohn, *2 Kings*, p. 72.

[9]Miscall, "Elijah, Ahab and Jehu," 79; see George Savran, "1 and 2 Kings," p. 153.

[10]Miscall, "Elijah, Ahab and Jehu," 80.

according to the word of the LORD spoken to Elijah" indicates that he acts as an instrument of Yahweh. But does Yahweh condone everything Jehu does in Jezreel? In the eighth century, through the prophet Hosea, Yahweh indicts the dynasty of Jehu for what happens here: "I will punish the house of Jehu for the massacre at [literally, "the blood of"] Jezreel" (Hos 1:4). In verse 11, Jehu's massacre moves beyond his charge to remove the house of Ahab. In an act that appears to be politically motivated, he kills **all his chief men, his close friends and his priests, leaving him no survivor.**[11]

8. Jehu Slaughters Relatives of Ahaziah and Those Who Remain from the House of Ahab (10:12-17)

10:12-14 Jehu sets out for Samaria and meets (literally, "finds" [מָצָא, *māṣā'*]) **relatives** [literally, "brothers"] **of Ahaziah** at **Beth Eked**. On the pattern of 1 Kings 13:24 and 20:36, where a lion from Yahweh *finds* (*māṣā'*, "happens upon") his victim, the use of *māṣā'* may imply that this meeting is not a coincidence (cf. v. 15). The name Beth Eked ("*house* of binding"), with Beth Haggan ("*house* of the enclosure," 9:27), reinforces the *house* motif in this narrative — the fall of the *house* of Ahab, which now encompasses the *house* of David, and the *house* of Baal.[12] Even though the exact location of Beth Eked is unknown, it is odd that they are north of Samaria.[13] Perhaps they are on a raid to retaliate for the assassination of their king. There also is some ambiguity in their words: **"We have come down to greet** [literally, "for peace"] **the families of the king and of the queen mother** [i.e., Jezebel[14]]." With only a change in vowels, "to greet" (לִשְׁלוֹם, *lišlôm*) becomes "to avenge" (לְשַׁלֵּם, *lᵉšallēm*).[15] Since

---

[11]Cohn, *2 Kings*, p. 73. Hobbs notes that Jehu may have murdered the very officials who participated in the death of Naboth (*2 Kings*, p. 127).

[12]Cohn, *2 Kings*, p. 73. House as a motif in chapters 9–10 ties together the key themes of the obliteration of the house of Ahab and the house of Baal in Israel (Garcia-Treto, "The Fall of the House," 47-48, 60).

[13]See Hobbs, *2 Kings*, pp. 127-128; Melvin Hunt, "Beth-Eked (place)," in *ABD*.

[14]Jezebel is the only queen in the northern kingdom to be named with the title "queen mother" (Cogan and Tadmor, *II Kings*, p. 114).

[15]Hobbs, *2 Kings*, p. 128.

they profess to be visiting "the families of the king and of the queen mother," they are at least aware of the deaths of Joram and Jezebel. Once more, the theme word *peace* (שָׁלֹום, *šālôm*) appears in this narrative (see comments on 9:16-23; 30-35), but Jehu is no messenger of peace.[16] Whatever their real intentions, for Jehu the Judeans pronounce their guilt by association. After ordering that they be taken alive, he **slaughters** (*šāḥaṭ*, a ritual sacrifice?; see comments on v. 7) all **forty-two** members of the company.[17] That he left no survivor (from שָׁאַר, *šā'ar*) is thematic (vv. 11[2×],14,17,21).[18] No one remains in the wake of the Jehu's wrath.

10:15-16 Leaving Beth Eked, Jehu *finds* (*māṣā'*) **Jehonadab son of Recab**, who, it so happens, is **on his way to meet him**. Jeremiah 35 indicates this man was a conservative, fervent adherent to the old ways. In the time of Jeremiah, Jehonadab is remembered as the patriarch who forged a clan that abstained from wine and refused to live in cities. Jeremiah praises the Recabites for obeying the command of their forefather, unlike Judah who refused to obey Yahweh's servants the prophets (vv. 1-19). That Jehonadab has set out to meet the usurper who is battling for Yahweh is certainly consistent with the account in Jeremiah. Also, in 2 Kings 10:23, Jehonadab joins Jehu in his efforts to eliminate Baal worship in Israel. An exilic audience, probably familiar with this conservative clan, recognizes the significance of the meeting. Jehu's confrontation with the house of Ahab attracts faithful devotees of Yahweh.

Consequently, this encounter has important implications for the story, which are highlighted in the exchange between the two men. It is unfortunate, however, that the layers of meaning for the broader story are obscured in the English text. The Hebrew literally reads, "Is your heart right [*yāšār*; cf. vv. 3,30], as my heart with your heart?" This is awkward in English. Provan suggests the following nuance:

---

[16]Nelson argues the violence of Jehu is Yahweh's way of restoring peace in Israel (*First and Second Kings*, pp. 202, 205-206; see also Olyan, "*Hăšālôm*," 660-668).

[17]Forty-two is also the number of the "children" who were cursed by Elisha, and may symbolically represent numerous victims (see n. 33, p. 297).

[18]Provan notices the resonance with the 7,000 in the days of Elijah (1 Kings 19:18), who remained (*šā'ar*) faithful to Yahweh (*1 and 2 Kings*, p. 217).

"Is your heart right? As (it is) with my heart, (is it) with your heart?"[19] The language calls attention to the *heart* and suggests meaning beyond this simple exchange. Yet, the question of the narrative is not the character of Jehonadab's heart — it is whether the *heart* of Jehu is *right* with Yahweh? In verse 30, Yahweh says that Jehu has "done well in accomplishing what is *right* [*yāšār*] in my eyes and [has] done to the house of Ahab all I had in mind [literally, 'in my *heart*'] to do." But in verse 31, the narrator says that Jehu did not keep the law of Yahweh "with all his *heart*." Jehu's heart is for Yahweh, but not completely. Since Jehu goes on to tell Jehonadab to **"come and see my zeal [קִנְאָה, *qin'āh*] for the LORD,"** a careful reader wonders if his *zeal* is completely *right* with Yahweh.[20] Elijah also claimed to be *zealous* (קָנָא, *qānā'*) for "Yahweh God Almighty" (1 Kgs 19:10,14), but did not remain in step with the God of Israel — first in retreat and then in overzealously going beyond Yahweh's judgment on Ahab (see comments on 1 Kings 19 and 21).[21]

10:17 Once he arrives in Samaria, Jehu **kills all who were left** [הַנִּשְׁאָרִים, *hanniš'ārîm*, 'the ones who remained'] **there of Ahab's family**. Again, *šā'ar* is used to characterize Jehu's purge. He leaves no *survivors* from the house of Ahab (cf. vv. 11,14,21). The narrator adds that this was done **according to the word of the LORD spoken to Elijah**. This is the word of Yahweh to Elijah in 1 Kings 21:28-29 that he would "bring [this disaster] on [Ahab's] house in the days of his son" (see comments on 2 Kgs 9:24-26).

9. Jehu Destroys Baal in Israel (10:18-28)

10:18-27 Jehu now moves to destroy the house of Baal and eliminate Baal worship in Israel. Before the people, he asserts, **"Ahab served Baal a little; Jehu will serve him much."** Whether this accurately reflects Ahab's religious fervor is unclear. In any case, Jehu pro-

---

[19]Provan also sees the connection with v. 30 and suggests that the theme is "who is on the LORD's side, who is in the right?" (ibid., p. 218).

[20]Sternberg frames this as a gap in the narrative, reflected in the question, "[Is] Jehu a madman or a zealot?" (*Poetics of Biblical Narrative*, p. 233).

[21]Cohn observes that Jehonadab in the chariot with Jehu balances the scene with Bidkar in his chariot when Jehu assassinates Joram (*2 Kings*, p. 74).

fesses allegiance to Baal and vows he will be more faithful than Ahab, the king who built the house of Baal and introduced the worship of Baal in Israel (1 Kgs 16:29-33). He proposes a **great sacrifice for Baal** to inaugurate a program of patronage, to which he invites **the prophets of Baal, all his ministers and all his priests**. To this point in the story, the reader shares the point of view of Jehu's audience in Israel. The new king looks like he will continue in the idolatrous ways of the house of Ahab — until the storyteller informs the reader that **Jehu was acting deceptively in order to destroy the ministers of Baal** (v. 19). This creative strategy has the effect of drawing the reader into the narrative and underscoring Jehu's deceptive act. There is also wordplay in the narrator's words. Jehu calls the assembly to destroy (from אָבַד, *'ābad*, "perish") the ministers (עֹבְדִים, *'ōb°dîm*, from *'ābad*; literally, "the ones who are serving") of Baal.[22] There is also grand irony here — that Jehu has called a *great sacrifice* to Baal. Instead, he will *destroy* (i.e., "sacrifice") the servants of Baal to Yahweh.

Jehu calls **"an assembly in honor of Baal."** From all over Israel, servants of Baal come; **not one** [לֹא נִשְׁאַר, *lō' niš'ar*, from *šā'ar*] **stays away**. The repetition of *šā'ar* suggests that, again, there will be no survivors (cf. vv. 11,14,17). The **temple** [literally, "house"] **of Baal** overflows with worshipers, as Jehu and Jehonadab enter **to make sacrifices and burnt offerings**. Jehu ensures there are no **servants of the LORD** in the assembly and stations guards around the temple. As soon as he finishes **making the burnt offering**, he gives the order: **"Go in and kill them; let no one escape."** Jehu's guards kill all of the worshipers and **throw their bodies** into an outer court.[23] The **sacred stone** (cf. 3:2)[24] and house of Baal are (literally) "torn down [נָתַץ, *nāthaṣ*]." The narrator adds that **the people have used it**

---

[22]Hobbs, *2 Kings*, p. 129.

[23]"The inner shrine of the temple of Baal" is an interpretation. In Hebrew, the phrase is "the city [probably referring to a wall around the temple] of the house of Baal," suggesting a walled courtyard around the temple (see Provan, *1 and 2 Kings*, p. 218; Hobbs, *2 Kings*, p. 130).

[24]Gray argues that that the second reference to the sacred stone (v. 27) was originally the "*altar* [מִזְבֵּחַ] (*mizbēaḥ*) instead of מַצֵּבַת (*maṣṣ°bath*), 'sacred stone'] of Baal" (*I & II Kings*, p. 558, note). If so, the text more closely parallels 1 Kings 16:32, where Ahab "set up an *altar* for Baal in the temple of Baal."

for a latrine[25] **to this day**. Savran perceptively observes that Elijah, who was concerned with turning the hearts of the people back to Yahweh, executed only the priests of Baal.[26] But more significant for the storyteller's indirect strategy, in the narrative that directly follows Jehu's revolt (when Jehoiada orchestrates a similar coup in Jerusalem in which the house of Baal is torn [*nāthaṣ*] down), only Mattan the priest of Baal is killed (11:18). In fact, in Jehoiada's coup, only two are eliminated — Athaliah and Mattan. By contrast, Jehu's revolution is a bloodbath in which he eliminates anyone he believes could be a political threat.

The reference to the house of Baal as a latrine ("place of excrement") parallels Jehu's statement (quoting Elijah) that "Jezebel's body will be like *refuse* on the ground" (9:37). The structure of the Jehu judgment narrative reinforces this connection and calls attention to the eradication of foreign worship in Israel, as follows:[27]

A. Jehu is anointed king (9:1-15).
  B. Jehu kills King Jehoram outside Jezreel (9:16-26).
    C. Jehu kills King Ahaziah in Beth-Haggan (9:27-29).
      D. *Jehu kills Jezebel in Jezreel (9:30-37)*.
  B′. Jehu massacres the house of Ahab in Jezreel (19:1-11).
    C′. Jehu massacres the kinsmen of King Ahaziah at Beth-eked (10:12-14).
      D′. *Jehu massacres worshipers of Baal and destroys house of Baal in Samaria (10:15-28)*.
A′. Summary of the reign of Jehu (10:29-36).

The parallel structure emphasizes episodes "D" and "D′," which suggests that the amount of narrated time spent on Jehu's bloodletting in Jezreel and Samaria crescendos in the death of Jezebel and the destruction of the house of Baal.

10:28 Laudably, the purge results in the elimination **of Baal worship in Israel**. The Hebrew text (MT) actually reads, "Jehu destroyed

---

[25]Following the *qere* ("what is read") in the margin of the Hebrew text. The consonants in the text are for "excrement" (מחראות, *mḥr'wt*), which is pointed with the vowels for "latrine" (מוֹצָאֹות, *môṣā'ôth*). See Hobbs, *2 Kings*, p. 130; Cogan and Tadmor, *II Kings*, p. 116.

[26]Savran, "1 and 2 Kings," p. 153.

[27]Adapted from Cohn, *2 Kings*, pp. 65-66 (italics added); cf. Garcia-Treto, "The Fall of the House," 54.

Baal from Israel." The destruction of the *house of Ahab* and the *house of Baal* deals a serious blow to the worship of Baal in Israel. However, the negative effects of the house of Ahab on Israel and Judah are not that easily undone (see 2 Kgs 17:16,19; 21:13). An exilic audience knows that the judgment of Jehu is only a preview of what will come for both kingdoms.

10. The Reign of Jehu Is Evaluated (10:29-36)

10:29 The narrator's assessment of the reign of Jehu is mixed. He should be applauded for removing Baal from Israel, **however** (רַק, *raq*, cf. 1 Kgs 3:2,3), there is a caveat. Jehu continued in **the sins of Jeroboam son of Nebat, which he had caused Israel to commit— the worship of the golden calves at Bethel and Dan.** He abolishes foreign idolatry in Israel but continues to support an idolatrous view of Yahweh when he does not **turn away** from Jeroboam's folly. For Jeroboam, this was enough to warrant a similar judgment from Yahweh (see comments on 1 Kgs 12:25–14:19).

10:30-31 The narrator now allows the reader to overhear Yahweh's commendation of Jehu. Because Jehu had **"done well** [טוֹב, *ṭôb*, "good"] **in accomplishing what is right** [*yāšār*] **in my eyes"** and **"done to the house of Ahab all I had in mind** ["in my *heart*"] **to do,"** Yahweh promises, **"your descendants will sit on the throne of Israel to the fourth generation."** Echoing Jehu's words to the leaders of Samaria ("choose the best [*ṭôb*, "good"] and most worthy [*yāšār*, "right"]," v. 3), Yahweh commends Jehu for doing what was *good* and *right* in his eyes. Jehu was the best and most worthy, but was he wholly committed to Yahweh? The reader has already had occasion to question whether the *heart* of Jehu was *right* with Yahweh (see comments on v. 15). The storyteller now plainly says, **Jehu was not careful to keep the law of the LORD God of Israel, with all of his heart**. In light of what Yahweh said to Jeroboam through Ahijah ("do whatever I command you . . . by keeping my statutes and commands"), when Jehu does not keep the law, he does not "do what is *right* [*yāšār*]" in the eyes of Yahweh (1 Kgs 11:38) — therefore, he does not merit an enduring dynasty like David. The narrator repeats the refrain: **He did not turn away from the sins of Jeroboam which he had caused Israel to commit**. Of Jehu, Turner writes,

"Regardless of the merit of the performance, only the righteous in heart get spiritual credit for their performance."[28]

And Jehu's incomplete heart for Yahweh also colors the accomplishments for which he is commended. Noticeably, and without precedent, Yahweh only rewards Jeroboam with four generations on the throne of Israel. When the prophet Hosea announces that Yahweh is about to punish the house of Jehu, he declares that it is "for the massacre [literally, "blood of"] at Jezreel" (Hos 1:4; see comments on vv. 9-11). Later in Kings, when Zechariah (who also did not turn away from the sins of Jeroboam) is assassinated by Shallum (who conspires [קָשַׁר, qāšar] against the house of Jehu, 2 Kgs 15:8-12) after only six months on the throne, the storyteller indicates that this happened "so the word of the LORD was fulfilled: 'Your descendants will sit on the throne of Israel to the fourth generation'" (v. 12). Ironically, Jezebel was correct. Jehu is Zimri (see comments on 9:31; cf. 1 Kgs 16:8-20).[29] The house of Jehu will end as it began, in treachery and bloodshed. As the house of Baasha was destroyed by Zimri because he became like the house of Jeroboam "and because he destroyed [the house of Jeroboam]" (1 Kgs 16:7), so the house of Jehu will be destroyed because he followed Jeroboam — and because of the way he destroyed the house of Ahab. The narrator commends Jehu, but in his indirect style allows the inconsistencies and ironies in his presentation (especially the ironic contrast with Jehoiada's coup to follow, ch. 11) to negatively frame the elimination of the houses of Ahab and Baal and "cast doubts on [his] motives as well as his methods."[30]

As a result, the author appears to be ambivalent toward the reign of Jehu.[31] To the contrary, in a rather calculated way the storyteller

---

[28]Turner, *Annual Lesson Commentary*, p. 61.

[29]See Savran, "1 and 2 Kings," p. 155.

[30]Ibid. Cohn writes that the narrator "sandwich[es] YHWH's praise in a sea of negativity" (*2 Kings*, p. 75).

[31]The narrator is often described as being ambivalent toward Jehu's reign (see, e.g., Savran, "1 and 2 Kings," p. 153; Cohn, *2 Kings*, pp. 75-76; Brueggemann, *1 & 2 Kings*, p. 403; Nelson, *First and Second Kings*, p. 205). While this is true in the sense that both positive and negative aspects of his reign are presented, such a characterization fails to see the sophisticated way the storyteller is wrestling with the "ambiguities" inherent in God working in human history.

is able to say again that Yahweh is using imperfect people to accomplish his purposes, but does not necessarily condone the way his word is enacted. Divine will and human will converge once more in judgment on the house of Ahab, but it does not follow that Yahweh was responsible for every detail in the bloodbath at Jezreel (see comments on 1 Kings 2). Yahweh often uses evil men to punish the wicked.[32] In the end, the house of Jehu reaps as it had sown. At the same time, Jehu's reform was noble, reflecting the heart of God. Worshiping any god but Yahweh incurs the wrath of the true God of Israel. But an exilic audience should also know that reform of the type Jehu sponsors is not enough. Instead of rescuing Israel from Baal and restoring a relationship with Yahweh, his purge only foreshadows the inevitable. Jehu's reform does not succeed, at least in part, because he does not follow Yahweh with all of his heart![33]

10:32-33 Without commentary, the narrator juxtaposes to his evaluation of Jehu a note about the decline of Israel during Jehu's reign. The narrated time for the reign of Jehu (the bulk of chs. 9–10) is only a minuscule part of his actual reign, yet surely reflects the character and spirit of his tenure as king. Now in a footnote to the story, the storyteller appends a historical note that reinforces (and frames) the negative implications of this account. That Yahweh begins **to reduce the size of Israel** indicates his displeasure with Jehu. The harm that Elisha saw from Hazael for Israel begins during his reign (cf. 8:12). Hazael takes from Israel the whole area of the Transjordan.

Extrabiblical sources shed some light on the underlying politics. On two annalistic accounts of Shalmaneser III (in the eighteenth and twenty-first years of his reign),[34] the king of Assyria records campaigns against Hazael. In the first inscription (841 B.C., the first year of the reign of Jehu[35]), he also reports accepting tribute from "Jehu,

---

[32]Turner, *Annual Lesson Commentary*, pp. 34-36.

[33]On the other hand, Josiah follows Yahweh with all of his heart, and his reform does not succeed in rescuing Judah from the sins of Judah's Ahab, the evil king Manasseh (see comments on 2 Kings 23).

[34]*ANET*, p. 280.

[35]This date is an important benchmark for the chronology of the kings of Israel and Judah. Twelve years prior to this, Shalmaneser confronted Ben-Hadad and Ahab at the battle of Qarqar (853 B.C.). After the death of Ahab, his sons Ahaziah and Joram reign twelve actual years before Jehu assassi-

son of Omri" (the Assyrian designation for the king of Israel). On
the famous "Black Obelisk of Shalmaneser" (probably corresponding with this inscription[36]), Jehu (or his representative) appears in
relief, prostrate before the king of Assyria. If this is Jehu, as many
believe, it is the only contemporaneous portrait that survives of a
Hebrew king. The accompanying inscription records gifts to
Shalmaneser of "silver, gold, a golden bowl, a golden vase, golden
tumblers, golden buckets, tin, a staff for a king, [and] hunting
spears."[37] Jehu must be securing the protection of Assyria against
Hazael. In the Tel Dan inscription, Hazael maintains he played a
role in the assassinations of Joram and Ahaziah, although his claims
are probably only braggadocio (see comments on 2 Kgs 9:27-28).
Apparently, shortly after becoming king, Jehu made overtures to
Shalmaneser to secure his throne against Hazael. After the twenty-
first year of his reign, Shalmaneser makes no other incursions west
against Damascus. In this vacuum, Hazael dominates the region and
takes the Transjordan from Jehu, to which the Tel Dan inscription
appears to allude (see comments on 9:27-28). Nadav Na'aman
believes that the archaeological evidence from excavations at Jezreel
suggests that Hazael destroyed Jezreel, which remained in ruins
through the Aramean domination of Israel.[38]

10:34-36 The narrator closes with his characteristic concluding
formula. The **other events** of his reign are found in the **annals of
the kings of Israel**. Jehu **rests with his fathers and** is **buried in
Samaria**. **Jehoahaz his son** reigns in his place. Since the narration of
Jehu's conspiracy did not allow a formal introduction to his reign,
the narrator closes with the note that **Jehu reigned over Israel in
Samaria . . . twenty-eight years** — not the forty years of a prosperous reign, nor an unusually short reign of a wicked king. The storyteller now turns his attention to the effects of the house of Ahab on
Judah. What does Jehu's purge mean for the house of David, which
has cast its lot with the house of Ahab? How can Yahweh's unconditional promise of an eternal throne now be realized?

---

nates Joram at Ramoth Gilead (Thiele, *Mysterious Numbers*, pp. 76-77, 103-
104; see comments on 1 Kings 11:41-43).

[36]See Cogan and Tadmor, *II Kings*, pp. 120-121.

[37]T.C. Mitchell, *Biblical Archaeology: Documents from the British Museum*
(Cambridge: Cambridge University Press, 1988), p. 47; *ANET*, p. 281.

[38]Na'aman, "Notes on the Excavation of Tel Jezreel," 126.

2 KINGS 11

J. REVOLT AND REFORM REVIVE JUDAH (11:1–12:21[22])

1. The House of David Survives Athaliah (11:1-21[12:1])

11:1-3 Turning to the house of David, the narrator draws the reader into the significance of events abruptly, with the statement that **Athaliah** [the first word in the Hebrew text] **the mother of Ahaziah . . . proceeds to destroy the whole royal family** [literally, "seed"]. With portentous consequences for the promise to David of an eternal throne (2 Samuel 7), like Jehu, Athaliah sets out to eliminate all pretenders to the throne.[1] The phrase "the *whole* royal family" reflects her intention and point of view. It will be six years before she discovers that the royal *seed* survives. Before that discovery, the house of Ahab **rules the land**. Athaliah is a daughter of Ahab, as the following "family tree" bears out:[2]

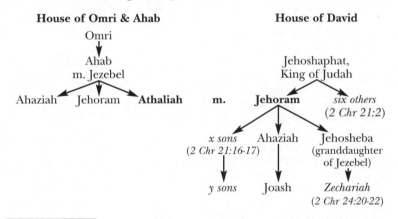

House of Omri & Ahab　　　　　**House of David**

Omri
↓
Ahab　　　　　　　　　　　　Jehoshaphat,
m. Jezebel　　　　　　　　　King of Judah

Ahaziah　Jehoram　**Athaliah**　**m.**　**Jehoram**　*six others*
(2 Chr 21:2)

x sons　Ahaziah　Jehosheba
(2 Chr 21:16-17)　　　　　(granddaughter
of Jezebel)

y sons　Joash　*Zechariah*
(2 Chr 24:20-22)

---

[1]For an insightful discussion of the similarities and differences between the two revolts, see Nelson, *First and Second Kings*, pp. 206-207, 214.

[2]Adapted from Hicks, *1 & 2 Chronicles*, p. 402 (following William Johnstone, "Guilt and Atonement: The Theme of 1 and 2 Chronicles," in *A*

Whether Athaliah is a daughter or stepdaughter of Jezebel, "there is a Jezebel in Judah, intent on doing what Jehu has done in Israel."[3] The Queen Mother rules, although the absence of a regnal notice indicates that the narrator considers her reign illegitimate.

The promise to David of an eternal throne hangs on the bare thread of a child. As Moses was rescued from Pharaoh, and the Messiah from Herod,[4] a child who embodies the promises of Yahweh is rescued from the clutches of Judah's Jezebel. **Jehosheba**, a sister of Ahaziah, snatches **Joash son of Ahaziah** from Athaliah and hides him in the **temple of the LORD**. The child is taken from his **bedroom** by his aunt and carried to the house of Yahweh, where he is safe from Athaliah.[5] In his brief outline of events, the narrator leaves an interesting gap here. For six years the child is undetected. The reader suspects because the queen's allegiance lies with the house of Baal. During the reign of the wicked Athaliah, the most secure "safe house" for the only surviving heir to the throne of David is the house of Yahweh, who must be protecting the child.

11:4-11 In the seventh year of Athaliah's reign,[6] **Jehoiada** appears without introduction, as he makes a **covenant** with the **commanders of units of a hundred, the Carites,**[7] **and the guards**. Even though he is the dominant actor in this episode, the reader does not

---

Word in Season: Essays in Honor of William McKane, ed. by J.D. Martin and P.R. Davids, JSOTSup 42 [Sheffield: JSOT Press, 1986], p. 120). Italics represent information found only in Chronicles.

[3]Provan, *1 and 2 Kings*, p. 219.

[4]See Brueggemann, *1 & 2 Kings*, p. 414; Nelson, *First and Second Kings*, p. 213.

[5]In the Hebrew text, "in a bedroom" appears to locate the place from which Jehosheba took "him and his nurse" (see Provan, *1 and 2 Kings*, p. 221). Hicks makes a connection with Samuel (1 Samuel 1–2), who grew up in the house of Yahweh at Shiloh (*1 & 2 Chronicles*, p. 404).

[6]The text does not give a regnal notice for the ascension of Athaliah or the length of her reign. This information is inferred from the plot and from the reference to the seventh year in v. 4. In his chronological system, Thiele counts her reign at seven years (nonaccession-year reckoning [*Mysterious Numbers*, p. 104]). In his system, Galil assumes that supporters of Joash would count his reign from the assassination of his father Ahaziah (*Chronology of the Kings*, pp. 47-48).

[7]The Carites (also in the Hebrew text of 2 Sam 20:23) may be the same as the "Kerethites" of 1 Kgs 1:38 (Provan, *1 and 2 Kings*, p. 221; cf. Hobbs, *2 Kings*, p. 139).

learn that he is a priest until verse 9. The Chronicler adds that Jehoiada is the husband of Jehosheba (2 Chr 22:11), shedding some light on why Joash is taken to the temple. The narrator's use of "covenant" anticipates the covenant that Jehoiada will shortly orchestrate between Yahweh, the king, and the people (v. 17). Jehoiada binds the men in an oath, before he introduces the child. Appropriate to his age and role in the story, Joash is introduced simply as **the king's son**, which also reflects the point of view of the participants in this scene. In fact, after verse 2, Joash is only named "the king's son" or "the king" until the summary statement in verse 21[12:1 in the MT] that "*Joash* was seven years old when he began to reign." In chapter 12, when the king is old enough to be an actor in the story, he is consistently named "Joash." The king is only an object, an agent, in the events that bring down the reigning queen of the house of Ahab in Judah. Jehoiada is the main actor, the one who initiates the coup against Athaliah.[8]

The underlying Hebrew for the instructions that are given to the guards is difficult to translate with precision. The upshot is that Jehoiada enlists the commanders of soldiers going off duty with those going on duty to protect **the king**. As Jehu positioned men around the house of Baal and commanded that no one should escape (10:24-25), so Jehoiada stations guards around the king and commands, **"Anyone who approaches your ranks must be put to death. Stay close to the king wherever he goes"** (v. 8).[9] The commanders assemble their men, and in a gesture that is surely designed to signify what is about to happen and motivate the troops, Jehoiada hands over to the commanders the weapons of King David.[10] However, the **spears and shields** of the NIV may not be the

---

[8]Naming in the Joash narrative has important implications for the composition of Kings. The author of the Joash narrative appears to have used archival sources for both the coup of ch. 11 and the repair of the temple in ch. 12, yet he "skillfully manipulated [them] for his own literary purposes" (Hobbs, *2 Kings*, p. 135; see p. 150). The obvious design in the naming of Joash in chs. 11–12 suggests that a literary explanation may lie behind naming elsewhere in Kings (see "Excursus: Ahab's Wars with Aram").

[9]Cohn, *2 Kings*, p. 78.

[10]Provan suggests another possibility, that the weapons were symbols of power to be given to the new king (*1 and 2 Kings*, p. 222), although, they are not mentioned in the coronation ceremony that follows (vv. 12-14).

weapons in view here. "Spear" in the MT is in the singular (though plural in 2 Chr 23:9), and שְׁלָטִים (*šᵉlāṭîm*, "shields" in the NIV) is rendered by some "quivers" and by others "bows."[11] In any case, under the charge of Jehoiada and with the arms of Israel's greatest king and founder of the dynasty, the only surviving son of David is about to be restored to the throne.

11:12-16 Jehoiada brings out "the king's son" and places on him a **crown**. The word translated "crown" (נֵזֶר, *nēzer*; cf. 2 Sam 1:10) also designates the Nazirite vow (from *nāzar*, "to dedicate"; see Num 6:1-21), indicating that the crown is in some sense a symbol of consecration.[12] The young king is also presented with the עֵדוּת (*ʿēdûth*, "testimony"), which the NIV translates **a copy of the covenant** (elsewhere in Kings translated [NIV] "requirements" [1 Kgs 2:3], "warnings" [2 Kgs 17:15], and "regulations" [23:3]; cf. "statutes," Ps 132:12). Whether this represents a complete copy of the covenant or a document that outlines the prerogatives and limitations of the king, it seems reasonable to assume that Moses' "law of the king" lies in the background[13] (as the NIV translation connotes). Moses charged, "When he takes the throne of his kingdom, he is to write for himself on a scroll a copy of this law, taken from that of the priests, who are Levites. It is to be with him, and he is to read it all the days of his life so that he may learn to revere the LORD his God and follow carefully all the words of this law and these decrees" (Deut 17:18-20). In the underlying Hebrew (MT) of verse 12, the last four verbs are plural. The people **proclaim him king**, **anoint him**, **clap their hands**, and **shout, "Long live the king!"**

As Adonijah and his company heard the sound (קוֹל, *qôl*) of the coronation of Solomon (1 Kgs 1:41-49), so Athaliah hears the uproar (*qôl*) and goes **to the people** at "the house of Yahweh." The narrator now relays the scene from Athaliah's point of view.[14] The queen sees

---

[11]For "quivers," see Hobbs, *2 Kings*, p. 141; for "bows," see Provan, *1 and 2 Kings*, p. 222. It is unlikely that this text refers to the bronze shields Rehoboam made to replace the gold shields taken by Shishak (1 Kings 14:26-27); contra Gray, *I & II Kings*, pp. 572-573.

[12]Since it is not certain that "crown" is intended here, Hobbs translates *nēzer* "the badge of office" (*2 Kings*, pp. 133, 141). Cogan and Tadmor use the word "diadem" (*II Kings*, p. 128).

[13]Brueggemann, *1 & 2 Kings*, p. 409; see Nelson, *First and Second Kings*, p. 209; Hobbs, *2 Kings*, p. 141; Cogan and Tadmor, *II Kings*, p. 128.

[14]Cohn, *2 Kings*, p. 79.

(רָאָה, *rā'āh*) and **there** [הִנֵּה, *hinnēh*] is **the king, standing by the pillar**. The narrator breaks frame and adds **as the custom was**. During the coronation ceremony, the king apparently by tradition stands beside one of the pillars of Solomon's temple, Jakin or Boaz — pillars that signify Yahweh as the source of security and strength for the king and people (see comments on 1 Kgs 7:13-32 and "Excursus: Solomon's Temple Viewed in Context"). The assembled crowd, including **the people of the land**, rejoices. The phrase "people of the land" may in this instance represent landed gentry who oppose the political and religious policies of the house of Ahab. Later, this group plays a role in Josiah's ascension to the throne (21:24; cf. 23:30,35; 24:14; 25:12,19).[15] Athaliah tears **her robes** and cries, **"Treason! Treason!"**[16] — as Joram cried, "Treachery, Ahaziah!" when he realized Jehu's murderous intentions (9:23). The allusion to the death of Joram reminds the reader of Elijah's prophecy concerning the extermination of the house of Ahab (1 Kgs 21:20-22). Jehoiada's conspiracy, however, does not take the bloody turn of Jehu's revolt, restoring "the house of David with a single execution."[17] Jehoiada commands the guards to take Athaliah away and kill anyone who goes after her. The narrator interjects that the priest had instructed them **"not to put [her] to death in the temple of the LORD."** Athaliah is taken and killed at **the place where the horses enter the palace grounds**, which calls to mind Jezebel, who was trampled by horses in her death (2 Kgs 9:33).[18]

11:17-21[12:1] Jehoiada makes a covenant between the LORD and the king and people that they would be the LORD's people. According to Moses, the descendants of Israel are a holy people to Yahweh in a covenantal relationship with him (cf. Deut 4:20; 7:6; 14:2,21; 26:18-19; 27:9), which because of Judah's apostasy must now be renewed. In fact, the language reflects a covenant renewal ceremony reminiscent of the covenant Joshua made with Israel at

---

[15]See Nelson, *First and Second Kings*, pp. 209-210; Cogan and Tadmor, *II Kings*, pp. 129-130; Cohn, *2 Kings*, p. 80. Although, in other contexts "people of the land" may represent the entire population of Judah (cf. 15:5; 16:15); cf. Hobbs, *2 Kings*, pp. 142, 144.

[16]Athaliah uses the word קֶשֶׁר (*qešer*, "conspiracy"; cf. 9:14; 10:9).

[17]Cohn, *2 Kings*, p. 80.

[18]Ibid.

Shechem (Josh 24:14-28).[19] At that time, Joshua admonished the people to "throw away the foreign gods that are among you and yield your hearts to the LORD, the God of Israel" (v. 23). Jehoiada also makes **a covenant between the king and the people**, which suggests "the consent of the governed" as well as the responsibility of the king to reign with justice and in righteousness (Psalm 72).[20] After finding the "book of the covenant," Josiah, standing in the temple beside "the pillar," will make a similar covenant with Yahweh, to which the people also commit themselves (23:2-3). In response to the covenant of Jehoiada, **the people of the land** move to **the temple** [literally, "house"] **of Baal**, which they "tear down" (יָתַץ, *nāthaṣ*). The echo of Jehu's demolition (*nāthaṣ*) of the house of Baal in Samaria is intentional (2 Kgs 9:27). With the fall of the house of Ahab, in both Israel and Judah, comes the destruction of the house of Baal. Yet, as Nelson points out, reform in Judah happens not through the prophetic word; it is brought about by the written word, the covenant. He writes, "God is at work even when there is no visible evidence of God's presence."[21]

In an effort to "throw away the foreign gods," the people **smash the altars and idols** of Baal and **kill Mattan the priest of Baal**. In stark contrast with Jehu's revolt, only the priest of Baal is killed. And he is killed by the people in response to the covenant they have made with the God of Israel, not for political reasons. In fact, the people's response to the covenant reflects an important theme in chapter 11. Jehoiada's revolt enjoys popular support — for the elimination of the house of Ahab and the house of Baal in Judah, and the restoration of the house of David.[22] For the inspired storyteller, this is a positive development in Judah, which differs markedly from the corresponding revolt in Israel. Cohn sums up the disparities between the two insurrections: "The contrast between the bloody, horrific massacres of Jehu and the swift, orderly coup of Jehoiada could not be sharper."[23] The disparity between the revolts puts Jehu

---

[19]See Provan, *1 and 2 Kings*, p. 220.

[20]This dynamic view of covenant underlies John Locke's idea of "the consent of the governed" (Brueggemann, *1 & 2 Kings*, p. 417).

[21]Nelson, *First and Second Kings*, p. 213.

[22]Ibid., p. 214.

[23]*2 Kings*, p. 80; see Nelson, *First and Second Kings*, p. 214.

in perspective and explains Hosea's invective against the massacre in Jezreel (Hos 1:4).

Jehoiada takes the young king in a procession from the house of Yahweh to the palace, where he takes **his place on the royal throne**. The narrator adds that **the people of the land rejoice**, and **the city is quiet** (שָׁקֵט, *šāqaṭ*, "at rest"). This may reflect political realities in Judah. The landed gentry who support the revolt rejoice, while the urban advocates of the house of Ahab hold their peace.[24] It is more likely, however, "the city was quiet" is meant to recall the promise of rest that accompanies commitment to the covenant. In Joshua and Judges, *šāqaṭ* appears in the phrase "the land had *rest*," which signifies "the restoration of the elemental, reliable, reassuring governance of Yahweh."[25] The promise of Solomon's kingdom of שָׁלוֹם (*šālôm*, "peace") resurfaces with the death of **Athaliah** and the restoration of the house of David. This happens in the person of the young king **Joash**, who is **seven years old when he** begins **to reign**. As the narrator revealed in his report on Jehoram's reign, Yahweh is not ready to destroy Judah. He keeps his promise to "maintain a lamp for David and his descendants forever" (8:19).

---

[24]Nelson, *First and Second Kings*, p. 210.
[25]Brueggemann, *1 & 2 Kings*, p. 413. Hobbs suggests that the "quiet" is the reason for the "rejoicing," (*2 Kings*, p. 144).

2 KINGS 12

2. The Reign of Joash Ends Up Less than Solomon
(12:1[2]-21[22])

12:1[2]-3[4] The regnal notice for Joash reinforces the reader's expectations for his reign. Perhaps Yahweh will restore the fortunes of the Davidic throne with the king he has established. Like Solomon, Joash reigns the forty years of a good king. The narrator even avers, **Joash[1] did what was right** [יָשָׁר, *yāšār*] **in the eyes of the LORD**. But just as in the introduction to Solomon's reign, there is a caveat: "Only [רַק, *raq*; "however" in the NIV], **the high places . . . were not removed; the people continued to offer sacrifices and burn incense there**" (see comments on 1 Kgs 3:2-3). The reader's expectations will not be realized. Worship on the high places symbolizes a lack of complete commitment to Yahweh and his covenant with Israel. Like other kings of Judah, the reign of Joash will not measure up to the standard set by David. Perhaps the negative qualification is also intended in the somewhat ambiguous phrase, **all the years Jehoiada the priest instructed him**. The Chronicler plainly demonstrates that after the death of Jehoiada, Joash turned against Yahweh, even to the point of executing Jehoiada's son Zechariah

---

[1]As the NIV text notes for 11:21[12:1] and 12:1[2] indicate, the Hebrew has two variant spellings, "Joash" (יוֹאָשׁ, *yôʾāš*) and "Jehoash" (יְהוֹאָשׁ, *yᵉhôʾāš*), for the king of Judah, and for the king of Israel in 13:9–14:27. While the different spellings may reflect vocalization (e.g., the shorter spelling for names in construct, with an inseparable preposition, or preceded by the direct object marker, etc.), as with Joram/Jehoram (see comments on 8:25-27), there are exceptions with no discernible pattern. The storyteller may again be suggesting that the kings of Judah and Israel are in one sense interchangeable. Later, he will disparage Judah for following the path Israel has taken (17:19). To avoid confusion, the NIV names the king of Judah "Joash" and the king of Israel "Jehoash," a format that will be maintained here.

(2 Chr 24:17-27). The young king is faithful only during the days of his mentor and father figure, Jehoiada the priest.

Important to the larger story, this brief introduction also establishes a frame for interpreting the reign of Josiah, who in many ways mirrors Joash. Josiah begins tò reign at eight years old and repairs the temple (22:3-7), as did Joash. He also "did what was right [*yāšār*] in the eyes of the LORD" (2 Kgs 22:2). But Josiah will remove the high places from the land and walk "in all the ways of his father David, not turning aside to the right or to the left" (v. 2). This contrast will establish even greater expectations for the reign of Josiah — that he will restore the kingdom of David and Solomon, which also will be unrealized.

12:4[5]-16[17] King Joash commands the priests to take the sacred contributions **to repair whatever damage** [בֶּדֶק, *bedeq*; vv. 6[2×],7, 8[2×],9,13; cf. 22:5] **is found in the temple**. That the king takes the initiative to repair the temple is commendable, but the narrator leaves a gap as to how the house of Yahweh has come into disrepair. The reader suspects neglect during the reign of Athaliah. Filling in the gap, at least in part, the Chronicler adds that "sons of that wicked woman Athaliah" broke into the temple and appropriated its sacred objects for Baal (2 Chr 24:7). The priests are to direct at least three types of offerings to the temple repair:[2] **the money collected in the census** [cf. Exod 30:11-16], **the money received from personal vows** [cf. Lev 27:1-34] **and the money brought voluntarily to the temple** [cf. Exod 35:4-29]. The statement in verse 5[6] that the priests were to **receive the money from one of the treasurers** is difficult to translate.[3] Whatever the exact meaning, the emphasis is again on using funds **to repair whatever damage** had been done to the temple.

---

[2]This follows if "the money that is brought as sacred offerings [הַקֳּדָשִׁים, *haqqŏdāšîm*] to the temple of the LORD" (v. 4) is in apposition with the three offerings named afterwards (as the NIV translates this verse). This phrase may, however, represent a fourth source of income, the money that was earmarked for the purchase of sacred objects (cf. v. 13[14]). See Hobbs, *2 Kings*, p. 152. The question is whether *haqqŏdāšîm* is "the sacred offerings" or "the sacred objects" (cf. v. 18[19]).

[3]For the range of views on the meaning of מַכָּרוֹ (*makkārô*, "one of the treasurers" in the NIV), see Provan, *1 and 2 Kings*, p. 225; Hobbs, *2 Kings*, pp. 152-153.

However, by **the twenty-third year of King Joash the priests still had not repaired the temple**. The storyteller leaves another gap here. How long did the priests ignore the king's order, and what were the reasons for their neglect? In any case, the chronological note may be more about Joash. That the king aggressively takes charge of the project in the twenty-third year of his reign, at age thirty (cf. 11:21[12:1]), may indicate that he has reached his "majority" and assumes complete control over the affairs of state. **Jehoiada the priest** appears now in a subordinate role, as he **and the other priests** are called before the king. They agree to use appropriate funds for temple repair and to contract the work out to others. While there is no indication that the priests were dishonestly misusing collections, they were not following the king's order to direct collections to the repair of the temple.[4] So, in part by contrast with Jehoiada and the priests, Joash emerges as a righteous king who is devoted to the worship of Yahweh and his house in Judah. The renovation of the temple is his program.

To comply with the king's order, Jehoiada places **a chest** with **a hole in its lid** for contributions. The location of the chest, **beside the altar, on the right side as one enters the temple**, has generated some discussion. A position beside the "threshold altar" in the inner court is consistent with the identification of those who had charge of putting collections into the box, "the priests who guarded the entrance [literally, 'threshold']."[5] If this is correct, there is no contradiction between Kings and the account in Chronicles, which places the box "at the gate of the temple of the LORD" (2 Chr 24:8) — and so there is no need to posit an accommodation to the Chronicler's day.[6] To the description of the collection process, the Chronicler adds, "A proclamation was then issued in Judah and Jerusalem" that the people should bring Moses' census tax for the repair of the temple (2 Chr 24:9).

The recent publication of an ostracon (an inscribed potsherd) from Iron Age Palestine may confirm the proclamation of Joash. Written in Old Hebrew script, the inscription represents a receipt for a contribution/payment for the temple and reads as follows:

---

[4]Brueggemann, *1 & 2 Kings*, pp. 420-421.
[5]Hobbs, *2 Kings*, p. 153.
[6]Contra Hicks, *1 & 2 Chronicles*, p. 412.

> According as Ashyahu the king commanded you
> to give to
> Zakaryahu silver from Tar-
> shish for the house of Yahweh:
> three shekels.[7]

The king's name Ashyahu is unattested in the Old Testament, but probably is a form of the name Joash/Jehoash or Josiah, where the theophoric element (*Yah/Yahu*[8] for "Yahweh") is reversed. So *Yo/Yahu-ash* ("Joash/Jehoash," "Yahweh has given") becomes *Ash-yahu*. *Y'ash-yahu* ("Josiah") contains the imperfect form of *ash*.[9] The scholars who published the ostracon date the inscription from pale-ographic analysis (the form of the letters) to the last half of the seventh century and the reign of Josiah.[10] Also on paleographic grounds, other scholars date the inscription to the latter part of the ninth century, probably from the time of Joash of Judah.[11] If the inscription dates to the time of Joash, it is the oldest reference to the temple ("house of Yahweh") outside the Bible. The name Zakaryahu (Zechariah) corresponds with the son of Jehoiada the priest during the reign of Joash (2 Chr 24:20), or with one of the temple administrators during Josiah's reign (35:8). Both Joash and Josiah take contributions for the repair of the temple. Only with Joash, however, does the biblical text mention a royal proclamation to secure funds for the repair (24:9).

When the chest fills, **the royal secretary and the high priest**[12] come to **count the money** and **put it in bags**. This description has been interpreted as representing the use of silver coins for exchange, reflecting a composition perhaps as late as the Hasmonaean dynasty

---

[7]Bordreuil, et al., "King's Command," 3.

[8]For the purposes of this discussion, standard transliteration is not employed.

[9]Bordreuil, et al., "King's Command," 4; see Shanks, "Three Shekels for the Lord," 31.

[10]Bordreuil, et al., "King's Command," 3.

[11]Shanks, "Three Shekels for the Lord," 31.

[12]The designation "high priest" (כֹּהֵן גָּדוֹל, *kōhēn gādôl*) is also appended to Hilkiah in 2 Kgs 22:4; 23:4. In 2 Kgs 25:18, Seraiah is named "head priest" (כֹּהֵן הָרֹאשׁ, *kōhēn hārōʾš*). Cogan and Tadmor argue that the titles were interchangeable in the First Temple period and do not indicate a later redactor (*II Kings*, p. 138).

in the second century B.C. Silver coins were not used widely for exchange until the Persian period. Reflecting this view, Arnaud Sérandour writes that the house of Yahweh inscription (i.e., the temple receipt, above) "contradicts" the biblical text, where silver for the temple "is never weighed . . . it is always 'counted,' 'added up,' or the 'total is worked out.'"[13] However, the language in Kings actually appears to imply weighing. In the Hebrew, the verb order is "they tied" (צוּר, ṣûr) and "they counted" (מָנָה, mānāh) the silver (v. 10[11]). Nelson perceptively suggests that this implies that the silver ingots and pieces of jewelry, etc., were tied in bags for weighing and then were counted.[14]

The silver is given to the overseers who pay the **carpenters and builders, the masons and stonecutters**. The description of the workers and their labor (vv. 11[12]-12[13]) is strikingly similar to the description of Solomon's work force for the construction of the temple (1 Kgs 5:15-18), but Joash does not measure up to Solomon when it comes to the precious temple objects, for which the collection is not used (2 Kgs 12:13[14]; cf. 1 Kgs 7:50).[15] The reference to utensils of silver and gold sets the stage for the sacred objects of his fathers that Joash gives to Hazael (2 Kgs 12:18[19]). In contrast with the priests, the workers need no oversight. They carry out their responsibilities **with complete honesty**. The narrator adds that **the money from the guilt offerings and sin offerings** (see Leviticus 4–5; Num 5:5-10) is not used for the repair. The priests can rightfully take what **belongs to** them (cf. 1 Sam 2:12-17).

12:17[18]-18[19] With no warning, the storyteller transitions to **Hazael king of Aram**, who attacks Gath and then moves toward Jerusalem. Joash responds by giving **all the sacred objects dedicated**

---

[13]Arnaud Sérandour, "King, Priest, and Temple," *NEA* 61 (March 1998): 6.

[14]Nelson, *First and Second Kings*, p. 211. Another suggestion is to read צוּר (ṣûr) as יָצַר (yāṣar) with the sense of "casting/forming." The silver was "melted down" and then counted (Hobbs, *2 Kings*, pp. 153-154; Cogan and Tadmor, *II Kings*, pp. 138-139).

[15]Provan, *1 and 2 Kings*, p. 224. For the parallels between Solomon and Joash, see also Nelson, *First and Second Kings*, p. 212. The apparent contradiction between v. 13[14] and the reference in 2 Chr 24:14 to the articles that were made for the temple may be explained by considering the Chronicles note as referring to "surplus funds" (Hicks, *1 & 2 Chronicles*, p. 412).

by his fathers—Jehoshaphat, Jehoram and Ahaziah, the kings of
Judah—and the gifts he himself had dedicated and all the gold
found in the treasuries of the temple of the LORD and the royal
palace to "Hazael king of Aram" in order to save Jerusalem. Instead
of turning to Yahweh, he strips the temple of its sacred objects and
empties the treasuries of Judah for Hazael. Like Asa (1 Kgs 15:18-
24), Joash is no Solomon. Instead of wealth flowing from Aram to
Jerusalem, as in the days of Solomon, the treasures of the kingdom
flow to Aram.[16] When Solomon finished the temple, he brought the
"sacred objects" his father had dedicated and placed them in the
temple (1 Kgs 7:51). Joash takes the sacred objects he and his fathers
had dedicated and sends them to Hazael. Also, a play on the word
הַקֳּדָשִׁים (haqqŏdāšîm, "the sacred offerings/the sacred objects") emphasizes the incongruity in his actions. In effect, the king of Judah
takes "the sacred offerings" (haqqŏdāšîm, 2 Kgs 12:5[6]) that were
given by the people and gives them (haqqŏdāšîm, "the sacred
objects," v. 18[19]) to Hazael. And when Joash sends the *treasures*
(אֹצְרוֹת, 'ōṣrôth) of the temple and palace to Aram, he foreshadows
what will eventually happen when the king of Babylon takes the *treas-*
ures ('ōṣrôth) of Judah to Babylon (24:13; cf. 14:25-28; 15:17-19; 2 Kgs
14:11-14; 16:7-9; 18:13-16; 24:10-13).[17] The prospects of a restored
Solomonic kingdom do not materialize.

12:19[20]-21[22] Almost in passing, in his usual formulaic concluding paragraph, the narrator mentions that **officials** (literally,
"servants") of Joash **conspire** [קָשַׁר, qāšar] **against him and assassinate him at Beth Millo, on the road down to Silla**. The identification of Beth-Millo and Silla is uncertain.[18] Beth-Millo may be related
to the "supporting terraces" (מִלּוֹא, millô') that Solomon constructed
(1 Kgs 9:24).[19] The narrator names the servants who assassinate the
king, **Jozabad son of Shimeath and Jehozabad son of Shomer**, without any critical remarks.[20] It stands out that each has the same name
("Yahweh has bestowed"), differentiated only by spelling (as in
Joram/Jehoram, Joash/Jehoash). Is it possible that the naming for

---

[16]Provan, *1 and 2 Kings*, p. 224.
[17]For the significance of the treasures, see Mullen, "Crime and
Punishment," 231-248.
[18]Hobbs, *2 Kings*, p. 156.
[19]See M. Görg, "Beth-Millo (place)," in *ABD*.
[20]Cohn, *2 Kings*, p. 84.

these comparatively insignificant characters (only agents in the story) is meant to suggest that Yahweh is bringing about the demise of Joash — he has "bestowed" death on the king?

The Chronicler adds information not given in Kings (2 Chr 24:17-27). After the death of his mentor Jehoiada, Joash turns away from Yahweh. The people abandon the temple and worship idols. Yahweh sends prophets and speaks through Jehoiada's son Zechariah (perhaps the one named on the "house of Yahweh inscription"; see above), but Joash does not listen. He orders Zechariah executed in the temple courtyard, a crime to which Jesus refers (Matt 23:33-36; Luke 11:47-51). By contrast, Jehoiada, out of respect for the house of Yahweh, had Athaliah executed outside the temple precincts.[21] Because Joash and Judah "had forsaken the LORD," Hazael comes up against Jerusalem, and Joash is wounded. His servants conspire against him and kill him in his bed, "for murdering the son of Jehoiada the priest" (v. 25). The Chronicler also adds that the conspirators' mothers were Ammonite and Moabite, suggesting Yahweh's foreign judgment on Joash.[22]

The author of Kings is not so explicit. He allows the grand ironies of the life of Joash to characterize his reign. The young king's reign begins with so much promise. He does right when he sets out to repair and restore the house of Yahweh but ends his reign by stripping the same house of its sacred objects to bribe a foreign king.[23] His reign begins when a righteous priest conspires to overthrow the wicked house of Ahab. His reign ends, as did the reigns of Joram, Ahaziah, and Athaliah, in conspiracy and assassination. Joash is **buried with his fathers in the city of David. And Amaziah his son succeeds him as king**. The Chronicler says that he was not buried in the tombs of the kings (2 Chr 24:25). The end accents the promising king's turn away from Yahweh.

---

[21]Hicks, *1 & 2 Chronicles*, p. 415.
[22]Ibid., p. 417.
[23]Brueggemann, *1 & 2 Kings*, p. 422.

2 KINGS 13

V. KINGS OF ISRAEL AND JUDAH TO
THE FALL OF SAMARIA (13:1–17:41)

A. YAHWEH BLESSES JEHOAHAZ AND JEHOASH OF ISRAEL
(13:1-25)

1. Jehoahaz Seeks Yahweh's Favor,
But Does Not Turn from the Sins of Jeroboam (13:1-9)

13:1-5 The house of Jehu in Israel continues with Jehu's son **Jehoahaz**, who begins to reign in the **twenty-third year of Joash son of Ahaziah** and **reigns seventeen years**. By repetition, the reader has been conditioned to anticipate what follows. As his father, Jehoahaz continues in **the sins of Jeroboam the son of Nebat, which he had caused Israel to commit** (cf. 10:28,31). For this, Yahweh's **anger burns** **against Israel**, and he keeps **them under the power of Hazael** and **Ben-Hadad** of **Aram**. This language especially mirrors the book of Judges, where Yahweh in his anger allows Israel's neighbors to oppress them, and then he raises up leaders *to deliver* them (see Judg 2:14-16; cf. 2:20; 3:8; 10:7; cf. 2 Kgs 24:20).[1] Unpredictably, Jehoahaz seeks (יְחַל, *yᵉḥal*, from *ḥālāh*) Yahweh's face (cf. forms of *ḥālāh* in 1 Kgs 13:6). Because Yahweh *sees* [רָאָה, *rā'āh*] **how severely the king of Aram is** oppressing [לָחַץ, *lāḥaṣ*] Israel, he hears and responds with **a deliverer for Israel. So the Israelites lived in their own homes as they had before** — perhaps the first reference to exile in Kings.[2]

---

[1]Hobbs, *2 Kings*, pp. 166, 172; see also Brueggemann, *1 & 2 Kings*, pp. 428-429, 435.

[2]Provan, *1 and 2 Kings*, p. 230.

The language of these initial verses echoes the Exodus account. At that time, Yahweh said to Moses, "I have seen [rā'āh] the way the Egyptians are oppressing [lāḥaṣ] them" (3:9; cf. Deut 26:7-9).[3] Prior to this, the Exodus narrator said that Yahweh "heard [Israel's] groaning [in Egypt] and remembered his covenant with Abraham, with Isaac and with Jacob" (Exod 2:24). In verse 23, the storyteller in Kings also appeals to Yahweh's covenant with the Patriarchs to explain his action on Israel's behalf. As in the days of the Exodus, Yahweh sends Israel someone to "deliver" (מוֹשִׁיעַ, môšîa', "a deliverer/savior", from יָשַׁע, yāša') Israel. Speculation as to the identity of the unnamed deliverer centers on a political enemy of Aram (e.g., the king of Assyria; see comments on vv. 22-25) or perhaps the prophet Elisha, whose name means "God/my God saves."[4] Elisha has delivered Israel in the past and indirectly does so in the days of Jehoash (vv. 10-20). Hobbs argues that the allusions to Moses recommend Elisha as the deliverer here.[5] However, since verse 22 says that Aram oppressed Israel "throughout the reign of Jehoahaz," the reference to a deliverer may anticipate the time when Yahweh "saves them by the hand of Jeroboam" (14:27).[6]

13:6-9 Nevertheless, Israel (as their king, Jehoahaz) does not turn aside **from the sins of the house of Jeroboam**. An **Asherah pole** remains in Samaria (cf. 1 Kgs 16:33). Since the worship of foreign gods is not mentioned here, this object may represent the goddess as a consort to Yahweh (see comments on 1 Kgs 14:14-16). Jehu destroyed Baal worship in Israel, but did nothing about the golden calves at Bethel and Dan (10:29) — and apparently also allowed Asherah to remain in the land. At the high places of Jeroboam and with an Asherah in Samaria, Israel continues in its idolatrous worship of Yahweh. As a consequence, the army of Israel is reduced to **the dust at threshing time**. The contrast between Jehoahaz's ten chariots and the two thousand chariots that Ahab marshaled for the battle of Qarqar[7] puts Israel's military situation in perspective. This assessment

---

[3]Hobbs, *2 Kings*, pp. 166-167.

[4]For a summary of interpretations, see ibid., pp. 167-168. Galil proposes a coregency with Jehoash and his father Jehoahaz in order to say that Jehoash is the deliverer referred to here (*Chronology of the Kings*, pp. 56-57).

[5]Hobbs, *2 Kings*, pp. 167-168.

[6]Cohn, *2 Kings*, pp. 89, 104.

[7]*ANET*, p. 279; see "Excursus: Ahab's Wars with Aram."

lays a foundation for the meeting between Jehoash and Elisha to follow (vv. 10-20a; see v. 14).[8] After Jehoahaz **rests with his fathers**,
Jehoash his son reigns in his place.

2. Jehoash Does Not Turn from the Sins of Jeroboam (13:10-13)

13:10-13 Jehoash begins his reign in the **thirty-seventh year of
Joash** in Judah and reigns **sixteen years**. A careful reader would
expect Jehoash to ascend the throne in the thirty-ninth year of Joash.
In verse 1, the narrator says that Jehoahaz became king in the twenty-third year of Joash and reigns seventeen years (= 39/40th year of
Joash). Thiele offers a reasonable explanation. During the reign of
Jehoash, Israel (and Judah during the reign of Amaziah) adopted an
accession year reckoning. The switch explains the discrepancy
between the two regnal notices (see "Introduction: Chronology").[9]

In the brief summary of his reign, the narrator records that, as
the kings of Israel before him, Jehoash continues in the sins of
Jeroboam the son of Nebat. Of his deeds, the storyteller only mentions the **war against Amaziah king of Judah**. In the subsequent
account of the reign of Amaziah (14:8-14), he will give a more
detailed description of these events. The regnal note that at the
death of Jehoash, **Jeroboam** (literally) "sat on his throne" may indicate coregency with his son before his death (see below). The same,
somewhat unusual (especially in regnal notes) expression is used of
Solomon, who apparently was coregent with his father before
becoming sole ruler of Israel (cf. 1 Kgs 2:12).[10]

---

[8]See Provan, *1 and 2 Kings*, p. 228; Hobbs, *1 and 2 Kings*, p. 169;
Brueggemann, *1 & 2 Kings*, p. 431.

[9]Thiele, *Mysterious Numbers*, pp. 105, 111-12; see Hobbs, *2 Kings*, pp. 184-
185.

[10]Hobbs, *2 Kings*, p. 185. Against this view, "sitting on the throne" is a
motif in the Solomon accession narrative that appears to reinforce the relationship between 2 Samuel 7 and the choice of Solomon to "sit on David's
throne" (cf. 1 Kgs 1:13,17,20,24,27,30,35,46,48; 2:12,19,24; 3:6; 8:20,25).

3. Elisha Predicts Victory over Aram (13:14-20a)

13:14 After completing the formal accounts of the reigns of Jehoahaz and Jehoash, the storyteller narrates the final episode in the story of the prophet Elisha. As in his investiture as prophet in place of Elijah (ch. 2), this scene stands outside the chronological frame.[11] **Elisha** is **suffering** [חָלָה, *ḥālāh*] **from an illness** from which he will die. The verb *ḥālāh* is the same root as the word used to describe Jehoahaz's overture ("Jehoahaz sought [*yᵉḥal*]") toward Yahweh (v. 4). With his word choice, the narrator subtly connects the two stories. In each, Yahweh's grace for Israel is demonstrated (cf. v. 23).

Jehoash king of Israel goes down to see Elisha, weeps over him, and cries, **"My father! My father! . . . The chariots and horsemen of Israel!"** The narrator offers no explanation for the king's behavior. He has, however, framed this story with a glaring portrait of Israel's depleted military force (v. 7). Now, the king's secret weapon, a power worth ten thousand chariots that has delivered Israel in the past (cf. chs. 6–7), lies on his deathbed. Jehoash unwittingly quotes the prophet himself, when Elisha *saw* the translation of Elijah: "My father! My father! The chariots and horsemen of Israel!" (2:12). In a brilliant stoke, the narrator on a literary level bookends the story of Elisha with a fitting epithet for the prophet, who embodied a double portion of the spirit of Elijah (cf. 2:9) and who served as Israel's protector and deliverer. Yet on the level of this scene, the king's exclamation indicates that he has the same fear for the future as Elisha at the loss of his "father."[12] However, the contrast between the two demonstrates his limited sight.[13] Elisha's statement meant he *could see* Elijah's translation, a sign that he would receive a "double portion" of Elisha's spirit. But Jehoash's statement is an exclamation of blind fear. With the repetition of this epithet for Elisha (i.e., "The chariots and horsemen of Israel!"), the king is situated as one whose faith is myopic. Like many of the kings of Israel before him, he apparently views the prophet primarily as a miracle worker (the one who delivers Israel). His faith is in the prophet, not in the God of

[11]Cohn, *2 Kings*, p. 87.
[12]Kissling, *Reliable Characters*, p. 179.
[13]Provan, *1 and 2 Kings*, p. 232.

the prophet who will rescue Israel in spite of the king's lack of faith (vv. 22-25; see comments on 6:24–7:20).

13:15-20a Through symbolic acts reminiscent of the resurrection miracles of the earlier prophet stories (cf. 1 Kgs 17:17-24; 2 Kgs 4:8-37) and reflecting shamanlike behavior (see comments on 17:21-23), the prophet predicts Israel's triumph over Aram. Elisha directs Jehoash with six imperatives ("get," "take," "open," "shoot," "take," and "strike"; vv. 15-18), to which the king dutifully complies.[14] Elisha's hands transfer his power to the compliant **king's hands**.[15] The prophet describes the arrow shot toward the east as **"the LORD's arrow of victory** [תְּשׁוּעָה, *t*ᵉ*šû'āh*, "deliverance/salvation"] **over Aram . . . at Aphek** [cf. 1 Kgs 20:26,30]." Jehoash will have complete (עַד־כַּלֵּה, *'ad kallēh*, v. 17) victory, but then in another symbolic act strikes the ground only **three times**. Elisha becomes angry. The king **"should have struck the ground five or six times."** Jehoash will not have complete (*'ad kallēh*, v. 19) victory over Aram. He will only defeat Israel's archenemy "three times." Although this scene raises questions about the character of Elisha (see below, "Excursus: Elisha in Context"), Jehoash *should have known* to strike the ground with more vigor (see comments on 1 Kings 20); he *should have seen* Yahweh's power over Aram. His actions belie his timidity and lack of sight/faith, to which Elisha reacts.[16] Victory will come for Israel, but *not completely* in the days of Jehoash (vv. 25; cf. 2 Kgs 14:27). After once more prophesying deliverance for Israel (cf. 7:1), the prophet dies.

4. The Bones of Elisha Revive the Dead (13:20b-21)

13:20b-21 The somewhat unusual story about the power in Elisha's remains is no more out of place than the other miracle stories in Kings. In fact, the episode reinforces one of the themes in

---

[14]Cohn, *2 Kings*, p. 88.

[15]Once more in a scene with Elisha, following the king's introduction (as "Jehoash king of Israel," v. 14), the reigning monarch is named "the king" (vv. 16,18), a literary device that highlights the role of the prophet in relationship with the king of Israel (see "Excursus: Ahab's Wars with Aram").

[16]Hobbs writes, "In the writer's view the limitation on the number of victories over Syria is a direct result of the lack of faith of the king" (*2 Kings*, p. 170).

the prophet stories of Elijah and Elisha. Through his prophets, Yahweh can restore life (cf. 1 Kgs 17:17-24; 2 Kgs 4:8-37). When some **Israelites** who were burying a man see **Moabite raiders** coming, they throw (from שָׁלַךְ, *šālak*) **the man's body** inadvertently on Elisha's bones, and **the man** comes **to life**. Provan suggests a play on the word *šālak*. In verse 23, the narrator says that Yahweh is not willing to "banish them [from *šālak*] from his presence." Later, he will say that because of their sins (17:7), Yahweh rejects Israel and "thrusts them [from *šālak*] from his presence" (17:20). Yet even then, an exilic audience can know that all is not lost (see below). The grace that Yahweh displays to Israel in the surrounding narrative comes from the power and prerogative of Israel's God. Even after the death of the prophet Elisha — and even after exile — there is the potential for life.[17]

5. Yahweh Shows Compassion on Israel (13:22-25)

13:22-25 In one of the more important paragraphs in Kings, the storyteller in exposition gives his theological slant on Yahweh's actions in behalf of Israel. **Throughout the reign of Jehoahaz**, **Hazael oppress**es (*lāḥaṣ*) Israel. But Yahweh chooses to be **gracious** and have **compassion** on his people — **because of his covenant with Abraham, Isaac and Jacob** (cf. Exod. 2:24; 3:7). For the first time, the narrator appeals to Yahweh's unconditional covenant with Abraham (see Gen 12:1-3; cf. 1 Kgs 18:36). Throughout Kings, Judah's relationship with the God of Israel is framed by his unconditional covenant with David (2 Samuel 7). In 2 Kings 8:19, the narrator reiterated that Yahweh "had promised to maintain a lamp for David and his descendants forever" (cf. 1 Kgs 11:36; 15:4). Now, he cites Yahweh's commitment to the Patriarchs as the reason for grace toward Israel. In addition, and unstated, Yahweh's promise to Jehu of a house of four more generations also lies behind his actions in behalf of Israel (cf. 10:30).[18]

---

[17]Provan, *1 and 2 Kings*, pp. 230-231. Hobbs suggests the miracle "is a fore-taste of the revival of the nation recounted in the following chapter" (*2 Kings*, p. 170).

[18]Provan, *1 and 2 Kings*, pp. 227, 229-230. For an excellent discussion of the relationship between the covenants of Abraham and David in Kings, see pp. 229-230.

The storyteller continues, **To this day** [literally, "until now"], **he has been unwilling to destroy them or banish** [from *šālak*] **them from his presence**. Yet, as already noted, in 17:20 the narrator will say that Yahweh "rejected all the people of Israel . . . and *thrust them* [also *šālak*] *from his presence*. However, if "to this day" has reference to the historical situation of the audience of Kings, as seems likely,[19] these incongruent statements together are a vehicle for the author's theological message of grace.[20] An exilic audience knows what happened to Israel. To them, the storyteller is intimating that, even in exile, Yahweh *has not banished them from his presence* — because of his covenant with Abraham, Isaac, and Jacob!

Yahweh's grace toward Israel occurs when Hazael dies. Jehoash **recaptures** [from שׁוּב, *šûb*] **from Ben-Hadad son of Hazael the towns he had taken in battle from his father** (cf. 10:32; 13:3,22).[21] The death of Hazael also corresponds with increased pressure on Aram from Assyria in the east. Adad-nirari III (perhaps the "deliverer" of v. 5) launched campaigns against the Aramean states, and the pro-Assyrian Zakkur king of Hamath and Luash rebelled against Aramean control. In approximately 796, Adad-nirari besieged Damascus,[22] apparently in the same campaign accepting tribute from "Joash of Samaria" (per the Tell al-Rimah stela, corroborated in the Calah inscription).[23] In this context, as Elisha prophesied, Jehoash defeats the king of Aram **three times**. In part, these victories may lie behind the later invective of Amos against Damascus (Amos 1:3-5): "I will send fire upon the house of Hazael that will

---

[19]Ibid., pp. 230, 232; Cohn, *2 Kings*, p. 89; cf. Brueggemann, *1 & 2 Kings*, p. 434. The phrase "to this day" can indicate the storyteller's use of sources (see comments on 1 Kgs 8:8). However, the phrase "until now" is rare in Kings (elsewhere only in 8:6) and in this text appears to refer to an exilic author's day.

[20]Provan, *1 and 2 Kings*, p. 230. Nelson represents the opposing view that Yahweh did not want to cast Israel aside, but his patience ran out (*First and Second Kings*, pp. 117-118).

[21]For a discussion of the view that the victory of Ahab over Aram (1 Kings 20) historically belongs to the time of Jehoahaz/Jehoash, see "Excursus: Ahab's Wars with Aram."

[22]See A.R. Millard, "Arameans," in *ABD*; Wayne T. Pitard, "Aram (place)," in *ABD*.

[23]See Cogan and Tadmor, *II Kings*, pp. 151-152; Linda S. Schearing, "Joash (person)," in *ABD*; *ANET*, pp. 281-282.

consume the fortresses of Ben-Hadad" (v. 4).[24] Jehoash also **recovers** [from *šûb*] **the Israelite towns**. For an exilic reader, the language of verse 5 resurfaces: "The Israelites lived in their own homes as they had before." As the bones of Elisha brought life, Yahweh's grace means the restoration (*šûb*=return; cf. 14:22,25,28) of Israel.

---

[24]The superscription to the book of Amos places his prophetic ministry during the reigns of Uzziah king of Judah and Jeroboam son of Jehoash king of Israel (1:1).

EXCURSUS

ELISHA IN CONTEXT

The last recorded episode in the prophetic career of Elisha (vv. 14-20a) reinforces questions about him that have surfaced through the course of the narrative. It is fair to say that the prophet is somewhat misleading in his dealings with Jehoash. After saying that the king would have complete victory over Aram, Elisha puts Jehoash through another test. The compliant king apparently passed the first by obediently following the instructions of the prophet. Not realizing that it was a "test," Jehoash strikes the ground only three times, causing an angry response from the prophet of Yahweh. The king's victory over Aram would not be complete! While the narrator appears to call attention to the king's lack of faith/sight in the way he retells the story (see comments on vv. 14-20a), this scene reflects a pattern of behavior on the part of the prophet in Kings that does not put him in a good light. In his interaction with Joram (ch. 3), Naaman (ch. 5), Hazael (ch. 8), and Jehoash (ch. 13), Elisha comes across as deceptive and somewhat patronizing. With good reason, Kissling calls attention to his "arbitrary and deceptive," "disingenuous" manner with Jehoash.[25] In terms of Elisha's characterization in Kings, he suggests that the prophet is not completely reliable.[26]

Kissling's reading is tempered by the role that deception plays in Yahweh's interaction with the kings of Israel. Just as the lying spirit operated in the enticement and death of Ahab (1 Kings 22), so Elisha enticed both Joram and Hazael (see comments on 2 Kgs 3:1-27; 8:7-15). Nevertheless, the prophet may be seen as having "an attitude" toward those in high places. Perhaps this is a human manifestation of his commitment to the disenfranchised in Israel (see comments on 4:1-7). The story of Elijah demonstrates that even prophets are fallible (see comments on 1 Kings 19, 21). Does Elisha's backtracking with Jehoash represent not Yahweh's intentions for Israel, but, instead, the prophet's own judgmental attitude toward the king — much like Elijah's attitude toward Ahab (1 Kgs 21:19-29)? In exer-

---

[25]Kissling, *Reliable Characters*, pp. 179-181.
[26]Ibid., pp. 149-199.

cising prophetic initiative, the grace that Yahweh has chosen to bestow on Israel is delayed until the time of Jeroboam, when Aram is completely defeated (2 Kgs 14:26-27).

At the same time, Elisha's prophetic career stands out as a vehicle of Yahweh's deliverance for Israel. For the storyteller in Kings, Elisha surely embodies the meaning of his name (אֱלִישָׁע, 'ĕlîšāʿ, "God/my God saves"). It is probably not just coincidence, for example, that the verb יָשַׁע (yāšaʿ, "to save/deliver") ties Elisha with Yahweh's victorious acts for Israel in 13:5,17.[27] Through Elisha, especially, Yahweh shows his grace and compassion for the descendants of Abraham.

But the storyteller has also crafted his narrative to say that the ministry of Elisha mirrors the career of Elijah. An analysis of the larger story suggests the following parallels:[28]

Elijah cycle — 1 Kings	Elisha cycle — 2 Kings
17:2-6 Elijah drinks from a wadi	3:9-20 Israel drinks from a wadi
17:8-16 Elijah multiplies oil and grain for widow	4:1-7 Elisha multiplies oil for a widow
17:17-24 Elijah resuscitates boy	4:8-37 Elisha resuscitates boy
18:20-39 Famine and the true God; miracle precipitates conversion	5:1-27 Leprosy and the true God; miracle precipitates conversion
19:1-3 Pursuit of Elijah; oath by pursuer	6:8-14, 31-32 Pursuit of Elisha; oath by pursuer
21:1-29 False witness denies man his land by royal directive	8:1-6 True witness rewards woman with her land by royal directive
2 Kings 1:1-18 Elijah sends oracle to mortally ill king	8:7-15 Elisha sends oracle to mortally ill king

Without doubt, this correspondence indicates literary design and suggests that in both these men of God, Yahweh was working mightily on behalf of Israel.

----

[27]Provan, *1 and 2 Kings*, p. 230.

[28]From Cohn, *2 Kings*, p. 92. Cohn's view that the Elisha narratives were originally connected with the kings of the house of Jehu, not the Omride dynasty (*2 Kings*, pp. 94-95; following Rofé, *The Prophetical Stories*, pp. 7-74), is transparently subjective, missing some of the literary features of the narrative and overlooking aspects of the story's plot. For example, the fact that the king of Israel often is not named in the Elisha narratives has a viable literary explanation — the prophet usually represents the narrative's focal point of view, reflecting the ideological perspective of the storyteller (see

In addition, the prophet Elisha prefigures the Messiah. As has already been delineated, the prophet Elisha mirrors the Messiah as a miracle worker and in his compassion and ministry for the poor (see comments on 4:1-7). As Elijah embodied the faith and power of the one who would come (see "Excursus: The Translation of Elijah in Context"), so Elisha's prophetic career epitomizes the work of the Messiah, whose name also means "God saves" (יֵשׁוּעַ, yēšûaʿ, "Yahweh saves," a form of "Joshua"). Provan insightfully suggests that the New Testament writers did not play up the many ways Elisha prefigures the life of Jesus because John is clearly identified with Elijah: "There would have been a natural desire within the church to avoid the suggestion that Jesus was John's successor in any sense that detracted from his pre-eminence."[29] This predisposition, however, does not take away from the similarities between Elisha and Jesus. In the life of this great man of God, Yahweh was working in Israel in a way that foreshadows what he would eventually do for all of mankind!

"Excursus: Ahab's Wars with Aram"). Also, Cohn's claim that the Elisha narratives "ignore the battle against the worship of Baal waged by Elijah during the reigns of the Omride kings" (Cohn, *2 Kings*, p. 95) overlooks the fact that Baal worship apparently declined in Israel after the death of Ahab and Jezebel, at least in terms of royal patronage. Joram, son of Ahab, moved away from the idolatrous worship of his parents, getting "rid of the sacred stone of Baal that his father had made" (2 Kgs 3:2).

[29]Provan, *1 and 2 Kings*, p. 234. For a good discussion of the ways in which Elisha prefigures the Messiah, see pp. 233-234.

2 KINGS 14

B. THE REIGN OF AMAZIAH FORESHADOWS THE END OF JUDAH (14:1-22)

1. Jehoash of Israel Defeats Amaziah of Judah (14:1-14)

The regnal notations for the first half of the eighth century in Israel and Judah (14:1-2,17,21,23; 15:1) present one of the more difficult chronological problems in Kings.[1] Thiele resolves the problems by positing coregencies for Jehoash and Jeroboam II in Israel (12 yrs.) and Amaziah and Azariah in Judah (24 yrs.), and with what he calls "dual dating" for the reigns of Jeroboam and Azariah. A coregency for Jehoash and Jeroboam is indicated by the subtle change in phrasing from 13:13 ("sat on his throne") to 14:16 ("reigned in his place") and the narrator's regnal synchronisms. For example, Azariah comes to the throne in the twenty-seventh year of Jeroboam, at the death of his father, and reigns fifty-two years (15:1). Since Azariah's father Amaziah died fifteen years after the death of Jehoash (14:17), when his son Jeroboam "reigned in his place" (v. 16), Jeroboam must have reigned as coregent with his father Jehoash for twelve years before his death (27 – 15 = 12). The coregency of Amaziah and Azariah in Judah is also suggested in the synchronisms. It is only fourteen years from the ascension of Azariah to the throne in Judah (27th yr. of Jeroboam) to the death of Jeroboam in his forty-first year (41 – 27 = 14). Then, 15:8 indicates that Zechariah became king at the death of Jeroboam in the thirty-eighth year of Azariah. So, Azariah must have ruled twenty-four years before his father Amaziah died (38 – 14 = 24). According to Thiele, Jehoash

---

[1]For a summary of approaches to what most have considered a conundrum impossible to reconcile, see Hobbs, *2 Kings*, pp. 184-185.

made his son Jeroboam coregent before going to battle against
Amaziah. After Jehoash breached the walls of Jerusalem, Amaziah
was taken prisoner to Samaria, and Azariah was placed on the
throne in Jerusalem. It follows that the length of reigns in 14:23
(Jeroboam's 41 yrs.) and 15:1 (Azariah's 52 yrs.) includes both the
years of the coregency and sole reign of the respective kings. In what
Thiele terms the author's "dual dating procedure," however, the
synchronisms (15th yr. of Amaziah and 27th yr. of Jeroboam) are to
the year each king becomes sole ruler of the land.[2]

Acknowledging that Thiele's "bold solution . . . fits the figures that
are given in the text," Hobbs argues that the coregency of Amaziah
and Azariah is less clear than that of Jehoash and Jeroboam. He challenges Thiele's version of the events of the story. In particular, it is not
clear from the text that Amaziah was taken captive for any lengthy
period. Nothing is said about his being one of the hostages taken to
Samaria, and the king apparently spends the remainder of his life in
Jerusalem, from which he flees when he learns of the conspiracy
against him. In 14:17, the narrator says that Amaziah lived fifteen
years after the death of Jehoash, but he says nothing about any captivity. Finally, a comparison with clear coregencies, like with Azariah
and Jotham (15:5), is "the main difficulty" with this theory.[3] In defense
of Thiele, Hobbs' objections to the imprisonment of Amaziah have a
rejoinder (see comments below), and Hobbs is inconsistent when he
allows a coregency for Jehoash and Jeroboam, which is deduced by
inference from comparing 13:13 and 14:16 and from the synchronisms, but rejects the coregency of Amaziah and Azariah because it is
not clearly indicated in the text.

14:1-4 In his synoptic presentation of the reigns of Israel and
Judah, the storyteller turns from Jehoash of Israel to Amaziah of
Judah, although the account of Amaziah will turn out to be as much
about the reign of Jehoash. **Amaziah son of Joash** (cf. naming v. 13)
becomes king and reigns **twenty-nine years** in Jerusalem, which
must have included a twelve-year coregency with his father Joash.[4]

---

[2]Thiele, *Mysterious Numbers*, pp. 106-118.

[3]Hobbs, *2 Kings*, p. 185; cf. Galil, who also sees a coregency with Amaziah
and Azariah (*Chronology of the Kings*, pp. 57-59).

[4]Thiele, *Mysterious Numbers*, pp. 113-116; see Cogan and Tadmor, *II Kings*,
p. 154; and comments above.

As in his assessment of the reigns of Asa, Jehoshaphat, and Joash (1 Kgs 15:11; 22:43; 2 Kgs 12:2), the narrator says that Amaziah does **what was right in the eyes of the LORD**.[5] Only, he does not do **as his father David had done** (cf. 1 Kgs 15:3-5,11), who remains the standard for the kings of Judah.[6] Also as the kings before him, Amaziah does not remove **the high places** (cf. 1 Kgs 15:14; 22:43; 2 Kgs 12:3). The statement that **in everything he follows the example of his father Joash** is somewhat ambiguous. His father turned away from Yahweh after the death of Jehoiada. Like his father, Amaziah will be assassinated in a conspiracy (14:19-20).

14:5-7 After securing his kingdom, Amaziah executes **the officials who had murdered his father** (cf. 12:20-21). In contrast with the revolts of Jehu and Athaliah, however, the new king does not put to death **the sons of the assassins**. In a noteworthy statement, the storyteller asserts that this was according to **the Book of the Law of Moses** and quotes Deuteronomy 24:16 that fathers and sons are to die for their own sins. Clearly, this interjection is a positive note in Amaziah's appraisal. The book of Deuteronomy stands behind the assessment of each of the kings of Israel and Judah (see, e.g., comments on 1 Kgs 2:1-4). However, the quotation from Deuteronomy also serves to frame other actions in the reign of Amaziah, which will serve to characterize him negatively (see below). Following the reference to the Law of Moses, the note that Amaziah defeats **ten thousand Edomites in the Valley of Salt and captured Sela** raises the possibility that the new king may restore the fortunes of Judah to the days of David and Solomon (see comments on 1 Kgs 22:47-49; 2 Kgs 3:4-8; 8:16-24). During the reign of Jehoram, Edom rebelled against Judah (8:20-22). David gave Israel its only other victory over Edom in the Valley of Salt (2 Sam 8:13-14).[7] In fact, in his next move,

---

[5]Solomon, the people of Judah during the days of Rehoboam, Jehoram, and Ahaziah of Judah are all said to have done evil in the eyes of Yahweh (cf. 1 Kgs 11:6; 14:22; 2 Kgs 8:18,27).

[6]The Chronicler replaces "as his father David had done" with "but not wholeheartedly" (2 Chr 25:2), which explains Amaziah's disastrous reign (see Hicks, *1 & 2 Chronicles*, p. 419).

[7]The location of the Valley of Salt is uncertain (Randall W. Younker, "Salt, Valley of [place]," in A*BD*). Sela is now generally identified with Sela', ca. 4 km northwest of Buseira (Wann M. Fanwar, "Sela [place]," in A*BD*). For both the Valley of Salt and Sela, see also Cogan and Tadmor, *II Kings*, p. 155.

against Israel (vv. 8-14), Amaziah may see himself as another David, uniting Judah and Israel once again.[8] The Chronicler expands on Amaziah's victory over Edom (2 Chr 25:5-16). Amaziah's army kills ten thousand and captures ten thousand, who are thrown over a cliff. Then, the king of Judah brings the captured gods of the Edomites to Jerusalem and worships them (v. 14). Accordingly, the expectation for a restored kingdom of Solomon will come to pass for Israel (1 Kgs 14:25), not for Judah.[9]

14:8-14 Following his victory over Edom, Amaziah challenges **Jehoash son of Jehoahaz, the son of Jehu, king of Israel**. With naming, the storyteller suggests ulterior motives and subtly characterizes the actions of Amaziah. In verse 13, the king of Judah is named **Amaziah king of Judah, the son of Joash, the son of Ahaziah**. Without exact parallel elsewhere in Kings, the double patronyms (i.e., "son of Jehoahaz, the son of Jehu," etc.) call attention to the fact that a son of Ahaziah is inciting a war against a son of Jehu, who assassinated Ahaziah of Judah on the way to Megiddo (9:27-28). While Amaziah exercises restraint in eliminating only the assassins who conspired against his father, when he challenges the king of Israel, he breaks the spirit of the Law of Moses (14:6; cf. Deut 24:16) that each one should be punished for his own sins.[10] Amaziah has a grudge against the descendant of Jehu who sits on the throne of Israel.

Jehoash responds with a parable of a **thistle**, a **cedar**, and a **wild beast**, intended to dissuade Amaziah from his aggressive intentions. While the specifics of the parable are perhaps debatable, the upshot is clear. Jehoash is warning Amaziah that if he continues in his aggression, Judah will be crushed.[11] The king's perspective, that Amaziah's **arrogant** behavior results from his victory over Edom, probably represents the point of view of the storyteller. Foreshadowing the end of the story, Jehoash asks, **"Why ask for trouble and cause your own downfall and that of Judah also?"**[12] Some suggest that the reference in the parable to **marriage** indicates that

---

[8]Hobbs, *2 Kings*, p. 186.

[9]See Provan, *1 and 2 Kings*, p. 237.

[10]Nelson, *First and Second Kings*, p. 219.

[11]Provan, *1 and 2 Kings*, pp. 238-239.

[12]Jesus may have had Amaziah in mind when he uses the analogy of a king going to war, to say that his disciples must "count the cost" (Luke 14:31-33); see Hobbs, *2 Kings*, p. 186.

Amaziah has proposed a treaty to be sealed by a marriage between the two houses, which is summarily rebuffed by Jehoash. However, there is no other indication of this in the story.[13]

Amaziah refuses to **listen**, so the two face each other at **Beth Shemesh in Judah**. This border town in the Shephelah guards the Sorek pass, a route from the Philistine plain to Jerusalem.[14] The Chronicler explains Amaziah's resolve as a reaction to rampaging Israelite mercenaries who are released from his service, without booty, before the attack on Edom (2 Chr 25:6-13). In any case, Judah is routed. As Amaziah captured (תָּפַשׂ, *tāphaś*) Edomites at Sela, Jehoash **captures** (*tāphaś*) Amaziah and marches on the capital, where he breaks **down the wall of Jerusalem from the Ephraim Gate** [exiting to Ephraim on the north] **to the Corner Gate** [on the northwest approach to the city].[15] The king of Israel takes **all the gold and silver and all the articles found in the temple of the LORD and in the treasuries of the royal palace**. He also takes **hostages** before returning to Samaria. Amaziah's aggressive behavior turns into defeat, which the Chronicler blames on his appeal to the gods of Edom (2 Chr 25:20) — not mentioned by the author of Kings. While the storyteller in Kings also does not specifically state that Amaziah is taken to Samaria, he does not say that he is released either. In the larger story, this episode clearly prefigures the exile of Jehoiachin, at which time treasures from the temple of Yahweh and the royal palace are also taken as booty (2 Kgs 24:8-17).[16]

2. The Reign of Jehoash Is Summarized (14:15-16)

14:15-16 The repetition of the concluding formula for the reign of Jehoash, in the heart of the account of Amaziah, is curious. For the most part, verses 15-16 are a quotation of 13:12-13, with one significant exception. In the account of Jehoash, the narrator says (lit-

---

[13]See, e.g., Thiele, *Mysterious Numbers*, p. 109; cf. Hobbs, *2 Kings*, p. 180; Provan, *1 and 2 Kings*, p. 238.

[14]Fredric Brandfon, "Beth-Shemesh (place)," in A*BD*.

[15]For the location of these gates, see Dale C. Liid, "Ephraim Gate (place)" in A*BD*; idem, "Corner Gate (place)," in A*BD*.

[16]Provan, *1 and 2 Kings*, pp. 236-237; cf. Mullen, "Crime and Punishment," 240-241.

erally), "Jeroboam sat upon his throne" (13:13). Yet, in the midst of his account of Amaziah, the narrator says (literally), "**Jeroboam his son** reigned instead of him" (14:16). The contrast reinforces the implication of the synchronisms that Jeroboam was for a time coregent with his father Jehoash.[17] But the repetition also has the effect of suggesting that Jehoash is the dominant personality in these events. In many ways, the story of Amaziah is as much about the king of Israel, who is framed in a more positive light — Jehoash dies peacefully, while Amaziah is murdered in a conspiracy. And ironically, during the reign of Amaziah, Judah comes under the control of Jehoash of Israel, as the nation will later come under the control of Nebuchadnezzar of Babylon.[18]

3. The People of Judah Conspire against Amaziah (14:17-22)

14:17-20 The storyteller now appends the concluding formula for the reign of Amaziah to his closing remarks on the reign of Jehoash. Without elaboration, he mentions that Amaziah **lived fifteen years after the death of Jehoash**, an innocuous statement that reinforces the view that Azariah (Uzziah) was coregent with his father Amaziah. The narrator does not say that Amaziah "reigned" for fifteen years after Jehoash (see above). For Thiele, this datum indicates Azariah was placed on the throne at the imprisonment of his father in Samaria. He must have been released at the death of Jehoash, returning to Jerusalem to live but not reign. For some reason, perhaps Amaziah's own political activities, an ambiguous "they" **conspire against him**, and he is murdered while fleeing to **Lachish** (ca. 45 km southwest of Jerusalem).[19] While this scenario is certainly plausible, and perhaps even probable, the narrator only gives a "bare bones" outline of the underlying events. The account is craft-

---

[17]Hobbs, *2 Kings*, p. 185; Thiele, *Mysterious Numbers*, p. 115 (see above).

[18]Provan, *1 and 2 Kings*, pp. 236-237. Provan (p. 237) also suggests that the chronological note about Jehoash in the midst of the account of Amaziah parallels the references to the regnal years for the king of Babylon in the story of Judah's final days (2 Kgs 24:12; 25:8).

[19]Thiele, *Mysterious Numbers*, pp. 113-116. The Chronicler adds that the conspiracy against Amaziah began when he turned from Yahweh (i.e., when he sought the gods of Edom; 2 Chr 25:27; cf. vv. 14-15).

ed, at least in part, to bring out the telling ironies of Amaziah's reign. Cohn observes that Amaziah flees (נוּס, *nûs*) toward Lachish, just as Judah flees (*nûs*, v. 12) before Israel. His body is *"lifted up* [וַיִּשָּׂא, *nāśā'*] on horses"* ("brought back by horse" in the NIV) as "his *heart* is *lifted up"* (*nāśā'*; "arrogant" in the NIV, v. 12) when he challenges Jehoash.[20] Amaziah's story is framed to show that another king of Judah with promise dies a violent death — and to foreshadow the end of this tragic narrative, when a king of Judah is taken captive to Babylon.

14:21 According to Thiele, Azariah is placed on the throne (at age 16) when Jehoash takes Amaziah captive. He argues that **the people of Judah** would have no need to take such action with the normal succession of the king's son at the death of the king, even though the placement of the verse suggests that Azariah ascended the throne at the death of his father. On the other hand, if verse 21 does not refer to the events surrounding Amaziah's capture, Azariah, if alive at all, would have been only an infant at Judah's defeat by Jehoash (16 yrs. old [v. 21] – 15 yrs. [v. 17] = 1). This would put a coregency with his father in doubt — and create havoc with the regnal synchronisms for this period of history. Whatever the exact course of events, Azariah becomes king **in the place of his father Amaziah**.

14:22 At first glance, the final verse of chapter 14 appears misplaced. It is almost as if the storyteller cannot withhold commenting on the accomplishments of Azariah,[21] which he will chronicle subsequently (without enumerating the king's activities, 15:1-7). On closer inspection, however, the note about Azariah may put an exclamation point on one of the themes of the account of Amaziah, which the NIV obscures. Provan calls attention to the fact that in Hebrew the text reads, "[Azariah] . . . rebuilt **Elath** . . . after *the king* [the NIV adds **Amaziah**] rested with his fathers." But is *the king* Amaziah or Jehoash? The phrase "rested with his fathers" most recently appears in reference to the death of Jehoash (v. 16). Is the storyteller saying that Azariah, as regent in place of his father Amaziah, is able to rebuild the port of Elath in Edom (cf. 1 Kgs 9:26) only at the death of Jehoash? Either way, the king of Israel is "the real power in the land"

---

[20]Cohn, *2 Kings*, p. 101.
[21]Brueggemann, *1 & 2 Kings*, p. 443.

during the reign of Amaziah.[22] At the same time, it is promising that Azariah rebuilds Elath for Judah (cf. 1 Kgs 9:26).

C. YAHWEH SAVES ISRAEL THROUGH JEROBOAM (14:23-29)

14:23-25 The account of the reign of Jeroboam is noticeably brief when compared with the duration and impact of his reign. He reigns **forty-one years** and **restores the boundaries of Israel**, yet as other kings of Israel does **evil in the eyes of the LORD.** He also does **not turn away from the sins of Jeroboam son of Nebat, which he had caused Israel to commit.**[23] The eighth century prophets Amos and Hosea demonstrate that Israel at this time was also characterized by social injustice and the worship of foreign gods (cf., e.g., Amos 5:11; Hos 2:17; 5:3-4). Indirectly, the Samaria ostraca, an archive of tax receipts found in an annex to the royal palace in Samaria, probably dating from the time of Jeroboam, reinforce this prophetic portrait of Israel. The receipts come from large estates, which appears to reflect the socioeconomic situation against which Amos railed. Also, in the ostraca the ratio of personal names compounded with Baal as opposed to Yahweh is higher than in the Bible, reflecting the "spirit of prostitution" addressed by Hosea.[24] Yet, in spite of his sins, Jeroboam restores the fortunes of Israel to the days of Solomon. The borders of Israel stretch from **Lebo Hamath** [or "Entrance to Hamath"[25]] **to the Sea of the Arabah** [i.e., the Dead Sea]. Politically, this must have happened with the assent of Assyria, in an effort to control Damascus.[26] For the inspired storyteller, these gains occur according to the **word of the LORD**, which

---

[22]Provan, *1 and 2 Kings*, p. 237; see Cohn, *2 Kings*, p. 101.

[23]Excavations at Tel Dan have documented extensive construction and renovations at the high place of Jeroboam (cf. 1 Kgs 12:25-33) during the first half of the eighth century B.C. and the reign of Jeroboam II (see Biran, *Biblical Dan*, pp. 191-206).

[24]See Dever, *Biblical Writers Know*, pp. 210-211. Ivan T. Kaufman observes, however, that the Baal names, except in one instance, belong to secondary, lower level men who work for owners who bear Yahwistic or non-Baalistic names, which he suggests may reflect sociological distinctions in Israel ("Samaria Ostraca," in *ABD*).

[25]See Cogan and Tadmor, *II Kings*, pp. 160-161; Hobbs, *2 Kings*, pp. 182-183.

[26]Cogan and Tadmor, *2 Kings*, p. 163.

comes **through his servant Jonah son of Amittai, the prophet from Gath Hepher** [cf. Josh 19:13], the only reference to this prophet outside the book that bears his name (cf. Jonah 1:1). The restoration of Israel to the expanse of the borders of Solomon (cf. 1 Kgs 4:21[5:1], 8:65; including Elath in Judah, 2 Kgs 14:22; cf. 1 Kgs 9:26) is enabled by the word of Yahweh!

14:26-27 The storyteller now explains the actions of Yahweh. The God of Israel sees **how bitterly everyone in Israel . . .** is **suffering**. There is **no one to help them**. Since Yahweh **had not said he would blot out the name of Israel** [cf. Exod 32:32-33; Deut 9:14; 29:20(19)] **from under heaven, he saves them by the hand of Jeroboam**. Repeating the sentiment of 13:23, Yahweh has not said he would destroy them. As he saw the oppression in Egypt (Exod 3:7) and how the king of Aram was oppressing Jehoahaz (2 Kgs 13:4), Yahweh sees the suffering of everyone in Israel. And, as he promised Jehoahaz a deliverer (מוֹשִׁיעַ, *môšîaʿ*, 13:5), Yahweh saves (from *yāšaʿ*) Israel through the reign of one who does evil in his eyes.[27] For the reader, the narrative has taken an unexpected course. Yahweh is silent in the defeat of a descendant of David, but acts as a *deliverer* for doomed Israel. Only divine prerogative can explain the direction the narrative has taken.[28] And, in a section of Kings where the word "return/restore" (שׁוּב, *šûb*) appears repeatedly to highlight the restoration of lands taken from Israel (13:25; 14:22,25,28), an exilic audience would be encouraged to anticipate once more the kingdom of Solomon — *restored* by the grace of Yahweh!

14:28-29 In his concluding formula for the reign of Jeroboam, the narrator mentions that the king of Judah **recovered** [*šûb*] **for Israel both Damascus and Hamath, which had belonged to Yaudi** (or "Judah"). The phrase "which belonged to Yaudi" is, literally, "to Judah in Israel." To overcome the difficult to comprehend "Judah in Israel," the NIV has the improbable Yaudi. Hobbs prefers an emendation to "to Judah *and* Israel,"[29] but Provan favors leaving the phrase as it is. He postulates that "'Judah in Israel' . . . could have been an Israelite designation for Judah during Jeroboam's reign."[30]

---

[27]See Cohn, *2 Kings*, p. 104.

[28]See Brueggemann, *1 & 2 Kings*, p. 449.

[29]Hobbs, *2 Kings*, pp. 183-184.

[30]Provan, *1 and 2 Kings*, p. 240. For a summary of interpretations, see also Cogan and Tadmor, *II Kings*, pp. 161-162.

By the grace of Yahweh, Jeroboam gains control over Israel's archenemy Damascus and Hamath. Yet, in spite of the optimism of Jeroboam's reign, the future is not promising for Israel. Because of the social injustice fostered by increased wealth and further stratification during the reign of Jeroboam, the prophet Amos proclaims:

> For the LORD God Almighty declares,
>   "I will stir up a nation against you, O house of Israel,
> that will oppress you all the way
>   from Lebo Hamath to the valley of the Arabah." (6:14)

> "The high places of Isaac will be destroyed
>   and the sanctuaries of Israel will be ruined;
>   with my sword I will rise against the house of Jeroboam."
>   (7:9; cf. vv. 10-11)

A careful reader of Kings also anticipates trouble for Israel. At the death of Jeroboam, **Zechariah** becomes king in his place, the fourth son of Jehu to sit on the throne of Israel (cf. 10:30).[31]

---

[31]See Brueggemann, *1 & 2 Kings*, p. 445.

2 KINGS 15

D. YAHWEH AFFLICTS AZARIAH OF JUDAH (15:1-7)

15:1-4 After the death of Amaziah, his son **Azariah** ("Yahweh helps [עָזַר, *'āzar*]"[1]) becomes king in Jerusalem. As indicated above, the **twenty-seventh year of Jeroboam** probably represents when Azariah begins his sole reign; his **fifty-two years** on the throne include his tenure as coregent with his father Amaziah (see comments on ch. 14). The refrain for the kings of Judah follows. Azariah does **right in the eyes of the LORD, as his father Amaziah had done**. There is no comment, however, on how he measures up to his forefather David (see 14:3; cf. 1 Kgs 15:3-5,11). **The high places** remain, on which **the people continue to offer sacrifices and burn incense** (replaced in Chronicles with a comment on the righteous influence of Zechariah; cf. 2 Chr 26:5[2]).

15:5-6 Without elaboration, the narrator says that Yahweh **afflicts the king with leprosy until the day he dies**. An obvious sign of divine disapproval, the storyteller offers no explanation. The Chronicler, on the other hand, fills this provocative gap with a detailed account of Azariah's pride before Yahweh. The king tries to assert his royal authority and unlawfully burn incense in the temple, only to be opposed by the priests and struck leprous by Yahweh. As a leper, he is barred from entering the house of Yahweh for the remainder of his life (2 Chr 26:16-21).[3] In quarantine, he lives **in a**

---

[1]The name appears as "Uzziah" without explanation in 15:30,32,34, although it has been suggested that Uzziah is a throne name, or the king's name when he becomes a leper (see Cogan and Tadmor, *II Kings*, p. 165). "Azaryau of Iaudu" in the annals of Tiglath-Pileser is now generally not identified with Azariah, but with a ruler from north Syria (Hobbs, *2 Kings*, p. 194; cf. Cogan and Tadmor, *II Kings*, p. 166).

[2]See Hicks, *1 & 2 Chronicles*, p. 427.

[3]See ibid., pp. 430-432.

separate house (literally, "in a house of freedom"[4]). **Jotham the king's son has charge of the palace and *governs* [שָׁפַט, *šāphaṭ*] the people of the land**. Azariah ends his reign as it began — only now he is coregent with his son. The narrator implies as much when he says Jotham "begins to *reign*" (מָלַךְ, *mālak*; not "govern") in the second year of Pekah (15:32).[5]

The numerous omissions to the lengthy and important reign of Azariah stand out. Other than the note about Elath (14:22), nothing is said about his wars, his building projects, or military defenses (cf. 2 Chr 26:6-15). Apparently, the storyteller in Kings is more concerned with Yahweh's actions than with the details of Azariah's reign. Ironically, Yahweh *helps* (*'āzar*) Israel through Jeroboam ("there was not one to *help* them," 2 Kgs 14:26) and curses with leprosy *Azariah*, whose name means "Yahweh *helps*." The God of Israel shows compassion to Israel because of his covenant with Abraham (2 Kgs 13:23), but what does his covenant with David (2 Samuel 7) mean for Judah? The insinuation in 14:22 was that perhaps during Azariah's reign the kingdom of Solomon would again be realized (when "he rebuilt Elath), but this does not occur.

15:7 The narrator completes this brief account with his typical closing formula, recording the death of the king. This event apparently impacted the prophet Isaiah, who testifies that "in the year that King Uzziah [i.e., Azariah] died" (Isa 6:1), he received his throne-room vision of Yahweh and call (vv. 1-13). When the NIV says that Azariah is buried **near them** [literally, '*with* his fathers'] **in the City of David**, the language is chosen to accommodate the Chronicler, who says that Azariah was buried in a field because of his leprosy (2 Chr 26:22). Josephus writes that the king was buried in his own garden (*Antiquities* ix.227; cf. 2 Kgs 21:18,26). A first-century-B.C. Aramaic inscription in Jerusalem that identifies the burial (or reburial) of "Uzziah king of Judah" appears to confirm the statement in Chronicles.[6] The report in Kings is simply an idiomatic way of say-

---

[4]Perhaps this carries the idea of "free from responsibilities," although, the term also occurs as a name for the underworld, an appropriate designation for the house of a leper, who is separated from society like the dead (see Cogan and Tadmor, *II Kings*, pp. 166-167).

[5]Hobbs, *2 Kings*, p. 195.

[6]Cogan and Tadmor, *II Kings*, p. 167, and fig. 5; Hobbs, *2 Kings*, p. 195.

ing Azariah was buried in Jerusalem. After Azariah's death, **Jotham his son** reigns in his place.

E. THE FORTUNES OF ISRAEL DECLINE PRECIPITOUSLY (15:8-31)

1. The House of Jehu Falls with Zechariah (15:8-12)

15:8-12 Sandwiched between accounts of the Judean kings Azariah and Jotham, the storyteller now chronicles the contrasting instability in Israel, which is reflected in a rapid succession of rulers.[7] **In the thirty-eighth year of Azariah king of Judah, Zechariah son of Jeroboam** (the fourth in the line from Jehu) comes to the throne in Samaria and reigns only **six months.** He does **evil in the eyes of the LORD, as his fathers,** and does **not turn away from the sins of Jeroboam son of Nebat, which he had caused Israel to commit.** The refrain in Kings that characterizes the kings of Israel is repeated once more (see comments on 1 Kgs 13:33-34) — and appears in the remainder of the chapter, with the kings of Israel, in a staccato fashion (vv. 18,24,28). In fact, the considerably compressed account of the fall of Israel that follows has the literary effect of signifying a precipitous decline that cannot be avoided.[8] The sins of Jeroboam are now coming to roost for the northern kingdom.

Shallum son of Jabesh conspires against Zechariah and **assassinates** him. If "son of Jabesh" means that Shallum is from Jabesh Gilead, his actions probably reflect intertribal conflict and insurrection across the Jordan, which apparently plays a factor in subsequent events (see comments on vv. 23-26).[9] As Shallum takes the throne, the house of Jehu comes to an end. The narrator puts closure on Zechariah's reign with the statement that **the word of the LORD spoken to Jehu** is **fulfilled: "Your descendants will sit on the throne of Israel to the fourth generation"** (cf. 10:30). The covenant with the house of Jehu has been fulfilled. The time is in sight, when Yahweh's word to Jeroboam that he "will uproot Israel from this good land . . . and scatter them beyond the River" (1 Kgs 14:15) will be enacted.

---

[7]See Brueggemann, *1 & 2 Kings*, p. 459.

[8]See Hobbs, *2 Kings*, p. 190.

[9]Thiele, *Mysterious Numbers*, pp. 124, 129-130.

2. Shallum Reigns One Month (15:13-16)

15:13-16 The conspirator **Shallum** takes the throne **in the thirty-ninth year of Uzziah** [i.e., "Azariah"] but only reigns **one month**. **Menahem son of Gadi** comes from **Tirzah** (see comments on 1 Kgs 14:17) to Samaria and **assassinates** Shallum. If Tirzah is the center of Menahem's power base, his revolt may represent rebellion against the usurper from the other side of the Jordan (see comments on vv. 27-31).[10] The **other events** of Shallum's reign, including his **conspiracy**, are **written in the book of the annals of the kings of Israel**, reminding the reader once more that the author is using reliable sources for his report. Noticeably absent from the account of Shallum is any reference to the sins of Jeroboam, probably because of the brevity of his reign (however, cf. 1 Kgs 16:15-20).

Before formally introducing the reign of Menahem, the story-teller cites his campaign against **Tiphsah**. Since the only known city by the name of Tiphsah is on the Euphrates, many scholars prefer "Tappuah" in the Lucianic recension of the Septuagint, a site on the border of Ephraim (cf. Josh 16:8). However, the reading in the Hebrew MT is plausible. Menahem may have been attempting to secure the northern border of the kingdom, which was extended to the Euphrates by Jeroboam (cf. 14:25,28).[11]

3. Menahem Gains Support from Assyria (15:17-22)

15:17-22 Spanning a length of **ten years**, **Menahem**'s more stable regime, though also **evil in the eyes of the LORD**, continues in **the sins of Jeroboam the son of Nebat**. Apparently, the new king is able to secure his kingdom through an appeal to **Pul**, a nickname for Tiglath-Pileser III **king of Assyria** (reigning from 745 to 727 B.C.).[12] Menahem gives the Assyrian king **a thousand talents of silver to gain his support and strengthen his own hand on the kingdom** (cf. 1 Kgs 15:16-20). Ostensibly, the king of Israel **exacts fifty shekels of silver** from **every wealthy man** in Israel for this purpose. Tiglath-Pileser withdraws from **the land**.

---

[10]Hobbs, *2 Kings*, p. 196.
[11]Ibid., p. 197; cf. Cogan and Tadmor, *II Kings*, p. 171.
[12]Cogan and Tadmor, *II Kings*, pp. 171-172.

Even though there are at least two references to tribute from Menahem to Tiglath-Pileser in the Assyrian's annals,[13] the underlying sequence of events is uncertain. Various dates have been suggested for Menahem's overture. Hobbs argues that the extant inscriptions do not correspond with 15:19-20. Difficult to translate, verse 20 can also be read as saying Menahem buys mercenaries from Assyria to enable his hold on the throne against a rival contender. The situation is not the payment of tribute by a vassal; Menahem is petitioning for intervention. In verse 20, for example, גִּבּוֹרֵי הַחַיִל (*gibbôrê haḥayil*, "wealthy men" in the NIV) can be translated "fighting men" (cf., e.g., Josh 1:14; 6:2; 8:3; 10:7). Hobbs construes the verse as saying that fifty shekels are given to each Assyrian soldier as payment for military services.[14] While at odds with the traditional reading of these verses, Hobbs' interpretation has in its favor that it emphasizes Menahem's appeal to Tiglath-Pileser, which is the central point in the text. Reading between the lines, the king of Israel secures Assyrian aid against an opponent in the Transjordan (see comments on vv. 27-31). At this behavior, the prophet Hosea scoffs, "[Assyria] is not able to cure you, not able to heal your sores" (Hos 5:13; cf. 7:11; 8:9; 12:1; 14:3). Later, Ahaz of Judah will employ a similar tactic against Samaria and Aram.[15] At his death, Menahem's son **Pekahiah** reigns in Samaria.

4. Pekahiah Reigns Two Years (15:23-26)

15:23-26 The synchronisms with the fifty-two year reign of **Azariah king of Judah** continue. **Pekahiah** begins his reign in the **fiftieth year** of Azariah, but reigns just **two years**. He also **does evil in the eyes of the LORD** and does **not turn away from the sins of Jeroboam**. One of his lieutenants, **Pekah** [a shortened form of Pekahiah, "Yahweh has opened the eyes"] **the son of Remaliah, conspire**s against him. In subsequent verses, Pekah's patronym ("son of Remaliah") almost always appears (15:25,27,30,32,37; 16:1,5; cf.

---

[13]See, e.g., *ANET*, p. 283; cf. Hobbs, *2 Kings*, p. 198; Cogan and Tadmor, *II Kings*, p. 172.

[14]Hobbs, *2 Kings*, pp. 198-200.

[15]Ibid., p. 199.

15:29), which calls attention to his lack of pedigree as an illegitimate claimant to the throne.[16] So, the cycle of conspiracy and assassination continues, about which Yahweh laments, "They set up kings without my consent; they choose princes without my approval" (Hos 8:4). With **fifty men of Gilead**, Pekah assassinates Pekahiah, perhaps along with some important officials,[17] **in the citadel of the royal palace**. That "men of Gilead" accompany him reinforces the view that he commands a rival regime across the Jordan (see comments on vv. 27-31). Pekah **succeed**s Pekahiah **as king**.[18]

5. Pekah Reigns, and Assyria Exiles Israelites (15:27-31)

15:27-28 The synchronism for the reign of Menahem presents a chronological problem that is impossible to solve with complete satisfaction (cf. the discussion of chronology for the first half of the eighth century, ch. 14; see "Introduction: Chronology"). **Pekah** becomes king of Israel **in the fifty-second year of Azariah** and **reign**s **twenty years**. In verse 30, the narrator closes the account of Pekah with a note that he is assassinated in the "twentieth year of Jotham." This is all well and good, until the reader discovers that Jotham only reigns sixteen years (15:33). And if Pekah the son of Remaliah dies in the twentieth year of Jotham, he is not alive to pose a threat to Ahaz, who succeeds Jotham on the throne of Judah (cf. 16:5-9; Isa 7:1–8:10).

Thiele's solution involves coregencies and dual dating. He believes Jotham was coregent with his father Azariah the last ten years of his father's reign, but also shares the throne with his son Ahaz at the end of his life. For Thiele, the comment in 15:37 that Rezin and Pekah begin to go up against Judah during the reign of Jotham implies as much. In 732 B.C., Damascus (and the Aram-Israel coalition) falls to Tiglath-Pileser. Therefore, the events of Isaiah 7–8 would have to fit into a four-year period at the end of Jotham's reign (ca. 735–732 B.C.), when he is coregent with Ahaz.

---

[16]Brueggemann, *1 & 2 Kings*, pp. 464-465.

[17]"Abrob and Arieh" is difficult to interpret. Many believe the phrase represents districts (cf. Deut 3:4,14) and was originally connected with v. 29 (see Hobbs, *2 Kings*, p. 200).

[18]Thiele, *Mysterious Numbers*, pp. 129-130.

So, coregency underlies the dual dating of sixteen and twenty years for the reign of Jotham (vv. 30,33). The twenty years includes Jotham's coregency with his son Ahaz.[19]

Turning to Israel, if Pekah begins his reign in the fifty-second (and final) year of Azariah, his twenty-year reign will outlast the reign of Jotham by eight years, even though verse 30 says that Pekah is assassinated in the twentieth (and final) year of Jotham's reign. (Thiele posits that Jotham's reign included ten years as coregent with Azariah, six years as sole ruler, and four years as coregent with Ahaz.) It follows that Pekah must have reigned concurrently with the preceding king(s) of Israel. To resolve the discrepancy, Thiele theorizes Pekah headed a rival "government" in the Transjordan for the twelve years of Menahem (10 yrs., v. 17) and Pekahiah (2 yrs., v. 23). He postulates that when Shallum, who is from Jabesh Gilead ("son of Jabesh," v. 13), takes the throne, tribes from across the Jordan rule Israel. With a power base in Tirzah, Menahem regains control and calls on Tiglath-Pileser to secure his rule in Samaria, against Pekah's opposition in Gilead.[20] For twelve years the northern kingdom is splintered. Then, with designs on Samaria, Pekah accepts a military appointment under Pekahiah. With the aid of fifty men of Gilead, Pekah assassinates Pekahiah and assumes control of both sides of the Jordan.[21]

Explaining many of the apparent discrepancies, Thiele's approach is not without its problems. Allowing that a rival reign for Pekah in the Transjordan is "attractive and certainly plausible," Hobbs calls attention to the fact that verse 27 appears to say that Pekah ruled twenty years "in Samaria."[22] He also is not convinced that Jotham was coregent with Ahaz, writing that it "creates a fiction for which there is not evidence at all in the text"[23] (apparently dis-

---

[19]Ibid., pp. 132-134.

[20]Some argue Pekah may have been an "agent" of Rezin (see Lawson K. Younger, "The Deportations of the Israelites," *JBL* 117/2 [1998]: 202; Wayne T. Pitard, "Rezin [person]," in *ABD*).

[21]Thiele, *Mysterious Numbers*, pp. 124-132. Galil believes "the datum that Pekah reigned for 20 years is erroneous." He postulates that Pekah had earlier been appointed as the official over Gilead and counted the years of his reign "retroactively" (*Chronology of the Kings*, pp. 65-66).

[22]Hobbs, *2 Kings*, p. 205.

[23]Ibid., p. 203.

counting Thiele's interpretation of 15:37[24]). And, a comment about
the synchronism of Pekah's reign with the last year of Azariah indicates that he does not accept Thiele's principle of "dual dating."[25]
More difficult for Thiele is the fact that his theory means Hoshea's
reign ends before the reign of Hezekiah, despite the synchronisms
between the two in 18:1,9,10. Thiele attributes these to "the editors
of Kings . . . who did not understand the dual dating for Pekah."[26]
One solution to this quandary is that Hezekiah begins his reign as
coregent with his father in the 720s before becoming sole ruler in
716/715 B.C. at the death of Ahaz (see comments on 17:1-2 and the
introductory comments to chs. 18-20).

15:29-31 During the reign of Pekah, **Tiglath-Pileser king of
Assyria** comes up against Israel and takes the northern provinces of
Israel, **Gilead and Galilee, including all the land of Naphtali**.[27] The
conquest of Gilead (in the Transjordan), in particular, is associated
with Tiglath-Pileser's campaigns against Damascus in 733 and 732
B.C. A reference in the king's annals generally corresponds to this
thrust,[28] although a formerly accepted citation to the "wide (land of)
[Naphta]li" has been shown to refer to Aram.[29] In the several military
assaults on the west from 734-732, Tiglath-Pileser incorporated the
coastal plain, the Galilee, and the Transjordan as Assyrian provinces.
The coastal city of Dor may have served as the administrative center

---

[24]See *Mysterious Numbers*, pp. 132-133.

[25]Hobbs, *2 Kings*, p. 205. For critiques of Thiele, see Hobbs, *2 Kings*, pp.
xliii-xliv; Galil, *Chronology of the Kings*, pp. 3-4; Dillard and Longman, *An
Introduction to the Old Testament*, pp. 158-159.

[26]Thiele, *Mysterious Numbers*, pp. 134-135.

[27]The phrase "Gilead and Galilee" may be a later gloss that summarizes
the regions affected (Cogan and Tadmor, *II Kings*, p. 174; see Younger,
"Deportations," pp. 207-209). For detailed analyses of the cities listed in
v. 29, see Cogan and Tadmor, *II King*, pp. 174-175; Hobbs, *2 Kings*, pp. 202-
203. In the ashes of the Assyrian destruction at Hazor, one of the cities mentioned in v. 29, archaeologists uncovered the shoulder of a storejar
inscribed with the phrase "belonging to Pekah," the king of Israel at the
time the city fell (Yigael Yadin, *Hazor: The Rediscovery of a Great Citadel of the
Bible* [New York: Random House, 1975], p. 183).

[28]Since there was a number of campaigns by Tiglath-Pileser to the west in
these years, the Assyrian and biblical references may not refer to the same
campaign (Younger, "Deportations," 208).

[29]*ANET*, p. 283; see Cogan and Tadmor, *II Kings*, p. 174; Hobbs, *2 Kings*,
p. 202.

of another province, as the archaeological record apparently confirms.[30] For the first time in Kings, descendants of Israel are **deported**. In one of Tiglath-Pileser's reliefs, captives are being exiled from the biblical city of Ashtaroth in the Transjordan (cf. Josh. 9:10; 12:4; 13:12,31). The Assyrian king claims to have exiled 13,520 from Israel, probably from Lower Galilee, which appears in the archaeological record as a decline in settlements.[31] Younger argues that the archaeological data suggest the deportations were "unidirectional," so Assyria could control trade down the Mediterranean coast unencumbered by a local populace (see comments on 17:24-41).[32] The prophecies of Ahijah (1 Kgs 14:15), Amos (Amos 4:1-3; 6:7; 7:17), and Hosea (Hos 9:3; 10:5-6; 11:5) are coming to pass. These verses also anticipate Ahaz's appeal to Tiglath-Pileser for aid against a Syro-Ephraimite coalition (see comments on 16:5-9). In that context, **Hoshea conspires against Pekah** and **assassinates** him, to which Tiglath-Pileser claims credit: "They overthrew their king Pekah and I placed Hoshea as king over them."[33] Hoshea begins his reign in the **twentieth year of Jotham** (see comments on vv. 27-28).

F. JOTHAM OF JUDAH DOES RIGHT IN
THE EYES OF YAHWEH (15:32-38)

15:32-38 Before narrating the fall of Samaria, the storyteller returns to Judah for the reigns of Jotham and Ahaz. **Jotham son of Uzziah** [i.e., Azariah] **king of Judah** comes to the throne in the **second year of Pekah** and reigns **sixteen years** (see comments on vv. 27-28). With his typical introductory formula for a king of Judah, the narrator includes the name of Jotham's mother, **Jerusha daughter of Zadok**, who may have been the daughter of a priest (cf. 1 Kgs 2:35).[34]

---

[30]See Younger, "Deportations," 203, 205; Ephraim Stern, "Dor," in *NEAEHL*; idem, "Dor (place)," in *ABD*.

[31]See Younger, "Deportations," 208, 211, 213. For a color photograph and description of the Ashtaroth relief, see J.E. Curtis and J.E. Reade, eds., *Art and Empire: Treasures from Assyria in the British Museum* (New York: The Metropolitan Museum of New York, 1995), pp. 62-63.

[32]Younger, "Deportations," 214, 224-27.

[33]*ANET*, p. 284.

[34]Hobbs, *2 Kings*, p. 204.

Perhaps she plays a role in the righteous character of her son the king. As his father, Jotham does what is **right in the eyes of the LORD**. Nevertheless, he also does not remove **the high places**. Of his achievements, on which the Chronicler elaborates (2 Chr 27:3-5), the storyteller in Kings only mentions that he **rebuilds the Upper Gate of the temple of the LORD**. In Kings, repairing the house of Yahweh is a righteous act (cf. 12:4-16; 22:3-7). For the reader, this one achievement symbolizes Jotham's reign. The Chronicler adds, "Jotham grew powerful because he walked steadfastly [in contrast with his father] before the LORD his God" (27:6).

Parenthetically, the narrator in Kings mentions that **the LORD** begins to **send Rezin** and **Pekah against Judah** (perhaps an indicator of coregency with Ahaz [see comments on vv. 27-28]). The crisis that is coming for Judah is from Yahweh.[35] A small change in the concluding formula reinforces the positive appraisal of Jotham's reign. The king is buried, literally, "**in the City of David**, *his father*." The spiritually disappointing reign of Azariah is followed by the righteous reign of Jotham, who is like his forefather David. However, the good influence of both Azariah and Jotham will be undone during the reign of Ahaz, who walks in the ways of the kings of Israel (cf. 16:3).

---

[35]Divine action is not cited for the advance of Tiglath-Pileser against Israel (Cohn, *2 Kings*, p. 110), although, it is certainly implied.

2 KINGS 16

G. AHAZ OF JUDAH FOLLOWS THE KINGS ISRAEL (16:1-20)

16:1-4 Ahaz son of Jotham king of Judah comes to the throne in the **seventeenth year of Pekah** at age **twenty** and reigns **sixteen years**.[1] In 18:2, the reader learns Hezekiah was twenty-five when he became king at the death of his father, which appears to imply Jotham was eleven when Hezekiah was born (20+16=36 at his death; 36−25=11 at Hezekiah's birth).[2] However, if Ahaz is twenty when he begins a four-year coregency with his father Jotham and then reigns sixteen years as sole ruler after his father's death, he would have been fifteen at the birth of Hezekiah, a more reasonable age to father a child.[3] **Unlike David his father**, Ahaz does **not do what was right in the eyes of the LORD** and **walks in the ways of the kings of Israel**. To this point in the story of Judah, Solomon (1 Kgs 11:6) and then Jehoram and Ahaziah (2 Kgs 8:18, 27), who were tied to the house of Ahab, are the only kings depicted as doing evil in the sight of Yahweh. Ahaz is the first to be described as "not doing what was right." Only Abijah (1 Kgs 15:3-5) and Amaziah (2 Kgs 14:3) are said to be unlike David. And only Jehoram, who married a daughter of Ahab, is portrayed as *walking in the ways of the kings of Israel* (8:18).[4]

Nevertheless, Ahaz goes beyond these kings. He **even sacrifices his son in the fire** [literally, "made his son pass through the fire," apparently an idiom for child sacrifice; cf. Deut 18:10; 2 Kgs 21:6;

---

[1]The name Ahaz is the shortened form, without the theophoric element, of Jehoahaz/Ahaziah ("Yahweh has seized"). Including Ahaz, five kings of Israel and Judah wear this name (cf. 1 Kgs 22:51; 2 Kgs 8:24-26; 13:1; 23:31).

[2]Hobbs, *2 Kings*, p. 212. Hobbs notices there is no mention of the queen mother — only here with Ahaz and in the account of Jehoram (2 Kgs 8:16-17).

[3]This point reinforces Thiele's thesis (see *Mysterious Numbers*, pp. 131-134; and comments on 15:27-28).

[4]Ahaziah is described as "walking in the ways of the house of Ahab" (8:27).

COLLEGE PRESS NIV COMMENTARY

23:10; and Jer 32:35; see comments on 23:10], **following the detestable ways** [תּוֹעֲבוֹת, *tôʿăbôth*] **of the nations the LORD had driven out** [from יָרַשׁ, *yāraš*] **before the Israelites** (cf. 1 Kgs 14:24; 21:26; 2 Kgs 17:8). The same language will be used to frame the reign of Manasseh (21:2-6). Moses had said that because of the "detestable practices" (תּוֹעֲבֹת, *tôʿēbōth*) of the nations in the land, like making their sons or daughters "pass through the fire," they would be "driven out" (from *yāraš*) of the land (Deut 18:12) — which an exilic reader knows happens to both Israel and Judah. In the narrator's review of his reign, however, Ahaz's wickedness crescendos when he **offers sacrifices and burns incense at the high places**. So far in Kings, the people are the ones who have been sacrificing *at the high places* (cf., e.g., 15:35). Ahaz is the first king of Judah, since Solomon (1 Kgs 3:3), to sacrifice and burn incense in person *at the high places*.[5] And, for the storyteller, this also mirrors the nations. With **on the hilltops and under every spreading tree**, he portrays Ahaz's high place worship as being like the nations, the very ones who were *driven out* before Israel in the days of Joshua (see Deut 12:2). A careful reader wonders what this will mean for Yahweh's promise to David (2 Samuel 7).[6]

16:5-9 Rezin king of Damascus and Pekah son of Remaliah king of Israel march against Jerusalem and **besiege Ahaz** (cf. Isa 7:1). Ahaz appeals to **Tiglath-Pileser** to **"save me out of the hand of the king of Aram and the king of Israel."** These two kings have aligned themselves against the Assyrian threat in the region and have marched **against Jerusalem** and **besieged Ahaz** (often styled the Syro-Ephraimite war). Their plan is to depose Ahaz and replace him with someone on the throne in Jerusalem ("the son of Tabeel," Isa 7:6) who will be well-disposed to their policies. The prophet Isaiah warns the king not to fear "these two smoldering stubs of firewood," for Yahweh says, "It will not take place, it will not happen" (7:4,7; see chs. 7–8). The king of Judah has three options: He can capitulate to Israel and Aram, petition Assyria for help, or trust in Yahweh to

---

[5]Cogan and Tadmor, *II Kings*, p. 186.

[6]Provan, *1 and 2 Kings*, p. 245. In Chronicles, Ahaz is characterized as the worst king of Judah, outstripping Kings' worst villain, Manasseh (Hicks, *1 & 2 Chronicles*, p. 437; for the different emphases in the Chronicles account, see pp. 437-449).

deliver Judah. Isaiah calls on "the house of David" to have faith in Yahweh as savior: "If you do not stand firm in your faith, you will not stand at all" (7:9).[7] With the sign of the "virgin birth" and the birth of the prophet's own son Maher-Shalal-Hash-Baz ("quick to the plunder, swift to the spoil"), Ahaz can know that within the span of a couple of years, the threat will disappear.[8]

A seal impression in clay (i.e., a bulla) has surfaced from the antiquities market that is inscribed with the name Ahaz: "Belonging to Ahaz [son of] Yehotam, King of Judah" (cf. v. 1). On the left side of the impression is a fingerprint that may be from the king himself.[9] This remarkable artifact is perhaps a direct connection with the story of Ahaz. The king of Judah may have used the same seal to ratify his treaty with Tiglath-Pileser on his trip to Damascus (see below). In the context of Ahaz's appeal to the king of Assyria, the prophet Isaiah says, "Bind up the testimony and *seal* up the law [i.e., Isaiah's prophecies concerning Ahaz] among my disciples. I will wait for the LORD who is hiding from the house of Jacob. I will put my trust in him" (Isa 8:16-17). The prophet chooses to trust in Yahweh; his disciples will see that his *sealed* testimony (i.e., prophecy) will come to pass!

Even so, the king of Judah takes the **silver and gold** from the **temple of the LORD** and **the treasures of the royal palace** to give as a *bribe* (שֹׁחַד, *šōḥad*, wrongly translated "present" in the NIV) to the king of Assyria. Taking treasures from the house of Yahweh foreshadows its

---

[7]Brueggemann, *1 & 2 Kings*, p. 466.

[8]The sons born to the "young woman of marriageable age" (עַלְמָה, *'almāh*, Isa 7:14) and to Isaiah (8:3) are signs to Judah (cf. 8:18). "Before the boy knows enough to reject the wrong and choose the right" (7:16) and "before the boy knows how to say 'My father' or 'My mother'" (8:4) both indicate the Syro-Ephraimite coalition would be defeated by Assyria within two years. Isaiah's son Shear-Jashub ("a remnant will return [*šûb*]," 7:3) and the child who would reign and be called "Wonderful Counselor . . ." (9:6-7) symbolize that Yahweh would save the house of David and restore Judah.

When Isaiah says that the young woman in the court of Ahaz would "give birth to a son, and call him Immanuel" (7:14), he is connecting Yahweh's actions for the house of David with his promise to Abraham: "Your wife Sarah will bear you [i.e., "give birth to"] a son, and you will call him Isaac" (Gen 17:19). By inspiration, Matthew sees this ultimately coming to pass in the birth of Jesus of the virgin Mary (Matt 1:22).

[9]Robert Deutsch, "First Impression: What We Learn from King Ahaz's Seal," *BAR* 24/3 (May/June 1998): 54-56, 62.

destruction and negatively characterizes the king.[10] Ahaz uses the treasures of Israel for a *bribe*, which further situates this wicked monarch (cf. Exod 23:8; Deut 16:19).[11] Tiglath-Pileser responds by **attacking Damascus, deporting its inhabitants,** and killing **Rezin.**

Correlating the biblical account with the Assyrian annals, Ahaz apparently appeals to Tiglath-Pileser during his campaign to Gaza in 734 B.C. Isaiah's meeting with Ahaz (Isaiah 7) must have occurred not long before then. The following year, the Assyrian king goes up against Israel (2 Kgs 15:29-30). In 732, Damascus is captured, and Rezin is killed, according to the word of the prophet Isaiah (Isa 7:14-16; 8:1-4). As Menahem appealed to Assyria (2 Kgs 15:19-20), with dire consequences ultimately for Israel, so Ahaz makes a similar move to save his kingdom.[12] Yet, his choice is shortsighted; it leaves out Yahweh — and therein seals Judah's fate. Brueggemann styles the unfaithful king "a quintessential non-truster who chose foolishly and destructively for his people."[13] Accordingly, the prophet says, "Yahweh will use [the king of Assyria as] a razor . . . to shave your head and the hair of your legs, and to take off your beards also" (Isa 7:20). Judah will suffer for Ahaz's lack of faith. Nevertheless, even then, God is *Immanuel* – he is with Israel (8:10; cf. 7:14; 8:8).

The note in verse 6, that **Elath** is taken by **Aram,** only later to revert back to the **Edomites,** also negatively frames the reign of Ahaz. His grandfather Azariah rebuilt Elath, Israel's southern outlet to the sea, and restored it to Judah (14:22), along with some of the grandeur of the age of Solomon. During Ahaz's reign, these gains are lost. Then, when the storyteller in verse 9 reports that the Assyrians **deport** the inhabitants of Damascus to their original home in **Kir** (Amos 9:7), he intimates a "reverse 'exodus'"[14] — no doubt suggesting the people of God can anticipate the same. For Israel, Hosea makes an analogous claim when he declares, "Ephraim will return to Egypt and eat unclean food in Assyria" (Hos 9:3; see comments on 1 Kgs 6:1; 14:14-16). The reign of Ahaz sets the stage for a similar consequence for Judah.

---

[10]Mullen, "Crime and Punishment," pp. 242-243.
[11]Cogan and Tadmor, *II Kings*, p. 188; Cohn, *2 Kings*, p. 113.
[12]See Hobbs, *2 Kings*, pp. 210-211, 214-215.
[13]Brueggemann, *1 & 2 Kings*, p. 473.
[14]Provan, *1 and 2 Kings*, p. 245.

16:10-18 Following the defeat of Aram, Ahaz makes a trip to **Damascus to meet Tiglath-Pileser**. Although not recorded in the Assyrian annals, the king's diplomatic expedition to the Aramean capital is historically plausible (cf. Jehu's audience with Shalmaneser III; see comments on 10:32-33). In Damascus, Ahaz sees an **altar** that he admires and directs **Uriah the priest** to build for him a similar one. Contrary to some interpretations, there is nothing in this episode that indicates Ahaz is complying with Assyrian directives. There is no extrabiblical evidence to suggest the Assyrians forced their gods on cowering vassals, and the altar the king of Judah covets is Aramean, probably the altar in the temple of Adad-Rimmon (cf. 5:18).[15] Ahaz "*sees* the altar" and decides he must have one of his own. With **detailed plans**, Uriah the (compliant?) priest constructs such an altar for the king in Jerusalem. On his return, Ahaz moves **the bronze altar** [cf. 1 Kgs 8:22,54,64] **that stood before the LORD** and replaces it with **the large** [literally, "the great"] **new altar**. He makes **offerings** and instructs Uriah as to the schedule of offerings on the altar. The storyteller adds that Ahaz modifies the **movable stands**, **the Sea**, and the enigmatic **Sabbath canopy** (2 Kgs 16:17-18; cf. 1 Kgs 7:23-36).[16] The king will use the bronze altar **for seeking guidance** (בָּקַר, *bāqar*).[17]

In recounting these events, the narrator draws attention to the offerings made by Ahaz the king. In fact, the chapter's concentric structure highlights the king's worship on the new altar:[18]

    A. Regnal summary introduction (16:1-6)

        B. King Ahaz sends tribute to Tiglath-Pileser (16:7-9)

            C. King Ahaz sends plans for the altar from Damascus to priest Uriah who executes them (16:10-11)

            X. King worships at the new great altar and moves the old bronze altar (16:12-14)

            C'. King Ahaz commands the priest Uriah to offer sacrifices and he does so (16:15-16)

---

[15]Cogan and Tadmor, *II Kings*, pp. 190, 192; Hobbs, *2 Kings*, p. 215; contra Brueggemann, *1 & 2 Kings*, p. 469; Gray, *I & II Kings*, p. 635.

[16]For the variety of ways scholars understand "Sabbath canopy," see Hobbs, *2 Kings*, p. 218.

[17]There is no reason to read *bāqar* ("to inquire/seek") as indicating divination (Cogan and Tadmor, *II Kings*, p. 189; Hobbs, *2 Kings*, p. 217; contra Gray, *I & II Kings*, p. 637).

[18]From Cohn, *2 Kings*, p. 111.

B′. King Ahaz raids the sancta of the temple because of the
    king of Assyria (16:17-18)
A′. Regnal summary conclusion (16:19-20)

When Ahaz makes offerings on the altar, he may be officiating in an
inaugural, dedicatory ceremony as David, Solomon, and Jeroboam
before him (cf. 2 Sam 6:17-18; 1 Kgs 8:63; 12:32; 13:1).[19]

Contrary to traditional interpretations, there is no emphasis on
foreign idolatry in this account. Nelson is correct when he calls attention to the fact that there is nothing out of the ordinary in what Ahaz
does when he sets up the new altar.[20] The offerings outlined by the
storyteller (vv. 13,15) are all appropriate for temple worship. Moreover, there is precedent for the king's actions. At the dedication of
the temple, Solomon consecrated the middle courtyard for offerings
because the *bronze altar* was too small. There, he "offered burnt offerings, grain offerings and the fat of the fellowship offerings," like Ahaz
(1 Kgs 8:64; cf. 2 Kgs 16:13). Later, in the reforms of Hezekiah and
Josiah, there is no attempt to dismantle Ahaz's altar. In fact, it even
appears that both these reformers use the altar that Ahaz set up (cf.
18:22; 23:9). Also, Isaiah describes the priest Uriah as a "reliable witness" (Isa 8:2), which is at odds with the view that this priest is com-
plicit with Ahaz in desecrating the temple offerings.

The contrast with the account in Chronicles reinforces this
observation. The Chronicler does not include the episode of the
altar. Instead, he emphasizes Ahaz's foreign idolatry. The king of
Judah worships "the Baals," "offers sacrifices to the gods of Damascus," and "builds high places to burn sacrifices to other gods" (2 Chr
28:2,23,25). In Kings, however, Ahaz is not portrayed as worshiping
foreign gods. When he officiates at the altar, for example, his
actions do not conflict with "the accepted practice of the Jerusalem
temple."[21] In fact, there is not anything Ahaz does that could not be
in worship to Yahweh. While obviously incongruent with the Law of
Moses, even child sacrifice (2 Kgs 16:3) could be enacted in his
name.

---

[19]Cogan and Tadmor, *II Kings*, p. 189; Gray, *I & II Kings*, p. 636; contra
Hobbs, *2 Kings*, p. 216.

[20]For the interpretation summarized below, see Nelson, *First and Second
Kings*, pp. 225-226.

[21]Cogan and Tadmor, *II Kings*, p. 192.

As is often the case, the storyteller's strategy is subtle. The attention he gives to the altar establishes a frame for reading the Ahazlike actions of Manasseh and the reforms of Hezekiah and Josiah, in which the altars of the high places throughout the land are dismantled (cf. 2 Kgs 18:22; 21:3-5; 23:9,12,15-17,20). When the Assyrians attack Hezekiah, the Assyrian field commander will say, "Isn't [Yahweh] the one whose high places and altars Hezekiah removed, saying to Judah and Jerusalem, 'You must worship before this altar [Ahaz's altar?] in Jerusalem?'" (18:22). This contrast puts in perspective the actions of Ahaz. While the righteous kings Hezekiah and Josiah set out to restore the temple worship laid out by Solomon, Ahaz is more interested in current religious trends and in satisfying his Assyrian overlord. Instead of restoring Solomonic worship, he dismantles furnishings commissioned by Solomon and in some way pays homage to Tiglath-Pileser. While the phrase **in deference to the king of Assyria** only modifies what Ahaz does to the "Sabbath canopy,"[22] it casts a shadow over all of his innovations. The king of Judah is more concerned with fashion and pleasing the king of Assyria than he is in pleasing Yahweh.[23]

An interesting use of naming underscores this focus. When Ahaz visits Tiglath-Pileser in Damascus, the storyteller names him **King Ahaz**, appropriate for the king of Judah operating on an international stage, even if it is only as a vassal. However, on his return in verse 12, he is named **the king** three times in succession: "*The king* comes back; *the king* sees the altar; *the king* approaches it and presents offerings [or "goes up"] on it." In the verses that immediately follow, *the king* is the understood subject of a string of action verbs ("offered," "poured," and "sprinkled"; v. 13). The narrator's use of naming has the effect of calling attention to his actions. What he does is on his own initiative; Yahweh is noticeably absent. The king's innovations are his own (in contrast with Solomon's innovations; see 1 Kings 8). Ahaz decides, for example, that the bronze altar will become an altar "for seeking guidance" — but he has not sought guidance in what he has done.

With Ahaz, Judah has a king who believes he can manipulate Yahweh, assuming for himself divine prerogative — like Jeroboam

---

[22]Hobbs, *2 Kings*, p. 218.
[23]Cogan and Tadmor, *II Kings*, p. 193.

and the kings of Israel who followed his apostasy (v. 3). As the storyteller moves to narrate the fall of Samaria, he has portrayed the king of Judah as a king who could sit on the throne of the doomed nation of Israel. The reader wonders if Ahaz has not secured for Judah a similar fate.

16:19-20 At his death, Ahaz is **buried with** [his fathers] **in the City of David**. "With his fathers" is an idiomatic way of describing death and burial. The Chronicler makes a point of saying that this wicked king is "not placed in the tombs of the kings of Israel" (2 Chr 28:27). **Hezekiah his son** reigns in his place.

2 KINGS 17

H. SAMARIA FALLS TO ASSYRIA (17:1-41)

In one of the more important chapters in Kings, the storyteller in chapter 17 narrates the fall of Samaria (vv. 1-6), explains in a sermonic style the reasons for Israel's punishment and exile (vv. 7-23), and portrays the resettlement of the land by Assyria (vv. 24-41). The anticipated judgment foretold by the prophet Ahijah finally comes to pass (1 Kgs 14:15-16), even though Hoshea does not follow the same evil course of the kings who were before him. The people have gone too far and cannot escape Yahweh's wrath. But the chapter also stands out for how the fall is framed. Unique to Kings, verses 7-23 represent a marked departure from the indirect style of the composition to this point. With language and thought borrowed from Deuteronomy, in exposition the storyteller carefully explains the reasons for the judgment on Israel. In much the same way Solomon's prayers at the dedication of the temple are theological discourse on the role of the temple in the life of Israel (1 Kings 8), the sermon offers theological justification for Yahweh's destruction of his people — only this treatise is couched in the narrator's voice. They have broken covenant and sinned against Yahweh. Yet, even such a straightforward excursus on Israel, like much of Kings, has another layer of meaning. It also explains why Judah suffers a similar fate — they follow the practices introduced by the kings of Israel (cf. vv. 13,18-20). So, those in exile who have suffered this disgrace should know to worship and keep covenant only with "Yahweh your God" (vv. 36-39).[1] When this interpretive frame is in place, the sto-

---

[1] It is possible to read vv. 24-41 as addressing a postexilic audience. Although, since there does not appear to be the same concern for the idolatry of the inhabitants of Samaria elsewhere in the postexilic literature, this is unlikely (ibid., p. 214).

ryteller has only to narrate the remaining episodes of the story of Judah to the time when they also are scattered among the nations.

1. Hoshea Is Seized, and Samaria Is Captured (17:1-6)

17:1-2 After describing the reign of Ahaz of Judah, who follows in the path of the kings of Israel (16:3), the storyteller turns to narrate the fall of Samaria. **Hoshea son of Elah** comes to the throne **in the twelfth year of Ahaz**. Yet, 15:30 says Hoshea assassinates Pekah in the twentieth (and final) year of Jotham, the father of Ahaz. Unless there is another, twelve-year coregency implied here (which doesn't correlate with the chronological notations in chs. 14–15), this synchronism clearly contradicts the earlier note.[2] Thiele believes a late editor of Kings, who did not understand dual dating or recognize the coregency (dual kingdoms) of Pekah with Menahem and Pekahiah, inserted this "artificial" note. Twelve years is exactly the length of time that, according to Thiele, Israel was splintered east and west (Menahem's ten years plus Pekahiah's two years). If Thiele is correct, it follows that the synchronisms for the reign of Hezekiah with Hoshea are also in error (18:1,9,10). A twelve-year coregency for Pekah in the Transjordan means Hoshea's nine-year reign ends before Hezekiah comes to the throne[3] — even though the repetition in 18:9-12 of much of the information in verses 5-6 has the effect of emphasizing that Samaria fell during the reign of Hezekiah.[4] One solution is that Hezekiah was coregent with his father Ahaz during the Assyrian assault on Samaria (see comments on 15:27-28 and the introductory comments to chs. 18–20). Nevertheless, with the available evidence (biblical and extrabiblical), it is impossible to make complete sense of the chronological notations in Kings.

Hoshea does **evil in the eyes of the LORD**, but **not like the kings of Israel who preceded him**. The statement reminds the reader of

---

[2]Gray emends the text to read "second" instead of "twelfth" in the MT (*I & II Kings*, p. 641), although there is little support for this change.

[3]Thiele, *Mysterious Numbers*, pp. 134-138. If Hoshea begins his reign in the twentieth year of Jotham (15:30), his nine-year reign would appear to be eclipsed by the sixteen-year reign of Jotham's son Ahaz as ruler of Judah (16:2).

[4]See Galil, *Chronology of the Kings*, p. 87.

Joram, who was not as bad as his parents, Ahab and Jezebel (3:2-3). Joram tore down the sacred stone of Baal that his father had made, but still continued in the sins of Jeroboam. Surprisingly, the characteristic "Jeroboam refrain" is missing for the reign of Hoshea (cf., e.g., 15:28). Does the storyteller mean to suggest by its absence that Hoshea turns from the sins of Jeroboam?[5] His restraint suggests an intentional gap that has the effect of framing the ensuing judgment. As in the case of Joram, reform is not enough to avert the calamity that is coming (cf. 9:24; 23:1-30). In spite of Yahweh's grace for Israel (13:23; 14:26-27), their sins have set them on a course that will not now be averted. Ironically, the king whose name means "salvation" (הוֹשֵׁעַ, hôšēaʿ; from yāšaʿ) will not be able to save Israel.

17:3-6 As indicated in the comments on 15:30, Tiglath-Pileser claims to have played a role in placing Hoshea on the throne of Israel, indicating that the king of Israel began his reign as a vassal of Assyria.[6] The author of the Kings account only mentions that Hoshea is **Shalmaneser's vassal** (literally, "servant"). Sometime during the reign of this Assyrian king, Hoshea withholds **tribute** and sends envoys to Egypt. **So king of Egypt** has engendered various identifications, including Osorkon IV and Tefnakhte I, "the Saite."[7] The essential point is that the king of Israel appeals to Egypt. Hoshea's actions recall the invective of the prophet Hosea: "Ephraim is like a dove, easily deceived and senseless — now calling to Egypt, now turning to Assyria" (Hos 7:11).[8] Later, Hezekiah apparently makes a similar appeal with disastrous results for Judah (18:21). Shalmaneser finds Hoshea a **traitor** (literally, "found in him a *conspiracy*," קֶשֶׁר, qešer[9]). Cohn astutely observes that this is narrated from Shalmaneser's point of view, which allows the author to

---

[5]See Provan, *1 and 2 Kings*, p. 247.

[6]*ANET*, p. 284.

[7]See Kenneth A. Kitchen, "Egypt, History of," in A*BD*; Edmund S. Meltzer, "So (person,)" in A*BD*.

[8]Hoshea's name appears on an eighth-century-B.C. seal ("Belonging to Abdi servant [i.e., 'official'] of Hoshea") in an "Egyptianizing style" — reflecting "important Egyptian cultural influence" in Israel (André Lemaire, "Name of Israel's Last King Surfaces in a Private Collection," *BAR* 21/6 [Nov./Dec. 1995]: 48-52).

[9]In its verb and noun forms, *qāšar/qešer* characterizes the kings of Israel (1 Kgs 15:27; 16:9,16,20; 2 Kgs 19:14; 10:9; 15:10,15,25,30; 17:4; for the kings of Judah, cf. 2 Kgs 11:14: 12:21[20]; 14:19; 21:23; 21:24).

avoid blaming Hoshea for the fall of Samaria. In the homily to follow, the storyteller claims that Yahweh is responsible for what happens to Israel.[10] Arresting Hoshea, Shalmaneser places him **in prison**
and **sieges Samaria** for **three years** (cf. 1 Kings 20, 2 Kings 6). After
which time, the city is **captured**, and the people **are deported**.

The king of Assyria settles the captives **in Halah, in Gozan on
the Habor River and in the towns of the Medes**. Halah and Gozan
indicate that some of the captives were exiled to the heart of
Assyria.[11] Israelite personal names have been found in documents
from Gozan, no doubt captives from Samaria.[12] Those taken to "the
towns of the Medes" probably had a more Spartan existence in a
border region. Sargon annexed territory belonging to the Medes in
716 B.C.[13] There is also clear evidence that Israelite deportees served
in the Assyrian military.[14] Samarians probably manned an elite chariot unit, and a deportee named Sama' from Samaria may even have
been a key advisor of Sargon. Israelite deportees were also probably
among the captives who built Sargon's capital of Dur-Šarruken
(Khorsabad).[15] Carved ivory plaques uncovered at Arslan Tash and
Nimrud probably include ivories taken during Assyrian military
campaigns against Israel.[16] Others were no doubt manufactured by
Israelite artisans exiled to Assyria.

Since the storyteller's theological aims restrict him to the highlights of the fall of Samaria, the exact sequence of events is difficult
to delineate precisely. In addition to the questions that emerge from
the text itself (e.g., "When was Hoshea imprisoned?"), extrabiblical
sources indicate that both Shalmaneser V and Sargon II participated in some way in Samaria's demise — in spite of the fact that only
Shalmaneser is mentioned by the author of Kings (vv. 3-4). The
Babylonian Chronicle (I, ll. 27-30) corroborates Shalmaneser's role

---

[10]Cohn, *2 Kings*, p. 117.

[11]Younger, "Deportations," 221-222. Younger shows that these destina-
tions correspond with information known about the reign of Sargon II
("The Fall of Samaria in Light of Recent Research," *CBQ* 61/3 [1999]: 461,
480).

[12]Cogan and Tadmor, *II Kings*, p. 197.

[13]Younger, "Deportations," 222-223.

[14]See *ANET*, pp. 284-285.

[15]Ibid., pp. 219-221; see Younger, "Fall of Samaria," 478.

[16]James D. Purvis, "Samaria (place)," in *ABD*.

with the notation: "On the twenty-fifth day of the month Tebeth, Shalmaneser (V) ascended the throne in Assyria [and Akkad]. He ruined/ravaged Samaria."[17] In as many as eight other inscriptions, however, Sargon claims credit for conquering the city, in one place naming himself "conqueror of Samaria (*Sa-mir-i-na*) and of the entire (country) of Israel."[18]

A variety of approaches has been tendered to reconcile these data. Dismissing the claims of Sargon, some argue that Shalmaneser alone captures Samaria and exiles its inhabitants to Assyria, as seems to be implied by the biblical text.[19] Others try to harmonize the Kings account with the data that clearly indicate Sargon played a key role. Galil believes verse 5 says only that Shalmaneser invades the "land of Samaria,"[20] at which time Hoshea goes out to meet the king of Assyria and is imprisoned. The Assyrians march against the capital of Samaria in 722 (the fourth year of Hezekiah, 18:9) and lay siege to the city. Only a few months later, Shalmaneser dies, and Sargon becomes king. As the new king moves to secure his throne, the city remains besieged by the Assyrian army (perhaps only a blockade with a reduced force). In the second year of his reign (720), Sargon completes the conquest of the city and exiles its inhabitants.[21] In another reconstruction, Cogan and Tadmor postulate that Shalmaneser imprisons Hoshea prior to an invasion in 724 or 723 B.C. The siege

---

[17]See Younger, "Fall of Samaria," 465; Galil, *Chronology of the Kings*, p. 84.

[18]*ANET*, p. 284; see Younger, "Fall of Samaria," 468-473; Galil, *Chronology of the Kings*, pp. 85-86.

[19]See, e.g., Thiele, *Mysterious Numbers*, pp. 163-168.

[20]For those who see the text implying two separate invasions by Shalmaneser, Hobbs is correct in suggesting that vv. 3-4 and 5-6 do not necessarily reflect separate military campaigns. These verse pairs are better read as parallel views of one campaign, first focusing on the king and then with an emphasis on the nation at large (*2 Kings*, p. 226; see Younger, "Fall of Samaria," 478).

[21]Galil, *Chronology of the Kings*, pp. 90-93. Both Galil and Cogan and Tadmor (based on Tadmor's research) date Sargon's destruction of Samaria to the second year of his reign (720 B.C.) in spite of the fact that his annals date the event to the year he began to rule (*ANET*, p. 284). But Sargon's accession year lasted only two months, and the following year he remained in Assyria. Apparently, scribes dated the campaign to his accession year so that the king would have a victory at the beginning of his reign (Galil, *Chronology of Kings*, p. 90; Cogan and Tadmor, *II Kings*, pp. 197, 200; see Younger, "Deportations," 217).

of Samaria ends during the winter of 722/721, with Shalmaneser's death coming shortly thereafter. Sargon assumes the throne, and the army withdraws from Israel as he consolidates his power. The Assyrian king returns in 720 and conquers the city, deporting 27,290 to Assyria.[22] With new editions of the relevant Assyrian texts at his disposal, Younger also believes there were two separate Assyrian assaults on Samaria, one by Shalmaneser that ends in an initial fall of Samaria in 722. Then, in a lightning campaign against the west, Sargon defeats a coalition of opponents in 720 and recaptures Samaria. Following the collapse of the city, a large number of Israelites are deported and resettled throughout the empire.[23]

Whatever the exact historical reconstruction, it does not follow that the Kings account is at odds with the actual sequence of events, or that the author of Kings did not have all of the pertinent information at his disposal (e.g., no idea that Sargon was involved).[24] The account of the end of the kingdom of Israel is another example where the writer's purposes are primarily theological and not a detailed history. In his cursory style, the storyteller in verses 5-6 telescopes the events surrounding the fall of Samaria that begin with the invasion of Shalmaneser and end in exile for Israel.[25] The deportation of Samarians to Assyria by Sargon is all part of a process that starts when Hoshea in his lack of faith in Yahweh turns to Egypt (vv. 3-4). That act precipitates Shalmaneser's response, which signals the beginning of the end for Israel. In his two-verse summary, the author is concerned with the fall and exile of Samaria, during the reign of Hoshea — which the following homily (vv. 7-23) will claim is effected not by the Assyrian kings, but by Yahweh!

---

[22]*ANET*, p. 284. See Cogan and Tadmor, *II Kings*, pp. 197, 199-200. Younger calls attention to the fact that the Great Summary Inscription lists the number as 27,290, while the Nimrud Prism has 27,280. He argues that the sum describes exiles "from both the district of Samaria and the city itself" ("Deportations," 218).

[23]Younger, "Fall of Samaria," 481-482.

[24]Contra Galil, *Chronology of the Kings*, pp. 93-94.

[25]Younger, "Fall of Samaria," 479; idem, "Deportations," 215.

2. Israel Is Exiled because of a Broken Covenant (17:7-23)

17:7-8 With Israel in exile, the storyteller moves to lay out the legal justification for Yahweh's actions against Israel in sermonic discourse. At the same time, he lays a foundation for interpreting the fall of Judah, with references to the similar track that the southern kingdom takes (vv. 13,18-19). For an audience in exile who knows what happened to both Israel and Judah, the treatise serves as a theological explanation for events and a call to remain faithful to Yahweh. Hermeneutically, the author accomplishes this by interpreting the Law of Moses with respect to Israel's rather checkered history. By way of introduction, verses 7-8 give an abstract of the whole discourse and offer the basic rationale for the demise of Israel. These things came to pass because the people **sinned against the LORD their God, who** *brought them up* [עָלָה, *'ālāh*] **out of Egypt from under the power of Pharaoh king of Egypt**. The language intentionally recalls the preamble to Yahweh's covenant with Israel and the Ten Commandments:[26] "I am the LORD your God who *brought you out* [from יָצָא, *yāṣā'*, "to go or come out"] of Egypt, out of the land of slavery" (Exod 20:2; cf. Deut 5:6). At the same time, the narrator's change in verbs from "brought out" to "brought up" adds an ironic turn. Because of their sins, the God who *brought up* (*'ālāh*) Israel from captivity in Egypt has allowed Assyria to *go up against* (*'ālāh*; vv. 3 ["*came up* to attack"], 5 [(2×) "*invaded*" and "*marched against*"]) Samaria and take his people back into captivity again.

Israel sins by worshiping (יָרֵא, *yārē'*, "fearing"; cf. 2 Kgs 17:25,28, 35,36,37,38,39) **other gods**, which was forbidden by the first commandment (Exod 20:3), and by following the **practices** [חֻקּוֹת, *ḥuqqôth*] **of the nations** Yahweh **had driven out** [הוֹרִישׁ, *hôrîš*, from *yāraš*] **before them** and that **the kings of Israel had introduced**. Instead of following the "practices" (*ḥuqqôth*, "decrees," v. 13) of Yahweh, they had chosen to go after the *practices* (*ḥuqqôth*) of the nations and their own wicked kings. Yahweh had given them the land *to possess* (יָרַשׁ, *yāraš*; cf., e.g., Deut 30:5,16,18; Josh 1:11,15; Judg 1:19; 2:6,21-23), *dispossessing* ("driving out," from *yāraš*; cf., e.g., Deut 4:38; 9:3-5; 11:23; 18:12) the abominable nations who were in the land before them. In Kings, *yāraš* functions as a key word in the

---

[26]Provan, *1 and 2 Kings*, p. 248.

story of Ahab and Jezebel to frame their evil influence on Israel (cf. 1 Kgs 21:15,16,18,19,26), which is now coming to fruition. In becoming like the nations, the people of God lost their right to remain in the land — so Yahweh *dispossesses* Israel and scatters them among the nations (cf. 1 Kgs 14:15; see comments on v. 24).

17:9-12 The discourse now moves to outline Israel's idolatrous practices, which in the eyes of Yahweh **were not right**.[27] At the top of the list, is worship on the **high places** that were built throughout the land, **in all their** *towns* ("cities," also in vv. 6,24,26,29). They also **set up sacred stones and Asherah poles on every high hill and under every spreading tree**. In Deuteronomy 12:2, Moses commanded them to "destroy completely" the places where the nations were worshiping, "on the high mountains and on the hills and under every spreading tree" (cf. 1 Kgs 14:23; 2 Kgs 16:4). **At every high place**, they **burned incense**; they also **did wicked things** and **worshiped idols**. Like **the nations whom the LORD had driven out** [גָּלָה, *gālāh*, "exiled/removed"] **before them**, they had become idolatrous. However, the gods of the nations are conspicuously absent in these verses (until v. 16). "Sacred stones and Asherah poles" represent male and female deities, but foreign gods are not named, leaving open the possibility that they were worshiping Yahweh and "his Asherah" as idols (see comments on 1 Kgs 14:14-16). When Israel became like the nations, they did more than worship other gods. They worshiped Yahweh in an idolatrous way. He became just another god to be manipulated and controlled with rituals, sacrifices, and offerings. And the high places especially fostered such an idolatrous view of Yahweh. At the high places, Israel mirrored the worship of the nations.[28]

---

[27]The connotation "secretly" for the verb חָפָא (*ḥāphā'*) in v. 9 is unlikely. Cogan and Tadmor suggest, "*ascribed* untruths" (*II Kings*, p. 205). Provan prefers, "*overlaid* things that were not right" (*1 and 2 Kings*, p. 251).

[28]Hobbs is correct in saying that high-place worship is found without negative commentary in passages like 1 Sam 9:16-24 (*2 Kings*, p. 232), but he is mistaken when he fails to see the negative characterization of high-place worship in Kings (except as it entails worshiping foreign gods). The high places do "become symbols of apostasy" (p. 232), but the issue is larger than foreign idolatry. When Jeroboam sets up high places with images for the God of Israel (and "his Asherah"), Yahweh is misrepresented, and his transcendence is compromised. At the high places, worship *to Yahweh* becomes idolatrous like the nations.

17:13-17 Both **Israel and Judah** were **warned** by Yahweh **through all his prophets and seers**. In Kings' characteristic style, where dialogue dominates, that message is recalled in Yahweh's voice: "**Turn** [שׁוּב, *šûb*] **from your evil ways** [דֶּרֶךְ, *derek*]. **Observe my commands and decrees, in accordance with the entire Law that I commanded your fathers to obey and that I delivered to you through my servants the prophets.**"[29] Moses' Law clearly passes judgment on the people and their sins, but Yahweh had patiently warned them to *repent* [*šûb*] and obey. In the string of phrases to follow, the verbs testify to Israel's *choice* to disobey Yahweh. They *would not listen*; *made* their necks *stiff* (like their forefathers who *did not trust* in Yahweh); *rejected* **his decrees, the covenant**, and his **warnings**; *followed* **worthless idols**; *imitated* **the nations**; and *did* **the things** Yahweh **had forbidden them to do**. They also *forsook* **all the commands** and *made* **for themselves two idols cast in the shape of calves and an Asherah pole** (see 1 Kgs 12:25-33; cf. Exod 32:4,8; Deut 9:12,16; Hos 8:5-6; 10:5-6; 13:2). They *bowed* **down to all the starry hosts**,[30] *worshiped* **Baal**, *sacrificed* **their sons and daughters in the fire**, *practiced* **divination and sorcery** (cf. Deut 18:9-14), and *sold* **themselves to do evil**.

The direction the people of Israel took was their own doing, yet the kings of Samaria contributed to the downfall. At least two allusions to kings of Israel from the preceding story stand out. Jeroboam altered worship in Israel and made the two calf-idols mentioned here (1 Kgs 12:25–14:20), which Hosea said would be taken from them in exile (Hos 10:5-6; cf. 8:5-6). And, when the narrator says, "[they] sold themselves to do evil," he is alluding to Ahab. Even though king of Israel, he "sold himself to do evil" ("urged on by Jezebel" and "going after idols, like the Amorites the LORD drove out [from *yāraš*] before Israel," 1 Kgs 21:25-26) and in the process sold out the people Yahweh had given him to shepherd. An obvious

---

[29]The phrase "my servants the prophets" appears in the commission of Jehu (see comments on 9:7).

[30]In this context, "all the starry hosts" (literally, "all the host of heaven") means worshiping the heavenly bodies (from a Canaanite background and not from Assyrian or Babylonian influence; cf. 23:4-5; Deut 4:19; 17:3). "The host of heaven" can also signify Yahweh's council or heavenly armies (cf. 1 Kgs 22:19; Josh 5:13-15). See E. Theodore Mullen, Jr., "Hosts, Hosts of Heaven," in A*BD*.

progression in Israel's sin is also indicated. The idolatrous worship that Jeroboam introduced devolved to bowing down before the host of heaven and the god Baal, and even to child sacrifice and sorcery — like the nations, whom Moses had warned them not to imitate (see Deut 18:9-13). Israel and her kings had broken covenant with Yahweh, and therefore legally deserved their fate. As Yahweh declared through the prophet Hosea, "Like Adam, they have broken the covenant — they were unfaithful to me there" (Hos 6:7). They gave themselves to *worthless* idols (הֶבֶל, *hebel*) — and they **became worthless** (*hābal*) in turn — **provoking** Yahweh **to anger** (cf. Deut 32:21; 1 Kgs 16:13,26).[31]

17:18-20 The writer shifts to delineate Yahweh's response. Yahweh is angry with Israel, and with Judah. The southern kingdom **followed the practices** (*ḥuqqôth*) of Israel (cf. Micah 1:13), who imitated the evil *practices* of the nations (cf. vv. 8,13). In fact, the language of verses 9-10,17 has its closest parallel with the description of the reign of Ahaz of Judah (16:3-4), and "starry host" and "sorcery" (vv. 16-17, not mentioned in the offenses of the kings so far) anticipate the sins of Manasseh of Judah to follow (21:3-6).[32] With this declaration, the entire sermon's invective turns on Judah. An audience in exile hears an explanation for the destruction of Jerusalem and the temple that Solomon built for Yahweh. And once more, verbs highlight the movement in the homily, as Yahweh acts. In his anger, he *removed* [from סוּר, *sûr*, "to turn aside"] **them from his presence**, *rejected* **all the people** [literally, "seed"] **of Israel**, *afflicted* them, *gave* **them into the hands of plunderers** [cf. Judg 2:14,16], **and** *thrust* **them** [from שָׁלַךְ, *šālak*] **from his presence**. The last phrase especially stands out. In 13:23, the storyteller affirmed that Yahweh had not been willing to "banish [from *šālak*] them from his presence," because of "the covenant he had made with Abraham, Isaac and Jacob." Apparently, Israel and her kings have gone too far, breaking the covenant Yahweh made with their fathers in the days of Moses. A reader in exile would now wonder about the covenant with

---

[31]The same phrase appears in Jer 2:5. Herbert B. Huffmon has demonstrated that Jer 2:4-13 is in the form of a "covenant lawsuit" ("The Covenant Lawsuit in the Prophets," *JBL* 78 [1959]: 285-295). Even though the lawsuit form itself does not appear in Kings, the storyteller is claiming that Israel is guilty of breaking covenant with Yahweh.

[32]Provan, *1 and 2 Kings*, pp. 248, 251.

Abraham — and the unconditional covenant with David (2 Samuel 7)! Have the sins of Israel and Judah nullified the promise to David that a son from his loins would have an eternal throne?

17:21-23 The sermon closes by underlining the cause that precipitated Israel's destruction. When Yahweh **tore** [קָרַע, *qāra'*] **Israel from the house of David** because of the sins of Solomon (cf. comments on 1 Kgs 11:26-40), Jeroboam chose to lead Israel another *way* (*derek*, "way/road," a key word in the story of Jeroboam; cf. 2 Kgs 17:13; see comments on 1 Kgs 13:33-34), causing them **to commit a great sin**. An echo of Aaron's "great sin" resounds (Exod 32:21,30, 31).[33] And, the refrain for the kings of Israel resurfaces, but now it emerges as an explanation for exile. When he set up the two idols to Yahweh, Jeroboam caused Israel to sin and set them on a course to ruin. With the verb *sûr* ("turn"), a recurring word in the Jeroboam refrain (cf., e.g., 2 Kgs 3:3; 10:29,31; 13:2), the narrator ironically casts Israel's fate. Since Israel and her kings **did not *turn* away** [*sûr*] **from** the sins of Jeroboam, Yahweh *caused them to turn* (*sûr*, **removed them** in the NIV; cf. v. 18) **from his presence**. This occurred even though he "warned [them] through all his servants the prophets" (v. 13). In his divine patience, Yahweh called on his people to *repent* (*šûb*, "turn/return," v. 13; also a key word in the Jeroboam story), but they refused. The delay in retribution could not continue. As Yahweh had *driven out* (*gālāh*) of the land the nations who were there before them (v. 11), he *exiled* (*gālāh*) Israel from the land he had given them. The audience in exile knows that, in spite of the promise to David, Judah suffers the same fate.

3. Samaria Is Resettled by Assyria (17:24-41)

Following the homily on the fall of Israel, one of the more curious sections in Kings appears, in which the storyteller describes the resettlement of the land of Samaria by the Assyrians. Foreign nationalities are exiled from their respective homelands to the region from which the people of Samaria are deported. This well-documented Assyrian policy was designed to assimilate conquered peoples into

---

[33]Cogan and Tadmor, *II Kings*, p. 206.

the empire and strengthen Assyrian control of its vast territories.[34]
But what is fascinating about this section of Kings is that the storyteller appears to be doing more than giving an historical account of
what happened in the territory of the northern kingdom after its
fall. In a rather long, healthy section that is dramatized with a report
to the king of Assyria and his response, the storyteller concerns himself with the religious practices of the people who resettle the land,
as if what matters most is that whoever lives in Israel must serve
Yahweh faithfully. Yet, by the end of the section, the reader suspects
that the storyteller has more in mind. His real concern is not the
abominable practices of those living in the land but the continued
faithfulness of his readers in exile.[35]

17:24 In exposition, the narrator begins by listing the nationalities from the broad expanse of the Assyrian empire who are resettled in the land, the **people from Babylon, Cuthah, Avva, Hamath
and Sephavaim**. These people inhabit the *towns* of **Samaria**, which
the storyteller apparently wants to emphasize (cf. "towns," v. 9; and
see below).[36] In the Nimrud Prism, Sargon claims, "I repopulated
Samerina more than before. I brought into it people from countries
conquered by my hands. . . . And I counted them as Assyrians."[37] In
the archaeological record, there is clear evidence that the Assyrians
rebuilt Israelite cities. Megiddo was reconstructed as the center of a
new Assyrian province on an entirely new plan that was uncommon
in Palestine. Dan experienced its greatest expansion since the Early
Bronze Age, and at numerous other sites Assyrian structures and
artifacts have been uncovered. Throughout the region, the material

---

[34]Cogan and Tadmor suggest, "This procedure, more than any other, created the new Assyrian empire" (ibid., p. 177). In contrast with the "unidirectional" deportations of Tiglath-Pileser (see comments on 15:29-30),
Sargon affects the typical Assyrian "bidirectional" policy of repopulating the
region with captives from other conquered lands, a policy designed to sta-
bilize the western border (Younger, "Deportations," 224-227).

[35]This view contrasts with those who see vv. 24-41 as designed to explain
the syncretism that existed in the north after the exile (cf., e.g., Hobbs,
2 Kings, pp. 227, 241).

[36]The fact that the designation "the Samarian" appears in the Assyrian
annals for Joash and Menahem, as early as the eighth century B.C., argues
against the view that "Samaria" is a new name for the Assyrian province of
the former state of Israel (Cogan and Tadmor, *II Kings*, p. 210).

[37]See Younger, "Fall of Samaria," 470.

remains reflect Assyrian influence. The open-court building design from Mesopotamia appears, for example, in the north in the last part of the eighth century B.C., replacing the typical Israelite four-room house. An Assyrian presence is also reflected in ceramics, seals, coffins, reliefs, and other categories of artifacts. In sum, the archaeology of this period demonstrates the Assyrian policy of rebuilding the towns of conquered nations,[38] which is also reflected in this text.

Then, with no fanfare, the narrator reports that these nations **took over** [יָרַשׁ, *yāraš*, "possessed"] **Samaria and lived in it** [literally, "in its towns"]. With his use of *yāraš*, the storyteller makes a bold claim. As already brought out (see comments on vv. 7-8), in the theology of the larger composition (Deuteronomy, and Joshua through 2 Kings) Yahweh has given Israel the land of Canaan to *possess* (*yāraš*). In order to give them the land that was promised to Abraham, Yahweh *dispossessed* (from *yāraš*) the nations from the land. Yet, Israel failed to *totally destroy* them (cf. Deut 7:1-11) and over time imitated their abominable practices. They therein lost their right to the land and are themselves now *dispossessed*.[39] The descendants of Abraham have been taken back into captivity, and Canaan has been returned to the nations. Subtly, with the use of a single word (*yāraš*), the narrator intimates the Exodus of Moses has been reversed, and the conquest of Joshua undone!

17:25-33 Because they do **not worship** [literally, "fear"] **the LORD** (cf. 1 Kgs 13:24 ff.; 20:35-36), Yahweh sends lions among the nations in the land. Framed in dialogue, a report reaches the Assyrian king that "**the people** [literally, "the nations"; also in vv. 8,11,15,29,33,41] who were **deported** [*gālāh*] **and resettled in the** *towns* **of Samaria** are being killed **because** [they] **do not know what the god of that country requires**." The king responds with a decree (represented in

---

[38]Ephraim Stern, "The Babylonian Gap: The Assyrians Impressed Their Culture on Israel . . . The Babylonians Left No Trace," *BAR* 26/6 (Nov./Dec. 2000): 45-51, 76; see Yigal Shiloh, "Megiddo: Iron Age," in *NEAEHL*; Biran, *Biblical Dan*, p. 261. Joseph Blenkinsopp challenges Stern's position that there was a contrasting "gap" following the Babylonian destruction of Judah ("The Babylonian Gap Revisited: There Was No Gap," *BAR* 28/3 [May/June 2002]: 36-38, 59; cf. Stern's rejoinder, "The Babylonian Gap Revisited: Yes There Was," *BAR* 28/3 [May/June 2002]: 39, 55).

[39]Hobbs writes, "the tables are completely turned" (*2 Kings*, p. 237).

dialogue) to resettle in Samaria one of the priests who had been exiled (*gālāh*) — to **"teach the people."** A priest returns, resides **in Bethel** (the location of one of Jeroboam's high places, 1 Kgs 12:29), and teaches **them how to worship the LORD.**[40] There is some irony in the fact that one of the Israelites exiled for not worshiping Yahweh correctly is brought back to teach the new inhabitants.[41] Yet, in spite of that instruction (or perhaps because of it), the nations make their own gods **in the several *towns* where they settled**. In fact, they worship their gods **in the *shrines* the people of Samaria**[42] **had made at the *high places*** [literally, "houses at the high places"; in the Old Testament only occurring in Kings; see 1 Kgs 12:31; 13:32; 2 Kgs 17:29,32; 23:19; cf. especially Jeroboam's "houses at the high places," 1 Kgs 12:31]. The people of the nations are at home in the Promised Land, worshiping in the *towns of Samaria* at the *high places* of Israel. A direct connection is being made with the word of Yahweh through the old prophet at Bethel: "For the message [of the man of God from Judah] declared by the word of the LORD against the altar in Bethel and against all the *shrines on the high places* in the *towns of Samaria* will certainly come true" (13:32). In the time of Josiah, the word of the man of God and the prophet of Bethel will come to pass (2 Kgs 23:15-20). The king of Judah will defile "all the *shrines at the high places* that the kings of Israel had built in the *towns of Samaria*" (v. 19). Before then, the exiled representatives of the nations worship their gods on the very same high places of Samaria. The people of the nations worship Yahweh, and, like Jeroboam, appoint **their own people to officiate for them as priests in the *shrines at the high places*** [cf. 1 Kgs 12:31-32]. In effect, the writer is insinuating that the high-place worship introduced in Israel by Jeroboam predisposed Israel to become like the nations.

After religious instruction from the priest in Bethel, the nations in the land **worship the LORD** but **also serve their own gods**, which are listed by the writer (vv. 30-31). Current knowledge about these

---

[40]Brueggemann suggests that this anticipates the mission of Ezra to Judah (*1 & 2 Kings*, p. 483).

[41]Cohn, *2 Kings*, p. 121.

[42]The text literally reads, "Samarians," only occurring here in the Old Testament. However, it is incorrect to read this term as "Samaritans," the sect mentioned in the New Testament (e.g., John 4). See Hobbs, *2 Kings*, p. 238; Nelson, *First and Second Kings*, p. 231.

deities is limited. The exiles from **Babylon** (destroyed after the revolt of Merodach-Baladan by Sennacherib in 689 B.C.[43]) worshiped the enigmatic **Succoth Benoth**. Joining Babylon in the revolt, the people of **Cuthah** were also exiled. Cuthah was the religious center for **Nergal**, the chief underworld deity in the Mesopotamian pantheon.[44] **Hamath** may be the Syrian city on the Orontes or a site in Elam, but the god **Ashima** is unknown. The gods **Nibhaz** and **Tartak** may be the Elamite deities Ibnahaza and Dirtaq, worshiped by the people of **Avva** (the Elamite city of Ama), although this is not certain. The location of **Sepharvaim** and the identity of the deities **Adrammelech** and **Anammelech** are also uncertain. However, since child sacrifice is associated with these two gods, מֶלֶךְ (*–melek*) in each name may represent Molech (see comments on 23:10-13).[45] After religious instruction, *exiles* in the land of Israel are *worshiping* (יָרֵא, *yārē'*, "fearing") Yahweh and *serving* (עָבַד, *'ābad*) **their own gods in accordance with the customs of the nations from which they had been brought** [*gālāh*]. Israel was to *worship* (*yārē"*) and *serve* (*'ābad*) only Yahweh (cf. Deut 6:13; 10:12,20).[46] For the reader, this description conjures up images of exiles from Israel and Judah, who are now scattered among the nations, also *worshiping* Yahweh — and *serving* the gods of the nations to which they have been exiled. Consequently, this section is ironic.[47] Yahweh is not simply a local deity who must be worshiped properly. In exile, the people must worship the God of Israel and all creation — exclusively (cf. 2 Kgs 5:15-18).

17:34-41 The phrase **to this day** indicates that at the time of the author's writing, these circumstances persist. It also connects this section with the sermon in verses 7-23 (cf. the same expression, [literally] "to this day," in vv. 23,41).[48] As in the homily, the language

---

[43]This information indicates the resettlement of Samaria progressed in phases over time (Cogan and Tadmor, *II Kings*, p. 209).

[44]For the fragmentary text of Nergal and Ereshkigal, see *ANET*, pp. 103-104.

[45]Cogan and Tadmor, *II Kings*, pp. 211-212; William J. Fulco, "Anammelech (deity)," in A*BD*; idem, "Nibhaz (deity)," in A*BD*; cf. Hobbs, *2 Kings*, pp. 238-239.

[46]Cogan and Tadmor, *II Kings*, p. 212.

[47]See Provan, *1 and 2 Kings*, pp. 250-251. Although, Provan does not consider the implications for an exilic community.

[48]Cogan and Tadmor, *II Kings*, p. 213.

that follows is drawn from Deuteronomy (vv. 35b-39). For example, the new inhabitants in the land do not **adhere to the decrees and ordinances, the laws and commands that the LORD gave the descendants of Jacob, whom he named Israel** (cf., e.g., Deut 5:31; 6:1; 7:11; 26:17; 30:16; however, "decrees, ordinances, laws, and commands" only appear together in 1 Kgs 2:3; 2 Kgs 17:34,37; 2 Chr 19:10; Neh 9:13; 10:30). They are not obeying the Law of Moses. Then, in the context of describing the practices of the nations in the land, the narrator adeptly transitions to the time when the God of Israel made a covenant with his people and quotes Yahweh (vv. 35b-39). Except, the charge occurs nowhere exactly like this in the Pentateuch. Hermeneutically, the author appears to be drawing on a variety of texts in a summary fashion (see, e.g., Deut 4:23; 5:2,6,15; 23:15; 30:16-17), which together declare that the "descendants of Jacob" (not just those living in the Promised Land) should not **worship other gods** or **forget the covenant**.

From a literary perspective, the change from the narrator's voice to the voice of Yahweh stands out. In the quotation, the people are addressed in second person, and Yahweh speaks in first person ("*You* [pl.] do not forget the covenant *I* have made with *you* [pl.]"). But Yahweh is also spoken of in third person (e.g., "To him you shall bow down"). The ambiguity has the effect of addressing more directly the audience in exile. The divine voice coalesces with the voice of the storyteller and speaks to an audience who has been exiled from the land: **"Worship the LORD your God: it is he who will deliver you from the hand of all your enemies."** The admonition is to refrain from worshiping the gods of the land to which they have been exiled. If there is any hope for deliverance, the people of Israel in exile must worship Yahweh. Only in him is there hope for return.[49]

Accordingly, the lengthy description of what happened in the land following the fall of Samaria becomes the point of application to the homily (vv. 7-23). Israel was scattered among the nations because of their many idolatries, which led to worshiping the gods

---

[49]Cohn is among those who miss the ironic nature of the composition. He writes that in vv. 24-41, "the writer sends [Israel] into literary exile, keeping his focus on the land that they vacated" (*2 Kings*, p. 120). Nelson, however, correctly sees this text as a "challenge" for the exiles "to avoid syncretism" (*First and Second Kings*, p. 232).

of the nations. Those addressed by the composition of Kings, the very ones exiled to Assyria and Babylon, must not succumb to the temptation to serve Yahweh *and* the gods of the nations. In a final observation, the storyteller asserts that the people of the nations in Samaria *would not listen*, continuing in their **former practices — worshiping the LORD, they were serving their idols.** Even in the day of the author (cf. vv. 23,34),[50] **their children and grandchildren continue to do *as their fathers* did.** If Yahweh is to be a savior for the descendants of Jacob in exile, they must not be "stiff-necked *as their fathers,*" who also "*would not listen*" and "did not trust in the LORD their God" (v. 14).

---

[50]In its final form, the composition must be dated at least as late as the mid-sixth century B.C., over a century and a half from the time of the fall of Samaria.

2 KINGS 18

VI. THE STORY OF THE FINAL DAYS
OF THE HOUSE OF DAVID (18:1–25:30)

A. THE PROMISE OF HEZEKIAH'S REFORM TURNS
PORTENTOUS FOR THE FORTUNES OF JUDAH (18:1–20:21)[1]

As already indicated (see comments on 17:1-2), the description of the reign of Hezekiah has chronological difficulties. Within the account itself, there are apparent inconsistencies. In 18:10 (see also 18:1-2), the fall of Samaria is dated to the sixth year of Hezekiah, which is synchronized with the ninth year of Hoshea king of Israel. Since Samaria fell to the Assyrians in 721/720 B.C., this would mean that Hezekiah ascended to the throne of Judah as early as 727/726 B.C. However, in 18:13 the storyteller dates the invasion of Sennacherib to the fourteenth year of Hezekiah. In view of the fact that Sennacherib's expedition against Judah is securely dated by extra-biblical sources to 701 B.C., this chronological notation situates the ascension of Hezekiah to 715 B.C., which would place his coronation well beyond the fall of Samaria to the Assyrians.

Several approaches have been taken to resolve the discrepancy:[2] (1) A few scholars have emended 18:13 to correspond with the other

---

[1]A parallel account of Hezekiah's reign, with minor variations, appears in Isaiah 36–38. The Chronicles account (chs. 29–32) differs significantly. Seventy percent of the account in Chronicles does not appear in Kings. For an outline of the differences between the Kings and Chronicles accounts, see Hicks, *1 & 2 Chronicles*, pp. 451-452. For an outline of the differences between Kings, Chronicles, and Isaiah in the account of the Assyrian invasion and related episodes, see pp. 483-484.

[2]The following outline of approaches is, for the most part, based on the summaries of Galil (*Chronology of the Kings*, pp. 98-100) and Andrew G. Vaughn (*Theology, History, and Archaeology in the Chronicler's Account of Hezekiah* [Atlanta: Scholars Press, 1999], pp. 8-14).

chronological notations in the account. For example, if "fourteenth" was originally "twenty-fourth," the chronological data are more consistent, though the fit is not exact.[3] (2) Others accept the accuracy of 18:13 and date the reign of Hezekiah from 715 B.C. Since the third military campaign of Sennacherib was the most significant military/political event during Hezekiah's reign, the chronological notation in 18:13 should be accepted as reliable (so, the fourteenth year = 701). For some, the reference to Tirhakah as "the Cushite King of Egypt" in 19:9 reinforces this dating and indicates that there were two campaigns by Sennacherib against Hezekiah (which have been combined by the author of Kings into one account). Tirhakah did not reign in Egypt until 690, which reinforces the lower chronology for Hezekiah's reign. It also suggests two Assyrian expeditions into Judah (in 701 and ca. 686), unless Tirhakah opposed Sennacherib as a general and not as the Pharaoh of Egypt (i.e., before his coronation in 690; see comments on 19:9).[4] (3) Another approach prefers the synchronisms in 18:1-2,9-10 that push the ascension of Hezekiah back to the third year of Hoshea. This interpretation corresponds with the view that Isaiah 14:28-29 indicates Ahaz and Tiglath-Pileser III died in the same year (727/726; however, this interpretation of Isaiah is by no means certain). The reference to Tirhakah, then, must be an anachronism, and the date for Sennacherib's invasion in the fourteenth year of Hezekiah cannot be accurate. Since fourteen corresponds with the fifteen extra years Hezekiah receives to equal the twenty-nine years of his reign ($14+15=29$; cf. 18:2), "the fourteenth year" originally must have been associated only with the miraculous healing story (20:1-11). A later redactor brought together the stories of Sennacherib's siege and Hezekiah's illness and dated them both to the fourteenth year of the king's reign. In a reconstructed sequence of events, Hezekiah ascends the throne in the 720s, becomes ill in his fourteenth year (ca. 713), receives an additional fifteen years, and is attacked by Sennacherib in 701 B.C.[5]

---

[3]See Gray, *I & II Kings*, p. 673.

[4]For the two campaign theory, see William H. Shea, "Jerusalem under Siege: Did Sennacherib Attack Twice?" *BAR* 25/6 (Nov./Dec. 1999): 36-44, 64.

[5]See Galil, *Chronology of the Kings*, pp. 102-104; Mordechai Cogan, "Sennacherib's Siege of Jerusalem: Once or Twice?" *BAR* 27/1 (Jan./Feb. 2001): 40-45, 69; Cogan and Tadmor, *II Kings*, pp. 228, 249-250.

(4) A final approach posits coregencies to explain the chronological discrepancies. For Thiele, the notations in 8:1-2,9-10 were added by an editor of Kings who did not understand the coregency of Pekah with Menahem (10 yrs.) and Pekahiah (2 yrs.), which explains the twelve-year discrepancy in the account of Hezekiah (ca. 727 vs. 715 B.C.). Thiele also theorizes that Manasseh was coregent with his father for the first ten or eleven years of his reign, placing his ascension in 698/697. This is necessary to account for the regnal data in Kings (99 years 6 months for the reigns of the kings from Manasseh to Jehoiachin) with the actual elapsed time from the proposed end of Hezekiah's reign (687/686) to Jehoiachin's imprisonment in 597 B.C. (= 89 yrs.).[6] Others resolve the chronological conundrum of Hezekiah's reign by positing a coregency with Hezekiah and his father Ahaz. Hezekiah becomes coregent with his father as early as 729/728 and assumes the throne as sole ruler at the death of Ahaz in 716/15. His twenty-nine year reign begins at that point, so that his fourteenth year is 701, the year of Sennacherib's invasion of Judah (see comments on 15:27-28; 17:1-2). This approach allows the synchronisms with the reign of Hoshea in 2 Kings 18:1,9-10 to stand, since they correspond with the period when Hezekiah was coregent with his father.[7]

Each of the proposals is flawed. There is little textual support for those who want to emend the chronological notation in 18:13. For the proponents of 18:13 as the reliable datum, the date of 715 B.C. for the ascension of Hezekiah is attractive and appears to correspond with the extrabiblical data. However, this approach disregards the tradition that Hezekiah began his reign in the days of Hoshea.[8] The view that Hezekiah came to the throne in the 720s (per 18:1-2,9-10) has the problem of explaining the reference to Sennacherib's invasion in the fourteenth year of Hezekiah (18:13). Attributing the notation to a redactor who conflates the invasion and illness stories has the effect of undermining the text, which

---

[6]Thiele, *Mysterious Numbers*, pp. 173-174.

[7]See Siegfried H. Horn, "The Chronology of King Hezekiah's Reign," *AUSS* 2 (1964): 48-52; Harold G. Stigers, "The Interphased Chronology of Jotham, Ahaz, Hezekiah and Hoshea," *BETS* 9 (1966): 88-90.

[8]The Chronicler indicates Hezekiah invited all Israel — north and south, after the fall of Samaria — to a Passover celebration in the first year of his reign (2 Chronicles 30; cf. 29:3).

connects the siege of Jerusalem and the miraculous healing of Hezekiah. The coregency approach has the advantage of explaining the chronological notations, so is the most reasonable course to follow. However, it does so without explicit justification from the text itself (e.g., a ten/eleven-year coregency for Hezekiah and Manasseh), other than the fact that "it works." With the available evidence, there is no completely satisfying solution to these chronological issues (see additional remarks in the comments below).

1. Hezekiah "Trusts" in Yahweh and "Pays Off" the King of Assyria (18:1-16)

18:1-8 The reign of **Hezekiah** (meaning "Yahweh has strengthened") is introduced with the standard regnal formula for the kings of Judah. However, his reign surpasses **all the kings of Judah, either before him or after him**. Later, when a similar statement is made about Josiah (23:25), the reader will wonder how the same thing could be said about both men. It is enough now to observe that in terms of his trust in Yahweh, there is **no one like him**.[9] He does **what is right in the eyes of the LORD, as his father David had done**. In a real way, this king is a true son of David, as allusions to David in the verses that follow will bear out. The careful reader wonders if perhaps the fortunes of Israel will be returned and the promise to David realized during the reign of this great king. And there is no caveat. Unlike the kings before him who allowed the high places to remain, Hezekiah **removes the high places, smashes the sacred stones and cuts down the Asherah poles**.[10] He also *crushes* (כָּתַת, *kāthath*) **the bronze snake Moses had made** (cf. Num 21:8-9). Cogan and Tadmor observe that *kāthath* is the same verb used in Deuteronomy 9:21 to describe the destruction of Aaron's golden calf (cf. Exod 32:20).[11] Parenthetically, the narrator adds that the people had been **burning incense to it**, calling it **Nehushtan** (in Hebrew a play on the

---

[9]See Gary N. Knoppers, "'There Was None like Him': Incomparability in the Books of Kings," *CBQ* 54/3 (July 1992): 411-431.

[10]In Hebrew, "Asherah pole" is singular (cf. 1 Kgs 15:13), which suggests to Provan that a certain object is in view (*1 and 2 Kings*, p. 254).

[11]Cogan and Tadmor, *II Kings*, p. 217.

words for bronze [נְחֹשֶׁת, *nᵉḥōšeth*] and snake [נָחָשׁ, *nāḥāš*]). In the ancient Near East, the serpent was often venerated as a god of healing. In the region of Syria-Palestine, numerous copper/bronze serpent figures have been found.[12] This first and only reference to Nehushtan in Kings emerges as a symbol of idolatry in Judah. In their worship to Yahweh, the people are acting like the nations around them. Hezekiah removes this obstacle to acceptable worship in Judah (cf. Deut 4:15-18).

Remarkably, the writer in Kings describes Hezekiah's reforms in just one verse (v. 4).[13] Enough is said to highlight the contrast between Hezekiah and his wicked father Ahaz, who is censured by the storyteller for his idolatrous practices. King Ahaz himself offered sacrifices and burned incense at the high places Hezekiah dismantles (see 16:4 and comments on ch. 16). Yet, with the emphasis on the high places in the preceding story of Judah, one would anticipate more detail on Hezekiah's reforms. Contrast with the Chronicler's account clarifies the storyteller's strategy in Kings. In Chronicles, most of the account concentrates on the reforms (2 Chr 29:3–31:21), with only one chapter dedicated to the events surrounding the campaign of Sennacherib (32:1-33). As mentioned, the author of Kings describes the reforms in one verse, the remainder of the account narrating the invasion and related events. Obviously, the two "theologians" have disparate purposes. While the Chronicler

---

[12]See Lowell K. Handy, "Serpent, Bronze," in *ABD*; cf. Hobbs, *2 Kings*, pp. 238-239.

[13]The reforms of Hezekiah (and Josiah to follow) should be understood as in no way effectively curtailing popular religion in Judah, which was syncretistic by nature (see Dever, *Biblical Writers Know*, pp. 196-197). In fact, Hezekiah may have addressed only sacrifices at altars other than at the temple in Jerusalem. At Tell Ḥalif, excavators uncovered a four-room domestic structure in which were found a shrine with two stone blocks (perhaps incense altars), a female pillar figurine, the base of a terra-cotta incense stand, and other related objects. The household shrine was destroyed during Sennacherib's invasion at the end of the eighth century, as the arrowheads and sling stones strewn across the stratum indicate (Oded Borowski, "Hezekiah's Reforms and the Revolt against Assyria," *BA* 53/2 [1995]: 151-152). These material remains probably reflect the syncretistic religious practices of many among the populace. The story of Kings will indicate that the reforms of Hezekiah and Josiah are not enough to cause God's people to return. Only exile will purge a remnant that can be brought back to resettle the land.

chooses to emphasize reform for his postexilic audience, the author of Kings wants to call attention to Hezekiah's response to the invasion of Sennacherib, the event that both politically and personally defines his reign. There will be more emphasis on reform during the reign of Josiah, who, in Kings, overshadows Hezekiah in this respect. For the author of Kings, Hezekiah's trust in Yahweh during the Assyrian crisis is the outstanding feature of his reign.[14]

Beyond any other king of Judah, Hezekiah **trusts** (בָּטַח, *bāṭaḥ*) in Yahweh, which in Kings functions as a key word in his story. The Hebrew *bāṭaḥ* occurs in Kings only nine times, all in the Hezekiah narrative (18:5,19,20,21[2×],22,24,30; 19:10).[15] However, the narrator's layered, ironic presentation will offer reasons for the reader to wonder if Hezekiah always trusts in Yahweh. The king also clings (דָּבַק, *dābaq*, **held fast** in the NIV) to Yahweh and does not turn aside from keeping the **commands the LORD had given Moses**. In Deuteronomy, *dābaq* is used to convey the idea of "holding fast to Yahweh" (cf. 4:4[adj.]; 10:20; 11:22; 13:4[5]; 30:20), which David's son Solomon was unable to do (cf. 1 Kgs 11:2). The king does not **cease** [סוּר, *sûr*, "turn aside"] **to follow** Yahweh, keeping the **commands the LORD had given Moses**. On his deathbed, David instructed Solomon: "Observe what the LORD your God requires: Walk in his ways, and keep his decrees and commands, his laws and requirements, as written in the *Law of Moses*, so that you may *prosper* [from שָׂכַל, *śākal*] in all you do" (1 Kgs 2:3). Hezekiah keeps the law. Yahweh is **with him**, and he is **successful** (from *śākal*) in whatever he does. So, Yahweh now has a faithful son of David sitting on the throne in Jerusalem. Yet, through the creative use of allusion, the narrator intimates that Hezekiah is more. "The LORD was with him; he was successful in whatever he undertook" parallels exactly a statement made about David: "In everything he had great success [from *śākal*] because *the LORD was with him*" (1 Sam 18:14; cf. 16:18; 18:12,14; 2 Sam 5:10; for other uses of the root *śkl*, see also 1 Sam 18:5,15,30).[16] In terms of his commitment to Yahweh and the Law of

---

[14]Knoppers, "Incomparability in the Book of Kings," 418; see Hicks, *1 & 2 Chronicles*, pp. 450-453.

[15]In Chronicles, *bāṭaḥ* appears in the Hezekiah narrative only once (32:10). See Hicks, 1 & 2 Chronicles, pp. 488-489.

[16]Provan, *1 and 2 Kings*, p. 253; cf. Hobbs, *2 Kings*, p. 253; see comments on 19:4,16.

Moses, Hezekiah is David. The king's victory over the **Philistines** reinforces this correspondence[17] (as other allusions in the verses to follow will secure). David and Hezekiah are the only kings who defeat the Philistines (cf., e.g., 1 Sam 18:27; 19:8).[18] The king's success even enables him to **rebel against the king of Assyria**.

When Hezekiah removes the high places, he is attempting to centralize worship in Jerusalem according to the injunction in Deuteronomy to worship at the *place* Yahweh would designate (see 2 Kgs 18:22; cf. Deut 12:1-28). For his religious fervor, he is listed among the good kings of Judah. He also may have been responding to the invective of prophets like Micah of Moresheth, who warned that Yahweh would punish Judah for their idolatrous practices (see Micah 5:10[9]-15[14]). In the time of Jeremiah, Micah is remembered for prophesying the destruction of Jerusalem, but Hezekiah sought Yahweh, who "relented" from the disaster that he had pronounced (Jer 26:18-19).[19]

Archaeological discoveries appear to corroborate Hezekiah's reforms. At Beersheba, for example, Yohanan Aharoni uncovered sandstone blocks, three with "horns" and a fourth with evidence that its horn had been broken off, that were used in the subsequent construction of storehouses. The blocks were apparently the pieces of a four-horned altar, which had been dismantled prior to the construction of the storehouses. On one of the blocks, the form of a serpent was carved in the soft stone (a representation of Nehushtan?). Since the storehouses appear to have been destroyed in Sennacherib's invasion of Judah in 701 B.C., the altar probably was demolished as part of Hezekiah's reforms.[20] At Arad, Aharoni also excavated an Israelite sanctuary from the time of the monarchy. The temple consisted of a courtyard and a sacred area with an inner chamber as a "Holy of Holies," in which were two standing stones (for Yahweh and his Asherah?) accompanied by a pair of horned altars for incense on the steps approaching the inner shrine. In the

---

[17]For the political setting for Hezekiah's campaign against Philistia to undermine Assyrian control in the west, see Cogan and Tadmor, *II Kings*, p. 217; Hobbs, *2 Kings*, p. 253.

[18]Provan, *1 and 2 Kings*, p. 253.

[19]See Cogan and Tadmor, *II Kings*, p. 220.

[20]See Dale W. Manor, "Beer-Sheba (place)," in *ABD*; Ze'ev Herzog, "Tel Beersheba," in *NEAEHL*; Dever, *Biblical Writers Know*, pp. 180-181.

courtyard stood a sacrificial altar of unworked fieldstones, measuring five by five cubits and three cubits in height — exactly the dimensions of the altar in Exodus 27:1. Although the stratigraphy of the site has been called into question,[21] in Stratum VIII a layer of fill covered the courtyard altar, which Aharoni interpreted as resulting from the reforms of Hezekiah. The incense altars appear to have been buried when the sanctuary was dismantled, indicating reverence for the temple's sacred objects.[22]

There are reasons to believe there may have been political ramifications to Hezekiah's reforms. Oded Borowski argues that the religious reforms must have been "part of Hezekiah's grand scheme which included preparations for the revolt against Assyria to gain independence."[23] When he centralizes worship in Jerusalem, the king also consolidates his political control over his realm and over its economy. Offerings pour into the capital, for which Hezekiah constructs additional storehouses (2 Chr 31:5-11). Political power now moves from local shrines and is concentrated in Jerusalem, yet the politically astute king provides for the priests and Levites whose income is lost by these reforms (2 Chr 31:15,19). In fact, Hezekiah's "grand scheme" appears to be exhibited in the much-discussed *lmlk* jar handles (stamped with *lmlk* [ילמ = לְמֶלֶךְ], "belonging to the king"), now securely dated to the late eighth century. These handles are generally believed to represent the centralized distribution of supplies in preparation for an Assyrian invasion. Hezekiah's overture towards the former subjects of the northern kingdom to observe the Passover in Jerusalem (2 Chr 30:1-2,6-12) would only further rein-

---

[21]David Ussishkin argues that the Arad temple was probably constructed in the seventh century and destroyed early in the sixth century after the reforms of both Hezekiah and Josiah ("The Date of the Judaean Shrine at Arad," *IEJ* 38/3 [1988]: 142-157). Herr associates the destruction of the sanctuary with the reforms of Josiah ("The Iron Age II Period," p. 161).

[22]See Dale W. Manor, "Arad (place)," in *ABD*; Dever, *Biblical Writers Know*, pp. 181, 183, Miriam Aharoni, "Arad: The Israelite Citadels," in *NEAEHL*; Miriam Aharoni, Ze'ev Herzog, and Anson Rainey, "Arad — An Ancient Israelite Fortress with a Temple to Yahweh," *BAR* 13/2 (March/April 1987): 16-35; Jesse C. Long, Jr., "Putting God in His Place," *GA* 132/2 (Feb. 1990): 37. For a photograph of the buried altars at discovery, see Borowski, "Hezekiah's Reforms," 151.

[23]Borowski, "Hezekiah's Reforms," 148.

force him politically.[24] The evidence suggests that the king of Judah consciously set out to restore the kingdom of Solomon.

Chronicles indicates that the reforms were begun in the first year of Hezekiah's reign, well before the Assyrian invasion in 701 B.C. (2 Chr 29:3; 30:13; as 2 Kgs 18:22 implies).[25] With the death of Sargon in 705, Hezekiah apparently seizes the opportunity to exercise his political independence by rebelling from Assyrian domination. It may have been during this time, if not before, that "Hezekiah's Tunnel" was constructed to carry water from the Gihon Spring to the western side of the city (cf. 2 Chr 32:3-4,30). The "Broad Wall" exposed to the west of the temple mount by Nahman Avigad in the 1960s and the recently discovered eighth-century wall that enclosed the Gihon Spring may have been constructed at this time to secure Judah's defenses against an Assyrian invasion (cf. 32:5-6).[26] Hezekiah's religious and political acts appear to have been intertwined, an idea that is not at odds with the biblical text. Following the comment that Yahweh was with Hezekiah and enabled his successes (v. 7), the narrator says **he rebelled against the king of Assyria and did not serve him**, insinuating that Hezekiah's rebellion is a choice to serve Yahweh instead of the king of Assyria, a theme which will resurface in the drama that follows.

18:9-12 Once more, the storyteller reminds the reader of the fall of Samaria (cf. 17:1-6). In these verses, he synchronizes Shalmaneser's assault on Hoshea and the northern kingdom with the reign of Hezekiah (for comments on the synchronisms with the reign of

---

[24]Ibid., pp. 148-153. The fact that a majority of shekel weights that have been uncovered in Palestine come from Judah in the mid-eighth to the seventh century B.C. suggests that Hezekiah may have introduced a program of royal standardization and supervision of commerce with his reforms (which was continued by Josiah). Dever suggests that serious reform would have attempted "to eliminate corrupt business practices by standardizing weights and measures under royal administration" (*Biblical Writers Know*, pp. 225-226).

[25]Hicks, *1 & 2 Chronicles*, p. 454; cf. Cogan and Tadmor, *II Kings*, pp. 219-220.

[26]Hershel Shanks, "Everything You Ever Knew about Jerusalem Is Wrong (Well, Almost)," *BAR* 25/6 (Nov./Dec. 1999): 20-29. Proponents of the two-invasion hypothesis argue that this construction was begun after the invasion in 701 in preparation for Sennacherib's anticipated return (see Shea, "Jerusalem under Siege," 36-44, 64).

Hoshea, see above). The repetition sets the stage for Sennacherib's invasion of Judah. It also frames Hezekiah's response to the king of Assyria. In the background of Hezekiah's actions lie the destruction and exile of the northern kingdom. For a first-time reader, tension is created. Will the king of Judah be able to triumph over the king of Assyria? Will his obedience to the law and commitment to Yahweh cancel out the anticipated effects of the reign of Ahaz? While Hezekiah in the end does overcome, an exilic audience knows that the righteous king will not be able to alter a similar outcome for Judah.

18:13-16 Sennacherib king of Assyria attacks all the fortified cities of Judah and captures them (for the role v. 13 plays in deciphering the chronology of Hezekiah's reign, see above). The almost identical language used in verse 9, which describes Shalmaneser's assault on Samaria, guides a first-time reader to anticipate the same fate for Judah.[27] Narrative tension increases. If Hezekiah is so righteous, how does one explain the king's plight?[28] In Sennacherib's annalistic account of the campaign against Judah, he echoes the biblical assertion that Hezekiah did not serve him (v. 7) and claims to have conquered forty-six fortified cities in Judah: "As to Hezekiah, the Jew, he did not submit to my yoke, I laid siege to 46 of his strong cities, walled forts and to the countless small villages in their vicinity, and conquered (them)." He also claims to have taken from Judah "200,150 people" as booty.[29] The list of cities suggests a strategy of eliminating opposition on the coastal plain and in the Shephelah (cf. Micah 1:10-16; Isa 1:7-8).[30] His siege and sack of one of the cities, the fortified town of Lachish (cf. vv. 14,17; 19:8), are well documented in the archaeological record. At the ancient site of Nineveh (Kuyunjik, Iraq), the nineteenth century explorer/archaeologist Sir Austin Henry Layard exposed the palace of Sennacherib, in which were found the now famous reliefs commemorating the conquest of Judah. The carved stone slabs that decorated one of the rooms of his

---

[27]Hobbs, *2 Kings*, p. 247. Verses 14-16 are missing in the parallel accounts in Isaiah 36 and 2 Chronicles 32, which Hobbs reasonably explains as being due to scribal error (pp. 247, 255).

[28]Nelson, *First and Second Kings*, p. 236.

[29]*ANET*, p. 288. The translation in *ANET* is from the Oriental Institute Prism, which parallels the Taylor Prism. The Rassam cylinder is somewhat more expansive (see Cogan and Tadmor, *II Kings*, p. 247).

[30]Hobbs, *2 Kings*, pp. 254-255.

palace[31] portray in various stages the siege and destruction of the city of Lachish (which protected the route to Jerusalem from the southwest), along with the subsequent capture and exile of defenders to regions beyond Judah. At the high point of the battle, the reliefs picture seven battering rams hammering the fortifications of the city as defenders throw objects, including stones, torches, and even a chariot, on the advancing Assyrian forces. Additional panels demonstrate the brutality of Assyrian siege warfare, with gruesome scenes of impaled corpses, captives flayed alive, and summary decapitations. In British and Israeli excavations at Tel Lachish, archaeologists have confirmed the conflagration with a massive layer of destruction debris, in which were found sling stones and arrow points littering the area of the assault. A massive siege ramp and a mass grave of approximately 1,500 individuals further elucidate the battle for Lachish and its carnage.[32]

In the context of the devastation wrought on Judah, Hezekiah sends a message **to the king of Assyria at Lachish**. In the message, Hezekiah admits, **"I have done wrong [**חָטָא**, *ḥāṭā'*, literally, 'I have sinned']. Withdraw from me, and I will pay whatever you demand of me."** The king's word choice is interesting. Is he in any way acknowledging that Judah's plight is the result of his indiscretions?[33] While the narrator has lauded the character of this righteous king of Judah, his actions in the events that transpire call into question his complete faithfulness to Yahweh. The king of Assyria demands from Hezekiah **three hundred talents of silver and thirty talents of gold**. In his account, Sennacherib claims to have taken in tribute "30 talents of gold, 800 talents of silver," and an array of other precious items.[34] The degree of correspondence between the accounts suggests that the Assyrian king is describing the same events.[35] As had

---

[31]The palace was completed ca. 694 B.C. with a work force that included Judean captives.

[32]See David Ussishkin, *The Conquest of Lachish by Sennacherib* (Tel Aviv: Tel Aviv University, The Institute of Archaeology, 1982); idem, "Lachish," in *NEAEHL*; Hershel Shanks, review of *The Conquest of Lachish by Sennacherib*, by David Ussishkin, *BAR* 10/2 (March/April 1984): 48-65; Dever, *Biblical Writers Know*, pp. 168-171; Jesse C. Long, Jr., "Confirming a Highway to Heaven," *GA* 138/3 (March 1996): 34-36.

[33]See Provan, *1 and 2 Kings*, p. 255.

[34]*ANET*, p. 288.

[35]Although, Sennacherib says that the tribute was sent "later, to Nineveh"

Ahaz (16:8), the king of Judah proceeds to give the king of Assyria **all the silver that was found in the temple of the LORD and in the treasuries of the royal palace**. He also **strips off the gold with which he had covered the doors and doorposts of the temple of the LORD for the king of Assyria**. No doubt for emphasis, the storyteller twice mentions that Hezekiah takes treasures from the house of Yahweh. Ironically, the Chronicler begins his account of Hezekiah's reforms with the note that the king "opened the doors of the temple of the LORD and repaired them" (2 Chr 29:3). Hezekiah now takes a symbol of that reform, the gold from the doors and doorposts of the house of Yahweh and in fear offers it in tribute to another "lord." Hobbs asserts that the king's act in effect cancels out the reforms.[36] The superlative account of Hezekiah's reign now turns sour. In the book of Kings, looting the temple and palace treasures is always a sign of disfavor, representing *a lack of trust* in Yahweh (cf. 1 Kgs 14:25-28; 15:17-19; 2 Kgs 12:18-19; 14:11-14; 16:7-9; 24:10-13).[37] When kings do not turn to Yahweh with complete trust, Yahweh's house often suffers. At the end of this story, Hezekiah is censured for showing messengers from Babylon the treasures of his kingdom. At the end of the larger story, Yahweh himself will take the treasures of the kings of Judah and of the temple Solomon built and give them to the king of Babylon — because of the sins of his people and their kings.

2. The King of Assyria Threatens Hezekiah
and Defies the God of Judah (18:17-37)

18:17-25 The narrator leaves not an inconsiderable gap between verses 16 and 17. In verse 16, Hezekiah paid Sennacherib tribute in gold from the temple, so that the foreign aggressor would withdraw from Judah. In verse 17, **the king of Assyria** sends representatives

---

(ibid.). For suggestions to explain the difference between the amounts in the two accounts (e.g., the Kings record may be incomplete), see Hobbs, *2 Kings*, p. 255; Cogan and Tadmor, *II Kings*, p. 229.

[36]Hobbs, *2 Kings*, p. 248.

[37]Mullen sees the "despoliation of the temple" notices as being connected with the failure to consolidate worship in Jerusalem, except in the case of Hezekiah, where it represents a lack of complete trust in Yahweh ("Crime and Punishment," 247).

with a large army to Jerusalem to force Hezekiah into submission. Missing in the story is what happened after the tribute was paid. To fill in the gap, some argue the author of Kings has conflated accounts of two invasions by Sennacherib. Verses 13-16 describe a campaign against Judah in 701 B.C., in which the king of Assyria retreated after tribute was paid. Following the Assyrian withdrawal, Hezekiah bolsters his defenses and makes overtures to Egypt for assistance, as he prepares for another invasion. From verse 17 through chapter 19, the story outlines events surrounding a second campaign against Judah, around 686 B.C.[38] While at first glance this view may seem improbable, the reader has already seen the story-teller telescope historical events for his theological purposes, when he describes the fall of Samaria and exile of its citizens in just two verses (see comments on 17:5-6). But the gap in the story could also be explained by other events, like some indiscretion on Hezekiah's part, which the storyteller has chosen not to relay. Either way, the reader is left with a break that has an important literary role in the story — in that it casts a shadow over the tribute that the king of Judah pays Sennacherib. Hezekiah pays a hefty sum of gold and silver and is not rescued from his plight. Whether the events narrated in verses 17 ff. transpire immediately on the heels of the tribute or several years afterward, the result is the same. The king of Judah "trusts" in tribute (and apparently in alliances) — in human, political means to alleviate his dire situation, without inquiring of Yahweh — and he ends up worse off than before!

The three eminent representatives from Sennacherib (the Assyrian titles are, literally, "viceroy," "chief eunuch," and "chief butler"; however, the titles may not represent their functions[39]) signify the gravity of their mission. **Eliakim son of Hilkiah the palace administrator** [literally, "who was *over the house*"], **Shebna the secretary,**[40] **and Joah**

---

[38]For a summary of this position, see Shea, "Jerusalem under Siege," 36-44, 64. Against the two-campaign theory, there are no annalistic inscriptions of Sennacherib that refer to a second campaign, although, his inscriptions for 688–681 B.C. are, for the most part, missing (see Cogan, "Sennacherib's Siege," 40-45, 69). Also, it is difficult to sandwich two invasions into Level III at Lachish. For a discussion of Tirhakah's role in this theory, see comments on 19:9.

[39]Cogan and Tadmor, "*II Kings*, pp. 229-230; Hobbs, *2 Kings*, p. 256.

[40]For Isaiah's judgment on Shebna for building an ostentatious sepulcher,

son of Asaph the recorder meet the Assyrian delegation **at the aqueduct of the Upper Pool, on the road to the Washerman's Field**. Ironically, this is the same place the prophet Isaiah met Ahaz with the message not to appeal for help from the Assyrians against the Syro-Ephraimite coalition (Isa. 7:3). Now, in the same location, the Assyrian king is demanding that Hezekiah submit.

The **field commander** (רַב־שָׁקֵה, *rab-šāqēh*, better understood as a member of the king's court, probably selected for his knowledge of Hebrew[41]) speaks for Sennacherib. He prefaces his speech with the messenger formula (**"This is what the great king, the king of Assyria, says"**). Through naming, he shows disrespect to the king of Judah, who is simply named **"Hezekiah,"** in contrast with **"the great king"** for Sennacherib. The narrator calls attention to the lack of respect by naming the king of Judah "King Hezekiah" in 19:1.[42] At the beginning of his speech, the field commander expresses the key question in the story: **"On what are you basing** [בָּטַח, *bāṭaḥ*, literally, 'trusting'] **this confidence** [בִּטָּחוֹן, *biṭṭāḥôn*] **of yours?"** On the level of event, the representative of the king of Assyria is trying to drive a wedge between Hezekiah and his subjects who are defending the city of Jerusalem (see below).[43] On another level, however, his speeches call into question Hezekiah's actions. In a rather brilliant way, the narrator allows the field commander to convey important information in the story and verbalize the question of the narrative. He has already said that, like no other king of Judah, Hezekiah *trusts* Yahweh. Nevertheless, the field commander raises questions about his trusting. (The verb "trust" [*bāṭaḥ*] occurs eight times in the Assyrian speeches/messages [vv. 19,20,21(2×), 22,24,30; 19:10].) Is Hezekiah **depending** (*bāṭaḥ*) on **military strength** to overcome the Assyrians, even *depending* [*bāṭaḥ*] **on Egypt** (for **chariots and horse-**

---

see Isa 22:15-25. Eliakim would replace Shebna as royal steward ("over the house"), which apparently happened by the time of the Assyrian invasion. The tomb of Shebna may have been found in the modern village of Silwan. In the shadow of the temple mount, the tomb bore an inscription with the title "over the house," which connects the Kings and Isaiah references to Shebna (see Dever, *Biblical Writers Know*, pp. 219-220).

[41]Cogan and Tadmor, *II Kings*, p. 230.

[42]Cohn, *2 Kings*, pp. 129, 133.

[43]For parallels of Assyrian representatives attempting to intimidate defenders, see Cogan and Tadmor, *II Kings*, pp. 242-243.

men, v. 24) for deliverance? The narrator has not informed the reader of such overtures, but since the field commander knows other information that is reliable (cf. v. 22), this appears likely. And it sheds more light on the actions of Hezekiah. The prophet Isaiah warned Hezekiah not to *trust* in Egypt: "Woe to those who go down to Egypt for help who rely on horses, who trust [*bāṭaḥ*] in the multitude of their chariots and in the great strength of their horsemen, but do not look to the Holy One of Israel or seek help from the LORD" (Isa 31:1; cf. 30:1-7).[44] A careful reader wonders if perhaps Hezekiah has gotten into this situation because he has not *trusted completely* in Yahweh.

A recently published artifact may bring to life Hezekiah's overtures toward Egypt. Impressed with the seal of Hezekiah, a clay bulla has surfaced (in the collection of Shlomo Moussaieff, the second such bulla to appear) with the inscription: "Belonging to Hezekiah, (son of) 'Ahaz, king of Judah" (or "Judah/Belonging to Hezekiah, [son of] 'Ahaz, King!). Also impressed on the bulla is a two-winged beetle (a dung scarab) pushing a ball of dung and mud. In the ancient Near East, the dung scarab represented the solar deity as the rising sun, which was also symbolized by the winged sun disk. On the *lmlk* jar handles, now securely dated to Hezekiah's reign, two-winged sun disks (and four-winged beetles) regularly appear. According to Frank Moore Cross, the image on the bulla is of Phoenician influence and signifies "the deity bringing salvation," as is reflected in Malachi 4:2: "The sun of righteousness will rise with healing in its wings."[45] Against this view, Meir Lubetski argues that the iconography on the Hezekiah bulla is Egyptian and reflects Judah's political posturing in an alliance with Egypt. Also, as the two wings symbolized pharaoh's control of Upper and Lower Egypt, so the symbol may have been chosen to signify Hezekiah's dominion over a united Israel (cf. 2 Chronicles 30–31). Lubetski adds that it is not a coincidence that the king of Judah names his son Manasseh,

---

[44]John T. Willis, *Isaiah*, The Living Word Commentary (Abilene, TX: ACU Press, 1980), p. 310; Hobbs, *2 Kings*, p. 257.

[45]Frank Moore Cross, "King Hezekiah's Seal Bears Phoenician Imagery," *BAR* 25/2 (March/April 1999): 42-45, 60; cf. Mark S. Smith, "The Near Eastern Background of Solar Language for Yahweh," *JBL* 109/1 (1990): 36-37.

the name Joseph gave his firstborn son in Egypt (Gen 41:50-51).[46] If the seal with the dung scarab represents the royal insignia for the reign of Hezekiah (reinforced by the *lmlk* jar handles), then it is plausible that the symbol also reflects Hezekiah's conscious move toward Egypt, which is discouraged by the prophet Isaiah and underlies the story of Hezekiah in Kings.[47]

The field commander's carefully crafted speech shifts to directly call into question Hezekiah's trust in Yahweh. In so doing, he transitions from speaking to Hezekiah (second person singular) to addressing the people (second person plural): **"And if you [pl.] say to me, 'We are depending [*bāṭaḥ*] on the LORD our God'—isn't he the one whose high places and altars Hezekiah removed?"** With this comment, the author opens a window onto internal Judean politics during Hezekiah's efforts to centralize worship in Jerusalem.[48] No doubt, the Assyrians have spies and informants among the populace.[49] Even though the king has made efforts to appease the priests who were economically displaced by the restructuring (cf. 2 Chr 31:15,19), there must have been strong opposition to his reforms. One can imagine the dissenting charge in Judah: "Yahweh has brought this calamity on us because Hezekiah has destroyed his high places and torn down his altars!"

---

[46]Meir Lubetski, "King Hezekiah's Seal Revisited," *BAR* 27/4 (July/Aug. 2001): 44-50. Referencing two newly revealed Hezekiah bullae decorated with a two-winged sun disk (with sun rays shooting from the top and bottom and Egyptian ankh ["key to life"] symbols on each side), Robert Deutsch believes that with the two-winged scarab and sun disk Hezekiah "was simply appropriating generally accepted icons of royal power and not importing meaning from either Phoenicia or Egypt" ("New Bullae Reveal Egyptian-Style Emblems on Judah's Royal Seals," *BAR* 28/4 [July/Aug. 2002]: 51).

[47]In the seventh and sixth centuries, seals from Judah are more aniconic (without images), perhaps indicating that the reforms of Josiah were more pervasive than the reforms of Hezekiah, as the author of Kings indicates (see Dever, *Biblical Writers Know*, pp. 236-237; and comments on 23:1-30). Although, Lubetski believes the decline in the use of images on seals, and especially the beetle as a royal symbol, reflects a change in political loyalties away from Egypt ("Hezekiah's Seal," 50).

[48]See Cohn, *2 Kings*, p. 130.

[49]Sennacherib mentions massive desertions from the king of Judah, which could also explain the field commander's strategy of undermining confidence in Hezekiah (*ANET*, p. 288).

In his initial speech, however, the commander saves his best weapon for last: **"The LORD himself told me to march against this country and destroy it."** For a modern reader, such a claim at first glance seems dubious, but for the Judeans within earshot, this would have been considered well within the realm of possibility. After all, Sennacherib's military successes in Judah must say something about Yahweh's role in recent events. Even more so, a careful reader suspects that the Assyrian king is correct. In the preceding homily, he has heard the writer claim that Yahweh, not the Assyrians, was responsible for the fall of Samaria (17:7-23). Commenting on the Assyrian invasion in 701, the prophet Isaiah makes a similar claim: "Woe to the Assyrian, the rod of my anger, in whose hand is the club of my wrath! I send him against a godless nation, I dispatch him against a people who anger me, to seize loot and snatch plunder, and to trample them down like mud in the streets" (Isa 10:5-6; cf. v. 24). Yahweh has decreed that Sennacherib tomahawk Judah and bring them down because of their sins.[50] Ironically, there is truth to the Assyrian's claim, even though his arrogance will shortly push Yahweh to act for Hezekiah.

18:26-37 The representatives from Hezekiah ask the commander to speak in **Aramaic**, not in **Hebrew** (literally, "Judean"), for fear of swaying **the people on the wall.** For the first time, the reader is told there are other Judeans overhearing the conversation.[51] The speech is not for Hezekiah. It is designed to foment insurrection among the people. The commander acknowledges that his message is also for those on the wall, who will suffer the same fate as Hezekiah and his government officials. In Hebrew, he directly addresses the **men sitting on the wall**, continuing his attack on Hezekiah: **"Do not let Hezekiah deceive you. He cannot deliver** [הַצִּיל, *haṣṣîl*, from *nāṣal*] **you from my hand. Do not let Hezekiah persuade you to trust** [*bāṭaḥ*] **in the LORD."** The field commander quotes Hezekiah as claiming that Yahweh will not give **this city into the hand of the king of Assyria.** The verb "deliver" (forms of *nāṣal*) stands out in the Assyrian's speech; this verb occurs thirteen times in Kings, twelve times in the Hezekiah story (18:29,30[2×],32,33[2×],34,35[2×];

---

[50]Willis, *Isaiah*, pp. 194-195.
[51]See Cohn, *2 Kings*, p. 131.

19:11,12; 20:6; cf. 17:39).[52] The repetition of this key word highlights an underlying question in the narrative: "Who will be able to *deliver* Jerusalem, Sennacherib or Yahweh?" In language reminiscent of Deuteronomy 8:7-9, the commander even declares that if the people surrender, they will be taken to **"a land of grain and new wine, a land of bread and vineyards, a land of olive trees and honey."**[53] In effect, he is offering another "promised land," if they would only surrender to the king of Assyria.[54] Sennacherib is claiming to have the power to give what Yahweh cannot give.[55] The choice is to submit to the king of Assyria and receive **life** instead of **death**!

Finally, after assailing Hezekiah, the commander moves to attack the God of Judah directly. The king of Judah is deceiving them when he claims, **"The LORD will deliver us** [from *nāṣal*]**."** He asks if the gods have been able to deliver any other nation from his hand. They were not able to save Samaria. Unstated is the implication that Yahweh was unable to deliver his people in the north. With such a record, **"How then can the LORD deliver** [from *nāṣal*] **Jerusalem from my hand?"** The battle is elevated to a contest between "the great king, the king of Assyria" and "the God of Judah." On orders from Hezekiah, **the people remain silent**, and his officials return in distress with word to Hezekiah, and **with their clothes torn**. The king's reaction will demonstrate that Hezekiah trusts in Yahweh to deliver.

---

[52]The Hebrew *nāṣal* also connects the Hezekiah story with the commentary on the fall of Israel (17:39). To be *delivered* from their enemies, the exiles must faithfully worship Yahweh their God.

[53]Hobbs, *2 Kings*, p. 259.

[54]Provan, *1 and 2 Kings*, p. 256.

[55]Nelson, *First and Second Kings*, p. 239.

2 KINGS 19

3. Hezekiah Turns to Yahweh (19:1-37)

19:1-7 The narrator turns his camera on Hezekiah. The king reacts by tearing **his clothes and put**ting **on sackcloth,** a sure sign of penance before God (cf. 1 Kgs 21:27-29; 2 Kgs 6:30). He goes up to the house of Yahweh and sends an impressive delegation to **the prophet Isaiah son of Amoz.** His words (prefaced by the messenger formula, "Thus says Hezekiah") reflect an unassuming humility and contrite spirit before the prophet of Yahweh: **"This day is a day of distress and rebuke and disgrace. . . ."** He wonders if perhaps Isaiah's God Yahweh has heard the representative of the king of Assyria **ridicule [חָרַף,** *ḥāraph*] **the living God.** His words expose an anguished heart and introduce one more allusion to his forefather David, who in the face of the Philistine giant cried, "Who is this uncircumcised Philistine that he should *defy* [*ḥāraph*] the armies of the *living God*?" (1 Sam 17:26; cf. vv. 25,36,45). A key word in the David and Goliath story, *ḥāraph* appears in Kings only in the Hezekiah narrative (19:4,16,22,23; occurring only thirteen times in Deuteronomy through 2 Kings), which demonstrates a clear connection with David's reaction to the Philistine champion. For Hezekiah, as for David, the foreigner's braggadocio is an affront to "the living God." In this way, the king of Judah becomes David as he pours out his heart to Yahweh's prophet Isaiah.

Hezekiah asks Isaiah to pray for **the** *remnant* [שְׁאֵרִית, *šᵊ'ērîth*] **that still survives.** With the word "remnant," he uses a word that has been subtly emphasized through the course of the story.[1] In its noun and verb forms, remnant/remainder (שָׁאַר/שְׁאָר/שְׁאֵרִית, *šā'ar/šᵊ'ār/ šᵊ'ērîth*) occurs twenty-four times in Kings (cf., e.g., 1 Kgs 15:29; 19:18;

---

[1]Provan observes that "remnant" has been thematic in the story of the northern kingdom (*1 and 2 Kings*, p. 261).

2 Kgs 7:13; 10:11; 17:18). A careful reader suspects, for example, there may be a connection between the remnant that has survived Sennacherib's invasion (and the Babylonian invasion) and the seven thousand Yahweh had *reserved* (*šā'ar*) to worship him in the time of Elijah (1 Kgs 19:18). A key theme also in Isaiah (see Isa 4:3; 10:19,20,21,22; 11:11,16; cf. Jer 23:3; 31:7; 44:2), it will play an even more important role at the end of the story of Kings (cf. 2 Kgs 21:14; 24:14; 25:11-12,22). No doubt, the remnant in exile would hear the king of Judah praying for their plight, as Solomon directly prayed for those who would be captive in a foreign land (1 Kgs 8:46-53).[2]

The prophet's response is encouraging. Prefacing his remarks with the messenger formula ("This is what Yahweh says"), Isaiah transmits a message in first person from Yahweh to Hezekiah: **"Do not be afraid of what you have heard [שָׁמַע, *šama'*]. . . Listen!** [*šama'*] **I am going to put such a spirit in him that when he hears** [*šama'*] **a certain report, he will return [*šûb*] to his own country, and there I will have him cut down with the sword."** Perhaps in some way like the "lying spirit" that enticed Ahab (cf. 1 Kgs 22:19-23), Yahweh is going to put a spirit in Sennacherib that will *entice* him to his own country, where he will be cut down (see below). But with play on the word *šama'* ("to hear"), Isaiah also intimates Yahweh will destroy the king of Assyria with his word.[3]

19:8-13 With a creative use of repetition that teases the reader, the narrator reports that **when the field commander hears [*šama'*] that the king of Assyria had left Lachish, he with**draws [*šûb*] **and** finds **the king of Assyria fighting against Libnah** (NW of Lachish; see comments on 8:22). And, Sennacherib **receives [*šama'*, "heard"]** **a** *report* **that Tirhakah is** coming out **to fight against him**.[4] Are the prophet's words coming to pass so quickly? Can the reader anticipate an Assyrian withdrawal? To the contrary, the king of Assyria does not

---

[2]See Knoppers, "Incomparability in the Books of Kings," 425.

[3]Cohn, *2 Kings*, p. 134.

[4]The reference to Tirhakah, who came to the throne of Egypt in 690 B.C., suggests for some that there must have been two campaigns against Judah by Sennacherib (see above; cf. Shea, "Jerusalem under Siege," 36-44, 64). However, Kenneth A. Kitchen argues that in 701, Tirhakah was sent by his ruling brother Shebitku to assist Hezekiah against the Assyrians. Since Tirhakah becomes king of Egypt by the time of the death of Sennacherib, he appears in Kings as the king of Egypt (*The Bible in Its World: The Bible &*

return (*šûb*) to his homeland. Instead, he reiterates his demands. Narrative tension is amplified. Perhaps the Egyptian response means that Hezekiah has appealed to Egypt in the meantime, which could nullify Isaiah's prophecy (see comments on 18:17-25). Sennacherib sends a communiqué to Hezekiah that questions the word of Yahweh: **"Do not let the god you depend on** [*bāṭaḥ*] **deceive you when he says, 'Jerusalem will not be handed over to the king of Assyria.'"** Once more, the theme of trust surfaces. The king of Assyria frames his ultimatum in terms of holy war. In a rhetorical question, he asks Hezekiah if he **"has not heard what the kings of Assyria have done to all the countries, destroying them completely** [from *ḥāram*]. **And will you be delivered** [from *nāṣal*]**?"** With his use of *ḥrm* (in Kings only in 1 Kgs 9:21; 20:42; 2 Kgs 19:11), the reader wonders if Yahweh has devoted Judah to destruction, much like the Canaanites who were to be totally destroyed in the days of Joshua (see comments on 1 Kgs 20:42). Sennacherib reminds the king of Judah that the **"gods of the nations that were destroyed by my forefathers"** were not able to **deliver** [from *nāṣal*] their kings. The clear message is that neither will Yahweh be able to deliver Hezekiah.

19:14-19 The reader now learns the latest communiqué has been conveyed by letter, which the king of Judah reads. Once more, the king goes to the house of Yahweh. Once more, the reader watches Hezekiah act (cf. vv. 1-4). In an ultimate demonstration of trust, the king **spreads** [the letter] **out before the LORD** and prays. His prayer is a window to the underlying man, demonstrating that his expressions of dependence on Yahweh are authentic. What the reader has suspected may have been only political posturing, in the final analysis, turns out to be genuine trust. His prayers (19:15-19; 20:2-3) also mirror the prayers of David and Solomon (cf. 2 Sam 7:18-29; 1 Kgs 8:22-53). For example, like David and Solomon, Hezekiah acknowledges that Yahweh alone is God, who rules over all the nations (2 Kgs 19:15,19; cf. 2 Sam 7:22; 1 Kgs 8:23).[5] The allusions to David and Solomon frame Hezekiah's actions and characterize him as a

---

Archaeology Today [Downers Grove, IL: InterVarsity, 1977], pp. 113-114; see Hobbs, *2 Kings*, p. 276; Cogan and Tadmor, *II Kings*, p. 248). For a response to the view that 19:9b-37 represents a separate account of 18:17-19a, see Hobbs, *2 Kings*, pp. 246-247, 268-269, 276.

[5]For additional parallels, see Knoppers, "Incomparability in the Book of Kings," 421-442.

righteous king. They also imply that, at least in this instance, Hezekiah is a king like the son promised to David.

Hezekiah declares that "[Yahweh] **alone** is **God over all the kingdoms of the earth**" and praises him as "the maker of **heaven and earth.**" He asks Yahweh to **"listen to the words Sennacherib has sent to insult [*ḥāraph*] the living God."** His language again echoes his forefather David (see comments on v. 4). In this instance, his concern is not just for himself but for the honor of his God. He acknowledges that the Assyrians have destroyed the gods of the nations. But in the same breath, he expresses his belief that **"they were not gods but only wood and stone, fashioned by men's hands."** Hezekiah asks, **"O LORD our God, deliver** [from *yāša'*] **us from his hand, so that all kingdoms on earth may know that you alone, O LORD are God."** Yet again, Hezekiah's response conjures up images of David, who challenged Goliath: "Today I will give the carcasses of the Philistine army to the birds of the air and the beasts of the earth, and the *whole world will know* that there is a God in Israel. All those gathered here will know that it is not by sword or spear that the LORD *saves* [from *yāša*]; for the battle is the LORD's" (1 Sam 17:46-47; cf. 1 Kgs 18:37).[6] By his actions and words, the character of the king of Judah is revealed — and through him the ideological viewpoint of the storyteller. The gods of the nations are not gods. Yahweh alone is God, the one who made heaven and earth. As David, the people of God must *trust* in him to save.

19:20-28 The king of Judah receives a reply from Yahweh through the prophet Isaiah: **"I have heard your prayer concerning Sennacherib king of Assyria."** Yahweh's response is framed as a poetic oracle in the mouth of Isaiah. The language is consistent with the prophetic speech in the book of Isaiah. For example, **the Holy One of Israel** is a characteristic title for Yahweh in Isaiah (cf. Isa 1:4; 5:19,24; 10:20; 12:6; 17:7; 29:19,23; 30:11,12,15; 31:1; 37:23; 40:25; 41:14,16,20; 43:3,14,15; 45:11; 47:4; 48:17; 49:7; 54:5; 55:5; 57:15; 60:9,14). The oracle chastises the king of Assyria as a proud minion who has **insulted and blasphemed** (cf. v. 6) the God of Israel, by ridiculing **the virgin daughter of Zion.** She **mocks** Sennacherib as he **flees.** Yet, the king of Assyria has done the bidding of Israel's God. Yahweh asserts, **"In days of old I planned it; now I have**

---

[6]Hobbs sees the allusions to David and Goliath, but he does not develop the connections for interpreting the story of Hezekiah (*2 Kings*, pp. 278-279).

brought it to pass, that you have turned fortified cities into piles of stone." Now, there is no doubt. Yahweh has decreed Sennacherib's assault on Hezekiah. It is from Yahweh (cf. Isa 10:5-11)! However, the king of Assyria has done so with **rage against** Yahweh. His **insolence** will not go unpunished. Yahweh affirms, **"I will put my hook in your nose and my bit in your mouth, and I will make you return [*šûb*] by the way you came."** As the Assyrians led captives into exile with hooks (cf. 2 Chr 33:11; Amos 4:2),[7] so Yahweh will send Sennacherib to his own country. Again, Yahweh promises to make the king of Assyria *return* (cf. v. 7).

19:29-34 For Hezekiah, Isaiah gives a sign that these things will come to pass (cf. the sign to Ahaz in Isa 7:10-25). In three years, following the devastation by the Assyrians, the people of Judah will **sow and reap, plant vineyards and eat their fruit.** Continuing with an agricultural metaphor (cf. v. 26), Isaiah announces, **"Once more a remnant [from *šā'ar*] of the house of Judah will take root below and bear fruit above. For out of Jerusalem will come a remnant [*šᵊ'ērîth*], and out of Mount Zion a band of survivors."** A *remnant* of the people will survive. But the remnant is not just those who remain in Judah. In similar language, the prophet proclaims in the book of Isaiah that a *remnant* in exile will *return* (*šûb*):

> A shoot will come up from the stump of Jesse;
>   from his roots a Branch will bear fruit. . . .
>
> In that day the Root of Jesse will stand as a banner
> for the peoples; . . . In that day the LORD will reach out
> his hand a second time to reclaim the remnant [*šᵊ'ār*] that
> is left of his people from Assyria . . . .
>
> He will raise a banner for the nations
>   and gather the exiles of Israel. . . .
> There will be a highway for the remnant [*šᵊ'ār*] of his people
>   that is left from Assyria,
> as there was for Israel
>   when they came up from Egypt" (Isa 11:1,10-12,16).

In the paragraph that prefaces Isaiah's account of Sennacherib's invasion, the prophet also declares: "And a highway will be there; it will

---

[7]For parallels, see Cogan and Tadmor, *II Kings*, p. 238.

be called the Way of Holiness. The unclean will not journey on it; it will be for those who walk in that Way; . . . But only the redeemed will walk there, and the ransomed of the LORD will *return* [*šûb*]" (35:8,9b-10a). The audience in exile should take heart. Yahweh will deliver a *remnant* of his people. The descendants of the captives pictured on their way into exile in the Lachish reliefs (see comments on 18:13-16) will experience a "second Exodus." Yahweh will reclaim the redeemed from exile, which happens when his people return from Babylon. In the larger canon of Scripture, however, out of the Root of Jesse the Messiah comes and delivers. On the day of Pentecost, those scattered among the nations return and are ushered into the messianic kingdom (the church) as they are baptized for the forgiveness of sins. The *highway* into exile becomes a *highway* of deliverance for Israel and for all the nations.[8]

Concerning Sennacherib, the prophet proclaims that the king **"will not enter** [Jerusalem] **or shoot an arrow here. He will not come before it with shield or build a siege ramp against it."** Since it is likely that the Assyrians have besieged the city (cf. 18:17; Isa. 29:1-4[9]), the oracle means that the Assyrian forces will not advance any further.[10] For the third time, Yahweh declares that Sennacherib will *return* (*šûb*; cf. vv. 7,28).[11] The king of Assyria **"will not enter this city."** The God of Israel will **"defend this city and save** [הוֹשִׁיעָהּ, *hôšî'āh*, from *yāša'*] **it."** And Yahweh takes this action for his "[own] **sake and for the sake of David my servant"** (cf. 20:6). When Hezekiah calls on Yahweh to deliver Jerusalem and demonstrates the trust that characterized David, Yahweh acts. He acts to defend his honor and to keep his promise to David.[12]

Yahweh's commitment to save Jerusalem, an obvious theme in the Hezekiah narrative, raises the question of the "inviolability of Zion." As a city holy to Yahweh, it must be indestructible. By the time of Jeremiah, this belief permeates Judean society (cf. Jeremiah

---

[8]Jesse C. Long, "Confirming a Highway," 34-36.

[9]Sennacherib claims to have laid siege to Jerusalem, surrounding it with "earthwork" (*ANET*, p. 288).

[10]Hobbs, *2 Kings*, pp. 272-273.

[11]Provan also sees "return" (*šûb*) as a theme in the story (*1 and 2 Kings*, p. 260).

[12]Hobbs, *2 Kings*, p. 282.

7), as is reflected in a seventh/sixth century bench tomb at Khirbet Beit Lei (seven miles east of Lachish):

> Yahweh (is) the god of the whole earth; the mountains of
>   Judah belong to him, to the God of Jerusalem.
> The (Mount of) Moriah Thou hast favored, the dwelling of
>   Yah, Yahweh.[13]

While one suspects that the deliverance of Jerusalem in 701 B.C. fostered such a notion in Judah, Olley demonstrates that trust in Yahweh, not the inviolability of Jerusalem, is what saves the city.[14] When Hezekiah in humility depends on Yahweh alone, he mirrors the heart of David, and Yahweh saves him. Also, the book of Kings in its final form undermines this view. In Kings, the election of the city of David is associated with Yahweh's promise to "establish" David's throne "forever" (2 Sam 7:16). To Jeroboam, Yahweh said, "I will give one tribe to [Solomon's] son so that David my servant may always have a lamp before me in Jerusalem, the city where I chose to put my Name" (1 Kgs 11:36). The story of Hezekiah recalls once more Yahweh's unconditional covenant with David, as Yahweh delivers Jerusalem. Even so, the exilic audience of Kings knows what Yahweh allows the Babylonians to do to the city. Yet again, through narrative, the writer raises the question of the Davidic covenant. With the city of David and Solomon's temple in ruins, how can Yahweh's promise to David be eternal?

19:35-37 The storyteller closes his account of Sennacherib's invasion by narrating events that confirm the word of the prophet Isaiah. Cohn observes that the sequence of verbs in Sennacherib's retreat (he "withdrew," "returned," and "dwelt") mirrors the verbs describing the approach of his messengers in 18:17, forming an inclusio around the siege narrative.[15] That very **night**, the angel of Yahweh kills **a hundred and eighty-five thousand** Assyrians.[16]

---

[13]Dever, *Biblical Writers Know*, p. 218.

[14]John W. Olley, "'Trust in the Lord': Hezekiah, Kings and Isaiah," *TB* 50/1 (1999): 59-77.

[15]Cohn, *2 Kings*, p. 139.

[16]Alan R. Millard compares the biblical account of Sennacherib's invasion of Judah with similar contemporary reports and determines that the reference to Jerusalem's deliverance by the angel of Yahweh in v. 35 should be considered as part of the narrative: "Neither on historical nor on literary

Contrast with the messengers (מַלְאָךְ, *mal'ak* = "messenger" and "angel") of the king of Assyria, who are powerless, is dramatic.[17] The king of Assyria sends messengers and besieges the city; Yahweh sends his messenger, and Sennacherib's army is devastated. Narrated from the point of view of the Assyrians who survive, when they awake in the morning, they are startled to see (הִנֵּה, *hinnēh*) **all the dead bodies**. As a result, as Yahweh said (vv. 7,28,33), Sennacherib **returns** (*šûb*) home to **Nineveh**. Sennacherib's own account is consistent with the biblical story. Of Hezekiah, he only can claim, "Himself I made a prisoner in Jerusalem, his royal residence, like a bird in a cage."[18] "The great king, the king of Assyria" (cf. 18:19) is not able to crush the Judean king, or prevail against the God who is "over all the kingdoms of the earth" (cf. 19:15). Provan writes, "'David' has once more overcome Goliath."[19]

The final scene in the siege narrative is an account of Sennacherib's death at the hands of two of his sons, **Adrammelech and Sharezer**. They **cut him down with the sword**, which is also according to the word of Yahweh (v. 7). Sennacherib's son **Esarhaddon** becomes king in his place. In his annals, Esarhaddon describes a confrontation with his older brothers for the throne, and his son Ashurbanipal claims to have punished the ones who killed his grandfather.[20] In confirmation of these basic events, the Babylonian Chronicle records that Sennacherib "was killed by his son in rebellion" (ca. 680 B.C.).[21] Ironically, Nabonidus of Babylon claims that Marduk "made [Sennacherib's] own son murder the king of [Assyria]."[22] The prophet Isaiah asserts: "When the LORD has finished all his work against Mount Zion and Jerusalem, he will say, 'I will punish the king of Assyria for the willful pride of his heart and the haughty look in his eyes'" (Isa 10:12).

---

grounds need it be detached and treated as a later addition" ("Sennacherib's Attack on Hezekiah," *TB* 36 [1985]: 76).

[17]Provan, *1 and 2 Kings*, p. 262.

[18]*ANET*, p. 288.

[19]Provan, *1 and 2 Kings*, p. 260.

[20]*ANET*, pp. 288-290.

[21]Quoted in Hobbs, *2 Kings*, p. 283; cf. Cogan and Tadmor, *II Kings*, pp. 239-240.

[22]*ANET*, p. 309; see Cogan and Tadmor, *II Kings*, p. 244.

2 KINGS 20

4. Yahweh Delivers Hezekiah from Illness (20:1-11)

20:1-6 The narrator begins the next episode with a loose connection with the preceding events (**In those days**), although the repetition of **"I will defend this city . . ."** in verse 6 (cf. 19:34) links these happenings to the deliverance of Jerusalem. If the king's illness did not come after the invasion, it could have occurred sometime during Hezekiah's preparation for the assault.[1] In another story where a king is ill (cf. 1 Kings 14 [Jeroboam], 2 Kings 1 [Ahaziah], and 2 Kings 8 [Ben-Hadad]),[2] the prophet Isaiah goes to the king with a word from Yahweh: **"You are going to die; you will not recover."** Weeping profusely, Hezekiah **turns his face to the wall and prays** — conjuring up images of Ahab (cf. 1 Kgs 21:4; where the Hebrew reads "he turned his face" for "sulking" in the NIV).[3] In contrast with Ahab, Hezekiah can pray, **"I have walked before you faithfully and with wholehearted devotion and have done what is good in your eyes."** The king has kept the charge of his forefather David to "walk in his ways, and keep his decrees and commands, his laws and requirements, as written in the Law of Moses . . . with all [your] heart" (1 King 2:3-4; cf. 18:3-8). Yahweh hears and acknowledges Hezekiah's prayer. Before the prophet leaves the palace, the word of Yahweh comes to Isaiah: **"I have heard your prayer and seen your tears; I will heal you. . . . I will add fifteen years to your life. And I will deliver** [from נָצַל, *nāṣal*] **you and this city from the hands of the king of Assyria."** Yahweh repeats that he will defend Jerusalem

---

[1]For the chronological implications in the arrangement of episodes in the Hezekiah account, see above.

[2]Cohn, "Convention and Creativity," 603-616; idem, *2 Kings*, pp. 59-60, 140-141.

[3]Provan, *1 and 2 Kings*, p. 263.

"for my sake and for the sake of my servant David." It is almost as if Hezekiah's prayer reminds Yahweh of his servant David, and his commitment to keep one of David's sons on the throne. Hezekiah does right with respect to the covenant with Moses, and Yahweh remembers his covenant with David.

20:7-11 The prophet directs the king's attendants: **"Prepare a poultice of figs."** The remedy cures the king. The word translated **boil** (שְׁחִין, *šᵉḥîn*) appears in the Exodus narrative (9:10-11) and is one of the curses of the covenant (Deut 28:27,35), which suggests that the malady is from Yahweh. Interestingly, Isaiah's action in this story more resembles the prophets Elijah and Elisha, than his prophetic role reflected in the book of Isaiah. The prescription also parallels ancient Near Eastern medical practices, indicating in this instance that the prophet is functioning somewhat like a physician, who as a prophet also mediates Yahweh's power to heal.[4] In contrast with Ahaz who refused a sign from the prophet (Isa 7:11,14), Hezekiah[5] asks for a sign. If this scene is not a flashback to a point before Isaiah applied the poultice, the king is apparently afraid that he will not experience a complete recovery.[6] To the prophet's proposition, he requests that **"[the shadow] go back** [שׁוּב, *šûb*] **ten steps."** Isaiah calls on Yahweh, who makes the shadow *return* (*šûb*) ten steps (cf. Josh 10:12-14). It is unclear exactly what is meant by the **stairway of Ahaz**. It may have been a sundial, but more recent interpretations

---

[4]See Hobbs, *2 Kings*, pp. 287, 291-292; Cogan and Tadmor, *II Kings*, p. 255. Margaret Barker marshals evidence that Hezekiah's malady was bubonic plague. In antiquity, for example, a fig poultice was a remedy for plague swellings. She suggests that the Assyrian army acquired the plague in Egypt (per Herodotus' story of the defeat of the Assyrians by mice [*Histories* 2.141]) before besieging Jerusalem. From the Assyrian messengers, the king of Judah acquired the disease, which was the cause of Sennacherib's retreat ("Hezekiah's Boil," *JSOT* [2001]: 31-42). If she is correct, the story of the king's disease is directly related to the invasion of Sennacherib, as the account in Kings implies (see p. 34).

[5]In v. 10, Hezekiah's name is spelled "Yehezekiah" ("Yahweh will strengthen").

[6]Provan, *1 and 2 Kings*, p. 264. The differences between the accounts of this miracle in 2 Kings 20, Isaiah 38, and 2 Chronicles 32 do not mean that the story is inauthentic (Hobbs, *2 Kings*, pp. 292-293). Cohn explains the temporal inconsistencies in the story (e.g., requesting a sign after he is already healed) as indicating personal (i.e., physical) and political deliverance (*2 Kings*, p. 143).

suggest that actual steps are indicated.[7] In any case, the God "who made heaven and earth" (cf. 19:15), at the request of the prophet Isaiah, performs a miracle for the king of Judah that demonstrates he alone is God — when he makes the shadow *return*.[8] Since *šûb* appears as a key word in Kings (see comments on 1 Kgs 13:33; 2 Kgs 8:1-6), is it too much to suggest that the storyteller is employing *šûb* once more with symbolic overtones? The God who caused Sennacherib to *return* (*šûb*) to his homeland (19:7,28,33,36) and made the shadow *return* (*šûb*) ten steps (20:9,10,11) could also cause the exiles to *return* from captivity in a second Exodus!

5. Hezekiah Shows Off the Treasures of Judah (20:12-21)

20:12-18 With the phrase **at that time**, the narrator connects the visit of the delegation from **Merodach-Baladan son of Baladan king of Babylon** with Hezekiah's recovery. The statement that **letters and a gift** are presented **because he had heard of Hezekiah's illness** also indicates the same, but probably does not represent the only reason for the messengers' mission. Merodach-Baladan ruled Babylon from 722 until Sargon deposed him in 710/709. He remained in exile until Sargon's death in 705 and reigned nine months before Sennacherib's first campaign in 704–703 terminated his hold on the throne. Sennacherib also waged war with Merodach-Baladan in 700, after which the former king of Babylon fled to the swamps from which he disappears from history.[9] Contrary to the view that the visit of the Babylonian delegation should be dated during his first tenure as king of Babylon (at the time of Ashdod's rebellion against Sargon in 713; cf. Isaiah 20 [as a way of resolving the chronological difficulties in Hezekiah's reign]),[10] there is no reason not to accept the storyteller's linkage between Sennacherib's invasion and Hezekiah's illness and the visit of the Babylonian delegation. If the embassy from Babylon were sent during Merodach-Baladan's second stint as king, it is reasonable

---

[7]Hobbs, *2 Kings*, pp. 293-294.

[8]Barker explains the movement of the shadow back ten steps by "a 75 percent eclipse of the sun over Jerusalem in the late afternoon on 6 August 700 BCE, lasting from about half past five until sunset" ("Hezekiah's Boil," 40).

[9]Cogan and Tadmor, *II Kings*, pp. 260-261; cf. Hobbs, *2 Kings*, p. 289.

[10]Cf. Cogan and Tadmor, *II Kings*, pp. 260-263.

to envision a delegation to secure western support against the Assyrians (as Hezekiah is preparing for Sennacherib's invasion). Hobbs argues that the evidence allows a visit "in or around 701 B.C.," after the king of Babylon was deposed for the second time. Whether Merodach-Baladan is actually king at the time of the visit is irrelevant.[11] It is also possible that the delegation is dispatched by Merodach-Baladan as late as 700, just after the deliverance of Jerusalem and before Sennacherib ends Merodach-Baladan's ambitions to retain the Babylonian throne. If the visit occurs just before the invasion, there is no inconsistency between the tribute Hezekiah pays to Sennacherib (18:14) and the treasures that appear in his storehouses in this episode. In any case, Hezekiah's illness must have been only pretense for an attempt to secure Judean support against Sennacherib.

The king of Judah shows [**the messengers**] **all that** is **in his storehouses . . . his armory and everything found among his treasures**. For emphasis, the narrator repeats that there was **nothing in his palace or in all his kingdom that Hezekiah did not show them**. Without elaboration, the narrator says the prophet Isaiah goes to the king and asks about the delegation. Hezekiah answers that the embassy from Babylon **"saw everything in my palace. . . . There is nothing among my treasures that I did not show them."** The repetition with exposition and in dialogue stresses the king's actions. A careful reader recognizes the emphasis and recalls the important role royal treasures have played in negatively characterizing Judean kings (see comments on 18:13-16). Isaiah responds with an oracle of doom from Yahweh: **"The time will surely come when everything in your palace . . . will be carried to Babylon."** This will include the king's **own flesh and blood** who will **become eunuchs in the palace of the king of Babylon**. The prophet's words anticipate the end of the composition of Kings, when Nebuchadnezzar takes the treasures of the palace and temple including the royal family to Babylon (24:8-17). Daniel and some of his companions are members of the house of David who serve the court in Babylon (Dan 1:1-7).[12]

However, missing in the word of Isaiah is any rationale for Yahweh's harsh reaction to Hezekiah. And neither does the narrator

---

[11]Hobbs, *2 Kings*, p. 289.

[12]See Rex A. Turner, Sr., *Daniel: A Prophet of God* (Montgomery, AL: Southern Christian University, 1993), p. 10.

offer a reason. Instead, he allows the inconsistencies in his presentation of Hezekiah to characterize this important king. Obviously, the storyteller ends his account of Hezekiah on a negative note. If the episode of the king's illness and the story of the envoys from Babylon occur prior to Sennacherib's invasion (perhaps in 713, better in 704/703), the writer has consciously rearranged the chronological events for his theological purposes. But if these events transpire after the invasion, the effect is the same. Hezekiah's reign does not alter Judah's course. This king of Judah stands out among those who were before and after him (18:5), but his *trust* in Yahweh does not forestall the destruction of Jerusalem. When he shows the emissaries from Merodach-Baladan the treasures of Judah, the reader can see a proud heart (cf. 2 Chr 32:25) that is *trusting* in treasures instead of the God who gave them.[13] According to Moses, the ideal king should not accumulate silver and gold (Deut 17:17).[14] It cannot be just coincidence that a story that begins with tribute in *treasure* (including silver and gold from the temple), which is not able to deliver the king, ends with a display of *treasure* that will one day fill Babylonian coffers. And, when the embassy from Babylon is viewed in terms of its political ramifications, Hezekiah emerges once more as a king who is relying on alliances to secure his political well-being. The story ends with the king showing off treasures and making an alliance. Hezekiah is not judged for the "stupidity" of showing his treasures to the king of Babylon — but for not *trusting* in Yahweh!

The storyteller has painted a complex portrait of Hezekiah. When he turns to Yahweh during the invasion of Sennacherib, he acts like David and merits the grace of God, but his virtuous acts are not enough. Even a righteous king, a reformer who stands above the other kings who have occupied David's throne, is not able to deter the calamity that is coming. Hezekiah is both an example of one who, like David, in an extraordinary crisis *trusts* in Yahweh, and a model of one who does not always *trust* in the God who delivered him. Hezekiah's *trust* saves Jerusalem. His *lack of trust* invites a prophetic oracle of judgment. Through the story of Hezekiah, an

---

[13]The Chronicler adds that Yahweh left Hezekiah to the envoys from Babylon "to test him and to know everything that was in his heart" (2 Chr 32:31).

[14]Hobbs, *2 Kings*, p. 294.

exilic audience is admonished to walk in the Law of Moses, worship Yahweh alone, remove themselves from the dangers of idolatry — and *trust* in Yahweh,[15] the one who caused Sennacherib and the shadow to *šûb*! Only when the exiles *repent* (*šûb*) and *trust* in him alone, is there any chance for *return* (*šûb*).

20:19 The king's response is curious: **"The word of the LORD you have spoken is good."** Then the narrator shares with the reader Hezekiah's inner speech: **For he thought** [literally, "and he said"]**, "Will there not be peace and security in my lifetime?"** (cf. 1 Sam 3:18). Delayed retribution appears once more in Kings. Yahweh is gracious; however, the king who receives his mercy appears to be more concerned with his own circumstance than with the fortunes of Judah. His last words in the story are consistent with his already revealed foibles and characterize him as a materially minded, selfish king.[16] But the peace and security Hezekiah receives will not last long. His evil son will ensure God's judgment on Judah.

20:20-21 In the formulaic conclusion to Hezekiah's reign, the narrator mentions among his achievements the **tunnel by which he brought water into the city**. This remarkable engineering feat, today known as "Hezekiah's tunnel," was apparently part of preparations for the Assyrian invasion (see comments on 18:1-8), which the Chronicler outlines in more detail (2 Chr 32:1-8,27-30). This great king of Judah **rests with his fathers**, a phrase which in Kings signifies a peaceful death. The Chronicler adds that he "was buried on the hill where the tombs of David's descendants are." He also records that "all Judah and the people of Jerusalem honored him when he died" (2 Chr 32:33).[17] **Manasseh his son** reigns in his place.

---

[15]Nelson also emphasizes the theme of trust for the exiles (*First and Second Kings*, p. 242; cf. Knoppers, "Incomparability in the Books of Kings," 425).

[16]See Provan, *1 and 2 Kings*, p. 265. Nelson interprets Hezekiah's words as representing grateful submission (*First and Second Kings*, p. 246).

[17]In addition, the Chronicler identifies as a source for his composition, "the vision of the prophet Isaiah son of Amoz in the book of the kings of Judah and Israel" (2 Chr 32:32).

2 KINGS 21

B. MANASSEH AND HIS SON AMON SECURE JUDAH'S FATE (21:1-26)

1. Manasseh Does Evil in the Eyes of Yahweh (21:1-18)

21:1-6 Hezekiah's son **Manasseh** does not walk in the righteous ways of his father, modeling more his grandfather Ahaz (ch. 16).[1] During his **fifty-five** year reign, he undoes the reforms of Hezekiah. His long reign may have begun as coregent with his father. This hypothesis is perhaps reinforced by the fact that he is only **twelve years old** when he becomes king.[2] The storyteller promptly informs the reader that Manasseh does **evil in the eyes of the LORD**. Up to this point in the story, only Solomon, Jehoram, and Ahaz of the kings of Judah have been portrayed as doing evil in the eyes of Yahweh (cf. 1 Kgs 11:16; 8:18,27; 2 Kgs 16:2). After the reign of Manasseh, only Josiah is described as "doing right" in his eyes (22:2). But Manasseh's sins are especially egregious. He **follows the detestable practices** [תּוֹעֲבוֹת, *tô'ăbōth*] **of the nations the LORD had driven out** [from יָרַשׁ, *yāraš*, "to possess"] **before the Israelites**. Moses had warned Israel not to participate in the *detestable practices* (*tô'ăbōth*) of the nations they were to dispossess (cf. Deut 12:31; 18:9,12). Early in his narrative (during the time of Rehoboam), the storyteller described the sins of Judah with the same language (1 Kgs 14:24). Ahaz also merits a similar description (2 Kgs 16:3). When the narrator uses the verb "to drive out/dispossess" (from *yāraš*), he not so subtly foreshadows what will happen to the people of Judah. If

---

[1]Provan, *1 and 2 Kings*, p. 266.
[2]Thiele postulates a ten to eleven year coregency for Manasseh with his father Hezekiah (*Mysterious Numbers*, pp. 173-174, 176-177; see introductory comments to ch. 18; cf. Hobbs, *2 Kings*, p. 304).

Manasseh influences Judah to behave like the nations, like Israel (the paradigm for Judah's downfall), the southern kingdom will lose their inheritance (see comments on ch. 17).

Like Solomon, Manasseh is a builder. However, he mirrors Solomon at the end of his reign, when he built high places for the gods of his foreign wives (see comments on 1 Kgs 11:1-13). Manasseh even *rebuilds* (literally, "turned back [*šûb*] and built [בָּנָה, *bānāh*]") **the high places his father Hezekiah had destroyed**. No doubt, the king is trying to earn the favor of those in Judah who believe Sennacherib's assault on Jerusalem was brought on by his father's "blasphemous acts" against Yahweh's high places (cf. 18:22). Manasseh also builds (*bānāh*) **altars in the temple of the LORD**, the place where Yahweh said, **"I will put my Name."** However, the altars the king of Judah builds are **to all the starry host** (cf. Deut 4:19; 17:3; 2 Kgs 23:5; Jer 7:18; 44:15-19),[3] to which he **bows down** and **worships**. He **erects altars to Baal and** makes **an Asherah pole, as Ahab king of Israel had done** (cf. 1 Kgs 16:31-33; 18:4). The king does not believe in Yahweh as the one true God.[4] The association with Ahab is ominous for Judah. Other parallels with Ahab will secure this connection and suggest that by allusion Manasseh is Judah's Ahab.[5]

The writer's catalogue of Manasseh's sins includes making **his own son**, literally, "pass through the fire" (see comments on 16:3; 23:10), practicing **sorcery and divination**, and consulting **mediums and spiritists** (like Saul, 1 Sam 28:3-25[6]). The language comes from Deuteronomy 18:9-13. Of these "detestable [*tô'ăbōth*] ways of the nations" (v. 9), Moses said, "Anyone who does these things is detestable [*tô'ăbōth*] to the LORD, and because of these detestable

---

[3]The "starry host" reflects worship of the heavenly bodies, which was common in Canaanite worship. There is no evidence to indicate that an Assyrian astral cult (or other Assyrian religious practices) was imposed on Judah. Contrary to earlier views, there is nothing in the account of Manasseh that cannot be explained by Canaanite influence on Judah (Morton Cogan, *Imperialism and Religion: Assyria, Judah and Israel in the Eighth and Seventh Centuries B.C.E.* [Missoula, MT: SBL and Scholars Press, 1974], pp. 42-61, 72-88; Cogan and Tadmor, *II Kings*, pp. 266, 272; Hobbs, *2 Kings*, pp. 305-306; see n. 30, p. 451 above).

[4]Provan, *1 and 2 Kings*, p. 267.

[5]See Hobbs, *2 Kings*, pp. 305, 311; Provan, *1 and 2 Kings*, pp. 267-268.

[6]Provan, *1 and 2 Kings*, p. 268.

practices [tô'ăbōth] the LORD your God will drive out [from yāraš] those nations before you" (v. 12; cf. 2 Kgs 17:16-17). In this frame of reference, the storyteller emphasizes Yahweh's visceral reaction to the tô'ăbōth of Manasseh. These initial verses are bookended with the statement that the king "does evil in the eyes of Yahweh" (see vv. 2, 15,16),[7] which **provokes him to anger** (from כָּעַס, kā'as, "to be angry"). The Hebrew kā'as is a key word in Kings, most often used to characterize Israel's apostasy (cf. 1 Kgs 14:9,15; 15:30; 16:2,7,13,26,33; 21:22; 22:54; 2 Kgs 17:11,17; 21:6,15; 22:17; 23:19,26).

21:7-9 The storyteller calls attention to the **carved Asherah pole** that Manasseh places (שִׂים, śîm, **put** in the NIV) in the temple. Yahweh had placed (śîm, v. 4) his Name in the house that Solomon built. In the same house, Manasseh places (śîm) an image of Asherah.[8] When he does this, Manasseh is most likely erecting an image of the goddess as consort to Yahweh (see comments on 1 Kgs 14:14-16). The king of Judah is worshiping foreign gods (vv. 1-6) and misrepresenting Yahweh before the people. As if the God of Judah were like one of the gods of the nations, an image of his consort now resides in the temple. The author's wording indicts the king. Manasseh sets up (literally) "the Asherah image/idol [פֶּסֶל, pesel]" ("carved Asherah pole" in the NIV). In the Ten Commandments, Yahweh directed, "You shall have no other gods before me. You shall not make for yourself an idol [pesel] . . . ." (Exod 20:3-4). To top it off, the king of Judah places the image in the house of Yahweh. Of this house, Yahweh said **to David and to his son Solomon, "In this temple and in Jerusalem, which I have chosen out of all the tribes of Israel I will put my Name forever."** When the storyteller repeats that it was Yahweh's choice to cause his Name to dwell in Jerusalem (cf. v. 4, both times in dialogue), he underscores the importance of Name theology in Kings (cf. comments on 1 Kgs 5:5; 8:27-30) and raises the question of Yahweh's unconditional covenant with David. The choice of Jerusalem and Solomon's temple was integral to Yahweh's promise to "establish the throne of his [i.e., David's offspring] kingdom forever" (2 Sam 7:13) — which is clearly reflected in Solomon's prayers at the dedication of the temple and is explicitly stated by Ahijah to Jeroboam (see 1 Kgs 8:6,44,48; 11:13,32-36).

---

[7]Cohn, 2 Kings, p. 146.
[8]Nelson, First and Second Kings, p. 250.

However, commenting on Manasseh, Yahweh in the same breath
also refers to his conditional covenant with Israel through Moses: **"I
will not again make the feet of the Israelites wander from the land
. . . if only they . . . will keep the whole Law that my servant Moses
gave to them."** Both the Davidic and Mosaic covenants come into
play.[9] Yahweh promised to establish David's throne forever, but the
people have not listened to (i.e., obeyed) Moses. Manasseh leads
them **astray**, so that **they do more evil than the nations the LORD
had destroyed before the Israelites**. As in the homily on Israel in
chapter 17, the writer is clearly laying out the legal case for the fall
of Jerusalem. An exilic audience knows that Judah suffers the same
fate as Israel and the nations who were driven out before them.
Nevertheless, while Judah deserves the same judgment, the covenant
with David looms over the composition. Apparently, Yahweh's
choice to put his Name in Jerusalem was not *forever*! A reader in
exile wonders if perhaps the sins of Manasseh have invalidated the
promise to David? The verses that follow make clear that it is God's
choice to destroy Judah — including the city of David, the place
where Yahweh caused his name to dwell!

21:10-15 As with the nation of Israel (cf. 17:13,23), Yahweh sent
his servants the prophets to Judah, whose message the narrator telescopes in dialogue: **"Manasseh king of Judah has committed these
detestable sins** [*tô'ăbōth*]. **He has done more evil than the Amorites
who preceded him and has led Judah into sin with his idols."**
Characterizing Manasseh's reign, *tô'ăbōth* appears again. And the
language conjures up images of Ahab, who "behaved in the vilest
manner [from תָּעַב, *tā'ab*] by going after idols, like the Amorites the
LORD drove out before Israel" (1 Kgs 21:26). In terms of his influence on Judah, Manasseh is Ahab. And, he also is Jeroboam. As
Jeroboam *caused* Israel *to sin* (causative of חָטָא [*ḥāṭā'*, "miss, go
wrong, sin"]; see, e.g., 1 Kgs 15:26; 2 Kgs 15:28; cf. 23:15), the
refrain that characterized the kings of Israel (see comments on 1 Kgs
13:33-34), so Manasseh in the same way *causes* Judah *to sin* [from
ḥāṭā'], "has led Judah into sin" in the NIV). In the composition of
Kings, Jeroboam and Ahab are responsible for setting Israel on a
path of ultimate destruction. Therefore, Yahweh declares, **"I am
going to bring** [causative of בוֹא, *bô'*, "come"] **such a disaster** [רָעָה,

---

[9]Cohn makes a similar observation (*2 Kings*, p. 147).

rā'āh] **on Jerusalem and Judah that the ears of everyone who hears it will tingle.**" Because the king and people have done *evil* (עַר, *ra'*; cf. vv. 2,6,9, 15,16), the God of Judah is going to bring *disaster* (*rā'āh*; cf. 1 Kgs 14:10; 21:21). The language also mirrors one of Jeremiah's invectives against Jerusalem and the oracle to Samuel concerning Eli (Jer 19:3; 1 Sam 3:11).[10] The judgment on Eli, in particular, lies in the background of Yahweh's words. The condemnation of Eli was framed in terms of royal judgment (against "his *house*," "family" in the NIV), which appears to function in the larger canon as a paradigm of Yahweh's judgment on the kings of Israel.[11]

In language reminiscent of Amos 7:7-9, Yahweh adds, **"I will stretch out** [נָטָה, *nāṭāh*] **over Jerusalem the measuring line used against Samaria and the plumb line used against the house of Ahab."** Jerusalem will be assessed by the same standards as those applied to Samaria. And the city of David will come up short. In another graphic image, Yahweh declares, **"I will wipe** [מָחָה, *māḥāh*] **out Jerusalem as one wipes a dish."** Because the people have **"done evil in my eyes"** and **"provoked me to anger** [from כָּעַס, *kā'as*, cf. vv. 6,17] **from the day their forefathers came out of Egypt until this day,"** Yahweh resolutely proclaims, **"I will** *forsake* [נָטַשׁ, *nāṭaš*] **the remnant of my inheritance and hand them over to their enemies."** The verbs stand out. The God of Judah promises to act ("I am going to bring," "I will stretch," "I will wipe," and "I will forsake"). The *remnant* (*šə'êrîth*) of his people that he delivered from the hand of Sennacherib (see comments on 19:29-34) will be given over to their enemies. Solomon's prayer, "May [Yahweh] never leave us nor *forsake* [*nāṭaš*[12]] us" (1 Kgs 8:57), will not be honored.

21:16-18 As if to place an exclamation point on his scathing assessment, the storyteller adds that Manasseh **sheds so much innocent blood that he fills Jerusalem from end to end**. Such a vivid portrayal suggests the king of Judah must have been a despotic ruler. In the Old Testament canon, there are no prophets from the time of Manasseh, a fact that probably reflects the tyrannical nature of his regime. According to Jewish tradition, Manasseh executed the prophet Isaiah by sawing him in two, a tradition which may be

---

[10]Provan, *1 and 2 Kings*, p. 267.

[11]Robert Polzin, *Samuel and the Deuteronomist*, pp. 51, 61, 68, 151.

[12]The Hebrew *nāṭaš* only occurs twice in Kings (8:57; 21:14).

reflected in Hebrews 11:37.[13] Provan observes that "it is no surprise to find Manasseh, who was 'like Ahab,' accused of the shedding of blood" (1 Kgs 21:19,35,38; 2 Kgs 9:7,26; 24:3-4; cf. Deut 19:10,13; 21:8-9).[14] The phrase "shedding innocent blood" can also refer to the oppression of the disenfranchised (cf. Jer 7:6; 22:3,17; Ezek 22:6 ff., 25 ff.).[15] Alluding once more to Jeroboam, the writer mentions again the king's **sin that he had caused Judah to commit** (literally, "his sin, which he caused Judah to sin [from *ḥāṭā'*]") — **so that they do evil in the eyes of the LORD** (cf. vv. 2,6,15). Manasseh's depravity is responsible for the wickedness of God's people in Judah.

Remarkably, in a fifty-five year reign the author of Kings chooses only to record Manasseh's sins. There obviously was much more that could have been said about Manasseh, which the record in Chronicles makes clear.[16] In fact, in some important ways the Chronicler's account differs significantly from Kings. The Chronicler records the Assyrians taking Manasseh captive with a hook in his nose and in bronze shackles to Babylon (ruled by Assyria at the time). Punitive actions against states participating in an Egyptian rebellion in 671 or the upheaval resulting from a revolt in Assyria in 648 would have been adequate reasons to call the king of Judah to task.[17] In Babylon, Manasseh "humbles himself greatly before the

---

[13]Carl D. Evans, "Manasseh, King of Judah," in *ABD*; Hobbs, *2 Kings*, pp. 305-308.

[14]Provan, *1 and 2 Kings*, p. 269.

[15]Cogan, *Imperialism and Religion*, p. 90; Cogan and Tadmor, *II Kings*, p. 269. Referencing the prophetic voice in Micah 3:9-11 and Jer 7:5-7, Brueggemann writes that "shedding innocent blood" broadly describes "acts of systematic, institutional violence whereby the powerful prey upon the weak and vulnerable in exploitive ways" (*1 & 2 Kings*, pp. 534-535).

[16]The archaeological record indicates that following the Assyrian assault on Judah in 701 B.C., Judah was more like a city-state with a much-reduced territory (e.g., with the Shephelah lost). During the reign of Manasseh, however, there are signs of recovery (Israel Finkelstein, "The Archaeology of the Days of Manasseh," in *Scripture and Other Artifacts: Essays on the Bible and Archaeology in Honor of Philip J. King*, ed. Michael D. Coogan, J. Cheryl Exum, and Lawrence E. Stager [Louisville, KY; Westminster John Knox Press, 1994], pp. 169-187).

[17]Cogan, *Imperialism and Religion*, pp. 67-70; Evans, "Manasseh, King of Judah" in *ABD*; cf. Hobbs, *2 Kings*, p. 309. Ashurbanipal was often lenient toward rebellious vassals (cf. *ANET*, pp. 296-297; see Cogan and Tadmor, *II Kings*, p. 271). Manasseh was a vassal of Assyria during the reigns of Esarhaddon and Ashurbanipal. Esarhaddon records employing Manasseh

God of his fathers" and prays. Yahweh hears and brings him back to Jerusalem. On his return, the king of Judah champions a reform in which he removes the image and the altars he had placed in Jerusalem and restores the worship of Yahweh. He commands the people to serve Yahweh, which they do. Only, they continue worshiping on the high places (2 Chr 33:10-17,19). However, for the author of Kings, Manasseh's repentance is apparently irrelevant to (not inconsistent with) the overall purposes of his composition. Concerning the two accounts, Hicks points out, "The two historians are using Manasseh to serve different ends. [Kings] uses his reign to justify the exile, but the Chronicler uses it to encourage his postexilic community." He adds, "The Chronicler focused on the individual while [Kings] is concerned about the nation."[18]

In this frame of reference, Manasseh's repentance and subsequent reforms are noteworthy, but his son Amon undoes any important gains. And, if reform is the remedy for Judah's sins, the reign of Josiah should have been enough to avert the judgment on Jerusalem. The author of Kings is an accomplished literary artist, and a consummate theologian, who is proffering an explanation (a "theodicy"[19]) for the destruction of Jerusalem and the temple where Yahweh caused his name to dwell. In his treatise, the kings of Israel and Judah set in motion events that culminate in the fall of Judah. The remnant in exile is suffering because of the sins of kings like Manasseh (who according to Kings is largely responsible for the exile; cf. 23:26-27; 24:3; Jer 15:4). While repentance and reform are necessary to restore a relationship with him, the audience of Kings must know that Yahweh is the one who will deliver his people. Those reading this composition in exile must wait on Yahweh. Perhaps he will yet keep his promise to David?

In his formulaic conclusion, the author of Kings takes one more jab at Manasseh. The king's other deeds, **including *the sin* he com-**

---

and other kings from the West to rebuild Sidon and to transport building materials to Nineveh for his palace (*ANET*, pp. 290-291). During the reign of Ashurbanipal, Manasseh supplied troops for an Assyrian campaign against Tirhakah of Egypt (*ANET*, p. 294; see Cogan, *Imperialism and Religion*, pp. 67-68; Cogan and Tadmor, *II Kings*, p. 265; Hobbs, *2 Kings*, pp. 303-304).

[18]Hicks, *1 & 2 Chronicles*, pp. 497, 500.
[19]See Brueggemann, *1 & 2 Kings*, pp. 537-538.

mitted (literally, "the sin which he sinned"), are written in the **annals of the kings of Judah**. At his death, Manasseh is buried in **the garden of Uzza**, the burial place for Manasseh and his son Amon. Provan wonders if there is an intentional association being made with Uzzah, who incurred Yahweh's wrath for irreverently reaching out to touch the ark of God (2 Sam 6:1-8; however, see comments on 2 Kgs 15:7).[20] **Amon his son** becomes king in his place.

2. Amon Walks in All the Ways of His Father (21:19-26)

21:19-26 As Ahaziah followed the example of his father and mother, Ahab and Jezebel (1 Kgs 22:52; cf. 2 Kgs 3:2), **Amon** does **evil in the eyes of the LORD, as his father Manasseh had done.**[21] In a short reign of **two years**, he also worships **idols** and *forsakes* **the God of his fathers** (cf. 1 Kgs 9:9; 2 Kgs 17:16). Like Jeroboam, he does not **walk in the way of the LORD** (see comments on 1 Kings 13). As a result, his **officials conspire** [קָשַׁר, *qāšar*] **against him**, which reminds the reader of the frequent turnovers in the northern kingdom (cf., e.g., 15:10,15,25,30). Subsequently, **the people of the land** (perhaps the landed gentry; see comments on 11:12-16) kill those who conspired [*qāšar*] against the king. What the narrator gives only a cursory treatment probably reflects underlying internal strife in Judah and political intrigue. In a palace coup, Amon may have been assassinated for his pro-Assyrian policies, or perhaps he simply resumed the tyrannical rule of his father.[22] The involvement of the people of the land implies their commitment to the Davidic dynasty (cf. 23:30,35).[23] Amon is also buried in the **garden of Uzza**, appropriately in the same garden as his father.[24] **Josiah his son** sits on the throne of David in his place.

---

[20]Provan, *1 and 2 Kings*, p. 269. Uzza may also refer to the garden of Uzziah (cf. Cogan and Tadmor, *II Kings*, p. 270).

[21]The Chronicler contrasts father and son: "Unlike his father Manasseh, he did not humble himself before the LORD" (2 Chr 33:23). See Hicks, *1 & 2 Chronicles*, p. 508.

[22]Reasons for the king's murder remain speculative (Cogan and Tadmor, *II Kings*, p. 276). For a summary of historical reconstructions, see pp. 275-276; Cogan, *Imperialism and Religion*, pp. 70-72.

[23]Hobbs, *2 Kings*, pp. 310-311.

[24]Cohn, *2 Kings*, p. 149.

2 KINGS 22

C. JOSIAH'S REFORMS CANNOT FORESTALL
THE FALL OF JUDAH (22:1–23:30)

1. The Book of the Law Is Found (22:1-20)

22:1-2 The narrator opens the story of **Josiah** with his typical regnal formula. Josiah is **eight years old** when he becomes king of Judah and reigns **thirty-one years** in **Jerusalem**. As is his custom with the kings of Judah, the storyteller adds that his **mother's name** is **Jedidah** ("beloved"). He may expect the reader to recall that Solomon was to be called Jedidiah ("beloved of Yahweh"; 2 Sam 12:25) — to demonstrate Yahweh's favor on the child born to David and Bathsheba (after their adulterous affair). Regardless, other allusions to Solomon in the account of Josiah will suggest an association and, by contrast, that Josiah is the son of David that Solomon was not. The storyteller declares Josiah righteous. He does what is **right in the eyes of the LORD** and **walks in all the ways of his father David**. Instead of walking in the path of his father Amon and his grandfather Manasseh, he follows the example of "his father David." Like Hezekiah, Josiah is a true son of David (see comments on 18:3). The language recalls David's instructions and Yahweh's pledge to Solomon that if he would "walk faithfully" (as had David), Yahweh's promise to David of an eternal throne would be realized, and Solomon would have a long life (1 Kgs 2:3-4; 3:3,5,14; 9:4; cf. 8:25,58; 11:4). Josiah does not **turn aside** [סוּר, *sûr*] **to the right or to the left** from following David, who did not "turn aside" (*sûr*) from "any of the LORD's commands" (1 Kgs 15:5; cf. Deut 17:20). By contrast, the kings of Israel did not "turn aside" (*sûr*) from the sins of Jeroboam, who caused Israel to sin (cf., e.g., 2 Kgs 3:3; 17:22). When this faithful king of Judah eradicates foreign worship in Israel and reestablishes the covenant between Yahweh and his people, by allusion he also becomes Moses for a restored Israel (as Solomon was Moses in instituting temple worship). Jeroboam had the opportunity to be Moses and deliver God's people from the pharaonic policies of Solomon, but instead became Aaron and led them into apostasy. A new Moses, and a true son of David, rescues a generation of Israelites from their forefathers.[1]

At this point, the account in Chronicles diverges from the storyteller's record in Kings.[2] Immediately following the introductory evaluation of Josiah's reign (2 Chr 34:1-2; =2 Kgs 22:1-2), the Chronicler records that in his eighth year Josiah "began to seek the God of his father David." In his twelfth year, he "began to purge Judah and Jerusalem of high places, Asherah poles, carved idols and cast images" (2 Chr 34:3). After summarizing his initial efforts at reform, the Book of the Law is discovered in the eighteenth year of Josiah's reign (34:8; as in 2 Kgs 22:3) — which is six years after the king had begun his religious reformation in Judah and in Samaria as far north as Naphtali. By contrast, in the Kings account Josiah's reforms come after finding the Book of the Law, which stimulates the restoration of pure worship in Judah. These differences reinforce what has already been observed, that the two accounts of the same underlying historical events have been framed to address specific concerns. In this instance, the Kings account appears to be "more topically driven than Chronicles."[3] Apparently, the Chronicler is especially interested in the personal dimension of Josiah's reform, while Kings is more concerned with Judah's communal response. The underlying circumstances may have been that Josiah was only able to effect real reform in Judah after the discovery and reading of the Book of the Law.[4]

22:3-13 The first dramatized scene in the account of Josiah in Kings occurs in the **eighteenth year of his reign**. The now twenty-six-year-old king sends **Shaphan** his **secretary** (or "scribe") to

---

[1]Provan, *1 and 2 Kings*, p. 220.

[2]The account in Chronicles differs significantly from the presentation in Kings, with important additions (and omissions). For a more detailed discussion of the differences between Kings and Chronicles, see Hicks, *1 & 2 Chronicles*, pp. 509 ff.

[3]Ibid., p. 512.

[4]Ibid., p. 509-513.

Hilkiah the high priest[5] with instructions for repairing the temple. The parallels with the temple repairs of Joash are obvious. For example, in both stories the people make contributions for the construction (1 Kgs 12:6[7]-10[11]; cf. 2 Kgs 22:4);[6] the "keepers of the threshold" are the priests who receive the funds (1 Kgs 12:9[10], "the priests who guarded the entrance" in the NIV; cf. 2 Kgs 22:4, "the doorkeepers" in the NIV); and there is no need to account for the money given to the workers, since (literally) "they are acting with fidelity [בֶּאֱמוּנָה, *be'ĕmûnāh*]" (1 Kgs 12:11[12]-15[16], "they acted with complete honesty" in the NIV; cf. 2 Kgs 22:7, "they are acting faithfully" in the NIV). More significant, the reference to the **carpenters, the builders and the masons**, along with the building materials they are to purchase for repairing (literally) the "breach" (בֶּדֶק, *bedeq*; 1 Kgs 12:6-9,13; cf. 2 Kgs 22:5) in the temple, has a direct parallel in the description of the temple construction during the reign of Joash (1 Kgs 12:11[12]-12[13]; cf. 2 Kgs 22:5-6). Both accounts call to mind the building activities of Solomon, who was Yahweh's choice to build for him a house (cf. 1 Kgs 8:15-21). These connections raise expectations that the glory of Solomon will be recaptured in the days of Josiah. An audience in exile, however, knows that, as in the reign of Joash, these prospects will not be realized (see comments on 1 Kings 12).

At the temple, Hilkiah informs Shaphan that he has found **"the Book of the Law** [vv. 8,11] **in the temple of the LORD."**[7] Whether the high priest actually found "the Book of the Law" or merely acts as if

---

[5]Two bullae (i.e., seal impressions) with the names of Shaphan's son Gemariah (cf. Jer 36:12,25) and Hilkiah's son Azariah (cf. 1 Chr 6:13[5:39]) have been found in the Babylonian destruction of Jerusalem (Tsvi Schneider, "Six Biblical Signatures: Seals and Seal Impressions of Six Biblical Personages Recovered," *BAR* 17/4 [July/Aug. 1991]: 28-31). Another son of Shaphan, Ahikam, supported Jeremiah (cf. Jer 26:24), and a grandson, Gedaliah, became governor of Judah after the fall of Jerusalem (cf. 2 Kgs 25:22-26; Jer 40:5-41:10). See Hobbs, *2 Kings*, p. 324.

[6]A recently published ostracon appears to be a receipt for a payment to the "house of Yahweh." Some scholars connect the inscription with the temple repairs in the time of Josiah, others to Joash (see comments on 2 Kgs 12:4[5]-16[17]).

[7]The Hebrew word order, with object first, calls attention to the discovery: "The scroll of the Book of the Law I have found in the House of Yahweh" (Cohn, *2 Kings*, p. 153).

he has discovered the book is not clear from the text.[8] The high priest, not the narrator, reports the discovery of the scroll. One can imagine a scenario where Hilkiah pretends to find the document in order to introduce the young king to the Law of Moses. With what is said about his father and grandfather, it is unlikely that Josiah was exposed to the Torah as a young man. Either way, by implication the reader learns that the worship of Yahweh has been imperiled by the wicked policies and practices of Manasseh. This narrative gap draws[9] the reader into the story and, at the same time, focuses attention not on the discovery, but on the king's response to the scroll that was found.

The extent of the book is also not clear from the text. The phrase "Book of the Law" first appears in Deuteronomy in reference to the teachings Moses gave Israel before entering Canaan (see Deut 28:58,61; 29:20; 30:10; 31:24,26; cf. Josh 1:8; 8:31,34; 23:6; 24:6; 2 Kgs 14:6; 23:24). The king was to have a copy of the Law to read "all the days of his life" (Deut 17:18). "Book of the Covenant" (23:2,21) occurs elsewhere only in Exodus 24:7 and in 2 Chronicles 34:30, the parallel account to the Kings narrative. In Exodus, "Book of the Covenant" refers to the law Moses received at Mount Sinai. The reforms that were inaugurated by Josiah, after hearing the words of this book (23:1-25), indicate that the document included the book of Deuteronomy (see below).[10]

When Hilkiah presents the scroll to Shaphan, he names it "the Book of the Law." After reporting to the king on the temple repairs, Shaphan casually mentions, "Hilkiah the priest has given me *a book*." The narrative delay in getting the scroll to the king (from Hilkiah to Shaphan to Josiah) dramatizes the action and creates suspense for the reader.[11] When **the king hears the words of the Book of the Law, he** tears **his robes**. Brueggemann notices a contrast between Josiah's response to the Book of the Law and his son's reaction to

---

[8]Provan, *1 and 2 Kings*, p. 271.

[9]Nelson correctly calls attention to the gap in the narrative (*First and Second Kings*, pp. 252-253).

[10]There is nothing in the story to suggest the view that the account of the discovery of the "Book of the Law" indicates the book of Deuteronomy was a product of the seventh century B.C. Hobbs writes, "The earlier certainty that this passage [i.e., 2 Kings 22–23] provides a cornerstone for the dating of Deuteronomy is now somewhat eroded" (*2 Kings*, pp. 316, 325; see "Introduction: Composition").

[11]Nelson, *First and Second Kings*, p. 255.

the scroll of Jeremiah. Josiah tears his garments; Jehoiakim tears the scroll (Jer 36:23).[12] The naming "the Book of the Law" represents Josiah's point of view. What was merely "a book" becomes the "the Book of the Law" after the king hears its precepts and warnings. When he sends his representatives to Huldah, he names the scroll "this found book" because its contents have not yet been verified.[13] The king's reaction to the reading is the focal point of view in the narrative. Apparently frightened by what he has heard, Josiah directs a delegation of high officials: **"Go and inquire of the LORD for me and for the people and for all Judah about what is written in this book."** Up to this point in the composition, kings have inquired of Yahweh only in illness or for military endorsement (cf. 1 Kgs 14:5; 22:5,7,8; 2 Kgs 1:2,3,6,16; 3:11; 8:8). The reading of the Book of the Law indicates to Josiah, **"The LORD's anger burns against us because our fathers have not obeyed the words of this book."** Even after hearing the word of the prophetess, however, the contents of the book are kept from the reader. Only when Josiah acts on what he has heard will its contents be made known.[14]

22:14-20 The delegation, including the high priest Hilkiah, goes to inquire of **the prophetess Huldah**. She is the only prophetess in the book of Kings, and nothing else is said about her in Scripture. The fact that she is married to an official who is **keeper of the wardrobe** (cf. 10:22) may indicate she is connected to the court and explain why the delegation is sent to her, instead of to a prophet like Jeremiah.[15] She is also close by, **in Jerusalem, in the Second District** (cf. Zeph 1:10). This may be the area enclosed by the "broad wall" when Hezekiah enlarged the city on the northwest (cf. Neh 3:8; 2 Chr 32:5).[16] Her prophetic word is divided into two oracles. In verses 15-17, the word of Yahweh concerns judgment on Judah and Jerusalem. Verses 18-20 address the faith response of Josiah.

The prophetess prefaces her word three times with the messenger formula: **"This is what the LORD, the God of Israel, says"** (vv. 15-16,18; "the God of Israel" occurs only in vv. 15,18). Josiah is first

---

[12]Brueggemann, *1 & 2 Kings*, pp. 545, 574.

[13]Cohn suggests "this found book" indicates its contents have not been verified (*2 Kings*, p. 154).

[14]Hobbs, *2 Kings*, pp. 319, 326; Cohn, *2 Kings*, p. 154.

[15]Hobbs, *2 Kings*, p. 327.

[16]W. Harold Mare, "The Broad Wall (place)," in *ABD*.

named **"the man who sent you"** and then **"the king of Judah."** That
he is not named "Josiah" creates some distance between the prophetess (and by extension Yahweh) and the king. Josiah is not responsible for the coming destruction. Nevertheless, Yahweh's judgment is
sure and severe. He is **"going to bring disaster** [רָעָה, *rā'āh*; cf. 21:12]
on this place [מָקוֹם, *māqôm*; vv. 16,17,19,20] **and its people, according to everything written in the book the king of Judah has read"**
(cf. Deut 28:15,45). Jerusalem, the *place* (*māqôm*) where Yahweh
caused his Name to dwell (cf. Deut 12:4; see comments on 1 Kings
8), will experience the wrath of God. Because the people have **forsaken** (עָזַב, *'āzab*; cf. 1 Kgs 9:9) Yahweh and worshiped **other gods**,
provoking him to anger (from כָּעַס, *kā'as*; cf. v. 13) by **all the idols
their hands have made**, Yahweh declares, **"My anger will burn
against this place** [*māqôm*] **and will not be quenched."**

Concerning Josiah, Yahweh says, **"Because your heart was
responsive and you humbled** [from כָּנַע, *kāna'*] **yourself . . . and you
tore your robes and wept in my presence, I have heard you."**[17] A
key word in Chronicles (cf., e.g., 2 Chr 32:26; 33:12,19,23), *kāna'*
("to be humble") in Kings only describes the repentance of Ahab (1
Kgs 21:29) and Josiah. As Yahweh noticed Ahab's contrition at
Elijah's word of judgment, he hears Josiah. The *disaster* (*rā'āh*) promised against the house of Ahab was postponed until "the days of his
son" (v. 29). The account of Ahab's repentance frames Josiah's
response to the Book of the Law. The judgment on Judah will not
occur during the reign of Josiah (cf. 2 Kgs 20:16-18).[18] Yahweh promises, **"Your eyes will not see all the disaster** [*rā'āh*] **I am going to
bring on this place** [*māqôm*]." Ironically, the storyteller has also
characterized Josiah's grandfather Manasseh as Ahab. Together,
these allusions guide the reader. Like the house of Ahab and
because of Manasseh, Judah's destruction will be total. However,
because he humbled himself, Josiah will receive mercy, but only for
himself.[19] In an expression of grace, the king will be "gathered **to his
fathers**" and "buried **in peace**" — before the catastrophe for Judah
from Yahweh, which is certain.

---

[17]The language of v. 19 ("that they would become *accursed* [שַׁמָּה, *šam-
māh*]") comes from Deut 28:37 (Nelson, *First and Second Kings*, p. 257).

[18]Provan, *1 and 2 Kings*, p. 272; Nelson, *First and Second Kings*, p. 256.

[19]Iain W. Provan, *1 & 2 Kings*, Old Testament Guides (Sheffield: Sheffield
Academic Press, 1997), pp. 92-93.

2 KINGS 23

2. Josiah Institutes Reforms and Renews the Covenant (23:1-27)

23:1-3 The narration chronicles the king's response. Calling together (literally, "he sent and *gathered*" [אָסַף, *'āsaph*]) **all the elders of Judah and Jerusalem**, King Josiah goes up to the house of Yahweh (as had Hezekiah, 19:1,14) with ["all"] **the men of Judah,** ["all"] **the people of Jerusalem, the priests and the prophets** and reads in the presence of *all* **the people . . .** ["all"] **the words of the Book of the Covenant.** The use of *'āsaph* ("to gather") connects Josiah's actions with Yahweh's promise that he would be *gathered* (from *'āsaph*) to his fathers (22:20).[1] In spite of the fact that Yahweh has decreed that Judah and Jerusalem will experience the wrath of Yahweh (and that the king will personally miss that judgment), the king calls *all* the leaders and *all* the people to renew their covenant with Yahweh.[2] The narrator names the scroll that was found "the Book of the Covenant" to intimate the nature and solemnity of the ceremony that the king orchestrates. In a covenant renewal ceremony that parallels the actions of Jehoiada after purging Judah of the wicked influence of the house of Ahab — and which is reminiscent of Solomon's dedication of the temple and Joshua's renewal ceremony at the end of his life (see comments on 1 Kings 8, 2 Kgs 11; cf. Josh. 24:1-28) — Josiah stands by **the pillar** of the temple and **renews the covenant in the presence of** Yahweh (cf. 11:12-24,17).[3] He calls on the people of Judah **"to follow Yahweh and keep his**

---

[1]Cohn, *2 Kings*, p. 155. Cohn also calls attention to repetition of "all" in these verses (pp. 155-156).

[2]See Nelson, *First and Second Kings*, p. 260.

[3]At the end of the story, the bronze from the pillars of the temple will be taken to Babylon, which symbolizes Yahweh's judgment on Judah for breaking covenant (2 Kgs 25:13-17).

commands . . . with all his heart and soul." Later, the narrator will say that there was no king in Judah who turned to Yahweh as Josiah, "with all his heart and with all his soul and with all his strength" (v. 25; cf. Deut 6:5; 10:12). As the king *stood* (עָמַד, *'āmad*) by the pillar and renewed the covenant, *all* **of the people** (literally) *take a stand* (*'āmad*, **pledged themselves** in the NIV) in the covenant. Josiah's influence is far reaching.

23:4-24 The storyteller now chronicles Josiah's purge of idolatrous worship in Judah, which reveals the content of the scroll that was found.[4] There is no indication in the narrative itself of political motivations for the reforms. Josiah's reign parallels the decline of Assyria. Following the death of Ashurbanipal in 626 B.C., the empire unravels. In 612, Nineveh falls to the Babylonians, and by 610/609, Assyria is no longer a world empire. In this context, it seems unlikely that Josiah's reform (in the eighteenth year of his reign = 622/621) represents a revolt against Assyrian rule. There is also no evidence to indicate that his reforms are directed against Assyrian cultic practices (e.g., the worship of astral deities) imposed on Judah. The reforms address Canaanite influences institutionalized by Ahaz and Manasseh. While there probably are political overtones to Josiah's purge, they are internal and not geopolitical. The author of Kings emphasizes the religious aspects of the reforms.[5]

The litany of objects the king **removes, tears down, burns, scatters,** and **desecrates** covers a wide range of religious paraphernalia. While some scholars have questioned the historical accuracy of this description, William G. Dever demonstrates "that recent archaeological data provide for the first time a credible historical-cultural context for this notoriously enigmatic passage [i.e., 2 Kings 23] in the Hebrew Bible."[6] Dever lists nine categories of religious practices

---

[4]Cohn, *2 Kings*, p. 156.

[5]Hobbs, *2 Kings*, pp. 322-323; Nelson, *2 Kings*, p. 253. For the question of Assyrian cultic influence on Judah, see Cogan, *Imperialism and Religions*, pp. 65-96. Brueggemann suggests that Josiah's Passover and move to take back northern territories may have been motivated in part by increased revenues for Jerusalem (*1 & 2 Kings*, p. 558).

[6]William G. Dever, "The Silence of the Text: An Archaeological Commentary on 2 Kings 23," in *Scripture and Other Artifacts: Essays on the Bible and Archaeology in Honor of Philip J. King*, ed. Michael D. Coogan, J. Cheryl Exum, and Lawrence E. Stager (Louisville, KY: Westminster John

reflected in the account of Josiah's reforms. The following chart outlines his discussion and serves as a convenient summary of the narrator's description of the purge.[7]

Cultic Activities in 2 Kings 23	Archaeological Record
Unauthorized priests (vv. 5,8,9,20)	On 7th/6th century ostraca found at the Arad temple/high place are names of priestly families known from the Bible. On two plates, the letters *qôph* (ק) and *kāph* (כ) probably represent the phrase "set apart to the priests."[8]
High places and standing stones (vv. 5,8,13,14,15-18,19)	Raised platforms/open air shrines at which were standing stones and altars are illustrated in the high place at Tel Dan, where the "shrine/house on a high place" established by Jeroboam has probably been found (with a raised platform and the remains of a large horned altar).[9]
Veneration of Asherah and her cult symbol (vv. 4,6,7,14,15)	Eighth century texts from Khirbet el-Qôm and Kuntillet 'Ajrud mention Asherah as the consort of Yahweh. The "articles" and "weaving" for Asherah (vv. 4,7) must have been for the deity. Pieces of linen and woolen textiles at Kuntillet 'Ajrud may reflect the enigmatic reference to weaving in verse 7.[10] The more than three thousand terra-cotta "pillar" figurines found throughout Judah (often in domestic contexts and tombs) surely represent Asherah as the

Knox Press, 1994), pp. 143-144. The pervasive nature of Josiah's reform may be reflected in seventh and sixth century Judean seals, which, in contrast with earlier seals, are without artistic representations (see n. 47, p. 476).

[7]The chart is adapted from Dever's list and subsequent discussion (ibid., pp. 147-158). The "Archaeological Record" column presents only the highlights of his article. For more details, see ibid. (and references there); Dever, *Biblical Writers Know*, pp. 159-243.

[8]See comments on 18:1-8.

[9]See Biran, *Biblical Dan*, pp. 159-233; and comments on 1 Kgs 12:25-33. For a survey of the high places at Dan, Tell el-Far'ah (North, Tirzah), Megiddo, Ta'anach, Beersheba, Arad, and Kuntillet 'Ajrûd, see Dever, *Biblical Writers Know*, pp. 174-187. At Bethsaida, a recently excavated ninth-century *high place in the gate* (see v. 8), with standing stones, a basin for libations, and a stela on which was carved a bull with crescent-shaped horns and sporting a short dagger, sheds some light on this cultic feature (see Rami Arav, Richard A. Freund, and John F. Schroder, Jr., "Bethsaida Rediscovered: Long-Lost City Found North of the Sea of Galilee Shore," *BAR* 26/1 [Jan./Feb. 2000]: 48-51).

[10]Garments may have been woven to decorate statues (Cogan and Tadmor, *II Kings*, p. 286).

mother goddess and consort of Yahweh (and also may function as talismans).[11] Verse six refers to a larger image (i.e., idol) of the goddess.

Proscribed altars and incense offerings (vv. 5,12,15-18)

Large altars are known from several sites (12th to 6th centuries), including the "Bull Site" in the territory of Manasseh, Dan, Arad, and Kuntillet 'Ajrud. A small altar with associated iron shovels (censers) was found at Tel Dan. Numerous small stone horned altars (10th–6th centuries) have been found at Israelite and Judean sites.[12]

Horse-and-chariot imagery, connected with solar and astral deities (vv. 4,5,11)

The worship of astral deities probably has Canaanite origins. Horse and chariot imagery represents the deity riding as the sun across the sky. In Iron Age Palestine, horse figurines are common. Seal impressions with horses (sporting a sun disk on their heads) and winged sun disks represent Phoenician, Aramean, and Neo-Assyrian influences on Judah. Terra-cotta horse figurines with sun disks between their ears were found in a cave in Jerusalem, in the shadow of the temple mount. Some female figurines appear to hold sun disks. With these horses, Yahweh may have been represented as a sun god (cf. Ezek 8:16).[13]

Temple prostitution (v. 7)

The translation "male shrine prostitutes" is open to question. The term may be translated "consecrated ones." The use of the term קָדֵשׁ (qodeš) for sacred objects in inscriptions from cultic contexts at Arad, Beersheba, and Tel Miqne/Ekron would support the alternate interpretation.[14]

Child sacrifice (v. 10)

There is no archaeological evidence of child sacrifice in Israel/Judah during the Iron Age. The Phoenician Topheth at Carthage in North Africa perhaps indirectly supports the biblical text, since the Phoenicians were "Canaanites" (see below).

---

[11]See comments on 1 Kgs 14:14-16; 2 Kgs 13:6-9; 21:7-9. For the pillar figurines, see Dever, *Biblical Writers Know*, pp. 192-193.

[12]See ibid., pp. 188-189.

[13]See J. Andrew Dearman, *Religion & Culture in Ancient Israel* (Peabody, MA: Hendrickson, 1992), pp. 89-90, 96; and below. A tenth-century cult stand from Taanach (decorated with a winged sun disk and a horse/bull) and an eighth century ostracon from Kuntillet 'Ajrud (painted with praying figures gazing into the sky) may represent Israelite worship of Yahweh as a sun god (J. Glenn Taylor, "Was Yahweh Worshiped as the Sun?" *BAR* 20/3 [May/June 1994]: 52-61, 90-91).

[14]See comments on 1 Kgs 14:22-24.

Magic (v. 24)	Magic is reflected in the numerous amulets and charms that have been found from the time of the monarchy and before. The Asherah figurines, mentioned above, probably reflect sympathetic magic as talismans for childbirth. Egyptian Bes figurines and Eye-of-Horus plaques may also represent a form of sympathetic magic to ward off evil. A hoard of *astragali* (i.e., knucklebones) in the 10th-century sanctuary at Taanach reflects divination. A "hand of Fatima" carved on the 8th century Khirbet el-Qôm inscription may be a good luck charm. A silver amulet from an Iron II tomb at Ketef Hinnom, on which was inscribed the Priestly Blessing of Numbers 6:24-26, even reflects the use of Scripture as magic.[15]
Tombs and burial practices (and bones for desecration; vv. 14,16,20)	Tombs in the hills surrounding Jerusalem have, for example, been verified at Silwan, where monumental tombs, apparently including the tomb of Shebna (cf. 18:18), have been found. The graves of the common people (v. 6) were probably simple pit graves.

Josiah's purge is carried out in the **temple** and around **Jerusalem**, in all the **towns of Judah**, in Samaria at **Bethel**, and in the **towns of Samaria**. The king directly attacks the worship of foreign gods, **Baal** and the astral deities, **the sun and moon, the constellations**, and **all the starry hosts** (see comments on 21:3).[16] He also exterminates (from שָׁבַת, *šābath*) **the pagan priests** (הַכְּמָרִים, *hak-kᵊmārîm*; only elsewhere in Hos 10:5; Zeph 1:4) who had been **appointed by the kings of Judah**. When the narrator uses *hakkᵊmārîm*, he appears to be distinguishing these priests from הַכֹּהֲנִים (*hakkōhănîm*), **the priests** who officiated at the high places **from Geba to Beersheba**[17] in the **towns of Judah** and in the **towns of**

---

[15]See Jesse C. Long, Jr., "God's Name Is Not Magic," *GA* 132/3 (March 1990): 53; Dever, *Biblical Writers Know*, p. 180.

[16]An Edomite shrine at 'En Ḥaṣeva (a fortress twenty miles southwest of the Dead Sea), in a seventh/sixth-century stratum, was intentionally destroyed in antiquity, perhaps as a result of Josiah's campaign against foreign cults (see Rudolph Cohen, and Yigal Yisrael, "The Iron Age Fortresses at 'En Ḥaṣeva," *BA* 58/4 [Dec. 1995]: 223-235; idem, "Smashing the Idols: Piecing Together an Edomite Shrine in Judah," *BAR* 22/4 [July/Aug. 1996]: 40-45, 48-51, 65).

[17]The phrase "from Geba to Beersheba" parallels "from Dan to Beersheba" and sets the boundaries for Josiah's restored Judah (Cogan and Tadmor, *II Kings*, p. 286).

Samaria (vv. 8,9,19-20).[18] The contrast suggests that the priests in this latter group are idolatrous priests of Yahweh. The priests (*hakkōhănîm*) of the high places in Judah (i.e., the Yahwistic priests) do not **serve the altar of the LORD in Jerusalem**, eating **unleavened bread with their fellow priests**, implying that Josiah strips them of their priestly prerogatives.[19] In Samaria, however, where the king does not have the political restraints one assumes that he has in Judah, Josiah **slaughters** *the priests* (*hakkōhănîm*) who worshiped on the high places (see below). In some important ways, the fervor of Josiah's purge mirrors Jehu (cf. v. 20),[20] even though comparisons with the more righteous Jehoiada are a better match. Both Jehu and Jehoiada eliminated Baal worship for a season.

The "foreign" worship that Josiah attacks includes child sacrifice, although scholars are divided over the meaning of **Molech** (occurring eight times in the Hebrew Bible; Lev 18:21; 20:2,3,4,5; 1 Kgs 11:7; 2 Kgs 23:10; Jer 32:25; cf. Acts 7:43). The traditional view is that Molech was an underworld deity who was worshiped by Judeans in a cult of the dead at the **Topheth, which was in the Valley of Ben-Hinnom**. Topheth (with an uncertain etymology and occurring nine times in the Hebrew Bible; 2 Kgs 23:10; Jer 7:31,32[2×]; 19:6,11, 12,13,14) is the biblical name for the place where the human sacrifices were made. It was probably located at the southern end of the city of Jerusalem at the intersection of the Hinnom and Kidron valleys.[21] The rival theory for the meaning of Molech argues that the word (from the Punic *mlk*) is a technical term for a type of sacrifice. This view appears to be supported by Punic inscriptions, classical descriptions of child sacrifice among the Carthaginians, and evidence of child sacrifice at Carthage, where burial urns with the remains of sacrificial victims (human and animal) have been

---

[18]Ibid., pp. 285-286. This interpretation contrasts with Provan, who does not see in the text any differentiation between priests. He writes that this distinction means there are "both orthodox and idolatrous high places functioning in the towns of Judah" (*1 and 2 Kings*, pp. 275-276). Provan misses the idolatrous nature of worship to Yahweh in Judah and Israel. There are both high places to foreign deities and high places to Yahweh, all of which are idolatrous!

[19]Hobbs, *2 Kings*, p. 334.

[20]Ibid., p. 336.

[21]Philip C. Schmitz, "Topheth (place)," in *ABD*.

excavated.[22] Since Molech includes the consonants for the Hebrew
מֶלֶךְ (*melek*, "king"), some believe Molech is a sarcastic distortion of
the name of the deity ("King," as בַּעַל [*ba'al*] means "Lord"). The
consonants of *melek* have been combined with the vowels from the
word בֹּשֶׁת (*bōšeth*, "shame," the same has been suggested for *tōpheth*).
However, this vocal exchange is now disputed.[23]

Whatever the exact meaning of Molech, the biblical text indicates that the practice of child sacrifice was of Canaanite origin
(Deut 12:31) and received governmental backing during the reigns
of Ahaz and Manasseh (2 Kgs 16:3; 21:6). Jeremiah associates child
sacrifice at the Topheth in Jerusalem with Baal worship (Jer 19:1-15),
which would support Canaanite influence on Judahite rites. At
Carthage, inscriptions in the "Topheth" cemetery to Ba'al Ḥammon
and Tanit (equivalent to the Canaanite goddess Astarte) indicate
Phoenician (i.e., Canaanite) roots and suggest an indirect connection between the oracles of Jeremiah and the practices at Carthage.
Child sacrifice at Carthage is evidenced from the eighth to the second centuries B.C. (spanning the prophetic career of Jeremiah).[24] In
Jeremiah's famous temple sermon, Yahweh declares, "They have
built the high places of Topheth in the Valley of Ben Hinnom to
burn their sons and daughters in the fire — something I did not command, nor did it enter my mind" (Jer 7:31; cf. 19:5). If Molech is a
term for a type of sacrifice, or perhaps the name of a god ("King")
that could also be applied to other deities, it is reasonable to consider that some of these sacrifices are directed to Yahweh.

Other aspects of the purge indicate how far idolatry permeates
Judean society. Beyond the worship of foreign gods, the worship of
Yahweh has become idolatrous (whether or not child sacrifice was
directed to Yahweh). An image of the goddess **Asherah** (probably the
one set up by Manasseh, 21:7) resides in the temple, apparently with

---

[22]For an overview of the Topheth at Carthage, see Lawrence E. Stager and
Samuel R. Wolff, "Child Sacrifice at Carthage — Religious Rite or
Population Control?" *BAR* 10/1 (Jan./Feb. 1984): 30-51.

[23]For more detailed discussions of the meaning of Molech, see George C.
Heider, "Molech (deity)," in *ABD*; idem, *The Cult of Molek: A Reassessment*.
JSOTSup 43 (Sheffield: JSOT, 1985); and references there.

[24]Stager and Wolff, "Child Sacrifice at Carthage," 36, 44-45. Andrew
Dearman emphasizes a connection between child sacrifice in the biblical
accounts and Ba'al Ḥammon at Carthage (*Ancient Israel*, pp. 90-96).

accompanying cultic personnel/devotees (cf. v. 7). There is little question that the goddess is being worshiped as the consort of Yahweh (see comments on 1 Kgs 14:14-16). In addition, **the horses that the kings of Judah had dedicated to the sun** indicates Yahweh was associated with and no doubt venerated as a sun god. Mark S. Smith cogently argues that a Yahwistic solar cult emerged in Judah at the influence of the monarchy.[25] For many in Judah, Yahweh is just another one of the gods of the land. The idolatrous view of Yahweh that Jeroboam introduced in Israel has become part of the fabric of Judean culture. The tribe of Judah has "followed the practices Israel had introduced" (2 Kgs 17:18-20; see comments on 1 Kings 13).

The writer's well-designed account of the reforms of Josiah resonates with the larger composition in other important ways.[26] References to **Ahaz** and **Manasseh** (v. 12) suggest that Josiah undoes what these two wicked kings had perpetrated on Judah. In addition, the righteous king desecrates **the high places that were east of Jerusalem on the south of the Hill of Corruption** [הַר־הַמַּשְׁחִית, *har hammašḥîth*]. This phrase, *har hammašḥîth*, is a play on "mount of ointment/olives" (הַר־הַמִּשְׁחָה, *har hammišḥāh*), which brings into this context the verb שָׁחַת (*šāḥath*, in various forms, "be corrupt/act corruptly/ruin/destroy") from Deuteronomy (cf. 4:16,25,31; 9:12,26; 10:10; 31:29; 32:5).[27] These are the high places **Solomon** built for **Ashtoreth, Chemosh**, and **Molech** (or Milcom) for his foreign wives

---

[25]Smith, "Solar Language for Yahweh," 29-39; cf. Taylor, "Was Yahweh Worshiped?" 52-61, 90-91. Steve A Wiggins argues against the view that Yahweh was identified with the sun in Israel ("Yahweh: The God of Sun?" *JSOT* 71 [1996]: 89-106; cf. J. Glen Taylor, "A Response to Steve A. Wiggins, 'Yahweh: The God of Sun?'" *JSOT* [1996]: 107-119; Wiggins, "A Rejoinder to J. Glen Taylor," *JSOT* 73 [1997]: 109-112). While Wiggins' cautions with respect to interpreting the biblical and extrabiblical evidence are constructive (especially with respect to the presentation of J. Glen Taylor), he is unconvincing in his discussions of 2 Kgs 23:11 and Ezek 8:16, which imply that by the time of the later monarchy in Judah there was a solar cult that was in some way associated with the worship of Yahweh (see Smith, "Solar Language for Yahweh," 29).

[26]Hobbs observes the correspondence between the reforms of Josiah and Joash, Hezekiah, and Jehu. The parallels suggest that Josiah's reform will not rescue Judah from judgment (*2 Kings*, pp. 320-321).

[27]Cogan and Tadmor, *II Kings*, p. 289; Provan, *1 and 2 Kings*, p. 276. Provan believes this wordplay parallels the substitution of the vowels for *bōšeth* ("shame") in the word Topheth (p. 276), which Nelson also sees for

(cf. 1 Kgs 11:1-11). Josiah also desecrates the **altar at Bethel, the high place made by Jeroboam son of Nebat, who had caused Israel to sin**, burning human bones on the altar. Once more, the narrator weaves into his story the refrain that characterized the kings of Israel (see comments on 1 Kgs 13:33-34). When the storyteller says Josiah **burns** the high place (and **the Asherah pole**) and **grinds it to powder** (v. 15), he intentionally conjures up images of Moses, who *burned* and *ground into powder* (and scattered the ashes on the water) Aaron's golden calf (Exod 32:20; Deut 9:21; cf. 2 Kgs 23:6). Josiah is Moses reincarnate, who destroys the abomination of Israel's Aaron, Jeroboam son of Nebat (see comments on 1 Kgs 12:25-33).[28]

The narrator explicitly says Josiah's actions are **in accordance with the word of the LORD proclaimed by the man of God who foretold these things**. The man of God prophesied, "A son named Josiah will be born to the house of David. On you he will sacrifice the priests of the high places . . . and human bones will be burned on you" (1 Kgs 13:2). Josiah burns the bones from tombs nearby on the altar to defile it (making it unfit for worship, v. 16; cf. v. 20), and he *slaughters* (חַבָז, *zābaḥ*, "slaughters for sacrifice") the priests who officiated at the high places in Samaria (no doubt including the altar in Bethel, v. 20) — all according to the word of the man of God. While consciously associating Josiah's destruction of the high place in Bethel with the word of the man of God from Judah, the storyteller also connects the king's actions with the word of Yahweh in more subtle ways. In the dramatized scene where the king notices the tomb of the man of God, which is narrated from Josiah's point of view,[29] the storyteller indirectly reinforces the role of Yahweh in these events. The king has been methodically accomplishing Yahweh's prophetic word, yet, he has to be told, "[The tombstone] **marks the tomb of the man of God who came from Judah and pronounced against the altar of Bethel the very things you have done to it.**" What Josiah has done has been on his own initiative; he has unwittingly carried out in detail the prophecy of the man of God, which implies that Yahweh is working through the faith response of

---

Molech and Ashtoreth (Nelson, *First and Second Kings*, p. 258), although, see comments on 23:10.

[28]Provan, *1 and 2 Kings*, pp. 273-274.

[29]Cohn, *2 Kings*, p. 159.

this righteous king. And, he has also unwittingly fulfilled the wish of the old prophet from Bethel[30] who had his sons bury him in the tomb of the man of God, apparently to protect his bones from the desecration foretold by the prophet (1 Kgs 13:31-32). The story has come full circle. The **word of the LORD** in the mouth of the prophet has come to pass — as has the word of the old prophet in Bethel. To his sons, the old prophet said, "The message [of the man of God from Judah] declared by the word of the LORD against the altar in Bethel and against all *the shrines on the high places* [literally, "houses at the high places"; in the Old Testament only occurring in Kings; see 1 Kgs 12:31; 13:32; 2 Kgs 17:29,32; 23:19] *in the towns of Samaria* will certainly come true" (1 Kgs 13:32). Josiah desecrates *the shrines at the high places* ["houses at the high places"] **that the kings of Israel had built in** *the towns of Samaria* (2 Kgs 23:19). In addition to undoing the evil influences of Ahaz and Manasseh, Josiah, as the quintessential royal reformer, reverses the apostasies of both Solomon and Jeroboam![31]

To further characterize Josiah as a righteous king, the storyteller records his great Passover. The king orders *all* **the people** to **"Celebrate the Passover to the LORD your God, as it is written in this Book of the Covenant."**[32] The account in Chronicles brings out the all-encompassing nature of this festival. All Judah and Israel participate in the feast. Josiah restores the kingdom to a time before the division at the death of Solomon (cf. 2 Chr 35:19). When the narrator in Kings refers to the Book of the Covenant, the reader recalls that Josiah has affected all these reforms because of the scroll that was found in the temple. To put his pious act in perspective, the narrator interjects that there has not been a Passover like the one Josiah celebrated **since the days of the judges** (cf. Josh 5:10-12[33]). This

---

[30]In v. 18, he is named "the old prophet who had come from Samaria," which signifies he is from the region of Samaria. A contrast is being made between the man of God from Judah and the old prophet from Samaria (Cogan and Tadmor, *II Kings*, p. 290).

[31]See Knoppers, "'There Was None Like Him,'" 428.

[32]Chronicles expands the account of Josiah's Passover (cf. 2 Chr 35:1-19). For a discussion of the role this Passover plays in characterizing the reign of Josiah in Chronicles, see Hicks, *1 & 2 Chronicles*, pp. 520-524.

[33]The Chronicler interprets "the days of the judges" to be "the days of the prophet Samuel" (2 Chr 35:18).

statement anticipates the assessment that there was no other king like Josiah.[34] The great Passover also connects Josiah once more with Solomon, who celebrated a great festival at the dedication of the temple (probably the Feast of Tabernacles; cf. 1 Kgs 8:2,65-66). But before giving a formal evaluation of Josiah's reign, the narrator returns once more to the king's purge. Josiah also removes **the mediums and spiritists, the household gods** [תְרָפִים, *t^ᵉrāphîm*; cf. Gen 31:19; Ezek 21:21(26-27); 1 Sam 15:23; Zech 10:2]**, the idols and the other detestable things** that were in Judah and Jerusalem. Echoes of the words of Moses in Deuteronomy pervade the narrator's description (cf. Deut 18:9-14; 29:16-17). All of this, the king of Judah does to fulfill **the requirements of the law written in the book that Hilkiah the priest had discovered**. Josiah is the faithful son of David who, according to his forefather's instructions, "keeps [Yahweh's] decrees and commands, his laws and requirements, as written in the Law of Moses" (1 Kgs 2:3).

23:25-27 In contrast with his account of Hezekiah, the storyteller bookends his story of Josiah with positive assessments (see v. 2; cf. 18:3-8).[35] His evaluation of Josiah is superlative. There was no other king like Josiah, **neither before nor after . . . who turned** [שׁוּב, *šûb*] **to the LORD as he did—with all his heart and with all his soul and with all his strength, in accordance with the Law of Moses**. At first glance, this statement contradicts the similar statement about Hezekiah. There was also no other king like Hezekiah, "either before him or after him" (18:5). However, Knoppers has shown that the storyteller is actually highlighting "specific features" in each king's reign. Hezekiah is singled out for his trust during the Assyrian invasion, and Josiah is unmatched in his reforms (cf. 1 Kgs 10:23-24; Deut 34:10-12).[36] But the language for Josiah indicates much more. Following Yahweh with all of one's heart not only is the essence of Torah (cf. Deut 6:5); it is also the conditional aspect of the covenant Yahweh made with David. To Solomon, David remembered the

---

[34]Provan, *1 and 2 Kings*, p. 274.

[35]Cohn, *2 Kings*, p. 152.

[36]Knoppers argues that this strategy suggests not redactional levels, but unity in the composition ("'There Was None Like Him,'" 411-431). Representing those scholars who miss the literary implications of the surface tension between the parallel accolades for Hezekiah and Josiah, Cohn calls it a "clear contradiction" (*2 Kings*, p. 161).

promise: "If your descendants watch how they live, and if they walk faithfully before me with all their heart and soul, you will never fail to have a man on the throne of Israel" (1 Kgs 2:4). Josiah is the faithful son of David who meets this high standard[37] — and who has taken Judah back to a time before the apostasies of Solomon and Jeroboam. Yahweh has raised up for David a faithful son to sit on his throne. Fulfilling the commandments with all his heart and undoing all of the evil his forefathers introduced, he is Israel's ideal king!

A careful reader is taken aback by the next statement. The narrator avers, **Nevertheless, the LORD did not turn away** [*šûb*] **from the heat of his fierce anger.**[38] Josiah is unsurpassed in turning to (*šûb*, i.e., "repenting") Yahweh with all his heart. Yet, Yahweh will not turn (*šûb*, i.e., "repent") from his commitment to punish Judah. Josiah's repentance cannot override the sins of Manasseh, who has *provoked* Yahweh **to anger** (from כָּעַס, *kā'as*). Yahweh says, **"I will remove** [from סוּר, *sûr*] **Judah also from my presence as I removed Israel."** The king of Judah does not "*turn aside* [*sûr*] to the right or left" from following "his father David" (22:2; cf. Deut 5:32; 28:14), but Yahweh will not *turn* [*sûr*] from his intention to destroy Jerusalem. In spite of his promise to David, the God of Israel declares, **"I will reject Jerusalem, the city I chose, and this temple, about which I said, 'There shall my Name be'"** (cf. 2 Sam 7:13). The reforms enacted by this most righteous king are not enough to alter Judah's course.

3. Josiah Dies Unexpectedly (23:28-30)

23:28-30 The concluding formula for the reign of Josiah begins innocently enough. The **other events** in his reign are written in the **annals of the kings of Judah.** Then the storyteller appends the shocking conclusion to Josiah's reign. Without explanation, the narrator records that **King Josiah marches out to meet [Pharaoh Neco king of Egypt] in battle,** but Neco **kills him at Megiddo.** The

---

[37]Hobbs makes a similar observation (*2 Kings*, p. 338).

[38]See Cohn, *2 Kings*, p. 162. Hobbs observes that the Mesha Stele uses the same language, when it records that "Chemosh was angry at his land" (*2 Kings*, p. 338; cf. *ANET*, p. 320).

Hebrew text does not say that Josiah was killed "in battle" (missing in the MT). The NIV is interpolating from the account in Chronicles (cf. 2 Chr 35:20-24). With the resulting ambiguity in Kings,[39] the narrator calls attention to the prophecy that Josiah would die in peace (cf. 2 Kgs 22:20; see below). On the level of event, the king of Judah is apparently trying to block Neco's attempt to rescue the declining fortunes of the Assyrian empire. The Babylonian Chronicle for 609 B.C. records that a large Egyptian force crossed the Euphrates and besieged Haran, by that time controlled by Babylon, but was unable to displace the Babylonians. The Chronicler adds that the Egyptians faced the Babylonian army "at Carchemish on the Euphrates" (2 Chr 35:20). Consistent with his anti-Assyrian policy, Josiah is attempting to keep the Egyptians from undermining Babylonian efforts to replace the Assyrians as a dominant world power.[40] Ironically, Yahweh will use Babylon to effect his wrath on Judah (cf. 20:16-18).

On a literary level, the tension intensifies. Through the prophetess Huldah, Yahweh promised Josiah that because he had *humbled* himself, he would be gathered to his fathers and buried in peace (22:18-20). Now, the king's **body** is being driven back (literally, "brought him *dying* [מֵת, *mēth*] from Megiddo"[41]) **in a chariot from Megiddo to Jerusalem**. It appears that Yahweh has also not kept his word to Josiah. However, allusions to Ahab, whose body was also driven back to Samaria in a chariot (1 Kgs 22:37-38), suggest that Josiah's death is an act of mercy.[42] In an expression of grace, Yahweh's judgment on Ahab's house was averted to the days of his son

---

[39]See Cohn, *2 Kings*, p. 162.

[40]For more details on the underlying historical events, see Cogan and Tadmor, *II Kings*, pp. 391-393, 300-301; Hobbs, *2 Kings*, pp. 339-340.

[41]The NIV drops the participle *mēth* from the translation, which leaves the impression of an inconsistency between Chronicles (dying in Jerusalem; cf. 2 Chr 35:24) and Kings (dying at Megiddo). Recognizing the participle ("brought him *dying*") eliminates the problem (Hicks, *1 & 2 Chronicles*, p. 527).

[42]Provan, *1 and 2 Kings*, p. 275. The Chronicler gives a different account, which is noticeably more negative toward Josiah. Disregarding the word of God in the mouth of Neco, Josiah disguises himself, is wounded by archers, and is placed in another chariot that carries him to Jerusalem, where he dies (2 Chr 35:20-24). The Chronicler obviously notices the allusions to Ahab in the Kings account, which he highlights in his narration of the death of Josiah (e.g., adding to his account that Josiah disguised himself and was killed by archers; cf. 1 Kgs 22:29-38).

because he humbled himself (from כָּנַע, *kāna'*) before Yahweh
(21:27-29). Even though killed in battle, he "rested with *his fathers*"
(22:40), the sign of a peaceful reign in Kings (see comments on
1 Kgs 22:44).[43] Josiah dies in battle, but his death is also an act of
grace. Because he humbled himself before Yahweh, the king is shel-
tered from the terrible calamity that is coming. As Yahweh
explained, "Your eyes will not see all the disaster I am going to bring
on this place" (2 Kgs 22:20). Josiah's death at the hand of the
Egyptians is peaceful, in comparison with the judgment that lies on
the horizon.[44]

But the tension in Josiah's untimely death only masks the conflict
in the larger story.[45] When the ideal king of Judah dies, with Yahweh's endorsement (cf. 22:20), there is little hope for Judah. And, as
with other reforms (most recently Hezekiah), Josiah's purge does
not result in deliverance for Judah. Both his reforms and his repentance do not divert Yahweh from his decision to punish Judah.[46]
Adeptly embodied in a single story, this is the tension in the larger
composition of 1 and 2 Kings — the tension between the justice and
mercy of Yahweh. And this underlying tension raises questions
about how Yahweh works in the world. Nelson writes, "The neat
theological formula which insists that righteousness leads inevitably
to success (1 Kgs 2:3) and repentance to forgiveness is fatally under-
cut. God's gracious promises to David and Jerusalem (23:27) are in
abeyance."[47] An audience in exile wonders if there is any hope for

---

[43]Being "gathered to one's fathers" generally signifies a peaceful death (cf.
Gen. 25:8); see Hobbs, *2 Kings*, p. 328.

[44]Nelson, *First and Second Kings*, p. 257.

[45]Missing the literary significance of Josiah's death, Brueggemann writes
that "the narrator apparently can think of nothing to say that would resolve
the [problem of Josiah's death]" (*1 & 2 Kings*, p. 561). The storyteller is actually saying a great deal in the way he narrates the scene of Josiah's death.
The underlying tension in the composition, which has been aggravated by
the untimely death of this model king, will find release by the end of the
story, when Jehoiachin is released from prison. There is still hope for Judah!

[46]Nelson, *First and Second Kings*, p. 255.

[47]Ibid., p. 260. In fact, in the larger story reform gives way to apostasy
(e.g., Asa and Joash give way to Ahaz; Hezekiah gives way to Manasseh; and
Josiah gives way to the four wicked kings at the close of the story). The failure of Josiah to alter Judah's course is not surprising (McConville, "Narrative and Meaning," 45).

the fulfillment of Yahweh's promise to David. If there is any hope for restoration, in Hobbs's words, "[It] must come from the same freedom [i.e., in which Yahweh acts to judge] to offer grace which is *dependent upon nothing*" (italics added).[48] If Yahweh acts, it will be because of his mercy. Josiah is buried **in his own tomb**, and the **people of the land** [see comments on 11:12-16; 21:19-26] **anoint** Josiah's son **Jehoahaz** as king of Judah.

D. YAHWEH'S PROMISE TO DESTROY
THE CITY OF DAVID IS REALIZED (23:31–25:30)

1. The Exile of Jehoahaz to Egypt Foreshadows Judah's Captivity (23:31-35)

23:31-35 Jehoahaz does not measure up to his father.[49] He is more like his namesake Ahaz, who was not like his forefather David (16:2). The young king does **evil in the eyes of the LORD, just as his fathers had done**, which is ominous for Judah. Allusions to Ahab in the Josiah narrative suggest that Judah will also fall in the days of his son. A careful reader wonders if the end has come. The end is near, but it will not come in the days of Jehoahaz, or Jehoiakim, but Zedekiah (all sons of Josiah).[50] The introductory formula is typical for the kings of Judah. There is no suggestion that the new king's mother is the daughter of the prophet **Jeremiah**. Although his prophetic ministry spans the period under consideration, Jeremiah does not appear in Kings. Jehoahaz reigns only **three months. Pharaoh Neco** incarcerates him at **Riblah in the land of Hamath**.[51] Only the barest historical details are given. Apparently, Jehoahaz is continuing the anti-Egyptian policies of his father,[52] so Neco eventu-

---

[48]Hobbs, *2 Kings*, p. 343.

[49]He is also named Shallum (cf. Jer 22:10-12; 1 Chr 3:15).

[50]Provan, *1 and 2 Kings*, p. 277.

[51]Riblah was located eleven kilometers south of Kadesh on the east bank of the Orontes. Neco made Riblah a headquarters for his campaign against the Assyrians. Later, Nebuchadnezzar uses Riblah as his headquarters in his campaign against Jerusalem (cf. 25:1-7; Jer 52:1-11); see Yoshitaka Kobayashi, "Riblah (place)," in *ABD*.

[52]Cogan and Tadmor, *II Kings*, p. 304; Hobbs, *2 Kings*, p. 341.

ally carries the Judean king **off to Egypt** where he dies (cf. Jer 22:11-12). In the extremely well-crafted literary masterpiece that is Kings, this event stands out. Symbolically, the *exile* of Jehoahaz to Egypt represents what Yahweh is ready to do to his people. He is about to send them back into captivity in Egypt.[53] Now, through taxation, the **silver** and **gold** their forefathers took from Egypt is returned (cf. Exod 3:22; 11:2; 12:35-36). The course on which Solomon set the nation has been realized (see comments on 1 Kings 11). Because of their abominations, the people of Israel have lost their right to the land, as had the Canaanites. The exiles in Babylon can only hope for a second Exodus to *return* (*šûb*) them to the land that was promised.

Neco places **Eliakim**, another son of Josiah, on the throne in place of **his father Josiah**. The narrator does not mention Jehoahaz, as if he never occupied the throne.[54] Probably corresponding with a pledge of loyalty,[55] the king of Egypt changes his name to **Jehoiakim**. In Hebrew, the change is slight, from "God will raise up" (אֶלְיָקִים, *'elyāqîm*) to "Yahweh will raise up" (יְהוֹיָקִים, *yᵊhôyāqîm*). In terms of the composition of Kings, however, the change is monumental. In the larger canon, name changes are usually significant (cf., e.g., Gen 32:22-32). Even though the Pharaoh of Egypt, and not Yahweh, affects this small modification of the king's name, the alteration has important literary significance. When Yahweh made his promise to David that he would establish his throne forever, he said, "When your days are over and you rest with your fathers, *I will raise up* (הֲקִימֹתִי, *hăqîmōthî*) your offspring to succeed you, who will come from your own body, and *I will establish* (הֲכִינֹתִי, *hăkînōthî*) his kingdom" (2 Sam 7:12). Yahweh promised to *raise up* David's offspring to succeed him and to *establish* his throne. One of his offspring, and a namesake of that promise (*yᵊhôyāqîm* [Jehoiakim], meaning "Yahweh will raise up"), has been raised to the throne. In the larger composition, the verb קוּם (*qûm*, "rise," in the Hiphil [causative], "to raise up") has been a key word in the scattered references to the Davidic

---

[53]Cohn notes the structural parallels between Judah under Egyptian domination (23:31–24:6) and Judah under Babylonian domination (23:8–25:7). The numerous parallels suggest that the storyteller has framed the story to say that the Egyptian conquest prefigures the Babylonian destruction of Jerusalem (*2 Kings*, pp. 163-166; see also Hobbs, *2 Kings*, p. 347).

[54]Cohn, *2 Kings*, p. 165.

[55]Cogan and Tadmor, *II Kings*, p. 304.

covenant (see 1 Kgs 2:4; 6:12; 8:20; 9:5; 15:4; cf. 11:14,23; 14:4). The promise to David resurfaces[56] — but will not be realized. Ironically, in spite of his name, Jehoiakim's reign is the beginning of the end for Judah. Yahweh is working to exile the people of Judah, including the descendants of David, to Babylon. Instead of delivering Judah, Yahweh *raises up* Nebuchadnezzar to punish the house of David. Foreshadowing what is to come, Jehoiakim's reign begins on a discordant note. He exacts heavy taxes of *silver* and *gold* from **the people of the land** (supporters of the Davidic dynasty who made Jehoahaz king, v. 30; see comments on 21:23) to pacify Neco in Egypt. At the end of the story, Nebuchadnezzar will take *silver* and *gold*, the treasures of Judah, to Babylon as booty (cf. 24:13; 25:15).

---

[56]When Jehoiachin (*y³hôyākîn*, "Yahweh will establish") ascends the throne, the reader recalls once more Yahweh's promise to David (see below). Jehoiachin is formed with the theophoric preformative *y³hô* (for the name "Yahweh") and the Hiphil imperfect of *kûn* (*yākîn*, "he will establish"). In 2 Sam 7:12, the verbs *hăqîmōthî* ("I will raise up") and *hăkînōthî* ("I will establish") are Hiphil converted perfects.

2. Jehoiakim Rebels against the King of Babylon (23:36–24:7)

23:36–24:7 Reigning **eleven years** in Jerusalem, **Jehoiakim** does evil **as his fathers had done**. Just as in the characterization of his brother Jehoahaz (23:32), the narrator conspicuously ignores the reign of his righteous father Josiah, which has no effect on the ultimate fate of Judah. Jehoiakim imitates his forefathers Ahaz and Manasseh, so in his days **Nebuchadnezzar**[1] **king of Babylon** invades the land of Judah. The founder of the Neo-Babylonian Empire, Nebuchadnezzar II took the throne at the death of his father, Nabopolasser, in 605 B.C. Before becoming king, the crown prince defeated the Egyptians at the battle of Charchemish (605) and summarily launched a series of military campaigns against Syria-Palestine. Ashkelon was conquered in December of 604. Sometime between the battle of Charchemish and the fall of Ashkelon, Daniel and his companions, of the royal family, are exiled to Babylon (cf. Dan 1:1-7; cf. 2 Kgs 20:16-19).[2] Jehoiakim capitulates and serves the king of Babylon for **three years**. Subsequently, the king of Judah *turns* (*šûb*, **changed his mind** in the NIV) and **rebels** [מָרַד, *mārad*; cf. 18:7,20] **against Nebuchadnezzar**, probably encouraged by a major Babylonian setback against the Egyptians in 601/600 B.C.[3] Jehoiakim's rebellion against Babylon mirrors his rebellion against Yahweh, who *sends* (שָׁלַח, *šālaḥ*) **Babylonian,**[4] **Aramean, Moabite and**

---

[1]His name is spelled Nebuchadrezzar in other texts, outside Kings, which more closely reflects his Assyrian name (see, e.g., Jer 21:2,7; Ezek 26:7).

[2]Daniel 1 dates the campaign to the third year of Jehoiakim (= 605 B.C.). The Babylonian records do not enable a more precise reconstruction.

[3]For the underlying historical details, see Hobbs, *2 Kings*, pp. 348-349; Cogan and Tadmor, *II Kings*, pp. 307-308.

[4]The Hebrew text uses the term "Chaldean" (cf. 25:4,5,10,13,24,25,26). By the time of these events, "Chaldean" is synonymous with lower

Ammonite raiders [גְּדוּדִים, *gᵉdûdîm*] **against** the king of Judah, as he had against Solomon (cf. Rezon's *gᵉdûd* or "band of rebels" in 1 Kgs 11:24).[5] The narrator explains that Yahweh *sends* [now with a different verb, שָׁלַךְ, *šālak*] **them to destroy** [from אָבַד, *'ābad*, "perish"; cf. Deut 28:51,63; 30:18] **Judah, in accordance with the word of the LORD proclaimed by his servants the prophets.** As Yahweh forewarned Israel by "his servants the prophets," so he warned Judah (see 2 Kgs 17:13,23; 21:10; cf. Jer 7:25; 25:4; 26:5; 29:19; 35:15; 44:4). Among those messengers was the prophet Jeremiah, through whom Yahweh charged: "What I did to Shiloh I will now do to the house that bears my Name, the temple you trust in, the place I gave to you and your fathers. I will thrust [from *šālak*] you from my presence, just as I did all your brothers, the people of Ephraim" (Jer 7:14-15; cf. 7:1-29; 26:1-24). When Jehoiakim burned the scroll of Jeremiah, Yahweh declared, "I will bring on [Jehoiakim, his children, his attendants] and those living in Jerusalem and the people of Judah every disaster I pronounced against them" (Jer 36:31; cf. 36:1-32).[6]

Before narrating the graphic scenes of Judah's final days, the storyteller repeats that Yahweh **removes** [from *sûr*] **them from his presence because of the sins of Manasseh,** which includes the shedding

---

Mesopotamia and Babylon. For a concise discussion of the Chaldean dynasties in Babylon (see Richard S. Hess, "Chaldea [place]," in *ABD*).

[5]The raiders may have been mercenaries hired by the king of Babylon (Hobbs, *2 Kings*, p. 349). The LXX omits "Yahweh" as subject in v. 2. However, if elided, Jehoiakim, not Nebuchadnezzar, would be the antecedent of the verb *šālaḥ*, which is implausible. Also, ascribing this action to Yahweh is consistent with the theology of the composition. The reading in the MT is preferred (Cogan and Tadmor, *II Kings*, p. 306; Hobbs, *2 Kings*, p. 349).

[6]Jeremiah also railed against Jehoiakim for a palatial palace he was building: "Woe to him who builds his palace by unrighteousness, his upper rooms by injustice . . ." (Jer 22:13; see vv. 13-19 and comments on 1 Kgs 7:1-12). This palace may have been excavated by Y. Aharoni and G. Barkay at Ramat Raḥel, a low mound north of Bethlehem that probably was a "country estate" for the royal house in Jerusalem. In Stratum VA, dated to the late seventh/early sixth century B.C., a new royal citadel evidenced ashlar masonry, palmate capitals, and a window balustrade with palmate columns and capitals, which had been painted red. The finds call to mind Jeremiah's prophecy, which refers to "a great palace with spacious upper rooms" and "large windows" that the king "decorates in red" (22:14). For these connections and a summary of excavations, see Dever, *Biblical Writers Know*, pp. 241-243; Yohanan Aharoni, "Ramat Raḥel," in *NEAEHL*.

of **innocent blood** (cf. 2 Kgs 21:9,11,16; 23:26). This statement calls
to mind the invective of Jeremiah against social injustice: "If you really change your ways and your actions and deal with each other justly, if you do not oppress the alien, the fatherless or the widow and do
not *shed innocent blood* in this place, and if you do not follow other
gods to your own harm, then I will let you live in this place, in the
land I gave your forefathers for ever and ever" (Jer 7:5-7).[7] Because
of Manasseh's abominable, oppressive practices, Yahweh is **not willing** [אָבָה, *'ābāh*] **to forgive** [סָלַח, *sālaḥ*]. Whereas the Chronicler indicates Yahweh forgave Manasseh for his sins (2 Chr 33:10-20), the
author of Kings blames Manasseh for the destruction of Judah and
Jerusalem. Apparently, Manasseh was unable to undo the damage he
had inflicted on Judah (see comments on 2 Kings 21). In any case,
there is even greater tension in the conflict with earlier statements by
the narrator in Kings. Concerning Israel, the storyteller maintained,
"To this day [Yahweh] has been *"unwilling [lō' 'ābāh]* to destroy
[Israel] or *banish* [from *šālak*] them *from his presence* [because of his
covenant with Abraham, Isaac and Jacob]" (13:23). In a similar statement about Judah, the storyteller declared, "For the sake of his servant David, the LORD was not willing [*'ābāh*] to destroy Judah. He had
promised to maintain a lamp for David and his descendants forever"
(2 Kgs 8:19). Yahweh was *unwilling* to destroy Israel and Judah. Now,
Samaria lies in ruins, and Yahweh is *unwilling* to *forgive (sālaḥ)* Judah.
Solomon's prayer that Yahweh *forgive (sālaḥ)* the sins of his people
Israel will not be answered (cf. 1 Kgs 8:30,34,36,39,50). Once more,
the storyteller indirectly calls attention to Yahweh's covenant with
David and dramatically heightens the tension in the story. Yahweh
appears to be ready to extinguish the lamp he had promised to maintain for David and for his descendants forever!

For the last time, the storyteller mentions **the book of the annals
of the kings of Judah.**[8] At his death, Jehoiakim rests **with his
fathers,**[9] and **Jehoiachin** [meaning "Yahweh will establish"] **his son**

---

[7]See Brueggemann, *1 & 2 Kings*, p. 571.

[8]It is possible that the annals ended with the reign of Jehoiakim (see
Cogan and Tadmor, *II Kings*, p. 307).

[9]Second Chronicles 36:5-8 records that Jehoiakim was taken to Babylon
(cf. Jer 22:19). While the phrase "rested with his fathers" is derived from
family-tomb burial practices, it becomes an idiom for death and does not
indicate that the king was buried in Jerusalem (cf. 1 Kgs 2:10). It is possible

becomes king in Jerusalem. The irony in the new king's name further underscores the tension in the story. Yahweh promised David that he would "*establish* [from כּוּן, *kûn*] the throne of [his descendant's] kingdom forever" (2 Sam 7:13). In the days of Jehoiachin, Nebuchadnezzar will come up against Jerusalem and exile a son of David to Babylon. To this concluding statement for Jehoiakim, the narrator appends an odd, almost out of place statement about Egypt (v. 7). When the king of Babylon comes up against Jerusalem, the king of Judah will get no assistance from the **king of Egypt**, who has been contained by Babylon (in the campaign of 604[10]). But the narrator has more in mind than the underlying course of events. The king of Babylon has taken from Pharaoh in Egypt **all his territory, from the Wadi of Egypt to the Euphrates River** — the territory Solomon ruled (cf. 1 Kgs 4:21,24; 8:65). The empire of Solomon has been given to Babylon.[11] It only now remains to be seen what will happen to the house of David and to the house Solomon built for Yahweh.

3. Jehoiachin Is Exiled to Babylon (24:8-17)

24:8-17 Like Jehoahaz, who was exiled to Egypt, Jehoiachin reigns only **three months** in Jerusalem. He follows in the ways of his father Jehoiakim, doing **evil in the eyes of the LORD**. After regrouping from his losses at the hands of the Egyptians (600/601 B.C.), **Nebuchadnezzar** advances on Jerusalem and besieges the city. **Jehoiachin king of Judah**, the queen mother, and the king's officers surrender to the king of Babylon, which saves the city from destruction. Now synchronizing events with the reign of Nebuchadnezzar, who is sovereign over Judah, the narrator records that **in the eighth year of the reign of the king of Babylon** he takes Jehoiachin prisoner. The Babylonian Chronicle recounts, "[Nebuchadnezzar] encamped against the city of Judah. On the second of Adar [= March 16] 597, he captured the city and seized his king."[12]

---

that the arrest of Jehoiakim was symbolic and that he was never carried to Babylon (see Hicks, *1 & 2 Chronicles*, p. 532).

[10]See above and Cogan and Tadmor, *II Kings*, pp. 307-308.

[11]Provan, *1 and 2 Kings*, p. 278.

[12]From Cogan and Tadmor, *II Kings*, p. 311; see Thiele, *Mysterious Numbers*, p. 190. Hobbs dates the capture to 16 February 597 (*2 Kings*,

Reminding the reader of Isaiah's promise to Hezekiah, the narrator adds that, **as the LORD had declared**, the king of Babylon takes **all the treasures from the temple of the LORD and from the royal palace** (cf. 20:12-21). What has been foreshadowed by the loss of treasure, at various points in the story, happens (cf. 1 Kgs 14:26; 15:18; 2 Kgs 12:19; 14:14; 16:8; 18:15; 20:13,15). The treasures include **all the gold articles that Solomon the king of Israel had made for the temple of the LORD** (cf. 1 Kgs 7:48-51). The wealth with which Yahweh blessed the house of David during the reign of Solomon (cf. 1 Kgs 3:1-15) is being given by Yahweh to the king of Babylon. **All Jerusalem**, including **officers, fighting men, craftsmen**, and **artisans** are exiled (גָּלָה, *gālāh*) — **a total of ten thousand**. Nebuchadnezzar also exiles (*gālāh*) Jehoiachin, a son of David who also bears the name of the promise ("Yahweh will establish"; see above). Exiled with him are his **mother, his wives, his officials, the leading men** in Judah, **seven thousand fighting men**, and **a thousand craftsmen and artisans**. The discrepancy between the deportation totals in verse 14 and verses 15-16 may be explained as references to different categories of exiles (cf. Jer 52:28-30). The ten thousand of verse 14 appear to be military officers and personnel. In verses 15-16, members of the royal family, some soldiers, and skilled craftsmen are exiled.[13] Apparently, the prophet Ezekiel was one of the captives taken at this time (cf. Ezek. 1:1-3). The Babylonian Chronicle records that Jerusalem fell in Nebuchadnezzar's seventh year (597 B.C.). No doubt, the exiles make their journey to Babylon in the following year (his eighth year, v. 12).[14] A cuneiform text from Babylon confirms Jehoiachin's exile. Dated to 592, the text records rations of food for *Ia-'-ú-kin/Ia-ku-ú-ki-nu*, "the king of

---

pp. 348, 351). The issues surrounding the chronological notations in the biblical accounts and the Babylonian records are difficult to solve. Thiele argues that understanding that reigns in some calendars are figured from the month of Nisan and others six months later in the month of Tishri explains many of the discrepancies (*Mysterious Numbers*, p. 180; cf. pp. 182-191). Galil posits that a key to unraveling the chronological notations is recognizing that the seventh year of Nebuchadnezzar was intercalated, where a month was added to adjust the lunisolar calendar (*Chronology of the Kings*, pp. 114-118; see pp. 109-114).

[13]Hobbs, *2 Kings*, p. 353. Hobbs suggests that the craftsmen were military engineers (p. 354).

[14]Cogan and Tadmor, *II Kings*, p. 311; Hobbs, *2 Kings*, p. 352.

Judah," and five of his sons.[15] Only **the poorest people of the land**
remain (שָׁאַר, šā'ar).

There is no concluding formula for Jehoiachin, who is in exile
(cf. 23:31-34; 25:27-30). The king of Babylon places the king's uncle
Mattaniah (another son of Josiah) on the throne in place of Jehoiachin. As Neco changed the name of his vassal (Eliakim to Jehoiakim,
23:34), Nebuchadnezzar changes Mattaniah's name to **Zedekiah**
(meaning "Yahweh is righteousness," or "Yahweh is my righteous-
ness/vindication"; cf. Jer 23:5-6). Yahweh's actions are righteous/
just, and, in spite of what the God of Abraham and David is doing
in Judah, he is their only hope for vindication/salvation.

After Jehoiachin and the captives are deported to Babylon, the
prophet Jeremiah sees a vision of figs. The exiles in Babylon are a
basket of good figs, which Yahweh watches. He promises, "I will
bring them back to this land. I will build them up and not tear them
down; I will plant them and not uproot them. I will give them a heart
to know me that I am the LORD" (Jer 24:5-6). Zedekiah and his officials, and the survivors in Judah and Egypt, are bad figs, a reproach:
"I will send the sword, famine and plague against them until they are
destroyed from the land I gave to them and their fathers (v. 10; cf.
vv. 1-10). While both kings receive judgment from Yahweh, in the
following events the fate of Zedekiah differs markedly from the fortunes of Jehoiachin.

4. Zedekiah Rebels, and Jerusalem Falls (24:18–25:26)

24:18-20a[16] The regnal formula for **Zedekiah** names his mother
Hamutal daughter of Jeremiah, indicating that he and Jehoahaz
were full brothers (cf. 23:31). He reigns **eleven years in Jerusalem**
(cf. 23:36) and does **evil in the eyes of the LORD, just as Jehoiakim**

---

[15]*ANET*, p. 308; cf. Cogan and Tadmor, *II Kings*, p. 311. The list may have
included two names in the lineage of Jesus, Jehoiachin (i.e., Jeconiah) and
his son Shealtiel (Matt 1:12). First Chronicles 3:17 indicates Jehoiachin had
seven sons. Seal impressions of Jehoiachin have also been found (Dever,
Biblical Writers Know, p. 172).

[16]Following a statement that marks the end of the words of Jeremiah, the
author of the book of Jeremiah appends an account of the fall of Judah and
Jerusalem that follows almost exactly the account in Kings (24:18–25:21,27-
30=Jer 52:1-27,31-34; cf. Jer 39:1-14).

had done (cf. v. 9). Before detailing the disaster that is coming, the narrator affirms that what happens **to Jerusalem and Judah** is because of the **anger** of Yahweh. His anger burns until **he thrusts** [from *šālak*] **them from his presence**. With wordplay, the storyteller calls attention to his assertion. Yahweh *sends* (*šālaḥ*) raiders against Jehoiakim (v. 2) and is *not willing* (*'ābāh*) to *forgive* (*sālaḥ*) Judah for the sins of Manasseh (v. 4). Now, the narrator declares Yahweh *thrusts* (from *šālak*) them *from his presence* (cf. Jer 7:14-15). In a masterful stroke, the language also brings in the author's commentary on the fall of Samaria (17:7-23). Yahweh was not willing (*'ābāh*) to *banish* (from *šālak*) Israel *from his presence* (13:23), yet, because of their abominations, he *thrust* (from *šālak*) "all the seed of Israel" *from his presence* (17:20; including Judah, v. 19; cf. 17:7-23). The homily on the fall of Samaria frames the account of the fall of Jerusalem. As Yahweh lost his patience with Israel, he has become impatient with the nation of Judah. They have followed the sins of Israel and, for the same reasons, will be exiled from the land of their inheritance.

2 KINGS 25

4. Zedekiah Rebels, and Jerusalem Falls (24:18–25:26) (Continued)

24:20b–25:7 Zedekiah **rebels** (מָרַד, *mārad*) against the king of Babylon, as had Jehoiakim (24:1; cf. 18:7,20), and incurs his wrath. The book of Jeremiah describes in more detail the weak and vacillating character of the Judean king and his participation in a conspiracy against Nebuchadnezzar, which was probably encouraged by an Egyptian revolt.[1] The prophet calls on Zedekiah to serve the Babylonian king, which he rejects (cf., e.g., Jeremiah 27). The Chronicler says Zedekiah "did not humble himself before Jeremiah the prophet" and "rebelled against King Nebuchadnezzar" (2 Chr 36:12-13).[2] The narrator in Kings chronicles Nebuchadnezzar's response. **In the ninth year of Zedekiah's reign, on the tenth day of the tenth month, Nebuchadnezzar king of Babylon marches against Jerusalem** (15 Jan. 588[3]). With this chronological note, the narrator calls attention to the significance of this event (cf. v. 27) and frames the siege, which continues into **the eleventh year of King Zedekiah.** The **famine** within the city recalls the siege of Samaria by the Syrians (cf. 6:24-31). **By the ninth day of the fourth month** (18 July 585[4]), the eighteen-month siege has become so

---

[1]For the occasion of Zedekiah's revolt, see Hobbs, *2 Kings*, pp. 354-355.

[2]For the last kings of Judah, the Chronicler abbreviates the reigns of Jehoahaz, Jehoiakim, and Jehoiachin (2 Chr 36:2-10). He adds to the theological evaluation of Zedekiah (36:11-14) and does not include the release of Jehoiachin from prison. Following a description of the fall of Jerusalem and subsequent exile (36:15-21), the Chronicler closes his composition with the Edict of Cyrus, an expression of God's grace and recommitment to the descendants of Israel (36:22-23). For the differences between the accounts in Kings and Chronicles, see Hicks, *1 & 2 Chronicles*, pp. 528-529, 534.

[3]Following Thiele, *Mysterious Numbers*, pp. 189-190.

[4]Ibid.

severe that (literally) "there is no bread for the *people of the land*." The phrase "people of the land" may represent elite, landed gentry, who are apparently supporters of the Davidic monarchy (see comments on 21:23-24). In excavations in Jerusalem, fecal material from an indoor toilet (reflecting an upper class domestic context) in a 586-destruction layer was found to have tapeworm and whipworm eggs, and was devoid of grain and legume pollen. These remains may reflect the famine, the shortage of fuel, and the unsanitary conditions of the siege.[5] At the dedication of the temple, Solomon prayed, "When famine or plague comes to this land . . . or when an enemy besieges them in any of their cities . . . and when a prayer or plea is made by any of your people Israel . . . then hear from heaven your dwelling place. Forgive and act" (1 Kgs 8:37-39a). Now, Yahweh is acting — against Jerusalem and the house Solomon built!

One letter in a group of ostraca (inscribed potsherds) discovered in a guardroom at Lachish may bring to life a reference in Jeremiah to two cities of Judah, Lachish and Azekah, that were holding out against the Babylonians: "And let (my lord) know that we are watching for the signals of Lachish, according to all the indications which my lord hath given, for we cannot see Azekah."[6] In Jerusalem, when **the city wall** is **broken through, the whole army** escapes **toward the Arabah** (i.e., toward the Jordan valley). The reader soon discovers that **the king** accompanies the fleeing army.[7] Zedekiah is captured **in the plains of Jericho** and taken to **the king of Babylon at Riblah** (cf. 23:33)**, where sentence** [מִשְׁפָּט, *mišpāṭ*, "judgment"] is **pronounced on him** (see comments on 25:28). On the level of event, his sentence is judgment for breaking his covenant/treaty obligations with the king of Babylon. For the storyteller, it is also judgment for rebellion against God. Is it just coincidence that the king is captured near the city of Jericho, the site of Israel's first victory in the Promised Land?[8] The Babylonians **kill** [שָׁחַט, *šāḥaṭ*] **the sons of Zedekiah before his eyes**. The Hebrew *šāḥaṭ* commonly occurs with the sense of "slaugh-

---

[5]Jane Cahill, Karl Reinhard, David Tarler, and Peter Warnock, "It Had to Happen — Scientists Examine Remains of Ancient Bathroom," *BAR* 17/3 (May/June 1991): 64-69.

[6]*ANET*, p. 322; see Robert A. Di Vito, "Lachish Letters," in *ABD*.

[7]"Zedekiah" may have dropped out of v. 4 (cf. Jer 39:4; 52:7); see Cogan and Tadmor, *II Kings*, p. 317.

[8]Provan, *1 and 2 Kings*, p. 279.

ter for sacrifice" (cf. 1 Kgs 18:40; 2 Kgs 10:7,14), which reinforces the narrator's view that this is judgment from Yahweh. Zedekiah and his sons are paying for the sins of Judah. After Zedekiah sees his sons slaughtered, his captors **put out his eyes**, bind him with **bronze shackles**, and carry him to Babylon.[9]

25:8-12 On the seventh day of the fifth month, in the nineteenth year of Nebuchadnezzar king of Babylon [i.e., 14 August 586[10]], **Nebuzaradan commander of the imperial guard** [literally, "chief cook," but with the sense of "bodyguard"] arrives to devastate Jerusalem, the city of David. Once more, the narrator synchronizes events with the reign of the Babylonian king (cf. 24:12). The detailed synchronism (i.e., "On the seventh day . . .") marks the infamous day. Nebuzaradan **sets fire to the temple of the LORD, the royal palace and all the houses of Jerusalem**. He also tears down **the walls around Jerusalem**. Archaeological excavations in Jerusalem have graphically demonstrated the enormity of the conflagration that enveloped the city, with evidence of burning and destruction by the Babylonians.[11] **The people who remained in the city, the rest of the populace**, and **those who had gone over to Babylon**[12] are **exiled** [from גָּלָה, *gālāh*]. The narrator once more calls attention to the remnant of the people who are left behind. Only the **poorest** *remain* (שָׁאַר, *šā'ar*; in 24:14; 25:11,12, 22[2×]; see comments on 19:29-36) to work the land.

25:13-21 The narrator's terse, almost matter-of-fact style in chronicling the destruction of Jerusalem masks the underlying tragedy and the larger significance of what occurs. For a Jewish audience, Yahweh has done the unthinkable. He has destroyed the city and house where

---

[9]Jeremiah 52:11 adds that he is put in prison. In the Kings account, only Jehoiachin of the kings of Judah is imprisoned (25:27: cf. 17:4).

[10]Following Thiele, *Mysterious Numbers*, p. 190; cf. Cogan and Tadmor, *II Kings*, p. 323 (16 August 586); Hobbs, *2 Kings*, p. 364 (July 586).

[11]A tower exposed by Nahman Avigad on the northern perimeter of the city evidenced burning and arrowheads, bringing to life the point in time when the wall was being breached. Similar destruction debris mark the excavations of Yigal Shiloh (in "the Ashlar House," "the House of Ahiel," "the Burnt Room," and "the House of the Bullae") and Benjamin Mazar (the "house of Millo"). For a summary of excavations, see Yigal Shiloh, "Jerusalem: Excavation Results," in *NEAEHL*.

[12]Judeans went over to the Babylonians at Jeremiah's urging: "Whoever stays in this city will die by the sword, famine or plague, but whoever goes over to the Babylonians will live" (Jer 38:2).

he caused his Name to dwell! In his typical, indirect way of telling the story, however, the storyteller puts an exclamation point on these events by describing what the Babylonians take to Babylon. They break up and carry away **the bronze pillars, the movable stands and the bronze Sea that were at the temple of the LORD**.[13] In addition, they take **all the bronze articles used in the temple service** and **all that were made of pure gold and silver**. The articles are enumerated (vv. 14-15). Calling attention once more to "the pillars, the Sea and the movable stands," **which Solomon had made for the temple of the LORD**, the narrator mentions that the bronze is **more than could be weighed**. The language intentionally calls to mind the description of the temple construction. Concerning the bronze for the temple, the narrator said, "Solomon left all these things unweighed, because there were so many; the weight of the bronze was not determined" (1 Kgs 7:48). The storyteller proceeds to describe in detail the two pillars, named Jakin (יָכִין, *yākîn*, "he will establish") and Boaz (בֹּעַז, *bō'az*, "in strength") in 1 Kings 7:21, each one **twenty-seven feet high**, with a **bronze capital . . . decorated with a network and pomegranates**. The brief sketch mirrors the longer description at the construction of the temple (7:15-22). Consequently, the pillars bookend the story of Kings and highlight the composition's central theme. To keep his promise to David to build him a house, Yahweh allows David's son Solomon to build for him a house, in which he causes his Name to dwell. Now that house lies in ruins, and the royal house is in exile. When the pillars are taken to Babylon, the prayer and promise their names represent ("that Yahweh *establish* Israel and her king in *strength*") fades (see comments on 1 Kgs 7:21 and "Excursus: Solomon's Temple Viewed in Context").

The **commander of the guard** takes prisoners, including some leading priests and royal officers, to Nebuchadnezzar at Riblah, where they are executed. The narrator appends a summary statement: **So Judah went into captivity** (from *gālāh*), **away from her land**. Since exactly the same thing is said about Israel (17:23b),[14] the reader can assume that Judah is exiled for the same reasons. The

---

[13]In Jeremiah, Yahweh declares that "the pillars, the Sea, the movable stands, and the other furnishings" would be taken to Babylon: "'They will be taken to Babylon and there they will remain until the day I come for them,' declares the LORD. 'Then I will bring them back and restore them to this place'" (Jer 27:19-22).

[14]Nelson, *First and Second Kings*, p. 263.

people have disobeyed Yahweh and brought on themselves the curses of the covenant, as Moses outlined: "Just as it pleased the LORD to
make you prosper and increase in number, so it will please him to
ruin and destroy you. You will be uprooted from the land you are
entering to possess" (Deut 28:63).

25:22-26 With the king and most of the rich and powerful exiled
to Babylon, the storyteller turns to chronicle events among the remnant of the people who remain in Judah. Nebuchadnezzar **appoints
Gedaliah**[15] **son of Ahikam, the son of Shaphan** (see comments on
22:3) to govern **the people he had left behind** (literally, "the people
who remained [šā'ar], whom Nebuchadnezzar caused to remain
[šā'ar]").[16] With the temple in ruins, the surviving army officers meet
Gedaliah at **Mizpah**, a holy place where Yahweh communed with
Israel in the days of the Judges (cf., e.g., 1 Sam 7:5-12).[17] Gedaliah
calls on them to submit: **"Serve the king of Babylon, and it will go
well with you."** Cohn suggests that this speech, as the only dialogue
in the account of the last days of Judah, represents the point of view
of the storyteller.[18] In any case, Gedaliah's message is not well
received. **Ishmael son of Nethaniah, the son of Elishama, who was
of the royal blood**, assassinates Gedaliah and his companions at
Mizpah **in the seventh month** [Oct. 586[19]]. The more detailed
account in the book of Jeremiah indicates Ishmael was an agent of
the king of Ammon (cf. Jer 40:7–41:16). After this, **all the people
from the least to the greatest, together with the army officers**, flee
to **Egypt**. In Jeremiah, the flight occurs after the prophet warns
them not to go to Egypt. Through Jeremiah, Yahweh promises to
bless them in the land of their forefathers: "I will build you up and

---

[15]The name "Gedaliah" has been found on a seal impression from the latter part of the seventh century at Lachish (see Edward R. Dalglish,
"Gedaliah [person]," in *ABD*; Cogan and Tadmor, *2 Kings*, p. 325).

[16]In Jeremiah, Gedaliah appears as a supporter of the prophet Jeremiah
(cf. Jer 26:24; 39:14: 40:1-6). For a more complete account of Gedaliah's
tenure as "governor," see Jer 40:7–41:18.

[17]The site of Tell en-Naṣbeh, ca. 12 km north of Jerusalem, may be the
location of Mizpah. A seal impression with "Jaazaniah servant of the king"
may be from the seal of "Jaazaniah the son of the Maacathite," who is mentioned in v. 23 (see M. Broshi, "Naṣbeh, Tell en-," in *ABD*; Jeffrey R. Zorn,
"Naṣbeh, Tell en-," in *NEAEHL*).

[18]Cohn, *2 Kings*, p. 171.

[19]Following Thiele, *Mysterious Numbers*, p. 191.

not tear you down; I will plant you and not uproot you, for I am grieved over the disaster I have inflicted on you" (Jer 42:10; cf. 41:16–43:13). In Kings, there is nothing of Jeremiah's oracle or the remnant's subsequent disobedience.

The account of Judah closes with a descendant of David (i.e., "of royal blood") orchestrating an assassination at Mizpah, as Solomon directed assassinations at the beginning of the story (cf. 1 Kgs 2:13-46). The people who remain flee to Egypt. Yahweh had told Israel they were not to go back to Egypt again (Deut 17:16). Moses also warned them, for breaking the covenant: "The LORD will send you back in ships to Egypt on a journey I said you should never make again" (Deut 28:68). Accordingly, the storyteller has framed the story of Judah to end with the people in Egypt. Physically, a remnant in Judah, **from the least to the greatest**, has fled to Egypt. Symbolically, the exiles are in Egypt as captives in Babylon. The Exodus of Moses has been reversed; the children of Israel are slaves once again![20]

5. Jehoiachin Is Released in Babylon (25:27-30)

25:27-30 The final four verses in Kings are a masterful conclusion to the composition. Without elaboration, the storyteller moves from the remnant in Egypt to Babylon, to the, by now forgotten, king of Judah who was exiled in the eighth year of Nebuchadnezzar's reign. That the narrator turns to Jehoiachin in exile calls attention to the fate of Zedekiah, who dies in obscurity in Babylon. The contrast between the two heightens the significance of the last event in Kings.[21] The fate of Zedekiah represents Yahweh's judgment on kingship in Judah. In the release of Jehoiachin, the house of David experiences Yahweh's mercy. The narrator locates the final episode **in the thirty-seventh year of the exile of Jehoiachin king of Judah** (561/560 B.C.). The chronological note echoes the synchronisms scattered throughout the composition and intimates that, even though in exile, Jehoiachin is the rightful king of Judah. In his accession year, **Evil-Merodach** (i.e., Amel-Marduk, son of Nebuchadnezzar) frees Jehoiachin from prison. Buttressing the connection with

---

[20]Nelson calls it an "un-exodus" (*First and Second Kings*, p. 264).
[21]Provan, *1 and 2 Kings*, p. 280.

Egypt — that Yahweh has sent Judah back into slavery in Egypt — the underlying Hebrew conjures up images of Joseph. Evil-Merodach (literally) "lifts the head of Jehoiachin from the prison house." When Joseph interpreted the dreams of the butler and baker, he said Pharaoh would "lift the head" of each one from prison. The butler would be restored to his original position; the baker's head would actually be "lifted" — which happens (Genesis 40: cf. vv. 13,17,19,20). Later, when he interprets Pharaoh's dreams, Joseph is released from the "round house" (a specific prison) and is raised to a position of honor (Gen 41:1-45; cf. 39:20), of which the king of Egypt says, "Only with respect to the throne [כִּסֵּא, *kissē'*] will I be greater than you" (v. 40). Along with other symbols of his new position, Joseph receives robes of fine linen (v. 42).[22] Speaking **kindly to him,**[23] Evil-Merodach gives Jehoiachin **a seat of honor** [*kissē'*, "throne"] **higher than those of the other kings who were with him in Babylon**. Of the exiled kings who are in Babylon, only Evil-Merodach has a higher position than the king of Judah. When he is released from prison, Jehoiachin also dons new garments, putting aside **his prison clothes**. The allusions suggest that, as he was an actor in the ancestral narratives, Yahweh is at work. Jehoiachin eats **at the king's table** and is given **a regular allowance** (literally) "all the days of his life." As Yahweh prospered Joseph and raised him from prison to a position of honor in Egypt, he has released Jehoiachin from prison in Babylon and given him a position above the kings who were with him in exile.

The narrative structure reinforces Yahweh's role in these events. In chapter 24, the narrator says Yahweh sent raiders against Jehoiakim, to destroy Judah (v. 2); the treasures of the temple and palace were removed as Yahweh declared (v. 13); and everything that happened to Judah and Jerusalem was because of Yahweh's anger (v. 20). In chapter 25, Yahweh is only mentioned in the phrase "house of Yahweh" (vv. 9,13,16). The statements in chapter 24 frame the events that are chronicled at the end of the story, which must

---

[22]See Cohn, *2 Kings*, p. 173.

[23]This expression may represent covenant language (see Cogan and Tadmor, *II Kings*, pp. 328-329; Cohn, *2 Kings*, p. 173). The phrase also parallels the statement about Zedekiah in v. 6 that (literally) "they spoke *judgment* against him" (Donald F. Murray, "Of All the Years the Hopes — Or Fears? Jehoiachin in Babylon [2 Kings 25:27-30]," *JBL* 120/2 [2001]: 255). The contrast calls attention to the favor toward Jehoiachin.

also be initiated by Yahweh — including the episode of Jehoiachin's release. In terms of structure, the king's liberation is clearly related to the other events in chapter 25. Evil-Merodach frees Jehoiachin on **the twenty-seventh day of the twelfth month** (2 April 561[24]). The day-and-month dating parallels the detailed notations in the preceding, systematic account of the fall of Jerusalem (25:1,3,8; cf. v. 25) and indicates the events are structurally related. The wording also implies that the release is a similarly significant event. However, in stark contrast to what preceded, the liberation of the king of Judah, at the hand of Yahweh, sounds a hopeful note.

In this frame of reference, additional allusions call to mind the promise to David. When David wanted to build a house for his God, Yahweh said that he would instead build a house for David; his son would build a house for Yahweh's Name to dwell: "I will raise up [קוּם, *qûm*] your offspring to succeed you, who will come from your own body, and I will establish [from כוּן, *kûn*] his kingdom. He is the one who will build a house for my Name, and I will establish [from *kûn*] the throne [*kissē'*] of his kingdom forever" (2 Sam 7:12-13; cf. v. 16). When the book of Kings opens, the promise to David underlies the story. With the use of the key word *kûn* (which in the causative means "establish"), the narrator indicates Solomon is Yahweh's choice. His kingdom is *established* (from *kûn*; see comments on 1 Kgs 2:12,46 and "Excursus: The Succession Story Viewed in Context"), and he builds a house for Yahweh (cf. 1 Kings 8). Now, the house where Yahweh caused his Name to dwell has been destroyed, and the reigning son of David is in exile. The people of Israel and Judah have broken the Mosaic covenant and have been returned to Egypt. Does this mean that the promise to David of an eternal throne has been nullified? Can an audience in exile have any hope that the kingdom might one day be reestablished?

Allusions to the promise frame the release of Jehoiachin. To begin with, the king in exile is a namesake of the promise. As already indicated, Jehoiachin means "Yahweh will establish [from *kûn*]." When he is named **Jehoiachin king of Judah**, the phrase (including the name) can be translated, "*Yahweh will establish* the king of Judah." Jehoiachin is the only king after Manasseh to have "king of Judah" appended to his name. In the context of the fall of Jerusalem, the

---

[24]Following Thiele, *Mysterious Numbers*, p. 190.

naming "king of Judah" places Jehoiachin on the same level with the "king of Babylon." But the storyteller is also making a play on his name. In verse 27, from the point of the name Jehoiachin, the Hebrew (including the name) can be read, "*Yahweh will establish* the king of Judah from prison."[25] Since prison in Babylon represents slavery in Egypt, the phrase suggests that Yahweh may yet deliver Judah. In fact, in the names of the son and grandson of Josiah, through whom the lineage continues, the verbs of the promise are maintained (cf. 1 Sam 7:12) — "Yahweh will raise up" (Jehoiakim) and "Yahweh will establish" (Jehoiachin). Ironically, Yahweh sends raiders against "Yahweh will raise up" (i.e., Jehoiakim) to destroy Judah, but, after exiling Judah and the house of David to Babylon, Yahweh releases "Yahweh will establish" (i.e., Jehoiachin) from prison in exile.

Two other allusions come in the last four verses. In verse 28, Jehoiachin is given (literally) "a *throne* [*kissē'*, "seat of honor" in the NIV]" that is (literally) "above the *throne* [*kissē'*] **of the other kings who were with him in Babylon.**" Yahweh promised that he would establish David's *throne* (*kissē'*). Finally, Jehoiachin eats **at the king's table** (literally) "all the days of his life," and he receives **a regular allowance** day by day, (literally) "all the days of his life." Repetition calls attention to "all the days of his life" (cf. Jer 52:34). In the Solomon narrative, the phrase is used to represent Yahweh's commitment to Solomon (cf. 1 Kgs 11:34) — so implies a similar commitment to Jehoiachin. However, in some key texts in Kings, "all the days" also corresponds with the "forever" of the promise to David, as the following chart bears out.[26]

---

[25]In the parallel to v. 27 in Jeremiah (52:31), "and he released him" appears in the last part of the verse, apparently to smooth out the awkward syntax (literally): "Evil-Merodach king of Babylon lifted up, in the year he became king, the head of Jehoiachin king of Judah, *and he released him* from the prison house." The absence of the phrase in Kings suggests that the author wants the reader to consider the reading: "Yahweh will establish the king of Judah from prison/exile."

[26]Murray misses the symbolic relationship between these phrases and points to "all his days" as indicating the limited and ambiguous nature of any hope in this passage ("Jehoiachin in Babylon," 262). In his rather pedantic approach, he also argues *kissē'* is hardly a throne and laments, "if only our text [i.e., 25:27-30] had provided . . . reference to a son for Jehoiachin" (pp. 261-262). Murray fails to see the significance of the name "Jehoiachin" ("Yahweh will establish") and appreciate the artistry in the narrative. The

2 Samuel 7:13	"I will establish the throne of his kingdom *forever* [עַד־עוֹלָם, *'ad 'ôlām*, **'forever'**]."
1 Kings 9:3	"I have consecrated this temple, which you have built, by putting my Name there *forever* [*'ad 'ôlām*, **'forever'**]."
1 Kings 11:36	"I will give one tribe to his son so that David my servant may *always* [כָּל־הַיָּמִים, *kol hayyāmîm*, **'all the days'**] have a lamp before me in Jerusalem, the city where I chose to put my Name."
1 Kings 11:39	"I will humble David's descendants because of this, but not *forever* [*kol hayyāmîm*, **'all the days'**]."
2 Kings 8:19	"Nevertheless, for the sake of his servant David, the LORD was not willing to destroy Judah. He had promised to maintain a lamp for David and his descendants *forever* [*kol hayyāmîm*, **'all the days'**]."

With "*all his days*," the storyteller raises the specter of the "*forever*" in Yahweh's promise. As Yahweh sustained Elijah (1 Kings 17), he provides for a descendant of David in exile. But with allusion (highlighted in the chart below), the storyteller intimates that Yahweh has also not forgotten his promise to David.

2 Samuel 7:13	"I will *establish* [from *kûn*]	the *throne* [*kissē'*] of his kingdom	*forever*."
2 Kings 25:27-30	"*Jehoiachin* king of Judah" = "*Yahweh will establish* [from *kûn*] the king of Judah."	Jehoiachin is given a *throne* (*kissē'*, "seat of honor" in the NIV) above the *throne* of the kings who were with him in Babylon.	Jehoiachin eats and receives an allowance *all his days*.

The story of Kings ends where it began — with the promise to David. Yahweh kept his promise by placing Solomon on David's throne and allowing him to build a house for his Name to dwell. Even when the descendants of David break covenant and follow in the path of the kings of Israel, Yahweh is not willing to forget the promise — until the abominations of Manasseh. At that point, even a righteous, repentant king, who meets the standards of the covenant and removes the apostasies of the kings before him, cannot turn Yahweh from his resolve to thrust his people from his presence — to send them back to Egypt.

---

constellation of allusions in this text declares that *Yahweh will establish* a son of the house of David!

The promise to David is not enough to rescue the people of Judah from their sins. Or is it? When a namesake of the promise is released in Babylon, a ray of hope glimmers for an audience in exile. The storyteller guides the reader to this conclusion, in part, through his characteristic use of allusion. As Provan demonstrates, the Ahab narrative frames the closing chapters of Kings. Because Manasseh is Ahab, the destruction of the house of David, like the house of Ahab, will be complete. And, because Josiah is also like Ahab, when he humbles himself before Yahweh, it will not happen in his days, but in the days of his son. Delayed retribution, the destruction of Jerusalem, occurs during the reign of Josiah's son Zedekiah. Nevertheless, when Jehoiachin is released from prison, he emerges from the annihilation of the house of David like Joash. Provan writes, "[Jehoiachin] survives like Joash, unexpectedly, in the midst of carnage; and he represents, like Joash during Athaliah's reign, the potential for the continuation of the Davidic line at a later time, when foreign rule has been removed."[27] In spite of Yahweh's judgment, the lamp for David has not been extinguished. Moreover, the allusions to Joseph intimate the same. In much the same way Joseph's head was lifted up in Egypt, the head of Jehoiachin is lifted up from "bondage" in Babylon. An exilic audience can take heart. As Joseph's deliverance foreshadowed what Yahweh would do for Israel through Moses, perhaps he will raise up another deliverer to bring about a second Exodus. Yahweh may yet keep his promise and establish the throne of David forever. An audience in exile must return to Yahweh, keep covenant, worship him alone, and trust in him as the God of their forefathers.

However, as the account of Josiah has made clear, deliverance comes not from obedience, but from the sovereign will and promise of God. Jehoiachin does evil like his father (24:9), so his release is based on "covenant promise."[28] Even Moses realized that deliverance would not be based solely on obedience. He saw that the curses of the covenant would be enacted, and the exiles would be brought back and their faith enabled by the power and promise of Yahweh:

---

[27]Provan, *1 & 2 Kings*, p. 92; cf. pp. 87-93; see idem, *1 and 2 Kings*, p. 280.
[28]Nelson, *First and Second Kings*, p. 269.

When you and your children return [šûb] to the LORD your
God and obey him with all your heart . . . then the LORD your
God will restore [šûb] your fortunes and have compassion on
you and gather you again from all the nations where he scattered you. . . . He will make you more prosperous and numerous than your fathers. The LORD your God will *circumcise your
hearts* and the hearts of your descendants, so that you may love
him with all your heart and with all your soul and live" (Deut
30:2-6; cf. 10:12-16).

Solomon's prayer that Yahweh might "hear from heaven and forgive
the sin of your people Israel and bring them back [šûb] to the land of
their fathers" (1 Kgs 8:34) may yet be realized.[29] The exiles must wait
on Yahweh! Only Yahweh can establish; only Yahweh can bring them
back — and circumcise their hearts to love and obey him. Hope for the
house of David, and the descendants of Abraham, lies in him![30]

For the Christian who has been blessed to see David's greatest
son, the story of Kings is a testimony to God's faithfulness. Yahweh
has kept his promise to David. Jesus reigns![31]

---

[29]McConville maintains that Deuteronomy 30 affirms, "The answer to
Israel's infidelity lies in God himself. He will somehow enable his people ultimately to do what they cannot do in their strength, namely, to obey him out
of the conviction and devotion of their own hearts" (*Grace in the End*, p. 137;
see idem, "Narrative and Meaning," 48). However, overlooking Solomon's
prayer in 1 Kgs 8:34 and the significance of *šûb* in Kings to signify both
repentance and return/restoration (see comments on 2 Kgs 8:1-6),
McConville argues that hope in Kings "is muted in that no specific expectation of a return to the land is expressed" (*Grace in the End*, p. 138; cf. p. 91).

[30]Cogan and Tadmor represent the popular, but rather bankrupt view
that vv. 27-30 are an addendum, "nonintegral to the book of Kings." They
write, "Rather than holding out the promise of salvation through the renewal of the Davidic dynasty, these verses are merely an epilogue by an exilic
writer who brought the narration of Jehoiachin's life up to date" (*II Kings*,
pp. 329-330). In the same vein, Murray argues that vv. 27-30 are "ambivalent" to decide "the fate of the Davidic monarchy and Judean people"
("Jehoiachin in Babylon," 264).

[31]In Matt 1:12, Jehoiachin appears in the lineage of Jesus as "Jeconiah." In
a note scribbled in the front of one of his well-worn Bibles, Rex A. Turner,
Sr., to whom this commentary is affectionately dedicated, has coupled Luke
1:30-33 and Acts 2:29-32 with 2 Sam 7:11-12; 1 Kgs 8:17-20; and 2 Chr 6:8-
11 as a reminder of the claim of Scripture, that Jesus was given "the throne
of his father David" (Luke 1:32).